Journey to the
HIGH
SOUTHWEST

A TRAVELER'S GUIDE

Seventh Edition

ROBERT L. CASEY
ILLUSTRATED BY JULIE ROBERTS

The Globe Pequot Press

GUILFORD, CONNECTICUT

The following publishers and authors have been kind enough to grant their permission for use of selected quotes from previously published material.

p. 156: National Geographic, "Our People, Our Past" by Albert Laughter, and "The Navajos" by Ralph Looney.

p. 416: Alfred A. Knopf, Inc. *Death Comes for the Archbishop* by Willa Cather. Copyright 1927 by Willa Cather. Copyright renewed 1955 by the executors of the estate of Willa Cather.

Text design by Nancy Freeborn
Illustrations by Julie Roberts
Interior photos: Photos on pp. xx 1 and 110–11, courtesy PhotoDisc; photo on pp. 236–37, by Robert Royem Photography, courtesy Durango & Silverton Narrow Gauge Railroad, Durango, Colorado; photo on pp. 336–37, by Rob Casey Photographer.
Maps created by Rusty Nelson; © The Globe Pequot Press.

ISBN 0-7627-2533-8

Manufactured in the United States of America
Seventh Edition/First Printing

To June and Pat, who went before—
To Liz, who will continue the journey—And to Mary,
whose loving support
and help made it possible to share
the journey with others.

CONTENTS

PREFACE TO THE
SEVENTH EDITION

The seventh edition marks the twentieth anniversary of *Journey to the High Southwest*. The extensive road trip that Mary and I took to update this edition revealed an unusually large number of changes. Chief among them were the additions of two new national monuments and a new national preserve. Canyons of the Ancients National Monument along the Colorado–Utah border near Cortez, Colorado and Kasha–Katuwe Tent Rocks National Monument south of Santa Fe, New Mexico, will delight travelers for decades to come. Meanwhile Valle Caldera National Preserve near Los Alamos, New Mexico, perpetuates for future generations nearly 90,000 acres of forest and high country meadows. And Grand Staircase–Escalante National Monument, highlighted in this book two editions ago, now has another visitor center in Cannonville, Utah. This location offers travelers good access to many of the monument's attractions.

Mary and I began our journey this time in Moab, Utah, where facilities for travelers are booming at an amazing rate. During our three nights in this small town we dined in a trio of restaurants that would be the envy of many larger cities. It can now be said with certainty that Moab is the good food hub for an area stretching south from Metropolitan Salt Lake City and Provo, Utah, all the way down to Flagstaff, Arizona.

Because history and culture of the High Southwest are a special emphasis of this book, we visited two cultural attractions in New Mexico, a state that has the highest percentage—28.6 percent—of residents who speak Spanish nationwide. The 22 acre National Hispanic Cultural Center in Albuquerque, New Mexico, with its evocative architecture, outstanding art museum, sculpture courtyard, performing arts center, library and genealogy center is well worth a visit.

Equally exciting to find, out on Museum Hill southeast of downtown Santa Fe, New Mexico, was the new Museum of Spanish Colonial Art where artworks and artifacts on exhibit exemplify a rich heritage spanning five centuries and four continents.

The High Southwest continues to be one of the most exciting places to travel in the United States.

May your Journey to the High Southwest be a memorable one.

ACKNOWLEDGMENTS

first I wish to thank my family, Mary, Rob, Dana, Chris, and Liz, for their support and encouragement. This effort would have been impossible without them. But I want particularly to thank Mary, whose unstinting effort helped make possible the timely completion of the last four editions.

I am deeply grateful to Julie Roberts for the fine illustrations she produced for the book.

Thanks go to Robbie Mantooth, a talented, energetic lifelong friend, for her assistance with this and other writing projects.

And thank you Mary and Jim Finney of Santa Fe, for being the most supportive and friendly hosts west of the Pecos.

There are some thank-yous not related to the tangible manuscript. I am extremely grateful to my parents, Pat and June Casey, who introduced me to the High Southwest. I am still in awe of my father's wonderful curiosity and special talent for befriending strangers, as he went knocking on unfamiliar pueblo or farmhouse doors. I am also indebted to my lifelong friend Jim Warram, who along with his parents invited me one summer to join them on a trip west. That memorable trip introduced me to the country west of the Rio Grande.

In the 1950s, when "Doc" (Dr. George Miksch Sutton) took some of us out to Oklahoma's Black Mesa country on the New Mexico border, he convinced us that the very western tip of the Oklahoma Panhandle was part of the High Southwest. There he taught us about mesas, buttes, and alcoves, and he introduced us to piñon jays, scrub jays, red-tailed hawks, and blue quail. I have had my eyes open ever since. In his sixties then, he shinnied up trees like a schoolboy to inspect bird nests, and he left us breathless and heaving behind him as he effortlessly negotiated steep inclines, probably with a twinkle in his eyes. Doc's timely suggestions about the early manuscript of this book's first edition before his death were most helpful.

I am greatly indebted to the many park rangers and park interpreters who patiently answered my many queries about the state and national parks and monuments listed in this book as well as the staffs of the region's many outstanding museums. I would also like to thank all of the authors mentioned in the bibliography whose works serve as part of the database for the book.

And thanks to the many readers of the previous editions of this book who not only expressed their appreciation of this kind of detailed travel guide but made many valuable suggestions about its revision. Some of these suggestions are included in this seventh edition.

INTRODUCTION

During several summers in the late 1940s, near the end of July when the Oklahoma sun had heated the asphalt to the point you could almost fry an egg on it and when even the largest of fans would not cool the bedrooms at night, we would pack the car and head for the high country in New Mexico. Sometimes on our way to Santa Fe or Taos, we went by way of U.S. Highway 66 through Clinton, Oklahoma; Amarillo, Texas; and Tucumcari, New Mexico, while at other times we headed west through the Oklahoma and Texas panhandles to Raton, New Mexico.

It was always the same. Early in the morning with the car windows rolled down as far as they would go, we began the long, hot daytime drive through the flat prairie, the superheated wind parching us to the bone. Occasionally the monotony was broken by a mirage ahead of us on the highway, where it actually looked like water was standing on the road. Or sometimes we would drive under an isolated cloud in the sky, a giant umbrella casting a protective shadow that screened us for a few miles from the sun's scorching rays. Although we headed west along what seemed to be a flat, straight road, we were actually gaining altitude slowly, mile by mile, so that by late afternoon we had gained more than 5,000 feet elevation. There it was hot, but not unbearably hot, for the dry country had finally wrung the last miserable bit of humidity from the air.

Just as the sun was beginning to set, the road began to climb noticeably, and we found ourselves in country altogether different from where we had been in the morning. We were now in a high desert surrounded by lofty mountain peaks looming in the distance. Immediately we flatlanders would try to spot patches of snow on those distant peaks, sometimes mistaking, in our eagerness, billowy white clouds for the real McCoy. The next thing we noticed was the sky. In the high, dry, clear air, it seemed bluer and brighter than we had known it, and it spread across the country with such immensity that it did not even look like the same sky we had at home. On the horizon that very blue sky dipped down to the earth, where it seemed to mingle with an infinite variety of multicolored landforms poking their tips right into its blue borders. As the road topped one high ridge after another, it seemed that we could see forever from those lofty viewpoints. There was a sense of boundless space and openness that was different from anything we had experienced before. Then, at some magic moment along that road as the sun made its magnificent exit behind the distant high mountains, the air suddenly chilled. For a few moments, exhilarated by the drop in temperature, we just gulped great deep breaths of that cool, high, dry air, pungent with the aroma of pine and sage. There in the deepening twilight and incredible silence of that big country, we knew we had reached the High Southwest.

I am not sure whether my love affair with the High Southwest began then at age ten with that first dramatic entry into the high country or whether it began earlier. For one day, sometime before that first trip to New Mexico, I had discovered, carefully wrapped and boxed in the attic of our home, a black pot that my parents had purchased in the late 1920s at one of the Indian pueblos along the Rio Grande north of Santa Fe. I recall being fascinated by the utter smoothness of that vessel's black, shiny surface. Over and over again my fingers traced the beautifully executed serpent design that encircled it, somehow trying to discover its meaning. I could not imagine how an object of such rare beauty could have been fashioned by hand from raw clay.

On my first trip to the High Southwest, I could hardly wait to visit that Indian pueblo to see how it was done. Sure enough, on arriving there I saw Pueblo Indian women hand-building and -decorating fine pots and firing them in open bonfires, just as their ancestors had done for nearly one thousand years before them. Those and other sights and experiences there left indelible impressions on my memory. One in particular stands out. In Spanish New Mexico that summer, I learned that the oldest public building in the United States was not along the East Coast but right there on Palace Avenue in **Santa Fe, New Mexico.** That jolting discovery fully awakened what must have been a dormant sense of prairie pessimism, for from that day on I never again fully trusted history books to tell it the way it really was. Later my pessimism seemed fully justified when I learned that the two oldest continually occupied villages or towns in the United States were not along the Atlantic seaboard as I had been led to believe but were

The Four Corners Area and North Central New Mexico

instead atop two high mesas, one in northeastern Arizona and the other in north-western New Mexico.

After that first summer I was hooked. I returned to New Mexico many times after that. And eventually I began journeying to the high desert and mountain country surrounding an area called the **Four Corners region,** where the borders of Utah, Arizona, Colorado, and New Mexico come together. In many ways this country was a continuation of the high country around Santa Fe and Taos. Dramatic thunderstorms pounded the ground on hot July and August afternoons, cooling and refreshing the air there just as they did in New Mexico. Pygmy forests of juniper and piñon were just as prevalent at certain altitudes there as they were in the Rio Grande Valley. I also found that the zoology and geology of both regions were quite similar. In both regions I walked isolated canyons, mesas, and mountaintops that offered a solitude I had never experienced before.

And there were cultural similarities too. Over time I learned that the ancient Indian culture in the Four Corners area, having given rise to the Pueblo civilization intact on the Hopi mesas today, also spawned the great Pueblo communities, which continue to flourish along the Rio Grande. Even the Navajo provided a link between the two areas. Their beginnings in the Southwest were centered not far from the Rio Grande. From there they eventually migrated west and settled in the Four Corners area where they live today. Historically the Spanish thought of the Four Corners high country as just another continuation of their New Mexico empire. They traversed its boundaries from one end to the other, dropping names wherever they went.

Within a few years I discovered that I had the same boundless enthusiasm for the Four Corners region that I had earlier for the Rio Grande Valley. I found myself visiting my favorite spots in both areas with relative frequency. Eventually I came to know all of the high country bounded on the east by New Mexico's Rio Grande Valley and on the west by Utah's canyon and plateau country as the High Southwest. To me it seemed to be an area that transcended state borders and local interests and begged to be explored as a whole. As time went on and I traveled more on this continent and beyond, the High Southwest became all the more precious, for I discovered that most of its exotic landforms and cultural features were not duplicated anywhere else in the world. Many of its indigenous people continue to live out a lifeway that has been in existence for almost a millennium, while some of its adopted residents have brought their sophisticated culture to its highest peak in the nationally recognized art galleries and the once well-known, prestigious opera house of the region. In many ways the High Southwest is a land of contrasts and paradoxes unparalleled anyplace else in the United States, perhaps in the world.

As interest in southwestern travel began to pick up, I was approached by several friends for travel advice to the High Southwest, since they had been unable to find a comprehensive traveler's guide to the region. About the same time, while having breakfast in Monument Valley one morning, I met several European travelers who told me of their frustration in trying to find a helpful, detailed, European-style guidebook to the Southwest's high country. And not long after that, on a busy

August weekend in Santa Fe, I took note of the large crowds there. It occurred to me that many of the people who returned there year after year possibly did not venture to other areas of the High Southwest because the last page of their guide-books ended just south of the plaza.

So I decided to write this book. It offers to the reader the broader perspective of someone who loves that high desert and mountain country yet who is an outsider. That perspective helps transcend local interests and state boundaries and allows for a unified approach to the High Southwest as a single geographic and cultural entity. So finally there is a traveler's guide that places most of the scenic and historical sights of the High Southwest between the covers of one book. The material included generally represents a balanced presentation of my favorite places to visit, which are easily accessible by the standard family automobile or by short walking or hiking trails.

The selected sights range from Santa Fe and Taos on the east to Bryce Canyon National Park on the west, and from Arches National Park on the north to the Hopi mesas and Flagstaff on the south. It covers some of the highest of the high country, from Red Mountain Pass, elevation 11,018 feet, and Telluride, Colorado, elevation 8,744 feet, to one of the lowest elevations of the high country, at Moab, Utah, elevation 4,000 feet. The book touches on Flagstaff, Arizona; Durango, Colorado; Santa Fe and Taos, New Mexico; and Mesa Verde National Park, Colorado. Yet it also details some of the more remote areas, including Grand Staircase–Escalante National Monument, Capitol Reef National Park, and Dead Horse Point State Park in Utah.

But not everything is included. I take full responsibility for omitting certain sights from this book, such as the Grand Canyon. The Grand Canyon is so well known, has had so much written about it, and is so heavily visited that it needs no further boosting from this or any other book. Although Chaco Culture National Historic Park is briefly mentioned in this guide, a detailed account of its ruins and how to see them will be added to future editions when a better all-weather road to the area is constructed. The wonderful high-mountain country around Red River and Eagle Nest, New Mexico, has been bypassed in favor of similar but higher-mountain country in southwestern Colorado. But that does not mean you cannot go there!

Besides the touring, accommodations, restaurant, and shopping sections of this book, I have tried to broaden the reader's perspective by detailing the **geologic and natural history** of some areas, while flushing out the **historical and cultural roots** of others.

Although it is possible to make a whirlwind trip and see all of the sights listed here in less than three weeks, most people will want to focus on the areas that interest them. Consequently I have divided the High Southwest into **four touring sections** that reflect what I feel are the major interest features of each region. **Section 1** details the exotic landforms for which the High Southwest is perhaps best known. The most intense concentration of these occurs in southeastern Utah. That section contains a geologic primer that will aid you in understanding what you see there, as well as in some of the other parts of the High Southwest. **Section 2,** in addition to providing a detailed touring and ceremonial dance and festival guide to the area's indigenous inhabitants, also details the history of their Indian ancestors who lived in the area. Nowhere in America can you experience both Indian past and present so acutely as on the Hopi mesas and the Navajo reservation in northeastern Arizona. But for many the High Southwest is intimately tied to the image of the American western frontier, including its prospectors, miners, and cowboys and its lofty mountains. Southwestern Colorado, the focus of **Section 3,** is the geographic location that evokes the history and ambience of the frontier West better than any other place I know, and it is there that the grandeur of the Rocky Mountains reaches its climax. **Section 4** concentrates on the cultural legacy of the Spanish, the first European explorers and settlers to penetrate the American heartland. You will see poignant evidence of their dynamic past wherever you go in north central New Mexico's Rio Grande Valley, and you will witness the unique lifestyle of their Hispanic descendants, who are the majority population in many of the towns there.

The **tours** in this book are, of course, suggested routes, and you can either use them or, with the information provided and a copy of the Automobile Club of Southern California's useful map "Guide to Indian Country" (see Bibliography: "Maps"), devise your own touring routes. The **narrative accounts** detail both some of the more adventurous and some of the less well-known sights. They are written to provide you with the particulars of an in-depth experience so that from the comfort of your armchair you can gain a good sense of what to expect in the High Southwest. Although the narratives are based on actual experiences and give you some idea about what can be accomplished in a half day or full day of touring or hiking, you may prefer to see more or less in a given period of time.

So choose the section or sections of the High Southwest that interest you, and proceed to use the enclosed maps and the **"Travel Access"** chart (see Practical Hints section) to help you make your plans. That chart and most of the information you will need to have a safe and successful journey are located in the **"Practical Hints"** section at the back of the book.

Although the Southwest tourist boom has brought higher prices to the region in general (and particularly to Santa Fe, Taos, Telluride, Flagstaff, and Durango), you will still find the Southwest a reasonably affordable place to travel. This book lists a wide range of accommodations, from inexpensive to very expensive. But its main focus is on moderately priced lodging that evokes the atmosphere of the Southwest.

No attempt has been made to rate the quality of the lodging except to point out that the author and his family and friends have either stayed in or inspected nearly all of the listings and found them to be more than satisfactory for the price category they represent. **Lodging** is rated according to the price of a room for two with private bath (before tax) during the more expensive peak months. These rates may escalate during major holidays or when popular local festivals and events are going on or during the height of the ski season in towns like Telluride, Colorado, and Taos, New Mexico. In categorizing bed-and-breakfast lodging prices, a downward adjustment has been made to their daily rates to place them on a par with traditional hotel and motel accommodations that offer no or minimal breakfast.

Dude ranches and resorts that offer the American Plan (meals and lodging) are not rated. With all establishments it is wise to ask about cancellation policies and how late in the day a credit card guarantee holds a reservation. The peak travel season in most areas is from Memorial Day through Labor Day, but April, May, September, and October are increasingly busy times. Make advance reservations for the peak season for some of the more remote locations like Monument Valley, the Hopi reservation, Canyon de Chelly, et cetera, where accommodations are sparse. Rooms are generally available in early spring and late fall without advance reservations, providing there are no special events attracting travelers to the area. Many of the lodging establishments give special rates to travelers affiliated with organizations like the American Automobile Association and the American Association of Retired Persons. The discount may be enough to offset much of the tax added to your bill. Mention your affiliation at the time you make your reservation.

The categories for lodging as outlined above are as follows: inexpensive, up to $90; moderate, $90 to $135; expensive, $135 to $200; and very expensive, $200 and up.

I have included many **Web sites** from which you can obtain e-mail addresses, as well as numerous **fax and toll-free telephone numbers.** If the toll-free number has changed, dial (800), (888), (866), or (877) 555-1212 to obtain the new number. Toll-free numbers and particularly Web site listings with their accompanying e-mail addresses may change often.

I have tried or visited nearly all of the cafes and restaurants listed here. Some have been favorites over the years. In many you will be able to enjoy the **food** of the region, including some interesting and well-prepared Southwest American Indian and Spanish New Mexican dishes. Although the price of a meal will vary according to what and how much you eat at a particular restaurant, a rough guideline to prices is presented throughout the book, based on the price of a three-course dinner for two (entree plus two of the following: salad, appetizer, or dessert) not including alcoholic or nonalcoholic beverages, tax, or tip. Only establishments that have a dinner menu are rated. Breakfast and lunch establishments and short-order eateries that are open in the evenings are not rated.

The categories for dining are as follows: inexpensive, up to $38; moderate, $38 to $68; and expensive, $68 and up.

It is my fondest hope that this will be a useful, hands-on guide for new travelers to the area. And, of course, I hope that veteran Southwest travelers will also find the book useful for planning trips to areas they had thought were too far away or too remote to visit, short-circuiting the several decades it took me finally to make the complete circuit of the High Southwest. If you see most of the sights that are listed in any one section of the book, you will have had a genuine in-depth High Southwest experience, which will include many places and tidbits of interesting and useful information not included in other guidebooks.

So after reading this book, should you travel to the Rio Grande Valley or the Four Corners area, keep an eye out for the ubiquitous High Southwest spirit. For whether you ride a horse at sunset through the sagebrush near Taos Mountain or take the chill out of an August evening with a piñon fire laid in the adobe fireplace of your casita in Santa Fe, whether you eat a lunch of posole, fry bread, and mutton stew in the company of our nation's first citizens on the Hopi mesas or take a walk up Capitol Gorge at Capitol Reef National Park to soak up the solitude there, you will be experiencing that omnipresent spirit of the American High Southwest, a spirit that well may hook you for a lifetime!

For this guide considerable effort has been made to provide the most accurate information available at the time of publication, but readers are advised always to check ahead, since prices, seasonal openings and closings, and other travel-related factors do change over time. Neither the author nor the publisher can be held responsible for the experiences of readers while traveling.

ONE

SOUTHEASTERN
UTAH

Canyon Country

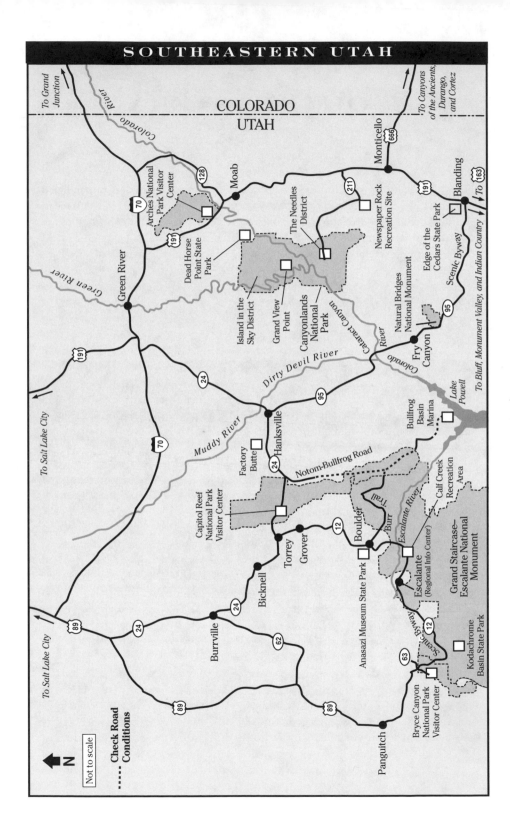

COLORADO
UTAH

To Grand Junction

To Canyons of the Ancients, Durango, and Cortez

Colorado River

Green River

Green River

To Salt Lake City

Moab

Monticello

Blanding

To Bluff, Monument Valley, and Indian Country

Arches National Park Visitor Center

Dead Horse Point State Park

The Needles District

Newspaper Rock Recreation Site

Edge of the Cedars State Park

Island in the Sky District

Grand View Point

Canyonlands National Park

Cataract Canyon

Natural Bridges National Monument

Fry Canyon

Colorado River

Scenic Byway

Dirty Devil River

Muddy River

Hanksville

Factory Butte

Bullfrog Basin Marina

Lake Powell

Notom-Bullfrog Road

Capitol Reef National Park Visitor Center

Calf Creek Recreation Area

Burr Trail

Escalante River

Grand Staircase-Escalante National Monument

Torrey

Grover

Boulder

Anasazi Museum State Park

Escalante (Regional Info Center)

Bicknell

Burrville

Kodachrome Basin State Park

Scenic Byway

Bryce Canyon National Park Visitor Center

Panguitch

To Salt Lake City

Not to scale

Check Road Conditions

N

128
70
191
211
666
163
95
191
24
95
24
70
24
12
12
62
63
89
24
89
89

INTRODUCTION

If you like scenic landscapes and are a naturalist at heart, the Utah Canyon Country awaits you with a store of wonders unparalleled anywhere else in the United States. Southeastern Utah is one of the few places in the world where the casual traveler can become acquainted with the history of the earth's crust in an effortless way, on paved roads that penetrate its heart. But if you like adventure, there are well-laid-out walking trails through this slickrock wilderness that will fill you with excitement at every turn.

You will explore zigzag canyons leading so deep into the earth that the walls reveal in their well-defined rock layers 300 million years of the history of the earth's crust. You will walk to the rims of sandstone canyons where, thousands of feet below, ancient rivers meet and flow on to the Pacific Ocean more than 1,000 miles away. In the bottom of some of those canyons, you will see weirdly eroded landscapes that you never imagined possible. Stone archways more than 100 feet high span desert expanses up to the size of a football field. Windows, larger than any human-made windows you have ever seen, open onto panoramas that defy the imagination. And you will see natural stone bridges spanning more than 100 feet that have already outlasted all the bridges human beings have ever made in Utah or any other place in the world.

The dry climate holds back the growth of vegetation, exposing the clear skeletal shapes of the rock. When vegetation does survive this aridity, it does so with a rare dignity and beauty. The barrenness around it sets it off like a piece of well-displayed art in a fine gallery. Birds, lizards, and insects are easily seen and identified, as there is so little cover to camouflage them. But more than anything else, you will see rock—for the earth's crust is sculpted to an infinite variety of shapes in this natural showcase. If you have ever wondered about the geologic forces that have shaped the earth, southeastern Utah offers a classroom rich in example. Although good paved roads lead to many fine sights, this is country where you will want to walk the trails to touch, feel, and examine each chapter of the story that nature has spread out for you.

Technically speaking, the land you will be traveling in southeastern Utah is part of a giant elevated rock table called a plateau. This giant plateau, almost as large as California and containing 130,000 square miles of high desert, is called the Colorado Plateau. It extends across the borders of four states—Arizona, New Mexico, Colorado, and Utah. The Colorado River for which it was named runs through it and drains it of its water. This high table land is at an average 5,000 feet above sea level. It is encircled on the north and east by the Rocky Mountains, while to the south and west the table edge drops hundreds of feet in stair-step fashion to the lower deserts and basins. But nature did not stop after building the

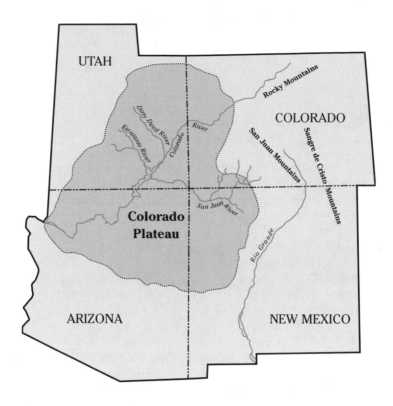

Colorado Plateau

main plateau. In southern Utah others soon formed atop the mother plateau, piggyback-style, producing some of America's highest—the Paunsaugunt more than 9,000 feet elevation and the Aquarius at 11,600 feet elevation. The Paunsaugunt contains delicately carved Bryce Canyon, while the Aquarius is home to Boulder Mountain, offering spectacular panoramas over the surrounding high deserts.

But the heart of the Colorado Plateau's scenic lands rests at lower elevations in southeastern Utah's Canyon Country. There, in 28,000 square miles of canyon and rock wilderness, nature has wrested unbelievable beauty from sheer rock. The scenery is so varied that a stunning array of names has been coined for the area. These include Red Rock Country, Sliprock Country, Standing Up Country, Rim Rock Country, and Panoramaland. Attesting to the uniqueness of the region, four national parks have been created to acknowledge the superb scenery and preserve it. A map of southeastern Utah reads like a who's who of national parks and monuments as it delineates Capitol Reef National Park, Canyonlands National Park, Arches National Park, Natural Bridges National Monument, and Grand Staircase—Escalante National Monument, while Bryce Canyon National Park flanks its western border.

Not allowing all of the scenic lands in its southeastern quadrant to be gobbled up by the federal government, the state of Utah has stepped in and preserved for your benefit even more scenic landscapes. Near Moab is a little-known slumbering giant, Dead Horse Point State Park, whose vistas over Utah's Colorado River Canyon easily rival those of the Grand Canyon to the south. Meanwhile Anasazi State Park at Boulder, Utah, and the Edge of the Cedars State Park at Blanding, Utah, preserve the heritage of the first people who roamed these canyons.

All of these parks are interconnected by good paved roads that pass through lands often as scenic as those set aside for preservation. This intense concentration of scenic parks in a relatively small area means that you can easily travel from one park to another in just a few hours. As you travel Utah's scenic roads, you will conclude that mile for mile southeastern Utah contains the most intense concentration of incredible, multicolored landforms in the world. You will see cliffs and buttes protrude skyward to heights that surpass the Sears Tower in Chicago and that dwarf the Eiffel Tower in Paris. Conversely you will see canyons that draw your eyes as far down as some mountains will pull them up, noting as some have said that much of the scenery in this corner of Utah's Canyon Country is "upside down."

Besides all this, southeastern Utah is a photographer's paradise. There even the most amateur of photographers come away with dramatic photographs of nature's handiwork. Professional photographers find ever-increasing challenges each time they visit. Tourists of all ages from many places enjoy this country. Of the nearly 1.5 million people who visited Bryce Canyon National Park during a recent year, several hundred thousand were from abroad, most coming from Europe and Japan. As you travel the scenic byways of southern Utah, you will hear visitors gathered in cafes, motel parking lots, and campgrounds talk about rocks, sunsets, sunrises, and vistas with such excitement that you would think they were talking about the final game of the World Series. You too may become a southeastern Utah fan after you follow the guideposts laid down in this section.

HISTORY

Although wonderfully scenic, the land in this area has often been too harsh for people to endure. Southeastern Utah is sparsely populated. The towns are small and have a "frontier" air about them. The ancient Indians, the early Mormon settlers, and the uranium "boomers," in that order, have left their mark on the land. Remnants of those past cultures are visible today. To aid in understanding those relics from the past and to gain a better understanding of the impact of human habitation on this region, some historical guideposts are helpful.

The first known inhabitants were Indians of the so-called Fremont culture, named by modern historians for the river that first attracted the Indians to the area. That ancient river, the Fremont River, was named for the American explorer John C. Frémont. The Fremont culture generally is regarded as a subdivision of the Ancestral Puebloan or Anasazi culture, most of whose people occupied Mesa Verde and other sites to the southeast. But the Fremont Indians lived farther to the north and west, occupying this region from approximately A.D. 950 to sometime before 1200. They grew corn and made dwellings and storage houses like the Ancestral Puebloans did. But unlike them, the Fremont People wore moccasins rather than sandals and were more dependent on hunting. Their dwellings, like the pit houses at Mesa Verde, were constructed by digging a hole in the ground. Then they placed basalt boulders in a ring around the pit. These served as a foundation for rock walls and corner posts, which supported the roof. They built storage houses for corn and other food high in the cliffsides.

You may see examples of these granaries along Calf Creek near Escalante, Utah, on the Hickman Bridge Trail at Capitol Reef, and at the Moki Ruin turnoff from Utah Highway 24, east of the Capitol Reef visitor center. Early archaeologists thought the small storage houses were the dwellings where the Indians lived and concluded that the people who lived in them must have been very small. They called these early people *Moqui* or *Moki*. The term is thought by some to have been derived from a Paiute Indian word meaning "little people," while others believe it is a term that drifted north from the Hopi mesas (see Section 2, "The Hopi: A Long and Continuous Past"). The term is still used today to label some of the remains of the Fremont culture. Possibly because of drought, internal conflicts, or fear of hostile marauding tribes, these people left southeastern Utah around A.D. 1200. It is thought that they migrated to the south, where they probably mingled with the Ancestral Puebloans, who are believed to be the forerunners of today's Pueblo Indians. The Fremont Indians left behind many fine examples of their culture through the medium of petroglyphs. You may see these on canyon walls in the Capitol Reef area, in the Escalante Canyon system near Calf Creek, and along the Colorado River near Moab, Utah.

Between the time the Fremont Indians left this area in the late 1200s or early 1300s and the time of the first white contact in the late 1700s there are many blank pages of history. It is thought that sometime after A.D. 1000 nomadic Indian tribes, hunters and gatherers from the Great Basin—that huge desert area to the north and west—migrated to the higher plateau land. It is possible they were responsible for forcing the Fremont people to abandon the area. These nomads are thought to be the forebears of the Utes and the Paiute Indians. The Utes claimed most of eastern Utah, but the Paiutes, who ranged over much of southwestern Utah, also pushed east as far as the Capitol Reef area, which they used for seasonal camps from 1600 on.

When the Ute Indians attacked Taos, New Mexico, in 1716, the Spanish defeated them and took some of the captured Indians into slavery, to be sold in Mexico. Thus began a practice that was to continue well into the 1850s. After this battle the Utes maintained contact with the Spanish traders, later acquiring horses, which allowed them to dominate the Paiutes. With horses they became aggressive raiders, not only stealing more horses and livestock but also stealing or buying Paiute Indian women and children for the flourishing Mexican slave trade. The Paiute women and children sold as slaves were used as domestics in New Mexico and New Spain. In return the adaptable Utes received wool blankets, horses, and guns or "thundersticks" with which they later exacted tribute from the Mexican traders along the Old Spanish Trail. With their aggressive actions they were able to so successfully fend off white settlement in southeastern Utah that the earliest permanent white community was not established until 1877, more than one hundred years after the first white people had entered the area.

The first documented white contact in Canyon Country came in 1765, when Juan María Antonio Rivera, under orders from the governor of New Spain in Santa Fe, New Mexico, led a prospecting and trading expedition north into Ute country. The route he established from Santa Fe into what is now southwestern Colorado became the eastern leg of the route later known as the Old Spanish Trail. It is believed that Rivera reached the Colorado River near the vicinity of today's Moab, Utah.

Eleven years later the priest at Zuni Pueblo, Fray Francisco Silvestre Vélez de Escalante, and his superior, Fray Atanasio Domínguez, set out from Santa Fe with a small expeditionary force. This group of ten, including the two priests, sought to find a land route for the establishment of a road from Santa Fe to Monterey, California, the two far-flung Spanish provincial capitals. They followed Juan Rivera's route into Colorado near the current towns of Durango and Dolores. They continued in a northerly direction until reaching what is now northern Colorado. From there they went westward to Utah Lake. At Utah Lake they hoped to traverse southward to the latitude of Monterey and head west to California. But with winter fast approaching, they gave up and headed back to Santa Fe five months later. Except where they crossed the Colorado River near what is now Glenn Canyon Dam at Lake Powell, they made a complete circle around Canyon Country. The maps from this great circle tour into Uteland, which were made by Bernardo de Miera y Pacheco, were published in 1811 by a German scientist, Alexander von Humboldt, who had come to New Spain from Germany around

1804. Although he never visited New Mexico, he did have access to the data supplied by the Spanish explorers, such as Pacheco, as they returned to Mexico City. His maps were instrumental in stimulating new interest in the region, as New Mexican traders spread into the recently discovered and mapped country and stepped up trading with the Utes.

By this time there was great interest in establishing a land route between Villa Real de Santa Fe de San Francisco (Royal Town of the Holy Faith of Saint Francis), known today simply as Santa Fe, and El Pueblo de Nuestra Señora de la Reina (Town of Our Lady the Queen of Angels), better known as Los Angeles. A number of variations on the Domínguez-Escalante route into Utah were tried in attempts to shorten the distance. Meanwhile routes from Utah west to California were being explored. It is not known precisely when or by whom the important shortcut through southeastern Utah was discovered. But finding the practicable crossing of the Colorado River near today's town of Moab, Utah, allowed the traders to bypass the difficult terrain of central and northern Colorado. The new route may have been discovered by Manuel Mesta, who at age seventy-five led an expedition deep into Ute Country in 1805. Some believe the honors should go to the Arze-Garcia party of 1813, while others credit the American mountain men for discovering this important shortcut. The result was a 1,200-mile route that came to be known as the Old Spanish Trail.

Although it was described as the longest, crookedest, most arduous pack mule route in the history of America and took more than two months to negotiate, the trail served as a major trade route for more than twenty years. Mules loaded with New Mexican woolens went west to San Gabriel and Los Angeles, while horses and mules from California were driven to Santa Fe. Paiute Indian slaves went both directions. By the end of the Mexican epoch in 1846 and the beginning of the California gold rush in 1848, this rugged trail, which had been forged segment by segment over several decades by brave and hardy souls representing a triad of cultures, fell into disuse as other, better routes to the West were established. But segments of the trail continued to play a role in Canyon Country history. Trappers, Mormon settlers, explorers, and scientists used it as a gateway to some of the remotest land in America.

With Spanish colonial restrictions removed after the independence of Mexico in 1821, American beaver trappers and mountain men began entering the Colorado Plateau and Canyonlands area in increasing numbers. In 1847 Brigham Young led his Mormon (Church of Jesus Christ of Latter Day Saints) followers west to settle in northern Utah. This area had been mapped only three years earlier as a result of a federal government expedition led by John C. Frémont of the U.S. Corps of Topographical Engineers. Frémont returned to the Colorado Plateau to explore the region of Canyon Country from 1853 to 1854 in his search for a shorter transcontinental railway route. During that expedition he mapped and surveyed parts of southeastern Utah, one of the last landmasses in the United States to be explored.

In 1855 the first white settlement in southeastern Utah was attempted when Brigham Young sent forty-two men down the Old Spanish Trail to the current site of Moab, Utah. On arriving in mid-June they immediately built a stone fort, dug irrigation ditches, planted crops, and began fulfilling their mission of preaching to the Ute Indians. This settlement, with all it implied, was too much for the Utes. Six months after they arrived, these hardy Mormon pioneers abruptly left and abandoned their settlement when three of their members were shot and killed outside the fort by a band of Elk Mountain Utes. It was twenty-two years later before another settlement was attempted in the area. That attempt stuck, giving birth in 1877 to the town of Moab, Utah, which would later become the county seat of Grand County, Utah.

In the late 1850s and 1870s, a number of trailblazers, cartographers, and geologists came into this area, recording what they saw. For the first time they recorded in their journals the scenic beauty of the area's unique rock jungles. They wrote in awe-inspiring terms of the beauty that abounded everywhere. One of these visitors was John Wesley Powell, who navigated and mapped more than 1,000 miles of the Colorado River in its serpentine and treacherous course from its source in Wyoming southwestward through the Grand Canyon. He left names on the land wherever he went. At one point, near today's Capitol Reef National Park, Powell's men saw the mouth of a river. One of the men wondered if this was a trout stream. His comrade is reported to have replied that it was not fit for trout because it was such a "dirty devil." The name stuck. The river became known as the Dirty Devil River. But unknowingly Powell had given different names to two different sections of the same river. In an earlier expedition along the Old Spanish Trail, some of his men had found an abandoned cache along a riverbank, the remnants of the earlier Frémont expedition. In honor of that group, they named the river the Fremont. Today the confusion continues. The upper section of the river is called the Fremont, while the lower segment just below where the Muddy River (also known as Muddy Creek) dumps its silty load is called the Dirty Devil.

Prospectors looking for gold entered southeastern Utah as early as the 1870s. The main route through the impenetrable rock barrier known as Capitol Reef was by way of a narrow passageway known today as Capitol Gorge. In the gorge the cliff walls rise hundreds of feet as the channel narrows to less than 20 feet. As the prospectors passed through, many carved their names on the cliff walls. For decades afterward many of the early pioneers inscribed their names on the same rock walls. Today those walls full of signatures, having withstood the test of time and the adversity of the elements deep in the protected gorge, are known as the Pioneer Register. Nearby and hundreds of years older are some Indian petroglyphs, telltale drawings reminding us who the first "pioneers" really were.

After the prospectors came the stalwart Mormon pioneers who began to settle in the Capitol Reef area along the Fremont River in the 1880s. Two structures remaining there today, Behunin Cabin and Fruita School, are testimony to the presence of the early white farmers who settled there. Later some of Capitol Reef's serpentine blind canyons served as hideouts for Morman polygamists, or cohabitationists, as they came to be known, who fled from the law. Today you may walk up remote Cohab Canyon, named for the fugitives who sought seclusion in its hidden recesses.

In the 1870s another Mormon pioneer, Ebenezer Bryce, built a cabin on a tributary that drained a large amphitheater or canyon of eroded rock. He has gone

Behunin Cabin, Capitol Reef National Park

down in history for his remark that the rock jungle near his homestead was a "helluva place to lose a cow." Not only that, but it was a marginal place to raise a cow, taking 200 acres of land to feed one cow or a few sheep. Bryce's rock jungle is known today as Bryce Canyon. He and other early settlers left this land of abundant rock and meager grazing long ago, for the sparsely vegetated land soon became overgrazed and increasingly subject to devastating floods known as "gully washers." The life on this land was too difficult for homesteaders. Time would prove that it was fit only for tourists.

But in other parts of southeastern Utah, the cattle industry thrived until the 1900s. It was given a boost by the arrival of the Denver and Rio Grande Western Railway in 1883. That line was a spur from the first transcontinental railway to link the East and West, which was completed with the driving of a golden spike near Ogden, Utah, in 1869. The train opened up Canyon Country to exciting times. Cattle rustling became even more profitable and, as one historian pointed out, if there were no cattle to rustle, there was always the train or a bank to rob. Like the Mormon cohabitationists, Butch Cassidy, Utah's own frontier Robin Hood, and other assorted outlaws hid out in the canyons of the Capitol Reef area. The Grand Wash Canyon was allegedly a favorite spot, as was a place east of there that was used so frequently as a hideout that it became known as "Robbers' Roost." Zane Grey, the famous western writer, has immortalized these rough-and-tumble days in several of his books.

By 1898 gold prospectors had discovered carnotite ore in the La Sal Mountains south and east of Moab, Utah. This greenish yellow ore, containing radon gas, vanadium, and uranium, began a small radium boom that ended in 1924. In the early 1900s a sample of radioactive ore from these deposits was sent to Madame Curie, who used it in her research on radium and radioactivity in France. After World War II, with the pressure of the Cold War, there was a push to find more uranium, and southeastern Utah became a target. Prospectors combed Canyon

Country in the 1940s and 1950s, but Charlie Steen, a down-on-his-luck Texas geologist, started it all in 1952. After several frustrating, hard-luck years of prospecting in southeastern Utah, he borrowed a drill one day in Moab to explore a hunch. He returned with an ore sample that must have shocked the Moab ore appraisers out of their boots. Steen had discovered a rich vein of uranium in his mine, soon to be called Mi Vida (My Life). This $60-million bonanza turned the peaceful Moab farm community of a few hundred souls into pandemonium. The boom had begun! The population of Canyon Country's largest town skyrocketed to more than 5,000. People lived wherever they could, in tents, barns, and even caves. After the uranium bonanza Moab settled back into a comfortable niche, until one of the world's largest supplies of potash was tapped in 1964. Once again Moab rode the crest of a miniboom. And when the potash industry leveled off, some of the economic slack was taken up by oil and gas exploration in several nearby areas. But that economic bright spot was dampened by the cyclical oil patch depressions.

To those visiting the area, it may not seem that industry has significantly marred the clean air of southeastern Utah. Yet old-timers say that the particulate-disbursing, power-generating, and coal gasification plants more than 100 miles to the south in northern Arizona have encroached on southeastern Utah's clear atmosphere.

Should more plants be built in the future, the pristine air that is this area's special province will definitely be threatened. On some days you can no longer see forever from some of southeastern Utah's former crystal-clear viewpoints. So do not wait too long to see Canyon Country. All of its wonder may not be there forever.

A GEOLOGIC PRIMER
TO SOUTHEASTERN UTAH

In addition to your appreciation of the beauty of the landforms in southeastern Utah, you may want to know more about the geology of the area. Rocks exposed to view in river gorges, steep canyons, high cliff faces, and soaring rock outcroppings have a fascinating story to tell. I traveled for many years in this country without studying the region's geology. That was a mistake, for when I finally boned up on the geology of the area, my appreciation deepened, making the land a friendlier, more interesting place to roam. Before, I saw cold, hard rock. Except for its shape I had little interest in it. Now when I see a sheer cliff wall in certain areas and recognize the Wingate formation, I immediately feel that I have found a trusted old friend. As a lay geologist I am not knowledgeable enough to identify all of the rock layers, especially when nature plays tricks and produces irregularities in the rock structure. But I am able to read some of the simpler stories the rocks have to tell. With a little practice you can do the same by having the following orienting text, figures, and charts at your fingertips. First comes a geologic history of the area. That is followed by a section focusing on three important rock features (shape, color, and distinctive surface characteristics) that are helpful in identifying specific rock and formation layers. By carefully observing these rock features and cross-referencing them with the chart in this chapter you should be able to identify many of the rock layers you see. Once you know the name of the rock layer, you can look it up in the appendix at the end of this section. There the prehistoric scenes of Canyon Country geology will emerge as you read how that particular rock layer was formed millions of years ago.

Geologic Overview

After walking a few miles in any direction in southeastern Utah's Canyon Country, you are apt to find yourself looking over the rim of an arroyo, a canyon, or a mesa, your forward progress stopped by the absence of land in front of you. You are confronted with a gaping chasm revealing many layers of rock in the side walls, descending to the depths below. One particularly dramatic and telling rim location is Dead Horse Point near Moab, Utah. There the role of time in the geologic process is illustrated graphically. From the rim of that 6,000-foot island in the sky, towering above the Colorado River 2,000 feet below, you are looking at nearly a dozen layers of rock that took about 100 million years to form. Focus your eyes on the Colorado River and its immediate banks and you are looking at a rock layer formed more than 275 million years ago.

As your gaze comes to rest on the rock directly under your feet, you might reflect that if you were standing there 170 million years ago, water from an ancient freshwater river would be flowing by your feet. It would deposit sand and silt that would eventually become the Kayenta sandstone you are standing on. But the stack of rocks under your feet and the rocks visible to you are only part of the original heap. At one time, beginning about 175 million years ago and ending less than 60 million years ago, there were another dozen layers that would have extended thousands of feet above where you are standing. At Dead Horse Point they have all eroded away over the past 10 million years, although near Bryce Canyon they are still intact. There you will walk on some of the very youngest rocks in Canyon Country, a mere 17 to 60 million years old.

So it has taken millions of years for most of the rocks you see in southeastern Utah to develop. Like a colorful, multilayered cake, one rock has been forming on top of the other for the past 275 million years. From the exposed banks of the Colorado River below Dead Horse Point State Park to the rim of Bryce Canyon, nature has created a rock pile thousands of feet high, containing about two dozen different rocks. The amount of time represented by the scenery boggles the mind and is almost incomprehensible to those of us living in a fast-paced world in which our patience is often tried by a delay of a few minutes or hours. But rock historians who understand the cadence of nature's pace use the word *period* to signify a unit of time lasting many millions of years, such as the Permian or Cretaceous Period. And they have coined the term *era* for a longer span of time encompassing several periods, like the Paleozoic or Cenozoic, to help us comprehend the enormity of it all.

Most of the rocks in the plateau stack are sedimentary rocks formed in an astounding variety of environments. These rocks began taking shape in ancient deserts, salty oceans, fresh lakes, boggy swamps, fertile deltas, vast floodplains, and the tidelands and streambeds that once covered this land. Sedimentary rocks are formed from grains or fragments of older rocks scrubbed off by erosion and washed by rivers downstream. Then, with accumulated masses of organic materials and sometimes volcanic ash, they were deposited at the edges of floodplains or shallow seas. Water seepage from above carried chemicals such as calcium and clay, which acted as cements binding the sediments together. But even with the proper ingredients, it took eons of pressure, heat, and chemical action to create the rocks we see today. Sediments containing particles of sand produce sandstone, while fragments of shells and other limy remains of marine creatures form limestone. Ancient mud and silt deposits, when well compacted, form shales. When less well compacted they form mudstones and siltstones. So paradoxically water, both fresh and salt, in copious quantities, has created the arid, skeletal landscapes you see today.

If the sediments that were laid down more than several million years form a layer of rock that is of uniform composition, that sedimentary rock is named both according to the sediments that gave it its origin and by the location where the rock was first studied. For instance, Navajo sandstone was named for the region where the rock was first studied, the Navajo reservation, and for the sediments forming the rock, ancient sands. But if the sediments making up a layer of rock are not of uniform composition so that the layer contains several different kinds of rocks, such as sandstone, siltstone, limestone, shale, or a conglomerate, the rock layer is called a "formation." Formations are named just like uniform rock layers.

For instance, the Kayenta formation is named after the location where it was first studied near Kayenta, Arizona.

But the climax of this geologic story does not begin until after the formation of the sedimentary rocks. It is a saga about the forces within the earth that began to shape the earth's crust. Twenty-two to 40 million years ago, molten rock pushed up the sedimentary rock of the plateau surface, doming it up thousands of feet, dotting the plateau with structures called laccolithic mountains. These scattered outcroppings, southeastern Utah's answer to the Rockies, include the Henry Mountains near Capitol Reef National Park, the Manti-La Sal Mountains east of Dead Horse Point State Park, and the Abajo or Blue Mountains south of Canyonlands National Park.

Lava boulders, Capitol Reef National Park

These mountains are the only mountains of igneous rock in the area. Igneous rock is formed from molten magma that has surfaced from within the earth. It is thought that these rocks contained the radioactive element uranium, which water leached from them and spread into the surrounding area where over millions of years it became a part of the sedimentary rock formations. And as if that was not enough, beginning about 10 million years ago, after the mountains were formed, dozens of consolidated layers of sedimentary rocks began to be slowly uplifted by forces in the earth's crust that are still not well understood. Over 5 million years at the rate of one-hundredth of an inch per year, the powerful pressures from within the earth raised thousands of square miles of flat lowlands from sea level to 4,000 feet and higher above the surrounding land.

These elevated flatlands are called tablelands and are the locations of many of the Southwest's high deserts or plateaus. During this time of upheaval, the land not only was raised to great heights but in some places was warped and bent and in other locations was tilted and contorted. In some instances huge blocks of the earth's crust fractured along fault lines and separated, opening the way for the further rising and development of higher but smaller plateaus like the Paunsaugunt. There on the Paunsaugunt, standing on the rim of Bryce Canyon, you may sense the full impact of this incredible story about the powerful forces within the earth. The infinite tonnage of the Claron Formation (formerly the Wasatch Group) rocks around the rim and below it were formed at sea level. Now they are with you, more than 8,000 feet above today's oceans.

The rest of the story, probably the last 8 to 10 million years, is of the final shaping of the structures you will see today. After the great uplifting of the plateau, the Colorado River and its tributaries—the Fremont–Dirty Devil, Green, Escalante, and San Juan Rivers—began to shape the land. Once a sluggish river, the Colorado became a forceful current. It began traveling mostly downhill from the newly formed Rocky Mountains at the eastern edge of the plateau and then picked up momentum as it descended, pell-mell, in its long journey down to the sea. With the land already fractured and ready for erosion, the increased flow of the river began the process of cutting down through the slowly uplifting sedimentary layers. It cut downward at approximately the same rate the land was rising so that today's riverbed that often is many thousand feet below the surrounding surface is, ironically, at about the same elevation it was when the whole process began.

In cutting down, the river exposed multiple layers of rock, creating the region's gorges and narrow slot canyons (canyons formed when streams cut through rock of the same composition from top to bottom) and initiating the development of the large-scale canyons. If you stand on the canyon rim at Dead Horse Point and look down, you will see the Colorado River as it flows through the canyonlands 2,000 feet below you. Draw an imaginary line out to the horizon from the rim where you are standing. For nearly 50 miles that line extends 2,000 feet above and parallel to the Colorado River bed below you. Once that empty space defined by your line would have been filled with solid rock, extending miles and miles to the horizon. Some have said that the real testament to the forces of erosion is not what you see, but what you do not see.

Throughout southeastern Utah erosion has created the vast, haunting spaces between canyon walls and the miles of open space between mesas and buttes that were once filled with solid rock. Literally hundreds of millions of tons of rock have been washed away by erosive forces. And it is still happening. It is estimated that the Colorado River, with its abrasive particles of sand and rock, erodes and washes away more than one million tons of sand and silt past any particular point every day. Even at that mind-boggling rate, the river washes away only 3 cubic miles of rock each century. These silts are now being deposited or laid down as sediments in today's freshwater lakes, filling Lake Powell and Lake Mead at alarming rates. After millions of years this sand and silt will be cemented into new sedimentary rock layers, to be studied and named by scientists of a future era.

But the river accounts for only part of the story of erosion by water. Although canyons are the children of rivers, the rivers do not play the only role. They may cut a gorge not too much wider than the river itself, but after that the forces of gravity and erosion take over. The river may undercut a cliff wall, but the root of a plant or tree or a wedge of ice may force a crack in the overhanging rock, which, with gravity's help, finally topples. In this way gorges widen into canyons. So the river begins the process by opening the sedimentary rock layers to weathering. Seasonal moisture then conspires to finish the job.

Even the final precision sculpting of arches, monuments, spires, pinnacles, mesas, buttes, and in some instances plateaus is mostly the result of falling seasonal water. So as many have pointed out, it is water that falls as snow over 10 million icy winters that seeps into fissures, freezing and expanding to further split the rock.

It is water in torrential downpours, driven by the gales of 10 million windy springs, and water falling in huge, heavy drops (as you may well experience in your summer travels) during the course of 10 million afternoon thunderstorms that pounds and abrades the rocks, which have no soil or vegetation to soften the blows. Rainwater courses down a path set by the cracks and fissures in the sedimentary rock. It scours the rock, dissolving the binding cements. It loosens grains of sand and washes them away, ever widening the cracks and fissures in the process, turning rivulets into gullies, gullies into washes, and washes into arroyos, lowering Canyon Country about 1 inch every 450 years. These are the major shaping forces for most of the scenery you will encounter.

But there are a number of phenomena you will see that are unexplained by this general summary. These include the lava boulders at Capitol Reef National Park, the unusual forces that created Bryce Canyon, and the great salt valley of the Moab region. Throughout Capitol Reef National Park, you will see round, black boulders strewn randomly about as though someone had turned loose thousands of bowling balls. The boulders are the result of volcanic activity that took place about 20 million years ago south and west of the park near Boulder, Utah. Although the lava flows did not reach Capitol Reef, black basaltic boulders did. They are erosional remnants of the lava that caps Boulder Mountain, also known as the Aquarius Plateau. They were pushed into the reef area by glacial meltwaters about 10,000 years ago after one of the last glacial ages. These forceful waters carried them many miles from their source, rounding and smoothing them as they tumbled along, depositing them in the Capitol Reef area. But nature did not stop its fanciful handiwork there. Many of the boulders, originally solid black in color, are now variegated, black and white. The white color that coats the boulder in interesting patterns is an alkali or lime coating that was deposited on those parts of the boulder's surface that have had contact with the soil over the past few thousand years.

Bryce Canyon is an exception to the rule that rivers are the mothers of canyons. At Bryce the Claron Formation, the colorful pink rock from which the hoodoos are carved and the pink cliffs are named, developed from iron-rich limy sediments between 63 and 40 million years ago. Later, that rock formation was subject to the same powerful uplift phenomenon from within the earth that affected the rest of the Colorado Plateau. As the earth rose, a series of north-to-south faults or zones of weakness in the earth's crust caused huge blocks of the crust to separate from one another. The Paunsaugunt fault was responsible for raising the land 2,000 feet above the surrounding level, creating the Paunsaugunt Plateau. This faulting and fracturing, rather than a river, opened the plateau cliffs to erosion, creating the unusual shapes you see today. Thus Bryce is not a true canyon but rather an escarpment at the very edge of a plateau. Erosion is eating away at the rim at a rate of about 1 foot every fifty years.

Most valleys are carved by the rivers that flow through them. But Moab Valley is different. Salt is responsible for creating its valley. Millions of years ago a salt deposit as big as Maryland and about 2.5 miles thick was laid down, a legacy of ancient landlocked seas. Lighter than rock and like putty when put under pressure, the salt ascended via numerous faults and other weak places in the sedimentary rocks, doming and warping their surfaces upward. The salt supported the rock much as a hand supports the glove that it fills. But as surface moisture seeped through the sedimentary rocks, it invaded the supportive salt structures, dissolving them. This removed the support from the surface, which then cracked and dropped, leaving vast, sheer-walled valleys or trenches. In areas like Arches National Park, the surfaces were cracked along the edges of the domes, in evenly spaced lines called joints. The forces of erosion have worked on these joints, gradually widening them to leave fins, vertical slabs of harder rock, standing in rows between open, eroded spaces. From natural recesses in these fins, erosion has caused the formation of arches.

Reading the Rocks

Now that you are acquainted with some of the ways sedimentary rocks are formed and shaped, the next step is to look at specific rocks and learn how to read their various clues. The accompanying chart (pp. 20–25) was devised to help in the identification of individual rocks or rock formations you may encounter. The chart details the age, thickness, color, characteristic shapes, surface features, fossil/mineral content, and some of the locations where the rocks can be seen. Having determined the identity of a rock layer that interests you, you may then turn to the appendix at the end of this section and read about environmental conditions prevailing when it was formed. You will discover that, paradoxically, the arid landscapes you see before you often had their origins in ancient freshwater lakes, saltwater seas, or verdant marshlands teeming with marine and other life-forms.

In order to identify a layer of rock, you must focus your powers of observation on four of its main features: shape, color, surface characteristics, and contents. By noting these features and cross-referencing them with the chart, you should be able to make a reasonably accurate identification. On the first try you may not be able to narrow the identification to a single rock or formation, since a number of the rocks have very similar features. But suppose you narrow your identification to two or three rocks on the chart. Most likely these rocks will appear at different levels in the geologic time column. If so, return to nature for more clues.

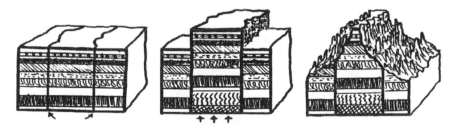

Bryce Canyon uplift and formation

Note the adjacent rocks above and below the rock you wish to identify. Cross-reference these features on the chart. A positive identification of one or both

Butte   *Mesa*

of the neighboring rock layers may resolve the ambiguity about the rock in question, for the latter will appear on the geologic time column just as it appears in nature. It can be identified as the rock just above, below, or sandwiched between the positively identified neighboring rock layers. It is not always possible to make a positive identification with the materials assembled in this book. There are complex geologic variables and exceptions to the usual patterns that this greatly simplified geologic primer does not accommodate. But this is a beginning to introduce you to some understandings that will, I hope, enhance your visit. If your interest goes beyond the scope of this primer, consult the geology references in the natural history section in the bibliography at the end of the book.

In order to read the rocks for clues to their identity, you must first look beyond their scenic beauty and focus on their physical characteristics. One of the most important features is rock shape. As you will recall, water erosion is instrumental in shaping the sedimentary rocks. But the precise shape sculpted by the water is determined by several factors within the rock layer itself. These include its thickness as well as how hard or soft the rock is. Harder rock layers contain more of the natural cements, such as iron oxide, silica, or calcium carbonate, while softer rocks contain fewer of these binding agents. In some rock layers the quantity of these natural cements varies throughout the rock so that some portions that are softer than others erode at a different rate, producing a variety of interesting shapes and in some instances, where the rock is very soft, creating pockets or tanks in the rock.

In addition to its hardness or softness, the shape of a particular rock layer is also affected by the hardness or softness of the rock layers immediately above and below it in the sedimentary rock stack. You will see these exposed alternating layers of hard and soft rock along the walls of canyons and on the steep sides and slopes of plateaus and mesas, formed either by faulting and uplifting of the land or by the action of a river cutting down on all sides of a landmass, leaving it elevated above the surrounding land. If the top of one of these elevated landmasses is composed of soft rock, it will erode away until a layer of erosion-resistant harder rock under it emerges to the surface, usually forming a flat protective cap over the rock layers below it. But since this cap may be many feet thick, it also serves as part of the vertical cliff wall.

Demoiselle

Monuments and spires

It is this flat-topped cap that gives this landform its name, because the Spanish thought that these flat-topped hills that were wider than they were high looked like tables or mesas. The slopes or sides of a mesa below the cap are often made of shales or softer sandstones. Over time even the durable cap of a mesa reduces in size, for as its softer base recedes with erosion, the edge of the cap rock is undermined. With nothing to support it and with the help of ice and root wedging, it eventually cracks, splits, and falls. As a mesa is shrunk in size by seasonal erosion, it may also be cut into smaller landforms by rivers and their tributaries. If these smaller mesa remnants are at least as high as they are wide, they are called *buttes*.

Further erosion may narrow a butte to a monument, tower, pinnacle, or spire. The shaft of a monument or spire is usually harder than the base on which it stands and, like a mesa or butte, is capped with a narrow rim of even harder rock. Erosion of the softer Claron formation rock under the cap may reduce a spire to a variety of interesting and weird forms called *hoodoo* rocks. Hourglass-shaped balanced rocks, delicate mushroom-shaped demoiselles, and strangely eroded pillars and pedestals are all hoodoo variants. Over time erosion finally topples hoodoo rocks to the ground. There they remain as boulders until further seasonal erosion demolishes them altogether, and they disintegrate into pebbles and finally into the sand you will walk on as you explore the surface of the Colorado Plateau.

Another example of the importance of hard-soft layering is in the formation of canyon walls. When canyon walls contain many alternating hard-soft layers stacked on top of one another, erosion proceeds at a different pace for each level, creating a stair-step effect as it shapes the sloping sides of the canyon. In Canyon Country sheer steep cliff faces of canyons are often of Wingate sandstone. Although it is topped by a rim of harder Kayenta sandstone, it rests on a base of softer Chinle formation rock, which erodes so easily that it undercuts the Wingate, leaving it extended unsupported in space. Eventually it splits off in giant pieces, leaving sheer, vertical cliffs.

Each layer of rock, then, erodes to characteristic shapes that aid in its identification. Other common shapes that aid in identifying a particular rock layer are as follows: badlands, rounded mounds, bluffs, ledgy cliffs, slopes, domes, fins, rounded walls, terraces, fluted cliffs, columns, ridges, towers, arches, windows,

Time	Rocks or Formation	Thickness	Sediments	Shape(s)
Cenozoic Era — Tertiary Period 63 million years ago	Claron formation (formerly known as Wasatch group)	600 feet	Limestones, siltstones, shale, sandstone	Spires, pinnacles, balanced rocks, intricate shapes (hoodoos)
Mesozoic Era — Cretaceous Period 135 million years ago	Mancos shale	3,500 feet	Shale with some sandstone and limestone	Fluted mesa cliffs, rounded mounds, badlands, smooth slopes
	Dakota formation	350 feet	Conglomerate, sandstone, shale	Low cliffs, bluffs, slopes
	Morrison formation	400 feet	Mudstone, shale, sandstone, volcanic ash	Hills, slopes, ridges
Jurassic Period 180 million years ago	Summerville formation	300 feet	Interlayered sandstone, siltstone, mudstone, shale, gypsum	Ledgy cliffs, slopes, open desert
	Entrada/ Moab tongue	150 feet	Sandstone	Low cliffs, sheer walled domes, petrified dunes
	Entrada/ slickrock member	350 feet	Sandstone, siltstone	Arches, rounded fins, domes, spires, bluffs, cliffs

Color(s)	Surface Features and Mineral/Fossil Content	Location(s)
Pink, red, white	Mammal bones	Bryce Canyon National Park.
Blue-gray, gray, black	Petrified wood, sea fossils (shark's teeth), quartz pebbles	Capitol Reef National Park. Between 8 and 30 miles east of visitor center along Utah Highway 24 to about 10 miles east of Caineville.
Light brown to white, gray, green	Fossilized oyster shells and ferns, petrified wood and bone, agate	Capitol Reef National Park. 12.5 miles along Utah Highway 24 from visitor center, then turn right on Notom Road 2 miles to see Dakota formation.
Variegated green, red, gray	Dinosaur bones, petrified wood and bone, agate, chert	I–70 and Utah Highway 24 junction and south of junction on 24 about 3 miles; east of U.S. Highway 191 just north of 191 and Utah Highway 313 junction; about 9 miles east of Capitol Reef National Park visitor center on Utah Highway 24 as road cuts through high ridge; and Wolfe Cabin area, Arches National Park.
Red-brown (definite brownish cast)	Ripple rock, mud crack casts, agate beds, thin horizontal bedding	12 miles south of Moab, U.S. Highway 191 cuts through this rock and at 14 miles appears to right of highway. Also, trail to Delicate Arch, Arches National Park.
White	Cross-stratified	Found in Arches National Park in Salt Valley and Klondike Bluffs areas and the top 4 feet of the crest of Delicate Arch.
Salmon, buff		Most of the arches in Arches National Park, including Delicate Arch; rock structures in Cathedral Valley, Capitol Reef National Park.

(continued on next page)

Time	Rocks or Formation	Thickness	Sediments	Shape(s)
Mesozoic Era — Jurassic Period 180 million years ago	Entrada/ Dewey Bridge member (related to Carmel formation)	100 feet	Siltstone, mudstone	Severely contorted shapes
	Carmel formation	650 feet	Siltstone, mudstone, shale, limestone	Red deserts, pedestals, or bases
Mesozoic Era — Triassic Period 230 million years ago	Navajo sandstone	850 feet	Sandstone (quartz sand)	Rounded humps; domes, knobs; sheer, high cliffs; butte forms; petrified dunes
	Kayenta formation	350 feet	Sandstone, shale, siltstone	Stone wall cap rock atop Wingate sandstone; ledgy slopes, small cliffs, natural bridges
	Wingate sandstone	357 feet	Sandstone	Sheer vertical walled cliffs with vertically cracked or fluted surface; towering spires; boulders litter slopes below

Color(s)	Surface Features and Mineral/Fossil Content	Location(s)
Dark red	Thin wavy bands of sediment layers, i.e., distorted horizontal layering or "wrinkling"	Arches National Park. In pedestal of Balanced Rock and in entrance of park, as well as in the Windows and Devil's Garden areas. Also, at base of Monitor and Merrimac Buttes along Utah Highway 313.
Gray-green to reddish brown	Occasionally cross-bedded	Not seen too frequently in this area. Forms the pedestal for Balanced Rock in Arches National Park. Also in outcrops 7.5 miles east of visitor center at Capitol Reef National Park.
Mostly white but may be lightly tinted with yellow, red, brown	Large-scale, high-angle cross-bedding; pterosaur and other tracks	Entire Escalante Canyon system. At Capitol Reef National Park, Capitol Dome, and base of Golden Throne. Buttes and domes rising above mesa at Dead Horse Point State Park and Canyonlands National Park. In Arches National Park, petrified dunes 6 to 6.5 miles from visitor center.
From whitish/grayish to dark reds and browns	Small-scale cross-bedding; dinosaur tracks	Throughout area caps Wingate sandstone cliffs; at Capitol Reef National Park forms Hickman Natural Bridge. Forms walkways at Dead Horse Point State Park and Grand View Point, Canyonlands National Park. Dinosaur tracks north and west of Moab on Utah Highway 279 (Potash Road).
Light orange to red-brown, pinkish	Often cross-bedded	Forms the high, sheer cliffs of Dead Horse Point State Park, Island in the Sky, Canyonlands National Park, and Capitol Reef National Park. High cliffs across highway from Arches National Park visitor center. Petroglyphs at Newspaper Rock, Canyonlands National Park region, are pecked on Wingate.

(continued on next page)

Time	Rocks or Formation	Thickness	Sediments	Shape(s)
Mesozoic Era — Triassic Period 230 million years ago	Chinle formation (includes Shinarump member)	650 feet	Shale, siltstone, mudstone, conglomerate, volcanic ash	Steep, ledgy slopes at base of Wingate cliffs; low, rounded hills
	Moenkopi formation	1,400 feet	Mudstone, siltstone, sandstone	Steep slopes with many protruding hard ledges; buttressed cliffs; low ridges; columns
Paleozoic Era — Permian Period 280 million years ago	Kaibab limestone	300 feet	Limestone	Deep in canyon walls
	White Rim sandstone	250 feet	Sandstone	Vertical or under-cut cliffs; balanced rocks, towers
	Cedar Mesa sandstone	1,200 feet	Sandstone	Vertical cliffs, natural bridges
	Cutler formation	1,400 feet	Sandstone, mudstone, shale	Strangely rounded walls, columns
Pennsylvania Period 310 million years ago	Honaker Trail formation	3,000 feet	Interlayered shale, limestone, sandstone	Near-vertical cliffs; narrow shelves, terraces

Color(s)	Surface Features and Mineral/Fossil Content	Location(s)
Variegated dark reds, browns, blue-green and gray-green	Marine fossils and fossilized plants, uranium	At Capitol Reef National Park and Dead Horse Point State Park and Canyonlands National Park, appears as grayish sloping base below Wingate sandstone cliffs. At Capitol Reef National Park, Shinarump caps Chimney Rock and makes up Twin Rocks. At Capitol Reef National Park, Slickrock Divide caps red Moenkopi. At location of Olyer Uranium Mine, Capitol Reef National Park.
Brick red (reddish brown)	Ripple marks, mud crack casts; occasional tracks	The base rock along highway between Fruita and Torrey, Capitol Reef National Park. Forms the base of Chimney Rock spire at Capitol Reef National Park. The ledgy slopes just above the white rim at Dead Horse Point State Park and Canyonlands National Park.
Grayish white		Visible only deep in canyon walls west of Fruita, Capitol Reef National Park, as viewed from Goosenecks Trail.
White	Cross-bedded layers	The White Rim as seen from Dead Horse Point State Park and Grand View Point, Canyonlands National Park.
White		White bands of the Needles, Canyonlands National Park. Base of north Sixshooter Peak and surrounding flatland, Canyonlands National Park.
Dark red		Along U.S. Highway 191, 0.5 mile north of Arches National Park entrance and north to Utah Highway 313 junction. Fisher Towers east of Moab. Red bands of the Needles, Canyonlands National Park.
Red, white, gray, or a combination of these	Marine fossils	Below Dead Horse Point State Park in Colorado River Gorge. Just beyond end of pavement of Utah Highway 279 (Potash Road), out of Moab.

Sandstone fins, Arches National Park

bridges, and pinnacles. Some of these shapes are self-explanatory, but a few need some elaboration.

A *badland* is a waterless area usually without vegetation, filled with monotonous, repetitive slopes and hills formed from soft, half-hardened rocks such as shales or limy siltstones. Badland topography has narrow gullies and sharp ridges and is often formed on the side of a plateau, hill, or mesa. You will see some incredibly beautiful badlands just east of Capitol Reef National Park near Caineville, Utah. You will also see giant rock walls with holes right through the middle of them. These holes are created by seasonal erosion and are called either arches or windows, depending on the perspective of the people who first discovered them. One person's "arch" might be another's "window."

Generally if the hole in the rock opens to the ground below, or if the hole is close enough to any of the rock's edges to influence its shape, it is called an arch. Windows are holes in the rock that are higher up from the rock's base. Their apertures are far enough away from the top of the rock that they do not affect the shape of the rock's edge. In Canyon Country arches form in Wingate, Navajo, Cedar Mesa, and Entrada sandstones.

The Entrada gives birth to most of the arches in Arches National Park. There the Entrada sandstone has been extremely fractured and jointed in the vertical plane by a variety of forces. Some believe that the vertical cracking in the Entrada began after the many layers of rocks that had previously formed on top of it eroded away. Experts think that the release of weight from above the Entrada caused it to slowly "rebound" or expand, thus creating many vertical cracks or faults in the rock. In other instances the joints or cleavage lines were thought to

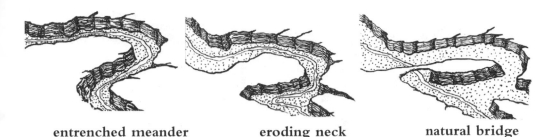

entrenched meander　　　　**eroding neck**　　　　**natural bridge**

Evolution of a natural bridge

have been caused by the collapsing of rock surfaces when their underlying salt support dissolved. But whatever the cause of the vertical fracturing, all are agreed that the next step involves seasonal erosion or weathering. Erosion eventually widens the cracks into narrow canyons, which separate the rock into vertical partitions called fins. *Fins* are relatively narrow sandstone walls that may be 100 feet tall and two or three times as long. Small recesses in the vertical surface of the fins are enlarged by erosion to formal coves or shallow caves. This process may occur on one or both sides of the fin. Eventually quarrying by water and ice persists until the fins are perforated. The perforations eventually enlarge to become graceful arches or high clerestory windows.

Natural bridges are also perforations of rock but are formed by running water instead of rain. These natural bridges occur on streams where rivers have gouged deep, winding curves known as *meanders*. The stream carves a great curve in its streambed, which comes back almost as if to meet itself before coursing on. At the point where it almost meets itself, it works away at the rock barrier to create a thin wall of rock between the curves. Eventually water on both sides of the thinning rock wall cuts and gouges away at it, until one day there is a breakthrough and the stream leaves its old curving course for a shorter, straighter one through the rock wall, flowing under a bridge of its own creation. Often you will see the old abandoned channel to the side of most natural bridges, as the river follows its new course under the bridge.

Window

After noticing the shape of the rock layers you wish to identify, note their color. This second identifying feature is a characteristic that makes Canyon Country rocks unique in the world. For nowhere else will you see the intense coloration of varicolored rock you see there. Rocks acquire color from the minerals they contain. Consequently a rock

Desert varnish

may have several colors, depending on where it is found. Iron in its many forms is responsible for most of the coloration you will see. In its oxide form it colors many of the red and red-hued rocks. In its other chemical states, iron creates some of the blacks, browns, yellows, grays, and greens you will see. Carbon gives a black or gray color. Manganese gives black, brown, red, and purple, while copper gives green. Grayish layers mixed with more colorful sandstone strata usually contain volcanic ash. This material fell on Canyon Country from the Arizona area, hundreds of miles south, where volcanoes were extremely active millions of years ago. White or whitish colors represent rock layers formed from relatively pure sand of beach, beach dune, or offshore sandbar origin. Red-hued layers within such sandstone represent land sediments rich in iron oxide that have been washed over the white sand by freshwater streams.

The white coloration you will see on some rocks is a superficial coating of alkali deposited on the rocks from the soil they have been in contact with. Sometimes alkali will coat level areas of the ground, giving the appearance of snow. Another colorful feature you often will see in Canyon Country is a huge streak of light brown to purplish black pigment on the side of a cliff. This phenomenon is called desert varnish. It looks like someone took a pail of varnish and poured it down the cliffside, leaving the face of the cliff dramatically streaked. Desert varnish at its darkest is thought to take thousands of years to form. Just what causes the black and brown streaks is somewhat of a mystery. The most common belief is that when it rains, a thin film of water rich in manganese and iron picked up from soils on the canyon rim or from the rock face itself streaks down the cliffs, coloring

Ripple rock   *Cross-bedded sandstone*

them. But more recent research has provided an alternative theory: Some think that much of the streaking on cliff walls is due to fine, windblown particles of clay that have settled on the rough, porous faces of the cliff walls. Then bacteria living there take manganese out of the environment, oxidize it, and emplace it on the rock surface, where it cements the clay and other particles that make up varnish to the surface. The result is a lustrous coating that resembles a burnished Pueblo Indian pot.

Rocks may also be colored by lichen or algae that grow on their surface, often imparting a green cast. And, of course, the colorful sandstones are greatly affected by the sunlight, giving off different hues at different times of the day. Some have said that at certain times of the day, the sandstones do not just reflect light but seem to glow as if they had their own light source.

Rock shape and color are the easiest identifying marks to use, since they can often be seen from a distance as you travel along. But the third rock characteristic requires a closer examination of the rock surface, for you will be looking for some identifying marks imprinted on the rock surface or captured within the rock millions of years ago. In your close-up examination of the rock layer, you will be looking for clues to the rock's history, such as cross-bedding lines, ripple marks, mud-crack casts, dinosaur tracks, and the fossils or minerals imbedded in the rock. When you find a rock surface feature, look it up in the rock identification chart under the "Surface Features" column. Then follow the column horizontally to the left to find the names of the rocks that are known to contain that feature. These rock features truly open windows on the prehistoric settings in which the rocks were formed.

When you walk up to a sandstone wall or a slab of sandstone on the ground, look carefully at its surface. The surface of some sandstone appears as if it was laid down evenly. But the surface of other sandstone is composed of many layers or strata sloping at different angles to one another, sometimes overlapping or interfingering. This cross-bedded or cross-stratified sandstone is thought to have been laid down during howling sandstorms millions of years ago when Sahara-like desert conditions prevailed in southeastern Utah. There, as winds changed direction, sand blew over already existing dunes, each new layer being deposited at a variety of cross angles to the previous layers. The cross-angle configuration in the sediments was then covered and preserved by the later formation of a shallow sea. Over time the protected sediments hardened to create the surface features you see today in these petrified sand dunes.

On the surface of some sandstone slabs, you may be fortunate enough to find ripple marks. This is a handsome feature with delicate, wavy ridges coursing across the rock surface. Mud and silt at the edge of a shallow sea, millions of years ago, were rippled by the water's action as it continuously advanced and retreated. The ripple pattern was preserved when it was buried under the forming sediments. After turning into rock it later was exposed to erosion, wherein the overlying sediments were washed off, revealing intact, after millions of years, the indelible evidence of an inland sea lapping at its own shoreline. From time to time you may see a surface feature resembling crinkled glass or mud cracks in a dry riverbed. These are fossilized mud cracks representative of shallow water conditions during prehistoric times. They formed in mud and silt sediments that were wet and then dried out, cracking in typical patterns. The cracks and depressions were filled by overlying sediments of a different type. When the sediments turned to rock and were exposed to erosion, the softer, original mud sediments washed away, leaving a cast of the cracks with raised edges in the more resistant covering layer. Other surface features to look for are dinosaur tracks, fossilized oyster shells and ferns, and petrified wood.

SEEING CANYON COUNTRY

Moab, Utah, is an excellent place to stay while seeing many of the sights in the eastern portion of this region. From there, by taking half-day or full-day trips, you can explore Arches National Park, Dead Horse Point State Park, Edge of the Cedars State Park, and two accessible areas of Canyonlands National Park. Moab is also headquarters for many raft trips down the Colorado River and is one of several meccas in the Southwest for mountain bikers.

But to see Natural Bridges National Monument; Capitol Reef National Park; the Anasazi State Park at Boulder, Utah; the sights around Utah Highway 12 Scenic Byway that are in Grand Staircase–Escalante National Monument; and Bryce Canyon National Park, it is best to spend several nights in the western portion of southeastern Utah. Utah Highway 12 Scenic Byway, one of America's most scenic paved routes, skirts the northwest boundary of southern Utah's newest national preserve, the 1.9-million-acre Grand Staircase–Escalante National Monument. This 100-mile-long stretch of highway leaves Grover and Torrey, Utah, near exotic Capitol Reef National Park; crosses through high forest and meadowland over the flank of Boulder Mountain (offering incredible views of the desert below); dips deep into the Escalante Canyon system; and winds through picturesque and remote southern Utah towns until it reaches Bryce Canyon National Park. And if you plan to visit Bryce Canyon, it is best to spend at least part of a day and a night there, since the changes in the sunlight best reveal its beauty. For more details about overnight stays at the National parks and monuments west of Moab, see "Staying There" at the end of this section.

Moab—The Hub of Canyon Country

Close to the **Colorado River** in a green valley surrounded by pink and red sandstone cliffs, Moab is on the way to or from most of the scenic sights of southeastern Utah. One of the lowest spots on the **Colorado Plateau** at 4,000 feet elevation, it is the largest town in Canyon Country, with a population of 4,600. It offers a wide range of good accommodations and several good cafes and restaurants. From early times Moab has exuded a western ambience because of its location on the edge of the slickrock jungles that surround it. It played host to prospectors of all sorts when the rocks around it yielded a wide variety of valuable minerals. And today Moab rides the crest of a recreational tourism boom fueled most recently by river runners and mountain bikers who find the surrounding slickrock trails irresistible.

Farmers, cowboys, and rustlers have walked its tree-lined streets along with outlaws like Kid Curry and Butch Cassidy. Cassidy once boarded the old Moab Ferry by force and took it across the Colorado River as he fled from the scene of his first bank robbery just over the border in Telluride, Colorado. With such an eclectic history, it is no wonder that Moab is the tolerant, open, and friendly place it is.

So do not hesitate to "bed down" a few nights in the western town of Moab. As you tour the national and state parks and monuments by day, you will return each evening to a bustling Utah town that now offers a plethora of attractive amenities. Away from the busy, urbanized sprawl of U.S. Highway 191, which bisects the town, you will find streets lined with giant old cottonwoods and in the spring fragrant catalpa. There you will see many of the early Mormon pioneer homes made either from hand-hewn red or brown sandstone blocks or from bricks molded from the local clays. These sturdy buildings must have offered a sense of security to the early settlers, who named their town after the Old Testament kingdom of Moab, a "far country" beyond the Jordan and Dead Seas, situated on the edge of Zion and surrounded by flat-topped mountains. The early Mormons must have felt that they too were occupying a remote country far from civilization as they established southeastern Utah's first white community smack-dab in the middle of the mysterious and foreboding Canyon Country in a valley ringed with flat-topped mesas.

Moab has three easily accessible and well-maintained parks. **Mill Creek Parkway** along Mill Creek provides several miles of an inviting, tree-shaded trail for pedestrians and bikers. From the west side of downtown, the paved trail passes under busy U.S. Highway 191 and stretches south to Cross Trails Park, finally ending at Rotary Park, which provides the usual park amenities, including picnic sites. The "City Park" or **Moab Park** is located several blocks west of U.S. Highway 191 at 400 North Street and 100 West Street. The Moab public swim center is also there, where, for a modest sum, you can take a dip on a hot summer day. Along Park Drive, on the south side of the park, is a large expanse of green grass rimmed by stately old trees shading a number of picnic tables under them. This oasis is a pleasant place to spend part of a warm summer evening slicing up and devouring watermelon purchased from one of the nearby grocery stores. More picnic sites are available in another tree-shaded park maintained by the Moab Lion's Club along the south bank of the Colorado River just east of U.S. Highway 191.

Take a brief tour of downtown Moab, where there are some interesting shops and craft stores, as well as the always instructive **Dan O'Laurie Canyon County Museum** at 118 East Center Street; (435) 259-7985. Moab is an excellent place to buy rock and mineral specimens, including petrified wood and certain fossilized plants and insects. You can purchase American Indian art and crafts, but you may also want to spend part of a day driving to **Blanding** or **Bluffs,** Utah, to the south and closer to Indian Country, where fine Indian jewelry, pottery, and weavings can also be found. For more information about Moab, write or visit **Moab Information Center,** a multiagency facility (National Park Service, United States Forest Service, Bureau of Land Management, Grand County Travel Council), corner of Main and Center Streets, Moab, Utah 84532; (435) 259–8825 or (800) 635–6622 or contact the Moab Area Travel Council, P.O. Box 550, Moab, Utah 84532; www.discovermoab.com.

Arches National Park

Arches National Park lies approximately 4 miles northwest of Moab just east of U.S. Highway 191. It contains in its 114 square miles of rock wilderness an amazing array of natural stone arches, windows, bridges, spires, and pinnacles. But the most remarkable features are its approximately ninety natural arches, whose varied and graceful spans are a photographer's delight.

Many of the more picturesque arches may be seen from the 18-mile paved road that starts at the visitor center and ends at Devil's Garden, elevation 5,355 feet. In addition, paved laterals from the main road lead into other parts of the park. From the visitor center the total round-trip driving distance of the main road and all of its laterals is 46 miles. Allow two and a half to three hours' driving time. At Devil's Garden and several other major stops in the park, relatively short, well-laid-out trails are available for your use. But because of the complex nature of the **Fiery Furnace Trail,** the recommended way to see this area of convoluted sandstone is to reserve space in person (there is a fee) on one of the twice-daily two- to three-hour-long guided walks (space is limited, so sign up early, as much as seven days in advance, at the visitor center).

A self-guiding booklet to the trails in the park that will lead you to many of its best-known sights and arches is available at the visitor center for a fee. One of these gems is **Landscape Arch.** It is the largest known natural stone span in the world, stretching more than the length of a football field. It is also one of the highest spans in the park, arching 105 feet above the ground. Yet another well-known arch in the park that has graced the covers of many magazines is unbelievably beautiful Delicate Arch. The foot trail leading to it is chock-full of excitement and scenic beauty at every turn and is the subject of the narrative that follows.

Many of the arches were known by the end of the nineteenth century. But it was not until the 1920s that a Hungarian-born prospector, Alexander Ringhoffer, became so enthusiastic about these scenic wonders that he alerted officials to their rare beauty, setting off a chain reaction that has led to their preservation. With the help of many local residents, the area achieved National Monument status in 1929 and National Park status in 1971. Since then the number of visitors to the park has been constantly on the increase. In a recent year nearly a million travelers enjoyed the park. In some years more than 15 to 20 percent of the visitors have been from other countries, the largest number coming from Europe, reminding us that the park's first enthusiast, the man who put Arches on the map, was European born. Information: Arches National Park, P.O. Box 907, Moab, Utah 84532; (435) 719–2299 (voice); (435) 719–2319 (TTY); www.nps.gov/arch.

Seeing the Park

After paying the entry fee, stop off at the visitor center. It offers a good natural history display and further augments this text on the formation of the arches and other geologic phenomena you will see. The center has many books on display that are for sale. Several free handouts about various aspects of the park are available for the asking. Above all, before you leave the center area, do not miss the

Landscape Arch, Arches National Park

excellent **Desert Nature Trail** nearby. Go out the front door and turn right. Walk a short distance toward the rising cliffs to the trail.

Although the common vegetation of the area is well marked, pick up a copy of the trail guide available there to read about some of the vegetation like single-leaf ash, squawbush, yucca, blackbrush, and Mormon tea. In addition, you will read about **cryptobiotic crust** ("hidden life") or so-called brown sugar soil, a common phenomenon in the high desert. This essential living crust consists of cyanobacteria, moss, fungi, and lichens. These minute organisms often form gardens that completely cover the ground, giving its surface a crusty reddish-brown to black look. Soil rich in these crusts absorbs more moisture, making it easier for plants to grow in this arid land. In addition, the crusts hold the soil in place, as well as providing it with nutrients. Visitors are urged to stay on the established trails in the park to avoid walking on this crust since it takes between 50 and 250 years for this fragile material to fully recover from trampling.

Before leaving the visitor center, you may want to purchase for a small fee a booklet entitled *Road Guide: Arches National Park*. This booklet is keyed to all the named pullouts and major sites of the park. You can do a quick auto tour of some of the major sites from the road and walk one or two of the trails in a long half-day. But to see and walk to most of the major sites in the park requires a full day or two half day visits. Some visitors stay for a week or more. If you travel from Moab to the park, tour the principal paved roads, and return to Moab, you will have traveled approximately 50 miles. Because of its relative low elevation, some parts of the park are like a hothouse in the summer. So prepare for your visit accordingly (see "Practical Hints" at the back of the book).

Cliffrose

The Adventuresome Trail to Delicate Arch: A Narrative Account

It is 7:00 A.M. here in Moab. We seem to wake up early in this land of bright morning light. But this morning we are awake a little earlier than usual as we eagerly anticipate our trip to Delicate Arch. Although we went there many years ago and have periodically reviewed the color slides we took then, there has been a strong urge to go back again to experience some of the magic of that magnificent landform that can be felt only in its presence. So today is the much-awaited day.

Although Moab is quiet this morning as we drive north out of town, my thoughts are racing. I have just finished reading Edward Abbey's stimulating book *Desert Solitaire*. The book recounts Abbey's experience as a ranger at Arches National Park many years ago. It is a well-written book, rich in descriptive language and filled with information about the plants, animals, birds, and rocks of the area. It is the best nature guide anyone could have for the Moab area, and I am eager to put it to use.

We cross the bridge over the Colorado River and the bridge over Courthouse Wash. Just yesterday afternoon we crossed this same bridge, pulling into the large parking lot on the right side of the road. Then we walked back on the graveled footpath and hiking route about 0.5 mile to the **Court House Wash early Indian rock-art site** at the base of the tall cliff up slope to the left. We spent nearly an hour there trying to spot some of the Barrier Canyon–style images on a panel of rock 52 feet long and 19 feet high that is on the National Register of Historic Places. We spotted some of the shadowy human forms unique to this style of rock art as well as animals that looked like bighorn sheep.

At the entrance to Arches, we pay our fee and then follow the excellent paved main road as it zigzags up the cliff face. In about 1 mile we stop at the first pullout to view the **Moab Fault.** From this vantage point a valuable geologic lesson is laid out before our eyes. At one time the heap of rocks we are standing on and the rocky cliffs on the other side of this narrow part of **Moab Valley,** across U.S. Highway 191, were part of the same contiguous rock mass. At that time there was no valley. There would have been no space for the railroad tracks, the highway, or Arches visitor center.

About six million years ago, forces in the earth's crust caused a fracture or a fault in the solid rockbed where the highway is now. The side we are standing on sank thousands of feet, while the side across the highway probably rose. This side ended up 2,600 feet—or almost 0.5 mile—lower than the other side. The space between the fractured and cracked walls was probably very small at first. The huge gap we see between the cliff walls this morning was created by seasonal erosion or weathering over millions of years. The fault extended south of here too, opening that area to weathering and the eventual creation of Moab's wide valley.

Moab Valley is a geographic oddball because the Colorado River runs perpendicular to it. Usually rivers run parallel to valleys, since most valleys are formed by the rivers that cut through them. But it was different for the Moab Valley. Although the Colorado River was there first, it did not create Moab Valley. The valley was formed as a result of the faulting and the weathering mentioned earlier. At that point the Colorado River, crossing the north part of the newly formed

Balanced Rock, Arches National Park

valley, might have left its channel to flow south down the valley. But that was impossible, for when the valley was formed, the land collapsed in such a way that the south end of the valley was considerably higher than the north end. The Colorado River was thus forced to cross the top of the valley, never really penetrating its long axis. Valleys and rivers that have this kind of relationship are called *paradoxical* valleys. From the bridge where we crossed the Colorado River this morning, the river flows through a gap in the valley's southwestern cliff walls a little more than 1 mile from the bridge. That gap, similar to a mountain pass, is called the *portal,* and it is there that the Colorado River enters its canyon system that stretches 270 miles before terminating just below the Grand Canyon in Arizona.

Now we turn our attention to the rock layers. I point out that the top layers in the cliffs across the highway look like Wingate formation rocks topped by Kayenta sandstone. But on this side of the road, those formations are nowhere in sight. They are still deep in the ground. What we see here on the surface are Entrada formation rocks and some Navajo sandstone, younger rocks that were formed on top of the Wingate and the Kayenta as the sedimentary rock pile was assembled. On the opposite side of the highway where we should see the Entrada and Navajo rocks and other younger rocks in the pile, we see nothing but blue sky. Those rocks that protruded for hundreds of feet were unprotected and were so vulnerable to weathering over millions of years that they have all eroded away. But on this side of the highway, the Entrada and the Navajo remain, for they were on the bottom of the heap, protected by still younger rocks like the Morrison, Dakota, and Mancos that topped them. Many of those younger, unprotected top layers that have eroded away here along the fault line can be seen in other areas of the park.

Content that we have learned something new, we pass in another mile the maze of rock fins known as **Park Avenue.** These fins resemble many American cityscapes as they reach skyward, blocking the sun in many places below them. In yet another mile we catch glimpses of the **Manti–La Sal Mountains,** the youngest rock mass in view, formed from the action of molten magma only 22 million years ago. **Mount Peale** at 12,721 feet is the highest peak in the La Sals. Now about 3.5 miles from the visitor center, we see **Courthouse Towers.** On a previous visit here we made a long stop, for it is a fine example of how erosional forces carve a variety of evolving forms from what was once a huge solid wall of rock called a *mesa* (see "Reading the Rocks"). Shortly we pass "petrified dunes" or cross-bedded Navajo sandstone and then pull over to look at **Balanced Rock,** about 9 miles from the visitor center. We all heave a sigh of relief that it is still here, for it looks like it could topple at any moment. And that will certainly be its fate

Double Arch, Arches National Park

when the attached, softer base weathers to a thinness that will not support it. If that 58-foot-tall, 3,600-ton, oblong, ham-shaped piece of Entrada sandstone ever takes a dive from its 73-foot-high rock perch, it is going to make a resounding noise when it smacks the ground below.

Just beyond Balanced Rock we bypass the spur road in the Window section of the park. Last year we took that road, traveling its nearly 3-mile length to the two parking areas where it dead-ends. From the first parking area, we followed a trail to see **the Spectacles** (**North Window** and **South Window**) and **Turret Arch.** From the second parking area, on the north side of the dead-end loop, we walked an easy 0.4-mile round-trip to view **Double Arch**—one of the most geometrically interesting arches in the region. Our kids remind me that on that route they saw the **"Parade of Elephants,"** a series of whimsically shaped stones resembling animals in a circus parade. Returning to the Windows' intersection with the main road, we continue on to **Panorama Point** with views out over **Salt Valley,** where some of the younger formations, such as the Morrison, which were eroded away along the fault line, can be seen. We pass the **Cache Valley Overlook** and reach the turnoff to **Wolfe Ranch** and Delicate Arch trailhead, about 11 miles from the visitor center. We recall that last year, when we had less time on our hands, we passed by this turnoff and continued on the main road past the **Fiery Furnace** area, with its maze of sandstone walls, to the **Devil's Garden** area at the end of the road. There, in a shaded picnic spot, we refreshed ourselves with food and drink from our small cooler before taking the somewhat level, 1.6-mile, one-hour round-trip walk along an "avenue" of smaller arches to a viewpoint

Fishhook or devil's claw cactus   *Bottle plant*

overlooking the world's largest natural rock span, **Landscape Arch.** But perhaps more than anything else, we remember returning, sweating hot, to our Moab motel for a refreshing swim.

Now we swing off the main road onto the **Delicate Arch** spur road where we can either continue on another mile to the **Delicate Arch Viewpoint** parking area, where distant views of the arch are possible after a short walk, or turn into the **Wolfe Ranch–Delicate Arch parking area.** We choose the latter since we intend to take the longer hike to the arch. There are only a few cars in the parking area this morning, which means we have beaten the crowds.

Before starting up the trail, we notice the green shale behind the parking area, which belongs to the Morrison, one of the youngest formations in the park. Ordinarily the Morrison is drab in color, but here it is tinted a beautiful shade of blue-green by the copper it contains. The Morrison was laid down more than 135 million years ago and often contains dinosaur bones. It is already very hot in this little valley this morning. We walk down to examine the ruins of Wolfe Ranch. The cabin, a small root cellar, the corral, and an old wagon are the only reminders that early settlers occupied this site from about 1888 or 1889 until about 1910. We marvel that they could have sustained themselves here for more than twenty years.

We cross the bridge that spans Salt Wash along the 3-mile round-trip trail to Delicate Arch. We stop on the bridge and look into the wash. We see the feathery leaves of the tamarisk shrub and a large clump of reeds growing out of the moist alkaline soil. We understand that there is quicksand under the wetter areas. On the other side of the bridge, just before the trail begins a steep incline, we follow a path to the left, a short distance below the cliff walls, to see a panel of rock art. The petroglyphs pecked in the desert varnish are of more modern origin than those we saw at Capitol Reef. The horse with a rider is the clue to the date. These carefully carved pictures were probably produced by the Utes after they had obtained horses from the Spanish. Except in pre-prehistory there were no horses on our continent until the Spanish arrived (see Section 2, "A Prehistory of Indian Country").

We return to the trail, which begins to climb. We will gain 500 feet in eleva-

Collared lizard   *Monkey flower*

tion by the time we reach Delicate Arch. We huff and puff up the excellent smooth trail, taking time to notice opuntia (prickly pear) and fishhook cacti as well as small clumps of luminescent green snakegrass and wispy Indian ricegrass that are on the left side of the trail. Soon the trail levels out. We stop to catch our breaths. It is already a little cooler just this far out of the valley as a gentle breeze hits our moist skins. My wife spots a small bottle plant to the right. We all admire its weird shape and see the bottlelike nodules along the stem just below each major branching point for which it is named. As we traverse this higher ground, there are good views of the surrounding Entrada sandstone eroded into many strange forms, and we see alcoves in the cliff walls streaked with desert varnish. We continue along the good trail on flat ground, passing several low areas in which the dirt is covered with white alkali, looking for all the world like newly fallen snow on this eighty-five-degree day.

Now the trail climbs again. This time it means business. But it soon levels out, offering good views back over the valley where we started. Pausing to catch our breaths, we notice several 8- to 12-inch-long lizards. One is a collared lizard with two black bands encircling its neck. My son thinks one of the other ones was a whip-tailed lizard with its characteristic orange-colored back. These lizards are having fun today, scurrying from rock to rock, occasionally crossing the trail. They are perfectly harmless and are a delight to watch. To the left we see giant alcoves or shallow caves in the sandstone. The backs of the caves are covered with dark desert varnish, but the seeps there have streaked the varnish with alkali, giving an interesting three-dimensional effect. We see the green "garden" under the seeps where tender, delicate, moisture-loving plants like maidenhair ferns, columbine, and monkey flower grow. Now the trail goes across a slowly rising plateau until we reach the next ascent. The trail for this next elevation gain is across the face of a huge sandstone outcropping called slickrock. It is not slick when dry but can become tricky when wet. We all have tennis shoes on today with good treads, but trail boots would offer more security for the less surefooted.

We feel the heat now, reflecting back up from the rock. We see a few black-blue ravens soaring above us as we stop for a cool drink from our canteens on

Twisted Donut Arch, Arches National Park

this waterless trail. Continuing on through the slickrock wilderness, the kids both yell at once, "There it is!" They have seen one of their favorite arches, **Twisted Donut Arch.** This small arch, 11 by 14 feet, magnificently frames Delicate Arch below and beyond it. We climb a few sandstone steps up to the arch and we are silenced by what we see. There is Delicate Arch on the far side of a smoothly rounded sandstone amphitheater, perched on the very edge of a canyon wall that plummets 500 feet to **Winter Camp Wash** below. In the background the snowcapped La Sal Mountains soar nearly 13,000 feet into one of the clearest blue skies imaginable. We sit down a few minutes in this comfortable place, which offers some shade and is exposed enough to catch a breeze if there is one. We drink more of our cool water—a must on a hike like this—and munch on candy bars, enjoying the relief from the intense sun.

We round the corner of Twisted Donut Arch and cautiously walk down the fairly steep, eroded sandstone bowl that dips gracefully to Delicate Arch. Slowly, almost reverently, we approach it. I feel the same tingling sensation in the back of my neck that I had when I first saw this beautifully carved piece of stone sculpture a few years ago. We stand directly under it and stretch our necks to see the roof of the arch, 45 feet above us. It is well named. Ironically this arch containing tons of stone has the appearance of floating on the edge of the canyon. There is a light, airy, delicate quality to it. How fragile it is we do not know, but it is an old arch carrying the patina of age gracefully.

How many more summer thunderstorms and winter frosts will it take before it topples? After all, nature creates beautiful spans like this and then works to level them. As we stand dwarfed by this monument to time, we slowly back away from it, trying to once again record on film what our senses will never let us forget. We walk back up the sloping surface of the amphitheater and take one last admiring look at it through Twisted Donut Arch. We comment that the thirty minutes we have spent up here this morning at the arch have more than compensated for the two days of driving it took us to get here. We walk back down the trail, arriving back at Wolfe Ranch about three hours after we started. We drive back to the main road with the air conditioner on full blast. We feel tired from the heat but exhilarated. The trail was as exciting as we had remembered it, and the sight of Delicate Arch was the kind of natural "high" we have come to expect here in the Southwest.

Dead Horse Point State Park

One of the major reasons people travel to Moab is to visit this state park perched on one long arm of a giant mesa sometimes called Island in the Sky. From Dead

Horse Point you will witness spectacular views out over the **Colorado River** and much of **Canyonlands National Park,** 2,000 feet below. This overview of what many call Utah's Grand Canyon rivals the vistas of another stretch of the Colorado River Canyon system seen from the rim of Arizona's Grand Canyon more than 250 miles to the southwest. The park, located 33 miles from Moab at an elevation of 6,000 feet above sea level, contains 4,630 acres of land. This land was set aside for the public in 1959 and is managed by Utah State's Department of Parks and Recreation. A small entry fee is required. The park contains an excellent picnic area. Its well-situated campground requires a fee. Water is available, but since it is hauled in from a source 70 miles away, you are requested to help conserve it.

Delicate Arch, Arches National Park

It is helpful to stop by the visitor center for orientation purposes. Inside there's a wealth of information about the geology and natural history of the area, while outside there is an instructive nature orientation trail nearby. The self-guiding booklet for the trail is excellent. From the visitor center it is only a short drive on to Dead Horse Point. There several markers and displays help explain the sea of rocks that unfolds thousands of feet below you. Information: Dead Horse State Park Visitor Center, P.O. Box 609, Moab, Utah 84532–0609; (435) 259–2614 or (800) 322–3770 for camping reservations; www.stateparks.utah.com.

Visiting the Colorado River and Dead Horse Point State Park: A Narrative Account

The daily thunderstorm was particularly vigorous this afternoon, leaving the August air fresh and dropping the temperature from the nineties down to the seventies. There are still some beautiful but ominous columnar cloud formations to the north. One of the darker ones appears to have a silver rim around it. And to the west an enormous rainbow crosses the sky, a poststorm phenomenon we have come to expect here in the High Southwest.

Deciding that the storm has passed, we prepare for our visit to Dead Horse State Park to view Utah's "Grand Canyon." We attempted this trip a few years ago but miscalculated the time and the distance, traveling halfway there only to discover that the sun was sinking rapidly and that our gas gauge was on empty. Confronted with the prospect of running out of gas on that remote mesa after dark, we did an about-face and dejectedly drove back to Moab, vowing to return someday. Today is the day. I check the gas gauge. It is nearly full. It is a little before 5:00

P.M. We have plenty of time to drive the 30-plus miles to the point and return before dinner.

As we head northwest out of town along U.S. Highway 191, the sun is low and to our left. We pass by many old cottonwood trees whose bright, almost acid green leaves give color to the whole valley, making it look like a shining desert oasis from a distance. We notice the contrast this evening between these green trees and the surrounding cliffs and bluffs of red, pink, off-white, and tan sandstone. A few seconds ago we passed the headquarters of **Navtec Expeditions,** run by the family of Doc Williams, a pioneer Moab physician who was instrumental in the development and preservation of the arches northwest of town as a national monument. At the very edge of town, on top of a hill to the right, we notice the restaurant Sunset Grill, formerly Mi Vida, the home of Charlie Steen, the Texas geologist who put Moab on the map with the discovery of his Mi Vida uranium mine in the 1950s. Then we pass a lovely old ranch home (converted to a restaurant), the residence of an early Mormon settler, nestled in the coolness of some tall cottonwoods.

Just beyond the northwest edge of town, the Colorado River comes into sight. Right on the banks of the Colorado is a park with a picnic and recreation area. We remember a fine Fourth of July evening spent there a few years ago, under an unbelievable canopy of stars. We stop to read the sign erected on the south side of the bridge. It tells about the early Mormon settlers and the establishment of **Grand County** in 1890, with Moab as the county seat. It emphasizes the importance of cattle and sheep grazing before Moab became the capital of the western uranium boom. It points out that Moab was the hub of Colorado River traffic years ago. But the sign does not reveal much about the **Ute Indians** who roamed and lived in this land for several hundred years before and after white contact.

No doubt the river's accessible banks served to water the horses the Utes acquired from the Spanish traders in the eighteenth century. But the Utes have been remembered in another way. This state did not forget its important Indian heritage. For when Utah became a state in 1896, it kept the name that had been on the land so long—the land of the Yutas, the Spanish name for the people of the area. Horses ridden by Spaniards probably found this river a welcome oasis in 1765. That year the first known white contact with this region was made by the Spanish soldier Juan María Antonio Rivera and his men. The road we are traveling tonight approximately parallels a segment of the **Old Spanish Trail.** Not far downstream from today's modern steel bridge is the site where a "practicable crossing" of the Colorado was discovered in the early 1800s. Which Spaniard, Mexican trader, or American trapper or mountain man made this discovery is unknown. But it is known that this crossing of the Colorado was a vital link in the Old Spanish Trail, joining the two far-flung cities of the northern Spanish Mexican empire, Santa Fe and Los Angeles.

It is now 5:30 P.M. The sun is still warm this evening. It is quiet. In this early evening stillness, we can imagine shouting men and hundreds of heaving animals swimming across this river. Perhaps the men are hanging on desperately to the newly constructed rafts to which the trade goods have been lashed. The swift undercurrent would have made an arduous day's work of this river crossing. Now we walk to the river's edge. This evening the river is flowing salmon red to brown,

Old Ranch House, Moab

looking for all the world like a vast stream of tomato soup. Some have character-
ized the river's muddy waters as being "too thick to drink and too thin to plough."
Stained by the minerals from the red rock surrounding it, it was first seen in the
High Southwest in the region of Arizona's Grand Canyon by members of Coronado's expedition in 1540. How it got its name is still uncertain. But one story has
it that it was named by a Spanish priest, Friar Francisco Garcés, in 1776. While our
Declaration of Independence was being framed, he debated about what to call this
reddish gruel. He did not name it the Rio Rojo or Red River. He was more precise. He named it the Rio Colorado or "reddish river." The name stuck.

The surface of the river appears smooth, but it has strong undercurrents along
this narrow passage above Moab as it cuts across rather than parallel to Moab Valley. At Arches this morning we learned how the Moab fault created this paradox.
From where we are standing, just a mile or so downriver, the Colorado flows
through a break or portal in the 800-foot-high cliffs and leaves the valley to enter
the Colorado River Canyon system. That almost 300-mile-long series of canyons
finally peters out just south and west of one of its most dramatic stretches, Arizona's Grand Canyon.

The segment of the Colorado River flowing in front of us originates about
300 miles northeast of Moab, near Grand Lake, Colorado, not far from Denver. A
little more than 32 miles downstream from us, it makes a great wild loop in the
canyon called an *entrenched meander* as it goosenecks its way around the rocks just

below Dead Horse Point, our destination this evening. From there the river drops 1 foot every mile for 30 miles until it reaches the confluence with its main tributary, the **Green River.** The Green River, flowing through most of eastern Utah, originates 700 miles northeast of the confluence in the Wind River region of southwestern Wyoming. Three miles below the confluence, rapids take shape as a prelude to the river's entry into **Cataract Canyon.** There the Colorado contains some of the wildest white water in the West, popular with rafting enthusiasts from all over the world. Calming itself at **Lake Powell,** the river then builds up steam as it churns through Arizona's Grand Canyon country.

As we return to the car, we discuss the fact that the river here at Moab, from the confluence up to its Colorado source, was once named the Grand River. In fact we are now in **Grand County,** Utah, named in the 1890s after this river. How the name got changed to the Colorado is a story with as many uncertain twists as the river itself. But it goes something like this: The Spaniards named the river they saw from the Grand Canyon the Colorado. The name stuck for that stretch of the river south to the Gulf of California. Later the Domíniquez-Escalante party were the first white men to come across a large river to the north. They named it El Rio San Buenaventura, the "river of good fortune." Known for a while by the American trappers as the Spanish River, the Spanish relabeled this river of good fortune, calling it the Rio Verde or Green River. To the northwest another large river was discovered, perhaps by French trappers. It was named the Grand River. At that time it was not known that the Green and the Grand joined to form the Colorado. In the 1860s Colorado Territory was formed. It was named after the great western river of the same name, which many thought ran through the territory.

Statehood came to Colorado in 1876, the same year that Captain J. N. Macomb's report of his 1859 Utah expedition was published. He had discovered the confluence deep in Utah's canyonlands where the Green and the Grand joined to become the Colorado. It was now clear that the Colorado River did not flow through Colorado. Embarrassed and increasingly sensitive to this discrepancy, Colorado pushed for renaming the Grand after the Colorado River that it joined. But to do so would have defied tradition. For in the 1890s the Federal Board on Geographic Names had established a policy of naming rivers after their longest tributary. According to this rule, the lower segment of the Colorado, that named by the Spanish, would have to be changed to the Green, since the Green River was the largest tributary. But eventually it was decided that historical precedence should rule, and the older name of Colorado was kept for the river below the confluence; no decision was made about naming the river above the confluence.

By 1920 the Colorado legislature, champing at the bit, declared that the river between Grand Lake and the Utah border would be named the Colorado. About the same time, the Utah legislature voted down a proposal to rename the Green River the Colorado. Jumping into the breach, the Colorado legislature convinced its Utah neighbor to name the 40-mile stretch of Grand River between the Utah border and its confluence the Colorado. Armed with this support, Coloradoans took the fight to Washington, D.C. There on July 25, 1921, Congress voted to change the name of the Grand River to the Colorado River. The people of Colorado now had possession of their namesake, while the people of Grand County,

View from Dead Horse Point

Utah, simultaneously lost theirs. The United States now had one river, its fifth largest, called the Colorado, that stretched deep from its mountainous interior to the Pacific Ocean.

As we drive across the bridge, we wonder if Grand County residents ever resented the change. Doubtful. It is more prestigious to be located on the banks of the Colorado River and to raft the Colorado River than some obscure tributary named the Grand River. But in spite of being well known, the Colorado River, unlike the Nile River with which it is sometimes compared, has not attracted settlement along its banks because of the rugged terrain around it. Except for the marinas and the recreational sites on Lake Powell and the "company" towns at Glenn Canyon Dam, Arizona, and Boulder Dam, Nevada, there is not a single, major commercial town along the river between Moab, Utah, and Needles, California, a distance of more than 1,000 miles.

Now everyone is wondering if we will ever get to Dead Horse Point. Approximately 10 miles northwest of central Moab, we reach Utah Highway 313, the road to **Dead Horse Point State Park** and **Grand View Point** in the **Island in the Sky District of Canyonlands National Park.** Immediately 313, a paved Utah Scenic Byway with bicycle lanes on each side, heads west 21 miles to the park through **Sevenmile Canyon.** It is scenic in its own right, bordered by tall, Wingate cliffs and numerous interesting rock formations. The road climbs out of the canyon in a series of steep switchbacks.

In about 4 miles we stop at one of several informative roadside pullouts along the way. We catch glimpses of two large, salmon-colored, flat-topped buttes to the northwest. We learn that they are named after the Civil War ironclad vessels, the *Monitor* and the *Merrimac*. The large butte to the west is called the **Merrimac,** while the smaller one to the east is the **Monitor.** The sheer cliff faces of both are of Entrada sandstone. They are each thinly capped with Summerville and Morrison formation rocks. Continuing on, the highway switchbacks through Kayenta sandstone ledges until, true to our geologic chart, we reach massive outcroppings of whitish cross-bedded Navajo sandstone, taking the form of smoothly rounded beehive mounds. As the road reaches the top of the switchbacks, it levels out on the mesatop, truly an Island in the Sky. Soon we enter a semibarren stretch of sand and grassland. To the right red slopes are studded with bright green Utah junipers. Just beyond them, about 7 miles from the U.S. Highway 191 junction, we pull off the highway to the left to look at the Bureau of Land Management exhibit. It describes the large alcoves we had just observed on the right side of the road. We too had noticed the white alkaline stains on the dark desert-varnished back walls of those alcoves creating a toothlike design, giving the illusion of white stalactites protruding from the alcove ceiling. Also from this vantage point we see the La Sal Mountains as well as row upon row of sandstone fins in the distance from which future arches will someday be formed.

The road continues on south with a very gradual incline. Piñon pines begin to appear along with Utah junipers. In this "pygmy forest" the trees are dwarfed due to a lack of moisture, poor soil, and widely fluctuating temperatures. These lovely trees, with interesting and contorted features, are small but very old. Trees with a diameter of 6 to 10 inches are often 150 years old, and some with only slightly larger diameters may be 250 to 350 years old.

We think of the wonderful aroma of piñon when its smoke fills the air in some southwestern communities on chilly fall and winter evenings, and we remember the first time we experienced the delightful, pungent smell of freshly cut juniper when we visited a Navajo Indian who was using that resilient wood for the construction of his hogan (see Section 2, "Monument Valley: A Narrative Account"). As the miles pass by, we look for cliff rose, yucca, and Mormon tea among the vegetation. We see many doves and a few desert cottontail rabbits. At a well-marked junction 14.5 miles from the U.S. Highway 191 junction, the highway continues straight on to Canyonlands National Park's Island in the Sky District and Grand View Point. The road to the left leads about 16 round-trip miles to Dead Horse Point parking area.

Reaching the park, we pay a fee at the entry station. We pass the excellent visitor center, which is closed this evening, and drive the short distance to the point. The view to the east is magnificent with the Manti–La Sals rising to almost 13,000 feet. We take time to look at our map and realize that in traveling this evening we have come full circle and a little more. Although we started our trip by driving northwest out of Moab, we are now several miles south of Moab but on a different plane, more than 1,000 feet above Moab Valley.

On the way to the parking area, we read an interesting story from the informative brochure. During the late 1800s cowboys used to herd the wild horses that roamed throughout the area across the narrow neck of land that separates the point from the mainland. The point served as a natural corral. Once the mustangs were on the point, the cowboys fenced the narrow neck off and captured the horses they wanted for their own use. The legend of Dead Horse Point states that a group of unwanted horses (culls or broom tails) were left stranded on the waterless point. They died there within sight of the Colorado River, 2,000 feet below. So now we know how this jutting peninsula of land, really a flat mesatop, obtained its name.

With the sun descending lower in the west, we pass through the narrow neck of the peninsula, only 30 yards wide, and begin to see for ourselves how this thin bottleneck could easily be blocked to create a natural corral. We park the car and walk—almost run—on the Kayenta sandstone to the rim. We are stunned by the view. Alone now—the sun dropping quickly, a slight breeze, utter silence—we gaze out over the point. As I stand there I know what it means to "see forever," 5,000 square miles of Canyon Country laid out before us. In the distance the Manti–La Sal Mountains lie to the east. They were named by the early Spaniards, who likened their snow-covered peaks to piles of salt. To the south are the **Abajo Mountains,** 50 miles away. Between those far-distant mountains of molten magma origin, time and erosion have carved an immense sea of canyons, labyrinths, and mazes. There are protruding towers, mesas, monuments, and monoliths in ever-changing colors—reds, purples, whites, pinks, and grays—as the sunlight casts lengthening shadows. The sheer cliffs expose almost every rock formation created in the Colorado Plateau over the past 250 million years.

Then my eye catches the river, serpentine-like, 2,000 feet below and 32 river miles downstream from Moab. Sometimes pink, sometimes brownish red, as it changes with the progression of twilight. It bullies and forces its way, cutting deeper and deeper through the sedimentary rock layers more than 1,100 miles from here to the shoulder of Mexico's Baja California, where, after being drained to the point of depletion by California's thirsty Imperial Valley, it trickles into the Pacific Ocean's Sea of Cortez, better known in this country as the Gulf of California. A mighty river, this "Grand," "Colorado," or whatever you want to call it. The fifth longest river in the United States demands respect as it makes a wild 180-degree turn, goosenecking around an enormous rock outcropping right before our eyes.

From up here on the point, the whole world is made up of sheer, steep cliffs, stratified walls, and stone staircases in multicolored layers. The Grand Canyon of the North, the Upper Grand Canyon, Utah's Grand Canyon—call it what you will, it is magnificent. We have been alone this evening until now, when one other visitor, a man from Germany, joins us at the rim. He is as awed as we are. Our mutual respect for what we are experiencing transcends the language barrier. Trading glances, each of us knows and understands what the other is feeling at this moment as we gaze out over the horizons of the High Southwest. Now the red sandstone is acid pink in color, while the sky behind it is a dark vibrant blue. An almost full moon is rising in the east. Here at the top of the peninsula, we feel we are at the

Spadefoot toads

fulcrum of the universe. As the sun goes down gradually in the west, the moon ascends slowly to the east, both lending their light to the panorama before us.

Far, far below we see a small whitish line curving and bending, a jeep trail left over from the uranium-fever days that now carries adventurers into Canyonlands National Park. Down to the east there are some human-made solar evaporation ponds used to recover potash. Much of what we are seeing from up here is Canyonlands National Park. Some say it is one of the best overviews of that park. Certainly it is one of the most accessible panoramic overlooks.

We notice a nice picnic area on the way back to the car. The rabbitbrush and snakegrass are taking on phosphorescent colors in the early twilight. Then we see a juniper loaded with bluish-purple, luminescent berries. It has been said that some of the rare beauty in this big country is to be found by searching out its smallness. Tonight, in the cool of the evening, we see an occasional white-tailed antelope, ground squirrel, and a few lizards scurrying about, although we see no kangaroo rats. As we drive out, the only car on the road, we see more doves and a few bluebirds. We notice on the road in front of us some small creatures. We stop to look. They are spadefoot toads, enjoying the rainwater that pooled this afternoon in some of the small holes beside the road.

The descent back down to U.S. Highway 191 is a treat—deep pinks and purples on the left with the full moon rising to the right. In front of us, directly north, intermittent streaks of lightning dance across the sky in both vertical and horizontal directions. We drive carefully, alert for any deer that might cross the highway. There is silence in the car as we drive back down to Moab. Each of us is reflecting in some way on the beauty and solitude we have experienced, thankful that this "grand canyon" is still pristine and reasonably untouristed. We arrive back in Moab at 8:30, 66 round-trip miles and three and a half hours later. Having feasted visually we are now ready to feast gastronomically!

Canyonlands National Park

Canyonlands National Park is the largest national park in Canyon Country. It contains in its 527 square miles some of the world's most isolated yet scenically beautiful rugged land. Once occupied by the ancient Indians, it was never thought suitable for settlement by white pioneers. The first known white man brave enough to walk through the heart of it and who lived to record his visit was Captain J. N. Macomb of the U.S. Topographical Corps, who led an expedition there in 1859. Scorched by the heat and jarred to the bone by the unevenness of the terrain, Macomb wrote tersely, "I cannot conceive of a more worthless and impracticable region than the one we now find ourselves in."

The expedition went up and down an endless series of "deep and great cañons," compelling Macomb to write, "I doubt not that there are repetitions and varieties of this for hundreds of miles." His expedition mapped the confluence of the Green River and the Colorado River, flowing through deep canyons in a riverbed rimmed with rocks of the Hermosa group, the oldest layers of the earth's crust to surface in the park. But Macomb was right. He had seen only the beginning of this up-and-down land. He never made it to the desolate heart of Canyonlands, a 30-square-mile area of hell on earth called the Maze. There a labyrinthian world of dry, desolate, skeletal rock creates an unbelievable concentration of canyons that twist and turn, divide and redivide like some baroque sandstone puzzle. But somehow those indomitable prehistoric Indians of the region eked out a living here, leaving pictographs of rare beauty on the canyon walls for modern-day adventurers to see and wonder about.

Understandably the area remained little visited a decade after Macomb's visit. Then John Wesley Powell, a one-armed Civil War veteran, led an expedition in search of a more direct rail route across the Southwest. He went down the Green River to the confluence and then on down the Colorado River, where he got the surprise of his life. Three miles below the confluence, the quiet river becomes increasingly rough. It moves faster and faster as the riverbed drops 8 feet each mile.

Then in one last giant step down, it races even faster as it drops 30 feet in 1 mile, deep in Cataract Canyon. Powell lived to tell about it, but several accompanying him on the expedition were killed by Indians before the expedition was concluded.

Seeing Canyonlands

This huge park of unusual beauty receives fewer visitors each year than the other parks in the region. But that is understandable. There are no roads that directly connect the park's several districts. Although these districts may appear close on a map, traveling between them requires anywhere from two to six hours by car, making it difficult to visit them all in a single day. And some of the sights within the park, like the Maze section, Monument Basin, the Totem Pole, Druid Arch, and Angel Arch, are beyond the reach of the average traveler. There are several good paved roads that take you to panoramic overlooks along the elevated rim of the Island in the

Totem Pole, Monument Basin, Canyonlands National Park

Sky section of the park and into the Needles area. But the roads to most of the major sights (including a wealth of Anasazi and Fremont early Indian dwellings and cliff art) are four-wheel-drive-vehicle roads. Some visitors, like Major Powell, prefer to explore the park by river; others choose to fly over it. But many hardy souls elect to hike through it. Moab serves as a base for many commercial tour companies designed to fit just about every adventurer's needs (see "Moab: Tours and Activities"). But for the average traveler with limited time and funds, the following two routes can be explored with great satisfaction. Information: Canyonlands National Park Headquarters, 2282 South West Resource Boulevard, Moab, Utah 84532; (435) 719–2313; www.nps.gov/cany.

Grand View Point—Island in the Sky District, Canyonlands National Park

Approximately 9 miles northwest of Moab, turn left from U.S. Highway 191 onto paved Utah Highway 313 at a junction marked DEAD HORSE POINT STATE PARK AND CANYONLANDS NATIONAL PARK, ISLAND IN THE SKY DISTRICT. Travel approximately 14.5 miles to the well-marked Dead Horse Point junction. The paved Canyonlands road continues straight ahead. To see all the sights listed here, you will travel on good, paved roads (except for 1.5 miles of unpaved road to the campground and **Green River Overlook**) 52 round-trip miles from this junction. From the junction travel 7.2 miles to the visitor center, through level high-desert grasslands. Along the route you will be rewarded with the views of three mountain ranges formed from molten magma upthrusts. The **Henry Mountains** rise in front and to the right, the Manti–La Sals loom behind you, and the Abajo Mountains appear to the left.

You will pay a fee (also good at Needles District), either at a kiosk on the road or at the visitor center, where there are exhibits, more detailed maps of the region, and helpful brochures relating to this section of the park. Some books about the area are for sale there also. From the visitor center continue along the Island in the Sky road past several scenic pullouts to the interesting **Mesa Arch Trail** at 6.4 miles from the visitor center. At the Mesa Arch trailhead, you can pick up an excellent self-guiding booklet that will lead you down the 0.5-mile loop trail. It identifies and explains most of the plant life along the way. At trail's end perched on the very rim of Canyonlands Park, 2,100 feet above the Colorado River, Mesa Arch, beautifully carved in the Navajo sandstone, frames the canyonlands below as well as the Manti–La Sal Mountains more than 35 miles away. This trail is somewhat confusing, so follow the rock cairn trail markers carefully and take note of your bearings. Do not let small children out of your reach because of the steep drop-off at the rim.

From Mesa Arch Trail parking lot the road junction is only about 0.3 mile. Take the left fork and continue south for 6.4 miles past a nice picnic area to **Grand View Point.** This overlook should not be missed. Although similar to the view from Dead Horse Point State Park, the vantage point there penetrates the park deeper, offering quite a different perspective. From the rim you see the cliffs drop to the **White Rim,** the top of a sandstone escarpment capped by White Rim, Cutler

Upheaval Dome, Canyonlands National Park

group rocks 1,250 feet below. That rim drops another 1,000 feet to the Colorado River, which is buried deep in the canyons and is not visible from this viewpoint. The 35-mile-wide basin you see was carved from the rock by the Green and Colorado Rivers with the aid of other erosive forces. The truly incredible view opens out to the **Abajo peaks, Cathedral Butte, North and South Sixshooter Peaks,** and the **Needles section** of the park. Immediately below is a view of the **Totem Pole.** This 305-foot-high spire of sandstone, one of the Standing Up Rocks in Monument Basin, looks like a miniature from Grand View Point.

Return by way of the same road to the junction with the Upheaval Dome and Green River Overlook roads to see one of the most peculiar geologic entities in Canyonlands Park. Drive northwest 5.3 miles to the **Upheaval Dome Overlook** parking lot. Just before reaching the parking lot, you will see **Whale Rock,** a very good likeness of that sea mammal sculpted by nature from Navajo sandstone. There is a primitive trail from Whale Rock overlooking Upheaval Dome crater. From the parking lot and pleasant, piñon-shaded picnic area, pick up the *Upheaval Dome Trail Guide* and walk 0.2 mile, mostly uphill, to a junction in the trail. One path leads to a viewpoint 0.5 mile to the left, while the other one leads to an overlook only 60 yards to the right.

What you see before you from either trail is a giant crater rather than a dome, the closest thing to a moonscape on earth that you may ever see. There in the center of a deep basin several miles wide, sharply angulated whitish green-gray rocks protrude upward. What happened there is still not entirely clear. Some believe this strange phenomenon was created by a meteor. Others hold that the creative force was salt. Under pressure from the thousands of feet of rock that had formed above it, salt the consistency of toothpaste oozed up through a weakened area of the earth's crust, pushing up the ten layers of rock above it to form a dome 3 miles wide. Six of the rock layers were so distorted by the movement that they were turned almost on edge. Eventually the surrounding area from which the dome rose slowly sank to form a trench or syncline around it.

Over the next 40 million years, erosion stripped away the overlying crust to expose the upturned and fractured faces of the domed rocks to further erosion. Near the center of the dome, the stack of upturned and broken rock eroded more easily, washing away into the canyon that extends from the fractured west wall of the crater. This created an inner void, an erosional basin 1,500 feet deep and 1 mile wide, circled by cliffs of the harder, more erosion-resistant Wingate sandstone. Today you will see, ringed by a floor of colorful Moenkopi formation rocks, the weird central core of Upheaval Dome with its multicolored, 500-foot-high, eroded, otherworldly spires extending from the White Rim, 1,000 feet below. Many of these gray-green rock forms are Organ rock shale.

The round-trip, nonstop walking time to the closer overlook and return to the parking lot is thirty minutes. Keep your eye open for black swifts in this area as they dart through the air. From the parking lot return to the main road. You have now seen most of the main sights except the **Green River Overlook.** Before you reach the junction with the Grand View Point road, turn right onto the Green River Overlook spur road, past **Willow Flat Campground** (fee; first come, first served; bring water and firewood) to the overlook. There you'll enjoy great views of the Green River in **Labyrinth Canyon.** From the junction you are 14.2 miles from the Dead Horse Point Road and 36 miles from Moab. From Moab allow well over two hours of round-trip driving time and two and a half hours of sight-seeing time. If you want to combine this trip with a visit to Dead Horse Point State Park, add another thirty minutes' driving time, plus an additional hour for seeing the sights. Information: Island in the Sky District Visitor Center; (435) 259–4712. Be sure to bring your own water, since none is available on the Island in the Sky. And fill your gas tank before leaving Moab.

The Needles District, Canyonlands National Park

The Needles District road is the only paved all-weather road that actually penetrates the canyonlands at eye level rather than at rim level. Although it will take you closer to many of the best sights in the park, like the Needles, it will not take you all the way to them. The end of the Needles District road is the beginning of numerous biking and four-wheel-drive-vehicle roads and hiking trails to some incredible landforms. Many of the hiking trails to those sights are generally long and strenuous and probably are not appropriate for the average traveler. What does this road offer the average visitor, then? It offers some spectacular views of the park at near-canyon level rather than rim level. It provides eye-level views of the Needles in the distance and several short but interesting nature trails through the slickrock.

From Moab drive south through beautiful red rock country that someone forgot to put in a national park. In approximately 39 miles you will reach a well-signed junction road to the right, Utah Highway 211, a Scenic Byway. The sign indicates that **Newspaper Rock Recreation Site** is 12 miles from the junction and Canyonlands National Park is 34 miles away. The first up-and-down 12 miles

Newspaper Rock, Newspaper Rock Recreation Site

take you to Newspaper Rock. Pull in the parking area to the right. Shaded picnic grounds are on the left side of the road. Walk a very short distance to the desert-varnished Wingate cliff face in front of you. You will see more petroglyphs than you ever thought imaginable, from the earliest prehistoric times through modern times, scratched in the sandstone. The variety is amazing. Even more amazing is that these writings are still intact. This unusually compact collection of petroglyphs is well worth viewing.

From Newspaper Rock the good paved road curves and winds as it begins the 22 miles to the park. The road, which follows **Indian Creek** as it flows from the Abajo Mountains to the Colorado River, eventually straightens as it enters a wide valley with many large cottonwoods. The road passes over several cattle-guards. These narrowly spaced, parallel pieces of pipe spook cattle belonging to the few ranchers in this remote valley and keep them from straying too far. The valley gives way to more open, picture-perfect western movie country as twin **Sixshooter Peaks** come into sight. These are really buttes, their unusual peaks carved from Wingate sandstone resting on Chinle and Moenkopi bases. Scenically this area somewhat resembles Monument Valley, Utah. Just before entering the park, you will pass a junction road to the north leading about 0.5 mile to the Needles Outpost (435–979–4007 or 435–259–8545), the only seasonal (mid-March to late December) watering hole, general store, and auto services facility (including four-by-four and jeep rentals) for miles around. At approximately 34 miles you will enter the park, where you will soon come to the handsome visitor center. Stop to see the natural history exhibits and bookstore, and pick up free maps and information folders about the area. There is a fee to enter the park (good at the Island in the Sky District also).

After leaving the visitor center, travel a short distance to the first parking area on the left, the **Roadside Ruin Nature Trail.** Pick up a self-guiding booklet

Rock cairn and scrub joy

from the box and walk the 0.3-mile loop trail to the **Anasazi Indian granary,** constructed of stone sometime between A.D. 950 and 1200. Along the trail you will see yucca, Fremont barberry, and big sagebrush.

Return to your car and drive about 0.5 mile to the junction of paved Salt Creek Road. Turn left, and in 0.6 mile turn left again onto a dirt road marked **Cave Spring Trail.** In about 1 mile enter the parking lot at the road's end. This is an interesting trail, taking you through some of the typical slickrock country at this elevation. In addition to the tips in the informative self-guiding booklet, you may wish to note several more important points. First, carry insect repellent. The wet nature of the springs attracts mosquitoes. Next, watch for cairns, small stacks of rocks that help guide the way. Part of the trail is over slightly steep sandstone slickrock. Finally, wear shoes that offer good traction. The trail is up and down, requiring two ladder ascents. One ladder has eight steps, while the other has twelve.

This 0.6-mile-long round-trip trail does bear out the notion that some of the beauty in this big country is found by searching out its smallness. Look for piñon pines whose bark has been stripped by porcupines. Look for pack rat nests in the cliff alcoves. It is hard to believe, but studies of some of these nests have established that they date back between 5,000 and 30,000 years, giving the pack rats at least squatter's rights to this area. And no doubt you will see numerous scrub jays and white-tailed antelope squirrels. Keep an eye out for rare golden eagles that may soar above. At the beginning of the trail is a large cave or alcove in the Cedar Mesa sandstone, its ceiling blackened from many kitchen fires. This cave served as a cowboy line camp, a temporary base for

Pack rat or desert wood rat

White-tailed antelope squirrels

cattle operations in the late-nineteenth and early-twentieth centuries.

Return to your car and drive back to the main park road. From there drive 1.5 miles to the junction with the Squaw Flat Campground and Elephant Hill spur road to the left and the Scenic Drive Road, past a picnic area, to **Pothole Point** and **Big Springs Canyon Overlook Trailhead,** straight ahead. Drive approximately 2 miles to the Pothole Point parking area. There a 0.6-mile loop walk out onto the sandstone flats gives good views of the spectacular Needles area, where you will see a forest of tall, red- (Cutler formation) and white- (Cedar Mesa sandstone) banded rock pinnacles. The self-guiding brochure obtained from the box in the parking area explains the formation of the potholes that surround you at every step. When a pothole dries up, the dirt in its bottom contains many microscopic eggs waiting for sufficient moisture to hatch. Sometimes when rainwater has stood in these usually dry rock basins for awhile, they may be filled with living creatures, such as fairy shrimp, snails, and horsehair worms.

Return to the road and follow it to its end, where there are good views out over the canyons. Not far from this point, to the southwest, hidden in the canyon, is the confluence of the Green and Colorado Rivers. From Big Springs Canyon Overlook Trailhead to the **Confluence Overlook** is an 11-mile round-trip hike over a "primitive" foot trail. Inquire at the ranger station before taking this hike. Drive 3.7 miles back to the junction and enter **Squaw Flat Campground** (twenty-six campsites; fee; first come, first served; water available spring through fall) and picnic area. Fine, shaded campsites backed up to nicely rounded Cedar Mesa sandstone bluffs are available there. From the southwestern section of the campground, numerous foot trails, many along dry creekbeds, extend into the park's most scenic sights, such as **Chesler Park,** with its grassy meadows, and **Druid Arch.** These are long hikes over rough country that should not be attempted in wet weather. The Druid Arch Trail is 11 miles round-trip. For further information about the hiking, mountain biking, and four-wheel-drive-vehicle routes, consult with a park ranger.

Having seen the major sights, return to Utah Highway 191 over the same road you came. From Moab this trip is a 170-mile round-trip drive that takes three-quarters of a day. If you are traveling from Moab south to Mesa Verde or Monument Valley, you might want to visit the Needles District on the way, early

Druid Arch, Canyonlands National Park

in the day, before proceeding south. Information: Canyonlands National Park Needles District Visitor Center; (435) 259–4711.

Permits (fee) are required for all overnight backcountry use throughout Canyonlands National Park and some remote day-use areas in the Needles District. For information about reservations for permits, call (435) 259–4351; www.nps.gov/cany. Many people make reservations months in advance since permits are limited, but permits are available to walk-ins on a space-available basis.

The Potash Road: A Scenic Byway to Dinosaur Tracks, Petroglyphs, and More

If you have an hour someday between major half-day trips or at the end of the day, be sure to sandwich in this scenic and educational trip close to Moab. Drive out of Moab across the Colorado River Bridge and then cross the Court House Wash Bridge to the junction of U.S. Highway 191 and Utah Scenic Byway Highway 279. Turn left onto paved Utah Highway 279, called the Potash Road. This well-engineered highway won an award some years ago as one of the most scenic drives in the country. In about 1 mile the Colorado River closely parallels the road as it prepares to exit Moab Valley. Both the river and you will enter **the Portal,** an opening in the cliffs on this side of the valley through which the river and the road enter the Colorado River Canyon system. The sheer walls are Wingate sandstone. The base of the walls rests on a variety of Chinle formation shales. At approximately 3 miles is a pullout to the left. A viewscope is zeroed in on **petro-**

glyphs and an **ancient Indian granary** on the steep canyon walls across the river. Binoculars are helpful.

At the next stop the sign says INDIAN WRITING. Pull off to the left side of the road. The petroglyphs are on the wall to the right. This is a very large, well-preserved gallery of many petroglyphs, possibly pecked in the desert-varnished Navajo sandstone wall by the Fremont Indians who flourished in this area and by the Utes who roamed this country later. This panel of petroglyphs is well worth seeing. The next well-marked pullout is to the right, marked by a sign that reads DINOSAUR. View tubes are fixed to reveal **dinosaur tracks** on a large slab of Kayenta sandstone on the cliffside above the parking area. More dinosaur tracks may be seen 23 miles north of Moab (on the east side of Highway 191 just north of Moab Airport) at the Sauropod Track Site. The next parking areas are for trails leading to **Corona and Bowtie Arches.** At 13 miles from U.S. Highway 191 is the **Jug Handle Arch** parking area. The configuration of Jug Handle Arch is interesting, since it occurs on a vertical plane and is one of the few known arches in this area to have formed in the usually resistant Wingate sandstone. At the end of the paved road to the right is the Moab Salt Plant and its nearby potash evaporation ponds, which can be seen from Dead Horse Point State Park. This 40-mile round-trip drive from Moab with stops takes about two hours.

The Scott M. Matheson Wetlands Preserve

On Moab's northwest side, the Nature Conservancy and the Utah Division of Wildlife Resources have made available to the public a virtual oasis in the desert. Touted as the only high-quality wetland along the entire length of the Colorado River in Utah, this 875-acre preserve hosts 175 species of birds at various times throughout the year, while beavers, river otters, frogs, and mule deer call it home most of the year. Hiking the well-laid-out trails from pond to pond to the observation posts at water's edge, you will walk alongside groves of Russian olives and Fremont cottonwoods, thickets of willow and tamarisk, and large clumps of cattails and bulrush. This unique slough on the outskirts of Moab is made possible by moisture from the La Sal Mountains to the east that finds its way, often through underground channels, to this unique spot. Bring binoculars. Allow at least an hour to explore—more if you are a naturalist at heart.

To reach the preserve, exit Main Street at McDonalds and drive north on Kane Creek Boulevard approximately 1.4 miles just past the entrance to Moab Skyride to the parking lot on the right side of the road. Park and follow the signs for your self-guided tour of the preserve. Open seven days a week from sunrise to sunset. Ranger-guided tours are given Saturdays at 8:00 A.M. March through May and September through November. Information: (435) 259–4629.

If you have seen all you want to see and have more time, you may want to take a trip down the Colorado River or a mountain-bike or a four-wheel-drive-vehicle trip into one of the more remote scenic areas around Moab. Half-day, day-long, and longer tours are available. Some of the tour operators are listed at the end of this section.

Rafting the Colorado: A Narrative Account

It is a few minutes before 9:00 A.M. We just arrived here at the raft tour office and are waiting for the bus that will take us 22 miles upstream from Moab to the launching site. We are well prepared for a day on the water in the July sun. In addition to camera and film, our day pack contains plenty of sunscreen. We all have sunglasses and hats with brims and are wearing shorts under our long pants. The rest—the water, lunch, and the waterproof containers for our valuables—are provided by the tour operator. We feel a little anxious this morning. No wonder. We have avoided doing this for years. Each year as we crossed and recrossed the narrow band of the Colorado River at Moab, passing the numerous signs advertising Colorado River trips, we discussed but quickly dismissed the possibility of such a trip. Somehow "rafting the Colorado" had always seemed connected with high adventure not suitable for a family with young children. But over time we came to know numerous ecstatic survivors of raft trips who extolled the safety as well as the fun, the pleasure, and the scenic beauty of such trips. So yesterday I took the plunge and made reservations for all four of us for today's oar-powered raft trip.

The bus arrives on time, and we climb aboard with about a dozen other hardy souls and several well-tanned raft guides who inspire confidence just by their weathered appearance, looking for all the world like veteran Huck Finns. The bus leaves U.S. Highway 191 at the bridge and turns up Colorado River Scenic Byway Utah Highway 128 as it takes us up the Colorado River Gorge, passing below the high rim of Arches National Park. Soon the gorge opens into wider valleys, offering striking views of such stone monuments as the **Priest and the Nuns, Castle Tower,** and the **Fisher Towers.** We are told that many of these sights have served as backdrops for a variety of western movies. At the launching site we exit the bus and explore, while our erstwhile river pilots prepare for the launching of the two large nylon and neoprene rafts, with their many individually inflated chambers. The river

Colorado River raft trip

rocks are fascinating. We ask about several of them and discover that our guides are well-educated natural historians. One particularly beautiful whitish rock with many parallel cross-striations is identified as a piece of oil shale, rounded and smoothed by the river's powerful grinding and cutting action. Our son finds several beached channel catfish that had given up the ghost of the silty water. The water is so thick with silt and debris today that it looks like gruel. It is almost surprising that it is wet! We are told that yesterday's big thunderstorm, the first in many weeks, has washed all kinds of matter into the river.

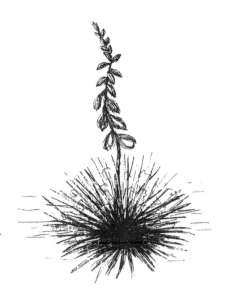

Yucca plant

The boats are ready. We are given life jackets and safety instructions before we board. Now that we are comfortably seated in the raft, our guide rows us skillfully into the main channel. He points out a variety of rock formations, including the Fisher Towers in the distance. He tells us that one of those towers, the **Titan,** is a 900-foot spire of ancient Cutler formation rock with a Moenkopi cap that stands up 300 feet taller than the Washington Monument. In a few miles we meet the first rapids, which slowly build up to the liveliest run on the trip, White Rapids. We hold on as the raft picks up speed, bouncing us up and down. The front of the raft is elevated some as we plunge through the rapids, Colorado River soup thoroughly spraying us. In the churning waters are small tree branches, medium-size burls of wood, detached juniper roots, pine cones, grass, and numerous small plants washed down from their native environments many miles away. Yesterday's storm must have cleared out every gully, wash, arroyo, and canyon for miles around. Now in calmer waters I reach over the side of the raft for a gnarled, twisted piece of wood. Success! It is a beautiful tree root smoothed to an exquisite fineness by the abrasive action of river and rocks. I place it on the floor of the raft, preparing for the next series of rapids. They are less intense and are followed by a wide, calm section of river where we pull ashore for lunch.

After exploring the shorelines and devouring a tasty lunch, we once again head for the main channel. The water is very still now, and the guide is forced to row. The sun is directly overhead, and we are grateful for our protective clothing. Soon we pull over to a wide, sandy beach where we see the bus waiting for us. This is the end of the trip. We have been on the raft for about five hours. While the boats are put back on the bus, we wade and swim a short distance from the beach. We are told to be cautious because of the swift undercurrents beneath the water's placid surface. We climb aboard our vintage bus and arrive back here at Moab around 4:30 P.M. Confident that we can survive the moderate rapids above

Moab, we are tempted to try a more difficult stretch of the river. Perhaps next time we will attempt Cataract Canyon!

Edge of the Cedars State Park Museum and the Dinosaur Museum, Blanding, Utah

If your travels will not take you farther south into Indian Country (see Section 2) and you would like to sample some of the region's Indian history, take a short day trip to **Edge of the Cedars State Park Museum,** Blanding, Utah, a focal point of Native American culture. Even if you are going south to Indian Country, this park, placed on the National Register of Historic Places in 1971, is well worth a stop.

Drive U.S. Highway 191 south 78 miles through Monticello, Utah, and the beautiful Abajo or Blue Mountains. In Blanding, make a stop at the instructive Blanding Visitor Center (435–678–3662) along United States Highway 191, on the north edge of town, before following the signed route to the state park on the northwest side of town. The monument is open (fee) daily except Thanksgiving, Christmas, and New Year's Day. It is located on the site of an Ancestral Puebloan Indian ruin that was occupied from A.D. 750 to A.D. 1220. An ongoing excavation and stabilization program is still in progress.

You can walk among several clusters of buildings and ceremonial ruins. The handsome visitor center houses an excellent museum, which contains dioramas and other well-designed exhibits showing how these early people lived. In addition, many artifacts from the ancient Indian site are on display. Be certain to visit the second floor, for there you will see the **Shumway collection,** another fine exhibit of early Ancestral Puebloan or Anasazi Indian pottery. This is a stunning collection and should not be missed. In addition, the museum now serves as a repository for Ancestral Puebloan pottery from the entire southeastern Utah region. These rare artifacts have been placed behind glass in visible storage so that they may be seen and appreciated by all. Besides the museum shop there are several Indian arts and crafts stores in Blanding (population 3,600). From Moab the round-trip driving time is approximately four hours. Information: Edge of the Cedars State Park Museum, 660 West and 400 North; (435) 678–2238; www.statepark.utah.gov.

The Dinosaur Museum in Blanding at 745 South 200 West is open from mid-April through mid-October. Fee. Large replicas of dinosaurs, a history hall of dinosaur movie memorabilia, and a time-line exhibit are housed in a contemporary building at the edge of town. The museum also includes casts of dinosaur tracks and the actual pelvis from a local dinosaur, the Blanding Giant. Information: (435) 678–3454.

Two Routes between Moab and Capitol Reef National Park

Capitol Reef is almost directly west of Moab, but to get there you must make an arc to the south or the north. The southern route, longer but more interesting, leads south from Moab to Blanding, Utah (see "Edge of the Cedars State Park Museum"), continuing south on U. S. Highway 191, 4 miles to the junction with paved Utah Highway 95. There are no towns from this junction to Hanksville Utah, 124 miles distant. Although gas is available at Fry Canyon, it is best to fill your tank at the junction. Utah Highway 95, an excellent paved road and a Utah Scenic Byway, provides incredible views of red rock country and mature pygmy forests as it courses northwest toward the Colorado River and Lake Powell. It cuts through spectacular Coombs Ridge, passes by several easily accessible Ancestral Puebloan sites, like Butler Wash Ruins, Arch Canyon Ruins, and roadside Mule Canyon Ruins, finally intersecting with Utah Highway 275, the 4.5-mile spur road leading to the heart of **Natural Bridges National Monument.** (For natural bridge formation see in this section "A Geologic Primer to Southeastern Utah.") The 8-mile loop from the monument's visitor center takes you to a variety of pullouts and scenic overlooks, allowing you to view the world's largest display of natural bridges. Allow about 1.5 hours for a leisurely reconnaissance of the monument, more if you wish to hike down some of the trails to the bridges. Information: Natural Bridges National Monument, HC60 Box 1, Lake Powell, Utah 84533; (435) 692–1234; www.nps.gov/nab.

From the National Monument turnoff, Scenic Byway 95 courses through remote Fry Canyon where there is a good cafe and comfortable lodging at **Fry Canyon Lodge** (see Staying There, page 99). From there the highway drops down into the Colorado River Basin, crossing the Colorado River at Cataract Canyon. As the highway winds out of the river basin, there are scenic pullouts that offer fine views of Lake Powell and Hite Marina. Continuing, it is only a short drive on to Hanksville, Utah, where there is a Bureau of Land Management visitor center on the west side of town, which has a pioneer water mill used for wood cutting and ore crushing on display. The Capitol Reef visitor center is only about thirty minutes away. Allow more than four hours driving time on this route from Moab to Capitol Reef National Park. Watch for icy conditions in cold weather.

For the northern route take paved U.S. Highway 191 from Moab to I–70 near Crescent Junction. Then travel west on I–70 past Green River, Utah, to the intersection of Utah Highway 24. Follow Utah Highway 24 south through Hanksville and Caineville to Capitol Reef. Along the way you may want to stop at Green River, the melon-growing capital of eastern Utah, approximately one hour out of Moab. It rests alongside the Colorado River's longest tributary and takes its name from that great river. It is an interesting, very small old Utah town that slumbers in the midday heat as the traffic whizzes by on nearby I–70. (That interstate connects Denver, Colorado, with I–15 to Las Vegas, Nevada, and Los Angeles, California.)

From Green River travel I–70 to Utah Highway 24 and turn south. The sights along Utah Highway 24 could very well be in a national park (see "Utah Highway 24 East of the Capitol Reef Visitor Center," later in this chapter). Near Hanksville, about an hour's drive from Green River, you will pass close to the junction of the **Fremont** and **Muddy Rivers** where they join to become the **Dirty Devil River** (see "History"). From Hanksville to Capitol Reef the driving time is less than an hour through some very scenic territory that includes good views of the moonscape badlands and Factory Butte, which stands taller than any of America's skyscrapers. Allow 2.5 hours for driving time between Moab and the Capitol Reef visitor center.

Factory Butte

Capitol Reef National Park

One hundred and fifty miles west of Moab, Utah, and 225 miles southeast of Salt Lake City is Utah's second-largest national park. It is one of the nation's most exotic but least-known scenic areas. Containing an unbelievable variety of landforms in its 378 square miles, the park stretches like an elongated teardrop for more than 80 miles from its northern border to the south, where its constricted tip comes within just a few miles of Lake Powell.

Within its borders the land ranges from 3,800 to 8,600 feet in elevation. It contains the 100-mile-long **Waterpocket Fold,** part of an elevated, elongated, and grossly distorted mass of rock that gives the park its name. Early prospectors trying to cross from east to west came face to face with this monstrous outcropping of rock rising from the desert floor, Utah's version of the Great Barrier Reef. Because it obstructed their forward progress and frustrated their journey westward, some of these fortune seekers who had previously known adventure on the high seas likened it to a reef rising from the ocean's floor. The reef was such an effective deterrent to travel that the lands west of it were some of the last to be explored and settled in the continental United States.

When the early explorers did penetrate the area in the 1870s, they were dumbfounded by what they saw, especially Captain Clarence Dutton, who reached the **Aquarius Plateau** (Boulder Mountain) area just southwest of Capitol Reef with the last exploration group formed to map unknown regions of the contiguous United States. Climbing to the lava rim on top and looking out over the weirdly eroded cliffs, the reef's Waterpocket Fold, and miles and miles of canyon and plateau country, he wrote, "It is a sublime panorama. . . . It is a maze of cliffs and terraces lined off with stratification, of crumbling buttes, red and white domes, rock platforms gashed with profound canons, burning plains barren even of sage—all glowing with bright colors and filled with sunlight." Later Dutton wrote, "The Aquarius should be described in blank verse and illustrated upon canvas."

Some have likened the Capitol Reef area to a symphony in sandstone. An unfinished symphony at that, with many variations on the theme. In Capitol Reef National Park, erosion continues to carve some of the most unusual features in Canyon Country, making liars out of the geology books. Canyons and cliffs take on sizes and shapes not found elsewhere. Even buttes, ordinarily easy to recognize, defy the norm and take on otherworldly shapes. One of Capitol Reef's most common butte shapes occurs when the Navajo sandstone erodes to the shape of a dome. The frequent occurrence of these symmetrical, sometimes 1,000-foot-high shapes, which resemble the domes on top of the principal government buildings in Washington, D.C., gives this national park the first part of its name, Capitol. And there are even variations on the dome theme. Many exotic rounded buttes have protuberant points, while others are squared off and look like cylinders standing on end. The Navajo Indians picked up on another unique aspect of the reef. They called it the "land of the sleeping rainbow." To them this long reef of geologic whimsy resembled a colorful sprawling rainbow, resting near the earth's surface, tinted by the multicolored Chinle shale, one of the most colorful rock layers on earth.

The scenic and geologic wonders of this area were first set aside for preservation in 1937 as a national monument. The monument received national park status in 1971. For a number of years, this remote, isolated park languished in solitude and peace, attracting loyal followers from Utah, California, and the Federal Republic of Germany (in that order during one year of heavy European travel to this country). But when the last segment of Utah Highway 12 was paved, opening an easy, all-weather route from Bryce Canyon National Park, the number of visitors to Capitol Reef increased so that in recent years the figure soared to more than 700,000. But this large park absorbs crowds easily, and even during the busiest summer months, there is a sense of peacefulness and remoteness not found at many of the other parks. You can still walk some of the park's less frequented short trails to unique scenic landscapes and have plenty of moments to yourself. That gas stations, restaurants, and motels have been removed from the park further enhances its sense of remoteness. The closest gas stations are near Torrey, Utah, 10 miles west of the park at the junction of Utah Highways 12 and 24. Information: Superintendent, Capitol Reef National Park, HCR70, Box 15, Torrey, Utah 84775; (435) 425–3791; www.nps.gov/care/.

Seeing the Park

The park is open all year. Two all-weather roads penetrate its north half. The paved road, Utah Highway 24, a Utah Scenic Byway, crosses it for 14 miles from east to west, while the paved Scenic Drive road probes its long axis for 12 miles. Both routes provide magnificent scenery from the road. But the park's uniqueness can best be appreciated by driving the short spur roads off the main roads and by taking short, safe walks into washes, slots, gorges, and canyons and over slickrock outcroppings to high canyon rims, natural bridges, and Indian ruins.

It is the special province of Capitol Reef that there are many interesting things to see concentrated in a reasonably compact area. This means that really long drives within the park are not required and that many locations of special interest can be revisited with ease. In addition, the scenic roads and trails there pro-

The Castle, near Capitol Reef National Park visitor center

vide an intimacy with the land you will not encounter elsewhere in the Southwest. If southeastern Utah is nature's classroom, then surely Capitol Reef is its hands-on laboratory.

In addition to the park's paved all-weather roads safe for family autos, there are miles of unpaved roads, often requiring special vehicles, that lead to remote sights of rare beauty.

The junction of Utah Highway 24 and the Scenic Drive road is the location of the Capitol Reef visitor center, elevation 5,400 feet above sea level. The center is dramatically situated across the highway and south of the **"Castle,"** an unusual Wingate butte with fluted and crenellated towers, sitting on top of colorful, ledgy Chinle formation slopes and fronted by a sculpted red Moenkopi base. These are three of the four most common rock formations you will see in the park. In addition to its setting, the visitor center provides an interesting ten-minute narrated slide show about the history and geology of the park. The display area in the center has some good natural history and cultural exhibits. Be certain to see the buffalo hide shields that were found within the park's borders. It has not yet been established who owned them. Probably they were made by either the Fremont Indians or the Utes who roamed this area in later times.

The center stocks many books for sale, offering a very good selection of information about the park and the Southwest.

Utah Highway 24 West of the Visitor Center

To gain an overall impression of Capitol Reef Park, you can do a fairly quick reconnaissance by traveling approximately 2.5 miles west of the visitor center to the **Panorama Point** and **Goosenecks Overlook of Sulphur Creek** junction. At the junction turn left and drive the short distance to the Panorama Point parking area. Walk to the viewing area, where you will find laid out before you the heart of the park, including the huge curving spine of Capitol Reef as it extends southward. Many of the whitish, swirling, rising domes, knobs, and cylinders are sculpted from the Navajo sandstone for which the park is best known. From this vantage point you can see why the reef presented such an impenetrable barrier to early settlers.

Beyond the reef to the southeast are the Henry Mountains; to the southwest is the Aquarius Plateau (Boulder Mountain). Return to the parking lot. Drive out the way you came for a very short distance to the dirt and gravel junction road taking off to the right to the **Goosenecks Overlook.** It is less than 1 mile long and easily passable. At the parking lot there are two trails. The shorter **Goosenecks Trail** leads 600 feet to a protected, fenced overlook of the **Sulphur Creek Gorge.** The second trail, labeled the **Sunset Point Trail,** extends about 0.33 mile, is double-wide (with a few benches along the way), and has been made as level as possible for those who are not steady on their feet.

The Goosenecks Trail leads through a veritable garden of Moenkopi rock as it follows the gorge rim at 6,400 feet elevation. The rim drops more than 500 feet to Sulphur Creek below, the dark reddish brown of the raindrop-pocked Moenkopi rim giving way to the contrasting whitish gray to tan layers of the Kaibab limestone. This is probably the only place where you will have a chance to see a broad expanse of the Kaibab limestone in southeastern Utah.

The sinuous, meandering curves made by Sulphur Creek deep in the gorge are called "goosenecks." As the creek sliced through this section of Miner's Mountain uplift, cutting its gorge, it kept the widely looping and curving course it had followed for millions of years across the surface of an ancient flat plain. As the land rose, the river cut down, much like an S-shaped cookie cutter. As it cut deeper, the river could not overflow its banks to reduce the curves. It became trapped in the deep recesses of its own curves. In other words, the meandering curves became entrenched. When entrenched curves are so close to one another that they almost

"Pastry" Moenkopi, rim of Sulphur Creek Gorge

meet, they are called goosenecks. These goosenecks are clearly visible from the rim.

As you walk along the longer Sunset Point Trail, keep an eye out for some interesting rock formations. Several giant slabs of Moenkopi have fallen in such a way as to produce forms that look like dolmens or ancient tombs. Other giant slabs show the separation of their formative layers, looking for all the world like cross-sections of flaky, multilayered pastries. Along this trail also look for such regional plants as Mormon tea, Utah juniper, piñon pine, and roundleaf buffaloberry. Return to Utah Highway 24 and turn left. Travel a little more than 0.5 mile to the well-marked **Chimney Rock** turnoff. Pull into the parking lot to view the spire that rises more than 400 feet from its base.

At one time this spire was attached to the nearby cliffside. The large gap you see between the two is a testament to the power of seasonal erosion or weathering (see "Geologic Overview"). The whitish cap on top of the chimney is a Chinle formation rock, Shinarump member. The Shinarump member is also the prominent feature of **Twin Rocks**, which can be viewed from a pullout 2 miles farther west on Highway 24. The shaft of the Chimney Rock spire and the eroded red beds in front of you belong to the Moenkopi formation. The 3.5-mile round-trip Chimney Rock Trail (allow two to three hours for this loop trail) takes off from this area and is rated as "fairly strenuous," gaining 540 feet elevation in 0.75 mile. From the ridge at trail's end are fine views of the reef face and Chimney Rock below. Return to Highway 24. Turn left and drive back to the visitor center junction. To drive and see all of the sights, excluding Chimney Rock Trail, along this segment of the highway takes about ninety minutes.

Now you can choose to continue on Highway 24, east of the visitor center, or take 20-mile paved round-trip Scenic Drive southeast alongside the face of the reef. Each of the next two segments as presented here will take half a day but can be seen piecemeal in a shorter span of time. For instance, just driving up the Scenic Drive road and back offers some good sights and takes only about an hour and a half. But taking any of the unpaved spur roads will take more time.

Scenic Drive Road

Turn right—or southeast—from the Capitol Reef visitor center and follow the signs along the Scenic Drive Road past the interesting **Blacksmith Shop** on the right and the **Ripple Rock Nature Center** on the left—a must-see educational stop if you have children with you. At 0.75 mile from the visitor center is the Picnic Area (Doc Inglesby Picnic Grove) and parking lot. On a hot day this area of the park is a veritable oasis. The translucent green of the giant old cottonwood trees (one with a girth greater than 20 feet) and the lovely old orchards watered by the ever-flowing Fremont River that passes nearby make this area a good resting spot for a picnic or camping. Both early Indians and white settlers recognized the amenities of this location. The settlers established the community of Fruita there. Even with the development of the park, traces of that early settlement area remain. From the picnic area you can take a footpath leading to a bridge across the river, then through the fruit orchards to the old **Fruita School House** across Utah Highway 24. The orchards still produce some of the largest, juiciest sweet

Utah juniper

cherries, peaches, apricots, pears, and apples you will ever taste, and if you are there during the fruiting season, you can pick a few of these morsels without charge as long as you consume them while you are in the orchard. You can pick fruit to take out of the orchard for a fee during the designated harvest season. Inquire at the visitor center. If you arrive in the spring when the orchards are blooming, the visual feast is free of charge.

Some afternoon if you want to "sit out" an afternoon thunderstorm, pull into the parking-picnic area. If it has been a "gully washer," as those storms often are, water will begin to cascade over the surrounding high cliff rims. Those instant waterfalls crash hundreds of feet down to the valley floor. After witnessing an event like that, you will never again question the role of seasonal water as the powerful shaping force of all that you see around you. Keep an eye out for colorful yellow-headed blackbirds and redwing blackbirds, as well as western bluebirds and black-billed magpies.

Just past the entrance to the picnic area and after crossing the small bridge over the **Fremont River,** to the right is the **Historic Gifford Homestead.** The turn-of-the-twentieth-century house is now a museum and store detailing the lifeway of the early Mormon pioneers in the area. Park at the picnic area and walk the short distance to the homestead. In the store local artisans have reproduced many of the handicrafts of the period; from time to time there are demonstrations of rag rug braiding, candle and soap making, tinsmithing, and pottery making. Special events are held at the Gifford House around Easter, Independence Day, September harvest time, and between Thanksgiving and Christmas. The Gifford House is open from late May through mid-October.

The Scenic Drive Road then passes by the pleasant **Fruita Campground** nestled on the right in the midst of orchards and lawns, a little more than 1 mile from the visitor center. On the left at approximately 1.2 miles is the **Cohab Canyon Trailhead** (see "History"). The trail is 3.5 miles round-trip and is rated as "strenuous" for the first 0.25 mile. It leads to a hidden canyon above the campground and a maze of narrow side canyons, ending just across Utah Highway 24 from the **Hickman Bridge** trailhead. In an additional 0.5 mile is the fee station where you can pick up a copy of the brochure titled *A Guide to the Scenic Drive*. Although the remaining portion of the main trunk road of the Scenic Drive is paved, it is narrow, winding, hilly, and without a center stripe. Always keep well to the right and obey the posted speed limit. Approximately 0.75 mile from the fee station, the road reaches the top of **Danish Hill,** where there is a paved pullout. This is a good place to stretch your legs and orient yourself to the surrounding country.

From the direction you have just come, look back to the northwest to nice views over the Fruita area. Across the road to the northeast are massive, steep, pinkish sandstone cliffs of the Wingate formation resting on greenish gray and purplish-appearing layers of Chinle formation rocks. They in turn rest on the dark reddish brown Moenkopi rocks that erosion has sculpted to a variety of interesting shapes. In the distance, to the south, all along the ridge of the reef are several strangely eroded outcroppings of whitish Navajo sandstone. Early settlers pulled no punches when they called one of the more prominent protuberances **Fern's Nipple.**

Continue south along the Scenic Drive approximately 1 mile to the unpaved spur road leading up **Grand Wash.** A *wash* is a dry water course larger than a gully and smaller than a canyon. When it rains, it is subject to flash flooding and can become a raging river capable of washing away everything in its path, including automobiles. Heed the sign and do not enter if rain is threatening. Just as you enter the wash, look carefully at the cliffside to the left, near the base. There you will see several old uranium mine tunnels, closed off with gates. Those mines are in the uranium-containing Shinarump member of the Chinle formation. Exploration for uranium was carried out in this area from 1904 up through the 1950s.

As you travel the 1.2 miles to the Grand Wash parking lot through the gap between the high, desert-varnished Wingate cliffs, you will notice an increasing amount of vegetation, particularly some fine stands of stunted Utah juniper. Also watch for Apache plum, Fremont barberry, rabbitbrush, and dwarf yucca. As you travel up the wash, you will catch glimpses of smoothly sculpted Navajo sandstone buttes in a variety of shapes along the skyline in front of you. Soon look for the pullout on the left. Here you can catch a view of **Cassidy Arch** high up to your left. You'll have to look hard to see the arch. Just before reaching the parking area is a sign marking a shallow depression in the rock wall to the right. This is **Echo Cliff.** Try it. It works.

From the parking lot a short and pleasant walk continues on up the wash leading 0.25 mile to the Cassidy Arch trailhead and 2.25 miles on through the wash to Utah Highway 24. The trail takes you through widely spaced junipers that offer good shade for a picnic on a hot day. In May the spaces between the junipers showcase a wide variety of wildflowers. As you continue along the trail, the sandstone appears "moth-eaten" in some areas. This honeycomb effect is caused by

erosion as water "melts" parts of the sandstone rocks that are not tightly cemented
together. Farther on you will see where erosion has gone wild, creating potholes and
gigantic vertical tanks in the sandstone the
size of phone booths. Many of these are large
enough to sit or stand in. The Cassidy Arch
trailhead sign is a good place to turn around,
unless you want to continue on through the
"narrows" for about 2 miles where the trail
slips between 500-foot-tall cliff walls that are
only 20 to 30 feet apart. Eventually the wash
will deposit you onto Utah Highway 24,

Rock wren

approximately 4.5 miles east of the visitor center. Another alternative is to take the
3-mile round-trip "strenuous" hike to Cassidy Arch (about 1,000 feet elevation
gain) in the Navajo sandstone. Whether Butch Cassidy, the outlaw, ever saw the
arch named for him is a matter of conjecture, but he did apparently frequent
Grand Wash, where he allegedly built a hideout shelter.

Return to the Scenic Drive road and turn left, following the road approximately 2.4 miles as it ascends gradually up to **Slickrock Divide,** paralleling a
gully to the right. The gully is filled with large slabs of Moenkopi rock, many having prominent "ripple marks" (see "Reading the Rocks"). Pull into the parking
area to the right. Slickrock Divide separates the Grand Wash and the **Capitol
Gorge** drainage areas and is named Slickrock because of the prominent smooth
sandstone outcroppings. It offers fine views of the reef, with many formations in
the Navajo sandstone visible above the Wingate cliffs. The land rising to the west,
called **Miner's Mountain,** is dotted with vegetation and is part of a large uplift
that extends from Sulphur Creek Gorge all the way up to this point. It was given
the name Miner's Mountain because of its uranium and copper deposits.

From the divide it is only a little more than 2 miles to the Capitol Gorge–
Pleasant Creek junction. Along the way you will pass the **Egyptian Temple,** a
structure, like Chimney Rock, carved from the Moenkopi and capped with the Shinarump member of the Chinle formation. In addition, you will see some light-
colored Shinarump boulders carved by nature into a variety of shapes, one
resembling a dinosaur. Just beyond the Capitol Gorge–Pleasant Creek junction are
a picnic shelter and orientation exhibit. Here the dirt and gravel road leads approximately 2 miles to the Capitol Gorge parking area and comfort station. Drive carefully on this rough road and do not enter if it is raining or a storm is threatening.

For eighty years this gorge, cut through the reef by water, was the only feasi-
ble route for wagons and autos to pass from one side of the reef to the other. Even
at that it was always fraught with difficulties. Flash floods and falling boulders made
travel through the gorge very difficult. As you travel down the gorge along the
2-mile unpaved road to the parking area, look for rock wrens, canyon wrens,
mountain bluebirds, and the seldom seen golden eagles. Although some eagles nest
in the high cliffs in the park, they seem to stay out of sight much of the time, relin-
quishing their airspace to the ravens that are commonly seen.

Erosional potholes and tanks

Soon the road passes between high Wingate cliffs rising abruptly on both sides. To the right is **Tapestry Wall,** where desert varnish (see "Reading the Rocks") has streaked the cliff walls with beautiful vertical designs. Also, as you drive along, look for evidence of cross-bedding in the sandstone next to the road. Much of the scenery along the sky-line, including the **Golden Throne** off to your left (as you return to the Scenic Drive), is sculpted from the smooth, cream-colored Navajo sandstone. A parking pullout is near a short trail leading to a viewpoint for the Golden Throne, one of the reef's best-known sculpted Navajo buttes and one of the most visible points along the reef, at 6,500 feet. In this area the cliff walls are in the Kayenta sandstone, topped by the Navajo. Drive on to the end of the road and the parking area.

From the parking area the **Capitol Gorge Trail** leads beyond the picnic shelter through the gorge's narrow walls (the "Narrows") for about 2 miles round-trip to the tanks where most visitors turn around. You will walk through areas where the cliff walls rise more than 800 feet above you. From the parking area signs also lead to the Golden Throne Trail, a "strenuous" 4-mile round-trip hike that gains more than 1,000 feet in 2 miles, offering clifftop views of the Golden Throne. Some say that this trail really penetrates the heart of the Capitol Reef country, offering incredible views of the awesome and beautifully eroded Navajo sandstone in all of its shapes and colors.

The 2-mile round-trip trail up the gorge is a flat one, the Kayenta rocks giving way to the Navajo sandstone. Farther down the gorge the Navajo will be at eye level. There again look for cross-bedded surface marks (see "Reading the Rocks"). These are sweeping lines on the rock's surface that intercept one another at varying angles, revealing the origin of this rock millions of years ago (see "A Geologic Primer to Southeastern Utah"). Notice how the Navajo cliffs erode to smooth, rounded shapes rather than the steep abrupt configurations of the Wingate sandstone. It is believed that if the Navajo rested on the same soft Moenkopi rock that underlies the Wingate, it too would fracture into giant pieces, forming steep cliffs. But the Navajo's base, the Kayenta, is harder and erodes more slowly, allowing subtle, rounded shapes to develop (see "Reading the Rocks," hard-soft layering).

As you walk down the gorge, you will soon pass **Fremont Indian petroglyphs** on the north cliff wall, and a little farther on at 0.5 mile you will reach the **Pioneer Register** (see "History"). Beyond the register beginning about 0.75 mile are the "tanks," erosional basins that collect water similar to those in Grand Wash. Water pockets like these are common throughout the "folded" and uplifted areas of Capitol Reef.

Return to the parking lot and drive back to the Scenic Drive road at the Y junction. Turn left onto the branch leading to Pleasant Creek. In about 1 mile from the Capitol Gorge junction, you will catch good views of the **Golden Throne** from a pullout to the left. Continue on approximately 2.3 miles to another Y junction. Bear right there and continue to keep to the right as you drive through the corrals of the old Sleeping Rain-

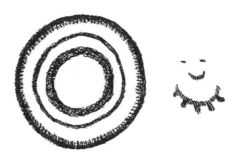

Fremont Indian petroglyphs

bow Ranch and on to Pleasant Creek. The road for conventional vehicles ends at the creek. There is plenty of space to park. (Note: Check on the condition of this dirt road at the visitor center before driving it.)

Hiking Down Pleasant Creek: A Narrative Account

It is 9:00 A.M. and the sun is already beaming down on us with a vengeance. We left our motel at 8:15, arriving at the visitor center just before 8:30. It took us only about thirty minutes to drive from the visitor center to the parking area here alongside Pleasant Creek. Today is going to be a scorcher. But for now it is very pleasant alongside this perennially flowing stream, aptly named Pleasant Creek. The stream has its origin up along the high escarpments of **Boulder Mountain.** There at elevations several thousand feet higher than here, rainfall is more plentiful, keeping this stream flowing year-round. Down here the precipitation is only a meager 5 to 7 inches a year. The stream has helped carve this beautiful wide valley and, like Capitol Gorge, has cut right through the reef. Cattlemen used to drive their herds to market along this well-watered route all the way to the old settlement of Notom on the east side of the reef, more than 6 miles away. The water is plenty cold. We were told that it is not drinkable, so we have our own water in quart containers in our day pack. Park officials recommend a gallon of water per person per day along backcountry trails like this one.

We douse ourselves with insect repellent and sunscreen and, with several water bottles in our day pack, head down the creek. There is not a maintained trail here, but intrepid travelers' boots have worn a path through the brush. Just north of us we notice a ranch house perched on the mesatop that extends like a peninsula into but above the valley. The site was once occupied by the early Indians of the region and later settled by Mormon pioneers. In the late 1930s it was developed and occupied by Lurt and Alice Knee, who along with other devotees helped put Capitol Reef on the map.

Now we leave the stream and walk across the valley floor to the high cliffs on the northeast side, just below the ranch. We reach the talus slopes below the cliffs and spread out as we search the cliff walls for some of the most unusual petroglyphs in southeastern Utah. Our daughter yells out first. Sure enough, she is

Tamarisk

standing in front of one of the petroglyph panels. We climb the jumbled heap of rocks to get a closer look. In one area we see several figures that look like "smiley faces." Now we see a number of concentric circles resembling a target with a bull's-eye. Unfortunately it is marred by someone's bullet. We have been told that many of these pictures may have been made by an ancient Indian stargazing and tracking cult. This may have been one of many "stations" in the Southwest to record the data of the heavens.

Even today the events in the heavens determine the time for planting and certain ceremonial functions for many Pueblo Indians. Perhaps the mouth in the "smiley figure" is a crescent moon and the two pecked holes above it are two stars or planets as they appeared in relation to the moon some starry night nearly 1,000 years ago. The concentric circles baffle us, but we do remember reading that they may represent the sun. My son notices some interesting animal and human forms, many of which we have seen in other locations. We marvel at the ability of these people to incise the rock so precisely with little more than a piece of chert or flint that has been "worked" into the shape of a chisel.

Looking at our watches, we pull ourselves away from other possible petroglyph discoveries and return to the creek to explore the valley farther downstream. We walk through sage, tamarisk, and willow. Monarch butterflies, as large as we have ever seen, flit nonchalantly in the purple tamarisk blossoms. One monarch, completely absorbed with the blossoms, catches my daughter's eye. She sneaks up behind it and is able to photograph it from less than two feet away. Now the valley's southern wall and the creek come close together as we enter Pleasant Creek's canyon. Soon the canyon walls narrow and block the sun. The shade is refreshing, for even at the lower elevations here in the park it is considerably cooler in the shade than in the sun. Now we reach an area where the creek narrows and flows down slippery sandstone steps. It drops a few feet at a time until it finally cascades into several large, deep pools before it continues its meandering course as Pleasant Creek.

It is 11:00 A.M., warm and getting warmer. We are sweating profusely. The pools look inviting. The cold water feels good as we immerse ourselves. The smooth sandstone creekbed is slippery, the water instantly refreshing. As the kids wade upstream, we dry off by stretching out on a huge slab of sandstone. The warm rock feels good on our cold, wet bodies as the hot sun beams down from a bright blue sky. Colorful butterflies flit from one side of the creek to the other. We relax completely. Scanning the horizon, we notice several massive, white domed-shaped rock formations looming in the distance against a backdrop of one of the bluest skies we have ever seen. With no other people around, we have the valley to ourselves this June day. We savor these moments of total solitude, unique on this earth, deep in the remote canyon recesses of Pleasant Creek, Capitol Reef National Park.

Utah Highway 24 East of the Capitol Reef Visitor Center

In many ways the drive east of the visitor center on paved Utah Highway 24 is one of the most satisfying in terms of gaining an overall impression of sights the park has to offer. It is one of the busiest sections of the park and can even be downright crowded midsummer. From the visitor center to the park boundary is about 8 miles. From there you may want to continue a few more miles on paved Utah Highway 24 to see an excellent "Moki" Indian ruin and the moonscape-otherworldly badlands around Caineville and Hanksville. That drive will reward you with a view of massive and famous **Factory Butte,** rising more than 1,500 feet above the desert floor. Several picnic sites both inside and outside the park dot the road from the visitor center to Caineville. Along the way there are many sights close at hand to the left and right of the road, but also keep your eyes focused on the skyline for magnificent views of the eroded white Navajo sandstone forms that have made this area so famous. The road follows the Fremont River most of the way. That river provides the essential moisture for the relatively lush vegetation and cottonwood groves you will see on the way.

From the visitor center drive east a little less than 1 mile through many pleasant, tree-shaded areas to the first pullout to the left. There you will find an old **one-room log schoolhouse** built in 1896 by Fruita's Mormon settlers and last used in 1941. The schoolhouse is furnished and there is a recorded historical message about the school. The next pullout a little farther on puts you within a few steps of being face-to-face with a fine panel of **Fremont Indian petroglyphs** pecked into the Wingate sandstone cliff wall. An elevated viewing platform extends the entire length of the panel. Tune to AM 540 on your car radio to learn more about this panel of rock art and the culture of the ancient Fremont Indian artists who executed this work. A little farther on and in front of you, the space

Fremont Indian petroglyph panel

between the walls of the Fremont Canyon at skyline level is filled with a symmetrically rounded whitish dome that is startling in its immensity. This is **Capitol Dome,** probably the best example of the domelike Navajo sandstone structures found throughout this park.

Approximately 2 miles from the visitor center is a large parking area to the left. This is the trailhead to **Hickman Bridge.** If you have time to take only one longer hike in the park, take this "moderate" 2-mile round-trip walk to see Hickman Bridge and an amazing array of other sights. The elevation gain is 400 feet in 1 mile. Carry water in the summer. The following narrative details this hike.

Hiking the Trail to Hickman Bridge: A Narrative Account

We just arrived here at the Hickman Bridge trailhead. It is now 4:00 P.M. The air is fresh, and it is a little cooler now as a gentle breeze pushes the last few clouds from the sky, remnants of this afternoon's thunderstorm. We notice that the Fremont River that so far has been to the right side of the road is now on this side of the highway. We drop a coin in the wooden box at the trailhead for a copy of a self-guiding booklet that will help us identify numerous plants and natural phenomena. We take notice of the handy comfort station.

Booklet in hand, we start out on the flat, well-maintained trail and follow it as it parallels the river. We sidestep small pools of water created by this afternoon's brief but heavy rain. We are impressed with the vegetation here along the river. Cottonwoods, willows, and tamarisk grow profusely. Especially tamarisk. Tamarisk or tamarix or salt cedar is a southern European, Mediterranean import that has its origins in the deserts of the Middle East. It was introduced into the Southwest early in the century as an ornamental and for erosion control.

Between 1910 and 1930, this pesky plant, whose abundant seeds have "wings" in the form of small tufts of hair, became established throughout the High Southwest as seasonal breezes spread the seeds everywhere. It is a beautiful plant when it blooms, and even out of bloom its sparsely filled juniperlike branches are attractive, lending a nice green color to many a dry and drab creekbed. But its growth has become so prolific that it is squeezing out native willow trees, and its moisture consumption is so high that it is now thought to be an undesirable plant in the arid Southwest.

Looking up, we see very little vegetation above the river. The river provides a narrow band of sustenance for life in this dry country. Now we pass by rabbitbrush, a fall-blooming plant that is found everywhere in this arid land. Rabbits use it for food and shelter. We also identify four-wing saltbush, with its distinctive winglike bracts and narrow leaves, and squawbush or skunkbrush, so named for its use by Southwest American Indian women for basket materials. Its malodorous plant stems give rise to its other, less attractive name. Now the trail begins to climb abruptly. Winding our way up the cliffside, we catch good views of Capitol Dome.

As we near the top, we catch sight of numerous rounded, black as well as black-and-white lava boulders, looking for all the world like randomly strewn bowling balls. They seem to be everywhere (see "Geologic Overview"). They are stuck here and there on the benches and ledges above the Fremont River that brought them here. My daughter spots a small, narrow-leaf dwarf yucca off the trail to the right near the **Whiskey Spring Trail** junction. The yucca may well have been the single most useful natural plant to both the early Indian and the settler. Amazingly the early Indian got beyond the yucca's warlike, bayonet appearance and found that the pods, flowers, and young stalks were edible. Strips of the inedible leaves were twisted into cords and used in sandals, mats, and baskets. Not wasting any part of the highly prized yucca leaf, the sharp tips of the leaves were used as needles. The early settlers discovered that yucca roots also supply a soapy lather when placed in water—instant desert shampoo!

Roundleaf buffaloberry

Staying to the left at the junction with the **Rim Overlook** and the **Navajo Knobs Trail,** we soon come to an area with vistas to the north. Looming up in front of us are several impressive Navajo sandstone monoliths. We take numerous pictures of these awesome rocks before going on. Now we spot a prickly pear cactus as well as a small, barrel-shaped fishhook cactus as we walk into a sparse pygmy forest of Utah junipers and piñon pines. We see a large clump of roundleaf buffaloberry with its jadelike leaves. In addition, we notice numerous tufts of Indian ricegrass. The early Indians harvested the seed heads by threshing them. Then they cooked the grain or ground it into meal. We also spot several nice specimens of Mormon tea. Mormon settlers brewed a tea from the tough, rounded stems of this plant.

The trail takes us onto the face of a large outcropping of sandstone. We travel over this slickrock easily with our tennis shoes. Now the trail parallels a wash. To the right our son spots a Fremont Indian granary, a construction of sticks and mud built in a small alcove in the cliff wall. These storage cysts, mistaken for the homes of early Indians, led to the misnomer Moki or Moqui, thought by some to mean "small person." Beans, corn, and squash, the staples of the early Southwest American Indian diet, were probably stored here, safe from marauding animals. As we continue up the wash, many potholes and water tanks at the bottom of the wash come into view. Some of these natural storage tanks can hold thousands of gallons of water. They are formed when sand and gravel abrasives, powered by the force of running water, scour the surfaces of rocks. Continued abrasion over thousands, even millions, of years dissolves the sandstone where it is less well cemented together and hollows it out into these huge pots and tanks.

Walking mostly over rock along a narrow twisty segment of the trail, we spot Hickman Bridge in the distance. We are surrounded by a sea of rock and are reminded of a passage about Capitol Reef written by Stephen Trimble: "Rock, it dominates your view of Capitol Reef. Naked, ungiving, overwhelming rock. Per-

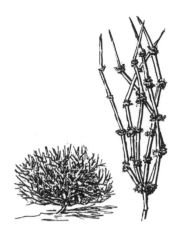

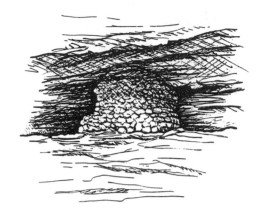

Mormon tea   *Granary, Fremont or Moki Indian ruin*

haps the feeling that the place arouses depends on that, the scarcity of life, the immensity of bare and broken rock." As we approach the bridge, we are awed by its presence. It is a huge but graceful stone semicircle spanning 133 feet between its bases. It is set amid a backdrop of rock slabs, boulders, and cliff faces—a true rock jungle. Now we are at the base and can appreciate its other dimension. This sturdy Kayenta sandstone bridge and its strong support average 15 feet in thickness. We notice the streambed under it. As it passes under the bridge, it continues its precipitous downward course.

At a high point immediately under the bridge, the inside of the arch is 72 feet above us. As we move east of the center of the bridge, it is nearly 125 feet above us. We feel completely dwarfed by its size. Now we discuss the difference between an arch and a bridge (see "A Geologic Primer to Southeastern Utah") and decide that this is a bridge, since the river runs under it. We assume the abandoned river channel followed a course west of the bridge before it created a hole and established its path through this sandstone wall. Originally known as Broad Arch, it was renamed for Joseph Hickman, who was instrumental in establishing this area as a national monument.

I climb back under the bridge and ascend the talus slope behind it to the west. I want a picture of our family framed by this giant hole in the rock wall. As I turn to look back, I am amazed by what I see. From this vantage point the true magnificence of this bridge is apparent. My family appears so small that I can barely see them as they stand under it. Rising in the background, perfectly framed by the graceful curving lines of the red stone bridge, is the massive presence of Capitol Dome. The light is perfect now; the scene beautiful if not poetic. I snap this perfect picture, compliments of Mother Nature.

Everyone is up here now. We stand in silence soaking it all in. As the sun begins to go down, the colors become richer with each passing minute. The bridge frames the white cap of the dome as it turns golden in the evening light, while the color of the sky behind it deepens to an incredible shade of blue. The silence is as powerful as the shapes and the colors. But we break the silence as we

View of Capitol Dome through Hickman Bridge

clamber noisily down the rock slopes back to the bridge and retrace our steps down to the trailhead. On the way down we catch an incredible view of **Pectol's Pyramid** across the highway to the south. We reach the car by 7:00 P.M., giving us ample time to drive back to Panorama Point to see the last rays of sunlight on Capitol Reef's west face.

Hickman Bridge Parking Lot to Hanksville

From the Hickman Bridge parking area, continue east on Utah Highway 24. In the next few miles are several parking areas offering views of many of the park's landmarks, such as swirling, pointed **Navajo Dome** with its pleated skirt base. Almost 4 miles from the visitor center is a shaded picnic area on both sides of the highway. There are picnic tables and toilets but no water. In less than 1 mile farther you will come to a parking pullout to the right that is at the end of **Grand Wash.** For those hiking through from the Grand Wash Trail off the Scenic Drive road, this is the exit. This 2.25-mile one-way trail can be walked in either direction. A little more than 6 miles east of the visitor center, on the right, is the **Elijah Behunin Cabin** and parking area. Built of sturdy sandstone blocks in 1892, this home is another testimonial to the hardy Mormon pioneers who attempted to settle near the **Fremont River.** After these pioneers had done much backbreaking labor to divert the river and then plant fields and orchards, violent floods washed away just about all their efforts in the third year of their residence. But that was not unusual, as this harsh land resisted most efforts to tame it.

About 0.5 mile farther up the road, almost 7 miles from the visitor center, is a parking turnoff to the left. There you will find a small falls cascading into a water hole. Notice the warning sign: DANGER. HAZARDOUS AREA. Heed the sign. Should you be tempted to enter the water, you do so at your own peril. Swimming is prohibited at this spot. Not only is there a dangerous undertow in the pool at times, but the sandstone when wet can be treacherously slippery.

About 8.5 miles east of the visitor center is the eastern border of the park, where wayside exhibits tell about the park. But do not stop touring there. The sights and the scenery continue even if the park does not. In another 0.5 mile is a shaded picnic area on the right. Then about 9 miles from the visitor center is the junction with the Notom-Bullfrog Marina Road. The road is paved approximately 5 miles beyond Notom (only a geographic place-name now and the location of a ranch) and unpaved much of the rest of the way.

Continue east on Utah Highway 24. In less than 2 miles, you will see a parking turnoff to the right labeled **Moki Ruin.** This is a picnic area as well. Close to the road, requiring only a short walk, is one of the best Fremont Indian granary structures to be seen in the area. Continue straight ahead until you cross the Fremont River, where you will begin to see over the next 4 miles some of the most distinctive landscapes in the Southwest.

Entirely different from those in the park, these Mancos shale badlands look like moonscapes with their wrinkled, fluted, blue-gray, pyramid-shaped structures lined up in rows for miles and miles. This scenery reaches a climax 5 miles east of Caineville where Factory Butte, with its crenellated towers, rises with great power and strangeness more than 1,500 feet above the surrounding desert. If you do not enter or leave Capitol Reef on this route, be certain you drive this far east. Near Factory Butte you are approximately 25 miles from the visitor center and 20 miles from Hanksville. Hanksville, 40 miles from the Capitol Reef visitor center and situated near the junction of the Fremont and Dirty Devil Rivers, offers gas and food. As you return to the visitor center from this eastern segment of Highway 24, you will be rewarded with some superb views from the highway that were not visible to you as you traveled in the other direction.

Remote Capitol Reef

The all-weather paved and dirt and gravel roads open up only a small part of the park's immense area to most visitors. Additional spectacular country can be seen on the network of four-wheel-drive and/or high-clearance-vehicle roads that more thoroughly cover the park. Some—like the Notom-Bullfrog Basin Marina Road to the Glen Canyon National Recreation Area and the Burr Trail Road to Boulder, Utah—connect the park to other locations. Others lead to remote areas of fossilized dinosaur bones and oyster shell beds, agate beds, and agate caves. Still others will take you face-to-face with several stunning monoliths in **Cathedral Valley**—like the **Temple of the Sun, Temple of the Moon,** and **Solomon's**

Butte—that have helped make the park famous. Road conditions change dramatically due to rain or snow. You should inquire at the visitor center before you start out for any of these destinations. The average visitor will probably feel more comfortable taking a half- or full-day jeep tour from a tour operator listed at the end of this section.

Utah Highway 12 Scenic Byway: From Capitol Reef to Bryce Canyon via Grand Staircase–Escalante National Monument

If you have the time, travel Utah Highway 12 Scenic Byway, approximately 100 miles from Capitol Reef National Park to Bryce Canyon National Park through sections of Grand Staircase–Escalante National Monument. This exceptionally scenic route offers dramatic views at almost every turn and takes you through remote southeastern Utah towns, where time seems to have stood still. This is perhaps the most interesting and scenic 100 miles you can drive in Utah's Canyon Country. The paved two-lane road takes you up to 9,400 feet elevation as it crests **Boulder Mountain** on the way to Boulder, Utah (see "Boulder Mountain, Boulder, Utah," below) and then plunges you deep into the Escalante Canyon system (see "Utah Highway 12 Scenic Byway Calf Creek Recreation Area: The Escalante Canyon System," below). The road then emerges from the canyon depths near the town of **Escalante, Utah** (population 800) with an interagency visitor center west of town and its restaurants, motels, and shops (see "Staying There," this section) before it winds by the **Escalante Petrified Forest State Park** 1 mile west of town. There you will find a small visitor center, self-guided trails (trail guide pamphlets provided) through an area laden with petrified wood, and a nice shaded picnic and camping area around a lake, **Wide Hollow Reservoir.** Information: Utah Parks and Recreation, P.O. Box 350, Escalante, Utah 84726; (435) 826–4466 or (800) 322–3770 for camping reservations.

From there the route passes through a number of small southeastern Utah towns until it reaches the road junction to **Kodachrome Basin State Park.** There you will find the informative Cannonville branch of the Grand Staircase–Escalante National Monument Visitor Center (435–679–8981). From Cannonville, travel 7 miles on a paved road to Kodachrome Basin State Park, where there are pleasant picnic and camping sites in the midst of unique freaks of nature called petrified geyser holes—eroded, white, misshapen plugs of stone and sediment standing upright everywhere you look (fee; 435–679–8562 or 800–322–3770). After **Cannonville** comes the interesting and historic old town of **Tropic** (population 450) with its shaded picnic areas and historic log-and-stone homes and roadside cafes and motels. Then Utah Highway 12 enters more scenic country and winds through a 5-mile segment of Bryce Canyon National Park before reaching the créme de la créme, **Bryce Canyon.**

Much of the scenery you will see along this route, such as at the **Calf Creek Recreation Area** deep in the Escalante Canyon system, is within the boundary of the **Grand Staircase–Escalante National Monument,** 1.9 million acres of sandstone canyon, plateaus, cliffs, and unique rock formations. Public use of this new monument is still under study, but it has been established that the Bureau of Land Management will oversee its use rather than the National Park Service. For more information about this monument, which contains in an area about the size of Delaware some of the wildest, most remote desert wilderness in the United States, contact the **Escalante Interagency Office,** 755 North Main Street, P.O. Box 246, Escalante, Utah 84726; (435) 826–5499; www.ut.blm.gov/monument/.

Utah Highway 12 is a scenic byway, not a speedway. Although it is a good, paved two-lane road, there are some segments with narrow to no shoulders. And some parts of the roadbed wind and twist and are without guardrails. Allow two and a half hours one-way driving time—and more if you plan many stops.

Boulder Mountain, Boulder, Utah

The Aquarius Plateau, from which Boulder Mountain tops out at 11,600 feet above sea level, making it the highest timbered plateau in North America with rushing mountain streams, wide green meadows, and great stands of quaking aspens and stately evergreens, offers a stark contrast to the park below it. Even on the warmest of summer days, the temperature up there is pleasant. The views of the surrounding countryside as described by Captain Dutton (quoted in the introduction to the "Capitol Reef" section) are truly magnificent. You can reach this genuine mountain country in less than an hour from the Capitol Reef visitor center on Utah Highway 12 from Torrey to Boulder, Utah. The road climbs Boulder Mountain to 9,400 feet before descending to Boulder. There are numerous pleasant places that you will find for picnicking along the way.

If you go as far as the summit, you might just as well continue on Utah Highway 12 to **Boulder, Utah,** approximately 50 miles from the Capitol Reef visitor center. Most popular tour books have missed this town. You should not. At 6,000 feet elevation this small farming and ranching mountain community (population 100), on the flank of Boulder Mountain, has the distinction of being the last town in the United States to have a road built to it. That was in 1938–39. Until then it was the only town in the continental United States to receive its mail delivery by pack mule and packhorse. The town is scenically situated among evergreen trees and numerous mounds and ridges of white Navajo sandstone.

But more importantly Boulder is the home of **Anasazi State Park Museum** (known to some as the Coombs Site). This was a distant Kayenta Ancestral Puebloan or Anasazi outpost on the northwestern frontier of that great ancient

Ancestral Puebloan dwelling, Anasazi State Park

culture (see Section 2, "A Prehistory of Indian Country"). The park is located on the site of a village dating back to somewhere between A.D. 1050 and A.D. 1200. The excellent visitor center on the site has some good displays of early Indian life portraying its culture from various perspectives. There are displays of artifacts found on the site as well. Outside, a six-room, life-size replica of an Ancestral Puebloan dwelling has been constructed on the path that leads to the excavated prehistoric village. There eighty-seven rooms have been unearthed by University of Utah archaeologists. A small entry fee is charged to walk the interesting self-guided trails (trail brochure provided) through the ruins of this ancient village. There are several shaded picnic tables convenient to the visitor center. Information: Anasazi State Park Museum, P.O. Box 1429, Boulder, Utah 84716; (435) 335–7308.

The **Burr Trail Road** intersects Highway 12 on the south side of Boulder. This 30-mile paved section of the Burr Trail through a highly scenic portion of the Grand Staircase–Escalanate National Monument is well worth the trip out and return to Boulder. There are picnicking opportunities along the way as the road courses by Deer Creek Campground into Long Canyon and passes by the Gulch. Just beyond the Gulch look for a pullout on the left near a large and prominent cottonwood tree, which marks a very short informal trail to a small but beautiful slot canyon. The desert varnish on the towering cliff walls near the mouth of the canyon is exquisite. Other spectacular views open up as the road heads west toward Capitol Reef National Park. When the pavement ends at the park border, it's time for the casual traveler to turn around. Only high-clearance and preferably four-wheel-drive vehicles in dry weather can negotiate the steep switchbacks snaking their way down to the Notom-Bullfrog Marina Road.

Boulder now offers very good lodging, making it a pleasant place to stay in this very remote and scenic Utah town.

Utah Highway 12 Scenic Byway Calf Creek Recreation Area: The Escalante Canyon System and Grand Staircase–Escalante National Monument

From Boulder, Utah, it is an easy 20-mile drive over paved Utah Highway 12 to the Calf Creek trailhead in the Escalante Canyon system. When you come this far, you know you are truly in some of the remotest country in the United States. Calf Creek feeds the Escalante River, the last river in the continental United States to be discovered and mapped. The Escalante Canyon system is conveniently situated between Capitol Reef and Bryce Canyon National Parks. This portion of the Grand Staircase–Escalante National Monument beautifully captures the spirit of the High Southwest.

Entering the canyon system from either direction is a dramatic event, as the road winds deeper and deeper through beautifully sculptured Navajo sandstone, each turn of the road revealing some new configuration and each approaching turn offering tantalizing views of some spectacle ahead. Down, down, down through layers of rock, until finally you see a lush green paradise with the **Escalante River** flowing through it. The early Fremont Indians found this little bit of paradise, as evidenced by the numerous storage huts and petroglyphs that

Lower Calf Creek Falls, Grand Staircase–Escalante National Monument

abound in this deep canyon system. Look for the sign to Calf Creek Falls Trail and Calf Creek Campground. Follow the road to the fee parking and day-use area and tree-shaded campground alongside Calf Creek. This is a good place for a picnic or just to take a stroll.

If you have time, take the 5.5-mile round-trip walk along the flat canyon floor to **Lower Calf Creek Falls.** A self-guiding booklet is available in a small box at the trailhead. The trail follows the creek as closely as possible as it winds up the canyon between sandstone walls that contain numerous alcoves, caves, and petroglyphs. Look for horsetail in the wetter areas. It is a plant that dates back to the dinosaur age and that thrives in the seeps and moist areas of the canyon floor. Occasionally you may find pieces of barbed wire, a reminder of the early white settlers who used this natural box canyon for pasturing their calves. Calf Creek, they called it. At the end of the hike you will be rewarded with the rare beauty of 126-foot-high Lower Calf Creek Falls. You can feel the cool mist of the falls and see the lush hanging gardens around it—the oasis penultimate of southeastern Utah. You should allow four to six hours for this round-trip hike. Information: Grand Staircase–Escalante Monument, Escalante Interagency Office; (435) 826–5499.

Bryce Canyon National Park

If you travel to Capitol Reef National Park or to the eastern border of Grand Staircase–Escalante National Monument, you will be within a few hours' drive of Bryce Canyon National Park, which rests just beyond the western boundary of Utah's southeastern quadrant. Although jammed with travelers during the summer months, this unique park should be visited if you have time.

It is Utah's smallest national park, yet yearly it receives the second-largest number of national park visitors in Utah. In recent years more than 1.7 million visitors (about one-third from other countries) roamed the park's 56 square miles. In the summer it is probably the most densely populated national park in Utah. Yet even at the busiest times, pockets of peace and quiet can be found. It is a park well worth seeing for its truly stunning, delicately carved sandstone landforms that offer a visual feast not found elsewhere in the High Southwest.

Bryce Canyon National Park straddles the eastern edge of the lofty **Paunsaugunt Plateau,** one of America's highest elevated tablelands. The park extends for 18 miles along the plateau's rim and high escarpments, providing you with superb views over the surrounding Colorado Plateau country more than 2,000 feet below. On a clear day the country unfolds in front of you as you look out from **Yovimpa Point,** elevation 9,105 feet. Eighty miles in the distance, you can make out the **Henry Mountains** in the northeast, while 90 miles away near the Arizona border, **Navajo Mountain** rises into view.

But the park is better known for its "badlands" or its erosional forms than it is for its views. Not a "canyon" in the true sense of the word, the delicately carved sculptured forms that have made the park so famous occur along the eroding cliff faces of the uplifted Paunsaugunt Plateau. Paunsaugunt is a Paiute Indian word meaning "home of the beaver." Most of the unusual and extremely delicate rock forms have been carved from the Claron Formation sandstone, one of the youngest in the sedimentary stack (see "Geologic Overview"). Its varied composition includes

Bryce Canyon National Park

Sego or mariposa lily (Utah state flower)

soft layers of silt and clay with very little calcium carbonate–binding cement, as well as hard layers of limestone and dolomite that are well cemented together. The differential weathering of those alternating hard-soft layers accounts for many of the unusual shapes you will see. Perhaps the word *exquisite* describes the eroded forms better. Some have called this crenellated escarpment a fairyland, as beautiful demoiselles, delicate spires, minarets, pinnacles, and weird hoodoos reach for the sky. Some of the formations are so unusual that you will probably be caught up in the game of "name it yourself." Why not? Others have.

Early on Paiute Indians, letting their imaginations run wild, read so much into these rock forms that they developed an enchanting legend about them. They believed this area was the home of exotic lizards, birds, and manlike creatures that fell into evil ways and were all turned into stone. Accordingly they named this area Unka-timpe-Wa-Wince-Pock-ich, which means "red rock standing like men in a bowl-shaped canyon." Settlers and early park visitors also unleashed their creative minds on these rock forms, coming up with the **Turtle, the Gossips, Alley Oop and Dinny,** the **Happy Family,** and the **Organ Grinder's Monkey.** And in one single leap of fantasy, someone called a large, stony presence **Queen Victoria.** This fascination with the park's landforms made it highly popular very early in the century. The area was set aside as a national monument in 1923. By 1928 the monument was doubled in size and was declared a national park.

One of the early surveyors of the park put aside his tripod long enough to write, "There are thousands of red, white, purple and vermillion colored rocks, of all sizes, resembling sentinels on the walls of castles, monks and priests in their robes, cathedrals and congregations . . . presenting the wildest and most wonderful scene that the eye of man ever beheld." The unusual and dramatic coloration of the landforms is due to the different stages of oxidation of iron and manganese that have stained and colored these once drab rocks. Bryce's highly colored rocks are extremely sensitive to the nuances of changing light. In the early morning you will see them change from a reddish brown to light gold with traces of purple, blue, and lavender. Around noon those hues are replaced with flaming yellows and oranges, as well as brick reds and tans. In the evening those colors change to the many shades of pinks and reds for which the park is most famous. Even clouds crossing the sun's path in the daytime change the coloration from yellows and oranges to reddish browns and rusts. Some formations are topped with white, giving the impression of a winter scene.

All of the colors stand in contrast to the fresh green provided by the stands of juniper, ponderosa and piñon pine, Douglas fir, spruce, and aspen that dot the canyon rims and floors. Add to all of this the intensely clear blue sky found at this extremely high elevation and you have a picture whose subtleties challenge even the best photographer's skill.

If you plan to stay overnight in the area, try to stay near the rim at **Bryce Canyon Lodge** or at one of the park's campgrounds nearby. Being close enough to walk a short distance to the rim easily and often to see the formations change color with the changing of the light will make your Bryce Canyon experience an even more memorable one. But rimside accommodations at the lodge must be made months in advance (see "Staying There," this section).

Bryce's high altitude, averaging more than 8,000 feet above sea level, means cooler day- and nighttime temperatures, a real bonus in the summer. Summer comes late with an explosion of wildflowers in late June and July. During those months you can see blue columbine, sego or mariposa lilies (Utah's state flower), yellow evening primrose, wild iris, and Indian paintbrush. More than 400 plant species grow in the park. In the winter the main park roads are kept free of the high-altitude snows as Bryce Canyon is covered with a mantle of snow providing it with yet another contrasting color. Information: Superintendent, Bryce Canyon National Park, P.O. Box 170001, Bryce Canyon, Utah 84717; (435) 834–5322; www.nps.gov/brca. Or if you are in the area, tune your car radio to AM 590 or 1610.

Seeing the Park

Although Bryce Canyon can be seen as part of a day trip from some other base location, its rare beauty is best appreciated by spending part of an afternoon, an evening, and part of a morning there. In that length of time, not only can you see most of the sights that have made Bryce Canyon so popular with travelers (particularly along the 5.5-mile **Rim Trail,** which follows the canyon edge from **Fairyland** to **Bryce Point**), but you can hike several interesting short trails into the heart of Bryce's beautiful badlands as well. The only entry point into the main section of the park is near its north border from Utah Highway 12.

Visitors may drive into the park all year, but during the busiest months optional shuttle buses are available from a staging area outside the park (near Ruby's Inn) to the visitor center and all major scenic stops. The park entry pass that includes unlimited shuttle use over several days is cheaper than the self-drive park entry pass for the same number of days.

At the visitor center you will find geology and natural history exhibits and can view a narrated slide show about the natural history of the park. A list of interpretive programs, ranger-led walks, talks, and campfire programs offered in the summer is also posted there. (Day visitors with trailers must leave them in the visitor center parking lot or the trailer turnaround south of the Sunset Campground. Campers should leave their trailers at their campsites while exploring the rest of the park.)

The best way to see the park is to first travel the 18-mile-long scenic road to its end point at **Rainbow Point** and **Yovimpa Point.** The speed limit is 35 miles per hour. Then as you leisurely return north, you can turn into the various overlooks and trailheads without having to cross in front of the oncoming lane of traffic.

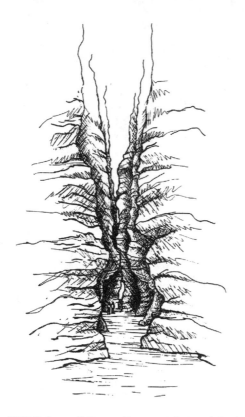

"Wall Street," Bryce Canyon National Park

At Rainbow Point take time to walk the easy to moderate 1-mile-long **Bristlecone Loop Trail** along the plateau top through a fir-spruce, bristlecone pine community. There you will see numerous bristlecone pines, a species known for its longevity and that is considered to be the oldest known living thing in the world. Some bristlecones in the West are nearly 5,000 years old. Allow about an hour. From a similar elevation, Yovimpa Point, 9,105 feet above sea level, offers excellent views out over the **Colorado Plateau** as far as New Mexico on the clearest days. From Yovimpa Point you can truly see forever.

Driving north back toward the visitor center take the spur road to both Bryce Point and **Paria Viewpoint,** which offer fine panoramas of the pink escarpment that is Bryce Canyon's signature sight. Vehicles longer than 25 feet are not allowed at Paria Viewpoint. Two longer trails, both "strenuous," begin at Bryce Point. One, the hike to the **Hat Shop** along the **Under-the-Rim Trail,** is 3.8 miles round-trip (about four hours hiking time, with a 900-foot elevation change) and takes you through a region rich in demoiselle erosional forms. The other, **Peek-a-boo Loop,** is a 5.5-mile round-trip trail (three and a half hours hiking time, with an 800-foot elevation change) that leads to views of **Alley Oop** and **Dinny, Three Wise Men, Bryce Temple, Cathedral,** and **Hindu Temple.** This trail also connects with the **Navajo Loop Trail** leading to **Sunset Point**. When horseback rides are scheduled along this or any other trail, hikers must give horses the right-of-way. Visitors should carry water on most trails below the rim and wear footwear offering good traction.

During May through September when the park is exceedingly crowded, parking spaces at some of the overlooks may be difficult to find. This is a particularly good time to use the park shuttle system. Since several of the overlooks (Inspiration, Sunset, and Sunrise) are reasonably close to one another, it may be wise to park at one overlook and use the excellent walking trail along the rim to reach the other overlooks. You may also park in the centrally located Sunset Motel Unit parking lot at Bryce Canyon Lodge.

Douglas firs growing out of gorge, Bryce Canyon National Park

The Sunset Point portion of the rim trail, elevation around 8,000 feet, gives you a breathtaking view of what makes Bryce Canyon such a special place. As you look out on the enormous amphitheater of delicately carved miniature canyons giving rise to thousands of fanciful shapes, you will begin to understand the powerful sculpting force of seasonal erosion.

The very rim you stand on is eroding away at the rate of 1 foot every fifty to sixty years. Continue to walk south along the almost level rim trail. The 0.5-mile section of trail between **Sunrise Point** and **Sunset Point** is not only fairly level but also paved, allowing handicap access to this particularly dramatic section of rim trail. Or you can choose to take the **Navajo Loop Trail** from the Sunset Point area, one of the favorite walks in the park. This trail is fairly strenuous (elevation change is about 520 feet) but is easy to negotiate. Just below the rim take the trail to the right. It descends several hundred feet below the rim by way of many well-designed switchbacks to a narrow gorge, called **Wall Street,** from which the trunks of several large Douglas fir trees rise more than 100 feet above the canyon floor between the narrow, 200-foot-tall canyon walls to the light above.

After Wall Street there are two trail junctions. Always stay to the left to complete the Navajo Loop. Along this route you will see the **Turtle, Camel and Wisemen,** the **Organ Grinder's Monkey, Thor's Hammer,** and the **Temple of Osiris.** Keep an eye out for round-leaved manzanita, mountain mahogany, and ocean spray, a few of the plants that thrive in this environment. Of course, at the end of this 1.4-mile round-trip loop, you must regain the 520 feet in elevation that you lost on the way down. There are places to rest along the way as the trail switches back up to the rim. This round-trip hike takes about one and a half hours.

Back on the level rim trail, you can walk a short distance south to **Inspiration Point,** which offers some different views of the amphitheater, or walk north to Sunrise Point, where the morning sun places much of the canyon in favorable light. From there you can take the **Queen's Garden Trail,** which leads 320 feet down into the canyon past views of Queen Victoria, **Queen's Castle,** and **Gulliver's Castle,** where, in addition to the rock formations, you will see several of the rare, almost extinct bristlecone pine trees. This is the easiest hike below the canyon rim, taking less than one and a half hours for the 1.8-mile round-trip excursion. It also connects with the Navajo Loop Trail. The **rim trail** goes on another 5 miles to **Fairyland Point** near the park's entrance station where there is an intense concentration of fanciful formations in a relatively small canyon. If you spend an evening at the park when the moon is bright, be sure to take a walk along the rim. You will see yet another variation on the theme of the canyon's ever-changing appearance.

And should you decide to stay longer at Bryce Canyon National Park, there are more than 50 miles of hiking trails to remote caves, hollows, canyons, prairie dog villages, and, of course, more of those weirdly eroded hoodoos! First-come, first-served overnight backpacking is available along the 22-mile-long Under-the-Rim Trail. A backpacking permit (fee) is required.

STAYING THERE

For some of the more remote areas of southeastern Utah, lodging and food are listed under one heading. But for Moab, where there are many choices, they are each listed separately. Generally you will take meals in a cafelike atmosphere or in a restaurant or dining room serving basic fare. Try to remember that your visit to southeastern Utah is to savor the visual landscapes. Let the visual feast compensate for some of your gastronomic needs. You will not, however, be entirely starved for quality food and superb cooking, for the scene is changing rapidly, especially in and around Moab, where several high-caliber restaurants, cafes, and dining rooms that would get along famously in any large American city have sprung up in the past few years.

Wine, beer, and cocktails are available in most areas covered by this book, except on the Indian reservations, where alcohol is illegal. The legal drinking age in all states is twenty-one. The most restrictive liquor laws are in Utah, where state liquor "package" stores are the only locations in which you can purchase liquor, wine, or beer with an alcohol content above 3.2 percent—except on Sunday and holidays, when they're closed. Only 3.2 percent beer can be purchased at food and convenience stores (depending on locality) but not wine. Restaurants with proper licensing may now serve wine by the glass or by the bottle and

mixed drinks if these are served in conjunction with food at tables or waiting areas. Although you can drink beer in a bar, you cannot be served mixed drinks or wine by the glass in a bar, except in certain easy-to-join private clubs.

Mountain bikers and visitors of all sorts may periodically fill the town of **Moab** from late March through early November, especially if one of the many scheduled special events is being held. During those times reserve lodging early because the 2,300 motel, B&B, and condo units can go quickly. And be aware that lodging prices escalate dramatically during special events. If you need additional lodging choices besides those listed here or the precise date of an event or festival or maps or books about the area, contact **Moab Information Center,** Center and Main Streets, P.O. Box 550, Moab, Utah 84532; (435) 259–8825 or (800) 635–6622; www.discovermoab.com. You can also call Moab-Canyonlands Central Reservations, which represents condo rentals and some but not all motels and B&Bs, at (435) 259–5125 or (800) 505–5343; www.moab utahlodging.com. Moab also has a hostel, the Lazy Lizard International Hostel (AAIH), 1213 South Highway 191, Moab, Utah 84532; (435) 259–6057. International visitors may exchange foreign currency at Zions Bank (435) 259-5961.

Amtrak (800–872-7245) makes

one stop a day in Green River, Utah, which is on the route of shuttle buses to Moab from Salt Lake City. Taxi or bus reservations are required. (See "Rental Cars and Taxi/Shuttle Service," this section.)

Moab, Utah

Lodging

The Gonzo Inn. This inn is located just south of the downtown shopping district yet far enough from Highway 191 to offer peace and quiet and vistas of the pink cliffs. This southwestern-style forty-three-room inn-motel with retro 1970s and industrial era influences is unique in Moab. You'll also go "Gonzo" over another plus: The inn is just a stone's throw away from the paved Mill Creek bike and walking trail. Most of the nicely furnished rooms have small outdoor patios or balconies. Some luxury suites are available. Continental-style breakfast is served in the breakfast area. Specialty coffees are available for a fee. Among the other amenities are a gift shop, heated pool, whirlpool, laundry, and bike storage. Information: The Gonzo Inn, 100 West 200 South, Moab, Utah 85432; (435) 259–2515 or (800) 791–4044; fax (435) 259–6992; www.gonzoinn.com. Moderate to expensive.

Greenwell Inn (Best Western). Open all year. One of the nicest and most comfortable older motels in Moab, a stone's throw from the Mill Creek bike and walking trail. The seventy-seven air-conditioned rooms with TVs, phones, and full bath facilities fill up fast. Queen and king beds are available in many rooms. Rooms farthest from U.S. Highway 191 are the quietest. Heated swimming pool and whirlpool. There are restaurants nearby. Information: Best Western Greenwell Inn, 105 South Main Street, Moab, Utah 84532; (800) 528–1234 (Best Western Reservations Center) or (435) 259–6151; fax (435) 259–4397; www.quinstar.com/green well. Moderate.

Cali Cochitta Bed and Breakfast. Located in central Moab is this historic-home-turned-B&B. With a former restaurateur at the helm, the breakfasts are hard to beat and the box lunches are special. Dinner also available. The three rooms, one suite, and three cottages are well tended. Hot tub. Information: Cali Cochitta Bed and Breakfast, 110 South 200 East, Moab, Utah 84532; (435) 259–4961 or (888) 427–8112; fax (435) 259–4964; www. moabdreaminn.com. Inexpensive to moderate.

Sunflower Hill Bed and Breakfast Inn. In a turn-of-the-twentieth-century home (plus an adjacent cottage)—and situated in a quiet neighborhood amid shade trees, grassy lawns, and flower gardens and within easy walking distance of downtown Moab—rests this B&B. There are eleven guest rooms and suites (one two-bedroom unit). All have private baths (some with whirlpools). In the sunny dining room, breakfast is served. Ask about age restrictions. Information: Sunflower Hill Inn, 185 North 300 East, Moab, Utah 84532; (435) 259–2974 or (800) 662–2786; fax (435) 259–3065; www.sunflower hill.com. Moderate to expensive.

Cedar Breaks Condos. The six Cedar Break Condos (at Center and

400 East) are located in a two-story building in a quiet location away from the highway but close to restaurants and shops. They are spacious and comfortable. Most have two bedrooms, living-dining room, and kitchen. Some have balconies. Information: Cedar Breaks Condos, 110 South 400 East, Moab, Utah 84532; (435) 259–5125 or (800) 505–5343; www.moabutahlodging.com. Inexpensive.

Canyonlands Inn (Best Western). In the heart of downtown Moab at Main and Center Streets yet situated so that most of the rooms offer peace and quiet. There are seventy-seven nicely furnished, air-conditioned rooms in this attractive two-story motel. Standard or deluxe rooms, heated swimming pool, fitness room, and a storage area for bikes make this a comfortable place to stay. Continental breakfast included. Information: Best Western Canyonlands Inn, 16 South Main Street, Moab, Utah 84532; (435) 259–2300 or (800) 528–1234; fax (435) 259–2301; www.canyonlandsinn.com. Moderate.

Rustic Inn. This budget inn is open all year and is located just off U.S.

Highway 191. Thirty-four air-conditioned rooms with TVs and telephones. All rooms with queen beds. This motel is in a quiet location. The large rooms are a bargain for the price. Heated swimming pool on the grounds. Information: Rustic Inn, 120 East 100 South Street, Moab, Utah 84532; (435) 259–6177 or (800) 231–8184; fax (435) 259–2642; www.moabutah.com/rusticinn. Inexpensive.

Kokopelli Lodge. You'll find these charming eight-in-a-line smaller units are just a short walk to downtown and yet off Highway 191, nestled around a shady courtyard with picnic possibilities. Each of the petite rooms are priced economically, and a continental breakfast is thrown in as well. Information: Kokopelli Lodge, 72 South 100 East, Moab, Utah 84532; (435) 259–7615 or (888) 530–3134; fax (435) 259–8498. Inexpensive.

Comfort Suites. Located less than a mile south of downtown is this seventy-five-room motel. The quietest rooms are in the back away from Highway 191. The spacious rooms have a microwave and a refrigerator. Indoor whirlpool and swimming

Moab, Utah

pool. Exercise room. Continental breakfast. Information: Comfort Suites, 800 South Main Street, Moab, Utah 84532; (435) 259–5252 or (800) 228–5150; fax (435) 259–7110. Inexpensive to moderate.

Redstone Inn. Located south of but within easy walking distance of downtown is this rustically handsome log motel with fifty-two rooms. The smallish rooms are furnished with either a queen or two standard beds, refrigerators, and microwaves. Most bathrooms have showers only. Guests have access to barbecue grill, picnic patio. Information: Redstone Inn, 535 South Main Street, Moab, Utah 84532; (435) 259–3500 or (800) 772–1972; fax (435) 259–2717; www.moabredstone.com. Inexpensive.

Adobe Abode B&B. Out by the Nature Conservancy's Scott M. Matheson Wetlands Preserve and across from Moab Skyride is this B&B. Its many interesting details, borrowed from both Indian and Spanish influences, have been lovingly crafted and incorporated into the design and decor. There are three guest rooms in a long wing that adjoins the common areas in the main house. Each room has its own special Southwestern signature. Hot tubs. Generous continental breakfast. Information: Adobe Abode, 778 West Kane Creek Boulevard, Moab, Utah 84532; (435) 259–7716; www.adobeabode. com. Moderate.

Pack Creek Ranch. This country inn is located 15 miles south of town (from U.S. Highway 191 turn left at mile marker 118, then right onto La Sal Mountain Loop Road). When you turn into the gate at Pack Creek

Ranch and see the tall mountains and pink cliffs in the midst of a green valley cut by a clear mountain stream, you may think you have died and gone to heaven. On this large ranch spread there are a variety of differently configured western-style cabins, all with kitchens and private baths, but no phones or TV, accommodating a total of sixty guests. One large cabin has four bedrooms. All cabins are nicely furnished. Some have fireplaces. A full breakfast is served in the handsome lodge dining room. Swimming pool, hot tub, sauna, Jacuzzi. Also available for a fee are massage therapy and trail rides. Information: Pack Creek Ranch, P.O. Box 1270, Moab, Utah 84532; (435) 259–5505; fax (435) 259–8879; www.packcreek ranch.com. Moderate.

Sorrel River Ranch Resort. Located just off Utah Scenic Byway 128 about 20 miles northeast of Moab (mile marker 17) is this 160-acre country club–like oasis on the banks of the Colorado River. In this beautiful natural setting are thirty-three luxurious units occupying log buildings alongside the river. Swimming pool. For a fee, massage, canoes, bicycles, and horseback rides. On site is the **River Grill Restaurant,** a scenic dining venue open to the public by reservation. Information: Sorrel River Ranch Resort, P.O. Box K, Highway 128, Moab, Utah 84532; (435) 259–4642 or (877) 359–2715; fax (435) 259–3016; www.sorrel river.com. Expensive.

Castle Valley Inn. This enviable spot with great vistas out to dramatic Castle Rock and red rock cliffs might seduce anyone to move to Utah. On eleven acres there are five nicely decorated rooms in the main house with refrigerators and three bungalows with kitchenettes. Two-night minimum sometimes required. Full breakfast included. Hot tub. From Moab take Utah Scenic Byway 128 east along the Colorado River canyon for 15.5 miles to the junction with La Sal Mountain (loop) Road/Castle Valley Road, where you turn right. After 1.5 miles turn right through Castle Valley gates and follow the signs 1 or so miles to the inn. Inquire about age restrictions. Information: Castle Valley Inn, HC64, Box 2602, Moab, Utah 84532; (435) 259–6012 or (888) 466–6012; fax (435) 259–1501; www.castlevalleyinn.com. Moderate.

Campgrounds

In addition to the campgrounds at **Arches National Park** (Devil's Garden, fifty-three sites; 435–259–4285), **Dead Horse Point State Park** (twenty-one sites; 435–259–2614 or 800–322–3770), and **Canyonlands National Park, Island in the Sky District** (twelve sites with no hookups at Willow Flat; 435–259–7412, ext. 10), there are several commercial campgrounds, including three just south of downtown. They are **Up the Creek Campground** (adjacent to the Mill Creek Parkway walking and biking trail), a walk-in campground for tents only (210 East 300 South; 435–259–6995), **Canyonlands RV Park** (144 sites; 435–259–6848 or 800–522–6848), and the **Moab K.O.A. Campground** (125 sites; 3225 South Highway 191; 435–259–6682 or 800–562–0372). Located 1 mile north of downtown is **Slickrock Campground** (144 sites;

Kit fox

435–259–7660 or 800–448–8873).

Out farther south of town is **Spanish Trail RV Park** and campgrounds (seventy-three sites; 435–259–2411 or 800–787–2751). **Kane Springs Campground** (sixty sites) is 4.5 miles from McDonald's on Kane Creek Road (435–259–8844). Nine miles north of town near Arches National Park is **Arch View 80 Camp Park** (eighty sites; 435–259–7854 or 800–813–6622).

Food

Center Cafe. Fine food lovers don't miss this aptly named restaurant with *Bon Appetit* and Zagat accolades, just off Main Street at 60 North 100 West; (435) 259–4295. This serious gourmet restaurant carefully prepares a seasonal menu. Begin with fresh asparagus risotto with goat cheese and tarragon, then choose an entree like sautéed pork loin with dried cherry compote and blue cheese soufflé. Tantalizing desserts and cheese plates. Breakfast Saturday and Sunday, lunch and dinner daily. Reservations advised. Expensive.

Bucks Grill House. Good food aficionados make a beeline to this ranch-style casual, family-friendly restaurant at 1393 North Highway 191; (435) 259–5201; www.bucks grillhouse.com. The food is American Western with south-of-the-border influences. Begin with duck tamale with adobo sauce and grilled pineapple salsa. Follow up with a roasted game hen with cornbread turkey chorizo stuffing, or spice-rubbed grilled salmon topped with citrus butter on a bed of chili rice, or the house specialty "cowboy steak"—spice-rubbed, pan-seared, topped with barbecue butter. Pasta dishes. Desserts and extensive wine and beer list. Dinner only. Moderate.

Desert Bistro. Don't miss this fine food dining spot smack-dab in the center of Moab at 92 East Center; (435) 259–0756. Start with tequila-cured salmon and chilled asparagus with roasted red pepper coulis. Then an entree like homemade avocado ravioli stuffed with Montrachet cheese and sun-dried tomatoes with shiitake mushrooms in white wine. Homemade desserts, wine, beer, and spirits. Dinner only. Reservations advised. Moderate to expensive.

Jail House Cafe. This is the place for breakfast in Moab—101 North Main; (435) 259–3900. Inside and out on the covered patio, try the ginger pancakes with Dutch apple butter, the chorizo three-egg scramble, or Southwestern eggs Benedict with country-fried potatoes. Omelettes. Fresh orange juice and good coffee. Daily until 12:00 noon.

Eklecticafe. A little farther out at 352 North Main; (435) 259–6896. Have Sunday breakfast or lunch any day inside or on the patio at this cheerful spot. The lunch menu carries the day with soups and salads, Indonesian curry wraps, Reubens, and beef or veggie burgers. Convenient box lunches also provide satisfying fare.

Slickrock Cafe. Enter the old historic building on the corner of Main and Center Streets and find a slick southwestern interior complete with its own "slickrock critter" logo; (435) 259–8004. Plenty of salads, burgers, and sandwiches to choose from for lunch and tasty pasta, fish, and chicken dishes for dinner. Microbrews on draft. Wine. Inexpensive to moderate.

Mondo Cafe. At 59 South Main Street in the Western Plaza right behind the Moab Information Center is this soup-and-sandwich coffeehouse where they do all of your favorite espresso drinks right. Breakfast items include freshly squeezed (right in front of your eyes) orange juice, hot chocolate, croissants, cinnamon rolls, waffles, egg dishes, and bagels; (435) 259–5551.

Sunset Grill. The views and spectacular setting may outshine the food; yet the combination is worth a visit; (435) 259–7146. In the former home of uranium king Charlie Steen way up on the cliffside at 900 North Highway 191, you can start with a Southwestern salad or Norwegian smoked salmon followed by Colorado lamb rack chops grilled with mint butter and served on a port-wine peppercorn sauce. Seafood and pasta specialties. Patio dining. Dinner only. Moderate.

Bar-M Chuckwagon. This live western show and cowboy supper venue 4 miles north of the entrance to Arches National Park off Highway 191 can be fun; (435) 259–2276 or (800) 214–2085. Barbecue chicken, beef, and Bar-M baked beans top the menu. Gunfights for an appetizer and a western music show for dessert. Reservations; www.moab-utah.com/chuckwagon.

Moab has two brew pubs that also serve light meals. Either place makes a nice lunch stop. Downtown is **Eddie McStiff's** in the Western Plaza; (435) 259–2337. South of downtown is the **Moab Brewery**'s microbrew pub at 686 South Main; (435) 259–6333.

Tours and Activities

Dan O'Laurie Museum. Located at 118 East Center, the museum is rich in historical detail and staffed by knowledgeable volunteers. Exhibits focus on prehistory, pioneer history, geology, uranium mining and milling, minerals, and gemstones. Upstairs gallery features the work of local artists. Book and gift shop; (435) 259–7985. Reduced hours in winter. Closed Sunday and holidays.

Moab's Skyway and Rim Trail. At 985 West Kane Creek Boulevard just north of 500 West Street is this quad chairlift that will take you 1,000 feet above Moab Valley to the Moab Rim, offering spectacular views of the Colorado River, the La Sal Mountains, and Arches National Park. Trails for walking and biking are at the top. Bikers can ride the Moab Rim Jeep trail; (435) 259–7799; www.moab-utah.com/skyway.

Canyonlands by Night and Day Tours. Scenic sound and light tours of the Colorado River by boat, starting around 8:00 or 8:30 p.m., May through October. Fee. Information: Canyonlands by Night and Day Tours, 1861 North Highway 191, P.O. Box 328, Moab, Utah 84532; (435) 259–5261 or (800) 394–9978; www.canyonlandsbynight.com.

Canyonlands Field Institute. Located at 1320 South Highway 191, this nonprofit educational organization, which focuses on conservation of the natural and cultural heritage of the Colorado Plateau region, offers a series of seminars and local day camps and field trips in and around Moab. Active Elderhostel river and land trips and custom trips may include rafting, jeeping, or hiking with pack stock. Information: Canyonlands Field Institute, P.O. Box 68, Moab, Utah 84532; (435) 259–7750 or (800) 860–5262; www.canyonlandsfieldinst.org.

Tag-a-Long Expeditions. River and four-wheel-drive-vehicle tours. Rubber rafts and other conveyances packaged for just about any tour you can imagine along the Colorado and its tributaries. One-day raft trips on the Colorado around Moab, as well. Just as comprehensive are the four-wheel-drive tours and jet boat–jeep combination to many canyonland sights. Information: Tag-a-Long Expeditions, 452 North Main Street, Moab, Utah 84532. Telephone: (435) 259–8946 or (800) 453–3292; fax (435) 259–8990; www.tagalong.com.

Lin Ottinger Scenic Tours. Four-wheel-drive-vehicle tours only. Tours into Arches and Canyonlands

National Parks, including visits to Monument Basin and the Totem Pole, special geologic, fossil, and rock-hunting tours, as well as many others. The owner and his staff's longtime experience in the area and knowledge about geology and dinosaurs make the cross-country jeep rides come alive. Information: Moab Rock Shop, 600 North Main Street, Moab, Utah 84532; (435) 259–7312.

Tex's Riverways. River tours only. Located 0.25 mile north of downtown Moab on U.S. Highway 191. Jet boat tours along the Colorado for a few hours or a day. Backpacker transport also provided to the Maze, Lathrop Canyon, and other remote sites. Also canoe rentals for unguided canoe trips. Information: Tex's Riverways, 691 North 500 West, Box 67, Moab, Utah 84532; (435) 259–5101; wwwtexsriverways.com.

Navtec Expeditions. This experienced tour operator, whose pioneer family helped put the Arches area on the map, provides scenic oar-powered raft half-day, full-day, and two-day trips, either white water or calm water. Also motorized rigid inflatable boat tours and fully guided jeep tours. Information: 321 North Main Street, P.O. Box 1267, Moab, Utah 84532; (435) 259–7983 or (800) 833–1278; fax (435) 259–5823; www.navtec.com.

Adrift Adventures. Half- and full-day Colorado River trips, horseback or jeep and raft combination tours. Tour canyonlands by jeep or jet boat. Information: 378 North Main Street, P.O. Box 577, Moab, Utah 84532; (435) 259–8594 or (800) 874–4483; fax (435) 259–7628; www.adrift.net.

Rim Cyclery. This outdoor store and bike rental stop is truly more than a bike shop. Information: 94 West 100 North Street, Moab, Utah 84532; (435) 259–5333; www.rimcyclery.com.

Rim Tours. This outfitter will take you on mountain bike tours of Utah's Canyon Country in and around Moab, Colorado's Rocky Mountains, and even Arizona's Grand Canyon. Information: 1233 South Highway 191, Moab, Utah 84532; (435) 259–5223 or (800) 626–7335; fax (435) 259–3349; www.rimtours.com.

Sherri Griffith Expeditions. This well-known tour outfitter at 2231 South Highway 191 specializes in overnight river-raft trips on the Colorado, Green, and Dolores Rivers. Also, combination mountain hike and raft tours. Information: Sherri Griffith Expeditions, P.O. Box 1324, Moab, Utah 84532; (435) 259–8229 or (800) 332–2439; fax (435) 259–2226; www.griffithexp.com.

Canyon Voyages Adventure Company. Besides river-rafting rentals and trips, these river runners also offer kayaking as an alternative—even a kayaking school. Information: Canyon Voyages, 211 North Main Street, Moab, Utah 84532; (435) 259–6007 or (800) 733–6007; www.canyon voyages.com.

Chile Pepper Bike Shop and Rim Tours. A bike rental shop, espresso shop, and mountain bike clothing company. Information: 515½ North Main, Moab, Utah 84532; (435) 259–4688 or (888) 677–4688; fax (435) 259–4643; www.chilebikes.com.

Poison Spider Bicycles. On the

north end of town this bike shop also rents mountain bikes and offers tours. Often a busy place, it seems. Information: 497 North Main Street, Moab, Utah 84532; (435) 259–7882 or (800) 635–1792; fax (435) 254–2312; www.poisonspiderbicycles.com.

Horseback riding. Available from these outfitters: Pack Creek Ranch, (435) 259–5505; Cowboy Adventures, (435) 259–7410; and Arch View Trails, (435) 259–7854.

Redtail Aviation Scenic Air Tours. Eighteen miles north of Moab, just off U.S. Highway 191 at Canyonlands Airfield. Information: Redtail Aviation Scenic Air Tours, P.O. Box 1004, Moab, Utah 84532; (435) 259–7421 or (800) 842–9251; fax (435) 259–4032; www.moab-utah.com/redtail.

Moab Golf Club. Located at 2650 South East Bench Road, this scenic golf course lets you tour yourself around eighteen holes; (435) 259–6488.

Rental Cars and Taxi/Shuttle Service

Bighorn Express. This shuttle to the Salt Lake City airport stops in Green River, Utah, going and coming, making it a possible link to Moab for Amtrak passengers. Call in advance for schedule. Advance reservations required; (435) 328–9920 or (888) 655–7433; www.bighornexpress.com.

Roadrunner Shuttle. This is an all-sport shuttle service for bikers, hikers, and others who need a lift somewhere; (435) 259–9402.

Thrifty Car Rentals. Rent cars,

four-wheel-drive vehicles, or vans at 711 South Main Street. A shuttle service to and from Moab airport and the Amtrak station at Green River, Utah. Information: (435) 259–7317; www.thriftycolorado.com.

Budget Rent-A-Car and Farabee 4 x 4 Rentals. Cars and jeeps at 401 North Main Street; (435) 259–7494; fax (435) 259–2997.

Fairs, Festivals, and Events

The precise dates and a complete list of Moab's annual events are available from Moab Information Center, Center and Main Streets, Moab, Utah 84532; (435) 259–8825 or (800) 635–6622; www.discovermoab.com. In nearby **Blanding, Utah,** check on such stellar events as **The Four Corners Indian Art Festival,** held annually in mid September at Edge of Cedars State Park Museum at (435) 678–2238 or the Blanding Visitor Center (435) 678–3662.

The tourist season begins early in March with the **Moab Skinny Tire Festival,** followed by the **Easter Jeep Safari** in late March or early April. April sees the major **Tour of Canyonlands Bike Race** and the **Moab Rod Benders Car Show.** In May there are the **Moab Quarter Horse** and the **Paint Horse Shows,** the **Moab Arts Festival,** and the **Friendship Cruise** (boaters cruise 196 miles from Green River, Utah, to Moab.) Early June sees the big, professional **Canyonlands PRCA Rodeo** as part of **Butch Cassidy Days.** A grand fireworks display on **Fourth of July** is followed by the **Four Corners Classic Horse Show** the last week of July. August sees the **Grand County Fair** with a rodeo and horse show. In late August/early September there's the **Moab Chamber Music Festival** using a grotto on the Colorado River as one of the venues. Cooler October ushers in the **Moab Rock, Gem and Mineral Show,** the **24 Hours of Moab Bike Race,** and, around Halloween, the **Canyonlands Fat Tire Bike Festival.**

Shopping

Southwest American Indian art can be found at numerous shops and galleries closer to Indian Country in nearby Blanding and Bluff, Utah.

Kokopelli Gallery and Lema Trading Company. Two locations: 70 North Main Street, (435) 259–5055; and 860 South Main Street, (435) 259–5942; www.lema trading.com. Although Moab isn't a center for American Indian art, some authentic pieces (Pueblo pottery, Navajo rugs, jewelry) can be found here.

Moab Rock Shop. Located at 600 North Main Street; (435) 259–7312. Much like a museum, except you can buy what you see. Specializing in rocks, minerals, and fossils of the area. The staff are regional geology experts. The four-wheel-drive-vehicle trips are legendary.

Back of Beyond Book Store. Located right downtown at 83 North Main Street; (435) 259–5154 or (800) 700–2859; www.moab.net/backof beyond. This highly regarded general bookstore offers an exceptional selection of Southwest and Colorado

Plateau titles, including many specialized guidebooks. There is an unusually comprehensive selection of books on natural history and environmental subjects, as well as in-depth selections covering archaeology, Southwest Indian, and western Americana titles, including the complete works of Edward Abbey.

Tom Till Gallery. This gallery at 61 North Main shows the work of a fine Southwest photographer whose stunning fine art landscape images capture your attention; (435) 259–9808 or (888) 479–9808; www.tomtill.com. Postcards of many of the images are also available. The Southwest has never looked better than it does as shot by this talented Moab photographer.

Arches Book Company. A new and used book store at 78 North Main; (435) 259–0782; www.arches bookcompany.com. It offers a wide selection of fiction and nonfiction and Southwest titles. Espresso bar on premises.

T.I. Maps, Etc. Located at 29 East Center Street; (435) 259–5529; www.moab.net/timaps. U.S. Geological Survey, four-wheel-drive and offroad, trail, raised relief, and satellite maps of the region. Also recreational guidebooks, science and nature books.

U.S. Highway 191 through Monticello, Utah, to Blanding, Utah, and Utah Scenic Byway 95

Either as a day trip from Moab to see Edge of the Cedars State Park and the Dinosaur Museum (see "Seeing

Canyon Country") or on your way to Capitol Reef National Park or Indian Country, Blanding makes a worthwhile stop. Blanding has numerous fast food outlets and several motels.

MD Ranch Cookhouse. Monticello is not in Moab, but it is on the way to Blanding. Either going or coming, stop for a meal (breakfast, lunch, or dinner) at 308 South Main; (435) 587–3299. This western-style restaurant with its A-frame ceiling and knotty pine paneling serves up excellent victuals: homemade soups, salads, and sandwiches for lunch and a tasty dinner menu with buffalo burgers, stew, steaks, chicken quesadillas, dutch-oven-style potatoes with onions and green chilies, bacon, and green pepper. Inexpensive to moderate.

Fry Canyon Lodge. If you are going to Capitol Reef National Park via Utah Highway 95 and Natural Bridges National Monument, consider spending a night in a very scenic area at this remote lodge—a solar-powered "country inn disguised as a classic desert outpost." It is the only building on the Scenic Byway's entire length of 120 miles between Blanding (a little more than an hour from Blanding) and Hanksville, Utah. With only ten rooms, advance reservations are often necessary. The five newest rooms, built perpendicular to the lodge, are very nice. Sometimes the cafe is open only to guests. Call ahead to check; (435) 259–5334; www.fry canyon.com. Dinner reservations advised. Inexpensive.

Capitol Reef National Park

There are no services in Capitol Reef National Park. To find accommodations, food, gas, and supplies, you must travel outside the park. You will find numerous accommodations and several good cafes nearby.

Most of the facilities near Capitol Reef National Park are in or around the small towns near the park. Torrey and Bicknell, Utah, 11 and 19 miles, respectively, from the Capitol Reef visitor center, offer services to the west along Utah Highway 24. Probably the most consistent facilities for food and lodging center on Torrey, Utah. If the motels and B&Bs are full there and in Bicknell, it is only 11 miles to Loa, where you will find several more food and lodging choices.

Groceries, gas, propane, diesel fuel, ice, and Laundromats can be found in Torrey. There is a medical clinic in Bicknell, while the nearest hospital is in Richfield, 75 miles west of the park.

For further information contact Superintendent, **Capitol Reef National Park/Visitor Center,** Torrey, Utah 84775 (435) 425–3791 or the Wayne County Travel Council; (435) 425–3365 or (800) 858–7951; www.capitolreef.org.

Lodging and Food

Best Western Capitol Reef Resort. On Utah Highway 24 is the closest lodging to the park, this one hundred–unit air-conditioned motel with all the amenities and a gift shop with sundries as well. Heated outdoor pool and hiking on the spacious 55 acres surrounding the resort. Horseback rid-

Badlands around Cainville, Utah

ing, tennis, jeep, and mountain bike rentals. The Red Cliff Restaurant on premises. Best Western Capitol Reef Resort, P.O. Box 750160, Torrey, Utah 84775; (435) 425–3761 or (888) 610–9600; fax (435) 425–3300. Moderate.

Rim Rock Inn. Next closest to the park is this twenty-room western-style budget motel offering great views. The smallish rooms are nicely appointed, all with private bathrooms. The eclectic Rim Rock Restaurant serves up western fare (435–425–3388; www.therimrock.com). Information: Rim Rock Inn, P.O. Box 750339, Torrey, Utah 84775; (435) 425–3398; or (888) 447–4676. Inexpensive.

Cactus

Wonderland Inn and Restaurant. Located just a few miles farther west atop a small rise at the junction of Utah Highways 12 and 24, 1 mile east of Torrey, is this very pleasant, well-appointed, and comfortable modern motel with fifty air-conditioned units, heated swimming pool, gift shop, and on-site restaurant. Information: Wonderland Inn, Torrey, Utah 84775; (435) 425–3775 or (800) 458–0216; fax (435) 425–3212; www.capitolreef wonderland.com. Inexpensive.

Sky Ridge—A Bed and Breakfast Inn. Situated on 72 acres and topping a high knoll near the junction of Highways 12 and 24 is this upscale B&B that offers magnificent views in all directions. The three-story gabled building has six guest rooms, all with private bath, some with whirlpool tubs, while another room has a private deck and hot tub. Hiking trails. Full breakfast. Information: Sky Ridge, P.O. Box 750220, Torrey, Utah 84775; call and fax (435) 425–3222; www.bbiu.org/skyridge. Moderate.

Cowboy Homestead Log Cabins. Just a few miles from the Utah Highway 12 and Highway 24 junction, alongside Highway 12 outside of Torrey, are these modern log cabins on a 150-acre historic ranch. These very nice cabins, which are lined up for great views of Boulder Mountain, have all the amenities, including cable TV, phone, and up-to-date kitchenettes. There are hiking trails, and because the owners are rodeo participants, horseback rides are also available (fee). Information: Cowboy Homestead Log Cabins, P.O. Box 750130, Torrey, Utah 84775; (435) 425–3414 or (888) 854–5871; www.cowboyhomesteadcabins.com. Inexpensive.

Austin's Chuckwagon Lodge. Located smack-dab in the middle of Torrey, Utah, is this handsome two-story, fifteen-unit motel of log construction, which gives it an Old West appearance. Some two-bedroom family cabins. Heated pool and whirlpool. Laundromat, a bakery (worth visiting), and general store on the premises. Information: Austin's Chuckwagon Lodge, 12 West Main, Torrey, Utah; (435) 425–3335 or (800) 863–3288; fax (435) 425–3434; www.austinschuckwagonmotel.com. Inexpensive.

Capitol Reef Inn and Cafe. Reaping the benefits of the wonderful old shade trees that grace many of southern Utah's small towns, the Capitol Reef Inn's off-the-road location seems idyllic. Perhaps that makes up for the modest, unassuming-looking units that appear to be a relic of a bygone age. These smaller units have been thoroughly refurbished and modernized so that the ten air-cooled rooms are very comfortable. Information: Capitol Reef Inn and Cafe, 360 West Main Street, Box 750100, Torrey, Utah

84775; (435) 425–3271; www.capitol reefinn.com. Inexpensive. Now to the **Capitol Reef Cafe** with its regional book and map store. The sounds of classical music and the gurgling espresso machine may send you into ecstasy. Fresh food prevails with breakfasts that are well prepared and either light or hardy, and lunches that are eclectic and good. Dinner entrees cover the gamut but almost always include broiled fresh local trout, steaks, and freshly baked bread. Delicious desserts. Wine and beer list. Inexpensive.

Cafe Diablo. This very nice, food lover's restaurant at 599 West Main serves a mostly southwestern menu. Innovative entrees like pumpkin seed–encrusted Road Creek trout with cilantro lime sauce accompanied by vegetables and wild rice pancakes dot the menu. Tasty desserts. Patio dining. Microbrews. Dinner only; (435) 425–3070; www.cafediablo. com. Moderate.

Brink's Burgers. Located at the east end of Torrey. An old-fashioned kind of hamburger stand with a modern twist and cafe seating as well. Good hamburgers and fries. Deliciously cold soft ice cream on a warm night; (435) 425–3710.

Robber's Roost Books and Beverages. Located in a handsome contemporary building at 185 West Main, Torrey, this specialty book and local handcraft store carries many outstanding Southwest titles (it's home to Entrada, a Capitol Reef support group) and a complete espresso bar. Here your specialty coffee drink will be made with care, the way you're used to; (435) 425–3265.

Campgrounds

In addition to the excellent campground just south of the visitor center in the park, there are several other campgrounds located in the surrounding National Forest Service and Bureau of Land Management lands.

Fruita Campground. One of the most pleasant campgrounds anywhere in the Southwest, the seventy units here are right in the park, less than 1 mile from the visitor center. First come, first served. The campground is beautifully situated in a lush valley under towering pink cliffs with large cottonwood trees and fruit orchards just steps away. And the Fremont River courses through nearby. The nice amphitheater sets the scene for evening programs prepared by the park personnel; (435) 425–3791.

Thousand Lakes R/V Park. Located just west of Torrey. A very pleasant setting with good mountain views at a cooler elevation of 6,800 feet. Thirty-eight units. Tent sites, full and partial hookups. Four-by-four rentals. Private; (435) 425–3500 or (800) 335–8995; www.thousand lakesrvpark.com.

Sunglow Campground. This campground is located 22 miles from the visitor center just out of Bicknell, Utah, 2 miles off Utah Highway 24. It rests at a cooler elevation of 7,500 feet. Seven units. Open all year. Fishlake National Forest; (435) 836–2811.

Singletree Campground. This campground is just off Utah Highway 12, the highway to Boulder, Utah. It is in the pines at 8,200 feet elevation and has thirty-one units. Farther south on the same road are Pleasant Creek and Oak Creek campgrounds with eighteen and eight units, respectively. Dixie National Forest. Telephone: (435) 425–3702.

Sand Creek Hostel/RVPark/ Campground. Just off Highway 24, Torrey, Utah, is this budget enterprise with eight beds in the dormitory, twelve RV spaces, and twelve pleasant, grassy tent sites; showers; rest rooms. Information: Sand Creek Hostel RV Park, 540 Highway 24, Torrey, Utah 84775; (435) 425–3577.

Events and Tours

Harvest Homecoming Days. Typically the last week of September, the Fruita area becomes a living museum as pioneer life is reenacted. Details at www.nps.gov/care.

Hondoo Rivers and Trails. Most of the remote sights north of Utah Highway 24 in Capitol Reef National Park and in other locations are not accessible by the standard automobile. Daily tours to places like Cathedral Valley and Hell's Backbone and multiday four-wheel-drive tours, including specialized rock art tours to remote locations like Barrier Canyon, are offered by this highly experienced tour outfitter. Bicycle shuttle service. Information and a detailed schedule: Hondoo Rivers and Trails, P.O. Box 750098, 90 East Main Street, Torrey, Utah 84775; (435) 425–3519 or (800) 332–2696; www.hondoo.com.

Wild Hare Expeditions. Located next to the Best Western Capitol Reef Resort. This outfitter offers full-day and multiday trips for hiking, mountain biking, backpacking, four-wheel-drive tours. Vehicle support. Information: Wild Hare Expeditions, 2600 East Highway 24, Torrey, Utah 84775; (435) 425–3999 or (888) 304–4273; www.color-country. net/~thehare.

Alpine Anglers Flyshop and Boulder Mountain Adventures. Located in Torrey. This full-service fly shop with professional guide staff offers day-long excursions or multiday fly-fishing pack trips with horses. Information: Alpine Anglers, 310 West Main, Torrey, Utah 84775; (435) 425–3660 or (888) 484–3331; www.canyon-country.com/alpine.

Grand Staircase–Escalante National Monument, Utah Highway 12 Scenic Byway, Boulder to Escalante, Utah

Should you need more detailed information about recent developments at Grand Staircase–Escalante National Monument, contact the Escalante Interagency Office, P.O. Box 246, Escalante, Utah 84726; (435) 826–5499. Or contact the monument at P.O. Box 225, Escalante, Utah 84726; (435) 826–5499. Or try the monument's Cannonville Visitor Center, 10 Center Street, Cannonville, Utah 84718; (435) 679–8981.

Boulder Mountain Lodge and Hell's Backbone Grill. Located at the junction of the Burr Trail Road and Utah Highway 12. One of the nicest places to stay in Southeastern Utah, the lodge's twenty handsomely appointed rooms are spread over several architecturally appealing buildings with lovely views of a large pond, wildlife sanctuary, and the surrounding countryside. Two two-bedroom units and two efficiencies. Information: Boulder Mountain Lodge, P. O. Box 1397, Boulder, Utah 84716; (435) 335–7460; (800) 556–3446; fax (435) 335–7461; www.boulder-utah.com. Inexpensive to moderate. The lodge's **Hell's Backbone Grill** is a grill and restaurant that stands out in this remote red rock country. Its specialty gourmet dinners featuring fresh salads, local red trout, complex pasta dishes, excellent steaks, and a dinner hamburger to die for are a destination for many. Breakfast and dinner. Reservations recommended. Moderate.

Escalante Canyon Outfitters. In Boulder, Utah, is this provider of the red rock wilderness canyon experience. Horses will carry your gear on multiday backcountry trips while you day hike and explore from the comfortable base camp. Information: Escalante Canyon Outfitters, P. O. Box 1330, Boulder, Utah 84716; (435) 335–7311 or (888) 326–4453; www.ecohike.com.

Red Rock'n Llamas. This llama touring and outfitting company located in Boulder, Utah, a short drive away on scenic Highway 12, offers four- and five-day eco-soft tours into the red rock canyons of the Escalante River and Capitol Reef. Also backpacking guide service and jeep tours. Information: Red Rock'n Llamas, P.O. Box 1304, Boulder, Utah 84716; (435) 899–1454; (877) LLAMA; www.redrocknllamas.com.

Escalante Outfitters Inc. and Bunkhouse. In the town of Escalante, if it's a good specialty coffee, a homemade pizza, or a fresh salad bar you want, or outdoor equipment, even liquor, head for the Escalante Outfitters, 310 West Main Street. What a treat! You can also bunk down there in petite log cabins with double beds or bunk beds, all sharing bathrooms and showers in a nice facility in the central courtyard for $30-plus per night. With all the Europeans staying there, you may have the opportunity to practice your German or French. But reserve ahead. Information: Escalante Outfitters, 310 West Main Street, P.O. Box 570 Escalante, Utah 84726; (435) 826–4266; fax (435) 826–4388; www.aros.net/~slick roc/escout. Inexpensive.

Escalante Grand Staircase Bed and Breakfast Inn. Located in Escalante along the main route through town. The four units out back are spacious and nicely furnished as is the one other room in the main house. A full breakfast is served in a western-style room off the kitchen. Hot tub. Mountain bike rentals. Information: Escalante Grand Staircase B&B, 280 West Main, P.O. Box 657, Escalante, Utah 84726; (435) 826–4890 or (866) 826–4890; fax (435) 826–4889; www.escalantebnb. com. Inexpensive.

Prospector Inn. Another good bet in Escalante is this large, modern, fifty-room motel. The rooms are modern, clean, and comfortable and have all of the amenities, including air-conditioning. Tour buses frequent this motel so reserve early. Information: Prospector Inn, 380 West Main, Escalante, Utah 84726; (435) 826–4653; fax (435) 826–4285. Inexpensive.

Ponderosa Restaurant. Located behind the Prospector Inn. This large all-day restaurant has a European/ American flair. Breakfast with Hungarian scrambled eggs with hashbrowns. The lunch menu has some delicious soups on it; salads and sandwiches are also available. The dinner menu ranges from T-bone steak to delicious stuffed cabbage rolls with sauerkraut. The service is excellent and great care is taken with the food here; (435) 826–4658. Moderate.

Escalante Outback Adventures. This adventure company offers 4 x 4 vehicle and hiking tours to archaeological sites and slot canyons as well as photo safaris to the region. Hiker shuttle available. Information: Escalante Outback Adventures, 325 West Main Street, Escalante, Utah 84726; (435) 826–4967 or (877) 777–7988; www.escalante-utah.com.

Bryce Canyon National Park

Lodging and Food

Bryce Canyon Lodge. Conveniently located in the national park just a short walk from the famous Bryce Canyon rim. Open the first of April to late October. There are 114 units nestled in the pines only yards away from the portion of the canyon rim detailed in the "Seeing Canyon Country" section. You may stay in one of the forty large historic stone and timber duplex "Western" cabins complete with gas log fireplaces, two double beds, private bath, and nice, wide front porches, or you can bed down in one of the attractive and spacious "motel" rooms with two queen beds, private bath, and small, private porch. There are seventy of these very nicely decorated and comfortable rooms located in two handsome two-story stone-and-timber buildings. No air-conditioning, as it is not required at 8,000 feet elevation. From any of the 114 units, you can view the birds in the pines or stroll over to the canyon rim.

The handsome lodge building, restored to the historic 1930s period, has two mammoth fireplaces, a spacious and pleasing dining room, a lobby area with a post office, an auditorium, and a large gift shop that carries curios and southwestern Indian crafts, particularly jewelry. The lovely informal dining room serves three meals a day and will fix box lunches on request. *Dinner reservations are necessary.* Call ahead the evening or morning before you arrive (435–834–5361) to reserve space. Snacks can be obtained at the General Store 0.5 mile north (follow the signs to Sunrise Nature Center). There is also a coin-operated Laundromat there. Horseback rides available (fee), as well as scenic van tours (fee). If you arrive before 4:00 P.M., you can avoid some congestion by checking in before the tour buses arrive. Reservation deposit required. Information: Xanterra Parks/Resorts, 14001 East Iliff Avenue, Suite 600, Aurora, Colorado 80014; (303) 297–2757; fax (303) 297–3175; www.Xanterra.com. For same-day reservations (lodge desk telephone): (435) 834–5361; fax (435) 834–5464; www.brycecanyonlodge.com. Moderate.

Ruby's Inn (Best Western). Located 1 mile from the park entrance near the junction of Utah Highways 12 and 63. Open all year. Of the motels outside the park, this is the closest one to it. There are 369 air-conditioned, modern units with queen and king beds located in several one- and two-story motel buildings around the spacious property. Heated indoor swimming pool. The Western Art Gallery sells Southwest Indian crafts, and there's a regional bookstore as well. There is also a general store with groceries, sundries, and a post office. Thirty-minute film processing is available. There are guided van and bus tours, car rentals, helicopter scenic flights, horseback rides, cookouts, bike rentals, and a Nordic Center in winter. The Western-style restaurant in the main lodge serves three meals a day, and in season there is a diner north of the lodge. Best Western Ruby's Inn, P.O. Box 1, Bryce Canyon, Utah 84764; (435) 834–5341 or (800) 468–8660; fax (435) 834–5265. Moderate.

Bryce Canyon Pines. Open all year. Located on Utah Highway 12, six minutes from the park entrance. Nicely located with good vistas out over the plateau countryside, the fifty units are nicely furnished and well maintained. Coin-operated laundry, heated swimming pool, restaurant, horseback rides. Information: Bryce Canyon Pines, P.O. Box 43, Bryce, Utah 84764; (435) 834–5441 or (800) 892–7923; fax (435) 834–5330; www.color-country.net/bcpines. Inexpensive.

World Host Bryce Valley Inn. If you're headed for Bryce from the east

Western cabin, Bryce Canyon National Park

on Highway 12, you may want to spend the night in the cozy little town of Tropic, only 10 miles from Bryce Canyon. Several well-run, basic restaurants are there but nothing fancy. There are also several roadside motels. Among them is the sixty-five-unit World Host Bryce Valley Inn and restaurant, **The Hungry Coyote,** which is popular with international visitors on tour. You'll find comfortable rooms and pleasant walking through the streets of this rural town after dinner. Information: World Host Bryce Valley Inn, 200 North Main Street, P.O. Box A, Tropic, Utah 84776; (435) 679–8811; fax (435) 679–8846; www.brycevalleyinn.com. Inexpensive.

The Grand Staircase Inn and Country Store. Located just steps away from the Grand Staircase–Escalante National Monument's branch visitor center is this twenty-six-unit, three-story motel, which serves as a jumping-off place to many of the region's interesting sites. Information: Grand Staircase Inn, 105 North Kodachrome Drive, Cannonville, Utah 84718; (435) 679–8400 or (877) 472–6346; www.grandstaircaseinn.com. Inexpensive.

Campgrounds

The park has two campgrounds offering a total of 218 sites. One, North Campground (open all year), is located just east of the visitor center;

the other, Sunset Campground, is 1 mile south of the visitor center. Both available on a first-come, first-served basis, no reservations. You are advised to arrive early in the day. Both have tables, fire pits, and nearby water and rest-room facilities. There is no water available between October 1 and May 1. Campers are required to bring their own firewood or purchase it in the park. There is a fourteen-day camping limit. A camping fee is levied. Groceries and coin-operated Laundromat are available at the General Store located in the Sunrise Point area. Showers are also available there. The North Campground can accommo-date small trailers, but hookups are not available. A fee dump station is available.

Outside the park you will find a campground and hookups at Ruby's Inn RV Park and Campground (200 sites, 100 with hookups; see Ruby's Inn Best Western). Sixteen miles east of Bryce Canyon in Cannonville, Utah, is the Cannonville Bryce Valley K.O.A. with sixty-four RV sites, five cabins, and sixteen tent sites. Showers, laundry, and swimming pool. Information: Cannonville Bryce Valley K.O.A.; (435) 679–8988 or (888) 562–4710; www.grandstaircase koa.com.

APPENDIX: PREHISTORIC SCENES OF CANYON COUNTRY GEOLOGY

During one of the very earliest periods in this region, the Permian Period, a series of shallow seas covered the area we now call the Colorado Plateau, laying down marine deposits of beach, offshore, and sand-bar sand (Cutler formation, Cedar Mesa sandstone, and White Rim sandstone). Meanwhile freshwater sediments accumulating in the tidal flats, following the retreat of the seas and sand dunes, 1,000 feet thick, began to be cemented into rock (Cutler, de Chelly sandstone). Then during the early Triassic Period, the sea retreated and the area became a broad floodplain, a tidal flat, and then later returned to a shallow sea.

During this time shallow marine, mudflat, and tideland sediments were laid down (Moenkopi). Then meandering streams and shallow lakes laid down sediments carried from the ancestral Rockies to the north and east of the vast, level floodplains. These were layered with volcanic ash from Arizona that dusted the land (Chinle).

During this prehistoric time when the vegetation was lush and today's tree-less land was covered with swamps and forests, the scene was set for the deposition of a yellowish hard sandstone, the Shinarump, a Chinle formation member. As time wore on and the timber died, fell, and decayed, it was the decaying wood that collected the radioactive mineral uranium that was leached by water from the igneous rock that had been thrust upward from the earth's interior to form the laccolithic mountains.

During the later Triassic Period, the land experienced an uplift, draining the seas and becoming a vast, Sahara-like desert. Forceful winds blew sands into deep drifts or dunes that over time became cemented into sandstone (Wingate sandstone). Later freshwater sediments were deposited by a system of sluggish streams that covered most of the country following the desert interval (Kayenta). But returning desert dunes, containing dry lakes, built up again. Time and mysterious geologic forces froze the dunes into immobile rock or petrified dunes (Navajo).

In the early Jurassic Period, the land tilted again and a shallow sea advanced and retreated many times. Rivers from the sea, flowing into lower areas, deposited a variety of marine sediments (Carmel formation). Then came a time of more tranquil activity during which the land was covered with a series of landlocked basins wherein marine mudflat deposits were made (Entrada/Dewey Bridge member). Forming out of marine tidal flats and the remaining reddish-colored desert dunes, soft siltstone and sandstones were laid down (Entrada/Slickrock member). From white dune sand of sea coastal origin, another variety of sandstone was formed (Entranda/Moab tongue). Then another shallow sea deposited marine origin sediments (Curtis formation). This was followed by another layer of coastal marine origin sediments (Summerville formation), which was deposited in the tidal basins and mudflats of the retreating Curtis Sea. This was the final and youngest of the great red bed sediments deposited in this region, aptly called Red Rock Country.

The land was again lifted in the later Jurassic Period to create a wide freshwater floodplain that eventually became a swampy lake. Reptiles were numerous in this environment during this Age of Dinosaurs. At the same time volcanic ash once again layered the region, and the freshwater lake and stream systems deposited several sediments (Morrison formation).

Then eighty million years ago, one of the newest layers began forming. This occurred with the slow encroachment of the sea in the Cretaceous Period. A multilayered sediment was laid down from erosion products from higher ground, by shale deposited from tidal lagoons and marshes, and by beach sand (Dakota formation). Then as the last Cretaceous sea alternately and sluggishly advanced and retreated, sometimes stagnating, it made deposits of marine origin (Mancos shale). During its fitful retreat from the area, this sea laid down marine, lagoon, and beach sand sediments (Mesa Verde formation). Now a whole new system of freshwater lakes began to build up in the late Cretaceous and early Tertiary Periods. Deposits of freshwater or brackish lake water were laid down (Claron formation), from which most of the rock shapes at incredible Bryce Canyon have been carved.

- TWO -
NORTHEASTERN ARIZONA

Indian Country

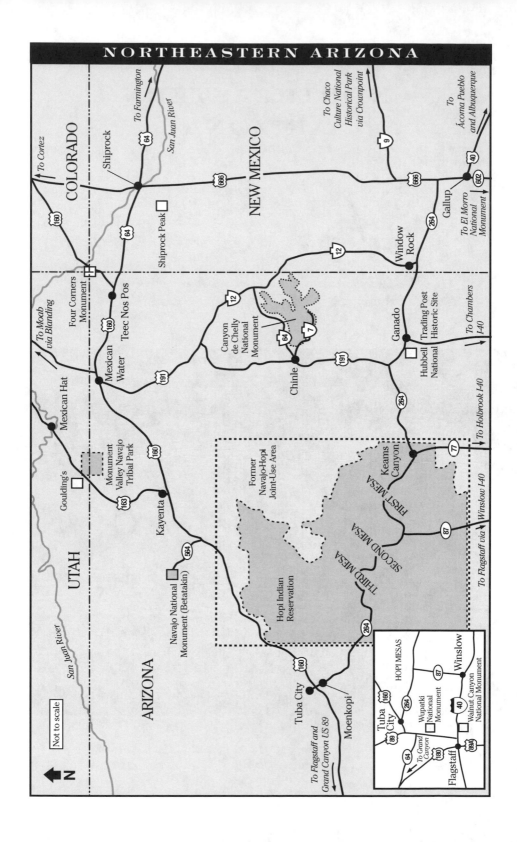

NORTHEASTERN ARIZONA

INTRODUCTION

Stretching south from the scenic sights of southeastern Utah, the Colorado Plateau extends into northeastern Arizona. The terms *remote* and *scenic,* which so aptly describe southeastern Utah, are also applicable to some extent in Indian Country. But it is not as scenic and remote as it is foreign and different. It is the scenery that boggles your mind in southeastern Utah. But it is the culture that surprises and astounds in this part of the Four Corners area. Some consider this area an undeveloped nation within a nation. Others have called it the land of room enough and time enough. But more than anything else, it is a region in which the people make the real difference. The land is not much more forgiving than the land that ran off the hardiest of the white settlers in Utah. It is not easy living in this arid, windblown, eroded country. But a sturdy group of people have learned to live with the harshness of the environment there, adapting their culture and lives to it . . . living in harmony with it. So with a sense of patience and understanding that has endured for generations, approximately 10,000 Hopi and 200,000 Navajo continue to live out their lives in the region.

The resilient Hopi live in the same villages and settlements and farm the same land their ancestors did in the twelfth and thirteenth centuries. The continuity of the present with the past is more evident with the Hopi than with any other cultural group in America. These very first Americans found white man's ways strange and from the time of white contact until now have maintained such a positive sense of identity that only a trickle of Western traditions, philosophy, and religion have penetrated the high Hopi mesas.

The adroit, adaptable, and tenacious Navajo have held onto and survived in this land, which they adopted much later in time. Forming a strong bond with the land, they fought vigorously against white intrusion, but it was a losing battle. When they were finally defeated, they were rounded up and marched to eastern New Mexico for "deprogramming." After that protracted social experiment failed, they were returned to their homeland. Although they had adopted a few white customs, they still retained the essence of their culture.

It is no wonder, then, that we speak of the Hopi Nation and the Navajo Nation. These independent and powerful cultures are very different from the rest of mainstream America. The melting-pot theory did not hold up there as it did with other distinct cultural groups. The Irish and Poles longed to become "Americanized," as did the Germans and Swedes. But these peoples, the first Americans, have had great faith in their roots and have clung to a lifeway that has enriched them spiritually for centuries.

So visiting Indian Country is like entering a different country. (See "Practical Hints: Meeting the Indians" in the back matter of this book.) Each time I visit and

113

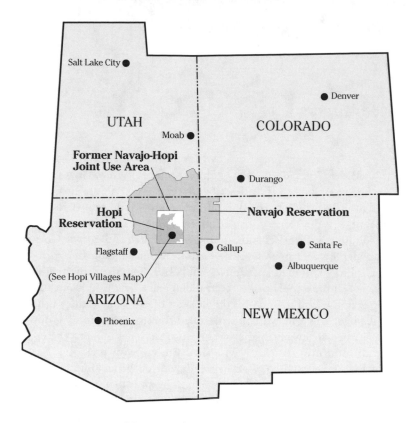

Navajo and Hopi Reservations

return home, I have trouble dealing with the cultural shock. I have crossed no oceans or international borders, yet when I travel to Indian Country, I experience a very foreign way of life. When I first traveled to this area, I would return home and begin to think about what I had seen. Women in bright long skirts and colorful blouses herding sheep across the highway. Indian men with braided hair gathering around a filling station, talking in a language unfamiliar to me. Road signs that point the way to Kin-Li-Chee, Beclahbeto, Teec Nos Pos, and Shungopovi and maps telling about the location of Dzilidushzhinih, Ziltahjini, and Dzilintsah peaks. Back home, 1,000 miles from Indian Country, it all seemed like a dream. I began to doubt that I would ever see these things again. Yet year after year, they continue to be there.

Although they have lived side by side for generations, the Navajo and Hopi are just as distinct from each other as they are from the rest of America. They come from different lines of descent, have a different history, speak different languages, and practice different religious and cultural ways. The Hopi, with about 900 years of continuous living in the area, speak a language belonging to the Uto-Aztecan language group. Many native people from Mexico speak a language derived from this same linguistic stock. The Hopi always have farmed and lived in villages. The Navajo, on the other hand, are relative newcomers to the Southwest. Some say they arrived as

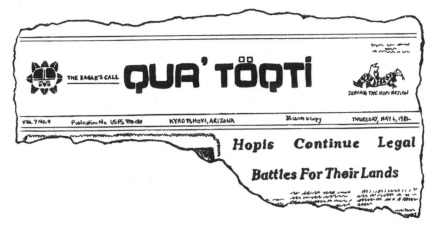

An example of a tribal newspaper

early as the 1400s, while others say late in the 1500s. They speak a language that derives from Athapascan linguistic stock. Today some of the native people in northern Canada, up to the Arctic Circle, and in the northwestern part of the United States speak languages derived from the same stock. The Navajo ancestors were hunters and nomads tending to live in widely separated family clusters rather than in villages.

How the Hopi and the Navajo came to be neighbors in conflict is an interesting story. Since around A.D. 1100–1300, the Hopi have continuously occupied a small parcel of rugged mesas and desert country in northeastern Arizona, which is surrounded by a vast no-man's-land. Today they occupy the same territory, but now it is completely surrounded by Navajoland. This has produced great conflict. Although conflict and enmity between the two groups goes back to the nineteenth century when the Navajo raided Hopi villages and encroached on their lands, it is neighbors disputing over land occupancy and ownership that keeps that conflict going today. In fact, you might read about it in one of the sporadically published Navajo or Hopi newspapers. In many instances the fire of conflict has been fanned by the U.S. government's well-meaning but misplaced efforts to help settle the land disputes that are behind most of the ill will.

The germ of today's conflict began in 1882 when President Chester A. Arthur gave the Hopi 2.4 million acres of land, which were west of the lands that had been granted the Navajo in 1868. This included lands they had occupied for generations. But the language of the Hopi grant stated that the lands were not only for Hopi Indians but for "such other Indians" that the government might "see fit to settle thereon." The farming- and village-oriented Hopi did not expand into the area surrounding the mesas. The restless, nomadic Navajo did. Not only did they fill the vacuum around the mesas, but they also made raids and encroached on the Hopi villages.

The Hopi complained to the government, for fear of being gobbled up by their neighbors. So in 1943 the government allocated 640,000 acres outright to the Hopi. Instead of being pleased the Hopi were offended, since they felt this would forever rob them of using or possessing the remaining 1.8 million acres from their earlier grant. Predictably the Navajo said they should be considered the "other Indians" mentioned in the 1882 grant and proceeded to occupy lands around the Hopi reservation. The conflict remained unresolved for years. Finally the courts designated the disputed area as a "joint-use" area. That is the way it appeared on most maps for years. But the failure of that solution was obvious from the beginning.

As the management and maintenance of the area became paralyzed by the dispute, the area began to look once again like a no-man's-land. Roads deteriorated and wells dried up. The ownership in the joint-use area became a source of conflict when the time came to issue leases to mine one of the world's densest deposits of coal there. The government came to the "rescue" again in 1974. That year Congress, in passing the Navajo-Hopi Land Settlement Act, authorized the partitioning of the disputed 1.8 million acres according to population and density and allocated funds for the relocation of members of one tribe living on land partitioned to the other tribe. In 1977 the courts drew up partition lines and ordered compliance with the 1974 law.

The drawing of the partition line in 1977 seemed easy enough on paper. But when the penciled line took the form of a five-strand barbed-wire fence stretching across 300 miles of desert, it caught thousands of Navajo and a few hundred Hopi on the wrong side. Thus began a massive relocation campaign by the government. The campaign began by stripping the "offside" Navajo of 90 percent of their sheep herds and forbidding them to construct permanent homes on the disputed land. Then the government sweetened the pot with promises of free housing and cash incentives. By the mid-1980s all but about 1,000 Navajo had relocated or had promised to do so. But those who had relocated to the government-provided tract homes in subdivisions outside of towns, on or near the reservation, did not fare so well. Uprooting them from their native homesteads was unsettling enough. But stripped of their herds and their land, they had no skills to generate income. Many who were uprooted did not speak or read English. Utility bills and property tax statements often went unheeded, since they were not written in Navajo. (For a parallel experience involving the Spanish in New Mexico, see Section 4, North Central New Mexico, "History.") Unscrupulous real estate entrepreneurs had a field day. Soon many relocated Navajo, who had given up their herds and had no urban job skills, were not only out of work but also homeless. The 1,000 or so Navajo who refused to relocate became even more adamant in their refusal when they saw what was happening to their newly relocated friends and relatives. Their staunch and well-publicized refusal to move from areas such as Big Mountain gained support from activist groups around the United States. As the legal deadline for completion of the relocation process loomed closer in 1986, it was apparent that a nasty confrontation was at hand. There were rumors that the government might use army helicopters and that the National Guard might be sent in to force the Big Mountain Navajo off the land. The Navajo heated up the dispute, contending that the government, in conspiring with the energy companies, had passed the 1974 partition and relocation act as a ruse to seize control of the land that was rich with coal and uranium deposits. The Federal Navajo-Hopi Relocation Commission wisely backed away from the deadline, using the excuse that relocation of the resistant Navajo was not practical until new houses could be constructed for them or until they could make a decision about where they wanted to be relocated. Even so, by the late 1990s there were still several hundred Navajo not yet relocated. Some have signed up to move from the partitioned lands, but for those who refuse to move, federal negotiators came up with a plan that would allow them to sign a seventy-five-year lease with the Hopi tribe. The Hopi in return will receive monetary compensation from the U.S. government. Meanwhile the Navajo have filed a complaint with the United Nations, charging that the government's policy of forced relocation violated their human rights.

The $400-million-plus tab for relocation has far exceeded the initial estimate of around $50 million. You may see evidence of this painful relocation as you travel through Indian Country.

HISTORY OF THE PEOPLE

first a word about the historical materials that follow. Much of our knowledge about this part of the Southwest has come from two sources. One is the anthropological and archaeological information stemming from the studies of the ruins found in the Four Corners region. This information is not always consistent, because in many cases there is wide disagreement between "experts" about what a certain piece of historical evidence means. There are many gaps in the historical chain of evidence, leading to much speculation about what may or may not have happened. Consequently I have presented in the brief summaries offered here what seems to be the dominant or prevailing view.

The second source of information comes from the people native to this area, the Hopi and the Navajo. Because they had no written language, there is a rich history available only in the oral tradition. Certain rites, prophecies, legends, and sayings are still handed down from the elders to the young people. Many white anthropologists, writers, educators, and others with a genuine interest in American Indians have interviewed numerous native people to learn about their history and culture. Much of the information has been published. The problem is that beyond a very general framework, the Indians have not told a consistent history to their white interviewers. There are many inconsistencies in the "truths" about American Indians that have been recorded by white authors.

It may be that the oral tradition has been inconsistent and that indeed there are several versions of the same myth or ritual going around among the Indians. Or, and I can believe this to be very likely, the Indians have told any tale that came to mind to their white interviewers, keeping the genuine and authentic details of the myths and legends to themselves. It's likely that important information has been hidden from the white man's view. But even if the published body of information does reflect the genuine views of the Indians about their own mythology and history, those data are quite often in conflict with current archaeological "evidence." Of course, the academicians generally imply that their "science" gives a more accurate picture than the Indians' oral history as told to white interviewers. Yet it should be remembered that the scientists are often at odds with one another in the interpretation of their "data." So read these pages of history as though they represent the best that we outsiders know at this time. These are the facsimiles of facts, not facts themselves.

A Prehistory of Indian Country

The history of the indigenous people of the Southwest brings us at once to the question of the emergence of early human beings on the North American conti-

nent. A popular theory is that sometime between 12,000 and 30,000 or
40,000 years ago, or perhaps earlier,
some advanced Stone Age people
came down from today's Asia in the
region of Siberia. They had fully
developed brains and a spoken language. In addition to their coppery
skins, dark eyes, black hair, and wide
cheekbones, they possessed distinctive, shovel-shaped incisor teeth.
They probably crossed what is now
the Bering Sea on either a land
bridge or a stretch of glacial ice, or
possibly at a later time they may
have crossed that 55-mile-wide
channel by boat. As they slowly
migrated southward, their travels

Atlatl

may have taken them along an ice-free corridor, either paralleling the eastern side
of the Rocky Mountains or stretching down the coast of Alaska through present-
day British Columbia.

After several thousand years, perhaps at a pace no faster than 10 miles every
year, these hardy people spread over this new land from Alaska to the tip of South
America, a migration trail more than 10,000 miles long. As they were heading
south, some of the animals native to North America were moving north. These
animals, including the camel and the horse, were dwindling in numbers as the
environmental conditions changed. They finally became extinct on this continent
as the new immigrants grew in numbers, slaughtering more of the animals as their
need for food increased.

In South America, where the ice from the great Ice Age receded first, the
wandering migrants took strong root, possibly 14,000 to 25,000 years ago or earlier in the fertile soil and warming climate of Patagonia. These earliest civilizations,
nurtured under less hostile conditions after the Ice Age, grew and developed until
they were the most advanced of the Asian immigrant civilizations of their time. As
the ice receded farther north, civilization in what is now Central America and
Mexico began to take shape and flourish.

In today's Southwest the ice melted somewhat later. Before the Ice Age was
completely over, a group of people who have come to be called the Clovis culture
was living in the Southwest some 11,000 to 12,000 years ago. They had developed
fluted spearpoints and a special spear-thrower called the *atlatl*. They hunted camels,
horses, and mammoths just east of the land you will be traveling through. The finding of their relics in New Mexico, especially their fluted spearpoints, is the earliest
irrefutable evidence for the existence of human habitation in the New World. Similar sites have been found at Naco, Arizona, and the Lehner sites in Arizona.

Next, the prehistorians tell us, a people called the Cochise emerged about
9,000 years ago in the Southwest. The name was taken from Cochise, Arizona, a

town in southeastern Arizona near which many of the artifacts of these people were found. This culture existed in that region for about 7,000 years until 500 to 300 B.C. These people were initially hunters, using the same types of weapons as the earlier Clovis people. But as it became drier and as other environmental conditions changed over time, the animals became extinct and the Cochise were forced to convert their lifestyle or perish.

They chose to change. In addition to hunting deer, mountain sheep, rabbits, and birds, they became food gatherers, seeking berries, seeds, and nuts. They used these natural vegetables until about 2000 B.C., when it is thought that they began to plant a primitive form of corn called "pod" corn that was probably introduced from meso-America, where it had evolved from natural grasses over a period of many years. The Cochise also learned about squash and beans from those great civilizations to the south.

Probably the adaptable and innovative Cochise desert culture spawned the next developing group, the Mogollon culture. And about the same time, the first Pueblo people, who may have had their roots in the Cochise culture but who probably developed from the early Desha and Oshara traditions of southeastern Utah and northwestern New Mexico, were settling in on the high desert. (For many years archaeologists and others have called these early people the *Anasazi*, the Navajo word for them translated to mean "the ancient enemies." But understandably that usage is now changing in favor of "Ancestral Puebloans," a name linking these early people to their modern descendants, the Pueblo Indians.) The earliest Ancestral Puebloan residents of the Colorado Plateau were first named "Basketmakers" in 1893 by Richard Wetherill. A local cowboy who previously had made some outstanding discoveries at Mesa Verde, Wetherill decided to explore a blind canyon stemming off Grand Gulch in southeastern Utah. There this unschooled archaeologist discovered a cave with ninety mummified bodies. Wrapped in fur blankets, they had large, exquisitely woven vegetable fiber baskets over their heads.

Kayenta Anasazi black-on-white storage vessel

These Basketmakers lived between A.D. 200 and 700 in the Four Corners region, their culture peaking between A.D. 500 and 700. Before A.D. 500 they used the atlatl spear-thrower and made snares and nets to trap field mice, gophers, rabbits, and prairie dogs. In addition to using yucca, cactus, and bulb plants, they grew corn and later beans and squash. Their houses, so-called pit houses, were built partially underground. They made superb, even somewhat ornate square-toed sandals, and the men wore their long hair divided into three sections, one on each side and one in the back, each section wound into thick bobs and tied in place.

In their drive toward domestication, they advanced the art of basket weaving to an all-time high. Crafting finely woven jars, trays, bowls, and baskets of all sizes

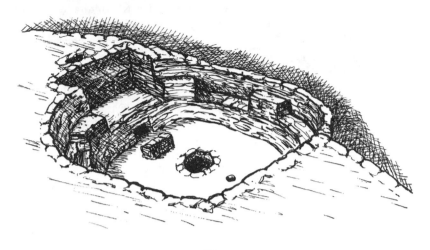

Kiva

and shapes, they also developed the intricate technique of coil weaving with binding splints. Weaving so finely that many of the vessels held water, they sometimes water-proofed their vessels further with pine pitch. It is thought that the development of the bean, which would have been difficult to eat when shelled and dried, led to the innovation of filling the woven vessels with water and then dropping hot rocks into them to raise the temperature sufficiently to cook and soften the beans.

The later Basketmakers developed fixed communities with permanent pit house structures 3 to 5 feet deep. These houses had a smoke hole in the roof and a covered entry hole on the side. Eventually the side hole was reduced to a ventilation-size opening, and the top hole was used for entry and exit. Between the fire pit, located in the middle of the house, and the ventilation hole was an upright piece of flat stone, a deflector stone. These pit houses also had a hole in the floor filled with clean sand. Some archaeologists speculate that these holes represented the *sipaapuni* or *sipapu,* through which the Pueblo people believe they made their first entry into this world. *Sipapus* are also found in underground ceremonial rooms called kivas, which evolved from these early pit house structures. At the acme of the Basketmaker period, the bow and arrow replaced the atlatl, and fire-resistant pottery began to replace the basket. Decorating their pottery with the same designs they used on their fine baskets, the Basketmakers used geometric lines, circles and dots, and animal figures. A favorite subject was the turkey. But unlike the first white settlers to the New World, the Ancestral Puebloans probably did not eat the turkey, for it, like the dog, was kept as a pet and its feathers were used for ceremonial purposes.

The Pueblo Culture, emerging from the Basketmaker tradition in A.D. 700, peaked in the so-called classic period between 1100 and 1300. When people think of the Ancestral Puebloan Culture, they often associate it with this period of time. For during those years all the people living in the high Southwest probably were Basketmaker descendants of the early Puebloans. Although the Ancestral Puebloans are sometimes referred to as the "Cliff Dwellers," archaeological evidence indicates that only certain groups spent the last fifty years or so of their one thousand years

Wild turkey

of existence as a cultural entity in that type of dwelling. For the most part they lived in communities in mesatop homes. Even when some of the people lived in the cliff dwellings, many others continued to live on top of the mesas (see Section 3, "Mesa Verde National Park") close to their corn and cotton fields.

As the Pueblo culture flourished, so did that of their neighboring group, those Cochise descendants, the Mogollon, who lived in the mountains south of the Colorado Plateau. Probably because of their proximity to the highly developed civilizations to the south, in the land that would eventually become Mexico, they were the first group in the region to make pottery. It is likely that they passed their advanced knowledge on to the early Basketmakers and their later Pueblo Culture descendants who took pottery making to heights never known before in the Southwest. It is possible that they borrowed other ideas from the Mogollon people, as well as from the Hohokam culture, another group who lived in the west and south. *Hohokam* is a Pima Indian word meaning "those who have vanished." They too were greatly influenced by the advanced cultures farther south, developing an elaborate irrigation and canal system. In addition to growing cotton and weaving garments from it, they learned to etch delicate designs on the surface of seashells with cactus juice, thus anticipating the discovery of that art in Europe by 400 years.

So the Ancestral Puebloan Culture developed not in isolation but most likely in conjunction with these other cultures as they traded back and forth over long distances. There is also evidence that from time to time some of these different groups actually commingled and lived near one another as they migrated throughout the Southwest.

The Sunset Crater–Wupatki area near today's Flagstaff was one such cultural frontier. For many years it had been thought that cinders and ash from the Sunset Crater Volcano eruption of A.D. 1065 blanketed the arid soil, creating a moisture-preserving mulch that greatly enhanced the productivity of the land. But more recent evidence points to a variety of factors that could have attracted diverse groups to live in the same area. These include enhanced farming productivity due to increased rainfall and newly discovered water-conserving farming practices, the evolution of the area as a crossroads for trade with a variety of other peoples, and a need to find new, arable land at a time when there was a general population increase in the Southwest. For whatever reason, when news of this farming bonanza spread, splinter groups from the Kayenta Ancestral Puebloans, the Hohokam, and possibly the Mogollon cultures moved into the area and lived side by side with each other and the area's native inhabitants, the Sinagua people, who themselves had migrated to this area many years before from what is now southeastern Arizona. After several generations this region became a melting pot for early southwestern culture. There is evidence that both goods and ideas were assimilated among the different groups. So with a touch of Mogollon here and a tinge of Hohokam there, the Ancestral Puebloans were able to develop a complex and productive society from a rich blend of cultural traits.

The Ancestral Puebloans have been grouped into subtypes by modern scientists. These subgroups are based on differences of geographic location, pottery, and architecture. Four of the major groups are Mesa Verde, Chaco, Kayenta, and Rio Grande. (Section 3 of this book details the Mesa Verde Ancestral Puebloans, while Section 4 covers the Rio Grande Ancestral Puebloans.) The remains of the Chaco area dwellings, located within a half-day drive of the places detailed in Sections 2, 3, and 4, are not so dramatically situated, but they are nevertheless some of the most extensive of the early Puebloan remains. Their buildings contained as many as 800 rooms and towered four and five stories high, exhibiting the finest craftsmanship on the Colorado Plateau.

But a few of the most compelling Ancestral Puebloan remains were left by the Kayenta group in the area covered by this section. Some of the most accessible remains of the Kayenta culture are found at Navajo National Monument just south of Kayenta, Arizona, and in Canyon de Chelly, the heart of Navajoland. Although the Kayenta seem to represent a less-sophisticated culture, the dramatic sites for their villages are unparalleled in the Southwest. And some of their handiwork, especially their pottery, is exceptionally fine.

In the mouths of great caves in steep canyon walls, the Kayenta Puebloans built multistory dwellings above the ground in addition to pit houses. Often they built several rows of buildings, each containing twelve to fourteen rooms, with some rows each reaching several stories high. When the Spanish saw apartment house villages like these in caves, on mesatops, and in river valleys, they called them "pueblos." Although early Pueblo Culture construction was of the primitive "wattle-and-daub" type, where rows of upright sticks were bound together with string and plastered with mud, by later Kayenta times stone construction had gained a strong foothold. Even at that the wattle-and-daub method continued to be used occasionally.

Most of the early walls you will see represent construction with stones and mortar. Verdant valleys and great groves of trees were scarce, but stones were plentiful. Work crews apparently gathered these rocks, mostly sandstone, and then shaped them using a sharp-edged piece of chert, a flintlike rock. After a deep groove was scratched in the sandstone rock, it was placed over a smaller rock or pebble, the fulcrum located at the incised groove. The groove was then tapped with a hammer rock directly above the pebble, usually breaking the building stone neatly to the desired size and shape. But the procedure was done somewhat carelessly among the Kayenta people, so the stones are not shaped as carefully or as uniformly as they are in Mesa Verde and Chaco structures. And the walls are not as straight nor the corners as uniformly square as those found at Mesa Verde and Chaco Canyon. The chinking between the rock was accomplished with mud mortar containing potsherds and pebbles for additional strength.

These sedentary village farmers planted seeds with digging sticks and diverted water to their crops through intricate trench systems. They harvested their crops and stored them in stone granaries. Using the *metate,* a flat rock with a concave

Wattle-and-daub construction

surface, and a *mano,* an oblong piece of stone held in the hand, they ground corn-meal. Although they wove clothes from cotton and continued to make baskets of high quality, more and more the Kayenta people turned their efforts to pottery. Using the coil-and-scrape method in which unsmoothed coils were systematically pinched, they developed beautiful and functional corrugated pottery, as well as pottery decorated with a variety of colors. Although black on white was commonly used, the Kayenta Puebloans are renowned for their polychrome pottery, wherein three or four colors were used. In several of the area's museums you will see examples of pottery with black, red, and white pigments applied in a variety of designs on top of orange, yellow, or buff bases.

As you stand on the canyon floor at Betatakin ruin and view the dramatic and complex structures built into the remote canyon alcoves and as you admire the graceful and even exquisitely beautiful pottery of the Ancestral Puebloans, you are aware that civilization was marching along there at a rapid pace, although it never reached the zenith of the prehistoric cultures in meso-America. A forceful, determined people had learned to master one of the harshest environments in the world by developing a lifestyle in harmony with nature rather than in conflict with it.

But then something happened. Sometime between the late 1100s and A.D. 1300, many of the early Puebloans sites you can visit were suddenly and abruptly abandoned. All aspects of everyday life were left just as they were the day their inhabitants abandoned them. It was as if one morning someone you knew left his house with only his clothes on his back, never to return again. The reason for this abandonment is not known, but it is speculated that a great and prolonged drought hit this already moisture-poor region whose soil had been depleted from overuse by the expanding population. This may have opened the way for a form of erosion called *arroyo cutting,* which further depletes the soil in canyon bottoms and lowers the water table. Others suspect that social tensions within villages resulting in divisive practices like cannibalism might have played a role in their abandonment.

| Kayenta | Mesa Verde | Chaco |

Ancestral Puebloan masonry styles

Faced with starvation, these people had no choice but to leave and search for more fertile living sites. So over a period of several hundred years, the Ancestral Puebloan people of the Four Corners area migrated to other locations. Some migrated to the Rio Grande Valley, joining the few early Indians who had lived there for several centuries, establishing the farthest eastern outpost of the Pueblo People, while others migrated south, joining migrants from elsewhere to establish the most southwesterly community, a pueblo known today as Zuni. It is thought that the Ancestral Puebloans in the Kayenta area who had spread as far north as today's Boulder, Utah (see Section 1, "Boulder Mountain and Boulder, Utah," Anasazi State Park Museum), also migrated south along with small groups from the Mesa Verde, Chaco, and other areas. When they reached the southernmost ridges and mesas of the Black Mesa, they stopped. Perhaps from this high outpost, seeing even more desolate regions below them to the south, they felt they must make their last stand. Besides, small groups of people had been in and around these mesa extensions for several hundred years and had no doubt discovered the life-giving springs and the moisture deep under the sands. The coalescence of many disparate early Puebloan groups into one unified Hopi culture is the next part of the story.

The Hopi: A Long and Continuous Past

There seem to be no breaks, no lost chapters between the Hopi's ancestral past and their present lifeway. This is supported both by Hopi mythology and by modern archaeology. Hopi mythology has it that the Hisatsinom, the ancestral, early Hopi, entered this, the Fourth World, at a sacred spot in the Grand Canyon region, near the confluence of the Little Colorado River and the Colorado River. They entered the world, as the story goes, through a *sipaapuni* or *sipapu* or a hollow reed in the ground. From this emergence they began their diverse and scattered migrations to the four directions, forming a "Sacred Circle" of settlements. They called themselves *Hopitue* or *Hopi,* which in their Shoshonean, Uto-Aztecan language means "well-behaved" or "well-mannered."

According to the myth they all eventually would reunite at the center of the Sacred Circle or the "center of the universe," where they would live out their lives until Purification Day and entry into the Fifth World. So after years of wandering, they finally did reunite near three mesa extensions of the Black Mesa. From the north came the Bear, Bluebird, and Spruce clans from Mesa Verde; the Snake Clan from Hovenweep in Utah; and the Flute society of the Horn Clan from Canyon de Chelly. From the west came the Fire, Water, and Coyote clans from Betatakin and Keet Seel. From the south came the Sidecorn, Cloud, Sand, Tobacco, Rabbit, and other clans from Homol'ovi near today's Winslow, from Wupatki near modern Flagstaff, and possibly from Casa Grande south of Phoenix. From the east came a few clans from Chaco Canyon and the Salmon Ruins area.

Both archaeological findings and Hopi mythology are in general agreement that many groups of people migrated to a single location at the south end of the Black Mesa, where they formed villages and the unified culture represented by today's Hopi. The archaeologists also tell us that even before this time, a number of people from surrounding areas had already migrated there, inhabiting Antelope Mesa, 15 miles to the east, as early as A.D. 700.

After the clans began migrating to the mesa area between 1100 and 1300, villages were formed. One of the first villages established below the mesas after the migration was ancient Messeba, which later became Schomopovi or Shungopavi when it was moved to the mesatop where it is today. By 1150 the first village to be established on the mesatop, Oraibi, was formed. Although sparsely inhabited today, this ancient community is probably the oldest most continually inhabited village or town in the United States. Later other villages were established along the terraces of the mesa edges and below the mesas.

Awat'ovi mural fragment

At the acme of the early pre-Hopi or Hopi civilization, there were more than forty villages populated by several thousand people. With intermarriage and time the people began the process of coalescing into a single culture. When this began to happen, smaller villages were abandoned in favor of larger, more centralized villages. In fact by 1300 thirty-six villages had been abandoned, the population concentrating in the eleven remaining villages, plus three new ones to be formed after 1300. Some of these larger villages had multistory buildings, plazas, and kivas, all mirroring the "cave dwelling" structure from which these people had so recently migrated.

Today's Hopi villages reflect many of these same organizational and architectural ideas. In the excavations carried out at Awat'ovi, a Hopi village founded in 1332, the link between the late prehistoric villages and the religious and ceremonial symbolism of today's Hopi was well established through the 200 painted murals found in about twenty different kivas. Most of the murals were removed from the excavation site, and a number were placed in the Museum of Northern Arizona located in Flagstaff, Arizona, where they are currently stored.

During this period when many disparate peoples unified and settled in larger, more densely populated villages, some kind of social organization was required. It is thought by scholars that this is the time ceremonial ritual was laid down, eventually leading to the establishment of the *katsina* or *kachina* cult. Where the cult had its beginnings before coming to the mesas is not known, but Hopi mythol-

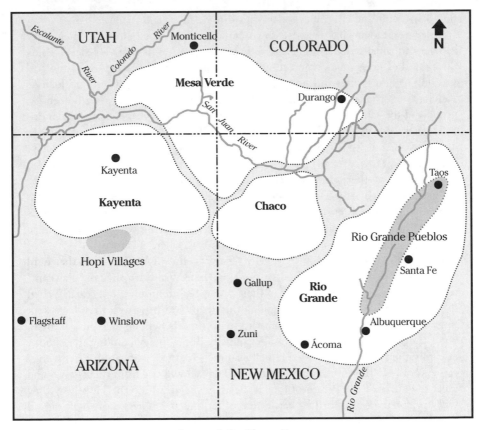

Ancestral Puebloan Groups

ogy and archaeological evidence point to an origin farther south. The Hopi depiction of gods with masks and costumes is very reminiscent of one of the other Uto-Aztecan groups, the Nahuatal-speaking Aztecs. Their culture, in what is now Mexico, flourished and peaked about the time scholars believe the Hopi were organizing themselves.

It was the development of the kachina cult that began to distinguish the Hopi Pueblo from other Ancestral Puebloan descendants, especially the ones who settled along the Rio Grande Valley. The Hopi believed the kachinas are ancestor deities who live in the San Francisco peaks, and they fervently believe that the kachinas will return yearly to the mesas with clouds of rain if the Hopi people have given them their due with sincere thoughts and prayers throughout the year. The kachinas are also associated with reproduction and the redistribution of food among the Hopi people. About the same time the kachina cult was established, the clan system developed, cutting across village boundaries and providing all the Hopi villages with a sense of harmony or unity not seen by the casual observer. The clan groups are matrilineal, meaning that a Hopi child is born into the mother's clan and knows the mother's sisters also as "mother" and their children as "brothers and sisters." The clan system, which may once have had as many as fifty clans within it, continues today with thirty active clans.

Secure in their villages and with constant ongoing development of their cere-monial and ritual system, the Hopi lived several centuries in relative peace. During this period of amalgamation and cultural growth, agriculture was expanded and coal was dug to heat homes and fire pottery. Then one day Pedro de Tovar and Juan de Padillo, two Spaniards, and their entourage arrived without notice on horseback, possibly at the easternmost and now extinct village of Kawayka. They had been dis-patched by Coronado from the Zuni village of Hawikuh in that year of 1540 to explore farther north (see Section 4, "History"). This first "white contact" must have confused the Hopi. For in Hopi mythology the story is told of two brothers who had the same mother: One brother had a light complexion, and the other was the color of Mother Earth. Each brother was given a stone tablet, and each tablet was marked with symbols portending the future. The older white brother took his stone and left the Sacred Circle for another land. The younger brown brother stayed in Hopiland and left his stone tablet at the Hopi mesas, where it is today.

There is an ancient Hopi prophecy related to this myth that states that until the other stone tablet is returned or until the True White Brother or "Pahaana" returns, the Hopi will lose interest in their language, ceremonies, and rituals. When the white brother returns, he will judge the people on how well they have kept their traditions. If they have not been faithful to their beliefs, he may punish them, but if the white brother stays, he will eventually dispel the evil among the people, becoming in effect their savior. He will lead the Hopi to Purification Day so they can enter the Fifth World, and on that special day all will rise from their graves and meet the Giver of the Breath of Life. If they have been true to the Hopi way, they will live forever on a purified earth, free of famine and illness. Love will prevail then, and there will be water everywhere. If this comes to pass, the Hopi people will at last not have to labor so much.

No doubt the Hopi, who had never seen a white man but whose legend had deified the idea of a white brother returning some day, wondered what to make of these unexpected visitors astride strange animals they had never seen before. But on this day the village chief sensed something more than a myth come true and drew a line that the white men were not to cross. The air was tense. A Spanish horse whinnied and moved suddenly. A fight ensued, and the Hopi were subdued. But the Spanish saw no riches, so they left and did not return for almost a century. By that time the Spanish had named these people living along the remote mesas the Tusayan, derived from the name Tucano, which they had given to one of the Hopi villages. In time the name Moqui was also given to the Hopi by the Spanish. This name was probably derived from a term used by other Pueblo people for their Hopi neighbors. But since the Spanish corruption of the term sounded like the Hopi word *Mokee*, which means "to die," it came to be spelled **Moki** as well as Moqui and took on a derogatory slant, especially when used by the Hopi's Span-ish enemies. (For another use of the term *Moqui* or *Moki,* see Section 1, "History.")

But the Hopi were not forgotten altogether, for in 1630 an edict came from the Spanish Franciscan order in Santa Fe. It declared that the Pueblo people, including the Hopi, needed to have their souls saved. In a short time the Spanish established a mission at the largest village, Awat'ovi. At that time there were only five or six Hopi villages and a population of around three thousand. A church was built there, and an intense effort to convert the Hopi was made for more than fifty years. But in 1680 the Pueblo people had had enough of increasing Spanish domination, and they revolted. The Hopi, who had never before or since been aggressive to other Indian tribes or whites, joined in. In a rare act of violence against others, they allegedly slashed the throats of the priests and hurled them over the mesa cliffs and then set about to destroy all evidence of the Spanish occupation. But ten years later the Spanish, who had finally been chased out of the Southwest altogether (see Section 4, "History"), returned and by 1692 had retaken most of the Pueblo villages of the Rio Grande.

With the return of the Spanish, most of the Hopi villages that had been established below the mesas moved to the mesatops, for they feared Spanish reprisals for harboring some of the Rio Grande Pueblo people who had fled for their safety to the Hopi mesas. There were enough of these immigrants to the Hopi mesas to form a new village, Hano, still in existence today. In 1699 the Spanish reestablished a tenuous foothold at Awat'ovi.

But the collaboration of Awat'ovi with the Spanish was not to be tolerated by the other villages. Consequently in 1700 civil strife occurred. The villagers of Oraibi and Walpi descended on Awat'ovi in the night, systematically killing most of the village men in the kiva and irreparably wrecking and burning the village to remove all traces of the Spanish. The women and children were captured and divided between the villages. In doing this the Hopi blotted out forever any dominant or meaningful Spanish influence on the mesas. Although the Spanish never gained a foothold there again, they did make peace with the Hopi late in the eighteenth century.

Since those early contacts the Hopi have had an ambiguous relationship with the white man. On the one hand, there has been the desire to find the True "Pahaana." On the other hand, the Hopi experience with all whites has been somewhat similar to their first experience with the Spanish. Other Spaniards, then Mexican traders, then American government officials, and finally some of the tourists on the mesas have duplicated the negative aspects of that first white contact. So the Hopi have learned to be a bit leery of whites, wondering who each white man is and what he wants. But perhaps there can be no rejection of all white people, for someday, as the legend says, the True White Brother will return and lead the Hopi to their paradise in the Fifth World.

Even though the Hopi rejected the Spanish, they nonetheless retained some of their culture. They learned from their enemies how to raise watermelons and peach trees. Within time wool replaced cotton in weaving, and sheep and goats introduced by the Spanish replaced antelope meat. For about another 100 years, the Hopi lived in security until a drought of major proportions hit the area between 1777 and 1780. Then in 1781 the legacy of white contact, smallpox, hit the villages. This deadly disease resulted in a massive depopulation of the villages. The survivors left the mesas temporarily to live with their friends, the Zunis and the Ácomas to the south. From about 1750 to 1863, raids by alien Indians exerted a disruptive influence on the Hopi. By 1853 another smallpox epidemic hit First Mesa, reducing the population by 50 percent. Between 1864 and 1868 another severe drought struck the area, forcing the Hopi once again temporarily to abandon their villages. This time the villages were abandoned almost completely.

Indian agents of the U.S. government began visiting Hopiland in 1870, and government-operated boarding schools were opened in that year. Desirous of "integrating" the Hopi with white society as soon as possible, Hopi children and their parents were bribed to increase school attendance with the stated goal of "reeducating" Hopi children to white ways. The idea was to break up the traditional lifeway. This interference from the U.S. government and certain religious groups split the Hopi into two warring factions reminiscent of the earlier strife at Awat'ovi. The Hopi began disputing among themselves as to who was following the Hopi way most diligently.

Because the disputes often centered on issues introduced by the U.S. government that were foreign to the Hopi way, the Hopi divided into two camps. One group came to be known as the "Hostiles," or those who were against government interference. The other group was known as the "Friendlies," or those who supported some of the changes wanted by the government. This split among the Hopi led not to loss of life but rather to the splintering of one group away from the other to form new villages. Old Oraibi felt much of the tension between old and new values. By 1896 the progovernment members and the antigovernment members of the village were holding separate ceremonies. By 1906 the tension had become so great that the two groups engaged in a "pushing" match, the loser having to leave the village. The Hostiles, or antigovernment faction, lost and split from Oraibi to form a new village, Hotevilla.

The white traders who came to the villages in the late 1800s began to affect the Hopi way drastically. Machine-made cloth began to replace much of the handwoven cloth. Even Hopi architecture was altered, in that the roof entrance was replaced by side wall doors. Around 1910 several new villages were formed below First and Third Mesas, and in 1943 land disputes with the Navajo began in earnest.

By 1943 the Hopi were wearing the clothing of the dominant white culture and were speaking and reading English. World War II found the Hopi fighting the war as well as helping out in worthwhile wartime industries off the reservation. Paved roads constructed in the 1950s and 1960s opened up the reservation to the outside world via the automobile. The mid-1980s saw the construction of the first high school on the Hopi Reservation. By the mid-1990s a sophisticated computer laboratory with Power Macintoshes was installed at the school, making it possible for Hopi students to access the Internet and initiate a school home page on the World Wide Web. With a high school on the reservation, many of the students who formerly traveled 160 miles round-trip each day to Holbrook or Winslow, Arizona, or who attended boarding school in Flagstaff, Phoenix, or California could, for the first time in this century, complete their secondary education close to home.

In spite of adapting to many modern ways, the Hopi have maintained the land and the villages their ancestors inhabited 900 years ago. They continue to resist being swept under by a wave of white modernism as one of the few Southwest tribes who have shunned casino gambling. In the face of great obstacles, elaborate rituals, ceremonies, and dances are still carried on by these people so diligently faithful to the hard but rewarding Hopi way.

The Navajo (Diné): Nomads and Survivalists

As mentioned in the introduction the Navajo are relative newcomers to the Southwest. They are Athapascan-speaking people who came from the north, where they occupied land near the Arctic Circle in the north and west of what is now Canada. No one knows why they headed south, but it is speculated that today's Navajo represent a group of these northern nomads and hunters who split off from the others and followed the buffalo south until they reached the plains of New Mexico, east of the Continental Divide. There these plains-dwelling people traded with Rio Grande Pueblo people in either the 1400s or 1500s and later moved and settled west of the Rio Grande on the Colorado Plateau. From there one group moved to the mountains south and east of the Colorado Plateau, becoming the predecessors of some of today's Apache Indians. Another group, staying on the Colorado Plateau, moved to the San Juan River watershed probably sometime in the late 1500s or early 1600s to an area abandoned earlier by the Ancestral Puebloans. They called themselves Diné or "The People," and they called this homeland where they settled (today's northwestern New Mexico, stretching from Farmington east to near Abiquiu) Dinétah.

Diné supplemented their hunting with farming. They learned about farming from their Pueblo neighbors, with whom they traded and whose villages they sometimes raided. It was there around Gobernador Canyon that much of Navajo religion and symbolism had its beginnings. For on top of Gobernador Knob, an ancient rock outcropping of molten magma origin, is the sacred spot where Changing Woman, the principal Navajo deity whose aging represents the progression of the changing seasons, was first found as a baby. Not far away at Huerfano Mesa, which the Navajos call "mountain-around-which-traveling-is-done," is the symbolic home where she was raised.

When the Spanish arrived in 1539–40, they made little mention of these people. But since they lived in small, clustered groups of extended families widely spread over this vast country, they were not as visible as the Pueblo people, who lived in more densely populated villages made of stone on top of high mesas. When the Spanish did finally encounter the more nomadic Indians, they called them *Apache,* a Spanish word possibly derived from the Zuni *Apachu,* which literally means "enemy." Later they found another group of Indians in northwestern New Mexico who were nomadic but who also farmed, and they named them *Apache de Navajo,* or literally "Apaches of cultivated fields." The Spanish borrowed the word *Navajo* from the Tewa-speaking Pueblo people, whose word *Navajo* means "great cultivated fields."

During the time of intense conflict with the Spanish in the late 1600s, which was detailed earlier in the Hopi section, many Rio Grande Pueblo people, such as those from Jemez Pueblo, fled westward seeking refuge with the Navajo in the San Juan River Basin. This period of Pueblo unrest greatly aided the Navajo. From the Pueblo émigrés they learned and incorporated many skills and ideas that enhanced their own lifeway. From the Pueblo people who brought their Spanish goats and their scrawny, spindly-legged, Spanish churro sheep with them, they learned about sheepherding. And Navajo women learned from Pueblo men how to shear sheep,

Navajo sheep and goats

make yarn, and weave it into blankets, skills the Pueblo people had learned from the Spanish.

Probably through close contact and intermarriage, they assimilated some of the ritual and religious ceremonies from the Pueblo people, as well as learning about pottery from them. The Navajo took to sheepherding as if they had been born to it. Later Spanish contact also offered "The People" another opportunity, the horse. Reintroduced to this country by the Spanish after becoming extinct in North America following the last glacial age, the horse became as one with the Navajo. Their nomadic instincts sensed bright possibilities in this new combination of horse and human.

With the ever-increasing need for new pasture for their sheep and under constant pressure from the hostile Utes to the north who attacked them often, the newly mobile Navajo were prodded to move steadily westward until they reached the Canyon de Chelly area by the early 1700s. There in the bottom of the canyon, they found seclusion, built their hogans, and cultivated fields that had been abandoned long ago by the early Puebloan people. The swift Spanish horse allowed the Navajo to step up their raids on other Indian villages for the purpose of increasing their animal stock. Their raids on the Hopi pueblos began an enmity that has lasted to this day. Later, unhappy with white encroachment on their lands, they raided white settlements, first Spanish, then Mexican, and later American. Their profligate raiding of Spanish settlements became such a problem that in 1805 the Spanish government sent an expedition led by Lieutenant Antonio de Narbona to quell them (see "The North Rim of Canyon de Chelly").

But the Spanish and later the Mexicans were unable to stem the tide of Navajo raiding. The harassed white settlers dubbed the Navajo the "Lords of the Earth." After this area became a part of the United States, the raiding intensified in the 1840s. In 1860 more than 1,000 Navajo attacked Fort Defiance. Alarmed white settlers demanded that the government do something. In 1863 Colonel Kit

Forked-stick hogan

Carson, previously a friend of the Navajo, was enlisted to systematically destroy Navajo orchards, fields, and hogans wherever he found them. In this way he broke the back of Navajo resistance so that in the winter of 1864, more than 8,500 starving, half-frozen, beleaguered Navajo (out of an estimated total of 12,000) surrendered and were forced to relocate to Fort Sumner in eastern New Mexico. Men, women, and children (all except babies and debilitated elderly) were forced to walk nearly 350 miles to a concentration-camp–like settlement in an area called Bosque Redondo on the Pecos River near the fort. This trail of tears has come to be known as the "Long Walk."

For four years the vanquished, uprooted Navajo eked out an existence on the ungiving land. They fell prey to white civilization's diseases and suffered from a shortage of fuel and good water. Many starved. Yet the unhappy but adaptable Navajo learned something from this experience. In addition to acquiring more knowledge about agriculture, they discovered the usefulness of wagons pulled by horses, and they learned to construct more long-lasting hogans, which would replace the earlier forked-stick hogans that have been dated from the early to mid-1500s. Introducing a style of dress you will still see in Navajoland today, the Navajo women, imitating the white officers' wives, began wearing long, wide, full-length skirts, which were either tiered or pleated. These skirts, often called squaw dresses or skirts today, were given to the Indian women at Bosque Redondo by missionaries who had collected cast-off, fashionable hoopskirts from the East and by military officers' wives who discarded this style of dress in anticipation of a new style. The Navajo women wore the skirts without the hoops, much as they do today. During this period the men began wearing pants from unbleached muslin they had received at the fort. They topped these with colored velvet shirts and tied bright satin scarves around their foreheads.

The experiment to deprogram the Navajo and to change them into an agricultural people was by and large an expensive failure. When the government finally

Hubbell Trading Post

recognized this, a treaty was signed between the government and the Navajo as an autonomous people. Because the preamble states that the treaty is between two sovereign powers, the Navajo have claimed to be a nation within a nation. Thus today they refer to themselves as the Navajo Nation. So in June 1868, after the Navajo were given 3.5 million acres of the lands they had formerly occupied around Canyon de Chelly, these proud people walked back home to resume their lives amid their cherished red rock canyons. Except for a few sheep and goats given to each family, the Navajo had to start over from scratch.

In the 1870s trading posts began to spring up on the new reservation. White traders attempting to befriend the alienated Navajo learned the Navajo language and often served as interpreters of white culture for them. The Navajo traded wool, rugs, silver, jewelry, and livestock for flour, coffee, utensils, and bright machine-made cloth. In some instances traders would advance credit as long as there was collateral. For collateral the Navajo pawned saddles, rifles, and jewelry. If the debt was not paid, the pawn was sold. But the debt often was paid in raw wool, woven blankets, and piñon nuts. The trading post of Lorenzo Hubbell, one of the most revered early traders, is still in operation today, thanks to the National Park Service (see "Back to Navajoland: Keams Canyon to Ganado"). Because of his great respect for the Navajo people, his counsel and guidance were well accepted by them.

By the late 1800s the Navajo once again were tending their flocks, their peach orchards, and their farms. White missionaries and schools came on the scene about this time. At the suggestion of the traders, the skilled women weavers, whose finely woven blankets were legendary by that time, began making heavier blankets called "rugs" that the traders could sell easily. These rugs represented an incredible array of startling geometric patterns, many of which were picked up by the Navajo weavers when they were incarcerated in the 1860s. (At Fort Sumner the U.S. government supplied their captives with more than 1,000 blankets of various designs from the looms of Hispanic weavers along the Rio Grande.) Navajo weaving became so popular that there was little left for their own personal use, so they began buying brightly colored, Oregon-made Pendleton blankets that the trading posts carried.

Meanwhile Navajo men further developed silversmithing skills learned earlier from Mexican silversmiths in the 1860s. The making and selling of beautiful silver and turquoise jewelry, along with the rugs, gave the tribe a new economic base. The Navajo themselves have a great affection for the jewelry they make, adorning themselves with it at ceremonies and social events, where jewelry is commonly seen as a sign of Navajo wealth.

Before the 1920s the U.S. government zealously wanted to "educate" the young Navajo so they could enter white society. Many Navajo children were sent away to boarding schools at an early age. Sometimes they were dragged kicking from their homes. Their long hair was cut short. The Navajo language was forbidden, and they were forced to learn English. In many cases the results were disastrous, producing people who could not live in either society. The emphasis has changed since the 1930s, with schools being provided on the reservation and with more emphasis on teaching children to live in both cultures. An increasing number of Navajo children attend day schools sponsored by the state-operated public school systems, religious missions, and the tribal government. In 1990, approximately 67 percent of all tribal members were Navajo speakers. Although today the number of native speakers has diminished, perhaps this will change now that bilingual education has become an integral part of the curriculum in some schools, especially those administered by the tribe. Still, because of bad roads and long distances, many Navajo children leave their homes at an early age to attend boarding schools sponsored by the U.S. Bureau of Indian Affairs.

The Navajo reservation, unlike other Indian lands, has continued to grow in size. Through executive order of the U.S. government and various congressional actions, numerous additions have been made to Navajoland. Since 1868 the reservation has increased fivefold or more, from 3.5 million to around 17 million acres. For a number of years, the Navajo population increased at a rate four to five times as fast as the national birthrate. Today, with 225,000 tribal members, the Navajo tribe is the seccond largest in the United States. Although full citizenship was conferred on all Indians, including the Navajo, in 1924, (rewarding them for their participation in World War I), they and all the other Indians in Arizona and New Mexico were not allowed to vote in state and national elections until 1948, when restrictive state laws were struck down.

As the Navajo population boomed, the population of their sheep and horse herds grew with them. The sparse land was heavily overgrazed by the early 1930s, and severe erosion was beginning to take its toll. The government started a stock reduction program that made little sense to the Navajo, whose prestige and very life were intertwined with their sheep herds. For the "good" of the Navajo people, government agents shot and killed thousands of animals, leaving their carcasses to rot. The Navajo were embittered, and once again a barrier of distrust with the U.S. government was raised. Over time programs to breed higher-quality, more wool-productive and meat-efficient sheep have been successful. But the Navajo

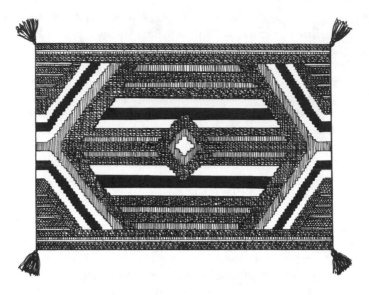

Navajo rug

began to realize that they could not live by sheep alone. Still an integral part of Navajo life, sheep have become less important economically, as more cattle have been introduced.

In 1934, under the Indian Reorganization Act, the Navajo were offered a constitution drafted by the U.S. government to help structure their tribal government. This constitution was voted down by the skeptical Navajo. Asserting their autonomy on the basis of the language of the preamble of the 1868 treaty, they formed their own council. They declared that they were a part of the United States yet separate, with full rights of self-determination.

The reservation took a quantum leap in terms of Anglo contact during World War II, when 3,600 Navajo served in the armed forces and 15,000 more were tapped for work in war-related industries. More than 400 Navajo Marine Corps recruits became well known during the war as "code talkers." They helped develop an intricate code crafted from the Navajo language, which they then used during the heat of battle to transmit secret messages about enemy troop placements. During the length of the war, the Japanese were never able to break the code. (Code talker museums can be visited in Kayenta and Window Rock, Arizona.) With these people returning after several years away, the reservation saw drastic changes. In addition, after World War II, uranium and oil were discovered on the reservation, further increasing white contact and helping to fill tribal coffers. Then the tribe began to develop business enterprises that included timber, power plants, and oil and gas production, as well as a park and recreational department staffed by Navajo rangers. Today, while debating the pros and cons of profitable casino gambling, the Navajo receive monies from strip coal mining in the Black Mesa and Four Corner operations, which generate power for the Southwest and southern Arizona. Ironically, in giving the Navajo their original land grant, the U.S. government thought it was giving away a piece of worthless land that nobody else would want.

In 1972 the government offered to let the Navajo begin to run their own reservation. The tribal government is represented on the local level by "chapter" houses throughout the reservation. Each district or chapter house elects a representative to the tribal council in Window Rock. The tribal government is headed by an elected chairman. The tribe has a police force, tribal court system, and tribal welfare department. Nonetheless the Bureau of Indian Affairs still has considerable authority over the tribe. Reservation lands, held in trust for the Navajo people, are managed by the U.S. Bureau of Indian Affairs. As individuals the Navajo do not own the land they occupy. Instead the tribe assigns traditional use areas to Navajo families, areas that are usually the lands the families have occupied for generations.

SEEING INDIAN COUNTRY

for most travelers coming up from the south or approaching Indian Country from the east or west via I–40, Flagstaff is an ideal stopping place before heading north to the Four Corners area. This relaxed, friendly city fast approaching 60,000 citizens is perched amid the pines at a cool 7,000 feet. But more than its cool climate and its western ambience, Flagstaff offers the visitor an outstanding introduction to and overview of the Four Corners Indian Country just to the north of it and serves as a major gateway to the **Grand Canyon.** Its **Museum of Northern Arizona** is a gem of a place, widely known for its focus on the early peoples of the Southwest and its ongoing involvement with the nearby Hopi, Navajo, Zuni, and Pai tribes. This forward-looking museum has often moved out of the staid, traditional museum role to become a dynamic force in the preservation of northern Arizona's Native American communities. The museum has reached out numerous times to offer its support and specialized services to its Indian neighbors to the north. In the 1960s the museum lent its assistance in obtaining National Historic Site status for the Hubbell Trading Post on the Navajo reservation. And in the 1980s the museum staff assisted the Hopi villagers of Walpi on First Mesa in identifying and preserving culturally significant artifacts as they stabilized and restored their village.

Even as far back as the 1930s, when it appeared that some of the Hopi crafts were languishing and losing their indigenous character, the museum initiated the legendary Hopi Artists Exhibition. Today, as part of the **Summer Heritage Program,** the museum celebrates all of the diverse cultures of the Colorado Plateau (see "Staying There: Fairs, Festivals, and Events"), showcasing separately each of the five cultures throughout the summer. These weekend marketplace events at the museum, with many of the artists in attendance, give visitors the opportunity to learn about Southwest American Indian and Hispanic cultures through the art represented there.

But the museum is not the only Flagstaff institution involved with the Four Corners Indian tribes. Resting on a large, handsome campus is **Northern Arizona University.**

This university, with nearly 20,000 students on its Flagstaff campus, also plays a major role in collaborating with and supporting these southwestern Indian cultures. Most importantly, the university provides a nurturing educational environment for the many Native Americans who are students there. In addition to offering courses in the Navajo language, bilingual instruction techniques are also taught to the benefit of both Hopi and Navajo primary and secondary school students.

The university also has many regional research-oriented programs, including its unique master's level Quaternary Studies Program, which takes an interdisciplinary approach to the last two million years on the Colorado Plateau; the Center for American Indian Economic Development; and the Bilby Research Center, where environmentally oriented research on the Colorado Plateau is carried out.

Northern Arizona University has many diverse programs besides the usual academic fare. Programs in the Forest Service Science Complex focus on ecology and management issues unique to the Southwest. The university's Park Ranger Training Program prepares and certifies park rangers for the National Park Service and the U.S. Fish and Wildlife Service. And in keeping with its mountainous location, Northern Arizona University's High Altitude Sports Training Complex has become renowned among national and international athletes. (See Northern Arizona's Web site at www.nau.edu.)

When visiting Flagstaff, you may have your first encounter with some of the Navajo and Hopi families who, in spite of a growing number of commercial stores and shops on the reservations, still come to Flagstaff, one of their favorite market towns, to shop and sell their crafts. Although Flagstaff's resident Native American population is small, on some summer weekends and over certain holidays and special university days, such as graduation, you will see so many Navajo and Hopi families that you will begin to think you are in the middle of reservation country rather than 50 miles to the south of it. And while visiting "Flag," as everyone likes to call it, take a trip to the casual downtown area, where you will see an egalitarian mix of Anglo businesspeople, ranchers, lumberjacks, and students, along with Southwest Indians of several tribes as well as some of the town's Hispanic citizens, who compose about 16 percent of the population.

Although influenced by the sophisticated Anglo sunbelt cities to the south, the remote "room enough and time enough" Indian cultures to the north, and the mix of mainstream America as it flows east and west on the interstate, Flagstaff has maintained an identity of its own. It has carved out a prominent position as the leading commercial and cultural city in northern Arizona. If not a beautiful city, Flagstaff is a genuinely warm and friendly western mountain town in a scenic high-altitude environment rich in history and tradition. So there is more to Flag than meets the eye of the one-night-stand traveler who drives bleary-eyed down Route 66 seeing only the city's sprawl of motels and fast-food joints. Flagstaff's true spirit lies off the interstate and its feeder arterials in the pleasant tree-lined residential districts, the restored historic downtown area, part of the Main Street USA program; and the surrounding ponderosa pine–clad hills and mesas that shelter pleasant parks and homes with stunning views of snow-clad mountains.

Despite its beautiful location, Flagstaff is quite different from its charming high-altitude sister city to the east. Unlike Santa Fe, Flagstaff did not develop slowly over several hundred years in a multicultural environment. Just about the time Santa Fe was being rediscovered and gentrified, the new town of Flagstaff was just beginning to find itself. So it is a relatively young city. Like many frontier towns, its settlement, although resolute and purposeful, was somewhat hasty. Its early growth and development yielded to the practical economical and geographic demands of the western frontier that spawned it.

In 1857 the U.S. government sent Lieutenant Edward F. Beale west to plot a practicable wagon road across New Mexico and Arizona (along the thirty-fifth

Using camels to help survey the High Southwest (1857)

parallel) that settlers could follow to California. In what was possibly one of the most unusual expeditions ever mounted in the west, Beale led twenty-five camels imported from Asia Minor through the High Southwest desert country. It was the first time a camel's hoof had touched American Southwest soil since prehistoric times (see "History of the People" and Section 4, "Seeing the Spanish Rio Grande Country"). One of the places they stopped to rest was near a spring not far from today's Flagstaff. Over the next few years, the newly blazed trail, called Beale's Wagon Road, was followed by many wagon trains heading west. Some stopped near the location of today's Flagstaff but then moved on. In the 1870s a group of fifty prospective settlers called the Boston Party rested near another spring in the same area. They found only one other settler there, Thomas F. McMillan, a rancher from Prescott who had come into the area to graze sheep. Together they celebrated the one hundredth birthday of the United States on July 4, 1876, by felling a pine tree, stripping it of its limbs, and attaching the stars and stripes to it. Other parties coming to the area continued the tradition so that when it came time to name a town, "flag staff" was chosen.

But the evolution from settling parties to town was to take longer. It was not until 1881 that a town was finally settled at Antelope Springs, just a little west of today's downtown Flagstaff. That year a giant sawmill was pulled into the area by oxen to begin cutting ties for the new transcontinental railroad that was being constructed along Beale's earlier route. The railroad arrived in 1882, and because of the steep grade at Antelope Springs, the rail depot was located about 0.5 mile east, adjacent to the new tracks. A new town developed there. Both "Old Town" at Antelope Springs and "New Town" grew up together until July 1884, when a fire burned down much of Old Town. From that time on New Town was the primary focus of growth, and it prospered until a disastrous fire in 1886 leveled most of its commercial core. Out of the ashes grew an even larger town, until the next downtown Flagstaff fire, in 1888. The town rebuilt again and, with the advent of running water, was not to be plagued by more fires.

Although earlier ranchers like Thomas F. McMillan had raised sheep in the area, pressure to raise beef did not come about until railroad and timber crews in the West began to demand more beef. Meanwhile the ranching and commercial opportunities of the area leaked to the East Coast, and by 1886 two members of the Babbit family from Cincinnati stepped off the train and began to make history. They, along with other family members who came later, developed an empire of retailing and ranching seldom equaled in the West. Defying tradition by successfully grazing both cattle and sheep, the Babbit family today still lays claim to hundreds of thousands of acres of deeded and permit land in their CO Bar Ranch and owns mercantile stores spread throughout Arizona, as well as a few trading posts and grocery stores on the Navajo reservation.

In the 1890s Flagstaff became the county seat of Coconino County, geographically the second largest county in the United States. Shortly thereafter Flagstaff was chosen as the site for a reform school. The lovely stone building constructed for that purpose was never utilized in that way. A teachers' school was established there instead, and eventually it evolved into thriving Northern Arizona University, one of the chief mainstays of Flagstaff's economy. In the mid-1890s the first tourists began coming to the area to enjoy its cool summer climate and take the stage line to the Grand Canyon. The **Weatherford Hotel** was built to accommodate some of the tourists after the local newspaper had cried loud and hard for more hotels and guesthouses. It was also in the 1890s that Percival Lowell (brother of American poet Amy Lowell), noted astronomer and internationally known expert on the planet Mars, decided the Flagstaff air was so clear that he would locate an observatory there atop a mesa west of town. His research, which led to the discovery of the planet Pluto, helped Flagstaff's observatory gain an international reputation among astronomers.

By the 1920s most of the downtown buildings had been constructed, and a stable community was developing when an economic slump hit the area. To bolster the community economically and take advantage of its unique location near the Grand Canyon and Indian Country, Flagstaff built a new rail depot and the **Monte Vista Hotel.** Indeed, the ploy to attract travelers worked, and a number of them stayed in the area. One such early traveler-turned-resident was Dr. Harold S. Colton, a zoology professor from the University of Pennsylvania. By 1928 this energetic natural historian had founded the **Museum of Northern Arizona** to preserve the natural and cultural history of the Colorado Plateau. The

The Monte Vista Hotel, Flagstaff, Arizona

museum has evolved into one of the finest in the region, with its focus on South-west archaeology and ethnology and its dedication to educating the public. Through her interest in art and ethnology, Mary-Russell F. Colton (Dr. Colton's wife) was instrumental in helping revive the crafts on the Hopi mesas, which had drastically declined in the early 1900s. Under her guiding hand Flagstaff became renowned as a nurturing center for southwestern Indian art.

By the late 1920s Flagstaff's main arterial, Santa Fe Avenue, became part of a national road system called the Old Trails National Highway. When the route was finally paved from Chicago to Los Angeles in 1932, it was designated as U.S. Highway 66, one of America's legendary thoroughfares. Over time it was dubbed the "Main Street of America" and "The World's Longest Traffic Jam" as it carried mid-America's impoverished Depression-era migrants west in the 1930s and their affluent vacation-bound children east in the 1950s and 1960s. With the explosion of automobiles after World War II and the development of Route 66 as the major east-west highway, Flagstaff's downtown business district dried up as the town's growth sprawled east and west along Highway 66. That sprawl is still evident today as dozens of motels, along with numerous convenience stores and shopping centers, line Route 66 and other major arterials near the exit ramps of the interstate highways. But in recent years with a shift in the city's economic base away from timber and toward Northern Arizona University (whose expanded summer programs offer a cool haven for hundreds of students) and tourism, there has been a renewed interest in the historic downtown area as well as the area south of the railroad tracks. The downtown development of the handsome new library in a beautiful parklike setting; **Heritage Square** and amphitheater with its Hopi-owned retail core; and the renovation of several downtown historic buildings to accommodate new restaurants, upscale shops, and galleries suggest that Flagstaff is on the move. There is now plenty of reason to spend more than just a quick "overnight" in Flagstaff as travelers discover the real charm and beauty of this high-altitude city and use it as a base to see many worthwhile sights in and around the city and the region.

Touring Flagstaff—A Few Short Tours

In less than an hour you can see much of downtown Flagstaff. Pick up a copy (fee) of the brochure *Flagstaff Downtown Historic Walking Tour* at the **Flagstaff Visitor Center.** Information: 1 East Route 66, Flagstaff, Arizona 86001; (928) 774–9541 or (800) 842–7293; fax (928) 556–1308; www.flagstaff.arizona.org.

If you are interested in the Southwest Indian cultures and the natural history of the Colorado Plateau to the north, you must visit Flagstaff's **Museum of Northern Arizona.** It alone is the most compelling reason to make a stop in Flagstaff. Described by the knowledgeable as one of the jewels of the museum world, this nearly seventy-five-year-old museum, beautifully situated in the ponderosa pines 3 miles north of downtown on U.S. Highway 180 (North Fort Valley Road), offers the best introduction to and reconnaissance of the region available anywhere. And across the road from the museum, the **W. S. Colton Research Center-Library and Photo Archive** offers veteran Southwest devotees a rare cache of information. The vast number of artifacts you will see in the museum are but a handful compared with the total collection stored in numerous nearby warehouses. Over the years the museum's large crew of dedicated staff-persons has been composed of some of the region's outstanding archaeologists, geologists, botanists, paleontologists, and anthropologists. Their special mission has been to present objects within the context of an articulated story line so that the viewer comes to understand not only the significance of a certain artifact but also how it relates to other artifacts from different time periods in the same culture. This special emphasis on education makes this museum a delight for both adults and children.

Before entering the museum you will see a sign marking the beginning of the 0.5-mile-long nature trail along the **Rio de Flag.** Step inside to get a trail guide, and then start off through the pines and down into the canyon, where markers point out important aspects of the flora and natural history of the Colorado Plateau that coordinate with many of the exhibits you will see inside. Should you not have time to follow this loop trail, you might spend a few minutes in the museum's picturesque central courtyard, where live flora specimens demonstrate six of the region's seven major life zones.

Upon entering the distinctive, native, gray-brown basalt stone building with its red-tiled roof, you will notice high ceilings supported by massive beams. The overpowering feeling of the Southwest provided by the architecture of the building is further enhanced by the view of the ponderosa pines and the San Francisco Peaks through the large picture window in the lobby. This is just the beginning of a museum adventure that will prepare you well for the Indian Country sights you are going to see, or help you fill in the information gaps you may have accumulated after touring the region.

The heart of the museum's permanent collection is the award-winning exhibit "Native Peoples of the Colorado Plateau," its content gathered from the several million anthropological artifacts in the museum's storehouses. There in the archaeology and ethnology sections, you will encounter one of the clearest and most comprehensive exhibits I know of relating to the history of the native peoples of the region. By using **time lines** the exhibit helps the visitor follow the development of many fascinating subjects, including the evolution of native foods. Mounted on the wall in the archeology section of this exhibit is a replica of one of the original mural fragments from the kiva or ceremonial chamber at Awat'ovi. Through the intricacy of this artwork, visitors gain an appreciation for some of the complexities of early American Indian societies. Elements from these remarkably sophisticated murals are found in many of the design motifs used today by Hopi potters, basket makers, and jewelers.

After viewing many ancient and historic artifacts in the archeology and ethnology galleries, the visitor is then introduced to exhibits tracing the development of Native American art. The Jewelry Gallery is resplendent with examples of Navajo, Hopi, and Zuni jewelry, while nearby are finely woven Navajo and Hopi textiles as well as a contemporary wall fresco done in the style of a kiva painting.

Elsewhere displays include permanent exhibits of the biology and geology/paleontology of the Colorado Plateau taken from the museum's sizable collection of biological, rock, fossil, and mineral specimens. The rooms containing these materials feature computer stations and state-of-the-art exhibits (like a life-size skeletal model of a carnivorous dinosaur known to have existed only in northern Arizona). Still another gem is the **Lockett Fine Arts Gallery,** featuring rotating shows derived from the museum's rich stash of paintings and sculptures, representing contemporary Native American and western Anglo artwork and artwork from outside sources. In the **Special Exhibits Gallery,** rotating shows are developed throughout the year. The **Branigar/Chase Discovery Center** contains the **Chase Gallery,** with rotating exhibits from the museum's permanent collection; and the spacious **Babbitt Gallery** displays art of regional interest, often by Native Americans.

The museum's bookstore has one of the most complete regional selections in the Four Corners region. And worth a visit almost by itself is the museum's outstanding gift shop, stocked annually with art from the annual Summer Heritage Program. The museum's **Venture and Discovery Programs** offer annually a series of regionally oriented youth and adult guided tours, seminars, and lectures.

The museum is open daily from 9:00 a.m. to 5:00 p.m. except Thanksgiving, Christmas, and New Year's Day (fee). To get there from Route 66 downtown, turn north onto Humphreys Street (U.S. Highway 180 North to the Grand Canyon), which then becomes Fort Valley Road. In approximately 3 miles you will see the sign to the museum, which is just left of the road. Information: Museum of Northern Arizona, 3101 North Fort Valley Road, Flagstaff, Arizona 86001; (928) 774–5213 or 5211; www.musnaz.org.

Nearby at 2340 North Fort Valley Road is the **Arizona Historical Society's Pioneer Museum,** where, in addition to Flagstaff memorabilia, you can see a replica of a frontier blacksmith's shop, as well as an early settler's cabin. Closed Sundays and major holidays; (928) 774–6272.

In addition to the Museum of Northern Arizona and the Pioneer Museum you may want to visit the well-known **Lowell Observatory,** located just 1 mile west of downtown on Santa Fe Avenue, at the top of Mars Hill at 1400 West Mars Hill Road. The visitor center is open daily but has reduced hours in the winter. The center offers video and slide lectures, guided tours, and a chance to view the heavens on some evenings. It is best to call to check on hours. Fee. Information: (928) 774–3358; www.lowell.edu.

And less than 6 miles west of downtown Flagstaff, perched up in the pines on a 200-acre site offering good views of the San Francisco Peaks, is the **Arboretum at Flagstaff.** A visit here takes you to the highest (7,150-foot-elevation) botanical garden in the United States that does botanical research. This living museum and plant research center focuses on the exhibition of plant materials native to alpine tundra, coniferous forest, and high desert, providing a superb introduction to the botany of the region. In addition, guided tours are led throughout the week. Besides the informative visitor center, the arboretum's gift shop offers native seeds, seedlings, botanical books, prints, and cards. From downtown Flagstaff take Old Highway 66 west for 2 miles to Woody Mountain Road (USFS Road 231), then south 3.8 miles on a good unpaved road to the center. Open daily April through early December. Closed mid-December through March. Information and current times: (928) 774–1442; www.thearb.org.

Half-Day Trip to Walnut Canyon National Monument

To whet your appetite for Indian Country, you may wish to take three hours out of your Flagstaff schedule to see a treasure trove of early Indian cliff ruins magnificently situated near the rim and down the steep walls of Walnut Canyon. Drive 7.5 miles east of Flagstaff on I–40 until you see exit 204, the exit to Walnut Canyon National Monument. From the exit travel 3 miles over an all-weather road to the monument's visitor center. Plan to spend some time in this informative center to view the natural history displays, particularly the botany exhibit, which is one of the best in the region. There are also displays of relics from the Sinagua, Hopi, and Navajo cultures. Petroglyphs, which are found in the canyon but are not visible from the hiking trail, are reproduced in the visitor center. They include the image of the humpback flute player who is associated with fertility and the abundance of crops.

From the visitor center (fee) you can take the **Island Trail,** a 0.9-mile round-trip hike on a 240-step paved path around a peninsulalike protuberance in the canyon wall. This island-in-the-sky provides magnificent vistas of this intimate canyon and its verdant vegetation, which includes groves of Arizona black walnut trees growing up alongside Walnut Creek 360 feet below the rim. The creek flows at a trickle nowadays because the water is held back in Lake Mary, which holds an important part of Flagstaff's scant water supply.

More importantly the Island Trail takes you directly to twenty-five of the cliff-dwelling rooms and provides visual access to approximately one hundred others. The Sinagua Indians, who may have assimilated into Hopi Culture, immigrated to this well-watered canyon from the Sunset Crater area sometime after A.D. 1125. They inhabited these dwellings until they abandoned them, sometime around 1250. It is thought that the Sinagua Indians who lived in the canyon left their former home when it became

Petroglyph, Walnut Canyon National Monument

overcrowded with opportunistic farmers from the other areas (see "History of the People," this section). Throughout the canyon the Sinagua built more than 300 rooms between 1125 and 1250. Using masonry techniques borrowed from their Anasazi neighbors, they constructed double-thickness stone walls at the openings of the many recesses and alcoves in the Kaibab limestone formation cliffsides. With the front walls closing in the recessed spaces, they then built perpendicular sidewalls, thereby closing up the sides and partitioning the long spaces into rooms.

The Island Trail descends via a series of good paths and stairs about 180 feet before it starts up again. Although it is only moderately difficult, you may find yourself huffing and puffing on the way back up. But rest assured, your tax dollars have purchased several nice benches along the way. As you walk you will see fossils, remnants from an ancient sea that covered this area more than 250 million years ago, as well as a wide variety of high-desert plants, such as yucca, cacti, barberry, Mormon tea, and, in the spring, Indian paintbrush. Parents should watch children carefully along the well-marked self-guiding trail, as it meanders close to the edge. An easier walk, the 0.7-mile **Rim Trail,** overlooks the canyon and meanders by early Sinagua rim-top structures. Information: Walnut Canyon National Monument Visitor Center, (928) 526–3367; www.nps.gov/waca.

Half-Day Trip to Wupatki National Monument via Sunset Crater Volcano National Monument

Another prehistoric Indian ruin you should not miss if you are in Flagstaff is the **Sinagua** Pueblo of **Wupatki,** located 38 miles to the northeast off U.S. Highway 89 North. This site is an easy half-day round-trip from Flagstaff or can be seen as you drive north toward Tuba City and Indian Country. On the way you will pass by the Sunset Crater cinder cone volcano and its associated lava fields. Leave Flagstaff by traveling east on Santa Fe Avenue past the Flagstaff Mall to U.S. Highway 89 North toward Page, Arizona. In approximately 15 miles from downtown Flagstaff, you will see the sign to Sunset Crater on the right. Travel approximately 2 miles to the **Sunset Crater Volcano visitor center.** The rim of the crater, about 1,000 feet above the surrounding surface, rises 300 feet above the crater floor. It is covered with reddish cinders colored by the oxidation of iron particles found in the area's basaltic rocks. This is in contrast to the remainder of the cone, which is black, due to the deposition of cinders from the more abundant nonoxidized basaltic rock. In both instances the cinders feel and look the same—typically lightweight and frothy in appearance. On the east side of the crater, deposits of gypsum, sulphur, and limonite, which evaporated out from the other gasses and steam, tint the multicolored rim yellow, purple, and green. Upon seeing this crater from a distance, the nineteenth-century American explorer John Wesley Powell could not help noting that at certain times of the day the rim seemed "to be on fire" and to "glow with a light of its own" much like a sunset.

But Sunset Crater, formed in A.D. 1065, is only the youngest of more than 500 cinder cones in the **San Francisco Peaks Volcanic Field,** which includes 2,200 square miles of cinder cones, lava flows, hills, and even the magnificent San Francisco Peaks themselves. Formerly a single, gargantuan volcano rising to more than 15,000 feet, the San Francisco Peaks were formed when the volcano collapsed a half-million years ago. These peaks, which dominate the Flagstaff skyline, can be seen from as far away as the Hopi mesas to the north and from much of the Navajo reservation. They are sacred to both groups. The highest peak, **Humphreys Peak,** which tops out at 12,633 feet above sea level, is Arizona's highest mountain. Before gracing these beautiful peaks with the name of their favorite saint, Saint Francis of Assisi, the Spanish had dubbed these volcanic outcroppings the Sierra Sinagua. The term means "mountains without water" and was coined because, in spite of their size, no major streams flow from them.

The Sunset Crater Volcano visitor center has an excellent geologic and seismological exhibit and a working seismograph. There are also exhibits focusing on the plants and insects of the area. There is a 1-mile-long, partially paved, wheel-chair-friendly loop trail—the Lava Flow Nature Trail—that bends through one of the lava flows. You will also be introduced to squeeze-ups, spatter cones, and lava blisters as you hike this informative self-guided trail. Although it was formerly possible to hike up to the rim of Sunset Crater, it is not allowed now, because heavy traffic

Sunset Crater, Sunset Crater Volcano National Monument

has caused serious erosion of the cinders. But the steep, 1-mile round-trip Lenox Crater Trail provides an opportunity to climb another cinder cone. Inquire at the visitor center. When driving, stay on the paved roads because driving on the cinders can be dangerous and is illegal. The park is open daily throughout the year (except Christmas Day) unless closed by snow. Fee; also includes entry to Wupatki National Monument. Information: Sunset Crater Volcano National Monument Visitor Center, (928) 526–0502; www.nps.gov/sucr.

From the Sunset Crater Volcano visitor center, you will drive northeast about 18 miles to Wupatki National Monument. The road winds through numerous lava formations, pygmy forests of piñon pine and juniper carpeted with black cinders, and finally wide-open country offering scenic vistas of the **Painted Desert** to the east. At 7.5 miles from the Sunset Crater Volcano visitor center is the Painted Desert Vista turnoff with its handy picnic area.

The ruins of **Wupatki Pueblo,** built of Moenkopi sandstone, rise from an open, exposed, and often windy section of the high desert. The multistory pueblo, once three to four stories high, contained more than one hundred rooms. It was erected by the Sinagua Indians following the volcanic eruption of A.D. 1065. The building techniques reveal traces of both Ancestral Puebloan and Hohokam cultures. The pueblo was occupied from A.D. 1100 to A.D. 1225. Housing more than 300 inhabitants, Wupatki or "Tall House," as the Hopi called it, was anchored on the east by an amphitheater and on the north by a ball court. It is the oval ball court unearthed in 1965 that gives this ruin its fame, as this feature is a rarity among the ruins found on the Colorado Plateau. It is a typical feature in the ruins found to the south in the Sonoran Desert area. There, however, the walls of the courts are made of adobe rather than masonry. In the Sonoran Desert area, the Hohokam, hearty desert dwellers and persistent irrigators, developed ball courts in many of their communities, as did their neighbors to the south in today's Mexico and Central America. The large, oval ball courts were used for a strenuous ball game that probably had religious significance. The presence of the ball court and evidence that parrots and macaws were kept at Wupatki are further testimony that this area was a melting pot for many groups of Indian farmers following the Sunset Crater eruption (see "History of the People," this section).

Wupatki National Monument contains more than 2,000 ruins in its 56 square miles of territory, and in its heyday it was populated by more than 4,000 residents. Several of the other ruins, such as Citadel and Lomaki, were built and occupied by Ancestral Puebloans and are easily visited just off the road northeast of Wupatki as the road stretches toward its northern junction with U.S. Highway 89. These early structures probably represent the southernmost settlements of the Kayenta Puebloans. The visitor center at Wupatki is well worth seeing. It contains a replica of an early pueblo dwelling, displays of prehistoric pottery found in the area, and an interesting natural history exhibit. Open daily. Fee; also allows entry to Sunset Crater Volcano National Monument. Information for all three Flagstaff area national monuments: National Park Service, Flagstaff Area Visitor Center, 6400 North Highway 89, Flagstaff, Arizona 86004; (928) 526–1157; fax (928) 526–4259.

Half-Day Trip to Oak Creek Canyon

The beginning of this popular 16-mile-long canyon, noted for its red rock formations and scenic beauty rather than prehistoric ruins, is located about 13 miles from Flagstaff. Like a long twisting slide, U.S. Highway 89A takes you from an elevation of 6,000 feet on the Colorado Plateau's southern rim through several life zones to an elevation of 4,500 feet on the bottomlands of Oak Creek in the Verde Valley. But more than that it takes you into another world represented by Sedona, an Anglo outlier of the sunbelt cities to the south. There elegant restaurants, resorts, galleries, and shops signal that you have left the quietude and remoteness of Indian Country far behind.

In the canyon, 21 miles from Flagstaff, is popular **Slide Rock State Park.** There, as the creek makes its rapid descent through the canyon, children of all ages wearing durable cutoffs slide with joy down the algae-covered slickrock chutes into quiet pools below. Watch for signs to the parking lot and recreation area on the west side of the highway about 8 miles north of Sedona. Sedona is less than 30 miles from Flagstaff, but the driving is slow because of the twists and turns in the road.

Winslow, Arizona: Half-Day or Overnight Trip to La Posada (Historic Railroad Hotel), the Meteor Crater, and More

For a mind-boggling experience straight out of the early part of the last century, travel U.S. Interstate 40, 60 miles east to Winslow, to tour the lobby and public spaces or spend the night at **La Posada Hotel** (corner of old Route 66 [Second Street] and Arizona Highway 87). Finished in 1930, it was the last of the great American Southwest railroad hotels. Unused as a hotel for more than forty years, this early Spanish rancho-style building with Mediterranean features typical of the Spanish Revival architecture of the day is now restored to all of its former splendor.

Enter the hotel and you'll stop in your tracks as you first glimpse the architect-designer's romantic vision of the Old Spanish Southwest. Explore further and let the magic and warmth of this beguiling hotel caress you with its gracious public spaces, enduring wooden beams, elegant polished stone and tile floors, intriguing wall murals, whimsical metal sculptures, and handsome Southwest-style chandeliers.

La Posada was the crowning achievement of American architect-designer **Mary Colter,** whose influence on twentieth-century American architecture and interior design increasingly is being appreciated. As architect designer for the Fred Harvey Company, her talented signature is still visible at the Hopi House, Bright Angel Lodge, Hermit's Rest, the Lookout, and Phantom Ranch at the Grand Canyon and to a limited extent at La Fonda Hotel in Santa Fe, New Mexico. Amtrak stops twice daily here. Information: La Posada Hotel; (928) 289–4366; www.laposada.org. (See Flagstaff "Lodging.")

You may even want to spend a few days exploring Winslow (population 9,500) and environs. Learn about Winslow's rail and ranching past as you tour several blocks of turn-of-the-twentieth-century homes on Williamson, Aspinwall, Warren, and Kinsley Avenues; call on the old Hubbell Trading Post building on West Second Street (home to the Arizona Indian Artists Cooperative); or visit the Old Trails Museum at 212 Kinsley for an in-depth look at early-day Winslow. These sights, centered around the old U.S. Highway 66 routes (Second and Third Streets) through town, tell you where Winslow has been. But a visit along the same routes past the contemporary **"Standin' on the Corner"** park to the upscale Seattle's Best coffeehouse and the newly refurbished historic Rialto Theatre on Kinsley Avenue between First and Second streets (home to the Winslow International Film Festival each October, 818–219–9339) tells you where it's going. Information: Winslow Chamber of Commerce and Tourism, 300 West North Road, Winslow, Arizona 86047; (928) 289–2434; www.winslowarizona.org.

Or strike out on a day trip from Winslow. Follow Arizona Highway 87 north a few miles to **Homolovi State Park** and visitor center where excavation (ongoing) on 4,000 acres has yielded more than 300 ancestral Hopi sites (602–542–4174). Continue driving farther north on Highway 87 for an hour to the **Hopi mesas and villages.** Follow Highway 87 south of Winslow to **Jacks Canyon,** frequented by rock climbers from all over the world. Travel an hour east on I–40 to **Petrified Forest National Park,** east of Holbrook, Arizona, where remains of a Triassic period forest and its creatures have turned to stone (928–524–6228; www.nps.gov/prfo). Travel I–40 west less than thirty minutes from Winslow toward Flagstaff to the **Meteor Crater** (a 570-foot-deep, 49,000-year-old crater that is a sight to behold) and visitor center with its **Museum of Astrogeology** and **Astronaut Hall of Fame** (928–289–2362).

Full-Day Trips to the Navajo and Hopi Reservations and the Grand Canyon

For years Flagstaff has served as one of the major gateways to the Grand Canyon. In fact it is estimated that several million or more tourists a year pass through the Flagstaff corridor on the way to the Grand Canyon. Should you want to travel to that scenic wonder of the world, you may want to consider a day trip there using Flagstaff as a base. If so, take the scenic route from Flagstaff to the canyon via Fort Valley Road (U.S. Highway 180). On the way out of town, you will pass by the Museum of Northern Arizona. The highway then takes you directly to the commercial hubbub and scenic center of the **Grand Canyon's South Rim,** a little more than 80 miles away. You can then return by way of the **Little Colorado River Gorge** and the **Cameron Trading Post** via Arizona Highway 64 and U.S.

Highway 89. The round-trip distance for this route is less than 200 miles. Alternatively you can spend the night on the south rim of the canyon in one of the dozen or so inns, lodges, or motels there, or incorporate a trip to the canyon with plans to explore Indian Country to the northeast. You can also drive to Williams, Arizona, 35 miles west of Flagstaff, to board a vintage (early 1900s) **steam train** for a day-long, round-trip **excursion to the Grand Canyon.** Amtrak now makes a stop in Williams on its way to and from Chicago and Los Angeles. Information and train reservations: (800) 843–8724; www.thetrain.com. For information about the Grand Canyon, contact Superintendent, Grand Canyon National Park, P.O. Box 129, Grand Canyon, Arizona 86023; (928) 638–7888; www.nps.gov/grca. For lodging on the south rim, contact Grand Canyon National Park Lodges, c/o Amfac Parks and Resorts, 14001 East Iliff, Aurora, Colorado 80014; (303) 297–2757; www.amfac.com; for same-day lodging (928) 638–2631.

Note: With around 5 million visitors some years at Grand Canyon, it is only a matter of time until private vehicles are banned from the park. In plans currently under study, visitors would park in large parking lots outside the park and be bused into the park for lodging, sight-seeing, and so forth. Check for the latest developments before visiting.

It is possible to use Flagstaff as a base for taking day trips into Indian Country. One recommended trip is to travel U.S. Highways 89 and 160 via Cameron, Arizona, to Tuba City, Arizona, the western capital of the Navajo Nation. From Tuba City you can travel on Arizona Highway 264 to the heart of the Hopi Mesas, returning to Flagstaff through the Painted Desert by way of Arizona Highway 87 (to Winslow, Arizona) and I–40. The round-trip mileage for this tour (all over paved roads) is approximately 270 miles.

Alternatively you can travel to Tuba City and continue north on Arizona Highway 160 to the intersection with Arizona 564, which takes you to Navajo National Monument and the magnificent Ancestral Puebloan cliff dwelling Betatakin. Round-trip mileage for this excursion is approximately 270 miles. Other sights, such as Monument Valley and Canyon de Chelly, which are farther from Flagstaff and require a considerable amount of sight-seeing time, are best seen by planning to spend more time there, possibly even overnight.

All of the aforementioned Indian Country destinations, their lodging and restaurant facilities, and a detailed discussion of their connecting routes are described in detail in the sections that follow.

The Navajo (Diné) Nation

Within the U.S. borders is a growing vibrant nation, the Navajo Nation. It is the most highly populated Indian reservation and the second largest tribe in the United States. Navajo reservation lands are as large as the states of Vermont, Massachusetts, and New Hampshire combined; twice the size of Israel; and as large as the state of West Virginia. They extend across the borders of three states, resting mostly in Arizona, where they comprise greater than 20 percent of that state's lands. These more than 17 million acres lie at a base altitude of 3,500 to 4,000 feet and ascend to more than 10,000 feet at Navajo Mountain. The reservation is sur-

Traditional hogan

rounded by four directional mountain peaks sacred to the Navajo. To the north is Dibé Nitsaa' or the La Plata Mountains in Colorado. To the south is Tsoodzil or Mount Taylor in New Mexico. To the east is Tsisnaajini or Blanca Peak in the Sangre de Cristo range in Colorado. To the west is Doko' oosliid or the San Francisco Peaks in Arizona. The eastern portion of the reservation is the most developed in a modern sense. But in the western reaches of the reservation, firewood must still be hauled and water carried 20 or 30 miles from paved roads to remote, traditional hogans that often have neither electricity nor plumbing.

The scenery almost rivals that found in portions of southeastern Utah, but the main reason to visit has to do with a culture who call themselves Diné or "The People" and their very different lifestyle, which permeates the land. I do not mean to say that the Navajo are living today as they did in the 1500s. That is certainly not the case. Modern civilization has made its mark. But where that has happened there has been a Navajo imprint, softening the blow and retaining a distinctive Navajo flavor. One of the first indicators that you are in a different country comes when you hear the Navajo language spoken or see the traditional Navajo home. It is called a *hogan,* which means "home" in Navajo. The traditional hogan you will see today is a rounded six- or eight-sided structure of logs, chinked with mud or clay. The roof is formed with cribbed logs and then covered with mud.

By building a many-sided structure, short logs, which are the only kind available in this land of "pygmy" forests, can be used to produce the maximum amount of interior space. As in a geodesic dome, there are no center supports and all of the interior space is open and usable. Always facing east to the rising sun, the door is the only source of light in some of the older, windowless hogans. The smoke from the open cooking and warming fire in the middle of the hogan is vented through a hole or pipe in the center of the rounded roof. In the more remote hogans, kerosene lanterns are still used when electricity lines or solar-powered electric

Navajo camp

generators are not available, and at night sheepskins are piled on the hard-packed dirt floor for sleeping.

The shape and style of the hogan is thought to reflect certain religious sites occurring in nature. A very early style of hogan, called the four-forked beam hogan, resembled an inverted cone or a mountaintop. It was thought that it was modeled after the holy mountain Gobernador Knob in northwestern New Mexico. Later, probably during the internment at Bosque Redondo in the late 1800s, the hogan changed to the perpendicular-sided hexagonal or octagonal structure. Some speculate that this shape was modeled after another of nature's creations, the holy place called Huerfano Mesa, also located in New Mexico.

Today even more changes are taking place in hogan construction. Although the basic rounded shape is being maintained, the walls are often framed in traditional modern style, and the cribbed, mud-plastered roof is giving way to modern structural and composition materials. Consequently you will see many interesting and innovative variations on the theme, showing the creative, independent, and adaptive forces at work among the Navajo.

Through the addition of extruding bay windows, modern skylights, and large sliding glass doors, the traditionally shaped hogan has taken on a new look in many areas. And, of course, television antennas adorn many hogans. You will also see alongside many hogans modern rectangular homes in the western tradition. But no matter what the shape of the hogan or house, the chimney remains resolutely in the center, because that is where the cooking fire has always been. Also you often see windowsills, doors, or roofs in various shades of blue. This characteristic is possibly derived from either the traditional Pueblo Indian or Spanish belief that the color blue helps keep evil or the devil away.

To the Navajo the hogan is more than a wall-less one-room entity warmed by a fire or stove in the middle. It is also a social place, a religious symbol, and a sanctuary where many Navajo ceremonies and rites are performed. According to Navajo legend the hogan was created first; then came the order and planning of all creatures. In the summer the dark hogan with its stale air gives way often to a brush shelter called a shade house or summer house. This breezy structure, often constructed of willows, provides shade from the hot sun yet allows air and light to penetrate.

So today as you drive along, you will see the modern version of a Navajo camp, a scene passed down from this ancient nomadic culture's long past. There may be a single, traditional, many-sided, geodesiclike dome hogan along with several other buildings. These may include a traditional modern or western home or a modern trailer home, as well as a summer house. The clustering of these various homes usually represents an extended-family living arrangement, which may include an elderly couple and their married daughters, along with their husbands and children.

Navajo silver squash blossom necklace

In the traditional family structure, a clan system is at work. Probably from their early contact with the Pueblo people, the Navajo adopted a clan system similar to that of the Pueblo. The Navajo, then, have a matrilineal society, with children being born into their mother's clan and property passing through the wife's clan. This usually includes the hogan and the land. It is said that the husband owns only his clothing, jewelry, and saddle. In this system fellow clan members are called "brother and sister" even though blood relationships may be distant.

The children and women of the traditional family often take care of the sheep, from herding and shearing to dyeing, carding, spinning, and finally weaving the blankets. The child-care and household duties belong to the wife, while the husband is the manager or trustee of the property and generally works in the fields growing corn, squash, and peaches, as well as tending to the horses and cattle. In the more remote sections of the reservation lacking modern conveniences, the men carry water and haul wood to the hogan.

So the Navajo hogan is at once the place where all aspects of living, including religious ceremonies, take place. But it is not for the dead. The Navajo fear the dead, and the hogan may be abandoned if someone dies in it. Often the dying person is removed from the hogan at the last minute so as not to contaminate the home. The Navajo believe that the dead person's ghost may be a threat to the living, for ghosts who appear at night can either chase people or make them ill. So it is best to die outside the hogan, and it is best to have someone else bury the dead. It is not even wise to speak the name of the dead person after he or she is gone. This Navajo aversion to the dead and superstition about death possibly played an important role in the preservation of the abandoned villages of the "Anasazi," which the Navajo discovered but never touched in the many years they lived in the San Juan River's Basin. The ghosts of those "ancient enemies" may have protected many great Pueblo structures. They were left unmolested for centuries, until the arrival of the early white settlers, who often plundered and destroyed valuable evidence from those pages out of the past. Moonlight requisitioning of Indian sites in the Southwest is still a considerable problem, even with many strict laws on the books to protect against such activity.

Off the highway, in trading stores and towns, the Navajo give other signals of their culture. Today you still occasionally see Navajo horses ridden sidesaddle by Navajo women in long colorful skirts or by a Navajo rancher in his cowboy garb. You may also see young Navajo boys riding bare-back, and sometimes you will see what the Navajo jokingly call the Navajo "convertible," the ubiquitous Navajo pickup that replaced the horse and wagon in the 1950s but that may never replace the horse in the more remote areas.

Modern clothing is replacing traditional dress for the younger children, but some middle-aged and older women wear traditional Navajo garb daily. Navajo men wear the adaptable clothes of the rancher, including cowboy boots and hats. This produces interesting comments from white children visiting the area for the first time. Once my son asked, "Dad, why are all the Indians here dressed like cowboys?" But at ceremonies the same men might wear dark velvet shirts and white trousers with bright satin or rayon scarves tied across their foreheads. As you overhear conversations in the trading posts, gasoline stations, or any of the places you have contact with The People, you will most likely do a double take. For the King's English alone is not for the Navajo. Most Navajo speak the Navajo language fluently. For many, English is a second language, which for some is spoken haltingly and with considerable accent.

More subtle differences from the white world also prevail. The Navajo religion and philosophy does not place much emphasis on material goods or on competition. There is a Navajo saying that a man can't get rich if he looks after his family right. This pretty well sums up the sense of sharing in the Navajo community. Of course, the Navajo like to wear and display fine silver and turquoise jewelry on their persons, and it is certainly true that they take pride in the number of sheep or cows they have. But having isn't everything there. Wealth often is counted in terms of sharing or knowing ritual songs or in taking care of one's family. The Navajo feel especially blessed in their land. Land that any travelers might consider barren and desolate the Navajo see as the most beautiful and magnificent land on earth. Much of it is, and a lot of that beauty is reflected in the Navajo people.

Yet it is a poor land. The land will support only one out of four Navajo. Overgrazing by sheep has so denuded this marginal land that many Navajo have switched from that traditional source of income to raising cattle. There are millions of acres of beautiful landscapes, but there is not enough productive land to support the needs of this, the fastest-growing Indian group in America. The average annual income on the Navajo reservation is considerably below that of the rest of the country. Unemployment, which hovers at the 40–50 percent level, contributes to the high level of poverty on the reservation. About 30 percent of the people don't have water or electricity to their homes, although some of those homes in remote locations have small solar electrical generators.

Although the people are poor, the reservation itself is one of the best-endowed Indian reservations in America. This land, often described by government agents many years ago as "worthless," has turned out to be richer than anyone ever imagined. For years the tribe received millions of dollars from the mining of oil, gas, uranium, and, more recently, coal. With the cuts in federal aid programs and the drastic slump in oil and gas prices during the mid-1980s, the financially hard-hit Navajo government began talking about making the reservation a haven for opportunity and private investment by wooing light industry to the reservation and promoting tourism. Income received by the tribe goes not directly to individuals but to the tribal government for the development of roads, dams, schools, and hospitals. The tribe engages in logging and operates sawmills, a utility authority, and the 100,000-acre **Navajo Agricultural Products Industry,** which includes massive irrigation projects. One of these, a 5,000-acre potato patch, makes the Navajo possibly the largest supplier of potatoes to the potato chip industry. The spending of tribal monies in this way has provided jobs for some Navajo families. Family wage-earners may work in the sawmill operation at Navajo, New Mexico, or the plants at Fort Defiance or Page, Arizona.

In addition, the reservation hosts several hospitals, health centers, and many medical clinics. There are numerous schools on the reservation, including the **Diné College,** with its two branches and four community campus centers. It was the first Indian-owned and -operated college for Indians in the United States. Other jobs are provided through the large bureaucracy of the **Navajo Nation's governmental center at Window Rock,** Arizona. Yet these opportunities do not provide enough jobs for the Navajo. Many drive daily to Flagstaff, Arizona, or Gallup, New Mexico, in search of work. Some live in the city during the week and return to their family on the weekends. Some never return, for the lure of modern amenities and opportunities elsewhere is so great that it tends to threaten the lifestyle you see today.

But some say that the independent Navajo will never be subsumed by the dominant culture. History bears out this notion. Spanish horses and other alien traditions were adopted by The People, yet they remained resolutely Navajo. There is little of the Spanish in their culture today. At Bosque Redondo they were programmed to live in settlements and become primarily an agricultural people like the Pueblo Indians. Today they do farm, but they also continue to raise sheep and graze cattle and live as their nomadic ancestors did, in widely separated family groups. Hospitals and clinics have been built, yet many Navajo prefer traditional healing ceremonies. Supermarkets have come to the reservation in the more populated areas, but small grocery stores and trading posts still continue to provide a social center and gathering place for the people who live in remote areas and are isolated from one another.

The pickup and other SUV-type four-wheel-drive vehicles you will see so often on the reservation have not anglicized the Navajo any more than the horse did in the seventeenth century. Look past the exterior of today's modern truck on the reservation. On the inside you will notice the braided hair of the father or grandfather and the long calico or sateen, tiered skirts topped by brightly colored velveteen blouses worn by some of the women, particularly the grandmothers. Observe some of the pickup beds where the kids ride. See the sharp bright eyes and quick smiles as they converse in their native tongue. They reflect that the beautiful Navajo tradition lives on. Be aware that the pickup may be headed to a particular spot of land where, on a warm summer's evening, a traditional Sing, such as the Enemy Way Dance, may be performed. Although this is a social dance where some of the traditional Navajo courtship rites will unfold, these so-called Squaw Dances may serve a curing function as well. The vehicles will come in slowly, pull off the highway, and park. The Diné gather and build a bonfire as darkness approaches. Not even the pickup or SUV sped up that wonderful slow, even tempo of Navajo life, which by comparison makes the average tourist look frenetic if not crazed.

In many ways the Navajo of today lives in two different worlds. In the same extended-family hogan complex, two cultures often live out their lives under one roof. One Navajo park ranger commented on how he had adapted to the dominant culture. He wrote:

I pushed myself to accept it. I live in two worlds. One is yours and one is my grandmother's. In our hogan, these two cultures live together under one roof.

There, although I often eat and drink like the white man, I am called by my Navajo name. We still call ourselves the Diné—the People. Our skin is brown like our mother earth. Our eyes are black like the universe at night. Our smiles are like the stars. And we speak like the voice of the wind.

This testimonial to the conflict of living in two worlds is amplified over and again in the half-dozen or so very engaging Navajo mystery novels by New Mexican author and journalist Tony Hillerman (see Bibliography). Although each of these absorbing books details different facets of the Navajo lifestyle, they almost all focus on the conflict and pain associated with bridging two disparate cultures in today's complex world. This conflict seems to permeate many aspects of Navajo life, and almost all Navajo families are affected.

One elderly Navajo woman whose children had left the reservation was heard to say that when her children and grandchildren returned home, they were afraid of the sheep and thought her hogan was a "dirty place." But the grandmother, who has herded sheep for decades and who still lives inside of and prays to the four sacred mountains, sees beauty wherever she goes. She does not see herself as being disadvantaged but rather feels rewarded that she can live out her life there. Perhaps when she is alone herding her sheep, under the giant, red monolithic sandstone memorials to time, she may chant a favorite old Navajo song:

I will be happy forever, nothing will hinder me.

I walk with beauty before me, I walk with beauty behind me, I walk with beauty below me, I walk with beauty above me, I walk with beauty around me, my words will be beautiful.

Information: Navajoland Tourism Office, P.O. Box 663, Window Rock, Arizona 86515; (928) 871–6436, 871–7371, or 871–6659; www.discovernavajo.com.

Monument Valley (Navajo)

Some call it the eighth scenic wonder of the world. Others refer to it as the land of "room enough and time enough." Still others know it as the penultimate in cowboy-Indian western landscape through such movies filmed there as *How the West Was Won, Stagecoach, Billy the Kid, She Wore a Yellow Ribbon, The Searchers, My Darling Clementine,* and *The Trial of Billy Jack.* But no matter what this area is called, it is impressive.

Resting on the **Colorado Plateau** at an elevation of more than 5,000 feet, Monument Valley is located close to the northern border of the 17-million-acre **Navajo Nation.** It lies in one of the most remote sections of the Navajo reservation, halfway between Mexican Hat, Utah, and Kayenta, Arizona, and 50 miles from the Four Corners Monument.

There, arising from the flat tableland, are more than forty named and dozens more unnamed red and orange monolithic sandstone skyscrapers jutting skyward hundreds of feet. Indeed, this valley of skyscraping monuments is not really a valley at all. Geologically the monuments sit atop a huge piece of uplifted ground, the **Monument Uplift.** What you see there testifies as much as anything to the mighty forces of uplift erosion and time in the Southwest. For there great expanses of Cutler formation rock, especially de Chelly sandstone, capped with Chinle formation rocks like the Shinarump or occasionally with Moenkopi rocks, have been carved into giant monuments found nowhere else in the world. And in the southern part of the valley, there are strangely shaped outcroppings of igneous rock of molten magma origin, like the magnificent El Capitan or Agathlan peak, an ancient volcanic neck or feeder pipe to a much larger volcanic structure that once rested here. As erosion continues its work, most of the monuments you see here today will be leveled to the ground over time. Until then this will remain a valley of rare beauty (see Section 1, "A Geologic Primer to Southeastern Utah").

In 1958, recognizing the unusual scenery there and desiring to protect it from any encroachment that could spoil it, the Navajo Tribal Council established Monument Valley as its first Tribal Park, originally setting aside approximately 30,000 acres of their reservation for it. Straddling the Utah and Arizona border, the park is primarily on the Arizona side. But which state it is in is a moot point, because all of the park (now at more than 90,000 acres) is on Navajo reservation lands, and the visitor center there is staffed by Navajo park rangers and Navajo assistants. The park receives approximately 400,000 visitors a year.

Monument Valley is home to many Navajo families who have occupied this territory continuously since the 1800s. Not even the persistent raids of Kit Carson in the 1860s rounded up all the Navajo living in Monument Valley and Hoskinnini

Mesa to the west. Consequently there were some areas where pastoral life and sheepherding continued uninterrupted throughout the nineteenth century.

In addition to the scenic delights Monument Valley offers, a brimful of historical and cultural gems awaits your exploration. The Ancestral Puebloans occupied this sector and abandoned it long before the Navajo arrived. More than one hundred archaeological sites of those ancient people have been found in Monument Valley. They left not only a legacy of building remnants but of flaked pieces of stones, potsherds, and magnificent petroglyphs as well.

But the drama of the landscape is somewhat overpowered by the people living there today. Far from the busy Navajo capital of Window Rock, Arizona, the Monument Valley inhabitants retain in their remoteness a staunch traditionalism that would be difficult to match anywhere else on the Navajo reservation. If you can stay in this area for a day or two, you will begin to see some of the people and their way of life unfold before your eyes. You may see Navajo women and their children tending flocks of sheep and goat herds close to or across the road. You will see numerous hogans and some of their modern counterparts being built alongside them. Some of these Navajo sheep have been inbred for so many generations that they sport strange genetic mutants, such as curled, double horns. You may catch a glimpse of young Navajo children riding bareback with the agility of West Coast Motocross racers. About dusk you may see an assortment of Navajo pickups and other vehicles parked along the side of the road where a Sing or ceremonial dance is to be performed. You will see brush shelters—called summer or shade houses—erected next to the hogans for the purpose of more comfortable summer living. And you will see Navajo women weaving their excellent rugs in intricate geometric designs. In many ways Monument Valley epitomizes what you will see in the areas depicted in the rest of Section 2. Scenery? Yes. But more than that a people, a culture whose coexistence with the harsh land there is more dramatic than the land itself, making the valley a wonder even without its scenic virtues.

As you turn off U.S. Highway 163 and drive several miles along the paved entry road to the Monument Valley visitor center, you will pay a fee at a kiosk. Offering a panoramic view of several of the valley's monuments, the visitor center—where vehicle and horse tours can be arranged—has a limited display-exhibit area, a seasonal restaurant (Hashke Neiniih), a snack bar, and a curio shop that sells a guide booklet to the park.

From the visitor center parking lot, a 17-mile unpaved loop road (rough and rutted in places—not for low-clearance vehicles) opens up great views of the monuments. Visitor are required to stay on the marked loop road. If the weather is clear and the road dry, the standard auto driven slowly and with caution should be okay. High-clearance four-wheel-drive vehicles make the drive much easier. Allow between two and three hours for the self-drive loop trip. If rain is threatening or the roadbed is wet, inquire at the visitor center before driving the loop road.

Alternatively you can hire a tour—either for a brief loop road jaunt or an extended several hours—on the spot at the visitor center or in advance from Kayenta (25 miles south), Mexican Hat to the north, or nearby Goulding's Ranch (see "Tours" at the end of this section). A tour provides peace of mind and allows

Monument Valley

you to concentrate on the scenery. The longer tours take you to petroglyphs, rock formations, and other sites off limits to the self-drive visitor. Information: Monument Valley Tribal Park, P.O. Box 360289, Monument Valley, Utah 84536; (435) 727–3353 or 727–3287; or Navajo Parks and Recreation Department, P.O. Box 9000, Window Rock, Arizona 86515; (928) 871–6647; www.navajonationparks.org.

While in the Monument Valley area, you may also visit the old **Oljato Trading Post** and **Navajo Museum** by following the paved road, Indian Route 42, for 9 miles from Goulding's Ranch (see "Shopping" this section).

Monument Valley: A Narrative Account

This morning as I pull back the drapes in front of the picture window of our motel room here at Goulding's Ranch, I see the faint shadow of the monuments to the east. I dress hurriedly to get outside so I will be ready to take some pictures when the light is just right. The air is cool against my face as I climb the talus slope below the high red rock cliffs just behind our room. I find a huge, flat-topped sandstone boulder, plop myself down on it, and wait for the prime moment. The silence out here this morning is deafening.

As I sit waiting, I think about the twentieth-century frontiersmen who first settled here. Harry Goulding, who died in 1981, is somewhat of a legend in these parts. He came here in the early 1920s. Shortly after that the Paiutes were moved out of this region. The Navajo were expanding their reservation then and wanted this area. The state of Utah put 640 acres or one section of land up for sale. Harry Goulding bought it for $2.00 an acre. Below a towering 600-foot red rock escarpment, Harry Goulding along with his wife, "Mike," pitched a tent and settled in. Soon he started a trading business, for a while trading goods out of the back of a horse-drawn wagon. In a few years he built a stone trading post and house that is now a wonderful and nostalgic museum. Goulding was known as an honest trader among the Navajo, who called him "Long Sheep."

Navajo boy, horse, and pony

Now there is enough light to see the long, black asphalt road, looking for all the world like a piece of decorative ribbon or a snake twisting its way to the east. With increasing light I can make out **Sentinel Mesa;** farther north, **Big Indian, Castle Butte, Bear and Rabbit, Stagecoach, King on His Throne,** and **Brigham's Tomb;** and, most northerly, **Eagle Rock.** I snap several pictures. A slight breeze comes up, and as the sun begins to ascend behind the monuments, the light changes dramatically, shifting colors over this broad panorama of the high desert and its rock projections.

The sun is up. The light is bright, and when I feel the sun's rays, already warm, I realize we must prepare for another typical July day with temperatures in the nineties. By now my family is up. We eat a hearty western breakfast at a window table where the view over the valley entertains us while we dine. Sitting near our table are two Belgian women and a family from France. Around the adjacent table this morning is part of a tour group from Germany. The atmosphere is warm and convivial. There is eager anticipation of the day's activities. We are going on a half-day tour deep into the valley. Others are going to a little gem of a place called **Mystery Valley**, an area particularly rich in prehistoric ruins.

We meet our guide for the day and one of the couples who will accompany our family of four in the open-air, four-wheel-drive vehicle. We are driven 5 miles over to the visitor center, where we spend some time looking at a geologic exhibit before heading into the valley. As we begin the trip, we are immediately glad we did not attempt to negotiate the park roads in our private vehicle. The road is badly rutted in places and, following yesterday's heavy rains, like a quagmire in other spots. So occasionally we divert from the road into the surrounding desert in order to make our way.

Shortly we reach a splendid area of high buttes and numerous monuments where many of John Huston's movies were made. There can be no doubt that this is the ultimate in "western scenery." Now we see a young Navajo boy riding bareback at a fast clip alongside the road. His pony is chasing along behind. Our driver hails him. He speaks Navajo and broken English. We ask him if we can take a picture. He agrees. We tip him, for our driver tells us that he will not allow his picture to be taken without a fee.

Navajo weaver

Now we seem to be in a forest of monuments not visible from the lodge. Rising 400 feet from the desert floor is a spire, hardly wider than our vehicle, that is called the **Totem Pole.** It is flanked by the **Yei-Bi-Chei** formation, which resembles a group of Navajo dancers. Soon we round a bend and come to a **Navajo encampment**. An extended family lives here. We stop and ask if we can enter one of the hogans. The response is friendly. A young Navajo girl about twelve or thirteen takes us into the hogan, where an upright loom is set up and an intricate tightly woven Navajo rug is in progress. It's cool inside the hogan. With the door open there is barely enough light to work by in this windowless structure. A sheepskin covers the hard-packed dirt floor where the weaver sits. As our eyes adjust to the darkness and we look around, the efficiency of the hogan architecture is evident immediately. Built somewhat like a geodesic dome, it has no center supports or joists, so all of the inside surface is usable. The hogan is noticeably cooler this morning than it will be this afternoon when the sun heats up the desert outside.

From here we head out cross-country. We are bounced and jostled around as we traverse this rough terrain. Shortly we come to another site, where a large hogan

Hogan under construction

Ancestral Puebloan petroglyphs

is being constructed. A young man and his friend are doing the work. Meanwhile his family is living in a recently built brush shelter for the summer, awaiting completion of the hogan. The aroma of the newly cut and peeled juniper wood is heavenly, and we ask if we may take a small chip. The gracious owner indicates yes with a broad smile and gives us a handful. He is pleased that we truly like what he is doing and indicates that he too likes to savor the pleasant aroma of juniper.

More cross-country. The way is very rough and bumpy now. We hold onto anything solid in the vehicle to keep from smashing each other. Then we arrive at the base of an enormous rock outcropping. A fantastic natural window high in its wall opens to the blue sky above. A short distance from here, we see an incredible number of petroglyphs carved through the desert varnish into the cliff wall. We stop and explore this area carefully. The sand under our feet yields potsherds from ancient times and pieces of chert that obviously have been "worked" and shaped by the former residents of this area. But the petroglyphs capture the day. With the sun to our back, good photographs are possible. I click away, using almost a roll of film as I move along the cliff wall to a variety of figures resembling goats, sheep, and turkeys and to stick figures of people as well as a host of other designs.

It is nearing noon, our time is running out, and it is very hot as we head across country along a rough trail down a dry creekbed. We seem to feel every boulder the truck laboriously negotiates. Along the way we stop at some incredible pink sand dunes, while our children climb part way up them and slide down. Sweaty and dusty, we arrive back at the ranch in time for lunch. We feel we have seen some magnificent scenery, but we are most pleased that we have been able to see close-up how the Navajo live. With this introduction to Navajo life, we feel we will more thoroughly enjoy the rest of our visit to Navajoland.

Navajo National Monument: Betatakin

From Goulding's Lodge in Monument Valley, drive south along paved U.S. Highway 163 25 miles to **Kayenta, Arizona**. Along the road you will see several interesting rock formations. One of them, on your left nearer Kayenta, is a towering formation of darker volcanic rock, **Agathlan Peak** or **El Capitan,** which rises to 7,100 feet elevation. The Navajo call this structure "Much Wool," derived from the times when The People scraped deer and sheep hides on the rough rocks at the peak's base, leaving an accumulation of hair or wool there. According to Navajo legend this is where the Two Came for Water Clan met up with the Western Water Clans, before journeying eastward. **Hoskinnini Mesa** looms to the west. Watch for sheep, goats, and cows along this somewhat narrow up-and-down road. If it is raining, do not negotiate this road until the rain subsides, for parts of the road, about halfway between Kayenta and Goulding's Junction, are subject to flooding. The signs that indicate this are to be heeded.

Kayenta, which in Navajo means "Spraying Water," is a sprawling town of nearly 5,000 inhabitants. In a wide-open location, where the wind seems to blow much of the time, this Navajo frontier town seems about as remote as any place in the United States. Yet with its schools and medical clinic, it is a useful and necessary shopping and trade center for this northwestern corner of the reservation. In addition, it serves as a rest stop and transportation hub for the many trucks along U.S. Highway 160 as they travel in and out of Arizona. Kayenta's pattern of sprawling growth makes it look larger than it actually is. Most of the

Agathlan Peak

growth has been on the north side, consisting of residences and modern buildings that blend reasonably well into the high-desert landscape. For many years there have been several motels that also offer food service. But with the development of the modern shopping center along the highway, with its pizza parlor, small shops, and large supermarket, travelers now stop in Kayenta to shop and soak up some aspects of contemporary Navajo living. Many visit the Navajo Nation's **Kayenta visitor center.** The modern building shaped like a traditional hogan dispenses Navajoland tourist information, displays Navajo cultural artifacts and historical exhibits, and sells Navajo arts and crafts, some of which are periodically demonstrated. Call (928) 697–3572 for additional information about hours and special Indian dance programs.

From Kayenta head southwest on U.S. Highway 160, a good paved, all-weather road. Look for Navajo sheepherders along this road. This is pretty country, as the road climbs through a pygmy forest of piñon pine and juniper to **Marsh Pass** (elevation 6,750 feet).

The canyons to your right are part of the **Tsegi Canyon** system. Tsegi Canyon consists of a large group of finger or dead-end canyons formed in the rock of Skeleton Mesa, which lies just east of **Navajo Mountain.** The small canyon that holds Betatakin Ruin to the south feeds into this canyon system. On your left is the northern portion of the **Black Mesa.** Coal is being mined there now. About 60 miles south the Hopi villages hug this mesa's high cliff walls as it abruptly ends at the desert's edge. This road is a bit windy and twisty, and large trucks often ply their way between Kayenta and Tuba City en route to Flagstaff, so the going can be slow.

About 19 miles south of Kayenta, you will come to a sign and junction road on the right leading to **Navajo National Monument.** Across U.S. Highway 160 from the junction is Black Mesa gas station and convenience store. Now head west on Arizona Highway 564, 9 paved miles through another pygmy forest of juniper and piñon pine. At the end of the paved road, elevation 7,268 feet, are a parking lot and monument visitor center. You are now several thousand feet above the elevation of Monument Valley. Your body will make you aware of the difference. You should also know that in summer the Navajo National Monument and the Navajo reservation (including Monument Valley) are on mountain daylight savings time, making them one hour later than the Hopi reservation and the rest of Arizona, which remain on mountain standard time.

I have seen many prehistoric dwellings in the Southwest, but the two that have inspired me the most are this one at Betatakin and Lowry Pueblo in Canyons of the Ancients, New Mexico, on the Colorado-Utah border. Neither suffers the congestion of Mesa Verde. In a recent year Navajo National Monument had around 90,000 visitors, a good percentage of whom were from abroad. There may be better ruins, larger ruins, or more intact ruins, but the dramatic site of Betatakin, coupled with its relative inaccessibility and solitude and its direct relationship to the Hopi villages to the south, makes it one of the major attractions in the Southwest. The monument, which has no fee, conducts tours of Betatakin ruin from approximately late May until early September. Allow at least five hours for this 5-mile round-trip hike. Navajo National Monument is also the departure point for **Keet Seel,** Arizona's largest and best-preserved ruin, with 160 rooms. There is a limited season. Only twenty people each day are allowed hiking permits for this rugged and strenuous 17-mile round-trip trek. Most hikers make it an overnight trip, staying one night at the primitive campsite, which has no potable water. Advance reservations and backcountry permits (free) are required (928) 672–2700. Confirm your reservation and permit no later than seven days before your visit or the permit will be canceled. During peak season reservations are accepted up to two months before the planned trip. Once at the site visitors must take part in a required Keet Seel orientation and are not allowed to enter unless accompanied by the ranger. All canyon trails are closed after the first snowfall and remain closed until all snow melts in the spring. The visitor center and the Sandal Trail (Ruin Overlook Trail), however, are open all year. For updated information: Superintendent, Navajo National Monument, National Park Service, HC71, Box 3, Tonalea, Arizona 86044–9704; (928) 672–2700 or 672–2706; www.nps.gov/nava.

Betatakin: A Narrative Account

After a filling, ranch-style breakfast at Goulding's this morning, we left very early and arrived here at the Navajo National Monument visitor center before 7:45 A.M. Yesterday we called from Goulding's to learn the exact time of the Betatakin tour, since tour time and frequency vary. The only tour today began at 8:15 A.M. We were told that only twenty-five people would be allowed on the tour (first come, first served), so we showed up before 7:30 A.M. The air is bracing this morning at this altitude. The small but well-run visitor center is a delight. It serves as a tour headquarters and museum for the three ruin sites, **Betatakin, Keet Seel,** and **Inscription House.** The last is closed because of its fragility. Most people come here to take the Betatakin tour. But I notice that a few people with advance reservations have come to hike the Keet Seel Trail.

We register for the Betatakin ruin tour (no advance reservations accepted) and, while waiting, view the excellent displays in the center. The exhibit of Kayenta pottery is one of the best I have ever seen, with some incredibly large pieces as well as some exquisite, smaller, polychrome pieces. The display reveals Anasazi life and migration and summarizes the evidence that links the Betatakin people to the Hopi. It is well done and instructive.

I learn from the museum exhibit material that the 600 acres making up this monument are on the Navajo reservation. The monument is named Navajo National Monument, but it is a U.S. government enterprise rather than a Navajo tribal enterprise. It was established as a national monument in 1909. The ruin we are to see today has nothing to do with the Navajo, except that it was discovered by migrating Navajo long after it was built. It belonged to a people whose descendants, the Hopi, have often been at odds with the Navajo. The name for this ancient Hopi-related ruin is *Betatakin,* a Navajo word meaning "Ledge House." The Hopi refer to the ancient dwellings in this area as *Kawestima,* or North Village, and to their ancestors who lived here as *Hisatsinom.*

Betatakin ancestral dwelling site

Fifty miles south of here are today's Hopi villages surrounded by and often ̈in conflict over land disputes with their age-old adversaries, the Navajo. Here Navajo rangers help protect Hopi history. All very confusing, I think, for first-time visitors. I vow that if I ever write a book about this area, I'll try to set the record straight. Although this part of the United States is referred to as "Indian Country," there are two very distinct Indian groups here. Understanding that makes many things clearer (see "Introduction to Northeastern Arizona" section).

With a little time left before the tour, we walk along a well-graded viewpoint trail, the **Sandal Trail,** 1 mile round-trip, to view Betatakin Ruin from the rim. At the beginning of the trail, we view a reconstructed example of a forked hogan, a Navajo sweat house, and a Navajo wagon. Then we pass the **Aspen Forest Overlook Trail,** a 0.8-mile round-trip walk descending steeply to a unique overlook of the trees along the canyon bottom (but not the ruin). On reaching the rim overlook at the end of the Sandal Trail, the ruin near the bottom of the canyon wall appears small in the distance. We are glad we have our binoculars with us.

At the appointed hour our ranger guide gathers us together and informs us that we are about to embark on a 5-mile round-trip, five- to six-hour tour. Sounds

Aspen leaves

easy. But she goes on to say that we will be descending 700 feet into the canyon in less than 1 mile. That means an elevation gain of similar proportions on the way back out. People with heart disease and physical problems that might be aggravated by this much exercise at this elevation (more than 7,000 feet) are urged to stay on the rim. We have been told to bring up to two quarts of water per person and to wear footwear suitable for hiking.

We caravan to the trailhead, then begin the descent. We are walking down into one of the finger canyons of the Tsegi Canyon system, part of the same canyon we saw at Marsh Pass this morning. In the distance looms Navajo Mountain, a sacred mountain and the highest point on the Navajo reservation. From this vantage point the canyon looks long and narrow as it disappears on the horizon. Looking into the canyon bottom, we observe the color of green I have come to associate with deciduous trees that receive ample water—a vibrant chartreuse green. As we near the bottom, I make out aspen, oak, and elder. Somehow it seems strange to see aspen in the canyon when none exist anywhere on the rim. Yet we are going from a high, dry, pygmy forest desert environment down into a moist valley environment, which contains Douglas firs (the tree that grows prolifically on the moist Northwest Coast of the United States) and horsetail, that ancient fernlike plant found in the West anywhere there is a lot of moisture.

We saw magpies and bluebirds near the road this morning, and already we have observed them and several ravens from the trail. Near the top of the canyon walls, we note the cross-bedded Navajo sandstone, and beneath it we see the purple-red of the Kayenta strata of rock. Deep in the canyons we are told that Wingate sandstone can be seen (see Section 1, "A Geologic Primer to Southeastern Utah"). We are also told that the Navajo sandstone is permeable, so that rainwater goes down through it until it hits the denser Kayenta stone. There the water stops its vertical descent and begins to seep horizontally on top of the Kayenta, until it reaches cliff faces or cliff bottoms, where it either emerges on the surface as seeps or springs or continues underground.

Finally when we reach the bottom of the steep trail, we sit and rest in the cool shade of the canyon forest. Although we won't actually enter the alcove, we are told by the ranger that this was a typical Ancestral Pueblo village of the Kayenta Puebloans, who lived here about A.D. 1260. They built and abandoned the village before 1300. Now as we walk along we top a small rise and from here can see the alcove for the first time. This naturally formed, erosion-carved alcove faces southeast. It is of magnificent proportions. It was probably right about this spot where John Wetherill, a Kayenta rancher and trader and younger brother of Mesa Verde's "discoverer," and Bryan Cummings, an anthropologist, acting on a tip from a Navajo friend, rode on horseback up this long finger canyon in 1909 and saw what we are seeing right now. The sight is overwhelming. The roof of the alcove is 500

Douglas fir

Horsetail

feet above the floor of the cave. Walking a little farther, we now catch a glimpse of many boxlike apartments, some several stories high and at different levels in this gaping aperture in the sandstone. There is silence as our group stands, transfixed. None of us expected to see anything quite this dramatic. The canyon is still. Only a gentle breeze sets the aspens quaking.

I wonder how they produced a small city deep down in this remote canyon. Not until this moment had it really struck me how innovative and hardworking the Ancestral Puebloans must have been to produce this edifice. Most of the village is very much intact after these 700 years. There are six tiers of rooms and a balcony of rooms high and to the back of the cave. We are told that some of the original 135 rooms were destroyed by a rock fall. At one time 150 inhabitants may have occupied this alcove. They farmed the narrow strip of land just below the village. We see a rectangular kiva similar to the ones in the Hopi villages. The tall mortar-and-stone tower was probably a granary for storing corn and other staples. We marvel at the tight construction, even though these people were not known to produce the finest of the Ancestral Puebloan buildings.

The high protective cliff roof shades the alcove from the hot midday summer sun like a huge umbrella. But in this region of cold winters, when the low winter sun shines, this alcove would catch most of those warming rays, and no doubt the stone would retain some of the heat. One hundred fifty noisy Ancestral Puebloans would have filled this empty alcove with a great vibrancy of sound and life. We explore for another thirty minutes or so. We view from a distance large hand-hewn timbers whose concentric rings, we are told, reveal that they were probably living trees here in this canyon sometime around A.D. 1100. We see soot from cooking fires that stained the apartment walls more than 700 years ago. We are gratified that there are only twenty-five of us down here rather than the masses who go tramping through some of the better-known cliff dwellings.

Now we begin the hard ascent back up the steep trail, equivalent to climbing the stairs of a seventy-story building. We take our time and enjoy the pleasant surroundings, chatting about our newly found discoveries. At the top we snack in the shade near the visitor center. We refresh ourselves before leaving for the Hopi mesas. We want to see and feel the relationship between the Hopi ancestors here at Betatakin and today's Hopi people. In just one day we will span the gulf of hundreds of years.

Navajo Trading Post Row and Tuba City

From Navajo National Monument return 9 miles to U.S. Highway 160; turn south. The road now follows **Klethla Valley,** once known as "trading post row" of western Navajoland. Along the road you will see ample evidence of the coal mining going on at **Black Mesa.** Some of the Hopi are concerned that the amount of water it takes to produce and transport coal will lower the water table of Black Mesa and cause a reduction in their farm production. This coal is being shipped by rail on the tracks that parallel the highway to fire generators at the **Navajo Power Plant** in Page, Arizona, which produces electric power for distant sites in Arizona and California.

Because this is one of the most remote sections of the reservation, you may see Navajo women in their colorful blouses and long, flowing skirts herding sheep on either side of the road. From now on you may begin to experience the feeling of being in a country with people whose customs are very different. A sense of timelessness begins to set in too, when you realize that you will be in one time zone in Monument Valley, mountain daylight savings time, and another zone by the time you reach the Hopi mesas, where the inhabitants are on mountain standard time.

In about 12 miles you will pass the junction to Page, Arizona. Twenty-eight miles farther down the highway are two large outcroppings of cross-bedded Entrada sandstone resembling elephant's feet.

Just 1 mile beyond **Elephant's Feet** on the left-hand side of the road is the old **Red Lake Trading Post.** The name of the post office near Red Lake is *Tonalea,* which in Navajo means "where water comes together." The old trading post was named for the small silted lake to the north of it. Established in 1881, the Red Lake Trading Post had several trader-owners before being permanently established at this exact site in 1891 by the Babbitt Bros. Trading Co. of Flagstaff, Arizona. Zane Grey often visited the old Red Lake post, and it is the setting for the first chapter of his book *Rainbow Trail,* published in 1915.

Trading posts like the Red Lake post, now a small, Navajo-run grocery store, and the historic Tuba Trading Post in Tuba City were an integral part of Navajo life for more than a century. Wood was so scarce in the old days that portions of the interior walls of the Red Lake post were constructed using boards emblazoned with the name Arbuckle Coffee Company, taken from that company's wooden shipping boxes. The proprietors will sometimes let visitors see their "Arbuckle" walls. With the numbers of trading posts dwindling these days, some of the functions of the old posts are carried out in a more modern setting not unlike grocery stores found in urban strip malls. Yet if you spend a little time in one of these modern "grocery posts" (like the **Tonalea General Store** along the highway about 0.25 mile south of the old Red Lake post), you will find among the more familiar goods special items that have been part of the Navajo trading post scene for more than a hundred years. There may be saddle blankets, galvanized buckets, large bolts of velveteen cloth, Indian arts and crafts, and a host of other items unique to the area.

Back on the highway notice the **San Francisco Peaks** beginning to loom up

The old Red Lake Trading Post, Tonalea

to your left as you drive approximately 20 miles to Tuba City, population 8,225, elevation 4,936 feet, where it's always very hot in the summer afternoon sun. But this vibrant and bustling center of western Navajoland, with its crowds of Navajo and their four-wheel-drive vehicles, is a good place to people-watch without being intrusive or feeling too self-conscious. So stop awhile. You may see Navajo women in ankle-length skirts with bright blouses and Navajo men in western garb with hair braided down their backs, all going about their daily business.

Tuba City, once occupied by Hopi people, was named for the Hopi leader Chief Tuvi, whose name was somehow changed into Tuba by early-day Washington bureaucrats. In fact the **Hopi village Moenkopi** lies just a few hundred feet east of the highway that bounds Tuba City on the east. The Navajo name for the town means "zigzagging water" because of the springs found in the area. Tuba City is the capital of western Navajoland and has a number of Navajo tribal services, including the always busy **Navajo Community Center** and a tribal law and order agency. It is also home to the U.S. **Public Health Service Indian Hospital.** There are several large grocery stores and trading posts there, as well as a good motel and several cafes. If you arrive around lunchtime, be sure to stop at the small Tuba City Truck Stop Cafe on the east side of U.S. Highway 160 near the junction of Arizona Highway 264, also known as Indian Route 3.

From the cafe's parking lot, you look east over the Hopi village of Moenkopi, just a few yards away. The cafe's specialty is the Navajo taco. Partake of one of these special tacos built atop Navajo fry bread, and you will know why this is one of the best eating establishments west of Window Rock.

Tuba Trading Post

Now with a taco or cold drink in hand, drive out of the glaring sun west into Tuba City proper to the shaded main street that runs alongside the historic **Tuba Trading Post,** about 1 mile west of U.S. Highway 160. This large, octagonal-shaped trading post has been on this site for more than one hundred years. Inside you will find some high-quality, handwoven Navajo rugs. And often excellent, well-crafted pieces of Navajo pottery and jewelry are available. Just outside the post is a traditional hogan that you are allowed to enter when the door is unlocked. Behind the trading post are the modern **Quality Inn Tuba City** and the **Hogan Restaurant,** which have put Tuba City on the map as a place to stay for a few days while touring the area. Be certain to observe the strictly enforced 15-mile-per-hour speed limit in sections of the town.

Drive back to the highway. Turn right onto U.S. Highway 160 and drive southwest for approximately 5 miles, where you will see an unpaved spur road (sometimes signed DINOSAUR TRACKS) taking off to the right or north of the highway, where there are usually some curio booths. In just over 0.2 mile, this road will take you within a short walk of a set of **dinosaur tracks,** compliments of the Mesozoic Era. Seventy-five miles to the south and west of Tuba City is **Grand Canyon Village.** Flagstaff is approximately 80 miles to the south of Tuba City. If you are headed to either destination, you might want to make a stop at the busy **Cameron Trading Post** on the **Little Colorado River,** 26 miles south of Tuba City. In addition to a motel and restaurant, there is a nice selection of regional Indian arts and crafts and a gallery section devoted to both historic and contemporary Indian art.

The Hopi World

High atop the Colorado Plateau in northern Arizona, another gigantic tableland is superimposed. It is called **Black Mesa.** From its origin in northern Arizona, it extends more than 60 miles to the south through much of Navajoland. At its southern end the mesa divides like fingers on a hand into several phalanges that extend high above the desert. At their tips where they abruptly end, the mesa cliffs drop 600 feet to the valley below. There the **Hopi villages** lie, many clinging to the edges of this rocky escarpment more than 6,200 feet above sea level. The mesatops, the terraces along the steep mesa walls, and the interconnecting desert between the three mesas constitute the small but significant Hopi reservation that encompasses 1.5 million acres, of which 911,000 are identified as Hopi partitioned lands. Many of the villages are as isolated from one another as they are from the rest of the modern world in this remote region of Arizona.

From these mesatop villages you can look out over thousands of square miles of brown and multicolored painted desert, punctuated with mountains, mesas, and buttes rising on the horizon. From these high promontories at night, the stars are the biggest and the brightest you will ever see, as though the mesas were stepping-stones to the heavens. For the first-time visitor who is willing to spend enough time to absorb some of the aura, this is heady stuff. There is a sense of mystery and eternity among these rocky, dry mesatops that are completely exposed to the full force of the elements.

What you feel may only be reflecting what the Hopi have known for almost 900 years. In Hopi mythology this is the Center of the Universe, *Tuuwanasavi*. This is the center of the vibrations of the world. This is the Sacred Circle, a holy place in tune with the Hopi universe. From here all the landmarks of the Hopi religious world are in full view. From the twin shafts of sacred Corn Rock close at hand to the mighty San Francisco Peaks looming in the distance more than 80 miles away, where the kachinas (Katsinam) live out their lives, you will view much that is sacred to the Hopi. To the southeast an extended ridge arises containing numerous small buttes and mesas (see White Cone on your map), giving the appearance of a notched calendar stick.

This is the Hopi calendar that only the village chiefs or appointed "sun watchers" are trusted to read. They watch this ridge carefully as the sun moves along it, as their ancestors have for generations before them. Especially they watch it in December as the sun moves from notch to notch, north to south, looking for the day when the sun reaches a particular spot along the ridge, reverses its direction, and begins heading north again, the harbinger of longer and warmer days. When the sun reaches a certain notch, a prayer is sung and the planting season begins. When it reaches still other notches, it signals the beginning of certain age-old ritual ceremonies and dances. Also in the distance are two curved buttes, the Giant's Chair and Montezuma's Chair. Sometimes they appear as one in the distance, like a giant pair of horns or wings. Horns like these are thought to transmit power from the heavens to the earth. At sites like these and others to the north, young Hopi men capture symbols of some of that power when they catch golden eagles for ceremonial purposes and bring them back to their rooftops and kivas.

If you drive through without stopping in this area on a hot summer's day, you will think you have not missed anything. All you will see is a certain drabness of brown rocks giving way to arid brown desert. Even *Maasaw*, the Hopi deity of life, death, and fire who led the Hopi into this world and who is their guardian, recognized that. In a Hopi legend he is quoted as saying, "My land is a wasteland. Look at it. There is nothing attractive. It is harsh land. However, if you are willing to live my way of life, you may stay here. Even though it is harsh land, beneath it

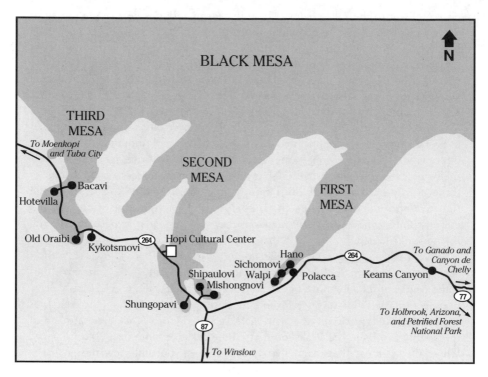

Hopi villages

are riches. For that reason do not ever allow it to pass into anyone else's hand."
Maasaw also prophesied that there the Hopi would "live in poverty but in peace."
After wandering in the four directions, the Hopi clans would, it was prophesied,
meet up eventually and settle on the mesas. So it is there that the Hopi took a
stand to live out their lives in this, the Fourth World, to await Purification Day and
entry into the Fifth World.

Maasaw was right. Beneath the land riches have been discovered. Coal and
uranium are now mined from the Black Mesa. But the real resources there are the
Hopi people, who have in the fastness of their subterranean kivas learned how to
use the land and the water wisely. Ironically this seemingly dry land has sustained
thousands of people for hundreds of years. For the early Hopi, the Hisatsinom, discovered that water at this southern end of the Black Mesa comes out in the form
of hidden seeps and springs along the mesa edges and below the mesas.

Black Mesa serves as a giant subterranean water reservoir, collecting rainwater from its extensive surface. The water filters through the permeable sandstone
and then courses between the rock strata to the Hopi mesas, where it waters the
small plots of farmland. Below the mesa sand dunes have piled up against the mesa
walls. These dunes act as an insulating blanket to help retain the water that seeps
from the bottom of the mesa. In these sandy areas the early Hisatsinom discovered
that 8 or 10 inches below the very dry-appearing surface was a layer of moisture
ready to be tapped for agricultural purposes. When they found that corn, beans,

and squash grew well there, they discovered a sustaining richness that far exceeds the value of any minerals being mined today.

But the dramatic setting of the Hopi villages is only one of the rewards awaiting the traveler. The other rewards are wrapped up in the most valuable resource there, the Hopi people, their history, culture, and religion.

By the time you get to the Hopi mesas, the colorful landscapes of Navajoland have faded to a dull, drab beige and brown. Jumbled heaps of rock make the land seem even more desolate. The people also seem less colorful. Simple, plain cotton dresses replace the long, colorful dramatic dress of the Navajo women. Khaki and polyester slacks replace the Navajo cowboy dress. A cotton scarf may be tied around the forehead, but there is no dramatic display of clothing, silver jewelry, or other adornments. But just as these dry mesas paradoxically give water from deep springs, the Hopi people project a richness that cannot easily be verbalized. The drama is so underplayed there that when it hits you, it is all the more powerful.

From deep in the kivas and the hearts and spirits of the Hopi come some of the most colorful and dramatically overpowering scenes I have ever witnessed. How can it be, I ask myself, that a man in simple, everyday modern dress, who by western and even Hopi standards holds a menial job, can undergo such a complete transformation that after only a few hours in the kiva, he becomes a figure of regal beauty and awesome power? As he ascends from the kiva to perform an intricate, ancient, complex dance, he commands the respect of all. For in Hopiland, respect is often tied to the Hopi way rather than to success in the modern world.

As it should be, the **Hopi way** will probably never be completely known or understood by an outsider. But from time to time, the outsider catches a glimpse of what it may be. The Hopi way is really a life pathway with several divergent branches. Each branch or byway demands some kind of special obligation or responsibility from the people. The various branches of the Hopi way are reflected in the organization of the Hopi culture and villages. Through the matrilineal clan system, the Hopi have certain kinship duties, responsibilities, and loyalties. Through the ceremonial societies and the religious leaders, the Hopi have certain responsibilities toward the religious and ceremonial life of the village, the Hopi community as a whole, and to humankind in general. To their villages the Hopi have certain secular responsibilities symbolized through the *kikmongwi,* the hereditary village father or chief, who in his autonomy gives way only to certain revered religious leaders regarding ceremonial functions. The Hopi also have certain social responsibilities to those in and beyond their own individual villages. In addition, they have certain agricultural or farming responsibilities to the family farm plots that have been handed down for generations on the mother's side of the family.

These highly structured and complex 900-year-old responsibilities and traditions were passed down through personal example, oral traditions, and many ceremonies and rituals. These responsibilities are for a lifetime, and with them go daily tasks to be fulfilled. Discharging one's responsibilities and performing one's immediate tasks are most important to living the Hopi way. A Hopi woman told me several years ago that she and her family could not go on vacation that summer, because her husband and sons had major roles in the ceremonial dances. This means that the family had to provide money for refurbishing costumes and to purchase

Hopi Kachina dolls

the many gifts to be given out by the clowns to the village people and its visitors. In addition, many hours are required in the kiva to learn and practice to perfection the very precise and intricate nine-centuries-old choreography that you may see performed in the village. Many dances reflect weeks spent in the kiva making ceremonial preparations. Many other hours are spent there patiently refurbishing the ceremonial masks and costumes. It has been said that the traditional Hopi may spend most of their lives in preparing for their ceremonial and other duties.

The rigors of the Hopi way begin early when a child is born into his or her mother's clan. Whether it is the Corn, Bean, Badger, Water, or any one of thirty or forty other clans, the Hopi child inherits the ceremonial and community responsibilities that were given to each clan years ago in exchange for the farmland each clan received. It is the duty of the mother's relations, especially her brother, to teach these duties to the child. As he grows up in the village, the child learns another set of obligations relating to village life, and he gains respect for the powerful village father or chief, the hereditary kikmongwi.

It is said that Hopi children know about music and dance from birth. Well they might, for almost from the very beginning they are exposed to a dazzling array of dances and ceremonies in the village plaza each year. During these times, especially during the kachina ceremonies, more responsibilities are taught. Kachina dancers give kachina dolls to infants of both sexes and later to the female children. The dolls, carved from cottonwood roots and then painted and clothed, not only are beautiful to look at and fun to play with but also serve an educational purpose. They introduce the young Hopi child to the power and sacredness of the kachina spirits by teaching her about the costumes, masks, and other details of these deities. At other times the dolls are occasionally given to older females as fertility symbols.

Between the ages of six and ten, both boys and girls are initiated into the kachina cult. At this time they learn the obligations of the kiva. They acquire a ceremonial father or mother who has been picked by the child's parents and who is from a different clan. The ceremonial parent has the responsibility of preparing the child for the rites of passage from childhood to adulthood. As the child reaches adulthood, he or she will be initiated into a priesthood or ceremonial society, such as Wuwtsim for men or Maraw for women, all a part of the Hopi spiritual world.

In addition to these social, religious, and ceremonial responsibilities, the Hopi child, especially the male, has been learning right along from his father the responsibilities of planting, nurturing, and harvesting good crops. If the term *Hopi* means anything to me, it means above all a people who excel in dry land farming. So it is no accident that a Hopi father will teach his son about corn, soil, water, and prayers for rain and good crops. Farming not only provides staples for the table but also provides products that are essential to the religious and ceremonial life of the Hopi.

The Hopi farmers raise a variety of products, but the one you will see most frequently in the fields is corn. Corn is not just a dietary staple there; it is an integral part of Hopi ritual and ceremonial life. Traditionally cornmeal, laboriously hand-ground from ears raised on nearby small farm plots, is a symbol of fertility and friendship and plays an important role in the marriage ceremony. Symbolically the Hopi speak of corn as "Corn Mother." An ear of corn is given to the newborn baby at birth, and corn pollen is used in christenings. Later the same child receives another ear at the time of initiation. In ritual dances cornmeal may be used as body makeup, while corn stalks and husks may be used in making the *paaho* or plumed prayer stick that is used in a variety of ceremonies.

Hopi cornfields are not like the ones in Iowa. And the corn is not the same either. A Hopi cornfield may be planted in very sandy soil and may be only from ½ to 10 acres in size. Even today tractors are used only sparingly to prepare the ground. Most of the planting is done by hand as the ancient Hopi did it centuries ago. The traditional planting stick is made from a sturdy stick cut from one of the high-desert shrubs and whittled to a wedge-shaped point on one end. Sometimes a short piece of pipe or metal is flattened at one end for the same purpose. The two yearly plantings are done by the boys and men on land belonging to the mother's clan, passed down through the female lineage for generations. The corn is planted 8 inches or more deep in areas where the soil is subirrigated and has good capacity to retain water and where it will receive good surface runoff. Prayers are said after the planting, and ceremonies are performed to ensure a good harvest. The patient Hopi farmer tends his corn diligently, with great care. More prayers are said to ward off too early or too late frosts, summer floods, drought, and wind- and sandstorms.

Hopi corn is short and stout and comes in a variety of colors, including yellow, red, white, and blue. These colors coincide with the Hopi symbols for the four cardinal directions. The colors that represent north and south, respectively, are yellow and red, while white and blue are the colors for east and west. It is blue corn that you will see used here and along the Rio Grande for various southwestern Indian foods. On the cob the kernels look bluish black, but when they are processed, they have a definite bluish cast. Hopi corn is descended from the "pod corn" that dates back to 2500 B.C. in the Southwest, wherein each kernel is individually sheathed, not looking too dissimilar from the seeds found in the heads of the wild grasses from which it was patiently developed.

Many dedicated people in the villages continue to live out the hard but rewarding Hopi way that has gained for the Hopi a reputation among their fellow Indians for spiritual purity and superiority. Even the neighboring Navajo and distant Pueblo tribes recognize the Hopi's spiritual pureness and often ask them to weave special ceremonial garments for them. But the drive toward purity of ceremonial life creates problems that may ironically lead to its demise in our modern world. For instance, other American Indian tribes feel no inhibition performing their dances away from the reservation, wherever their people may be. But the Hopi do not do this. A Hopi must return to the sacred ground of the mesas for his religious ceremonies. It is only in this setting that these ceremonies are held. It is only in village kivas that they are practiced. So understandably modern jobs are cutting into ceremonial life. It is hard if not impossible for a Hopi to take several weeks off from an hourly job so he can return to the mesa to prepare for the ceremonies. Consequently some of the villages have given up some of the more intricate ceremonies. Others, though, like **Shungopavi** and **Hotevilla,** remain steadfast.

This decline of the Hopi way and ceremonial life is firing once again the age-old controversy of being "true" to the Hopi way. The "Hostiles" of yesterday are known today as "Traditionalists" and the "Friendlies" of the early 1900s are known as the "Progressives." The Traditionalists are opposed to mining coal on Black Mesa and are against the introduction of industries on the reservation. They are against the quest for new homes, cars, and economic development in general. And when disrespectful tourists with camcorders or cameras or intrusive entrepreneurs and researchers push too far, they spark, from time to time, the cyclic flames of isolationism among the Hopi. Suddenly ceremonial dances are closed to non-Indians, and certain villages may limit or prohibit entry to visitors for a period of time.

Many of the Hopi feel that all this modernization will detract from spiritual responsibilities (so far no gambling casinos appear on the Hopi reservation). The Progressives, however, believe that modernization can occur with certain modifications so as to preserve most of the cultural and spiritual life of the tribe. Many of these differences are played out in the activities of the Tribal Council. The council was mandated by the U.S. government to represent the whole reservation. It was hoped that it could help unite the politically independent villages. Although each village is supposed to elect representatives to the council, not all villages are represented there. These elected representatives are frequently in conflict with the hereditary village chiefs, who often go their own way. But the council has been useful in presenting a united front for the reservation in its legal battles centering on land disputes with the Navajo.

Change is evident as you drive from one mesatop village to another, but it is not overpowering. Many of the older mud-plaster-and-stone homes are being replaced with homes made of manufactured concrete blocks and other modern building materials. Electricity has been installed in most of the villages. There is an increasing amount of indoor plumbing. Cars and four-wheel-drive vehicles seem abundant. Hopi men and women dress, for the most part, like all Americans. But as the new comes in, the old remains. Early in the morning a few of the Hopi women who are nurses depart for work in their white uniforms, while some of the older women carry buckets of water to their homes from a communal faucet and still other Hopi women prepare to fire their pottery in the age-old method, using sheep dung for fuel. Some of the men in hard hats depart from the village in pickups, headed for work 100 miles or more away, while other men can be seen weaving ceremonial garb or carving kachinas in their homes. Today you still will hear the friendly chatter of a community starting the day. And you will see in the center of things, integrated with village life, the ancient religious kiva, its ladder reaching skyward from the heart of the village.

Without a doubt the Hopi have an unshakable sense of identity. On the mesas today a Hopi can point to a certain cornfield, a special rock, or even a particular house and say with assuredness that his ancestors farmed this field, frequented that spot, or lived in that house for more than nine centuries. These rocky escarpments are home to the Hopi. Their agelessness renders a sense that this is a sacred spot. I am sure I am not the only visitor who experiences a tingle up and down his spine as I approach this high tableland from the desert below, or who is drawn back time and again to these mesas. The mesas, the villages, and the people are likewise magnets for the Hopi themselves, holding a sense of mystery and sanctity. Those Hopi who have left their mesa homes for jobs outside frequently come back home for good. Those who have left and live elsewhere in the Southwest often journey hundreds of miles to return to the mesas, seeking the personal fulfillment found in watching or participating in the various age-old dances and ceremonies. Information: Hopi Cultural Preservation Office, P.O. Box 123, Kykotsmova, Arizona 86039; (928) 734–6636 or 734–2113; or Hopi Public Relations Office P.O. Box 123, Kykotsmovi, Arizona 86039; (928) 734–3283; www.hopi.nsn.us.

The Hopi Villages

Starting just east of Arizona Highway 160 at Tuba City is Moenkopi, the first of twelve recognized Hopi villages you will encounter as you travel from west to east over a span of about 70 miles. Each of the villages will be described in its order of appearance. All are situated on or just off Arizona Highway 264, also known as Indian Route 3.

Moenkopi (Hopi: "running water all the time"). One of the largest of the Hopi communities, Moenkopi was not founded until the late 1800s, when villagers from Old Oraibi left that increasingly crowded village to form a new village. But this was not new territory for the Oraibi Hopi. They had planted corn in the fertile fields around Moenkopi Wash for generations. It is said that villagers in those early days ran the 45 miles between Oraibi on Third Mesa to their fields of corn, beans, squash, and melons at Moenkopi.

Moenkopi is the only Hopi village not situated directly on or beneath Black Mesa and is widely separated from the other villages. It is actually divided into two village units, Upper Moenkopi and Lower Moenkopi. Upper Moenkopi is one of the least traditional villages, as it snuggles up to the busy main north-south highway in this region and the Navajo tribal center of Tuba City. Lower Moenkopi is more traditional, as the kachina cult is still followed there and the village women continue to make fine wicker baskets.

As you are leaving Moenkopi, you will see for the first time on your journey, on the east side of the village just above the wash, homes made mostly of stone and plaster. These represent the kinds of homes found in most of the Hopi villages farther east. You will also see fields of Hopi Indian corn for the first time on the sides of the wash. Notice the short but sturdy stalks, and remember that these fields and others like them have grown corn and sustained the Hopi people nearly a thousand years.

Third Mesa (45 miles east of Moenkopi)

Bacavi (Hopi: "place where the reeds grow"). This village was founded during the troubled times of the early 1900s, when the internal conflict between the "Friend-lies" and the "Hostiles" at Old Oraibi became so intense that several dissident groups split from that village to form new villages. In 1909 some of the dissident villagers who had left Old Oraibi in 1907 to settle Hotevilla decided they wanted to return to Old Oraibi. Old Oraibi refused to let them come back, so they formed this new village. It sits well into the mesatop and has good springs, providing moisture for its arable fields. This very traditional village has the reputation of having some of the best ceremonial dancers in Hopiland. The women here weave wicker baskets of high quality.

Hotevilla (Hopi: "a slope of junipers" or alternatively "a scraped back," referring to the topography of the land here at the mesa's edge). This village was formed in 1906 by a "hostile" or anti-U.S. government group who, after great conflict with the progovernment faction, lost a "pushing match" and left Old Oraibi to form this new village. With naturally irrigated farmlands spilling below the village on the mesa's terraces, this village on the mesa's edge, the Hopi's largest, is well worth a visit. The terraced fields are most impressive and strongly resemble Oriental terraced fields as they descend the slopes behind the village. This community has the reputation of being the most conservative and traditional of all the villages. It is the village that most staunchly defends the ancient Hopi way. Some Hotevilla men still put up their hair in the old style with a bob in the back and square cut bangs in the front. The women make excellent wicker baskets.

Old Oraibi (Hopi: "place of ourai," a type of rock). Years ago when the village population was dwindling and only very conservative, older Hopi resided here, this village was frequently closed to non-Indians. But today, following an influx of new residents, the active part of the village is open and the public is invited to visit a gallery or two selling Hopi art and crafts. The oldest part of the village is still off-limits to visitors. This was the first mesa top village, settled about A.D. 1125 to A.D. 1150. It has remained occupied since that time, claiming the title of the oldest, most continuously occupied village or town in the United States. Although it is definitely the oldest mesatop village and the oldest continuously inhabited village in the same location, there is some dispute as to whether it is the first Hopi village. At one time Oraibi, with its narrow streets and multistoried buildings, must have definitely had an urban scale.

New Oraibi or *Kykotsmovi* (Hopi: "place of the hill ruins"). This somewhat sprawling, modern settlement at the base of Third Mesa accommodates the **Hopi tribal offices.** A gas station and a food store are also located there. Formed around 1910, this and other valley villages became modernized much more quickly than the mesatop villages. From here at New Oraibi or from the highway just west of New Oraibi as you enter town, you can look back to the west and catch glimpses of Old Oraibi and the ruins of the old church in the distance on the mesatop, as well as its terraces stepping down to the desert below.

Second or Middle Mesa (5 miles east of Third Mesa)

Shungopavi (Hopi: "water place where reeds grow"). Although some Hopi identify Old Oraibi as the first Hopi village, others would point their finger at Maseeba and its modern-day counterpart, Shungopavi. It is believed by many Hopi that Maseeba was the first village to be formed by the people known today as the Hopi. It was established in the 1100s, below Second or Middle Mesa. The village moved several times and, after the Pueblo Revolt in 1680, surfaced on the mesatop as today's village of Schomopovi or Shungopavi. Some call this venerable village the "Vatican" of the Hopi world. In the middle of the Sacred Circle, the center of Hopiland, it is situated at the tip of Second Mesa with a commanding view over the desert and the sacred Hopi monuments to the south.

Second Mesa juts its fingerlike projection farther into the desert than any of the other mesas. Being on Second Mesa is more like being on an island in the sky, rather than on a peninsular extension of a larger mesa. There is a certain sense of timelessness there, and from its vantage point all of the visual cues to the Hopi universe can be seen. This is a commanding position, with the site of old Maseeba just below Shungopavi's ridge. Although many of the ancient stone and stucco houses are being stabilized or replaced with new cinder-block homes, traditional village life is very much intact. Second Mesa women still make beautiful coiled baskets, while some of the men continue to weave beautiful ceremonial garments and sashes and carve kachina dolls. This village is the site of many dances. Ceremonial traditions are carried out here with diligence and rare beauty.

Shipaulovi (Hopi: "place of mosquitoes"). This village was formed by a dissident group of Shungopavi villagers when that village moved to the mesatop. It also has a commanding view from its mesatop position. Unfortunately in the past few years, modern housing built by the U.S. Department of Housing and Urban Development below the mesa has attracted most of the villagers away from the mesatop. The village is now almost abandoned, except when it is used for ceremonial purposes and dances. The women make coiled baskets there.

Hopi coiled basket

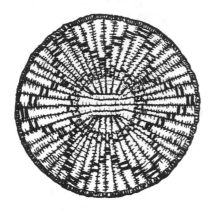

Hopi wicker plaque   *Hopi pot*

Mishongnovi (Hopi: "place of the dark man"). Settled around A.D. 1200, it was moved to the mesatop after the last Pueblo Revolt. It is one of the best-situated villages. The twin shafts of the sacred Corn Rock, visible for miles around, are just above the Mishongnovi graveyard on the terraces below the village. Many of the traditional rough-hewn rock houses can be seen there. As at the other Second Mesa villages, the women there make well-crafted and artistic coiled baskets and plaques.

First Mesa or East Mesa (8 miles east of Second Mesa)

Polacca (Hopi: "butterfly"). This is a modern suburban village founded by Thomas Polacca, a Hano village resident who moved down from the mesa in the early 1900s. Today this suburban offshoot of the three mesatop villages is home to many fine Hopi potters. It is an active, busy community and seems to grow every year as residents move from the mesatop to this more accessible location below the mesa.

Hano or **Tewa** (Hopi: "place of the eastern [Tewa] people"). This village was formed after the Pueblo Revolt by Tewa-speaking Rio Grande Pueblo people who immigrated to escape Spanish reprisals after the Pueblo Revolt. Over the years they have assimilated completely with the Hopi. They learned the Hopi language, but the Hopi at Walpi never learned Tewa. Since the original Hano villagers brought their highly developed pottery skills from the Rio Grande Pueblos, some of the best Hopi potters, including the renowned Hopi potter Nampeyo, have come from this village.

Sichomovi (Hopi: "hill place where flowers grow"). This village (sometimes called "Middle Village") is the newest on First Mesa, being formed as a suburb of Walpi sometime after 1700. It lies between Walpi and Hano up on the mesa. Since Sichomovi is a satellite village or colony to the older village, Walpi, its residents join with the Walpi villagers for many of the ceremonial society functions.

Walpi

Sichomovi is also a **pottery** village, and there pottery for sale signs are often seen in the windows of the houses.

Walpi (Hopi: "place of the gap"). Perched at the very tip of First Mesa, tiny Walpi is the most dramatically situated of all the Hopi villages, appearing to be an extension of the mesa itself. Its stone-and-mud-plastered buildings hug the narrow ledge above precipitous cliffs on all sides. The village was founded in 1417 but did not move to the tip of the mesatop until sometime between 1680 and 1690. Except for Sikyatki, an earlier, now extant village founded a little to the north below the mesa, Walpi is the oldest First Mesa village—and the smallest. A few stepped-back multistory buildings in the village shape to a somewhat pyramidal form that for some echoes the pyramids of the Aztecs. Unquestionably this is the most visually stunning of the Hopi villages. Walpi has undergone stabilization and some reconstruction. Because many of the centuries-old buildings were deteriorating, the Economic Development Administration spent about $500,000 to restore many of the weakened walls. Rock was cut by hand from the mesa itself, just as in ancient times, in order to be true to Hopi tradition. At Walpi you can see the *kiska*, a covered passage between the buildings used frequently in ancient times to interconnect parts of the village to the plaza. Walpi, with its stunning location, is truly a five-star village of the world. To visit Walpi, and usually Hano and Sichomovi as well, you must have a guide, which can be arranged after following the signs to the First Mesa Consolidated Villages Tourism Program on the mesatop; (928) 737–2262; fax (928) 737–2347.

Visiting Hopiland: A Narrative Account

Refreshed after a cold drink in Tuba City, and with a full tank of gas, we head back into the glaring sun and drive east on Arizona Highway 264 to the Hopi mesas.

We quickly drive through **Moenkopi,** the first and most removed of the Hopi villages, separated from the other villages by 45 miles of Navajo grazing lands and some of the controversial partitioned lands. We note the newer homes built at Upper Moenkopi, and toward the west end of Lower Moenkopi, farther down the wash, we see the old stone-and-mortar houses handsomely situated above the fertile valley of green cornfields. There is more green here than we have seen all day. The villages are quiet this hot afternoon. We reflect that Moenkopi Wash, which provides the moisture for the corn we see, is a tributary of the Little Colorado River. Not far from here, about 25 miles south, the Little Colorado empties into the Colorado River not far from the Grand Canyon. At the confluence of the two rivers is the ancient *sipaapuni* or the place in Hopi mythology where the Hopi people entered this, the Fourth World, from the Third World, through a hollow reed. From that sacred point, according to Hopi legend, they began migrations that would eventually take them to the mesas 45 miles east of here.

Between 14 and 15 miles from the Tuba City–U.S. Highway 160 junction, we see a windmill off to the left and come to a rough unpaved spur road heading toward it. A few years ago we explored this unmarked dirt road (do not enter if the road is wet or a storm is threatening), which, after crossing the cattle guard, leads to **Coal Mine Mesa Rodeo Grounds,** a parking area, and picnic tables. In the absence of any no-trespassing signs, we spread a picnic lunch on one of the tables along the rim of dramatic **Coal Canyon** (also known as Coal Mine Canyon), recognized for the stunning, variegated coloring of its beautifully sculpted escarpments. It is sometimes referred to as the "Little Bryce Canyon." But the Navajo, whose medicine men allegedly extract multicolored sands from the canyon, call it Ha Ho No Geh ("too many washes") Canyon. Here and in other spots like it on or near the Black Mesa, nature has opened up canyon walls to reveal vast seams of coal. For centuries the Hopi used coal obtained from canyons like this one. But today we decide to bypass it, since the best viewing times are in the early morning and late afternoon, not midday. Now the road climbs gradually until we reach a sign, 40 miles from Tuba City, that tells us we are entering Hopiland. In just a few more miles, we reach **Third Mesa.** A little farther on we pass two spur roads. The road to Bacavi is to the left, and the road to Hotevilla, to the right. We remember that a few years ago, we visited Hotevilla in search of a wicker basket. We were greeted diffidently by several people in the plaza of this very traditional village. We did not feel unwelcome, but we did feel that we had to put our best foot forward and do nothing disrespectful. The woman we were looking for that day wasn't home. Although we did not linger too long, we found Hotevilla to be one of the more interesting villages and were quite impressed by the terraced gardens behind the village.

A little farther on we pass an outlet for high-quality Hopi art, **Monongya Gallery.** A few seconds later we pass a spur road leading to **Old Oraibi.** There is a sign beckoning visitors to shop for **Hopi arts and crafts** there. The highway now descends into the valley between Third and Second mesas, offering views of Old Oraibi in the distance off to the right before entering **Kykotsmovi** or **New Oraibi,** a thriving modern community complete with a gas station and grocery store. This is the home of the Hopi Nation's headquarters. Continuing on toward

Second Mesa, we pass the **Hopi Civic Center** on the right before starting up fairly steeply to the top of Second Mesa. To the left is the **Hopi Arts and Crafts Guild Shop,** with the Second Mesa campground separating it from the **Hopi Cultural Center and Motel.** I pull into a parking space. As usual, several Hopi seeking refuge from the afternoon sun are standing in the shade provided by the buildings. After registering in the motel, I return to the car to drive it around to the other side of the complex, where our room is located. I put it in reverse and start to back out. Bang—crash! I receive a tremendous jolt, and my seat is knocked back a notch or two. I turn to see what happened. I have backed into a steel light pole.

As I sit trying to gather my wits, an older Hopi man comes out of the shade and ambles slowly to the car window. For a few minutes he just stands there quietly and looks at me. I think to myself, "Maybe he thinks I'm the True Pahaana." Then in a friendly but definitely serious way, he admonishes me for drinking too much that time of the day "in all of the heat." Defensively I try to explain that I'm just fatigued from the long drive and hot weather and that I have had nothing to drink. He smiles as though to say, "Sure you haven't," and goes back to stand in the shade.

I get out of the car to see what damage I've done. To my relief the dent and blue paint left on the pole by my car are matched by an artful array of other varicolored dents up and down the pole, looking for all the world like a Hopi version of the totem pole. I am relieved that I have done only what others who have parked in the same space before me have done. After checking in I walk to the air-conditioned room, drink a large glass of ice water, and take a siesta. In this

Hopi clowns—Koshare, watermelon kachina, and mudhead kachina

country there is indeed a time just to stand quietly in the shade or take a siesta!

Rested, I inquire at the desk if there are any dances this weekend. The desk clerk replies that a dance is about to begin at Shungopavi and that if we hurry we can get there in time. Shungopavi is an easy five-minute drive away. We arrive at Shungopavi, where the streets of the village are the stage and the roofs are the grandstands. While waiting for the dancers to emerge from the kiva, we remember last year we observed an outstanding ceremony that would make a born-again Hopi out of anyone. We saw some of the most dramatically costumed dancers we have ever witnessed, as they surfaced from the top of the kiva, their feet moving with staccatolike cadence as they danced their way into the plaza. We heard some of the strongest, most other-worldly sounds that we had ever experienced and then witnessed the dancing and chanting of some extremely complex rhythms, by a group of more than fifty of the Hopi faithful.

With two golden eagles in full view, tethered on the adjacent rooftop; with costuming that matched and excelled anything we had ever seen at the Santa Fe Opera; and with the buzz of the chorus gaining in momentum and speed, filling the air with that ancient music, we felt ourselves transformed, mesmerized, goose bumps forming, spines tingling. The Hopi around us were equally serious, showing great reverence and respect for this primordial enactment. Then came a break in pace, and the clowns emerged in the plaza, throwing gifts of food, cigarettes, candy, and even toys up to the crowds on the rooftop and in the plaza. There was laughter then as everybody reached out to catch the generous gifts from the clowns. That day we were treated warmly and hospitably by our Hopi hosts, who even helped at one point to clear a viewing path for our youngest so he could see what all the fun was about.

With that as background we are looking forward to today's Snake Dance. The same village, the same plaza. The same intense afternoon heat. The sky is clear and the air is quiet, the audience hushed, as members of the Antelope society emerge from the kiva in full, glorious costume. The sense we have is of strange creatures emerging from the bowels of the earth. With intricate rhythms the Antelope society chants and dances in place, while the Snake society members dance with snakes. Sidewinder rattlesnakes and other poisonous and nonpoisonous snakes from the Colorado Plateau are all here in their natural state.

We are told that these snakes were caught on and around Second Mesa many days ago and have been kept in the kiva until today. The handling of the snakes and the rhythmic chant builds to a crescendo as the snakes are placed in the handlers' mouths. Now with human teeth pressing their midsections just below their heads, their bodies suspended in space, the snakes writhe with fangs bared as they turn their heads back and forth perilously close to their handlers' faces. But with great patience each handler's accomplice, the guide, bends down, intently following every move of the snake's mouth, using the power of his eagle's feather to divert the snake and its poisonous fangs from the handler's face.

The audience is quiet, reverent. We and the other *pahaanas* present are seeing a harmony between man and nature we have never witnessed or ever thought possible. We gaze with great concentration now as the drama unfolds before us, and we forget the heat, forget that we had failed to buy sunglasses. The events in the plaza transfix us. There is a silent reverence among us, the spectators, white and Hopi alike. No carnival atmosphere here. This is the holiest of the holy.

The dance continues, lovingly, intensely. It is now almost 6:00 P.M. A shadow passes over the plaza. I look up and see large clouds forming in the distance as a huge black cloud moves toward Second Mesa. Now the wind begins to come up as the dance is about to conclude. Large raindrops start to fall. After being sanctified with cornmeal, the younger members of the Snake Clan grab up the snakes and race pell-mell out of the plaza toward the mesa's edge, where they release the dozens of snakes to the four directions, back to nature, grateful to them for helping to bring the rain. Now it is raining torrents. We rush to our car and head back to the motel. Dry, inside, we comment on how welcome this rain is on this August Saturday evening in Hopiland. We too are thankful to the Antelope and Snake society members, as well as nature's snakes, for this wonderful moisture they have brought through their hard work and diligent efforts.

(Please note: The Snake Dance has been closed to non-Indians for some time. For more information about Hopi dances, see "Staying There—Hopi Ceremonial Dances.")

After an excellent Hopi dinner of *posole,* lamb, and fry bread, we take a walk. The rain has stopped; the air is clean and is at its purest. The early evening sky is absolutely clear and the bluest of blues. The sun is sinking in the west, and at 6,200 feet altitude, it is becoming much cooler. We walk down the road a short distance, and then follow a path through the scrub to the mesa's edge. Far below us is the desert floor stretching out to the **Painted Desert** to the south. We look straight down. There are ledges and cliffs and piles of rock all the way down to the valley floor.

It is very quiet now. A hawk is circling above us. Strewn on the ground around us are some of the most unusual pieces of sandstone we have ever seen. These contorted rocks look as if they had been cooked in a pressure cooker, their insides bubbling up and then popping, leaving jagged edges and craters in all assortments of shapes. Sitting on this high escarpment, we sense the respect the Hopi have for their beautiful mesas. It doesn't take too much imagination to turn some of the square-topped mesa buttes in the distance into villages and, with a little more imagination, step back almost 1,000 years to when the Hopi first occupied these mesas. It is so quiet now that maybe, if we listen carefully, we can hear the distant sounds of a village full of life. Our reverie is abruptly ended with the realization that twilight is fading fast into darkness. As we make our

Snake Dance

way back to the motel in the evening silence, we have a sense that we are reentering civilization from some prehistoric time where we have stood on the edge of the universe and felt the vibrations of the Hopi world.

Visit to a Hopi Village: A Narrative Account

This morning after breakfast we visit the **Hopi museum** here at the cultural center. For a small fee we view a display of both new and old crafts and absorb some interesting historical points. At the **Hopi Arts and Crafts Silvercraft Cooperative Guild** about 100 yards away just beyond the campground, we spot a pot we particularly like, but it is being held for another buyer. We inquire about the pot's maker and discover that she lives on First Mesa. We ask if it is all right to visit her there. We are told that she sells from her home and sometimes takes special orders from there. We receive instructions about finding her home.

Following Arizona Highway 264 across the top of Second Mesa, we pass **Shungopavi** and then drop to the valley below, where to our left another high spur of Second Mesa protrudes. Atop this promontory are the old villages of **Sipaulovi** and **Mishongnovi.** Near the junction of Arizona Highway 87 to

Winslow and Flagstaff, we pass the Secakuku Trading Post complex with a supermarket and the Hopi Fine Arts gallery-shop. In a few miles First Mesa looms up on our left. It is narrow, steep, and dramatic, rising abruptly from the desert floor.

At first we do not see **Walpi,** the village on the western tip, but as we get closer we understand why. Its rock-and-mortar buildings blend perfectly with the mesa, looking almost like an extension of the mesatop. Now we notice wisps of smoke coming from the very top of the mesa and wonder if a Hopi potter is firing her wares this morning. About 13 miles from the cultural center at **Polacca Village,** we come to a sign on the highway: FIRST MESA VILLAGES. Turning left, we see another sign pointing left up the hill to Walpi, **Sichomovi,** and **Hano.** Then a sign welcomes us to First Mesa villages. It reads, in part, RESPECT OUR PRIVACY. ABSOLUTELY NOT PERMITTED: PHOTOGRAPHY, RECORDING, HIKING FOOT TRAILS, REMOVAL OF OBJECTS, SKETCHING, DRAWING—CLAN LEADERS. We now start up the paved road to the mesatop. There is a sheer drop-off on the downside. We hug the rock-strewn cliffside, just in case we meet another vehicle. About halfway up is a sign to a road off to the right, leading to a parking area for vehicles other than autos. We pass a few Hopi girls walking down the road; they smile and wave. We have heard that these eastern villages are the most receptive and friendly to strangers. Finally at the top we drive through the narrow streets of Hano or Tewa village to Sichomovi.

We follow the signs directing visitors to stop at the **First Mesa Consolidated Villages Tourism Office.** Here we park, check in, and are assigned a tour guide for our nearly hour-long tour of old Walpi and First Mesa Villages (fee). When the villagers are extra-busy with ceremonies on summer weekends, tours may not be given. Check with First Mesa Tours, (928) 737–2262, weekdays between 8:00 A.M. and 5:00 P.M. Many homes have small cardboard signs in their windows advertising pottery and kachina dolls. The morning comes peacefully to these mesa villages where children are already playing outside their stone-and-mortar houses. Several approach us selling **pottery.** We ask to see more and are taken to an open screen door. The child calls his mother. She greets us warmly and invites us inside. We see her wares and talk with her briefly about life on the mesa. Our children purchase a small pot from her daughter. In another room an older Hopi man is carving a kachina doll from a cottonwood root. He tells us that the root is becoming very expensive and hard to get. Formerly he traveled more than 100 miles to get his own but now has to rely on others for his supply. Some of the completed kachina dolls in the room are exquisite. Most are for sale, but a few of the special ones will be given at the right time to some very lucky Hopi child.

Soon we find the potter whose name had been given to us at the cultural center. She is dressed in a cool gingham dress and flat shoes, firing pots out at the edge of the mesa. The open fire that she tends carefully is burning with intensity, the flames licking the air. Occasionally she backs away from the fire when the wind blows the smoke into her eyes. We notice how the rock ledge we are standing on drops off precipitously to the desert below. The smoke spirals upward and curls off the mesa as it floats high above Polacca below us. She is firing three large pots this morning, she says, and using sheep dung for fuel. She points to the valley below and tells us that is where she used to gather the dry dung fuel. Now she has to buy it.

She invites us to her house, which also serves as her "studio." There are pots drying in the sun outside. After she tells us about digging her clay and making the slip she uses to coat the pots, she shows us several yucca brushes she uses to apply the decoration. These well-designed pots made by the coil method are thin-walled and as smooth as glass. There is no need for pottery wheels here in Hopiland! Although she does not have the shape we are looking for, she says she can make it for us.

We talk about prices. She sells for a little less than the craft stores on Second Mesa, but not much less, and she tells us she is amazed how much she is receiving for her pots, compared with what she used to sell them for. We all agree that in the past she received too little for the amount of work and time she puts into a pot. She is just now getting adequately compensated. So now, for the first time, she is making enough money to "put back" for her grandchildren's education. We thank her for her hospitality and return to the tourism center.

Our tour guide leads us a few paces across the "gap" or *walpi* into Walpi Village. There are houses several stories high, all built of stone from the mesa. We see one pyramidal-shaped complex of stone-and-mortar houses, which we learn has been occupied since around 1690, and we see the *kiska,* or passageway, under it dramatically cutting through this stony edifice. We are glad to see that the restoration work here was done with care and that extra efforts are

Snake Rock, Walpi

being taken to preserve this unusual village. After about forty minutes our guide returns us to the tourism center. Back in the car, we start the descent to Polacca. We are thankful for good brakes and go as slowly as we can on the way back down to the highway. We reflect that these three villages perched up on the mesa, safe in former times from revengeful Spanish and marauding Navajo, are reasonably safe today from modern tourist hordes. With considerable regret we turn east, leaving the Hopi villages behind as we head for **Keams Canyon,** 11.5 miles east of Polacca. We stop at Keams Canyon, primarily a government town, for gas, lunch, and a cool drink in the pleasant **Keams Canyon Trading Post, Cafe, and McGee's Indian Art Gallery.** We are always amazed by the excellent Indian handicrafts found here. Today we skirt the town where a bank, a motel, the Indian Health Service Hospital, and the Hopi Indian Agency are located, as we leave this otherworldly setting of the Hopi Nation and head 43 miles east to **Hubbell Trading Post** near Ganado, Arizona.

Back to Navajoland: Keams Canyon to Ganado and on to Window Rock and Canyon de Chelly

Heading east from Keams Canyon on Arizona Highway 264, you will come to the junction with U.S. Highway 191, which leads 32 miles north to Chinle, the gateway to Canyon de Chelly. This is a good time to tune your car radio to AM 660 (KTNN, Window Rock) to hear the Navajo language spoken. Continue 4 miles east past the junction to a sign indicating **Hubbell Trading Post.** Turn right and follow the dirt road across the bridge of the **Pueblo Colorado Wash** a short distance to the trading post. Park in front of the old stone-wall building. This National Historic Site is definitely worth a stop.

Although the Navajo mistrusted many whites, they never seemed to stop revering "double glasses" or "Old Mexican" as they affectionately called him. Don Lorenzo Hubbell began trading at Ganado in 1876. When he died in 1930, he was buried on top of a small hill overlooking the trading post, next to his wife, two sons, a daughter, and his very close Navajo friend Many Horses.

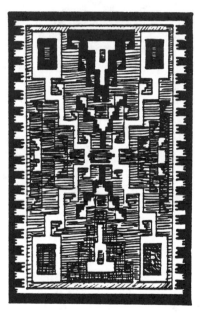

Navajo rug

His respect for the Navajo and their way of life led to their respect for him. When the Navajo returned from their Long Walk in the late 1880s, Hubbell, more than any other white person, helped them get through that difficult transition time. He served many roles for the Navajo. He translated and wrote letters for some and helped settle family quarrels for others. He helped in time of sickness and acted as interpreter of the government and its policies. Moreover, he helped set the standards in color and design that would bring the best market price and continuous business to the Navajo weavers. To this day the Hubbell Post is still operating. Owned by the U.S. National Park Service since 1967, it is operated on a nonprofit basis by the Southwest Parks and Monuments Association. It is still a functioning trading post and, in my estimation, still carries one of the best supplies of Navajo rugs in the area.

On entering the post you find yourself in a somewhat dark, rectangular space closed on three sides by counters. This space is called a "bullpen." It contains all kinds of necessities of living, including large bolts of the rayon and velveteen cloth Navajo women use for making their skirts and blouses. To the right and through a doorway is a room leading to the "rug room." There you will see one of the largest and best supplies of Navajo rugs anywhere on the reservation.

Return to the parking area, for on the west side of the complex is a small visitor center run by the park service; (928) 755–3475; www.nps.gov/hutr. There you will find historical exhibits and an excellent selection of books relating to the area.

Navajo Tribal Council Building and Window Rock

But the central focus is several **weaving looms** that are used daily during the summer by neighboring Navajo women. They do beautiful work, and they are often helpful in describing what they are doing and how they do it. The park service has done an outstanding job in preserving the old traditions of the post yet adding some unique educational features that are in harmony with the setting. Inquire at the visitor center about **guided tours of Hubbell's home.** The tour vividly reveals the way of life of the early white traders. Besides, on the home tour you will see many handsome old Navajo rugs as well as many mementos of the early West.

From the trading post return to Arizona Highway 264. A few miles east is the settlement of **Ganado,** elevation 6,400 feet, population 2,500. The town is named after one of the old Navajo chiefs, Ganado Mucho, who signed the 1868 treaty between the Navajo and the government. A Presbyterian mission and hospital are located there. To the north of town are the buildings of the area's parochial schools. Continue east from Ganado 28 miles to **Window Rock,** capital of the Navajo Nation. There is considerable traffic along this road, since it leads to the eastern, more populated region of the reservation. Near the junction of Indian Route 12 and Arizona Highway 264 is the sprawling commercial center of Window Rock (Navajo: *Nee Alneeg,* or "Earth's Center"), population 3,300.

Coming up to this junction, you can see Window Rock in the red sandstone formations to the northeast, and you will pass the Navajo fairgrounds and rodeo site on your right. On the northeast corner of the intersection is the main shop of the **Navajo Arts and Crafts Guild,** and just down the road beyond the tribally owned motel is the excellent **Navajo Tribal Museum Library and Visitors Center** (505–871–7941), depicting many aspects of the Navajo way of life. Books and journal reprints pertaining to the Navajo culture can be obtained there. You may wish to visit the tribal government seat just north of Indian Route 12, located beneath the beautiful natural window in the red sandstone formation there.

This window in the rock is the source of the town's name. This gaping hole in the rock and the spring below it are important in Navajo ceremonial rites. There are some early Ancestral Puebloan structures just below the window. But

more important than geologic and archaeological treasures is the large administration headquarters for the entire Navajo Nation. Of special interest is the well-designed Navajo Tribal Council Building, shaped like a hogan and containing murals depicting the history of the Navajo tribe.

From Window Rock you are 92 miles from the historically rich mesatop Ácoma Indian Pueblo (which rivals Old Oraibi for "oldest city" honors) and 164 miles from Albuquerque, mostly by way of U.S. I–40. And **Chaco Canyon's Chaco Culture National Historic Park** is 110 miles to the northeast, the last 20 miles being over a very rough unpaved road that is not negotiable with a standard car during wet weather. Call the visitor center at the park (505–786–7014) or visit www.nps.gov/cheu for updated information about road conditions and whether any new all-weather roads have recently been constructed to the park.

Leaving Window Rock, head north on the Fort Defiance Road, Indian Route 12. This excellent paved, all-weather road will take you to Canyon de Chelly. Along this road you will see a more modern version of Navajo life than you saw in the west. Small clusters of modern homes and trailers have sprung up. At certain hours the traffic can be fierce. In 5 miles a spur road to the left leads to Fort Defiance. Today **Fort Defiance** is a bustling, picturesque, modern community with no remains of the old fort (once called Fort Canby) that Kit Carson used for headquarters and that served as an early-day "concentration camp" for the Navajo he rounded up for the Long Walk. There are a number of tribal agency offices in Fort Defiance. Return to Indian Route 12 and drive north through beautiful forested ponderosa pine country, dotted with lakes. Approximately 50 miles from Window Rock, turn left at the junction of Indian Routes 12 and 64. Now drive 25 miles to the Canyon de Chelly National Monument visitor center, paralleling the north rim of Canyon de Chelly most of the way. If you have time, you might want to tour the north rim (see "The North Rim of Canyon de Chelly").

Canyon de Chelly

The Rio de Chelly and its tributaries descend from their origin in northeastern Arizona high in the **Chuska Mountains,** which are known locally as the "Navajo Alps." They have carved one of the most spectacularly beautiful canyon systems in the world. Canyon de Chelly is not the largest, deepest, or widest of canyons, but it is one of the best-proportioned and most aesthetically attractive canyons you will see anywhere. In addition to being a canyon whose size humans can relate to, it is a canyon with a human element. Wherever you look into Canyon de Chelly and its tributary canyons, there is evidence of human existence. Whether it is the ancient apartmentlike cliff dwellings that dot the floor and walls of the canyon or the hogans, cornfields, and peach orchards in the canyon bottom being actively farmed today, you know that the canyon has given warmth and shelter to people for generations. Somehow Canyon de Chelly National Monument epitomizes the geography in this area, beautiful landscapes that have been enhanced by people who have known how to blend in and live with their environement.

The canyon and its three branches measure more than 100 miles long. The

three tributary canyons of Canyon de Chelly are **Canyon del Muerto** and **Black Rock Canyon** to the north and **Monument Canyon** to the south. You can follow this canyon from its shallowest westernmost part about 30 feet deep to its deepest, southeasterly part where it plunges 1,100 feet into the earth, revealing eleven million years of geologic history and more than 1,000 years of human history.

From its barren and dry sandstone rim, you will observe a lush oasis of green cornfields, large trees, and flowing water far below. It is this sense of contrast that adds another unique dimension to Canyon de Chelly.

Canyon de Chelly National Monument, more than 130 square miles in size, was established in 1931. Historically the Navajo have called it *Tsegi,* meaning "rock canyon." *De Chelly* is a Spanish corruption of the Navajo word *Tsegi.* The canyon contains more than one hundred early Indian sites dating from A.D. 350 to 1300. Some are in shambles, others are still standing, and several appear untouched by time. The steep and extensively varnished canyon walls are filled with some of the richest and best Ancestral Puebloan and Navajo rock art in Arizona. Because Canyon de Chelly is more remotely located than many other canyon sites, you can view all of this in relative peace and quiet.

For a geologic view of how canyons on the Colorado Plateau form, see "A Geologic Primer to Southeastern Utah" in Section 1. Specifically most of the rock you see at Canyon de Chelly is sandstone by the same name. It was formed from ancient sand dunes and is dramatically cross-bedded in places. A harder rock, the more durable Shinarump conglomerate of the Chinle formation, makes up the rim of the canyon and overlies the de Chelly sandstone. In a few areas, such as the visitor center and the first overlook, you will see the

Canyon bottom, Canyon de Chelly

Chinle sandstone on top of the Shinarump. Although it has eroded away almost every place else, leaving a predominantly Shinarump rim, the softer Chinle sandstone still rests on top of the Shinarump there.

The canyon and its environs are owned by the Navajo people, so all tourists are guests of the Navajo. During the summer months, a large number of Navajo and their families farm in the canyon bottom, living there daily or on weekends. Although its cool, watered recesses make it a fine place to spend much of the day during the hot, dry summer, there are virtually no inhabitants during the winter, when snow makes access difficult. Cold winter air often is trapped in the canyon bottom, which is so deep in places that the low winter sun never penetrates it. Up on the rim as well as in the canyons, you will see plenty of Navajo life. Hogans in camps or clustered settlements can be found in and around the town of Chinle, which is just a few miles from the canyon.

Seeing Canyon de Chelly

Chinle, elevation 5,500 feet, population 5,300, is the place to mark on your map if you want to tour Canyon de Chelly. *Chinle* in Navajo means "running out," for it is there that the Rio de Chelly emerges from its deep canyon recesses. Chinle is a sprawling Navajo settlement with schools, medical clinics, gas stations, a bank (with ATM), and a few cafes. Southeast of town, about 2 miles on Indian Route 7, is the educational **Canyon de Chelly visitor center.** In the summer **Navajo jewelers** often are at work. Just outside the center are a Navajo hogan that you may enter and examine and a self-guided plant walk. Inside the center is an excellent visual display of the geology, natural history, and history of the canyon. Since you are not allowed to travel in the canyon without a park ranger or authorized guide, stop at the visitor center if you plan any extensive travel on the canyon floor. There is one exception to this rule. The **White House Ruin Trail** winding down to the canyon floor is a foot trail that you may travel unescorted.

From the visitor center drive down the hill and follow the signs to **Cottonwood Campground** and the **Thunderbird Lodge.** The campground is one of the most tempting on the Colorado Plateau, as it is nestled at the outlet of the canyon in a grove of shady cottonwood trees. During the summer park rangers present lectures and slide shows about the canyon in the evenings. Just beyond the campground the Thunderbird Lodge is another oasis. Formerly the site of the old Chinle Trading Post (1896), it is now a haven for those wishing to explore the canyon. There you will find motel accommodations, a crafts shop, and a Navajo rug room, as well as a good and economical cafeteria, open to the public. The motel office is also headquarters for four-wheel-drive-vehicle tours into the canyon. Half- or full-day tours may be arranged there. Full-day tours also enter **Canyon del Muerto.** From nearby concessionaires it is possible to take guided horseback trips to White House Ruin and other destinations. Binoculars are essential if you want to see well the striking rock art on the canyon walls from the various rim viewpoints.

The canyons to be viewed are somewhat Y-shaped, with the visitor center and motel located at the bottom of the Y where the river exits the canyon. From this

White House Ruin

main stem you can choose to follow the left branch or the right branch of the canyon. The left branch (following Canyon del Muerto) is known as the **North Rim,** and the right branch (following Canyon de Chelly) is known as the **South Rim.** It is possible to tour both branches and be on your way to another destination after about five hours of viewing and walking time. Or you could easily spend several days there. The choice is yours.

If you are particularly ambitious and short of time, it is possible to view the South Rim, then the North Rim, visit Window Rock, the Hopi villages (fleetingly), Tuba City, and be in Monument Valley by 10:00 P.M.—if you dare! Information: Superintendent, Canyon de Chelly National Monument, P.O. Box 588, Chinle, Arizona 86503; (928) 674–5500; www.ups.gov/cach.

The South Rim of Canyon de Chelly: A Narrative Account

Last night we arrived at Thunderbird Lodge about 7:30 P.M., checked in, and immediately drove 2.5 miles up the South Rim to see the canyon at sunset from **Tsegi Overlook.** On the way over we saw several Navajo homesites, complete with hogans. The view from Tsegi was startlingly beautiful. Standing on that high rim, we saw a broad expanse of canyon, the buff reds of the Navajo sandstone giving way to the pink, mostly sandy canyon bottom more than 275 feet below us, where we could make out a Navajo hogan and cornfields. As the sun dropped and a slight breeze came up, the colors became even more dramatic. A few minutes later we were back at the lodge, where we ate a filling and plentiful meal at the convenient cafeteria. Navajo tacos topped the list. After dinner we browsed in the well-stocked craft shop, located in the building adjacent to the cafeteria, made inquiries about local artisans, and then went outside to sit under the stars beneath the giant cottonwood trees. Another star-studded, comfortably cool night here on the Colorado Plateau.

It is now 8:00 A.M. We have finished breakfast and are ready to return to the South Rim. As we drive to the South Rim road, we realize that the canyon at its westernmost end is only 20 or 30 feet deep. We make a quick pass at Tsegi Overlook where we were last night and continue on to **Junction Overlook** at 3.9 miles. We stop for another view. It is still cool this morning, but the sun is warming things up quickly. We walk over to the rim. We notice that the canyon is considerably deeper here than at Tsegi. Here we see the junction of Canyon del Muerto, which stretches 26 miles to the northeast, and Canyon de Chelly directly below us.

Canyon del Muerto, or "Canyon of the Dead," was named by a Smithsonian expedition member in 1882, when numerous remains of prehistoric Indian burials were found there. About the same time the well-known archaeologist Cosmos Mindeleff visited Canyon de Chelly. He wrote about "first ruin," which we see this morning to the left and on the far side of the canyon. His writing helped spread the word to both Americans and Europeans about this unique part of the Southwest. About the same time Karl May in Germany was writing fantasy stories about the American Indians and the southwestern "desert." These writings, plus the many western movies filmed in the Southwest that have been so popular in Europe, have greatly influenced the visitor population here. Last night at dinner and this morning at breakfast, there were more visitors from Germany and France than from the United States. We mused to ourselves that many Americans go traveling in Europe without even seeing what the Europeans consider a prime attraction in this country.

Shrub live oak

At 6.4 miles we reach **White House Overlook.** We scurry down to the rim to see what is in store for us. This is a stunning overlook, down and across the canyon. For up from the sandy canyon bottom just beyond the **Rio de Chelly,** emerging from the brilliant green of the cottonwoods on the opposite wall of the canyon, is **White House Ruin.** Although there is a multistoried pueblo at the base of the cliff, it is the configuration of the cliff ruin directly above in a large alcove that gives this pueblo ruin its name. After some debate we decide we have time to take the 2.5-mile round-trip hike 600 feet down into the canyon to see the ruin. We bring our day pack with water bottles and a small first-aid kit.

We follow the well-marked trail sometimes called the "Women's Trail" because this section of the canyon's rim offers such easy access into the canyon that Navajo women can take their sheep up and down it. The trail starts down fairly rapidly. But we are all doing fine, even though some of us have on tennis shoes rather than boots. As we begin our descent, we notice it is 8:30 A.M., and the day promises to be hot.

This morning we comment on how bare of vegetation the rim is. But as we start our descent along the cliffside, we are aware of considerable and varied plant life, as well as signs of animal and bird life. The trail is wide, the tread is good and not at all "scary" as we had anticipated. The trail cuts first northwest and then southeast as it switches back and forth on the gentle descent. There are piñon pines and junipers on both sides of the trail, and we see many large sandstone rocks displaying the cross-bedding of the de Chelly sandstone, representing those vast "frozen" sand dunes of ancient times that were sculpted and hardened by nature into these surreal rounded masses. To our right, adjacent to the trail, is an ancient gnarled tree, its trunk shaped like a contorted piñon. But its moisture-preserving leaves, tough, green, and serrated like a holly tree, help us identify it as a shrub live oak. Above, two ravens we had spotted earlier are now soaring in the currents rising from the canyon. Walking along we spot some well-defined animal tracks in

the sand and, after some controversy, identify them as belonging to the gray fox. Now near the end of the trail, we enter a small, dark, and pleasantly cool tunnel in the sandstone; it ends in a few yards at the bottom of the canyon, putting us face to face with a Navajo farm and hogan.

Canyon wren

As we look back up, extending our necks to see the route we have traveled, we see no evidence of a trail, just a jumbled heap of boulders and rocks on a slant, topped by the steep edges of the ridge. Quickly but quietly we walk past the hogan so as not to disturb the occupants. For about the length of a football field, we walk in packed sand across the river bottom, dodging a few trickles of water but continuing to move forward as we watch for quicksand, a hazard here in the canyon bottom. On the other side of the canyon floor, we step up the small bank into a thicket of tamarisks and Russian olives, both imports that have become pests. As we emerge from the thicket through the willows into the cottonwoods, we find the trail to the ruin. Even with the summer sun at its zenith, there is considerable shade down here this morning in the deep recesses of the canyon. Although the shade makes it cooler, it is still humid here by the riverbed. We are told that in the winter cold air is trapped down here, and as icy winds blow through the canyon, it becomes a veritable freezer, for even the elevation of the canyon floor is a lofty 5,500 feet.

We find a comfort station—a welcome set of bathroom facilities—just below the ruin, near the historical markers. Several hundred people apparently lived in this multistoried apartment house constructed around A.D. 1100 by the Ancestral Puebloans. It was built in two sections along the lower part of the 600-foot south-facing canyon wall. In the well-preserved upper section is a central room with a long wall that was mud-plastered many years ago. This distinctive wall gives the ruin its name, for it stands out as a prominent, white, crenellated tower set behind and rising above the two structures in front of it. The signs below the ruin tell us that the first white man to record seeing the ruin was U.S. Army Lieutenant James Simpson, in 1849, while the first authoritative archaeological exploration and map of the ruin were made by the well-known archaeologist Cosmos Mindeleff.

We look over the structure in some detail. We realize that years ago it was a story or two taller than it is now. A small ladder connected the roofs of the lower complex to the alcove units above. On the wall between the upper and lower structures are several large, well-executed petroglyphs. The cliff face above the upper ruin provides a good example of desert varnish (see Section 1, "Reading the Rocks"). On the ground, buried in the sand, are numerous pieces of flaked chert, obviously worked by hand in making arrow points. We also see many potsherds in the sand. They belong to the ruin and to the Navajo owners, so we leave them where they belong.

We are the first ones down here this morning, so we sit in the sun by the ruin, surrounded by solitude, and try to reconstruct what life down here would have been like. If we raise our voices, they echo and reverberate off the canyon walls. No doubt the fifty inhabitants (including children) along with their turkeys and dogs would have raised quite a din in the echoing depths of Canyon de Chelly. We realize why the Ancestral Puebloans may have felt safe here and why the Navajo used the canyon to hide from the Spanish, Mexicans, and later Americans who attempted to retaliate and punish them for their injurious raids to white settlements. A few inches under the hot dry sand, we feel moisture, the lifeline of the earlier peoples in the canyon and the reason the Navajo still farm the canyon bottoms. We have read that somewhere in this vast labyrinthian canyon, on some obscure wall, is the locust sign of the Hopi Flute Clan, placed there before they migrated south to the mesas. We look again carefully at the building techniques and observe elements of Hopi architecture that we have seen at Walpi and in parts of Shungopavi. The tree-ring data from the roof logs here go back as far as A.D. 1060, while the latest date found here is 1275.

We turn now to cross the canyon bottom so as to make our ascent. Several canyon wrens dart in front of us. The way up is a little more challenging, an elevation gain of 600 feet in less than 1.25 miles. We stop to rest from time to time. The sun is warm, and as our thirst increases, we are glad we have our water bottles. As we hike up, many people are just coming down. It is a little like a mini–United Nations. First a couple from Japan. Then three young men from France. Now we pass a couple from Germany. Occasionally we stop to sip a little water and then push forward and upward. We pass several other people before we reach the top, but only one of them is an American! Now on top we rest on a large sandstone rock, literally gulping water.

We are glad we have been able to enjoy the solitude of the ruins by ourselves, and there are even a few apologies from some family members for the disgruntle-

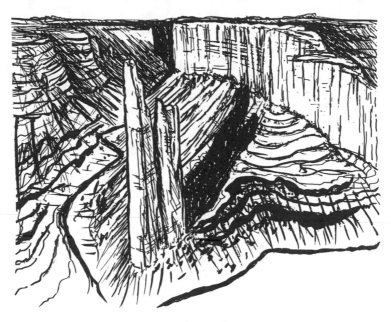

Spider Rock

ment they had expressed in having to get such an early start this morning. We notice that our round-trip hike, plus our stops and wandering, has taken us about three hours. It is just after 11:00 A.M. as we sit here enjoying the little breeze that has come up. We return to the car to find that all is well. We had been warned that we should take our valuables with us, place everything else out of sight, and lock the car when walking any of the trails. Too bad, but a reality that has to be dealt with here and in the trailhead parking lots in the Cascades and Sierras as well.

Back to the South Rim drive, we reach **Sliding Rock Overlook** in another 6.5 miles. On the short walk to the rim, we look for some of the aquatic life we have been told we would see in the numerous water-filled potholes or sandstone basins along the trails. Even though these are very fresh pools, and perhaps for that reason, we are unable to spot any fairy shrimp, spadefoot toads, or other interesting aquatic specimens. Now at the rim we see a small ruin on a narrow ledge across the canyon. This ruin has yet to be excavated. We return to the rim road and drive 9 miles farther to the turnoff to the parking lot at **Spider Rock Overlook.**

After walking 200 yards to the rim, we are awed by what we see, for protruding 800 feet straight up out of the canyon bottom is Spider Rock, with its cap reaching within just 200 feet of the rim. It towers magnificently, like a sentinel post, above the junction of Canyon de Chelly and Monument Canyon. It is a geologic remnant of the downcutting of the two canyons. For often in areas where two canyons merge, a lone, isolated spire remains, somehow missed by the onslaught and ravages of the rapierlike streams of water that cut through the stone around it. The Navajo call this 230-million-year-old monument to rock history *Tse Na'ashje'ii,* or "Spider Rock." It is the home of the Navajo deity, *Na'ashje'ii Asdzau,* or "Spider Woman," who in Navajo mythology is thought to live at the top of the taller of the two needles, while "Talking God" lives on top of the shorter spire.

To the left and on the far side of the canyon is another spire called **Speaking Rock.** From here with our binoculars we see a few Ancestral Puebloan sites across the canyon to the left of the overlook. A volcanic plug, **Black Rock,** is visible on the horizon a little to the left of Spider Rock. Now as we turn to walk back to the car, our son spots a large bird soaring in the air currents above the canyon. With the binoculars we identify it as a golden eagle, a rare find here and a nice end to our tour of the canyon. We return to the South Rim road and drive 22 miles back to the lodge for a refreshing lunch before heading on to the North Rim.

The North Rim of Canyon de Chelly

From the visitor center travel northeast on Indian Route 64, 5.4 miles to the turnoff to **Ledge Ruin Overlook.** Park your car and take the short walk to the rim. Across Canyon del Muerto, about 100 feet above the canyon floor, is a complex of twenty-nine rooms. Archaeological evidence from ceramic fragments suggests that the ruin was probably occupied from 1050 to 1275. Another short trail leads to a different overlook with views of **Dekaa Kiva.** You will see it high above the canyon bottom in an alcove. Although the kiva looks isolated today, it should be noted that the alcove directly to the west contains Ancestral Puebloan remnants and that the two alcoves were probably connected by a toe- and hand-hold trail. It is thought that this was probably a male ceremonial chamber, since it contains remnants of weaving looms, which it is thought were used solely by the Ancestral Puebloan men. A sign at this overlook explains early pit house structures.

Now return to the highway and drive 1 mile to **Antelope House Overlook Turnoff,** then 2 miles to the parking area. Park and walk 0.25 mile to the rim, keeping to the right. Below and to the right is the site of the ninety-one-room, four-story Antelope House. It acquired its name from the well-executed pictographs of antelopes on the canyon wall to the left of the ruin. Binoculars help here. These **antelope drawings** were done by a well-known Navajo artist, Di be Yazhi, in the 1830s. The other wall pictures were done by the Ancestral Puebloans. Occupied from A.D. 693, the site includes circular kivas and a main plaza. It was abandoned before the great drought sometime before 1260, probably because of flood damage it incurred because of its location near the river bottom. Its fleeing residents have probably become members of today's Hopi and Zuni Indians. There is some evidence to suggest that the area was used sporadically by the Hopi after 1300, probably for the purpose of growing crops in the summer.

Just across the wash from Antelope House is the **Tomb of the Weaver.** It is also in an alcove about 50 feet above the canyon floor. This single burial site contained the mummy of an old man who was probably a weaver. He was buried with a blanket made mainly of eagle feathers. In addition, a bow and arrow with numerous foodstuffs were found, such as cornmeal, corn on the cob, salt, piñon nuts, and beans. Under the feather blanket was a finely woven cotton robe, along with a skein of cotton yarn more than 2 miles in length. The tools of his trade, including a spindle whorl, were also found buried with him.

Now walk a little farther around the rim to the display sign for **Navajo**

Fortress. The word *fortress* refers to the single, high red stone butte on the other side of the canyon. The Navajo often had good reason to hide from whites seeking retribution after devastating Navajo raids. This was a fine place to retreat. Although not visible from the rim, a trail ascends to the top of the fortress. The trail is segmented, so as the Navajo climbed from one level to another, they could pull the ladder up behind them. While some pulled ladders, other Navajo hurled rocks at the enemy from behind stone fortresses built at each level. This was truly an effective defense system.

After returning to the highway, drive 5.3 miles to **Mummy Cave Overlook** turnoff. In about 0.5 mile turn right a short distance to the overlook parking area. From the rim you will see Mummy Cave across the canyon. This cave was so named because a U.S. archaeological expedition in the late 1800s discovered two mummies in the talus slopes below the ruins. The Navajo call this site *Tsvy Kini* or "House under the Rock." Some believe that the people who occupied this site were migrants from Mesa Verde, and certainly the three-story tower is reminiscent of that kind of architecture. There are fifty rooms and three kivas in the largest, eastern alcove. It is thought that access was via a hand-and-toe trail up the face of the cliff from the top of the talus slope. Excavations there have revealed evidence of Basketmaker habitation since A.D. 100.

Return to the spur road and turn right to **Massacre Cave** and **Yucca Cave** parking areas. Massacre Cave tells even more dramatically the history of conflict between the Navajo and whites. For there in 1805 the Spanish military leader Lieutenant Antonio de Narbona led a Spanish expedition from Santa Fe into Canyon de Chelly, hoping to halt the Navajo raiding on Spanish settlements as they spread east. Receiving word that the Spanish, along with some Zuni Indian allies, were on the march, the Navajo took refuge in a remote cave 500 feet high up on the canyon wall yet several hundred feet short of the rim. This cave, which you can easily see, is 300 feet long and 8 feet wide at its widest point. Protected from the rim by the angle of the cave's roof and from below by large rocks at the rim of the cave, about 150 Navajo, including many women and children, climbed the arduous route and took refuge there that day.

Exactly what happened is not known, but it is said that by the end of the day, Narbona's force had spotted the hideout and his sharpshooters had massacred 115 Navajo. Narbona supposedly delivered the ears of eighty-four Indians to the government in Santa Fe. Navajo legend asserts that only twenty-five of their people were killed there. The rest were captured. It is thought that Narbona's men fired from the spot where the overlook is, after one of the elderly Navajo women had given their position away by shouting taunts at the soldiers in the canyon below. Indeed the cave was safe from the canyon rim directly above it but not from its flanking rim.

A short walk farther along the rim leads to **Yucca Cave viewpoint.** This small early Puebloan structure is the last of the sites you can see from the North Rim road. From there you can either return to the visitor center or continue northeast on Indian Route 64, 13 miles to the junction with Indian Route 12, leading to Window Rock to the south or Lukachukai and Mexican Water to the north. Just south of this junction is **Diné College at Tsaile.** The handsome, modern, octagonal multistory building echoes the design of the Navajo hogan. The museum—**Hatathle Gallery**—is a must to see if you are in the area. One exhibit floor is devoted to a detailed, beautifully presented history of the Navajo people, while another exhibit floor often features rotating exhibits representing other Indian tribes. The gift store offers rugs, jewelry, baskets, and pottery made by students (and others) and is an excellent source for Navajo crafts. There's also Navajo culture bookstore; (928) 724–6600.

From Chinle to Mexican Water, Teec Nos Pos, and the Four Corners Monument

The drive north of Chinle on U.S. Highway 191 leading 63 miles to the junction with U.S. Highway 160 is one of the best routes to view the scenic and everyday life of today's Navajo. Although less crowded and more traditional than the Window Rock area, this stretch is not quite as remote as the Monument Valley region. This north-central portion of the Navajo reservation is still in transition and retains a rich cultural flavor alongside some of the best scenery in Navajoland. Just 12.6 miles north of Canyon de Chelly is the community of **Many Farms.** The Navajo call this location "Water Stringing Out." It is indeed such a well-watered place that there are many carefully tended and productive farms there, making it the breadbasket of the reservation in terms of its arable land. Many of the acres are irrigated, providing a belt of green when the rest of the country is brown and dry.

The road soon gives way to beautiful red rock country, dotted with Navajo hogans and farms. There are enough hogans of all shapes, sizes, and descriptions strung out along this route on both sides of the highway to make you a hogan expert by the time you complete this route. You may see flocks of sheep or goats alongside the road being tended by Navajo women and children. Where U.S. Highway 191 meets U.S. Highway 160, you have a choice. You can either go west through remote but fairly scenic country to Kayenta or head east 31.2 miles to Teec Nos Pos.

At Teec Nos Pos junction, turn north onto U.S. Highway 160 for a geography lesson you will not soon forget. At approximately 6 miles you will see a sign marking the spur road to the **Four Corners Monument.** Turn left and follow the short distance to the road's end and a large parking lot. Fee. Almost every day many Navajo are there, selling jewelry and other items to the tourist trade from booths set up around the parking area and small visitor center. This is the only place in the United States where the borders of four states are so aligned that you can be in all four states at one time. Walk up to the monument, place both feet in two of the four quadrants. Now comes the hard part—bend over and place each hand in the remaining two quadrants. You are now literally standing, squatting, or perhaps "panting" in four states at one time.

From there you can either continue north into southwestern Colorado and northwestern New Mexico (covered by Section 3 of this book) or retrace your steps to U.S. Highway 160 and 64 and head southeast to Shiprock, New Mexico. On the way you will see a most impressive geologic monument, 1,700-foot-high **Shiprock.** This volcanic plug or throat has fins of igneous rock running north and south that resemble wings. There are numerous Navajo legends concerning this rock that the Navajo call "Winged Rock." Although its soft volcanic rock represents a dangerous challenge, it was first climbed in 1939 by the California Sierra Club. Topping out at 7,178 feet, this imposing rock structure was named by early white settlers who thought it resembled an old windjammer under full sail. Indeed, in the evening just before sunset, after a hot summer's day, an optical illusion is created that makes it appear as though this monolith is rising off the desert floor and floating.

All along U.S. Highway 64, you may see oil well pumps as they bring barrels of "black gold" to the surface. In several areas, particularly around **Red Mesa,** you will see traditional hogans within a few yards of these pumps. The royalties from these wells go to the Navajo tribal government. At 26 miles from the Teec Nos Pos Junction is the sprawling modern community of **Shiprock, New Mexico.** There amid the traffic and the suburbanlike sprawl, you will note that the northeast corner of the reservation has not been able to resist some of the less desirable aspects of modern white culture. Nonetheless the Shiprock Trading Post and the Foutz Trading Company are still excellent sources for Navajo handicrafts.

From Shiprock you can travel 25 miles to Farmington, New Mexico, entering the southwestern Colorado/northwestern New Mexico geographic area. Alternatively you can head north on U.S. Highway 666, 41 miles to Cortez, Colorado, another gateway to that area.

Or to reach the sights in north central New Mexico you can drive south 92 miles to Gallup, New Mexico, and then 138 miles east on U.S. I–40 to Albuquerque via Acoma Pueblo. **Acoma Pueblo** can also be reached on a more scenic route from Gallup, New Mexico by traveling south on New Mexico Highway 602 to New Mexico Highway 53, which leads west several miles to **Zuni Pueblo** and circles east passing by **El Morro National Monument** (see secton 4, "North Central New Mexico History") and the **El Malapais National Monument** lava fields before meeting up with U.S. I–40 at Grants, New Mexico, about 15 miles from the Acoma Pueblo turnoff.

Or you can drive from Shiprock 40 miles east to Bloomfield, New Mexico, and then 167 miles southeast on U.S. Highway 550 (New Mexico Highway 40) to Bernalillo, New Mexico, where you are just a short distance from either Albuquerque or Santa Fe. Along this route, just south of Nageezi, New Mexico, is a 5-mile-long spur road to the west (County Road 7900) that deteriorates into a usually rough 16-mile dirt road (County Road 7950/7985) that leads to **Chaco Culture National Historical Park.** Before setting out to Chaco Canyon, call the park visitor center (505–786–7014) for an update of this road's condition.

STAYING THERE

Lodging

The total tour of northeastern Arizona covered here is more than 500 miles in length. Accommodations outside of Flagstaff are limited. But some of these accommodations are real gems that place you in the midst of settings that evoke the scenic and cultural essence of this area. If you are going to travel in this area in the busy spring, summer, or early fall season and where you stay and what kind of room you get make a difference, it is imperative to reserve ahead of time. Contact the establishment of your choice before you begin your trip, and tie down your reservation either by credit card guarantee or personal check. This way your room will be held for you no matter when you arrive. In lieu of any of the above, arrive before 4:00 P.M. on the day you want to stay, and inquire about space and the possibility of any cancellations. There are almost always cancellations, but there are almost always people wanting those cancellations during the peak travel season. Many tourist-oriented facilities on the high desert do not operate full services or are closed from mid-November through February. If for any reason you are traveling in this area in the winter months, you should check ahead of time to determine what facilities are open. And, of course, be prepared for episodic snow and winter conditions as late as April or early May.

Food

Restaurants outside of the Flagstaff area are sparse. Most of them are listed with the lodging they are associated with. A few independent cafes are listed separately. In Indian Country there are some special foods you may want to watch for. Staples of the Navajo diet are mutton stew, fry bread, fried potatoes, coffee, and soda pop. A popular dish is the Navajo taco. This is a piece of fry bread covered with a variety of condiments, including lettuce, tomatoes, beans, and either a chili or tomato sauce.

On the Hopi reservation keep an eye out for posole. Posole is corn that resembles hominy. The Hopi also relish stews and have their own version of fry bread. Look for the excellent pik'ami pudding made of cornmeal. And if you have the chance, try the piki bread, a small bluish cylinder of paper-thin bread resembling parchment paper rolled up into a scroll. This is a real delicacy. It is made of blue cornmeal, which is spread thinly on a stone griddle. After cooking just a few seconds, it is deftly lifted and rolled while soft.

And remember that alcohol (possession or consumption) is illegal on Indian reservations.

Hopi Ceremonial Dances

The Hopi value their privacy and conduct religious ceremonies throughout the year. Each village determines which dances may or may not be open to non-Indians. Dances usually are held on Saturday, with an occasional extra dance on Friday or Sunday. Several villages have closed most of their ceremonial dances (Kachina [or Katsina]), Snake, and Flute Dances) to non-Indians. Many of these dances occur throughout the summer. However, some women's and social dances (Butterfly Dances, etc.), which are held in late summer or fall, remain open.

Up to date dance information is hard to come by. The best bet is to contact the Hopi Cultural Center Motel, one of the Hopi tribe's cultural preservation or public relations offices or individual village tribal offices listed in "Staying There: The Hopi Reservation Telephone Numbers" section, or the Flagstaff visitor center. If you are on the Hopi mesas, check for notices on the door of the Hopi Cultural Center Museum or at the motel desk.

The interesting annual Hopi Ceremonial cycle begins with the Hopi New Year, at the time of the winter solstice, December 21. The Soyal Ceremony begins the cycle. During this time of longer days, as the sun starts back north again, the symbol of renewed life is further reinforced as a single kachina returns from his underworld home in the **San Francisco Peaks,** a harbinger of more deities to come in future months. And this is the beginning of the six to seven months in which the kachinas take the responsibility for village ceremonies from the Bear Clan.

Some of the kachinas are said to represent the dead, and some are cloud kachinas, who can bring rain; others are thought to be intermediaries between the Hopi and their gods. The kachina dancers are symbolic representations in human form of the kachina deities and conse-
quently resemble otherworldly beings with their masks and elaborate costumes. It is said that the kachina dancers are so well prepared through meditation and purification in the kiva that they feel themselves to be not just impersonators but actually personifications of the 250 to 300 different kachinas. During Soyal prayer sticks or paahos are exchanged among the villagers to honor the return of the kachinas and to wish for each other's well-being.

By February so many kachinas have returned that the largest kachina ceremony, Powamu or the Bean Dance, is staged. As many as 200 kachina dancers may appear at this time, thereby dramatically announcing the return of most of the kachinas to the village. During this ceremony beans are sprouted in the warm nurturing environment of the heated kivas, while the cold winds howl and snow blankets the plaza outside. This symbolic act presages the richness of the coming growing season. If the beans sprout well and grow tall in the kiva, then it follows that the corn will be strong and grow tall in the summer. But the concern is not just for crops. There is also a deep concern for renewed spiritual life as young children are initiated into the kachina cult. During this time the carved kachina figures or dolls are given to the young girls of the village, while other gifts are given to the boys.

Following Powamu is a constant series of kiva and plaza dances, as well as races in late winter and early spring. During some of these more social dances, marvelously costumed Hopi represent their neighbors or enemies. From May through July there are kachina dances almost every weekend

Museum of Northern Arizona, Flagstaff

in one or more of the villages. From April through July there are a variety of dances for good weather and good crops. They are often held on Saturdays so that the Hopi who live off the reservation can return to see them. The public is often welcome.

The kachina or katsina dances culminate with the **Niman or Home Dances** held the last three weekends in July in several of the villages. This, the second most important ceremonial during the year and the last of the masked dances, is held to thank the kachinas for their help in producing crops that are ripening by then and to bid them good-bye as they leave their villages for their spiritual home in the San Francisco Peaks for the remainder of the year. When the kachinas leave, responsibility for the ceremonial cycle returns to the Bear Clan. Usually on the third weekend of August, the Snake-Antelope

Dance occurs, alternating with the Flute Dance every other year.

In September the Women's Society performs several dances, including the **Knee High Dance** in late September and the **Basket Dance** around the middle of October. Morningtime **Butterfly Dances** are also performed during this time. The Hopi year ends in late November when the Men's Societies seek the solitude of the kiva to initiate young Hopi men into the important ceremonial societies and to pray for the renewal of life in a ceremony called Wuwtsim. With new initiates to keep these centuries-old ceremonies going, the new year is greeted once again with the Soyal Ceremony.

But not every traveler visiting Hopiland will want to or be able to spend the time to attend one of the Hopi ceremonial dances. You must be prepared to sit or stand at least two or three hours in the afternoon sun on a rooftop that you reach by climbing a ladder. If you are not there very early, all the good viewing positions will be taken and you will have to rubberneck it for the afternoon. The dances are well attended, and the crowds, which can be fierce, somehow materialize out of what appear to be deserted mesas and underpopulated villages.

If, however, these factors are not obstacles and you are willing to attend with peace in your heart, as the Hopi say, and in a sense to become a Hopi for an afternoon, you will have an unforgettable experience.

Shopping (Consumer Tips for Buying Indian Arts and Crafts)

In the late 1920s and early 1930s, my parents made several forays over rough, dusty, unimproved roads to the Pueblo villages along the Rio Grande Valley in New Mexico. The Pueblo Indians there, like those in western New Mexico and Arizona, had not too many years earlier discovered their "roots" in nearby archaeological diggings. They were greatly influenced by the art of their Ancient Puebloan ancestors; hence beautiful pottery once more became a hallmark of the native southwestern people. In those days some amount of trading still went on. My father took candy (especially jelly beans) with him, for in the more remote areas, candy was quite a luxury for the Indians. With some cash and candy, he acquired numerous pottery pieces, which have been treasured by my family ever since. Later he took me back to the same Pueblo villages, where I can vividly remember buying small pots from children my

own age in the dusty plazas of the pueblos. Still later and with greater appreciation of Indian crafts, I have taken my family to the doorways of Indian homes along the Rio Grande and on the Hopi mesas in the search for fine handcrafted items. Today with good, paved village-to-town roads in Arizona and New Mexico, a number of excellent craft shops are available along major highways, as well as in the center of some Indian villages. And, of course, just as earlier in the century, it is still possible to buy from the doors of the homes of the craftspersons.

But most travelers will probably make their purchases in one of the many convenient shops or galleries that specialize in Indian crafts. These shops, found in the major towns and cities, serve as marketplaces for today's Indian craftspeople. There the traveler will be aware, possibly for the first time, not only of the wide assortment and variety of crafts to choose from but of the large selection available of each of the different types of crafts. And it is probably there too that the traveler will first be aware of the price structure of authentic Indian-made crafts in today's marketplace. The confusion that comes from trying to make a single purchase from so many items and the "sticker shock" that so many travelers experience after looking at a few price tags are two of the complexities in today's market that were not present twenty or thirty years ago. In today's market Indian craftspeople receive fair prices for their skillful and time-intensive work. These prices, which allow for adequate but not excessive compensation, along with the personal satisfaction that comes from the increasing popularity and recognition of their work, have led to today's thriving southwestern Native American art movement. This country's indigenous traditional craft movement is no longer dying on the vine as it was when rugs and pots were sold for a pittance. In fact southwestern Indian arts and crafts have become so popular that the marketplace has attracted not only manufacturers of legitimate curios and souvenirs but opportunistic and unethical individuals as well, who by their dishonest but well-publicized abuses have hurt the reputation of the southwestern Indian arts and crafts movement and instilled an unfortunate element of doubt and skepticism in the mind of the unknowledgeable buyer. That is too bad. With a little planning most travelers alert to the problem of either manufactured or handmade imitations from this country or abroad should fare quite well in purchasing an authentic craft item to fit their budget. So arm yourself with some basic knowledge about the crafts you are interested in (for starters read the para graphs that follow), obtain a list of reliable shops (some thought to be reliable are recommended in this book), and proceed to search for the item that captures your heart and soul and yet fits your pocketbook. There is a wide range of prices available in today's expanded market. Do not hesitate to shop and cross-compare among the numerous reliable dealers on your list. You deserve to pay the lowest price possible that still provides the dealer and craftsperson with a fair but not excessive profit. A good dealer recognizes this. For ultimately the viability of the southwestern Indian arts and crafts movement rests on satisfied buyers like yourself who enthusiastically spread the good word about the beauty and pleasure derived from our country's most popular indigenous artwork.

You will see two broad classes of "American Indian made" items. In some shops you will be presented with an overwhelming array of commercially made items, which can be classed as souvenirs and curios. Although these items may be evocative of Indian Country and the American Southwest and some are produced by hand in other countries, most are manufactured in assembly-line fashion in this country or abroad for the Southwest tourist market. Some of them may actually be made by small manufacturing companies on or near the reservation, where local Indians apply stereotyped Indian designs to production-line pieces. Most of these items are not expensive to make and do not command the price of Native American handcrafted work. The other broad class of items is authentic one-of-a-kind pieces meticulously handcrafted by individual southwestern Indians using techniques and designs handed down through several generations in their families or villages. The difference in both quality and price of these two broad classes of "Indian-made" items is in most instances marked. But sometimes the imitation pieces are not clearly or accurately labeled and are pawned off, at higher prices, as genuine American Indian handmade crafts. Although there is nothing wrong with buying a piece that is manufactured or handmade in another country, you need to make certain that the price you pay reflects the origin of the item and does not carry the price tag of the more expensive, time- and labor-intensive American Indian craft item. Usually the differences are relatively easy to spot if you can spend just a little time to educate yourself. If you have time before your trip, use the bibliography in this book or, with the help of your local librarian, find books that illustrate with good color photographs examples of authentic Indian handcrafts. There are also a number of consumer guides that can help you sort out the differences. Alternatively when you reach Indian Country visit one of the museums listed in the text and spend some time there acquainting yourself with the real McCoy. You will find that for the most part a spirit and dynamism live in the better southwestern Indian handcrafted pots, rugs, and baskets that cannot be duplicated by commercially made look-alike items.

If you are in the market for an authentic Indian craft item, a basic knowledge of how the craft is created will help you choose the piece that best suits your needs and your pocketbook. You will see authentic handcrafted items ranging from less expensive pieces created by younger artisans just learning their trade to very expensive, museum-quality showpieces handcrafted by master artist-craftspeople whose work is so extraordinary that it would be classified as fine art by almost anyone's standards. There seem to be no hard and fast rules for determining the price of a handcrafted piece. But in general the more craft hours applied to producing the piece, the higher the price. Other factors that determine the prices may be the artists' skill, experience, and reputation (in that order), as well as the cost of the materials (silver and turquoise for jewelers, bags of dried sheep dung for some potters). To have some idea of the time involved in making a Navajo rug or a pottery vessel, I will explain here the time-consuming, labor-intensive steps used to create these two forms of Native American art.

Weaving. The weaver usually raises her own flock of sheep and goats. After shearing, the raw wool is cleaned, carded, spun, washed, and then dyed with either natural or manufactured dyes. If natural dyes are used, there is additional time in gathering the plant material and processing the dyes. The rug is then woven on a hand loom. Generally the intricate pattern is woven from memory. The preparation and weaving time for a 3-by-5-foot rug may be nearly 400 hours. Usually a tighter weave represents both more advanced skill and more time. Today a growing number of weavers are purchasing ready-made yarns in order to achieve more refinement in the final product. Of course, this saves a great deal of time. You should be on the alert for Navajo rug look-alikes or imitations from Mexico that use Navajo designs. It is certainly all right to purchase these rugs, as long as they are properly labeled and priced according to their method of manufacture and country of origin.

Pottery. The traditional potters in this century have dug their own clay from a special place on the reservation, processed it by hand, and then hand-built the vessel, giving it shape by using the coil-and-scrape method. After the clay slowly dries, the potter makes a slip from clay and water and applies it to the vessel's walls. The slip may then be meticulously burnished or polished with a smooth round stone or a piece of plastic. Pigments are prepared from both mineral and vegetable materials (depending on the color desired), and the pot is then decorated using yucca brushes to apply the design. Once the design has been painted on the vessel, it is then taken outdoors, where it is fired in a bonfire fueled by manure, usually dried cow or sheep dung. This traditional painstaking method of firing pots is very tricky because of the difficulty in controlling the intensity of the fire. Many pots can be lost in the process. The walls of traditionally fired pots are porous and should never be filled with water. Many of the older potters are still producing their work using all the steps just mentioned. But some younger potters are taking shortcuts by firing their work in electric kilns, using commercial clays, or wielding manufactured paintbrushes rather than yucca brushes. All of these changes reflect the desire to produce finer work and to save time. But it is sad to see the diminished use of bonfire firing, for there are wonderful (albeit unpredictable) surface changes that occur with that kind of firing that can never be duplicated in an electric kiln. Some Southwest potters have abandoned the coil-and-scrape method of hand-building the vessel and are now slipcasting pieces (making them in molds, production-line-style), hand-decorating them, and firing them in an electric kiln. These pieces are best classed as souvenir items and should not bring the price of a handcrafted piece fashioned in the traditional way.

Jewelry. Just a word about Indian jewelry. It is here that the "buyer beware" dictum should be applied in full force. Some aspects of the Indian

jewelry market have become so confusing that at times not even reputable, knowledgeable dealers can always be certain of a piece's authenticity. In order to sleep well at night, some dealers purchase bulk silver, turquoise, and coral, which they then parcel out to Indian jewelers who ply their trade either individually or in small workshops under the dealer's supervision. Through this arrangement dealers can best protect their reputations and consumers are certain of getting what they are paying for. Most Indian jewelers make their jewelry by hand, but they use modern machines and tools to help them in their tasks, just as their Anglo counterparts do. The consumer should buy jewelry only from a reliable dealer or a recommended source. And if you are going to buy very expensive jewelry, it might be best to have it evaluated by another dealer or a knowledgeable gemologist.

Whether you are seeking a gem-quality piece or just a nice piece of relatively inexpensive cast or hammered silver jewelry, it may be useful to know about some of the materials used in making Indian jewelry. Sterling silver is 92.5 percent pure silver. Generally it is marked in some way indicating that it is sterling silver. Yet I have seen pieces that are sterling that have not been marked. Coil silver is 90 percent pure and should be slightly less expensive than sterling. The next cheapest form of silver is silver plate, a mixture of nickel and silver that is much cheaper than the other two kinds but is often the silver of choice for certain items that receive a lot of wear, such as money clips. Turquoise is one of the most difficult minerals to evaluate. On today's market there are

Navajo silver concha belt

three types of turquoise. Natural turquoise or gem turquoise is by far the most expensive and is becoming increasingly difficult to find. Probably the most common variety of turquoise you will see on the market today is stabilized turquoise. This non–gem-quality but genuine turquoise is chemically treated to make it harder and more durable, because it is too soft in its natural state to be used in jewelry. It is, of course, less expensive than gem-quality turquoise and because of its availability is one of the more popular and common types you will see. It can be easily confused with gem-quality turquoise. The next type, reconstituted turquoise, is not turquoise at all but rather an aggregate of other mineral or plastic particles dyed to look like turquoise. It is very cheap. Do not think you can judge the difference between these three types of turquoise. Do rely on the judgment of a knowledgeable jeweler, dealer, or gemologist if you are contemplating the purchase of an expensive piece of jewelry. Equally difficult to determine are the authenticity of coral in jewelry pieces and the authenticity of workmanship in the hand-carved stone fetishes in necklaces. Some fetish pieces are being mass-produced cheaply in the Philippines and should not demand the high price of carefully crafted Zuni fetish pieces.

Increasingly Indian artists are bringing innovative new designs and techniques to their work. These innovations are often in the form of contemporary treatments of older designs that reflect the unique viewpoint of the artist. These pieces, although different from those produced in the past eighty years, are all a part of the evolving culture of the Native American people in the Southwest. The life of the Indian crafts movement depends both on artists who preserve the old teachings and styles and on those who incorporate new ideas with the old methods. The high-quality contemporary work of today may well become the standard for the "traditional" work of tomorrow.

Navajo Arts and Crafts

The Navajo make beautiful and finely crafted jewelry. In addition to turquoise and coral necklaces, look for the popular silver and turquoise and coral combinations found in bracelets, concha belts, and in the squash blossom necklaces. Less well known are Navajo sand paintings and the fragile Navajo pottery, brown in color because of its glazing with piñon pitch. In addition, the Navajo weave beautiful sashes and make purses constructed out of woven materials. From willow (sumac) gathered along desert streams, the Utah Navajo weave incredibly beautiful ceremonial-style baskets using complex geometric patterns that often tell a story. They also

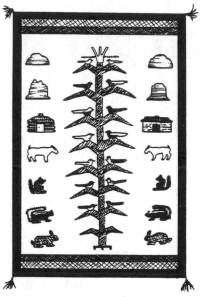

Navajo pictorial rug

make a few baskets covered with piñon pitch to make them waterproof. These baskets often have small handles made of horsehair.

But the tightly woven, durable, well-designed Navajo rug is probably the most sought-after item. Not too many years ago, trading posts in each corner of the reservation carried rugs woven only in that area. Today almost all trading posts carry a variety of rugs. Because of paved roads and better communication, Navajo weavers may travel all over the reservation trying to get the best price for their fine work. Also, with increased communication, the weavers in one region may often weave a rug that has been the specialty of another region. And today throughout the reservation, some weavers incorporate into their work mohair from the Angora goats in their herds. Although mohair gives a rug a softer look and feel, many weavers dislike it because the longer fibers of the silky mohair

often blur or obscure the sharp edges of a complex design. The following are some of the rug types you will see in most of the shops listed below.

Ganado Type Rug. This famous rug, often known as "Ganado Red," is what most people think a Navajo rug should look like. Traditionally it is a tightly woven, mostly aniline-dyed rug with a bright red background enclosed by geometric crosses, diamonds, and stripes, all in colors of gray, white, and black. Today gray often replaces the red background, but the bright reds are still present.

Crystal Rug. These rugs are thought to be some of the finest on the reservation. These distinctive rugs are borderless and are woven from wool dyed with the soft browns, golds, and oranges of the vegetal dyes. The vegetal dyes are the ones the weavers extract from native plants.

Two Gray Hills Rug. These popular, high-quality, expensive rugs, woven east of the Chuska Mountains in New Mexico not far from the Chaco area, combine beautiful natural tones of brown, black, and white wools (the sheep are often bred to produce the color needed) to create most of the design, which is then bordered by black, aniline-dyed wool, providing a fine contrast for the more subtle colors. The design focuses on the intricate central panel, which often is triangular or diamond shaped.

Yei Rug. These rugs have traditionally been woven in the Lukachukai area and in the Shiprock area. They depict the *Yei* gods of the Navajo religion. Mostly aniline dyes are used, and they may be bordered or unbordered. The Yeis woven in the Lukachukai area are heavier and better suited for the floor, while the Yeis woven in the Shiprock area make excellent wall hangings.

Teec Nos Pos Rug. These rugs are usually very busy and intricate in their design and are woven mostly from brightly colored aniline dyes.

Wide Ruins Rug. This is another rug that is woven with wool that has been colored with vegetal dyes. Mostly borderless, these rugs contain endless combinations of subtle, natural colors using a variety of forms of arrows, chevrons, and squash blossoms in the design motif.

Storm Pattern Rug. Originally a pattern found in the Red Lake area, it is now found throughout the reservation. This bordered, highly symmetrical rug contains mostly aniline dyes in bright colors. The designs include zigzags, diamonds, swastikas (an ancient Indian symbol referring to the four directions), arrows, and stepped terraces. Red and black as well as yellow and black combinations are in evidence. Some of these bold designs are now being made with more subtle vegetal dye colors.

Hopi Arts and Crafts

The quality of crafts in the Hopi villages is extremely high. In the various shops on the reservation, you can purchase some of the finest handwoven sashes being made in the Southwest today. These tightly woven pieces are made by the Hopi men, as are the beautifully carved and decorated Hopi kachina dolls that are carved in all of the villages. If you want a Hopi

Hopi sashes

kachina doll, you will find the prices and selections very good on the mesas. Several young Hopi woodcarvers are also making some outstanding contemporary pieces. In addition to these crafts, Hopi men make the handsome Hopi overlay silver jewelry in a stunning series of shapes and designs. Other Hopi artists design and craft beautiful contemporary jewelry. But possibly the acme of all Hopi handwork is reached by the Hopi potters working in the tradition of the renowned Hopi potter Nampeyo, who revived pottery making on the mesas. The delicately beautiful, hand-coiled Hopi pot is often intricately designed and is usually of the highest quality. The walls of some of the pots are so thin that they almost ring when tapped gently. Some Hopi potters also use a surface decoration called corrugation, an old Ancestral Puebloan pottery technique wherein the fingernail is used to make a series of small pinch marks in the unsmoothed coils of the wall of the vessel. And then there are Hopi baskets. There are probably no finer baskets being handwoven today in the

Southwest than those on the Hopi mesas. The varieties of baskets, including the unique coiled baskets, and where to find them, are listed in the subsection on Hopi villages in the "Seeing Indian Country" section.

Flagstaff, Arizona

In addition to the dozens of accommodations clustered around the freeway interchanges and along Route 66, Flagstaff also offers lodging in several quieter, more ambient locations near the charming, revitalized Downtown Flagstaff–Historic Railroad District. With Heritage Square as a focal point, the downtown area offers numerous restaurants, shops, and galleries, making it a major attraction that is not to be missed. Spend time meandering through downtown, including the surrounding older residential districts and the "Bohemian" section south of Route 66 to experience the flavor of a genuinely hospitable Southwestern town.

And while you're downtown, stop by the very helpful Flagstaff Visitor Center in the Old Santa Fe (now Amtrak) Rail Depot, a Tudor Revival building on the corner of Route 66 and Beaver Street. Information: 1 East Route 66, Flagstaff, Arizona 86001; (928) 774–9541 or (800) 842–7293; fax (928) 556–1308; www.flagstaff.az.us or www.flagstaffarizona.org.

For information on all three of the Flagstaff area's national monuments, pay a visit to the Flagstaff Area National Monument Information Center, 6400 North Highway 89; (928) 526–1157. Open daily except major holidays.

Flagstaff's accommodations fill rapidly during special events (see "Fairs, Festivals, and Events," p. 222). If your travel plans coincide with any of those dates, plan to make reservations well ahead of time. Flagstaff Central Reservations may be of help when lodging is hard to find. Information: (928) 527–8333 or (800) 527–8388; fax (928) 527–4272; www.flagstaff-rooms.com. And check at the Visitor Center for the newest B&B accommodations, because they are definitely on the increase.

Train noise, soothing and nostalgic to some but a nuisance to others, is more noticeable in hotel and motel rooms closer to the rail tracks. Many lodging facilities have rooms away from the tracks that aren't bothered by the noise, whereas others have taken measures to dampen the noise. You may want to inquire.

In addition to two budget hotels—the Monte Vista and the Hotel Weatherford—in the historic downtown area, Flagstaff has two **youth hostels: Grand Canyon International Hostel,** 19 South San Francisco; (928) 779–9421 or (888) 442–2696; fax (928) 774–6047; www.grandcanyonhostel.com; and **Motel Du Beau International Hostel,** 19 West Phoenix Avenue; (928) 774–6731 or (800) 398–7112; fax (928) 774–4067; www.dubeau.net.

Besides the many fast-food eateries located around Flagstaff, several fine restaurants are now available in this Arizona mountain city, offering excellently prepared food, served in pleasant surroundings that often evoke the spirit of the region.

And you will note that Flagstaff is also a transportation hub served by **Amtrak's Southwest Limited,** America West Express air shuttle from Phoenix, and Greyhound long-distance

Depot, Flagstaff, Arizona

bus service to the Phoenix airport and destinations along I–40. Should you arrive without a car, Flagstaff has convenient lodging and good food service within walking distance of the bus and rail stations. Taxi service is available from Pulliam Memorial Airport, where there are also rental car services. Flagstaff public transit, Mountain Line (928–778–6624), offers bus service within Flagstaff. As the southern gateway to the Colorado Plateau and Indian Country, Flagstaff is home to several tour and expedition services offering excursions and adventure trips to the Grand Canyon and the Four Corners area, including most Indian Country destinations. The city itself hosts many premier fairs, festivals, and events, which are detailed in this section.

Because Flagstaff is at the crossroads of several different highways and interstate freeways and is divided down the middle by the transcontinental Burlington Northern/Santa Fe Railroad tracks and further subdivided by hills and mesas, some orientation to this sprawling city is useful. It is helpful to know that I–40 passes to

the south of the town and south of Northern Arizona University. It intersects with I–17 on the west side of town near the university, while Flagstaff Mall anchors the east side of town. U.S. Highways 89, 150, and 66 merge into one and become Route 66 (also known as Business I–40), Flagstaff's major east-west arterial, which divides the town north and south. Downtown Leroux Street runs north and south, dividing Flagstaff east and west. U.S. Highway 89A (Beulah Boulevard) coming up from Oak Creek Canyon merges with traffic from the I–17 and I–40 interchange exits to become Milton Road, which then intersects and merges with Route 66. The San Francisco Peaks, the high mountains that can be seen from many places in town, are to the north. Be alert for the one-way streets in the downtown area.

Lodging

Birch Tree Inn B & B. Located only 0.5 mile from downtown, this pleasant B&B in a turn-of-the-

The high-altitude Abert squirrel

twentieth-century home is tranquilly situated on a tree-lined residential street near downtown and across from a park with tennis courts and walking trails in the nearby national forest. The five rooms (three with private bath and two that share a bath) are wonderfully comfortable. Downstairs guests may relax by the fire, enjoy a game of billiards, or indulge in tea and snacks, which are served in the late afternoon. A tasty full breakfast is prepared by the friendly hosts who run this excellent establishment. Information: Birch Tree Inn, 824 West Birch Avenue, Flagstaff, Arizona 86001; (928) 774–1042 or (888) 774–1042; fax (928) 774–8462; www.birchtreeinn. com. Inexpensive to moderate.

Inn at Four Ten B & B. This well-run bed-and-breakfast inn, located in a handsomely refurbished home (vintage 1907) in an enviable location just 3 to 4 blocks from downtown and the rail station, offers views of downtown Flag from its elevated perch above the historic downtown area. All of the nine exceptionally well-decorated rooms have private baths, minifridges, and coffeemakers. Seven rooms have fireplaces and three have Jacuzzi tubs. The public rooms are light and airy. A full

breakfast is served. Also patio and gazebo area. Information: Inn at Four Ten B&B, 410 North Leroux Street, Flagstaff, Arizona 86001; (928) 774–0088 or (800) 774–2008; fax (928) 774–6354; www.inn410.com. Moderate to expensive.

Weatherford Hotel. Situated in the heart of downtown Flagstaff in what may well be the most attractive of the downtown historic structures with its handsomely restored second-story balconies is this budget hotel, which caters to the traveler who just wants the basics without any frills like telephones and televisions. There are five clean, quaint, smallish rooms with private baths decorated in charming turn-of-the-twentieth-century style, three rooms with shared bath, and very inexpensive dormitory-style hostel accommodations. Downstairs is Charly's Pub and Grill and upstairs the Zane Grey Ballroom and Bar, which also hosts private parties and opens onto the double-tiered outdoor balconies. If you're a light sleeper it's best to ask for a quiet room. Information: Weatherford Hotel, 23 North Leroux, Flagstaff, Arizona 86001; (928) 779–1919; fax (928) 773–8951; www.weatherford hotel.com. Inexpensive.

Monte Vista Hotel. Also downtown is this other historic hotel, built in 1926. In a prime location, it is now a budget hotel. The Monte Vista offers fifty rooms and suites, most with TVs and private baths (some share a bath down the hall). Rooms vary in decor and condition. It is wise to take a look at your assigned room before checking in. Information: Monte Vista Hotel, 100 North San Francisco Street, Flagstaff, Arizona 86001; (928)

779–6971 or (800) 545–3068; fax (928) 779–2904; www.hotelmonte vista.com. Inexpensive.

Lynn's Inn B&B. This historic two-story brick home is in a residential area four blocks from the downtown shopping area and near City Park. The two guest rooms and one suite with their original pressed tin ceilings are decorated with turn-of-the-twentieth-century antiques. The light-filled sun porch in the back is where a full breakfast is served. Information: Lynn's Inn, 614 West Santa Fe Avenue, Flagstaff, Arizona 86001; (928) 226–1488 or (800) 530–9947; www.lynnsinn.com. Inexpensive to moderate.

Dierker House Bed and Breakfast. Just a few blocks west of downtown, this centrally located home offers both the convenience of downtown and the privacy of a residential district. The modest, older, Victorian-style house with its antiques-filled rooms offers three bedrooms, all sharing a bath. Well-prepared breakfast included. Information: Dierker House Bed and Breakfast, 423 West Cherry, Flagstaff, Arizona 86001; (928) 774–3249. Inexpensive.

ComfiCottages of Flagstaff. Located close to the downtown area are five one- to four-bedroom older reconditioned homes that provide the visitor with the unique experience of living in Flagstaff for a day or two. All cottages have kitchens, and breakfast foods are provided. Most are easy walking distance to downtown restaurants. The one at 710 Birch is the closest. Information: ComfiCottages of Flagstaff; (928) 774–0731 or (888)774–0731; www.comficottages.com. Moderate.

Comfort Inn. This motel with eighty-five air-conditioned units is near downtown and the university and somewhat secluded from the nearby shopping strips. The heated swimming pool, whirlpool, and motel entrance face the pines, allowing this modern motel to evoke the feeling of being farther out of town than it really is. The lobby gives way to a large public room with a fireplace and comfortable seating. The rooms are reasonably spacious, and twenty come with a wet bar, refrigerator, and microwave. Information: Comfort Inn, 2355 South Beulah Boulevard, Flagstaff, Arizona 86001; (928) 774–2225 or (800) 490–6562; fax: (928) 774–2225. Inexpensive.

Radisson Woodlands Hotel Flagstaff. This handsomely designed hotel, with its 183 air-conditioned units, rests atop a hill, giving it a fine view of the mountains around Flagstaff. It is also within walking distance of the university. The handsome but ever-busy lobby gives way to several restaurants, including the very nice Woodlands Cafe and Lounge, and Sakura, a Japanese restaurant. Heated pool, exercise room, sauna, and whirlpool. Information: Radisson Woodlands Hotel Flagstaff, 1175 West Route 66, Flagstaff, Arizona 86001; (928) 773–8888 or (800) 333–3333, fax (928) 773–0597; www.radisson.com. Moderate to expensive.

Fairfield Inn by Marriott. On a hill overlooking Milton Road and the university is this 135-unit Marriott motel, which can really pack 'em in. It is a no-nonsense, less-than-charming establishment, yet it has all the amenities one might need, including a heated outdoor swimming pool and well-lighted work desks and data ports in the smallish rooms. Information: Fairfield Inn Flagstaff, 2005 South Milton Road, Flagstaff, Arizona 86001; (928) 773–1300 or (800) 228–2800; fax (928) 773–1462. Inexpensive.

La Quinta Inn and Suites. This large 128-room multistory motel near Northern Arizona University (South Beulah Boulevard via South Milton Road and Forest Meadows Street) is close in, yet has some mountain charm provided by all the high-altitude pines that flank it. There is a heated pool and whirlpool. Some suites have computer workstations, and televisions are equipped with video games. Small pets allowed. Information: La Quinta Inn, 2015 South Beulah Boulevard, Flagstaff, Arizona 86001; (928) 531–5900 or (800) 531–5900; fax (928) 214–9140. Moderate.

Days Inn East. Located east of downtown just far enough off East Route 66 to dampen the road noise but within earshot of the rail tracks. Rooms at the back and closer to the ground are the quietest. This no-frills, three-story motel with fifty pleasant rooms (some with refrigerators) has an indoor Jacuzzi and serves a limited continental breakfast. Information: Day's Inn East, 3601 Lockett Road, Flagstaff, Arizona 86004; (928) 527–1477 or (800) 435–6343. Inexpensive to moderate.

Hampton Inn East. Located on Lockett Road adjacent to the Days Inn East and having the same proximity to the rail tracks is this three-story fifty-six-room motel with indoor pool and Jacuzzi. A generous continental breakfast is served in the lobby. Information: Hampton Inn East, 3501 East Lockett Road, Flagstaff, Arizona 86004; (928) 526–1885 or (800) 222–2052. Inexpensive to moderate.

Budget Host Saga Motel. An inexpensive motel on old Highway 66, this establishment has twenty-nine air-conditioned rooms with TVs. Heated swimming pool and playground. Information: Budget Host Saga Motel, 820 West Route 66, Flagstaff, Arizona 86001; (928) 779–3631 or (800) 283–4678. Inexpensive.

Little America Hotel. Situated on 500 pine-covered acres (with a walking and jogging trail) near I–40 (exit 198), this hotel is one of Flagstaff's best. Follow Route 66 east and turn north on Enterprise Road to 2515 East Butler Road. This superbly managed hotel with its brick facade and white gables has 245 air-conditioned, spacious, somewhat overdecorated rooms, many overlooking pine groves and mountains. Some suites with fireplaces and saunas. Flag's citizens use this hotel for weddings, anniversaries, and other special occasions. Heated outdoor swimming pool. Gift shop. Coffee shop. For finer fare there is the Western Gold Dining Room. This motor hotel fills up fast. Information: Little America Hotel, P.O. Box 3900, Flagstaff, Arizona 86003; (928–779–7900 or (800) 352–4386; fax (928) 779–7983; www.littleamerica.com. Moderate.

Residence Inn by Marriott. These 102 units out on the east side of Flagstaff are just a hop, skip, and a jump from the public golf course. Each unit is a well-designed living space and contains a small kitchen. There is a central courtyard with a heated swimming pool and an enclosed exercise room. Complimentary beverages are offered in the evening. Nice views. Small pets allowed. Information: Residence Inn by Marriott, 3440 North Country Club Drive, Flagstaff, Arizona 86004; (928) 526–5555 or (800) 331–3131; fax (928) 527–0328. Expensive.

Around Flagstaff: Winslow, Arizona, and Munds Park, Arizona

Motel in The Pines. If Flagstaff is overbrimming on a spring or summer weekend and lodging is hard to come by, try this pleasant, quiet, and very adequate twenty-two-room motel about twenty minutes south of Flagstaff using exit 322 off Interstate 17 at Munds Park, Arizona. Here you are truly in the Ponderosa Pines. Some units have kitchen and fireplaces. Small pets allowed. Restaurant is nearby. Information: Motel in the Pines, P.O. Box 18171, Munds Park, Arizona 86017; (928) 286–9699 or (800) 574–5080. Inexpensive.

La Posada Hotel and the Turquoise Room Restaurant. This outstanding historic railroad hotel, an oasis on 6 acres of landscaped grounds, is in Winslow, Arizona, about an hour's drive from Flagstaff (see "Seeing Indian Country; Flagstaff; Winslow, Arizona: A Half Day or Overnight Trip to La Posada..."). Designed by Mary Colter, one of America's first women architects, this handsomely restored hotel from the 1930s makes for a pleasant stop. The spacious public rooms—including the spectacular lobby with its collection of antiques and fine art, the orangerie, the large ballroom, the game room and distinctive gift shop, and the shady outdoor verandas—all make La Posada a very special place to stay. The thirty-eight rooms and suites (once the destination for America's rich and famous), all with private baths, have been comfortably updated with television and air-conditioning. Amtrak still stops at La Posada's doorstep each morning on the way to Chicago and in the evening en route to Los Angeles. A special treat at this hotel is the **Turquoise Room** with its martini lounge, espresso bar, and restaurant (928–289–2888). The restaurant, featuring Fred Harvey dishes from the 1930s and contemporary Southwest cuisine, is open for breakfast, lunch, and dinner (closed Monday). It is a must if you are anywhere near Winslow. For lunch or dinner appetizer, try the signature dish, a velvety black bean and cream of corn soup with red chili cream. From the wood-burning grill, follow with Wapiti farm-raised sauteed elk medallions and sour cherry sauce on a bed of Minnesota wild rice medley or a beef brisket plate with red caboose mashed potatoes and horseradish cream. Wine and beer list, fresh lemonade, and delicious desserts. Information: La Posada Hotel, 303 East Second Street (Old U.S. Highway 66), Winslow, Arizona 86047; (928) 289–4366; fax (928) 289–3873; www.laposada.org. Inexpensive (restaurant moderate).

Campgrounds

For additional campground information call (800) 365–CAMP.

Flagstaff Grand Canyon K.O.A. This K.O.A. is located 5.5 miles out on the northeastern fringes of town just beyond Flagstaff Mall on U.S. Highway 89. Use exit 201 from I–40 to find this large, modern, multifacility campsite in the pines. It includes some camping cabins for rent. There are two hundred tent and recreational vehicle sites spread out over 20 acres. Reservations recommended; (928) 526–9926 or (800) 562–3524; fax (928) 527–8356; www.co.coconino.az.us/parks.

Woody Mountain Campground and RV Park. Located at 2227 West Route 66 is this 25-acre upscale facility. with outdoor heated pool, a sandwich shop, and more; (928) 774–7727 or (800) 732–7986; www.woody mountaincampground.com.

Fort Tuthill Coconino County Park. Located 3 miles south of town just off I–17 (exit 337) and just off U.S. Highway 89A, the Oak Creek Canyon–Sedona Highway. The 30-acre park has nature trails, racquetball courts, ninety tent sites, and fifteen recreational vehicle sites; (928) 774–3464 or low season at (928) 774–5139; www.co.coconino.az.us.

Bonito Campground. Located near Sunset Crater Volcano Visitor Center 12 miles north of Flagstaff on U.S. Highway 89 and then 2 miles east on Forest Road 545 is this National Forest Service campground with forty-four sites in the pines for tents and recreational vehicles; (928) 526–0866 or call (800) 365–CAMP for other NFS campgrounds.

Pineflat Campground. Sixteen miles south of Flagstaff and just off the scenic Oak Creek Canyon–Sedona Highway (89A) is this

National Forest Service campground with fifty-eight sites for tents and recreational vehicles. Swimming in the creek, nature trails, and fishing are some of the extras. Reserve ahead of time. If this campground is full, ask about Cave Springs and Bootlegger campgrounds immediately to the south; (877) 444–6777.

Meteor Crater RV Park. Stay near the crater in one of the seventy-one landscaped pull-through spaces with full hookups and private rest rooms and showers; (928) 289–4002 or (800) 478–4002; www.meteorcrater.com.

Food

Cottage Place. You'll receive a warm welcome at this excellent award-winning dinner restaurant located in an early-twentieth-century home south of East Route 66 and the railroad tracks. Take Beaver Street immediately west of the Amtrak station and after 2 blocks turn onto Cottage Place (126 West Cottage Place); (928) 774–8431; www.cottage place.com. If you want to sample the best-prepared food in Flagstaff, make a reservation for dinner here. With a full and well-selected wine and beer list, the Cottage Place offers up dishes like rack of lamb, Cottage Place cassoulet, duet of duckling a l'orange and pork schnitzel. And the excellent fresh seafood menu tantalizes with dishes like fresh scallop sauté en croute. Superb soups and salads. Vegetarian specialties. Outstanding desserts. Reservations recommended. Dinner only. Closed Monday. Expensive.

Buster's. Located at 1800 South Milton in Green Tree Village shopping center southeast of downtown at 1800 South Milton Road (U.S. Highway 89A), (928) 774–5155. This casual lunch and dinner restaurant serves delicious fresh seafood and mesquite-grilled meats. Buster Keaton, the restaurant's namesake, probably never ate this well or this creatively. The luncheon menu features soups, salads, hamburgers, and sandwiches, while the dinner menu offers chicken Sonoma, veal piccata, shrimp Monterey, and a variety of salads and desserts. There are also omelettes and fruit dishes. "Kid's stuff" is for those under twelve. Sunday brunch. The modest wine list is well selected. Inexpensive to moderate.

Monsoon on the Rim. This informal, fun, New Asian–fusion eatery located downtown in Heritage Square, on the corner of LeRoux and Aspen (928–226-8844) is open daily for lunch and dinner. From lettuce wraps and pot stickers to spicy crunchy calamari, luau chicken, sizzling tilapia, and Korean garlic steak, you can't go wrong. Ditto for **Monsoon,** this restaurant's other location at 1551 South Milton Road (928–774–2266). Moderate.

Josephine's. A few blocks from downtown is this good-food restaurant that occupies a very handsome converted historic Flagstaff residence located at 503 Humphrey Street (928–226–0910). With a couple of pros in the food business running things, this modern American bistro serves Asian, Southwest, and traditional American lunches and dinners. Hours may change (call ahead), but typically open for lunch on Tuesday, lunch and dinner Wednesday through Saturday and open Sunday for barbecue. Moderate.

Charly's Pub and Grill and the Exchange Pub. Located downtown at 23 North Leroux in the historic Weatherford Hotel; (928) 779–1919. Although the nicely renovated, cozy space that houses the restaurant is reminiscent of the late 1890s, it is the modern western spirit of the place that hooks you. Or possibly it is the crowd of regular locals who seem to love this place that gives it so much life. The menu has a Southwest flair with an excellent assortment of sandwiches, delicious homemade soups, and salads for lunch. Breakfast includes many old favorites, like pancake and waffle specialties. For dinner there are steaks, prime rib and fresh seafood. Homemade bread, soups, and pies. Open daily. Inexpensive to moderate.

Arizona Donut Factory. Some morning if you're downtown, cross the tracks to 2 South Beaver (928–779–7077) and have one of the fresh, scrumptious, and creative donuts they make here and a cup of java. You'll be glad you did.

Beaver Street Brewery and Whistle Stop Cafe. Located south of the rail tracks near NAU at 11 South Beaver Street #1 (928–779–0079) is this large, very casual lunch and dinner establishment featuring soups and appetizers like soft pretzels and Arizona quesadillas. Also fondues, salads, sandwiches, and their specialty gourmet wood-fired pizzas. Good beer and wine list. Espresso. Desserts. Outdoor patio dining in the summer. Inexpensive.

Alpine Pizza. Located at 7 North Leroux in the historic district area; (928) 779–4109. This casual cafe turns out a variety of delicious pizzas, as well as lasagna and sandwiches. Outdoor streetside dining, weather permitting.

Cafe Espress Cafe-Bakery. Located at 16 North San Francisco Street; (928) 774–0541. With many vegetarian selections, this is a good place to catch up on the local scene at breakfast or lunch. Breakfast naturally features freshly baked breakfast rolls as well as omelettes. Lunch includes soups, salads, and sandwiches on home-baked breads. Espresso and cappuccino are served through the day and evening. Limited outdoor dining, weather permitting.

Late for the Train. Near downtown's Heritage Square at 107 North San Francisco Street and on Grand Canyon route Highway 180 (Fort Valley Road) is this very good coffeehouse, which roasts its own and features specialty coffees, homemade pastries, and sandwiches; (928) 779–5975 for North San Francisco Street Shop and (928) 773–0308 for Highway 180 shop.

Black Bean Burrito and Salsa Company. Located downtown in the Gateway Plaza, a pedestrian corridor and courtyard between Route 66 and Aspen Avenue; (928) 779–9905. This eatery, with both inside and outside seating, serves up original southwestern concoctions that befit the name of the place. Enjoy selecting from a wide variety of burritos and tacos made from fresh ingredients and accompanied by gourmet wraps and custom-made sauces.

Tea and Sympathy. Serves delicious soups, salads, and sandwiches and a fine selection of teas, scones, and desserts—breakfast, too—in a pleasantly cheery, redecorated older home downtown at 409 North Humphreys; (928) 779–2171. Open Wednesday through Sunday.

Horsemen Lodge. One mile east of Flagstaff on Highway 89 North is this well-established steak house that is known for its ambience and for having the best steaks in the area; (928) 526–2655. The pine log building houses numerous large rooms where rib-eye, T-bone, and sirloin steaks are served to what sometimes seems like an endless number of hungry eaters who return over and again to this steak mecca. The ambience is just like you would imagine a western steak house to be. Barbecue ribs, chicken, and even seafood are done on the oak pit. But, ah, the steaks. Children's menu. Dinner only. Closed Sunday (and Monday in winter) and major holidays. No reservations. Moderate.

Jackson's Grill At the Springs. Located about 4 miles from downtown on the route to Sedona, you'll find this oasis of American country dining in a peaceful clearing in the forest at 7055 North Highway 89A (928–213–9350). Pizza comes from the brick oven, and dishes like spit-roasted-glazed pork loin chops from the grill. Also barbecued baby-back pork loin ribs and daily fresh seafood specials. Lunch during the busy season. Dinner year-round inside or out on the view patio. Bar and wine list. Closed Monday. Moderate.

Tours and Activities

Museum of Northern Arizona Ventures and Discovery Programs. Ventures (May–October) offers a series of adult, small-group hotel-based Excursions (educational programs to locations on the Colorado Plateau and beyond, requiring only easy to moderate hikes); Explorations (outdoor learning opportunities with vehicle support and base camps, requiring moderate to strenuous day hikes); and Expeditions (remote area camping trips reached by boat or hiking). Discovery Programs (April–September) feature unique hands-on activities, workshops, classes, and tours for students of all ages interested in experiencing the arts, sciences, cultures, and history of the Colorado Plateau. Information: Museum of Northern Arizona Ventures and Discovery Programs, Education Department, 3101 North Fort Valley Road, Flagstaff, Arizona 86001; (928) 774–5211, ext. 209 or 220; www.musnaz.org.

Northern Arizona Shuttle and Tours, Inc. Shuttles to the Phoenix airport and the Grand Canyon. Tours to surrounding attractions around Flagstaff can also be arranged. Information: Northern Arizona Shuttle and Tours, Inc., 1300 South Milton Road, Suite 117, Flagstaff, Arizona 86001; (928) 773–4337 or (866) 870–8687; www.nazshuttle.com.

Open Road Tours, Inc. This company offers full-day tours to nearby sights, including the Grand Canyon or Grand Canyon Railway Depot, Williams, Monument Valley, and the Meteor Crater. Also shuttles to the Phoenix Airport. Information: Open Road Tours, Inc., 1 East Route 66, Flagstaff, Arizona 86001; (800) 766–7117.

Canyoneers, Inc. This major whitewater rafting concern offers a variety of trips on the Colorado River through the Grand Canyon; (928) 526–0924 or (800) 525–0924; www.canyoneers.com.

Arizona Raft Adventures. This enterprise also arranges Colorado River and other Arizona river trips. Information: Arizona Raft Adventures, 4050 East Huntington Drive, Flagstaff, Arizona 86004; (928) 526–8246; www.thecanyon.com/azra.

Absolute Bikes. Mountain bike rentals can be arranged here. Information: Absolute Bikes, 18 North San Francisco Street, Flagstaff, Arizona 86001; (928) 779–5969.

Vertical Relief Rock Gym. Indoor rock climbing–sport climbing is provided at this facility located at 205 South San Francisco Street, Flagstaff, Arizona 86001; (928) 556–9909; www.verticalrelief.com.

Flagstaff Urban Trails System. Hike, bike, or jog through quiet and scenic Rio de Flag, just a few seconds from the hustle and bustle of the summer tourist scene. Parking located on the south side of town off Leary Street. For further information call Flagstaff Parks and Recreation Office at (928) 779–7690. A recommended trailhead for mountain bikers begins in Buffalo Park off Cedar Avenue; www.flagstaff.az.gov.

Elden Pueblo. Near Mount Elden, just minutes from downtown

View of Monument Valley from Goulding's Ranch

Flagstaff, is this rich archaeological site that has been under excavation for many years. Native American artifacts from this site date back more than 800 years. Information: Coconino National Forest Archeology Section, 2323 East Greenlaw Lane, Flagstaff, Arizona 86004; (928) 527–3475 or 527–8762; or the NAU Learning Center; (928) 523–8797.

Elden Hills Golf Course. Take exit 201 from I–40 east and follow the signs along Country Club Drive to this picturesque course at 2380 North Oakmont Drive, which is surrounded by pines and offers vistas of the mountains. Information and tee times: (928) 527–7999.

Flying Heart Ranch. Located 4.5 miles north of Flagstaff just off U.S. Highway 89. Guided, hourly, half-day, and full-day horseback trail rides in the Coconino National Forest through wildflower fields and to panoramic viewpoints. Information: (928) 526–2788.

Grand Canyon Mule Trips. One-day mule trips into Grand Canyon to Plateau Point or overnight mule trips to Phantom Ranch in the canyon bottom alongside the Colorado River are offered by this outfitter. Reserve well in advance; (928) 638–2401 or Xanterra Parks and Resorts Reservations (303) 297–2757.

Fairs, Festivals, and Events

The Northern Arizona Book Festival. This diverse gathering of acclaimed authors is usually held during the second week of April. The festival features readings, poetry slams, panel discussions, workshops, and book signings; (928) 774–9118; www.flagstaffcentral.com/bookfest.

The Coconino Center for the Arts Festival Schedule. The Coconino Center for the Arts on Fort Valley Road, under the aegis of Flagstaff Cultural Partners, is the venue for several interesting activities. Trappings of the American West, from the last week of May through the second week of June, showcases painting, sculpture, saddles, and other related western art and culture trappings. The Wool Festival and the Folk Festival take place in early June. Information: Coconino Center for the Arts, 2300 North Fort Valley Road (U.S. Highway 1880); (928) 774–8861; www.drycreekarts.com; or Flagstaff Cultural Partners; (928) 779–2300; www.culturalpartners.org.

Pine Country Pro Rodeo. This professional rodeo takes place the third weekend of June each year. It provides a lot of real western thrills. Located at Fort Tuthill County Park; (928) 526–9926 or (800) 842–7293.

The Heritage Program Enduring Creations Celebrating Colorado Plateau Artists. Sponsored by the Museum of Northern Arizona, this late spring and all-summer-long program kicks off in May with the weekend-long Marketplace sales and cultural events, outdoors in the museum's parking lot. The Festival of Hispanic Arts and Crafts (traditional and contemporary Hispanic woodcarving, tin work, etc.) is the last weekend in May, followed by the Hopi Show (pottery, weavings, baskets, and jewelry) around the Fourth of July, the Navajo Show (Navajo rugs, pottery, baskets, and jewelry) the last weekend in July/first weekend in August, the Zuni Show (fetishes, jewelry, and pottery) the first weekend in September, and the Annual Festival of Pai Arts the third week of September. Information: Museum of Northern Arizona, 3001 North Fort Valley Road (U.S. Highway 180), Flagstaff, Arizona 86001; (928) 774–5213; www.musnaz.org.

Heritage Days and the Fourth of July Celebration. Held the last weekend in June through the Fourth of July is this celebration of Flagstaff's history. Events include a parade, the Route 66 Car Show, the Pioneer Day Festival, and the Coconino County Horse Races at Fort Tuthill County Park; (928) 774–4505 or (800) 842–7293.

The Arizona Highland Celtic Festival. This event is a pan–Celtic celebration featuring athletic demonstrations, dancing, and music (much bagpiping); (800) 842–7293.

Flagstaff Summerfest. Held over the last weekend in July or the first weekend in August at Fort Tuthill County Park, this juried arts and crafts show selects more than 200 artists from the West to sell their art. In addition to food booths, there's a barn dance and country-and-western music; (480) 968–5353.

Annual Coconino County Fair. This annual event, held at the nearby Coconino County Fairgrounds, draws folks from all over this huge county for contests, competitions, and just plain fun. Usually held around Labor Day weekend in early September (928–774–5139).

Flagstaff Winterfest. This festival in the month of February features more than one hundred events, including sled dog races; Nordic, alpine, and snowboarding events; concerts; historic walks through town; and more; (928) 774–4505 or (800) 842–7293.

Theatrikos. For theatergoers this community theater group regularly serves up productions featuring comedy, history, satire, and drama at the downtown Flagstaff Playhouse, 11 West Cherry; (928) 774–1662; www.theatrikos.com.

Shopping

Museum of Northern Arizona Gift Shop. 3101 North Fort Valley Road; (928) 774–5211, ext. 208 or (928) 779–1703. This shop is known for purchasing the best southwestern Indian arts and handcrafted work available. You will find many unique items here. Although beautiful craftwork from other tribes is available, the shop's extensive selection of Navajo, Hopi, and Zuni jewelry; Hopi pottery and kachina dolls; Navajo rugs; and Hopi weavings is exceptional. The gift shop's reputation is impeccable, so you can be certain that what you buy is the real thing. The museum also has a **bookstore** with a large selection of regional books and periodicals for sale, including current and back issues of the museum's own outstanding magazine published in conjunction with nearby National Parks, *Plateau Journal: Land and Peoples of the Colorado Plateau.* The museum is on Arizona Highway 180 just 3 miles north of Flagstaff city center, among the ponderosa pines.

The Old Main Art Gallery. An eclectic selection of contemporary fine art (including ceramic, sculpture, and glass) by regional artists can be viewed at this gallery on the Northern Arizona University campus at the corner of Knowles and McMullen Circle. Rotating exhibits; (928) 523–3471; www.nau.edu/artgallery.

Art Barn. Housed in a building adjacent to the Coconino Center for the Arts is this large arts and crafts shop with a bronze foundry located on the premises. This art emporium has a little bit of everything, from sculpture and wall art (depicting scenes and themes of the region), Indian crafts, and jewelry to contemporary pottery and crafts from the Flagstaff area; (928) 774–0822.

The Artists' Gallery. 17 North San Francisco Street; (928) 773–0958. More than forty local artists, some associated with Northern Arizona University, are represented in this fine arts and crafts cooperative. Wall art, ceramics, glass, and pottery.

Old Town Gallery. 2 West Route 66; (928) 774–7770. Located downtown, this gallery features a wide variety of fine American Indian wall art, sculpture, Mata Ortiz pottery, and jewelry; www.flagstaff.az.us/otg.

Puchteca Indian Gallery. 20 North San Francisco; (928) 774–2414. This downtown gallery stocks a good selection of handwoven Navajo rugs, pottery, and jewelry from around the Four Corners area.

Winter Sun American Indian Art. 107 North San Francisco Street; (928) 774–2884. This shop fills a small downtown space with American Indian teas, herbs of many kinds, pottery, kachinas, and other Native American art.

Babbitt's Backcountry Outfitters. Located on the corner of San Francisco Street and Aspen Avenue (928–774–4775) is this outstanding purveyor of outdoor climbing, camping, and hiking clothing and equipment. High quality, latest technology.

Babbitt's. 15 East Aspen Avenue; (928) 779–3253. A specialty shop for the fly fisher that provides all the essentials to hook a big one and stocks clothing and gifts as well.

Telephone Numbers

Flagstaff Visitors Center. 1 East Route 66. (928) 774–9541 or (800) 842–7293; fax (928) 556–1308; www.flagstaff.az.us.

Flagstaff Public Transit. (928) 779–6624 #1.

Amtrak. (928) 774–8679 or (800) USA–RAIL.

American West Airline. (800) 235–9292.

Sun Taxi Service. (928) 774–7400 or 779–1111.

Budget Rent-a-Car. (928) 213–0156, 779–5235 or (800) 227–3678.

Enterprise Rent-a-Car. (928) 774–9407 or 526–1377.

Hertz Rent-a-Car. (928) 774–4452 or (800) 654–3131.

National Car Rental. (928) 774–3321 or 779–1975.

Northern Arizona University. (928) 523–9011 or 523–1628; www.nau.edu.

Municipal swimming pool. (928) 779–7690.

Elden Hills Golf Course. (928) 527–7999.

Coconino National Forest. 2323 East Greenlaw Lane; (928) 527–3600 or 527–3491.

Arizona Snowbowl and X-Country Flagstaff Nordic (ski) Center. (928) 779–1951; www.arizonasnowbowl.com.

Weather conditions. (928) 774–3301.

Road conditions. (928) 779–2711.

Snow report. (928) 779–4577.

Monument Valley
Lodging and Food
Goulding's Lodge and Tours. Goulding's is the only accommodation in the valley and just a few minutes away from the monument's entrance. It is situated directly beneath soaring 800-foot red sandstone cliffs and offers panoramic views out over the valley and its many monoliths. The older ranch building is now a museum, and the sixty-plus air-conditioned lodging units are in typical motel style.

All three meals can be taken in a dining room that also offers fine vistas. The menu offers everything from Navajo tacos to steaks. The dining room is often closed January and February; limited hours December. Alcoholic beverages cannot be sold on the Navajo reservation. Curio and craft store. Heated indoor swimming pool. Tours to Monument Valley. A convenience store with gas pumps, a Laundromat, and a car wash just down the hill from the motel units. In the summer the ranch, which is in Utah, is on mountain daylight time (as is all of the Navajo reservation), while Arizona, immediately to the south of the Navajo reservation, is on mountain standard time. Information: Goulding's Lodge and Tours, Box 360001, Monument Valley, Utah

Goulding's Lodge, Monument Valley

84536; (435) 727–3231; fax (435) 727–3344; www.gouldings.com. Expensive.

Hampton Inn of Kayenta. This three-story motel located in Kayenta, Arizona, on U.S. Highway 160 has seventy-three rooms with Southwest furnishings. The lobby and dining room also use the Southwest motif and are warm and inviting public spaces. The dining room offers several Navajo specialties alongside traditional American and Southwest fare. There's a heated outdoor pool, a large gift shop, and an adjacent 2.5-acre Navajo Cultural Center. The Navajo code talkers exhibit is at the Burger King next door. Information: Hampton Inn of Kayenta, P.O. Box 1217, Kayenta, Arizona 86033; (928) 697–3170; (800) HAMPTON; fax (928) 697–3189. Moderate.

Holiday Inn—Monument Valley. Located in Kayenta, Arizona, at the junction of U.S. Highway 160 and 163, 24 miles from the entrance to the Monument Valley visitor center, this two-story motel with 160 rooms offers more beds than any other motel in the region. All rooms nicely furnished and air-conditioned; some with views and a few with two bedrooms. The bustling lobby of this motel (which fills rapidly during the tourist season) accesses the gift shop and the spacious, airy dining room done Southwest style. There Navajo waitstaff serve up for lunch and dinner, the best assortment of traditional Navajo dishes in the area (Navajo taco, Navajo lamb stew, fry bread, etc.). Still, standard American dishes prevail. Breakfast. Heated outdoor pool and wading pool. Coin laundry. Information: Holiday Inn—Monument Valley, P.O. Box 307, Kayenta, Arizona 86033; (928) 697–3221; fax (928) 697–3349. Moderate.

The San Juan Inn. Located 25 miles northeast of the Monument Valley visitor center on U.S. Highway 163. This older budget-option motel is dramatically situated along the banks of the San Juan River. It has thirty-six air-conditioned rooms (five two-bedroom units) with TVs and an adjacent restaurant. Information: San Juan Inn, Box 535, Mexican Hat, Utah 84531; (435) 683–2220 or (800) 447–2022; fax (435) 683–2210. Inexpensive.

Desert Rose Inn. Located on the south side of Bluff, Utah, 42 miles from Monument Valley, this is a handsome two-story, thirty-six room inn that has log beams and gallery porches and several detached log cabins nearby. Each room is handsomely furnished in Southwest style with all the amenities, including satellite TV, and data ports, plus each has a view of the surrounding red rock country. Hot tub. Conference facility. Information: Desert Rose Inn, 701 West Highway 191; (435) 672–2303 or (888) 475–7673; fax (435) 672–2217; www.DesertRoseInn.com. Breakfast and lunch can be taken at the **Twin Rocks Cafe and Trading Post** on East Navajo Twins Drive (435–672–2341), while dinner can be enjoyed in a pleasant setting nearby at the **Cow Canyon Restaurant and Trading Post** where the menu offers up tantalizing southwestern dishes. Cow Canyon Restaurant is open from April 1 through November 30, closed Tuesday and Wednesday. Reservations advised; (435) 672–2208. Inexpensive to moderate.

Campgrounds

Mitten View Campground.
Located 0.25 mile southwest of the Monument Valley Tribal Park visitor center. Inquire at visitor center. Space available on a first-come, first-served basis for the one hundred tent and recreational vehicle units. Fee. But groups of ten or more can make reservations; (435) 727–3287 or (435) 727–3353.

Goulding's Monument Valley Good Sampark Campground.
Located a short distance west of Goulding's Lodge in scenic Rock Door Canyon with fine panoramas of Monument Valley. Fifty sites with full hookups available. Rest rooms. Showers. Convenience store and gas pumps nearby. Heated indoor pool. Open March 15 to October 15; (435) 727–3231.

Tours

Crawley's Navajo Nation Tours.
Offers custom four-by-four tours of Monument Valley and surrounding sites as well as overnight camping jeep safaris. Information: Crawley's Navajo Nation Tours, Box 187, Kayenta, Arizona 86033; (928) 697–3463; fax (928) 697–3734.

Goulding's Lodge and Tours.
Goulding's offers half-day tours to Monument Valley and full-day tours to Monument Valley and Mystery Valley in a variety of four-wheel-drive vehicles. Tours operate only if minimum numbers of adult passengers are reached. Tours for children are near half the adult price. Advance reservations are recommended but are not essential if space is available. Information: Goulding's Lodge and Tours, Box 360001, Monument Valley, Utah 84536; (435) 727–3231.

Roland's Navajoland Tours.
Take a two- or three-hour, full-day, or even an overnight tour to Monument Valley sights in open-air four-by-four vehicles. No passenger minimums required. Information: Roland's Navajoland Tours, P.O. Box 1542, Kayenta, Arizona 86033; (928) 697–3524; fax (928) 697–3374.

Shopping

Oljato Trading Post and Museum.
This post in a remote area just a short drive northwest of Goulding's is on the National Register of Historic Places and continues the fine tradition of trading with Navajo on the reservation. A selection of Navajo rugs, baskets, pottery, and jewelry as

well as grocery supplies. Information: Evelyn Yazzie Jensen, P.O. Box 360416, Monument Valley, Utah 84536; (435) 727–3210; www. a-aa.com/monumentvalley.

Navajo Arts and Crafts Enterprise. Located in Kayenta, Arizona, near the junction of U.S. Highways 160 and 168, this Navajo Nation–operated craft store sells smaller affordable Navajo rugs and has a good selection of Navajo jewelry. Yarn and other weaving supplies for local Navajo weavers are sold here. Information: Navajo Arts and Crafts Enterprise, Kayenta, Arizona 86033; (928) 697–8611; fax (928) 697–3369.

Twin Rocks Trading Post. Located 42 miles northeast of Monument Valley in Bluff, Utah. This Southwest American Indian post carries one of the best selections in and around Monument Valley of Navajo rugs, baskets, jewelry, and other Native American art forms. Worth the trip. Information: Twin Rocks Trading Post, Box 330, Bluff, Utah 84512; (435) 672–2341 or (800) 526–3448; www.twinrocks.com.

Cow Canyon Trading Post. In Bluff, Utah, just off Highway 163. One gallery space holds fine art photographs; in another you'll find the best in Zuni Indian fetishes and pottery plus many fine contemporary Southwest Indian art forms, including Navajo pottery. Worth a visit. Information: Cow Canyon Trading Post, P. O. Box 88, Bluff, Utah 84512; (435) 672–2208; www.zunifetishes.com.

Betatakin (Navajo National Monument)

Campgrounds

Navajo National Monument Campground. Located amid piñons and junipers near the Betatakin visitor center at a cool elevation of 7,286 feet are thirty tent and recreational vehicle sites without showers and hookups. First-come, first-served system. Open year-round, weather and funds permitting. No fee; (928) 672–2366.

Tours

See this chapter's earlier "Seeing Indian Country" section, "Navajo National Monument: Betatakin."

Tuba City and Cameron, Arizona

Lodging and Food

Quality Inn Tuba City. Located in an enviable part of Tuba City just behind the Tuba Trading Post is this modern two-story motel that offers more comfort than you could ever imagine in the western capital of the Navajo Nation. There are eighty air-conditioned rooms, all with queen beds and TVs. Hogan Restaurant adjacent. Information: Quality Inn Tuba City, Box 247, Tuba City, Arizona 86045; (928) 283–4545. Moderate.

Hogan Restaurant. Conveniently located between the historic Tuba Trading Post and the Quality Inn, this restaurant serves from a modern air-conditioned building somewhat reminiscent of a large hogan. The food is basic American, with some Mexican and southwestern regional dishes with a Navajo twist. Takeout available; (928) 283–5260. Moderate.

Tuba City Truck Stop Cafe. This modest little place down on the highway near the junction of U.S. Highway 160 and Arizona Highway 264 with a view east toward the Hopi village Moenkopi serves up the best Navajo taco around; (928) 283–4975. Inexpensive.

Cameron Trading Post, Motel, and R.V. Sites. In a scenic location in view of the Little Colorado River, this historic complex of buildings is a welcome haven. One large sandstone building houses a wide selection of both good-quality and curio Indian arts and crafts, a convenience/general store with everything from animal crackers to galvanized buckets, and a restaurant. Open for breakfast, lunch, and dinner. The Navajo tacos are legendary here. Traditional American and Mexican favorites as well. Nearby the **Cameron Trading Post Collector's Gallery** offers the best of museum-quality new and old Navajo rugs, jewelry, Pueblo pottery, etc. The motel, close to the river, has sixty-plus units. Many of the second-story units have views. The rooms are decorated and modern in all respects. Four units have kitchen facilities. Information: Cameron Trading Post and Motel, P.O. Box 339, Cameron, Arizona 86020; (928) 679–2231 or (877) 221–0690. Moderate.

Fairs, Festivals, and Events

Western Navajo Nation Fair. Tuba City, Arizona. The western Navajo community hosts this large fair, similar to the other tribal fairs, on the second or third weekend in October; (928) 283–3285.

Shopping

Tuba Trading Post. Located 1 mile west off U.S. Highway 160. Navajo rugs, Navajo jewelry and pottery, southwestern Indian baskets, Pueblo Indian pottery, and kachinas are all available, as is cold soda pop. Information: Tuba Trading Post, P.O. Box 237, Tuba City, Arizona 86045; (928) 283–5441.

The Hopi Reservation

Lodging and Food

If the Hopi Cultural Center Motel (following) is full, the best alternative lodging choice is to drive either 65 miles south via Arizona Highway 87 to Winslow, Arizona, to stay at La Posada Hotel, a unique gem of a place (see Flagstaff Staying There, "Lodging") or drive 55 miles west on Arizona Highway 264 to Tuba City, Arizona, to the Quality Inn (see Tuba City Staying There, "Lodging and Food.")

Hopi Cultural Center Motel and Restaurant. If you plan to explore the Hopi mesas and villages, you may want to stay here, the only accommodation on the Hopi mesas. The Hopi, with the help of Arizona architect Ben Gonzales, erected this interesting complex of buildings, which evokes the ancient Hopi architectural style in a modern way. From the exposed second-story porches, you can see forever out over the high desert, while in the enclosed courtyard you feel a sense of the protection and comfort

Hopi Cultural Center Motel and Restaurant, Second Mesa

offered by the village plazas. Over the years the motel has periodically lapsed into disrepair, followed by rejuvenation efforts that bring it back to or above par. Even at their worst, when the rooms get to the well-worn stage, they are usually clean and comfortable enough. You may want to look at your assigned rooms before checking in.

The restaurant offers friendly service in a very pleasant, usually well-maintained dining room. The Hopi waitresses serve food that is Hopi-American, making the *tunosvongya,* or menu, interesting. Be sure to try items such as the *posole,* fry bread, and special lamb stew, as well as the blue cornflakes and the *sa kwa vi ka viki,* or blue cornmeal pancakes.

The adjacent **museum** (fee) is informative; (928) 734–6650. It tells the history of the Hopi people and displays some of the traditional crafts. In the summer the cultural center and the Hopi reservation are on mountain standard time rather than mountain daylight time. Reserve well ahead of time, especially on weekends. Children age twelve or younger stay for free with their parents. Information: Hopi Cultural Center Motel, P.O. Box 67, Second Mesa, Arizona 86043; (928) 734–2401; www.hopionline.com. Moderate.

Campgrounds

There is a modest campground adjacent to and operated by the Hopi Cultural Center and Motel as well as another campground, tribally operated, at Kykotsmovi. Inquire at the Keams Canyon Shopping Center about directions to several picnic areas located in the canyon there.

Fairs, Festivals, and Events

(For information about the Hopi ceremonial and social dances, please refer to the text at the beginning of "Staying There.")

Tours

(See "Flagstaff: Tours and Activities," this section.)

Shopping

Monongya Gallery. Situated in view of Arizona Highway 264 on Third Mesa just west of the turnoff to Old Oraibi. This excellent shop has carefully selected Hopi pottery, kachina dolls, and jewelry. Information: Monongya Gallery, P.O. Box 287, Old Oraibi, Arizona 86039; (928) 734–2344 or (928) 734–2544.

The Hopi Arts and Crafts Silvercraft Cooperative Guild. Located just west of the Hopi Cultural Center and Motel. This shop carries a selection of Hopi overlay jewelry, Hopi pottery, baskets, rattles, and kachina dolls. Information: Hopi Arts and Crafts Silvercraft Cooperative Guild, P.O. Box 37, Second Mesa, Arizona 86043; (928) 734–2463.

McGees Indian Art Gallery. Located just west of Keams Canyon on Arizona Highway 264 in the Keams Canyon Shopping Center complex. This very reliable, fairly priced shop carries a wide selection of Hopi, Navajo, Ácoma, Zuni, and other handcrafts from the Southwest. Ask to see the museum-quality Indian arts gallery. It is a good place to see some of the best of what is available in Indian jewelry, pottery, and especially kachina dolls. Good regional book and card selection. Information: McGees Indian Art Gallery, Box 607, Highway 264, Keams Canyon, Arizona 86034; (928) 738–2295; www.hopiart.com.

Telephone Numbers

Hopi Tribal Switchboard. (928) 734–3000.

Hogan, Canyon de Chelly

Hopi Office of Public Relations. (928) 734–3283; www.hopi.nsn.us.

Hopi Cultural Preservation Office. (928) 734-6636 or 734–2113.

Hopi Cultural Center Museum. (928) 734–6650.

Hopi Cultural Center Motel. (928) 734–2401.

Museum of Northern Arizona. (928) 774–5213.

Hopi Village Community Development Offices (for visiting status, dance information, and so on): **Bacavi office:** (928) 734–9360; **First Mesa office:** (928) 737-2670; **Hotevilla office:** (928) 734–2420; **Kykotsmovi office:** (928) 734–2474; **Mishongnovi office:** (928) 737–2520; **Moenkopi office:** (928) 283–5212; **Shungopavi office:** (928) 737–7135; **Shipaulovi office:** (928) 737–2570.

Canyon de Chelly/Ganado

Lodging and Food

Thunderbird Lodge. This is the ideal base from which to explore the surrounding canyons and early Indian ruins. Located in a lovely spot near the mouth of the canyon, less than 0.5 mile down the road from the visitor center and near the campground. The lodge, with seventy air-conditioned rooms with TVs, is an oasis in a grove of cottonwood trees. The older motel units built from native stone in the 1920s circle a tree-filled, grassy courtyard. The atmosphere is peaceful, and the staff is friendly and helpful. The novel idea of a cafeteria-style restaurant is worthy of praise. Children will be delighted with the choices, which include some Navajo favorites, as well as excellent French toast for breakfast. The cafeteria is also open to the public, and many Navajo from the surrounding area come to eat here. It occupies the old (late 1800s) trading post. The walls of the handsome cafeteria dining room display a spectacular assortment of fine Navajo weavings (all for sale) and glass cases containing miniatures. The lodge owners and their staff are well informed about the area (see "Tours"). On several evenings each week in the summer, park rangers at the nearby campground give a series of talks about the Navajo culture. Information: Thunderbird Lodge, Box 548, Chinle, Arizona 86503; (928) 674–5841 or (800) 679–2473; fax (928) 674–5844. Moderate.

Holiday Inn Canyon De Chelly. Right along the entry road to the monument from Chinle, this Southwest-style, 106-unit, air-conditioned, full-service motel is within easy walking distance of the Canyon de Chelly visitor center. The management has thought of most everything here, providing a heated swimming pool, meeting rooms, a gift shop (Garcia Trading Post), and a spacious restaurant. Many rooms with two double beds. Information: Holiday Inn Canyon De Chelly, P.O. Box 1889, Chinle, Arizona 86503; (928) 674–5000 or (800) 234–6835; fax (928) 674–8264; www.basshotelsinn. com. Moderate.

Best Western Canyon De Chelly Inn. If the Thunderbird and Holiday Inn are full, as is often the case, you can try this standard one-hundred-room air-conditioned motel with TVs and telephones. It is located just out of Chinle 0.25 mile east of Arizona Highway 191 and only 3 miles from the visitor center and the canyon. The motel has a restaurant. Information: Best Western Canyon de Chelly Inn, Box 295, Chinle, Arizona 86503; (928) 674–5875 or (800) 327–0354; fax (928) 674–3715. Moderate.

Thunderbird Lodge

Campgrounds

Cottonwood Campground. This campground at Canyon de Chelly National Monument is superb. It is beautifully situated in the trees at the mouth of the canyon. There are picnic tables, nature trails, and nightly campfire programs presented by the park rangers. First-come, first-served arrangement for the ninety-six tent and recreational vehicle sites; (928) 674–5500.

Spider Rock RV and Camping Too. A Navajo-owned and -operated site 10 miles east of the visitor center on South Rim Drive. No hookups; (928) 674–8261.

Tours and Fairs

Central Navajo Fair. In late August Chinle is the site for a rodeo, carnival, and traditional dances; (928) 674–5664.

Thunderbird Tours. Navajo guides lead tours from Thunderbird Lodge in large, twenty-four-passenger, open-air four-wheel-drive vehicles through the bottom of the canyon year-round. There are opportunities to get close-up views of White House Ruin, Mummy Cave, Antelope House, and Navajo Fortress. Half-day (both morning and afternoon) and all-day tours are generally available. Information: Thunderbird Lodge, Box 548, Chinle, Arizona 86503; (928) 674–5841.

Other tours. You may hike or drive your own four-wheel-drive vehicle into the canyon if you are accompanied by an authorized guide provided by the information desk at the visitor center (928–674–5500). Formal inter-pretive morning and afternoon hikes offered by the Tsegi Guide Association can also be arranged at the visitor center as can Canyon Hiking Service (928–674–1767) hiking tours and night walks (located 0.25 mile north of Thunderbird Lodge). De Chelly Tours (928–674–5433 or 674–3772) offer Unimog group and photography jaunts and overnight camping tours. There are fees for all guide services. You may also enter the canyon by horseback. Hourly, half-day, day-long, and more extensive overnight horseback trips are available. Arrangements can be made at the visitor center or with one of the approved concessionaires, such as Justin's Horse Rental and Canyon Tours (928–674–5678), or Totsonil Ranch Tours (928–755–6209).

Hubbell Trading Post National Historic Site. This historic but still active trading post is located 35 miles south of Chinle just outside of Ganado, Arizona. Daily tours of Hubbell's home, lasting about thirty minutes, are free of charge and offered several times throughout the day. There you will see paintings of some of Hubbell's rug designs, which Hubbell displayed inside the post as models to guide the Navajo weavers. In addition, there is almost always something interesting happening at the visitor center, which is in the small building to the right as you drive up to the post. Often Navajo weavers or other craftspeople will be at work demonstrating their considerable expertise. Information: Hubbell Trading Post, Box 150, Ganado, Arizona 86505; (928) 755–3475; www.nps.gov/hutr.

Shopping

Thunderbird Lodge Rug Room and Craft Shop. Located next door to the cafeteria. This shop features a wide selection of Navajo and other Indian jewelry, crafts, and curios. A separate rug room features a variety of styles of Navajo rugs. Information: Thunderbird Lodge, Box 548, Chinle, Arizona 86503; (928) 674–5841.

Hubbell Trading Post. Hubbell offers one of the consistently best selections of handwoven Navajo rugs and Navajo jewelry in the Southwest. The quality control is excellent, which means that Bill Malone, the trader here, really knows what he is doing. The large rug room holds just about every type of Navajo rug, ranging from less expensive saddle and half-saddle rugs to both new and old museum-quality rugs and tapestries. If you want to invest in a Navajo rug but know little about the subject, this is definitely a safe place to buy. You can trust the dealer's judgment. The post also has one of the best selections of Navajo piñon pitch-glazed pottery available, as well as a nice selection of Navajo sashes. Information: Hubbell Trading Post, Box 388, Ganado, Arizona 86505; (928) 755–3254.

Window Rock, Arizona

Lodging and Food

Navajo Nation Inn. If you need a place to stay on the east side of the Navajo reservation, try the tribally owned Navajo Nation Motor Inn. Modern in appearance, it has fifty-six air-conditioned units. Heated swimming pool. Cafe on premises (with Navajo specialties spread throughout the menu) and several fast-food cafes nearby. Information: Navajo Nation Inn, P.O. 2340, Window Rock, Arizona 86515; (928) 871–4108 or (800) 662–6189; fax (928) 871–5466. Inexpensive.

Fairs, Festivals, and Events

Annual Navajo Nation Fair. After the July Fourth celebration (dance, powwow, rodeo, and fireworks) comes this celebration held in early September. The Navajo Queen is selected, and ceremonial dances are performed. Both weaving and silversmithing are demonstrated, and those crafts are for sale. Information: Navajo Nation Parks and Recreation, P.O. Box 9000, Window Rock, Arizona 86515; (928) 871–6478; www.navajonation. parks.org.

Shopping

Navajo Arts and Crafts Enterprise. Located just beyond the northeast corner of Window Rock's main junction (intersection of Arizona State Highway 264 and Navajo Route 12) is this very large, tribally owned Navajo crafts shop. You will find Navajo rugs and an extensive selection of Navajo jewelry. At times you may find pine pitch-covered Navajo baskets and piñon pitch-glazed Navajo pots. In addition, the shop handles a variety of posters, cards, and books. Information: Navajo Arts and Crafts Enterprise, P.O. Drawer A, Window Rock, Arizona 86515; (928) 871–4090.

Navajo Museum, Library, and Visitors Center. Just off Arizona Highway 264 east of the Navajo Nation

Inn in a large modern building reminiscent of a giant hogan is this museum center and library, which specializes in the history of the Navajo. Indoor and outdoor performance areas; arts and crafts, book and gift shop, library; and a snack bar. Nearby is the Navajo Nation Zoo. Information: P.O. Box 1840, Window Rock, Arizona 86515; (928) 871–7941.

Telephone Numbers

Navajoland Tourism Department, P.O. Box 663, Window Rock, Arizona 86515. (928) 871–6436 or (928) 871–7371; fax (928) 871–7381; www.discovernavajo.com.

Navajo Parks and Recreation, P.O. Box 9000, Window Rock, Arizona 86515; (928) 871–6647; www.navajonationparks.org.

Gallup, New Mexico

Lodging and Food

El Rancho Hotel and Motel. If you're heading southeast from Window Rock and need a place to stay, the historic El Rancho Hotel and Motel (exit 22 from I–40) along old Route 66 in Gallup, New Mexico, is a treat. Built in 1937, it soon became a resting place for the Hollywood stars making movies in the area. The two-story lobby with its 1930s-style Southwest decor and a mezzanine whose walls are filled with movie memorabilia and art is stunning. Most of the ninety-eight air-conditioned rooms are smallish, not luxurious by today's standards yet surprisingly comfortable. But the charm is big, with many rooms carrying the name of a famous studio personality. Book a room in the old hotel portion, not the motel addition. The pleasant El Rancho restaurant is open for breakfast, lunch, and dinner. High-quality Navajo art on the wall is for sale. The adjacent Gallery of Arts sells the full range of Indian arts and crafts. Information: El Rancho Hotel and Motel, 1000 East Sixty-sixth Avenue, Gallup, New Mexico 87301; (505) 863–9311 or (800) 543–6351. Inexpensive.

Fairs, Festivals, and Events

Annual Intertribal Indian Ceremonial. Red Rock State Park, Gallup, New Mexico. This world's fair of the American Indian world is held for four days, including the second weekend in August. In addition to the sale of Indian arts and crafts, there are Indian dances, parades, and rodeos. Information: Gallup Intertribal Indian Ceremonial, 226 West Coal Avenue, Gallup, New Mexico 87311; (505) 863–3896 or (800) 233–4528.

Shiprock, New Mexico

Shopping

Foutz Trading Company. (505) 368–5790.

Shiprock Trading Company. (505) 368–4585.

Fairs, Festivals, and Events

Northern Navajo Nation Fair. Shiprock, New Mexico. Held in early October, this three-day event includes a rodeo and dancing; (505) 368–1081.

- THREE -
SOUTHWESTERN COLORADO
AND
NORTHWESTERN NEW MEXICO

Rocky Mountain Frontier Country

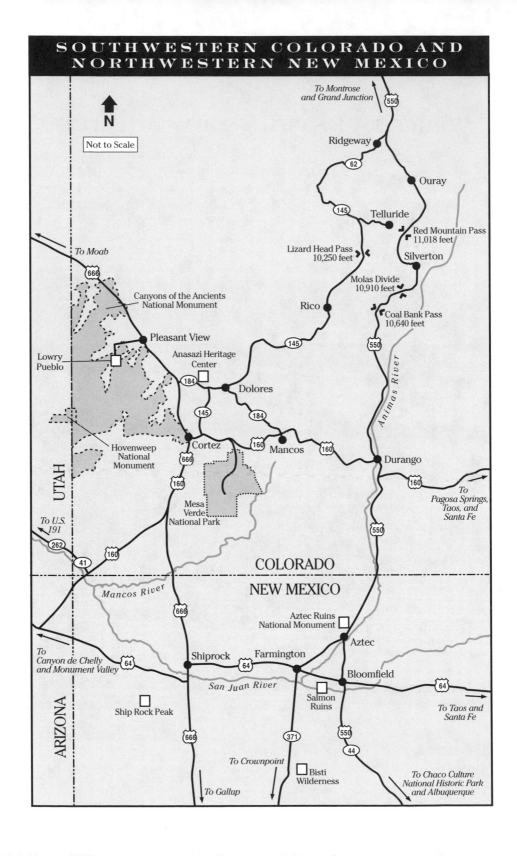

SOUTHWESTERN COLORADO AND NORTHWESTERN NEW MEXICO

N

Not to Scale

To Montrose and Grand Junction

550

Ridgeway

62

Ouray

145

Telluride

Red Mountain Pass 11,018 feet

Lizard Head Pass 10,250 feet

Silverton

Molas Divide 10,910 feet

To Moab

666

Canyons of the Ancients National Monument

Rico

145

Coal Bank Pass 10,640 feet

Pleasant View

Lowry Pueblo

Anasazi Heritage Center

184

550

Animas River

Dolores

145

184

Hovenweep National Monument

Cortez

666

160

Mancos

160

Durango

160

To Pagosa Springs, Taos, and Santa Fe

UTAH

Mesa Verde National Park

To U.S. 191

262

41

160

666

550

COLORADO

NEW MEXICO

Mancos River

Aztec Ruins National Monument

To Canyon de Chelly and Monument Valley

64

Shiprock

64

Farmington

Aztec

Bloomfield

64

San Juan River

To Taos and Santa Fe

ARIZONA

Ship Rock Peak

666

Salmon Ruins

371

550

44

To Crownpoint

Bisti Wilderness

To Chaco Culture National Historic Park and Albuquerque

To Gallup

INTRODUCTION

If it is a taste of the wild and woolly West you want, head straight to southwestern Colorado. There in that mountainous, historically rich quarter-slice of the Four Corners treat, you will see ghosts of the area's colorful past at every turn and will experience as pure a culture of western ambience as you will find anywhere in the United States. That ambience stems from a long history of western frontier traditions forged in the fiery hell-bent-to-leather years between the end of the Civil War in 1865 and the turn of the century. Those colorful but tumultuous years had their beginning when news of the mineral-rich **San Juan Mountains** spread like wildfire across the country, igniting an unprecedented stampede of fortune seekers to southwestern Colorado.

Those early prospectors, dropping out from all walks of life, came from everywhere imaginable, their carefully concealed life savings staked on their hopes and dreams of striking it rich. These robust men were not the least bit shy about their motives. Along the way west to Colorado, they spread the word, talking so openly and excitedly about where they were going and why that you would have thought they had been hired by a chamber of commerce or some New York advertising agency. Those who traveled in covered wagons must have thought of their wagon covers as canvases, stretched and ready to paint. For with crude brushes they daubed on those semicircular mobile billboards, in large, bold letters for all to see, the slogan "San Juan or Bust."

Even now the San Juan Mountains continue to excite and tantalize modern-day fortune seekers. Whenever gold and silver prices shoot up, parking spaces along the wide streets of southwestern Colorado's towns fill with a variety of four-wheel-drive vehicles, as merchants do a land office business selling gold pans and other prospecting paraphernalia. Local property owners pull their hair as scores of strangers and out-of-staters stomp across their land searching for gold, trying to hit pay dirt in "them thar hills and streams."

But in recent years most commercial mines have closed due to low metal prices. Should prices ever again go through the roof in this cyclic boom-bust business, local miners may once again pick up their hard hats and go to work. Even around Farmington, New Mexico, just to the south, where "black gold" and natural gas led to cyclic booms for a number of decades (more than 11,000 oil and gas wells were spudded and completed in the area), the emphasis is off the oil patch and back to a more steady economy based on agriculture and mining as it seeks industrial development and nurtures a budding tourism industry.

But you will still see part of southwestern Colorado's lively past in the scores of old mining shafts, fallen-down shaft houses, mining trams, and pyramidal heaps of mine "garbage," or *tailings,* that dot the mountainsides. Many of these mining ghosts, perched on the cliffsides in some of the most remote and inaccessible locations imaginable, can be viewed from modern highways that follow the routes of the narrow old mining roads of yesteryear, blasted mile by arduous mile out of solid rock. Be thankful that a few inches of smooth-as-silk asphalt separate you from those narrow dusty trails of the 1880s that were so rough and rutted that they snapped axles like matchsticks and shredded prospectors' tough leather boots like they were paper. And when they were wet, stretches of those old roads were so boggy that men, pack animals, and stagecoaches sank ankle- and axle-deep in oozing mud.

But the highway is not the only place you will come face-to-face with southwestern Colorado's exciting history. You will also meet its past if you travel on the **narrow-gauge steam train** that has huffed and puffed its way from Durango to Silverton since the 1880s. It got its start in 1882 when, after months of back-breaking, death-defying labor, the rails were finally laid over some of the North American continent's roughest terrain. The past also lives on in many of the buildings you will see and hotels and saloons you may visit in the old boomtowns, which were built when this was the rough-and-ready Wild West. Those were the days when, it is said, one hundred men were killed almost every month by either stray or intended bullets. That was when lynching sprees followed on the heels of hastily organized vigilante groups and when desperadoes like Butch Cassidy and lawmen like Bat Masterson walked the very same streets you will be exploring.

Memories of the past are even closer at hand when you stay in some of the old hotels and inns. Relics of the boom days of the 1880s and 1890s, they still offer comfortable lodging for tourists who are prospecting for memories of the Old West. And as you drive along from town to town, you will catch glimpses of working "cowboys" in the lower valleys carrying out their cowpunching activities just as their fathers and grandfathers did before them. In the small towns, you will see many of the local citizens wearing cowboy hats and boots purchased in stores that were selling those duds long before it was fashionable to dress like a cowboy. These citizens, from all walks of life, are modern western Americans whose broad smiles and spontaneous "howdy"s and "hi"s are part of a western tradition of openness that reflects the wide valleys and broad vistas you will see at every turn.

In spite of the honest-to-goodness authentic past of this area, much has been refurbished and embellished in the past decade to attract the tourist. Since the tourist "lode" was discovered around 1968, it has been mined with great enthusiasm. The same creative western ingenuity that saw the settlement of this area is now directed at the visitor. Much of the restoration is in very good taste. But the hokey, the cheap, and the claptrap have also crept in. Fortunately, for every curio place there are at least a dozen other genuine, rewarding experiences for the traveler.

The area is so beautiful and historically rich that it is easy to sort the wheat from the chaff. For this is no Disneyland! It is a land forged by the indomitable courage, patience, and hard work of the early settlers. For every road or trail blasted from the mountainsides, for every foot of railroad track laid, and for every mine dug, there were hundreds of men who lost their lives. Blinding snowstorms, avalanches, rockslides and crumbling rocky ledges, desperadoes, gamblers, stray or intended bullets, and high-altitude pneumonia all took their toll. Indeed, as many have noted, death was the sidekick of every man, woman, and child who sought fortunes and a new life in this mountainous western stronghold.

Yet when you pull into **Durango,** the area's largest town and tour base, to find heavy traffic at certain times of the day, crowded eating establishments, and already booked overnight accommodations, you may begin to wonder where the past is hiding. But you will not wonder too long, for soon you will begin to sense a certain frontier excitement in those "boom" tourist season months that, along with the genuine warmth and friendliness of the local people, offsets much of the commercial atmosphere.

Even though tourism is important to southwestern Colorado towns like Durango, they have a past that goes beyond today's throngs of summer visitors, a past whose economic base relied on the land: beef cattle, pinto beans, alfalfa. And on mining and the railway. Today during the quieter "off-season" months when most southwestern Colorado towns return to a more relaxed style of western life, the refreshing warmth and resourcefulness of their people are palpable.

Although the overwhelming cultural essence of this section is that of white western America, you may want to travel to this region to seek out another chapter in the history of America's first citizens. Before the explorer, before the prospector, miner, settler, and cowboy, the Indians, the **Ancestral Pueblo People** inhabited the lower mesas and river basins of southwestern Colorado and northwestern New Mexico. This dry land has helped preserve in a magnificent state of intactness the homes of those early inhabitants at **Mesa Verde,** Colorado, Pleasant View, Colorado **(the Lowry Pueblo in Canyons of the Ancients National Monument),** Aztec, New Mexico **(Aztec Ruins National Monument),** and the **Salmon Ruins** just outside of Bloomfield, New Mexico.

While this area is rich in remnants of the Indians' past culture, you will see little of their traditional way of life in southwestern Colorado today. You may catch a glimpse of a few Navajo from Arizona and New Mexico in traditional dress, as they bring goods to sell at one of the trading posts in Cortez or Farmington, but that is about it. The **Utes,** a once powerful group who proudly roamed this land after the Ancestral Puebloans but before the Spaniards, Mexicans, and Americans, were divided and placed on two small reservations removed from most of the major tourist traffic. For many years they lived a modern agrarian life, donning traditional dress only for special ceremonies a few times a year. But recently the Utes have been more visible to travelers through their casinos and commercial enterprises.

THE SETTING

The rich cultural heritage of southwestern Colorado has unfolded in a spectacular setting. From the Four Corners Monument at an elevation of 4,500 feet, the desolate, sparsely populated high desert of the Colorado Plateau gives way to rolling hills and rich farmlands in southwestern Colorado. This transition zone has been dubbed the "Pinto Bean Capital of the World" for its prodigious production of that southwestern American staple. From there the plateau continues to rise, even as numerous mesas and small plateaus arise from it. Then, through pine-clad foothills, the Colorado Plateau ascends to higher, lusher valleys—the Dolores, the Mancos, and the Animas, where cattle graze in pastures of rich, abundant grass. As it continues to ascend into the foothills, the Colorado Plateau comes to an abrupt halt. For there it meets the towering sheer walls of the Rocky Mountains, whose lofty peaks stand as great sentinels on the eastern edge of the plateau overlooking the high desert to the west for hundreds of miles. These mountains impart to southwestern Colorado its most unique physical characteristic. For to meet the Rockies there is to see them at their most majestic, rugged, bare-bones best.

Some have said that the mountains of southwestern Colorado, with their incredibly steep and weirdly eroded angular faces and with their wildly descending deep canyons, make the rest of Colorado's mountain country pale by comparison. The country is literally standing on its end with such an intense concentration of 12,000- to 14,000-foot peaks that the concept of "flat" has been squeezed right off the face of the earth. In the 600 to 700 square miles that constitute San Juan County, the flattest, widest spot is a small piece of land 1 mile wide and less than 2 miles long between the two old mining towns of Silverton and Eureka.

Technically speaking, the mountains you see around you are part of an unbelievable long and high rock outcropping resulting from three cataclysmic upheavals, the last one occurring just seventy-five million years ago. The Rockies extend from the Bering Sea in northwest Alaska to central New Mexico, dividing most of the North American continent into two watersheds. East of the line known as the Continental Divide, all rainfall and snowmelt courses its way to the Atlantic Ocean. West of that line nature's water eventually reaches the Pacific Ocean. At Silverton, Colorado, you will be only 5 miles west of the Great Divide. There you will see the Animas River as it courses southward to the San Juan River, which empties into the Colorado River, which flows on down to the Pacific Ocean's Gulf of California. A few paces east of that mountainous dividing ridge, the rains and snowstorms feed rivers such as the Rio Grande. It snakes its way along the Rio Grande Valley, skirting Santa Fe and passing Albuquerque as it courses on to El Paso, Texas. There it forms the border between the United States

Continental Divide

and Mexico, before emptying into the Atlantic Ocean's Gulf of Mexico.

The Rockies reach a show-stopping climax in Colorado, which boasts more than fifty peaks higher than 14,000 feet, culminating in the grandest of them all, Mount Elbert near Leadville, Colorado, which at 14,433 feet is the highest mountain in the whole Rocky Mountain chain. Not far from Mount Elbert, the Continental Divide makes a distinct turn to the southwest. There it enters southwestern Colorado, riding on the ridge tops and towering peaks of the San Juan range, which sweeps more than 100 miles from east to west and 70 miles from north to south. Its soaring, rugged peaks, like Uncompaghre Peak, Colorado's sixth highest at 14,309 feet, form a barrier that has delayed settlement and kept this region remote. Even today the only gateways from the east to southwestern Colorado's San Juan region are over mountain passes that top out at higher than 10,000 feet.

The San Juan range generally is thought to extend as far west as a line drawn between Durango and Ouray. Although many people refer to the mountains west of there as the "San Juans," they are actually parts of three separate ranges of magnificent proportions that nudge the eastern border of the Colorado Plateau and finger out westward onto the high desert. Southwest of Ouray, Colorado, around Telluride, are the San Miguel Mountains, boasting Mount Wilson at 14,246 feet and Diente Peak, which at 14,159 feet was the last of the 14,000-foot peaks in the Rockies to be scaled by climbers. To the south of there are the Rico and the La Plata Mountains.

Hesperus Peak, which looms above the La Platas, is one of the four sacred directional peaks of the Navajo. Its snowfields spawn rivers that flow many miles southward to the ancestral home of the Navajo in today's northwestern New Mexico. According to Navajo legend the La Plata range was fastened to the earth with a rainbow. Then "The People," as the Navajo call themselves, spread a blanket of darkness over the mountain and decorated it with obsidian. On a very clear

Aspen grove   *Blue columbine*

day, the La Platas are visible from as far distant as Boulder Mountain (Aquarius Plateau) near Capitol Reef National Park. This is a distance of more than 150 miles as the crow flies.

In addition to the human relics of bygone days, you will see an incredible array of flora as you ascend from one "life zone" to another. If you take the mountainous Silver Circle trip, along the San Juan Skyway from Durango through the old mining towns, you will ascend in this up-and-down land, in just a few miles, from 6,500 feet to more than 11,000 feet, passing through four life zones and possibly five if you do any day hiking from the road. Since temperature diminishes three degrees for each 1,000 feet of elevation gain and moisture increases proportionately at higher altitudes, the flowers and trees and other living things are different at various levels or zones of elevation.

In fact going up 1,000 feet is like driving north approximately 200 miles. So if you drive or hike high enough, you will see vegetation that resembles that found in the Arctic at sea level, more than 2,000 miles north. From the Four Corners Monument, one of the lower elevations in the High Southwest at 4,500 feet, to Red Mountain Pass, between Silverton and Ouray at 11,018 feet, you will travel through four life zones and be in easy view of the fifth one. From 4,500 feet to 6,500 feet near Durango, you will travel through the zone called the Upper Sonoran or Plains Zone. In addition to the piñons and junipers in this belt, you will also see willows and cottonwoods, as well as some cacti and yuccas. From 6,500 feet elevation to 8,000 feet, you will travel through the Foothills or Transition Life Zone into the ponderosa pine–Gambel oak belt, while from 8,000 feet elevation to 10,000 feet you will sometimes see in this Douglas fir–aspen belt called the Canadian Life Zone a few Colorado blue spruce, the Colorado state tree. But that tree is more common as you drive over the higher mountain passes into the spruce, subalpine fir belt, which occurs between 9,500 feet elevation and 11,500 feet.

Large trees like the Engelmann spruce thrive in this, the highest, coldest, windiest, and wettest zone in which trees will grow, where the rainfall may exceed 30 inches a year compared with 8 to 10 inches at lower elevations. Living at this elevation is similar to living in Canada's Hudson Bay area, ergo the Hudsonian Life Zone. From the high mountain passes, you will look up to see timberline beginning between 11,500 feet elevation and 12,000 feet, ascending to a point where the air is so rarified and dry, the winters so windy, cold, and severe, and the soil so rocky that larger, upright trees cannot grow there. Only tundra and low-lying mat-forming plants such as sedge and dwarf willow, similar to the vegetation found in the Arctic at sea level, survive there. Consequently timberline is sometimes called the Arctic Life Zone.

Spring breaks early near the Four Corners Monument, sometime around late February or early March. But similar signs of the sap's rising do not occur in the high mountains until June or later. There, in July or August, a splendid profusion of wildflowers can be seen, including the delicately beautiful Colorado state flower, the blue columbine. You may also observe red columbine, Indian paintbrush, alpine forget-me-nots, and dozens of other species in the wildflower meadows.

HISTORY

The first known people to leave a mark on southwestern Colorado were America's first and foremost masons and apartment builders, the Ancestral Puebloans. They occupied the deserts, river valleys, and mesas of this region for more than 1,000 years, building structures that have weathered the test of time. (Their history is well detailed in this book in Section 2.)

After the Ancestral Puebloans abandoned the area in the late 1200s or early 1300s, history's pages are blank. Sometime after they left but before the Spanish arrived, the Ute Indians inhabited much of this country. Seminomadic, they no doubt hunted in the higher mountains but made their camps at lower, warmer elevations. It is not known exactly when the Utes met up with the Spanish. But probably sometime in the 1700s, they acquired Spanish horses and from that time on distinguished themselves as aggressive warriors and raiders of the first rank. Doggedly they held onto their territory, frequently menacing the Spanish settlements in northern New Mexico. Rugged, hostile mountains, plus aggressive, hostile Utes, had a lot to do with the slow encroachment of white settlers into this region.

The ever-restless, ambitious Spanish were the first whites to visit southwestern Colorado as they sought gold, pelts, and Indian slaves. In 1765, under orders from the Spanish governor in Santa Fe, Juan María Antonio Rivera led a prospecting and trading party up the Dolores and Uncompaghre Rivers to the Gunnison River. Near the Dolores River in southwestern Colorado he found some insignificant silver-bearing rocks, and it is thought that it was he who named the mountains nearby the Sierra de la Plata, or the Silver Mountains. This expedition and others to follow left names on the land that are the only reminders we have today that the Spanish once explored this region.

Rivera found little of commercial value that would interest his superiors in Santa Fe. But he did open up a route that would soon lead to the establishment of the Old Spanish Trail (see Section 1, "History"). Some of the men in Rivera's party made additional trips into Colorado after 1765, leaving many other names on the land. In 1776 one of the men who had accompanied Rivera earlier, André Muñiz, acted as a guide for the Domínguez-Escalante expedition. That party entered southwestern Colorado in search of a route west to California, traveling near today's towns of Durango and Dolores. Along the way they camped at the base of a large green mesa that today carries the name Mesa Verde. They observed and were the first whites to record the discovery of an Ancestral Puebloan archaeological site in southwestern Colorado. That site, near Dolores, Colorado, is known today as the Domínguez and Escalante Pueblo Ruins and is the location of the excellent Anasazi Heritage Center (see "The Lowry Pueblo National Historic Landmark–Canyons of the Ancients National Monument: A Narrative Account").

Some of the names you will find on your map were dropped on the land during that expedition. When a member of Escalante's group injured his hand when he fell from his horse while fording a river, the Spanish explorers dubbed the river *mancos,* meaning "one-handed or crippled."

By the early 1800s American mountain men and trappers were exploring the area in their quest for beaver pelts. Men like Peg-leg Smith were outfitted with supplies in the crossroads trapping town of Taos, New Mexico. From there they would head west to Colorado's San Juan, Dolores, and San Miguel Rivers. These adventurous American trappers were a tough bunch. They, possibly more than any other whites, penetrated deeply into the mountain fastness of southwestern Colorado, bringing back invaluable information about the area and helping to find new routes through the mountains. One of the trappers, William Becknell, the "Father of the Santa Fe Trail," camped in the area of Mesa Verde, where he found pottery shards, stone houses, and other Ancestral Puebloan remains.

By the late 1820s a more direct route northwest from southwestern Colorado which crossed the Colorado River at Moab, had been discovered, leading to the opening of the Old Spanish Trail in 1830. The Ute Indians became very active in the expanding trade business, providing slaves to Mexican traders and often obstructing trade caravans, demanding payment for crossing their territory. It is also possible that a few prospectors found their way across this area in the 1840s, headed for the California gold rush. The next recorded visitor was Captain J. N. Macomb, who entered southwestern Colorado in 1859 with a United States government exploratory party.

Then when gold was discovered in 1859 and 1860 in eastern Colorado, fortune seekers headed west in large numbers. Learning from the Indians that there might be gold in the San Juan Mountains, Charles Baker, a veteran of the gold rush in eastern Colorado, led a prospecting party over the Continental Divide. The relatively flat valley they explored with the Animas River flowing through it became known as Baker's Park, site of today's Silverton, Colorado. Baker's dogged determination kept the group prospecting in spite of their meager findings. Finally in the fall of 1860, the discouraged group moved downstream to a site in the Animas Valley about 17 miles north of today's Durango. Although they found little gold there, they did build some of the first log cabins in southwestern Colorado. Disappointed and with mounting concerns about trespassing in Ute territory, they abandoned the site after a few months. They headed back to Fort Garland, Colorado, where they discovered that civil war had broken out. Baker left the area to enlist in the Confederate army. But the San Juan was still firmly entrenched in his mind as a region that would some day cough up millions.

When the war was over in 1865, Baker returned to the San Juan Mountains with several other men. They explored the Gunnison, Animas, and La Plata Rivers, looking for gold. Once again they found little to encourage them. Most of his party deserted this stubborn, determined man and headed for home. But Baker pushed on. Only when the group had dwindled to Baker and two others did he finally give up and head home. But on the way out of the San Juans, as he was trespassing on Ute territory, Baker was killed by the Utes. His two companions narrowly escaped.

Historically most of today's state of Colorado was Ute country. But with the rush of American settlers into eastern Colorado, the United States government removed the Utes from the lands east of the Continental Divide. They were "given" the lands west of the Rockies in 1868. From that time on the Utes became increasingly territorial. Prospectors who worked the streams west of the divide were taking great risks. Nonetheless men like Baker continued to trespass in their search for gold.

The next attempt to find gold in southwestern Colorado was led by Calvin Jackson. With a large group of men, he left Prescott, Arizona, in 1869. Harassed by Indians every step of the way, some of the group were killed. Others abandoned the expedition. Only eight made it to southwestern Colorado. Arriving in the dead of winter, they holed up in the cabins that Baker's group had abandoned. Their efforts to locate a promising source of gold were equally unsuccessful. Nonetheless from Baker's time on word had spread that some gold had been found in the area. Baker's vision of gold in the San Juans, more than his insignificant discoveries there, served as the kernel for rumors that grew into tall tales that kept the prospectors coming to the area.

Fed by just such rumors, Miles T. Johnson entered the western San Juans in 1870 and prospected in the Baker's Park area. There, after months of searching, he found the first profitable mineral lode in the San Juans in remote Arrastra Gulch, 3 miles northeast of today's Silverton. Somehow he was able to keep his gold strike a secret. But two years later when he packed his ore out, news of his Little Giant Gold Mine spread. A slow boom was on. Besides Arrastra other gulches were being explored and given colorful names such as Maggie Gulch and Minnie Gulch. By 1873 nearly 4,000 claims had been staked in this remote mining region, hundreds of miles away from civilization.

Prospectors had to be hardy souls to conquer the ruggedness of these mountains with their steep, sheer rock walls and precipitous canyons. These men were subjected to rock slides, dangerous ledge trails, and early snows with deep drifts that lasted until summer. Snow slides frequently sent down tons of snow in killer avalanches. Horses on steep trails would bolt, throwing their riders into gulches hundreds of feet deep. Attacks by bears were not unheard of. Death from exposure in this land of unpredictably extreme weather was a constant hazard. It is no wonder that the rush to the San Juans was said to be one of the most difficult migrations ever chronicled in western history. The early prospectors, miners, and settlers were said to have needed courage, patience, and strength in this remote land. But they also needed "white lightning" or its facsimile to bolster their courage, judging from the scores of saloons that sprang up in the sparsely populated mining camps.

In addition to these hardships, this was still Indian land west of the Rockies. The prospectors were trespassing and therefore subject to harassment by the Utes. In 1872 the great Ute chief Ouray rejected an attempt by the government to get back some of the lands it had given the Indians in 1868. But in 1874 Ouray saw the handwriting on the wall and did agree, in the Brunot Agreement, to give up a piece of land 60 by 75 miles in size that included the prime mineral areas. The Utes were paid 12 cents per acre for these 3 million acres of especially valuable land.

With the Indians no longer posing a threat, hundreds of fortune seekers

Early-day prospector

thronged to southwestern Colorado. The stampede had begun with the onset of serious mining in 1874. But by 1875 the boom was really on. Pioneer wagons from the east headed west carrying the slogan "San Juan or Bust." The principal route into this remote region was over the Continental Divide at Stony Pass (see Section 4, "The Setting"). At an elevation of 12,000 feet, it was one of the meanest and most difficult passes to negotiate in the Colorado Rockies.

The descent on the west side of Stony Pass was especially precipitous, the wagon road dropping 2,300 feet in the first 2 miles. This was the way many pioneer prospectors came in, and it was the exit route for the ore-laden pack trains. Sometimes these pack trains contained as many as 150 plodding burros, each laden with 200 pounds of ore on the way out or coal and supplies on the way in. But the burros were not the only beasts of burden subject to such misery. Oxen pulled their heavy loads in crudely made wagons whose wooden wheels crushed and groaned over the rough terrain.

Though it was gold most prospectors searched for, it was silver they found. With the discovery of more and richer deposits of silver, the area became known as the "Silvery San Juan." In the dramatic mountain-rimmed valley called Baker's Park, a town was born. The first cabin was built in 1871. The mining camp of Silverton, elevation 9,032 feet, was platted in 1874 and is the oldest major settlement in the San Juans. A hotel was built in 1874, and by 1875 a newspaper was established in Silverton. Today the *Silverton Standard and Miner* stakes its own "claim" as the longest continuously published newspaper west of the Continental Divide.

It has been said that in the 1880s wherever there was a rumor and a hole in the ground, a mining settlement would pop up. The small settlements were called *camps.* The ruins of these camps can be seen today, for they are the ghost towns of

False fronts

southwestern Colorado. Around Silverton many camps sprang up overnight in the gulches of the Animas River. Camps such as Howardsville, Eureka, Animas Forks, and Mineral Point were at extremely high altitudes. A story is told about a man in Animas Forks, just north of Silverton, who was arrested for drunkenness and brought to court. The judge levied a fine of $10 plus costs. Refusing to pay, the man said he would appeal to a higher court. The exasperated judge retorted that there was no such thing as a higher court, that at 11,300 feet, his was the highest court in the land. Today stories like this and nostalgic memories are the only remains of many of these camps. Most of them have disappeared completely through the ravages of time and weather.

But Silverton remains. It lives up to its reputation as "the mining town that never quit." There as in other mining towns, one-story buildings were constructed with their fronts higher than the building itself. False fronts, so typical of the early western towns, lent a touch of elegance to these rugged frontier settlements, offering partial compensation for the miserable living conditions. Wooden sidewalks so familiar in western movies were a necessity to keep from sinking knee-deep in the mud during certain times of the year. Saloons and places to buy liquor mushroomed in overwhelming numbers. At one time Silverton had thirty-four watering holes. Eventually hotels, restaurants, assay offices, churches, and schools completed the scene. Over and over again necessity was the mother of invention. Drinking water was frequently carried by a dog team pulling a wagon in the summer and a sled in the winter. Mail in the winter was often brought in by men on skis. Because these early towns constructed of wood were extremely subject to fire, Silverton wasted no time in bringing in the first hook-and-ladder fire truck over Stony Pass in 1878.

Thus far the mining activity described is that of men from the East heading west to find their fortunes. Ironically another thrust into southwestern Colorado was going on at the same time. On the West Coast veterans of the 1849 gold rush to California began to look east with greedy eyes to the Rockies they had bypassed a decade earlier in their pell-mell rush to Sutter's Mill. In 1856, almost one hundred years after Rivera passed by the La Plata Mountains, a Captain Moss left California to explore the west slope of the Rockies. He found good traces of minerals at the mouth of the La Plata River, possibly not far from where Rivera had passed. He returned in 1873, no doubt aware of the new mining activity in the Silverton area. He obtained good samples of quartz, which were predictive of lode mining. Because he was in Ute territory at the time, he negotiated a treaty with the Utes, who gave him permission to mine and farm a piece of land in the La Plata region, 36 miles square. For this permission he paid the Indians one hundred ponies and many blankets. With treaty and mineral samples in hand, he returned to San Francisco and enlisted the patronage of a wealthy man, Tiburcio Parrott. Captain Moss and his party returned to the La Plata River well equipped. They were responsible for discovering the first gold and silver lode there in 1875, which they called the Comstock. Another boom was at hand, and Parrott City, named after Moss's benefactor, was born.

The year 1875 was significant for southwestern Colorado. For in that year major discoveries were made near today's Ouray and Telluride. Restless prospectors from Silverton began spilling over the mountains looking for more riches. And they found them in another parklike valley, cut by the Uncompaghre River. By 1876 Uncompaghre City, later called Ouray, was rapidly expanding. In one spot, called the Mineral Farm, gold ore was found lying on the ground. Like digging potatoes, only a hoe or shovel was needed to reap the golden harvest.

In Ouray as in all the mining areas, both fortune and misfortune occurred. Fortune often meant hitting it big. There were numerous rags-to-riches stories there. One of the most famous ones concerns Thomas Walsh, the immigrant son of a poor Irish farmer who discovered gold in the form of telluride ore in the discarded tailings and waste dumps of other miners. Walsh's Camp Bird mine became one of the richest in the region. From its proceeds he bought his daughter the famous Hope Diamond.

In the summer of 1875, new discoveries were made in the San Miguel region. Later two towns cropped up. San Miguel City was the first, followed by Columbia. Columbia, later renamed Telluride for the rare sulphurlike element telluride found in the gold ore there, became the center for the area that included mines with such exotic names as the Smuggler, the Liberty Bell, the Tomboy, and the Hidden Treasure. Later, in 1879, a boom came to Rico. This area had been explored earlier in 1866 by a party of Texans and in 1869 by another group. But not until 1879 was a rich deposit of silver found nearby on Nigger Baby Hill, which got its unfortunate name because the rocks on the hill contained large quantities of black oxide of manganese. That year men in Silverton, Ouray, and the San Miguel areas dropped their picks and shovels and headed for Rico. Within a month more than 600 people had gathered there. Twenty-nine buildings, seven saloons, and four assay offices were quickly constructed to serve the new citizens. One of the newspapers in a neighboring town commented on how fast the town developed and stated that the town had "gotten there before it was sent for."

Otto Mears's toll road

With discoveries at Rico the Silver Circle was complete. From this time on more lodes were discovered around the already established mining camps, and thousands of tons of ore were shipped out by mule and oxen trains. In the 1870s a man by the name of Otto Mears, later called "the pathfinder of the San Juans," began building a series of toll roads connecting the major mining centers to one another and to the "outside." In less than ten years Mears engineered and built 450 miles of toll roads over this rugged up-and-down country, roads that were used by thousands of mules and burros, horse-drawn stage wagons, and panting prospectors. The toll road fees varied, but over one short stretch from Silverton to Ouray, later to be dubbed the Million-Dollar Highway, the fee was $5.00 for a four-horse stagecoach and $2.00 for a single rider and horse. With increasing traffic on the new toll roads, stagecoach robberies became commonplace.

Southwestern Colorado was booming. More and more people were attracted to the San Juans. In spite of the new roads and frontier settlements, the harsh land continued to mete out punishment. Many who came west were not really prepared to face the harsh life there. It is said that the first preacher in Ouray walked into town one winter in a blizzard, clinging to the tail of his donkey. He feared he would freeze to death if he sat quietly and rode the animal. Others soon became frustrated with the difficulty of everyday living in this cold, unforgiving high-altitude country. K. C. Gillette was one of those early prospectors who became frustrated and left. The story is told that as he was shaving himself one morning, his hands were shaking so much from the cold that he cut himself. In anger and frustration, he threw the razor to the ground, chipping the finely honed blade. The idea of a razor you could throw away after each use occurred to him. He abandoned the prospects of the riches in southwestern Colorado for the industrial denizens of the East. There he found other riches in marketing his Gillette throwaway razor blades.

In 1869 the transcontinental railway was completed at Promontory, Utah. With the main east-west connection completed, north-south spur lines from towns like Denver could be considered. The Denver and Rio Grande Railway was organized in 1870. By 1871 it was constructing track from Denver south and planning to extend it through Santa Fe and Albuquerque to El Paso. But as the silver boom in southwestern Colorado grew by leaps and bounds, a railway was needed there. The Denver and Rio Grande stopped its southerly march and made an abrupt turn west to accommodate this new lucrative market in southwestern Colorado.

There were other railways competing for the San Juan bonanza. But the Denver and Rio Grande, with its narrow-gauge, 3-foot-wide tracks, outpaced its standard competition, whose 4-foot-8-inch-wide tracks took longer to lay and when

Narrow-gauge train beside water tower

finished were more difficult to negotiate around the steep mountain curves than the narrow-gauge tracks. The new tracks went from Alamosa in eastern Colorado, over Cumbres Pass, zigzagging along the New Mexico–Colorado border to Chama, New Mexico (see Section 4, "Taos: Tours, Museums, and Activities"). There they turned northwest to the new smelter-railroad town of Durango. Twenty-seven hundred men laid 150 miles of track across some of North America's roughest territory in just a little more than seventeen months.

The workers lived in railroad camps. These were rough-and-tumble affairs. Merchants, following the camps as they moved along, sold vast quantities of whiskey. Heads fuzzed with liquor led to loose tongues, which sparked quarrels and fights. It was said that in one camp alone, thirteen men died of bullet wounds in less than a month. Desperadoes followed the camps and robbed unsuspecting workers indiscriminately. Snow, mud, and rock slides were the terror of all. In spring, fall, and winter, several feet of snow and ice had to be cleared before the ground could be exposed to lay the railroad ties.

Men worked under these conditions, as well as along narrow rock ledges inches away from precipitous 1,000-foot-deep "sudden death" canyons. This was more than most workers had bargained for. The desertion rate was astronomical. Many went home, and others dropped off the line and homesteaded in Colorado's rich agricultural valleys. But replacements were always available from Chicago, St. Louis, and Kansas City. There was no lack of men wanting to go west to find their fortunes. By the time the century was over, more than 1,635 miles of narrow-gauge rail line had been laid in the Rockies.

The track reached the new town of Durango in July 1881. Founded in 1880, this rugged town was ready for the railroad. It had passed through some of the growth pains of a new town and had begun to settle down a bit. In May, before the railroad came, an ordinance was passed that was intended to bring tranquillity, if not law and order, to the new town. The ordinance stated that any person carrying or concealing a pistol, bowie knife, dagger, or other deadly weapon would be fined no less than $5.00 and no more than $35.00. There also was evidence that Durango was hoping to boom someday and become a peaceful community. Newspapers advertised for young women to come to this manly town, and, sure enough, young ladies began arriving from all over the country.

While the track was being laid to Durango, the route from Durango to Silverton was being surveyed. Steel instead of iron rails were used on this 45-mile stretch of track that had an elevation gain of 2,000 feet. The train chugged into Silverton in July 1882, after nine months of backbreaking track-laying work. Silverton, settled in 1873 and incorporated in 1876, had 600 hardy souls on hand to greet the new train.

It is often pointed out that although many of these southwestern Colorado towns got their starts from mining activities, they did not really flourish and grow until after the railroad came in. By 1885 Silverton's population had grown from 500 to 2,000 and would eventually expand to 5,000. With the new railway it became possible for Silverton's citizens to reach Denver, the acme of civilization, in just under thirty hours. As time went on Silverton, Colorado, became increasingly "civilized" and connected with the rest of the United States. With the railway white prospectors and entrepreneurs realized for the first time the riches that had eluded the early Spanish conquistadors in the High Southwest.

As the mining communities boomed and rejoiced in the prospect of new riches, the earliest inhabitants of the region had fallen onto bad times. By 1879, with more and more white settlers pushing into Colorado, the Utes became a nuisance to the United States government. At the Ute agency near Grand Junction, Colorado, a man by the name of Nathan C. Meeker had become the Indian agent for the region. It was his view that the Indians should learn to farm. Not understanding that these were proud, seminomadic hunters who thought of farming as women's work, Meeker took their lack of interest as a sign of active resistance. He retaliated by plowing up the Ute horseracing track, thinking that if he could discourage the Utes from their favorite gaming activity, they would farm. That was the straw that broke the camel's back. The Utes retaliated with a vicious attack on Meeker's agency, killing Meeker and nine others.

This incident was all the United States government needed to purge all the Utes from the potentially rich mining and farming areas in western Colorado. The Ute removal agreement of 1880 spelled the end to traditional Ute life. Under the force of arms, the Utes were literally run out of northwestern Colorado into Utah, where they were placed on the small Unitah-Ouray reservation. The Utes in southwestern Colorado were driven from their green valleys to the arid and less desirable lands on the very southern border of Colorado adjacent to New Mexico. There they were placed on two reservations, the Southern Ute Indian reservation southeast of Durango and the Ute Mountain reservation just south of Mesa Verde. The land the Utes were forced to evacuate was occupied almost immediately by miners, while sheep and cattle ranchers homesteaded the lush grazing country north of the Ute reservations.

Ranchers from Texas had known about Colorado for some time. In 1866

Colonel Charles Goodnight, known as the "Father of the American Cowboy," drove 2,000 Texas longhorns to the rich grazing meadows in Colorado. Their profitable enterprise soon became known as Colorado's second gold rush. The first large cattle operation reached the San Juan area in 1875. Before this time the only meat in the developing mining and railroad communities came from mountain sheep or trail-worn oxen. The Colorado prospectors, miners, railroad workers, and large segments of the United States Cavalry wanted beef.

Numerous cattlemen flocked to Colorado. Pretty soon range wars and rustlers completed the cowboy scene. In addition to problems with rustlers changing cattle brands, there were also feuds over innocent mistakes involving brands. In one instance two ranchers whose operations were miles apart in the Durango area came to discover that they had the same brands. The cattlemen's "law of the range" prevailed. One of the ranchers was forced to change the brand on 22,000 head of cattle! For months the air must have been redolent with the smell of burned cowhide. Later the land was found to be suitable for sheep, a discovery that set the scene of numerous feuds between sheepmen and cattlemen. Just as many of the mines came to be owned by English syndicates, so many of the large cattle operations were eventually supported by English money.

Many who worked on the railroads and some who had come to find riches in minerals were impressed with the richness of the land. The Homestead Act, which had been passed in 1862, and the shipment of barbed wire into the area by 1878 attracted more and more settlers to the region. Homesteading 160-acre tracts, they cleared the land, built log cabins, brought in chickens and pigs, and planted orchards and crops. Potatoes, cabbage, tomatoes, and other vegetables grew extremely well. Apricots, peaches, and plums also flourished there. Not since the 1200s when the Ancestral Puebloans lived there had such a stable and productive farm people settled in this region.

But eventually feuds broke out between the wide-ranging cattlemen and the barbed-wire-loving homesteaders, who erected fences everywhere to protect their crops from the stampeding hooves of cattle. By the early 1880s the open range was quickly becoming a memory of the past. Nonetheless, in the Dolores area the cattle business was still so good that the bank there once recorded the highest per capita deposits in the United States. But that boom faded in a few decades when the cattlemen realized they had badly overgrazed the land. In doing so they had killed much of the formerly abundant grass. Eventually the bare land became eroded and many of the cattlemen moved out.

But the scene was being set for another boom that over the years would send millions of people flocking to the area, far surpassing the earlier mining and cowboy stampedes. The findings of an ancient culture in southwestern Colorado by Fray Escalante and his men were probably buried in some dusty diary stashed in Mexico when, almost one hundred years later, in 1874, William Henry Jackson, a member of a United States Geological Survey party, tromped through the Mancos Valley looking for cliff dwellings rumored to be in the area. Jackson, a photographer, recorded sighting one ruin that he labeled "Two Story Cliff House." The picture of this ancient stone building, later printed and distributed in the East, led to another kind of "rush."

Colorado cowboys

Although curiosity seekers from the East descended on the area in 1875 and in some instances recorded their findings of ruins, it was not until 1888 that the bonanza really got its start. In that year Richard Wetherill and Charles Mason, ranchers from Mancos, stumbled onto Cliff Palace, a multistoried dwelling up on Mesa Verde. The artifacts they found were astonishing. They immediately began a campaign to let the world know of their rich strike. In 1890 they took a collection of their Ancestral Puebloan artifacts to Durango. The exhibition failed. The busy miners and smelter operators were not interested. Undaunted, they went on to Pueblo, Colorado, where they were ridiculed. In Denver they were met with indifference. Nonetheless the word was out, and people began coming. By 1906, partly through the persistent efforts of the women's societies in Durango, the importance of the Wetherill find was so firmly established that Mesa Verde National Park was created by that great perpetrator of national parks, Theodore Roosevelt.

The late 1880s and 1890s saw the further development and refinement of the railways in the region. Silverton soon became the only town in the United States with four separate narrow-gauge rail lines serving it. In the 1890s another narrow-gauge line, the Rio Grande Southern, was completed. More than 162 miles of track were laid, giving birth to another railroad town, Ridgway. The route from Durango through Rico to Ridgway was so rugged that 130 bridges were needed to complete the line. With these new rails in place, all the ores dug in southwestern Colorado now could be brought to Durango's smelter. Between 1890 and 1891 the mineral output of the area was so prolific that even the railroads could not move the ore fast enough.

But the Silvery San Juan and its booming growth were shocked perilously when the silver panic of 1893 hit. That year the United States Congress voted for a gold standard, and the government stopped buying silver. With silver demonetized the silver crash was inevitable. Fortunately for the Colorado miners, a rich gold strike was made that same year in eastern Colorado, at Cripple Creek. Since some gold had been found in the San Juans from the 1860s on, efforts to find more

Galloping Goose

were intensified. These were so successful that by 1897 half the mineral output of the area was in gold. But that did not keep William Jennings Bryan from making an impassioned plea for the silver standard in 1896 in front of the Sheridan Hotel in Telluride. By this time, though, lead and copper were also being produced, along with the increasing quantities of gold. By the turn of the century, the area had a new moniker, the Golden San Juan.

Mining reached its peak between 1900 and 1912. At that time San Juan County boasted 5,000 people. The story is told that in 1904, when Andrew Carnegie stopped in Grand Junction, Colorado, on a rail trip, a messenger from Silverton was on hand to tell him how badly a library was needed in that rapidly growing town. Carnegie was apparently impressed, as he donated $10,000 for the library. It was built in 1905 and still stands today. But by the 1920s many mines had either slowed down or closed down as the boom began to fade. Towns began to dwindle in size, many of them barely surviving the depression of the 1930s.

The Rio Grande Southern also had problems. It had to discontinue its passenger trains, replacing them with **"galloping geese."** These contraptions were made from parts of old buses and cars and fitted with flanged wheels. They carried small amounts of freight and a few passengers to Ridgway and Telluride. One of the better-known vehicles was the *Casey Jones,* which had a Cadillac engine, a cowcatcher, and, of course, flanged wheels. Another popular "goose" had a Pierce Arrow engine. By 1952 the Rio Grande Southern Railway had shut down altogether, although some mining activity continued to sputter along. But there was renewed interest in the area when uranium ore was mined from the vanadium plant in Durango during World War II. From this material U-324 was refined to be used in the atom bombs that were dropped on Hiroshima and Nagasaki in 1945. But by the 1950s many of the boomtowns were already aging ghost towns. Eventually, in 1952, the Durango to Silverton Railway was forced to suspend year-round operations. But summer operations continued, for by that time a trickle of tourists had begun to discover the region.

Dormant since 1938, the Sunnyside Mine at Eureka, near Silverton, was reopened in 1959, and the American Tunnel was dug from Gladstone to Eureka. This mining operation, once rated as one of the largest gold producers in Colorado, has been intermittently open and closed over the years, depending on metal prices, and no longer sustains Silverton's permanent population of approximately 700. Over the past few decades, the area has become better known to the rest of the country because of the numerous movies that were made in and around the historic towns of southwestern Colorado, including such popular westerns as *True Grit, Tribute to a Badman, How the West Was Won, The Denver and the Rio Grande, The Tracker,* and *Night Passage.* Parts of *Ticket to Tomahawk, Naked Spur,* and *Around the World in Eighty Days* were also made there.

In 1961 residents of Durango and Silverton, the railway companies, and the Interstate Commerce Commission saved the last regularly scheduled narrow-gauge line in the United States from extinction. Of the original several hundred miles of track between Alamosa and Silverton, only the 65 miles linking Chama, New Mexico, and Antonito, Colorado, and the 45-mile link between Durango and Silverton remain today. In a recent year more than 200,000 passengers rode "the rails to Yesterday." Fortunately Silverton, Ouray, and Telluride have all been designated as either National Historic Landmarks or Districts, so much of their frontier atmosphere has been saved. The much-dreaded snow that claimed so many lives in the early days now provides a new and important source of economic renewal for the region as skiers flock in vast numbers to Telluride and Durango Mountain Resort at Purgatory.

SEEING ROCKY MOUNTAIN FRONTIER COUNTRY

Durango, population 14,000, lies nestled in the Animas Valley, surrounded by the foothills of the San Juan Mountains. With the Animas River flowing through the center of town and evergreen-forested hills and high mountain peaks visible in all directions, Durango is attractive by the very nature of its location. At an elevation of 6,512 feet, it offers an ideal summer climate for residents and visitors. Moreover, its location is suited ideally for a base from which to view most of the sights listed in this section. From late spring through early fall there are many tourists, and accommodations can sometimes be tight. In spite of these two shortcomings, Durango is an enjoyable place to stay, and its historic genuineness shines through on segments of Main Avenue, as well as along nearby tree-lined residential streets, like East Third Avenue, where you may feel transported to another century.

This is a town with a fascinating Old West history. With a little imagination you can see and feel the old, wide-open, rowdy kind of a place Durango used to be. Although Silverton was the center of the precious-metal boom of the 1870s, its mountain fastness made it an impractical smelter and freight center. The officials of the Denver and Rio Grande Railroad looked for a site along the lower **Animas River** as being more congenial to their interests. For there coal deposits had been discovered, along with lime and iron deposits. With coal readily available for fuel, a large smelter plant could be built to serve the entire region. So in 1879 the smelter at Silverton was brought down the mountains by mule train. A new smelter was built at a site 2 miles south of Animas City, the only community established in the lower **Animas Valley,** following an earlier attempt at settlement by Charles Baker and his group farther up the river in the early 1860s. Eventually the new smelter site location and the site of the first rail terminus in southwestern Colorado was given the Spanish name "Durango" by railroad officials.

Although it seems unusual that this Anglo rail town was given a Spanish name, it is even more ironic that the name was not derived from neighboring Spanish New Mexico, whose citizens had traversed this region for more than a century. Instead it is thought that the name was imported from Mexico, where the widely traveled Colorado territorial governor **Alexander Hunt** had visited. While there he had been impressed with a thriving, prosperous city named Durango, which was a mining and commercial city whose mountainous location next to a river was similar to that of the new town to be built in southwestern Colorado. For, you see, Durango is a word of Spanish-Basque origin meaning "well-watered place." Perhaps the Denver and Rio Grande officials who named the town took

Durango

Hunt's suggestion, hoping that somehow their new town would become as prosperous and successful as its namesake in Mexico.

In 1880, with the railroad under construction from Alamosa, Colorado, to Durango, the town was laid out. Many of its first inhabitants were veterans of the Leadville, Colorado, gold rush. By the spring of 1881, Durango's population had swelled to more than 1,000 somewhat thirsty citizens: Durango had fifty-nine saloons and other establishments where liquor could be obtained, and it was said that Durangoites drank the Winchester way, "fire and repeat." Above the sea of saloons, one lone church lifted its modest steeple to the sky that year, but it was not much of a moderating influence in that violence-prone town. Cowhands, gamblers, prospectors, and railway workers mingled together in an explosive sea of mud, tents, shanties, saloons, and dance halls.

One gang of outlaws was so violent that a vigilante committee was formed to curb their excesses. Naming themselves the **Committee of Safety,** these 300 men decided to close in on the gang. But before they could do so, a gambler shot and killed a local citizen in one of the saloons. Taking the law in their own hands, the vigilantes apprehended the gambler. Then, meting out frontier justice, they hanged him from a tall pine tree right in front of the post office that same night. The next day the Durango newspaper reported the incident in the following poetic terms: "A ghastly sight it was! A scene never to be forgotten. The slight wind swayed the body to and fro. The pale moonlight glimmering through the sifted clouds dotted the ghastly face of a ghostlier pallor. The terrible retribution stopped not in its pursuit. The foully murdered man was revenged ere the day in which the deed was done had flown."

There are ghosts of Durango's historic past wherever you go in this mountain town. Many of the original buildings were destroyed in the **disastrous fire of 1899.** The pine tree where the lynching was performed was just west of the railroad tracks on Ninth Street. The larger smelter on the Animas River was located just across from today's **Durango and Silverton Narrow-Gauge Railway** depot. Every western

Animas City Pioneer Cabin, Durango

town has sporting houses or houses of prostitution. Some of Durango's most famous houses were located near the corner of Narrow Gauge Avenue and Eleventh Street. These houses of ill repute carried such colorful names as the Hanging Gardens of Babylon and the Silver Belle. One obviously more reputable house was called Mother's. The top floor of the Strater Hotel served the same function more informally and was for many years known as the Monkey Hall.

The site of the first platted city in the Animas Valley, **Animas City,** is located just a few blocks off U.S. Highway 550, or Main Avenue, where the railroad tracks cross Thirty-second Street. That old town was annexed to Durango in 1948. But even today the visitor can see a few remnants of Animas City. The old Animas City School House, now the Animas Museum (Durango's history museum) is on a site to where an 1870s pioneer log cabin and a postrailroad structure, the Peterson House, have been moved.

Another of Durango's earliest landmarks is easier to find. **The Strater Hotel** has been situated on the same site, the corner of Seventh and Main, since the day it was constructed in 1888. It is testimony to Durango's rich past and thriving present. By 1885 Durango's population had reached nearly 3,000 and was growing by leaps and bounds. An ambitious twenty-year-old by the name of Strater came to Durango and saw the need for a fine hotel. With few funds but lots of grit, he constructed the Strater House, a fifty-room hotel with wood-burning stoves and comfortable furniture. The hotel, much enlarged, has been in continuous operation under local ownership since that time. Now beautifully restored to its past grandeur and possibly beyond, it is an anchoring Durango landmark.

When the first railroad came to Durango in the summer of 1881, a silver spike was driven at Ninth Street near the location of today's depot. Today the oldest railroad car on the narrow-gauge trip to Silverton is coach and baggage car 212. Built in 1878, it is the oldest railroad car in Colorado. The wooden interior of handsome ash and the original oil side lamps are today's reminders of a not-too-distant past. Numerous other old cars make the 45-mile run to Silverton. In case you wondered,

Diamond Belle Saloon

the car just behind the locomotive is the tender. It carries eight tons of coal and 5,000 gallons of water. The fireman shovels coal from the tender into the firebox. Water is pumped into the boiler from the tender, where the burning coal in the firebox makes steam by heating the water. The steam is diverted into cylinders, which push the pistons. Since the pistons are connected to the wheels by means of rods, the wheels begin to turn and the trip to yesteryear begins.

Durango has a number of nice parks for picnicking. My favorites are **Schneider and West Side Park** along the Animas River, just off Roosa Avenue between Ninth and Fifteenth Streets, and **Fassbinder Park** located just off Main on Seventeenth Street and Park Avenue. A nature and jogging trail, the **Opie-Reams Nature Trail,** parallels the Animas River from Alamo Drive north to East Third Avenue at Twenty-ninth Street. The trail is reached from Main Avenue by turning east 1 block past Twenty-first Street at the Vagabond Inn onto Alamo or by turning east onto Thirty-second Street to reach East Third Avenue.

If Durango's early history intrigues you, pay a visit to the **Animas Museum** (also known as the Animas School Museum or Durango's History Museum). The museum is located at Thirty-first Street and West Second Avenue, just off North Main Avenue (U.S. Highway 550) where the sign points the way to the old schoolhouse. The first floor of the museum-schoolhouse contains a turn-of-the-twentieth-century classroom displaying a nostalgic collection of early educational artifacts and teaching materials. In addition, the museum gift shop offers an excellent selection of regional and southwestern Colorado books, plus a small but well-chosen assortment of Southwest Native American crafts and historical memorabilia. Upstairs is a series of nine archaeological exhibits focusing on Durango's legacy by following a time line from Ancestral Puebloan times through the lifestyle of the area's nomadic Ute Indians and to the area's mining and Victorian times. Well worth a visit, the museum is open daily between mid-May and early October and is either closed or on a reduced schedule the rest of the year. Call for hours (970–259–2402; www.frontier.net/~animasmuseum). Useful historic walking tour brochures are available at the museum or at the **Durango Area Chamber Resort Association** visitor center. Mailing address: P.O. Box 2587, VG (Visitors Guide), Durango, Colorado 81302; (970) 247–0312 or (800) 525–8855; www.durango.org. It is located in a parklike setting along the Animas River south of town at 111 South Camino del Rio (U.S. Highway 550 South) in a modern building identified by an old steam locomotive parked nearby.

Another interesting side trip is a visit to **Fort Lewis College,** located on top of a hill east of town, offering fine views over the Animas Valley. The college's museum, also home to the **Center for Southwest Studies,** has displays of Southwest Native American artifacts. There is also a picnic area on the campus. Access to the college is from Main Avenue, where you turn south onto Eighth

Street. Drive up Eighth Street to Eighth Avenue and follow the signs all the way to the college.

Still another interesting side trip is a visit to the **Durango Fish Hatchery** and the **Durango Wildlife Center**. Here you can tour the grounds of one of the oldest (circa 1893) fish hatcheries in Colorado. This active hatchery produces about 1.5 million subcatchable trout and 210,000 catchable trout a year, fish that will eventually stock fifty-six streams and at least sixty-five lakes and reservoirs in southwestern Colorado. The show pond contains some unbelievably large specimens and a unique self-feeding device. The wildlife center focuses on the wildlife of Colorado, from birds to elk, and, as a showcase for the Colorado Division of Wildlife, gives a history of early trapping techniques as well as current efforts toward preservation. To reach the facility from downtown, drive north on Main Avenue, cross the bridge over the Animas River, and take the first right. Follow the signs to the site. For more information call either the wildlife center (open daily May to November) at (970) 259–3009 or the Durango Fish Hatchery at (970) 247–4755.

There are a variety of shops, stores, and galleries in Durango offering everything from fine Indian crafts, cowboy clothes, and railroad memorabilia to cheap curios. Durango's many restaurants are generally of high caliber and serve up some of the best food you will find in the whole Four Corners area. As in the old days, the bars and saloons are plentiful, many of them capturing the atmosphere of a bygone century. Early morning and late evening are excellent times to walk the streets to absorb some of Durango's genuine historic atmosphere. And if you happen to be in Durango on a warm summer night when the moon is full and the silhouettes of the surrounding mountains are visible, listen for the sounds of muffled voices and tinkling glasses coming up from the entrance of the **Diamond Belle Saloon** at the Strater Hotel. As you walk up to the entrance and push open the swinging doors, see if you do not have the distinct sensation of entering a time warp, a sense of being transported to another Durango, an earlier Durango, more than one hundred years ago.

Traveling the Silver Circle: A Narrative Account along the San Juan Skyway

Last night at dusk we arrived in Durango from Albuquerque, New Mexico. The first two motels we tried were full, but fortunately we found a room at the edge of town. After a late dinner we walked the moonlit streets and viewed the Rockies, dramatically silhouetted above the low-rise profile of the town. No skyscrapers here. Just two- or three-story buildings, some with the modified false fronts that are so typical of old western towns like this one. It was a quiet, unhurried evening as we strolled through the quiet streets.

But this morning things are different. Summer visitors crowd the streets, and the traffic is heavy for a town of 14,000 residents. On our way to breakfast at the Strater Hotel, we note that there is a chill in the air this bright August morning. Over the breakfast table we make our plans for the day and then adjourn to the beautiful old hotel lobby where I inquire at the registration desk about a room for tonight. Fortunately there is a cancellation. In a quick trip up to our room, we find

Durango and Silverton Narrow-Gauge Railway

it handsomely Victorian-style, with antique walnut furniture. The kids are impressed with the ornate handcarved headboard and the claw-foot bathtub.

With assurance of a bed tonight, we prepare to leave Durango to tour the "Silver Circle," a 260-mile round-trip drive on the **San Juan Skyway,** a National Forest Scenic Byway (www.SanJuanSkyway.com), which will take us on an all-paved loop through the heart of some of the highest and most ruggedly scenic parts of the Rockies to the silver boomtowns of the late 1800s. The highway is well engineered and easy to drive. This morning we saw the **Durango-Silverton narrow-gauge train** depart the depot. The shrill sound of the steam whistle and accompanying puffs of smoke made us sad we were not aboard. We had tried to get reservations before coming to Durango, but even three months ago the train was fully booked for today. Last night and this morning we inquired about cancellations, but earlier birds got the few canceled seats. So our plan this morning is to drive to Silverton and attempt to get seats for our children on the return trip to Durango, since we understand that some of the morning passengers make a one-way trip on the train, either spending the night in Silverton or returning by bus to Durango. We will complete the Silver Circle loop by car.

We leave downtown Durango driving north on Main Avenue, or U.S. Highway 550. On the way out of town, we pass the sign to the Animas Museum (Animas School House Museum), reminding us of our instructive visit there on a previous trip. Soon we are in the countryside north of town and on our way to the mountain fastness of the San Juan range of the Rockies.

Just out of Durango we enter a particularly wide, beautiful section of the Animas River Valley. Valleys like this one are typical of the Colorado scene. With the narrow-gauge tracks to our right, we glimpse views of the Animas River as it meanders through the valley. Today in its peaceful setting, it does not seem to live up to the dramatic name the Spanish gave it, the Rio de las Animas, or the "River of Lost Souls." We see numerous ducks flying up from the river and several red-wing and Brewer's blackbirds along the road, as one graceful red-tailed hawk soars above us.

As we gain altitude and the valley narrows, small ranches and summer homes dot the valley floor. They are colorfully backed by red rocks with dark green pines and junipers dotting their tiered, ledgy slopes that rise to meet the sheer cliff walls behind them. Green grasslands, tall ponderosa pines, and small blue ponds and lakes help complete this idyllic scene. Horses and sheep graze idly in the lush meadows, as trout rise in the lakes, leaving their telltale ripples in the shape of small concentric rings. In these rich green meadows, which the Ute Indians must have prized before the coming of the white settlers, we note the barbed-wire fencing nailed to spindly juniper posts. Barbed-wire fences like these, hastily erected by early homesteaders on their newly deeded lands, sometimes brought those early settlers into violent conflict with the region's first cattlemen, who fought to maintain the "open

range." Sadly we note the increased ski, tourist, and housing developments in this once quiet valley. But it's not yet too commercial for our favorite high-desert bird, the magpie, which goes sailing in front of us and across the meadow to our right, dressed in formal black and white.

Now as this excellent highway takes us farther up the valley, we gain altitude slowly but surely, until we catch fine views of **Windom Peak,** elevation 14,091 feet, one of the many "fourteeners" we will see today. Nearing **Hermosa,** Colorado, we see an old wooden water tank, used to replenish the water

Magpies

supply of the narrow-gauge steam locomotives. Just beyond Hermosa we cross the narrow-gauge tracks for the first time. We reflect that just a little north of here, the region's first prospector, Charles Baker, and his party made a bridge across the Animas River and established the first settlement in the western San Juan Mountains, a place that was occupied only a few months before it was abandoned. In another few miles the narrow-gauge tracks cross under the highway, and it is here that the train takes its own course to Silverton as it heads through the **Animas Canyon Gorge** rather than paralleling the highway.

Now the road ascends rapidly, taking us into increasingly beautiful high-mountain country, where spruces cover the high slopes and where for the first time today we see isolated stands of aspen. Now about halfway to Silverton, we see a bonanza of high peaks cropping up in the distance all around us. We pass by several small mountain lakes as well as large **Electra Lake.** Almost 24 miles from Durango now, we pass the **Purgatory Ski Area** road and are reminded, as we see the many ski cabins in the area, that skiing has made Durango and this valley an active center for travelers, even in the winter.

Just beyond the Purgatory road, the peaks that seemed so distant are now staring us in the face, including 12,972-foot **Engineer Mountain** and 14,086-foot **Mount Eolus.** Now we drive over **Coal Bank Hill Summit** at 10,640 feet,

Narrow-gauge train in Animas Canyon

more than 4,000 feet higher than Durango. On the other side of the pass, we get better views of Engineer Mountain, but the sight that takes the scenic award for the day is magnificent **Twilight Peak,** topping out above 13,000 feet. As we travel now just below the 11,500- to 12,000-foot timberline, surrounded by this sea of craggy, bare, unforgiving "thirteeners" whose crevasses still hold some of last winter's snow, we have that exhilarating feeling of being on top of the world. Surrounded by barren rock in all directions, we know that this is the heart of a mountain chain that could not have been named anything else but "Rocky."

We continue our ascent to lofty **Molas Pass,** elevation 10,910 feet. No wonder they call this route the San Juan Skyway: In several places there are sheer dropoffs beyond the shoulders. But the wide road is well engineered; in all of our driving today we have had to negotiate only a few horseshoe curves. We see bluebirds flit over the tarns from one stunted alpine tree to another and a few brave chipmunks scurry across the road. As we descend past **Molas Lake,** we observe more stands of Colorado blue spruce, the Colorado state tree, and mountains clad with stately Engelmann spruce.

Now we descend rapidly into a zigzag course to **Silverton.** In a few miles we spot that old mining town far below us to the right, nestled in a small valley surrounded by high peaks. The valley is named **Baker's Park** after Charles Baker, the first prospector to enter this area. As we stop to soak in this dramatic view, we notice Indian paintbrush just off the roadside. Descending farther, we get a view of the valley, 1 mile wide and 2 miles long. We are told it is the flattest piece of land in San Juan County. Not only is the valley flat, but it is also treeless, dry, and almost desolate looking in contrast to the green mountainside. The aerial view from here allows us to see the road we are traversing 1 or 2 miles ahead as it snakes its way down to what, at elevation 9,318 feet, is the oldest continuously inhabited community in southwestern Colorado.

Chipmunk   *Blue spruce*   *Indian paintbrush*

Silverton occupies the western side of this very flat valley. Five miles to the northeast over a passable road when it is not wet is one of Colorado's largest and best-preserved ghost towns, **Animas Forks.** From our high perch we see Silverton's symmetrical gridiron street system laid out before us, looking more like a piece of graph paper than a town. The Animas River courses through the valley just south of town, its red-streaked banks testimony to the iron oxides being washed down from the surrounding red mountains. We can see a series of roads leaving Silverton, extending like spokes from a hub, eventually winding through the numerous gulches that have produced an unbelievable amount of wealth over the years.

But according to Navajo legend, these gulches produced more than mineral wealth. That legend states that somewhere in this convoluted mountain country around Silverton, perhaps up one of these gulches, the Dineh or The People first emerged into the world from a hole in the ground. Snowmelt and water in these gulches spawn the Animas River, which flows 70 miles south into northwestern New Mexico to the **San Juan Basin,** near where the Navajo made their ancestral home in **Gobernador Canyon** (see Section 2, "The Navajo (Diné): Nomads and Survivalists").

We drive across the flat valley floor and cross iron-laden, red **Mineral Creek,** as we enter Silverton. We crane our necks looking at the mountains that encircle us. High and to the northwest is **Anvil Mountain;** to the northeast are **Boulder** and **King Solomon's Mountains.** To the southeast is **Kendall Mountain,** and to the southwest are **Sultan** and **Grand Turk Mountains.** Silverton's streets are wide and flat and still mostly unpaved. After all the up-and-down driving we have done this morning, it seems strange to find such a level piece of ground perched up here in the heart of the mountains. Just before entering town we visit the very nice Silverton Chamber of Commerce Visitors Center: P.O. Box 565, Silverton, Colorado 81433; (970) 387–5654 or (800) 752–4494; www.silverton.org. We make some inquiries, pick up a few helpful brochures, then drive into town.

As we focus on the town, we are instantly taken with the frontier, western character of this place. There are not any horses, but there are not many new vehicles either. The few cars and trucks, most of older vintage, are pretty well banged up from their use on the mountain backroads. Main Street, or Greene Street, is paved, but the few side streets and auxiliary streets are not. Even the pavement we see seems about to return to dirt, as it is fairly well covered in spots with dust and

United Church of Silverton

gravel. A cool breeze is blowing and whipping up the dust in the streets. Although we see several buildings with typical western false fronts, we particularly notice some of the elaborate Victorian buildings and quaint churches that gave the mining camps an aura of elegance.

We decide to tour the public rooms of the **Grand Imperial Hotel** on Main Street, built in 1882. Restored to much of its former glamour, it is well worth seeing, particularly its massive mahogany bar, the oldest in the region. Crossing the street, we walk by the **Teller House,** built in the early 1900s as a guesthouse and still used in that capacity today. The courthouse and the library were also built in the early 1900s. Today it is difficult to imagine that this was once such a wealthy and well-known area that financial syndicates in England bankrolled many of the mines and even built some of the buildings here.

Exploring the town, we are drawn immediately to the boxy tower and spire of the **United Church of Silverton.** It is Silverton's oldest, the first church being erected on this site in 1880. The simple design of the church, with its two multi-level, peaked roofs and its tall, pointed bell tower, almost seems to echo the shape of Kendall Mountain looming up behind it. Whether intended or not, a wonderful symmetry exists here between the natural and the man-made lines. As we leave the church, we note the galvanized metal roofs on many of the houses and speculate that they must make quite a din in the middle of a Rocky Mountain hailstorm.

We enjoy seeing the **San Juan County Museum,** located in the old jail next to the County Court House, before heading toward the rail depot. I recall the story that led to hiring **Bat Masterson** as sheriff of Silverton. In the 1880s the sheriff from Durango came up here looking for two desperadoes. He ordered Silverton's night marshal to help him out. The Silverton marshal saw several suspicious-looking men standing in front of a dance hall. When he approached them, they both opened fire, killing the marshal. The enraged citizens formed a vigilante committee. That night they caught and lynched an apparently innocent man. The desperadoes escaped. Because of incidents like this, the town of Silverton decided to hire Bat Masterson, the famous lawman from Dodge City, Kansas. Masterson was able to chase most of the undesirables away from Silverton, and the town became more peaceful after that. We look at our watches and realize that it is about time for the train to return to Durango. We inquire and find that space is available. Our children hop aboard. The train spews great clouds of cinders and smoke as it prepares to leave the station. With a final shrill whistle blast, it is off.

Walking back to the car, we are aware of numerous shops for the tourists. We see everything from rock and railroad memorabilia shops to craft and curio shops and several nice galleries and restaurants. This town of almost 500 residents must rely increasingly on tourism—not only the trainloads of passengers who spend a few hours here before returning to Durango but new ventures like the Silverton Ski Area, a lift-accessed backcountry ski area.

We regret we cannot linger a little longer here, but we have seen much of what the town has to offer and are eagerly anticipating the next 24-mile stretch of road to **Ouray,** which some claim to be one of the most scenic drives in Colorado. Driving out of town, we follow the signs to U.S. Highway 550, which parallels **South Mineral Creek** a few miles. Along the creek we come across some of the most extensive mining ruins we have seen today, backed by the orangy red hillsides. Now the highway starts up as though it meant it. Before this road was paved, one of the local newspapers described segments of it as being dangerous even to pedestrians. It went on to say that the grade was four parts vertical to one part perpendicular. We allow as how its designer, Otto Mears, was quite an engineer, as we drive along today's wide, paved, but curving, climbing road. Although the stretch from Durango to Ouray is often touted as the **Million Dollar Highway,** the term was first used for this stretch of road between Silverton and Ouray. No one quite knows why the "Million Dollar" name was coined. Some say it was because the construction of the modern road in 1923 over these few rugged miles was so astronomically expensive. Others say that it was because the gravel used for the roadbed was later discovered to be like a rich placer deposit, containing enough gold to be worth $1 million or more.

Now climbing more steeply, we reach 11,018-foot **Red Mountain Pass.** This area is loaded with large numbers of old mines on the left and right of the highway, as well as up and down the mountainsides and up just about every gulch. Many of these mines are in absolutely unbelievable locations, hugging the vertical faces of steep rocky cliffs. We see phantoms of the boom days everywhere we look. Old shaft houses and other ghost relics of the mining heyday remain to remind us of this area's mineral riches. With the limited technology available in the 1800s, it is a marvel that this heavy mining equipment could have been lugged hundreds of feet up to these cliff-hanging sites. We are impressed that those fortune seekers worked hard for what they got—if they got anything at all!

The afternoon sun gives the mountains an incredible redness, bringing out different shades of red and orange in the rocks. No problem figuring out how these mountains got their name. Now in a series of switchbacks, we descend the other side of the pass. One of the first things we see is the sign leading to the Idarado Mining Company's mine, formerly one of Colorado's leading copper producers. In a few miles we come to a relatively flat area called **Ironton Park,** where we spot a water *ouzel* or dipper, bounding along the surface of the water. This valley was named in honor of the mineral that has so generously stained the dirt, rocks, mountains, and rivers in this area. Even the stream is orange as it runs through the marshy meadow here. We are reminded that there were towns all along this route, as well as stagecoach stops. The mines were named for the loves, fantasies, hopes, and fears of their discoverers. The names are as colorful as the soil and the prospectors who named them: the Micky Breen, the Yankee Girl, the Orphan Boy, and the National Belle.

Now in a few more miles, after two exciting double-horseshoe curves, the

Mining relics

highway takes to a ledge or a shelf that was blasted out of the vertical side of the mountain by the indomitable Otto Mears in 1883. He called this testament to the power of dynamite the **Rainbow in the Sky Highway.** There was literally a pot of gold at both ends of this rainbow—and in between as well! The original ledge was very narrow, barely admitting a stagecoach, and it was steep, with a grade of 21 percent. As I ride the brakes down the pass, I am grateful that the slope of this modern highway is only 6 percent. I look up and see huge sheer rock walls to my right. Sometimes out of sight and hundreds upon hundreds of feet down on the left is the river. Someone once described this view as looking into the jaws of death. The speaker wasn't far from wrong.

In a few more miles, we round a curve and come face to face with an over-whelming view of a lush, green-clad valley hundreds of feet below us, encircled by high peaks. We know in an instant from this high perch that we are looking at our destination. **Ouray** is often called the "Switzerland of America," and no won-der. Deep in this mountainous amphitheater is Ouray town, surrounded by red rock ledges and cliffs arising from the valley in stair-step fashion to the lofty heights of the surrounding peaks. Just 2 miles from Ouray, we stop at **Bear Creek Falls.** This spectacular waterfall plunges 227 feet into the canyon below. It was right around here that Otto Mears placed his tollbooth, collecting $5.00 for stage-coach and horses and $2.00 for a horse and rider, as men and animals traveled the new road linking Silverton and Ouray.

With the dramatic pass we have just negotiated and with Ouray in front of us, we reflect that we are pleased to have come this far rather than just stopping at Sil-verton. It seems impossible, but the scenery is getting better and better. Now as we descend rapidly, each curve brings the town closer into view. In Ouray we see a

Beaumont Hotel, Ouray

pleasant western town that exudes warmth and a sense of community. About the only sign of life we see this afternoon is the **Uncompaghre River** as it flows lustily through the town. But this perennial river is more than just a place to catch a fish or two or cool your tired and dusty feet; it is responsible for turning this valley a shade of green not seen for miles around. The 700-plus full-time residents here (striking a nice balance between retirees and young families with children) have chosen not only a well-watered place to live but a cool haven at 7,800 feet elevation.

In many ways Ouray is our favorite family-oriented Colorado mountain town. It is old, western, and yet very civilized. After all, we recall, Ouray has depended on tourism quite a bit longer than the other nearby towns, so making travelers comfortable and happy seems to come naturally in Ouray town. The few days we spent here several years ago in this mountain oasis, with its many historic Victorian-style buildings, were a relaxing, enjoyable experience we would like to repeat. But today we have time only to see a few favorites like the **Box Canyon.** Instead of driving in from the first switchback south of town along U.S. Highway 550, we turn left from Highway 550, or Main Street, just as we enter town and then turn onto Third Avenue. We decide to park our car near the river and walk the short distance up to **Box Canyon Park.** Paying a small entry fee, we take the lower, shorter trail down into the canyon bed at the base of the 285-foot falls, rather than the trail to the top. This 21-foot-wide "canyon" is really more of a gorge or a slot than it is a canyon. The narrow trail, partly over a suspension type of bridge, leads us deeper and deeper into the earth, the deafening pounding of the water becoming louder with each step. Now so close to the falls that the spray is hitting our faces, we look up as far as we can see to where the water starts its long course downward. By the time it gets down here, it has a tremendous force.

Old fire station, Ridgway

If you want to witness the power of water, this is the place to come. As we stand here looking at this marvel of nature, one of the locals tells us that the water for the large hot springs swimming pool north of town is piped from this location.

As we walk back out, we comment that this is one of the finest natural sights in southwestern Colorado. We stop and rest for a few minutes at the pleasant picnic tables before walking back to the car. Driving through town we notice more renovations of older buildings than we had remembered. Several of our favorite buildings, the historic **Beaumont Hotel** and the **Saint Elmo Hotel** built in the 1890s, are still very much intact. We recall that this town too had money and that one of its more fortunate and flamboyant citizens, Thomas Walsh, pulled so much gold out of his Camp Bird Mine that when he went to buy the pricey Hope Diamond, it was like buying glass at the dime store.

Now we turn off Main to the right and drive up Sixth Avenue, where we pass the excellent **Ouray County Museum,** which details much of the mining history of the region. We turn left onto Fifth Street and see the Wiesbaden Hot Springs Spa and Lodge. A few years ago we walked from the motel lobby down into a series of subterranean chambers below the motel to bathe in a natural grotto filled with hot springwater. Less soothing but just as fun are the many hikes that radiate out into the mountains from Ouray. We remember particularly the short hike we took to 200-foot-high **Cascade Falls,** on the trail by the same name, which begins at the end of Eighth Avenue. We return downtown and stop for a short time at one of the several fine regional arts and crafts galleries.

Sorry that we do not have time to stay and eat dinner, we drive north out of town, passing the huge mineral hot springs swimming pool that is breathtakingly situated so that, as you stand neck-deep in warm, soothing water, you can look out on an array of peaks that would cure even the most homesick Swiss immigrant. We note that the helpful Ouray Chamber Resort Association (P.O. Box 145, Ouray, Colorado 81427; 970–325–4746 or 800–228–1876; www.ouray colorado.com) is located next to the **Ouray Hot Springs Pool.** As we drive on north, we discuss the pronunciation of the name that lies on the mountains and river here and that used to label the town until Ouray citizens discarded that long

Corral outside Telluride, Colorado

Ute name for a shorter one, Ouray, to honor the great Ute chief. In Ute, *Uncompaghre* means *unca* for "hot," *pah* for "water," and *gre* for "spring." Breaking it down this way, we come up with a pronunciation that satisfies us.

On the 10-mile drive to **Ridgway,** the road first parallels the glistening Uncompaghre River. Then we pass lush meadows that provide feed for horses and cows. Rustic ranch houses become part of the scenery as we move away from the mountains into the open country around Ridgway, altitude 6,985 feet. Ridgway, formerly a sleepy little town at the junction of U.S. Highway 550 and Colorado Highway 62, is now a bustling place billing itself as "the Gateway to Colorado's Four-Season Wonderland" (including the **Ridgway State Recreation Park**) and the northern point of entry to the San Juan Skyway. Its modern visitor center (providing information, films on the area, and a gift shop; 970–626–5181 or 800–220–4959; www.ridgewaycolorado.com), near the Colorado Highway 62 junction, its revitalized commercial area, and its newer shopping areas, lodging facilities, and restaurants all provide the visitor with many necessities and niceties—especially when visitors flock through Ridgway on the way to see wildflowers in bloom in the summer or to take in the turning of the nearby aspen forests in the fall. Once a rail and transportation center in the nineteenth century, this old ranching town still retains much of its western flavor, as we discover when several youngsters on horseback race furiously by the old fire station that is now an **art gallery.** The red front and bell tower of the old rock-walled fire station are set off beautifully by the exceedingly lush green park across the street. The scene looks so inviting that we stop to stretch, sit, and eat a snack in the park before moving on to **Telluride.**

The ascent is gentle as we head west on Colorado Highway 62 to Dallas Divide, Placerville, and Telluride. Just a few miles out of Ridgway, we come to a rise that gives us a view over a vast valley, rimmed with a stunning array of peaks. We have seen powerful mountain scenery all day, but this scene stops us in our tracks. I get out with my camera and click away, hoping to capture the essence of what we are seeing. These **Uncompaghre Mountains** are truly magnificent. The highest peak, rugged and foreboding at 14,100 feet, is **Mount Sneffels,** named for the volcano in Jules Verne's

Victorian home, Telluride

Journey to the Center of the Earth. We linger a little longer before continuing up to **Dallas Divide,** named for U.S. Vice President George Mifflin Dallas, who served under President James K. Polk. The divide tops out at 8,735 feet. Now heading down the other side, we pass through the remains of **Placerville,** established in 1876 as a mining camp but pretty well wiped out by fire in 1919.

We turn southeast onto Colorado Highway 145, following the **San Miguel River** for most of the remaining 12 miles to Telluride. From a few miles outside of town, we catch our first view of Telluride across wide **San Miguel Park** in a 6-mile-long glacier valley at the foot of numerous rock walls, rising precipitously to **Ajax, Telluride,** and **Ingram Peaks.** Just about 2 miles out, we glimpse another view of town, framed in the foreground by a few weathered old buildings and corrals. This is the approximate location of old San Miguel City. Founded in 1876, it was the first mining camp in the area. In the same year another little camp called Columbia cropped up. Being closer to the mining area, it grew up and outstripped San Miguel City. In time the name Columbia was changed to Telluride. Today's city, at 8,744 feet elevation, has around 1,600 permanent residents and is listed in the National Register of Historic Sites. As we drive farther toward town, we see ski condominiums spreading out from the **Historic District.** In 1972 Telluride was chosen as the site for a major ski development. The winter snow that was so oppressive to the early miners is now viewed as a form of "white gold," bringing new life and money to this otherwise snowbound town, which can receive up to 200 inches of snow in one season.

We stop briefly at **Telluride Visitor Services** (P.O. Box 653, Telluride, Colorado 81435; 970–728–4431 or 888–355–8743; www.visittelluride.com), located on the west side of town in an attractive modern building containing a restaurant and grocery store. As we drive in on the main street, Colorado Avenue, we immediately are impressed that Telluride is a little larger than both Silverton and Ouray. Numerous homes and older buildings reflect the richness of past bonanza times, while row after row of condominium units tell us that this town is in the middle of a ski boom. The mines, which produced the early opulence, were christened with names as colorful as their discoverers: the Pandora, the Smuggler, Hidden Treasure, the Tomboy, and the Liberty Belle are but a few. And at one, the Gold King, a Telluride citizen developed the world's first successful line to transmit alternating current. Driving through town we reflect that had this been 1889, the very road we are on might have been the escape route for **Butch Cassidy**'s first bank robbery after he and two cohorts looted the San Miguel County Bank, making off with $22,500. Emboldened by this success, Cassidy repeated his stellar performance over and over again, becoming one of the West's most notorious outlaws.

After parking we get out of the car and stand for a few moments, just taking in the high peaks encircling three sides of the town like a giant stage set. **Ingram Falls,** 3,000 feet above us, plummets several hundred feet down the rocky face of **Ingram Mountain.** Although it is several miles away, that mountain seems to be just at the end of the street. To the right of this impressive falls is another cascade of water that is even more breathtaking. **Bridal Veil Falls** streaks 450 feet down another vertical rock wall and takes the record as the highest unbroken waterfall in Colorado. We are told that in the summer, hang gliders descend from lofty **Ajax Peak,** elevation 12,785 feet, to land here on Colorado Street in front of the Sheridan Hotel.

Next to the courthouse we see the Galloping Goose with its Pierce Arrow parts. It has been on display here permanently since 1951, when it was mothballed following the removal of the narrow-gauge tracks. In the early days passengers arriving at Telluride were greeted by a stationmaster who would yell out, "To Hell you ride." But there is no hell in this pleasant mountain community today. Time spent in this old town with its fascinating array of nineteenth-century buildings, already restored or in the process of restoration, is nothing but pleasure. We walk from the old courthouse to the Sheridan Hotel next door. This three-story hotel, built in 1895, is one of the nicest we have seen all day. It was in front of this shrine in the "City of Gold," as Telluride was sometimes called, that William Jennings Bryan made several of his famous speeches, including a version of his "Cross of Gold" speech, in support of the silver standard in the late 1800s.

Adding to the sense that some kind of boom is going on here now, Telluride is very busy today. There are many young people gathering in front of the cafes and on the street corners. Yet in spite of all the people we seem to be the only ones in a hurry. While the atmosphere is more laid-back than bustling, the scene here has changed considerably from our first trip to Telluride a few years ago. Then it seemed Telluride still had one foot in the 1960s. Hardly so today, we think, as we wander through tony, very upscale specialty shops, boutiques, and galleries and view the phenomenal growth of multistory condominiums and hotels sprawling right down to the river and beginning to fill the valley to the west. From the standpoint of summer travelers, it would be sad to see the historic section of town dwarfed by the slick modern development built to support ski tourism. We hope that a healthy balance between the old and the new will be kept, since much of the more recent aggressive development has targeted **Mountain Village,** a Vail-like ski resort scene 5 miles southwest of Telluride resting at a lofty 9,450 feet.

From the material we picked up at the visitor information center, we note that the Telluride area (including Mountain Village), which is a popular skiing destination and bills itself as the "Summer Festival Capital of the United States," continues to boom with an ever-increasing number of places to stay, capable of housing several thousand guests. Nearly fifty restaurants, cafes, and bars offer food and drink, and numerous upscale shops, gift stores, and galleries are a shopper's delight. We walk down a few blocks from Colorado Avenue to the 2.5-mile-long San Miguel River Trail along the banks of the **San Miguel River,** which at this point in its journey is a beautiful mountain stream. We sit down on the grassy banks and just soak it all in. In every direction we look, there are elements of magnificence and beauty we have not seen in the other mountain towns along our route today. There are outstanding views in every direction. And just across the river the steep mountainside, cut with hiking and ski trails, is lush with a dense mixture of conifers and aspen. **Bear Creek Trail** beckons us to explore it, but we will have to wait for another day. No wonder everyone wants a piece of the action here. When we first came in this afternoon, we drove just east of town to **City Park.** There we walked in a huge area of open space dotted with tennis courts, walking paths, picnic benches, and an outdoor concert stage, which serves as a platform for the jazz, bluegrass, and rock musicians who perform here during Telluride's many summer festivals. After a few more minutes listening to the cold, rushing mountain water, we reluctantly get up, leave the riverbank, and walk back to Colorado Avenue.

We look at the clock in the courthouse tower and realize that it is 5:30 P.M. and time to go if we are to be back in Durango to meet our kids for dinner. Although we have to leave Telluride the way we came in, we alter our route a little by driving up a few streets to one of the dirt roads heading in the same direction. In this somewhat residential part of town, we see a beautiful, brightly painted Victorian-style home absolutely covered with "gingerbread." Although the house seems out of place in this rugged country, it lends a touch of elegance to this rocky glacial valley.

Now at the junction, approximately 3 miles from town, we interrupt our westerly course and turn left onto Colorado Highway 145 heading south to New Ophir and Rico. In just a few miles we pass the spur road to the left leading to Mountain Village. From there the highway rises steadily, and soon we see in the distance **Sunshine Peak** at 14,000 feet and **Mount Wilson** at 14,246 feet elevation. Shortly we see **New Ophir** along the road, with its mining and railway relics just off the road. There are a few homes, some old buildings, and a post office here. We remember reading a story about a postman who, on Christmas Eve in 1883, set out from Silverton with the Christmas mail for Ophir. He never made it. Two years later his body was found with the mail sack still strapped to his back. Some crushing Christmas Eve avalanche had done him in.

From New Ophir we pass through some of the prettiest forest land we have seen yet. Lining the road are beautiful groves of aspens, or "quakies," as the cowboys used to call them in their attempt to describe the way their leaves move with the wind. We pass by **Trout Lake** with its thick grove of aspens leading up the slope to timberline. Beyond there we see some of the most contorted peaks we have come across today. A half-moon is rising above these mountains this afternoon, visible even in the bright blue sky. The road takes us in a traverse around these peaks so that at one point we view them end on. We are struck by the peak on the very end, **Sheep Mountain,** elevation 13,182 feet. It is almost perfectly triangular in shape, and for a moment, the way the shadows are falling on it, it looks like an ancient pyramid in this high alpine country.

We now cross Lizard Head Pass at 10,250 feet elevation. It's very wide open up here on top of the pass. We stop to take in the quiet isolation this afternoon. The tops of 13,000-foot peaks look close enough to touch, once again giving us

Lizard Head Peak

that special feeling of being on top of the world. The map reveals that many of these mountains surrounding us are part of the **San Miguel range.** Looming up now on the right is the grotesque rock formation for which the pass was named. **Lizard Head Peak,** at 13,113 feet elevation, looks at first glance like some giant brooding bird sitting on a rock pedestal. I attempt to absorb more fully what I am seeing. Gazing at the strange rock formation in the fresh, rarefied mountain air, I have that spine-tingling sensation that comes when the senses are overwhelmed. I remember that it also caught the eye of a member of the Hayden expedition in 1874. Hayden commented that the pass was "marked by a curious monument of trachyte 290 feet high." Curious indeed. It looks like a giant pagan bird or lizard god sitting there. With great dignity, its awesome commanding presence rules the surrounding valleys, mountains, and sky. Viewed with some imagination, the stately spruce and fir lined up in the foreground look like loyal subjects standing at attention before the awesome figure above them. I know now that, for me, this is the most exhilarating experience of the day. For the third or fourth time in my life, I am experiencing at this moment a "Rocky Mountain High."

With insufficient time to hike the several-miles-long trail to Lizard Head, we descend Lizard Head Pass, following the **Dolores River** to **Rico.** We notice numerous anglers along the Dolores River, rated as one of the nation's top one hundred fishing streams. At Rico we see a town that has many of the old buildings of the mining days. A modest church, the plain fire station, and the many tin-roofed homes are quite intact. Although the great boom that occurred here in 1879 is definitely over, several restored older buildings indicate that Rico, like so many Colorado mountain towns, is on the threshold of a tourism boom. But if silence is golden, then this town is indeed *rico,* or "rich," as the name implies! This afternoon everything is relatively still and quiet here.

In another 35 miles we pass through **Dolores,** an active, thriving agricultural and cattle town of around 800 people where there is a monument marker detailing the Domínguez-Escalante expedition through here in 1776. It is now quite clear, in this broad valley of rolling hills and wide vistas, that we have left the mountainous mining terrain for cattle country.

Just south of Dolores we notice a sign to the outstanding **Anasazi Heritage Center** (a must if you are in the area) a few miles away, west along Colorado Highway 184. But before reaching that intersection, we turn left off the San Juan Skyway to take a shortcut east along Colorado Highway 184 to **Mancos.** On the way we pass through a beautiful region of valleys and lakes, seeing numerous resorts and guest ranches. Mancos is quiet this evening. From the beginning it has been a farming and ranching community, somewhat removed from the great mining bonanza higher up and to the north, although some disgruntled miners were among the first to homestead the fertile grasslands here. Fishing and horseback riding as well as its proximity to Mesa Verde are bringing many tourists here, sparking a miniboom in this area where most of the matchsticks in the United States have their origins. They are split from aspen wood, logged from those quaking groves high up on the slopes of the mountains. From the Mancos Valley we have a good view of the **La Plata Mountains** and Mount Hesperus at 13,232 feet.

The last few miles take us back to Durango, where we arrive shortly before 8:00 P.M. The narrow-gauge train arrived from Silverton around 6:30. We find our children sitting happily in that grand old lobby of the Strater Hotel, eager to tell us about their return rail trip from Silverton. At dinner, more than eight hours and 230 miles after we left Durango this morning, we share our tales of the Silver Circle. As we end our day, the old train depot, visible through the restaurant's windows, reminds us again that southwestern Colorado's past is very close to the present.

Indian Past: The Ancestral Puebloan Circle Tour

Unquestionably the essence of southwestern Colorado rests in its rich frontier history and its modern western ambience. Yet the area is best known here and abroad for its ancient Ancestral Puebloan cliff dwellings in **Mesa Verde National Park, a World Cultural Heritage Site.** This was the first national park in the United States to be dedicated to the preservation of human heritage. So it is a historical park dedicated to the Ancestral Pueblo People, also called the Anasazi, who, for unknown reasons, began to leave the mesas in small numbers, possibly as early as the eleventh century, building to a mass exodus in the thirteenth century that left the mesa deserted by A.D. 1300. And they never came back. So when you visit Mesa Verde and its immediate environs, you will not see any American Indians whose ancestors lived on the mesa. It is thought that the Mesa Verde people eventually migrated to other areas, resurfacing on the Hopi mesas and in the Rio Grande Valley, where they became the ancestors of some of the Southwest Pueblo Indians you will see in those areas. (The history of the Ancestral Puebloan and the speculative reasons for their leaving this area have been reported in Section 2 of this book, and the discovery of Indian ruins in the Mesa Verde region has been discussed in the history portion of this section.)

More than 750,000 people visit Mesa Verde each year. There are many reasons for you to do the same. The cliff dwellings are easy to reach. In a small area there is a rich concentration of well-preserved and in some cases restored ancient multistoried living quarters in large caves or alcoves along the cliff walls. The talks by the rangers are interesting and educational. The scope of the dwellings is magnificent. The crowds, the signs, the erected fences, the restrictions, and the prohibitions are the necessary distractions. Visiting off-season in October or April (less chance of snow than in winter) or during the winter months, you'll find the park

Mesa Verde Ancestral Puebloan pottery

blessedly more peaceful. The trade-off is that many fewer sites are open to visitors during the shoulder and winter months and most interpretive programs are not operating then. Schedules can change, so if you're coming off-season, call ahead to get the latest information. But do not miss Mesa Verde, especially if you will be unable to see the Ancestral Puebloan cliff dwellings at Betatakin or at Canyon de Chelly.

Mesa Verde National Park

Mesa Verde National Park was founded in 1906 with the primary purpose of preserving what remains of the structures of the Ancestral Pucbloans, who had inhabited the area. The rediscovery of those early Mesa Verde dwellings in 1888 by local ranchers, the **Wetherill brothers,** eventually brought considerable attention to the area. The Wetherills, whose observations sometimes presaged future scientific discoveries, are largely credited with putting "Mesa Verde" on the maps. Compatible with the spirit of the times, they enthusiastically promoted their discovery by exhibiting and selling the "relics" they found at Mesa Verde and other southwestern sites both to nearby and far distant museums and individuals. In 1891 a Swede, Baron Gustav Nordenskiold, performed the first systematic excavations of Mesa Verde, opening the way to future archaeological expeditions. But upon leaving to return to Sweden, Nordenskiold crated up box after box of invaluable relics to take home with him. The people of Durango protested this move and tried, through the courts, to block shipment of the antiquities. There was no law to support their protest. The unhampered removal of artifacts continued until the **Federal Antiquities Act** (see "Practical Hints: Meeting the Indians" in the back matter of this book for more on this subject) was passed in 1906, prohibiting the removal of ancient artifacts, and the park was established. By that time many fine, intact relics had disappeared from the site. Nonetheless other fine artifacts have been found since that time, and many of them are on display at the **Chapin Mesa Museum.**

The park contains approximately 52,000 acres. There are more than twenty major dwelling sites open to the public that have been excavated and stabilized. Of these only five are cliff-dwelling sites. But there are hundreds more that are inaccessible and not open to the public. From 1908 to 1922 **Spruce Tree House,**

Cliff Palace, and the **Sun Temple** were stabilized. The authenticity of some of these changes made in the name of "stabilization" has been questioned, since documentation found in the archaeological field notes often does not back up the reconstruction that was done. Nonetheless these reconstructed sites are well worth seeing. Yet it is satisfying to know that the research and excavation being done these days employs the best of modern know-how and technology so that mistakes made in the past will not recur.

With the exception of food service at **Spruce Tree Terrace** (open year-round), lodging, food, and gas on the mesatop are available only from spring to late fall. Gas is also available below the mesa at **Morefield Campground.** Dates of these services can change from year to year, so check with the park. And except for Spruce Tree House, the cliff dwellings are closed in the winter. **Wetherill Mesa** can be visited only from early June through either Labor Day or late September. Again, check with the park.

Corrugated pottery vessel

Durango makes an excellent base for a day trip to Mesa Verde National Park, Cortez, Colorado, and the remains of **Lowry Pueblo** in **Canyons of the Ancients National Monument** at Pleasant View, Colorado. You can also use Cortez and Mancos as bases for a similar day trip. But if you want to stay up on Mesa Verde, lodging is available in season there, and a campground is provided near the entrance below the mesa.

From Durango drive west on U.S. Highway 160, the San Juan Skyway (a National Forest Scenic Byway) 35 miles to the Mesa Verde turnoff. At the entry booth you will pay a fee and receive some information about the park. It is 21 miles to the major ruin sites over a narrow but paved mountain road that is often so congested and has so many sharp curves and steep grades that it takes about forty-five minutes to travel it. The speed limit in the park is 35 miles per hour or sometimes less. It is strictly enforced. After dark, be particularly cautious, for deer seem to think this road is also theirs. Information: Mesa Verde National Park, Mesa Verde, Colorado 81330; (970) 529–4465; www.nps.gov/meve/; or Far View Visitors Center; (970) 529–5036. After entering the park tune your car radio dial to AM 1610 for updated park information.

Seeing Mesa Verde National Park

When you arrive at the park's entry station (fee), you are at the north end of Mesa Verde. As the mesa reaches southwest, it, like the Hopi's Black Mesa, is cut by many deep canyons so that the southern edge fingers out above the desert below, creating several islands in the sky. Each of these island fingers of Mesa Verde is also called a mesa. The two that you may visit are **Chapin Mesa,** named after an early amateur archaeologist, and **Wetherill Mesa,** named for the ranchers who were the first white men to "rediscover" the early dwellings on the mesa. The structures on

Chapin Mesa were restored early in the last century, while those at Wetherill Mesa were not restored until the 1950s and 1960s.

From the entry station the winding and twisting road ascends up the north escarpment of the mesa, gaining almost 1,000 feet in elevation by the time it reaches Morefield Campground. From the campground (gas, food, and craft outlets), the road passes through stands of ponderosa pines, where you will see evidence of the Bircher wildfire of July 2000. After a short tunnel it begins the climb to the mesatop. At 6.4 miles from the entry station is the **Montezuma Valley Overlook,** with splendid aerial views north and west out over Cortez, Colorado and the Colorado Plateau. Both the valley and its major city, Cortez, were named by early settlers who thought that Aztecs from Mexico had built the many old dwellings that lay on the land.

Still climbing, the road reaches the mesa's top at elevation 8,512 feet, where there are a turnout and parking area. This is **Park Point.** Take time to stop here, for an unobstructed, one-of-a-kind, 360-degree aerial view of some of the major sights on the Colorado Plateau. The viewpoint at the end of an uphill trail, dotted with benches, takes only five minutes to walk. If it is a clear day, when you reach the top you will be rewarded by how far you can see. Sixty miles to the north and west are the Abajo or **Blue Mountains** in southeastern Utah, and on the horizon 110 miles to the north are the **Manti–La Sal Mountains** near Moab, Utah. Only 45 miles away is one of southwestern Colorado's famous fourteeners, **Mount Wilson,** elevation 14,246 feet. To the south, rising from the desert floor on the Navajo reservation in northwestern New Mexico, is a rugged giant of a monument, **Shiprock,** whose fractured top rises 1,700 feet into the sky. And in the same direction, 90 miles away in Arizona, are the **Lukachukai Mountains.** With views out over four states, Park Point adds an extra dimension to this geographic region known as the Four Corners.

Ponderosa pine

From this high point the road descends approximately 5 miles to the **Far View Visitor Center** (970–529–5036), a modern circular building. Open seasonally from late spring through mid-autumn, 8:00 A.M. to 5:00 P.M., the visitor center offers helpful information services and has on display museum-quality Indian arts and crafts of the region. All visitors should stop at the visitor center since admission tickets (first-come, first-served basis; fee) to hour-long tours of Chapin Mesa's **Cliff Palace** and **Balcony House** and Wetherill Mesa's **Long House** can only be obtained there. These dwelling sites cannot be visited without a ticket. At 1:00 P.M. when all of that day's tickets are sold out, you may purchase advances tickets for the next day's tour only. Visitors are allowed to tour only one of the above Chapin Mesa dwellings each day. Ranger-led tours begin every hour or every half hour depending on the season. Visitors with tickets should be at the tour site ten minutes early. When the visitor center is not open, visitors should proceed to the Chapin Mesa Museum for information (970–529–4475). If you plan to spend a full day at Mesa Verde, you may have time to see a few sites on both mesas. But half-day visitors will probably only have time to see the ruins on Chapin Mesa.

In general the Wetherill Mesa dwellings stabilized later in the century. Profiting from the application of more advanced archaeological techniques, they represent more accurately the way things were. But the Chapin Mesa structures, while thought by some to be overly restored, are more dramatic and, because there are more of them, render a fuller, more varied picture of early Ancestral Puebloan life. They are also easier to reach, since the Chapin Mesa road is relatively easy to negotiate and in most instances takes you right up to the short walking trails accessing the early dwelling sites.

The Wetherill Mesa parking lot is reached via a slow, 12-mile drive from the visitor center over a typical mountain road with lots of twists, curves, and steep grades. The road is only open Memorial Day through Labor Day between the hours of 8:00 A.M. and 4:30 P.M. Vehicles weighing more than 8,000 pounds GVW and/or are more than 25 feet in length are prohibited. Sandwiches and cold drinks are available on Wetherill Mesa. From the parking area you can walk a short distance to take the 0.5-mile self-guided tour of the cliffside dwelling **Step House** (containing ruins from two periods in the Ancestral Puebloan time line) or board the tram or minibus for the short ride to the cliff dwelling **Long House** (a dramatic ruin second only in size to Cliff Palace and containing a large central plaza), where you will join a 0.5-mile, round-trip ranger-guided tour. From there you can board the bus again to reach the starting point for a 0.75-mile self-guided tour of **Badger House Community,** four clusters of pit houses spread out on the mesatop.

To the right of the Far View Visitor Center, a ridge offering good views, is the **Far View Lodge** (800–449–2288) with its dinner-only restaurant. There is an Indian arts and crafts shop there, and one at the Far View services center, adjacent to the cafeteria (breakfast, lunch, and dinner) and the mesatop's only gas station. (For information about buying Southwest Indian arts and crafts, see the "Shopping" sections in Sections 2 and 4.)

As you drive south from the visitor center to see the major ruins on Chapin Mesa, look for an access road to the left of the highway at approximately 1.3 miles. There is a sign on this road marking the road to the **Far View Sites Complex,** but it is south of the spur road and faces south. Although these cliff-top dwellings are apparently intended to be seen upon exiting the park, seeing them on the way in places the cliff dwellings you will first see on Chapin Mesa in better chronological perspective, providing an excellent introduction to them. So turn left and follow the road a very short distance to the Far View area, where there are remnants of mesatop pueblos that preceded the cliff dwellings in time.

Because it is often bypassed by visitors as they rush pell-mell to and from the more famous sites, this site offers some solitude the others do not. You can wander in relative peace, letting your eyes explore several ruins of the Pueblo III or Great Pueblo Period, which spanned the years A.D. 1100 to 1300. Some of the structures had additions of up to three and four stories, as the Ancestral Puebloans slowly abandoned many smaller village sites to live together in larger communities. As the population increased, these new rooms were added, no doubt without the modern-day fear of reassessment and higher taxes. The Puebloans seemed to dote on these mesatop pueblos, living in comfortable villages like this until, inexplicably, they abandoned some of them in the thirteenth century and new homes were built in great alcoves in the cliffs that were occupied only for a short time.

Take time to view the hand-hewn rocks in the walls of **Far View House,** carefully cut to rectangular building-block size and then shaped with exactness to fit the corners and curved walls (see Section 2, "A Prehistory of Indian Country"). Mud mortar, sometimes containing strengtheners such as small rocks and pot-sherds, was then used sparingly to cement the building blocks together. Contem-

plate how people who did not have the benefit of the wheel carried the thousands of tons of sedimentary rock and the huge Douglas fir timbers for roof supports that were required to construct multistoried apartment buildings containing more than fifty rooms and several kivas or ceremonial chambers.

Erecting these huge buildings with the limited technology available at the time is a truly amazing feat. If you have more time, you may want to walk a few hundred feet to another ruin, **Pipe Shrine House,** circa A.D. 900 to 1300, or take the short footpath to **Far View Tower,** one of fifty-seven tow-ers of unknown function that once were scattered across the mesatop.

Returning to the main road, turn left and continue a little more than 3 miles to the four-way stop, following the signs to the Chapin Mesa Museum and Spruce Tree House. Although it is hard to comprehend,

Masonry walls and doorway,
Far View House

you are now at the same elevation as when you entered the park at the entry sta-tion. This section of the park has picnic tables, rest rooms, a lunchroom and small grocery store, an excellent bookstore, and an Indian arts and crafts shop. Be cer-tain to take time to see the **Chapin Mesa Museum,** a real gem, which contains many of the artifacts that have been excavated and removed from the sites you will be seeing. In addition, displayed on the walls of the museum's auditorium are six wall mural paintings. They were executed by eight historically significant Ameri-can Indian artists who were associated with the Santa Fe Indian School in the 1920s and 1930s. Julián Martinez, one of the artists, was the husband and co-worker of Maria Martinez, the renowned San Ildefonso potter. And another of the artists, Jack Hokeah, was Maria's adopted son. Now take time to see the museum's ceramic collection. The size and design work of the ceramic pieces on display are truly stunning. Also be certain to see the lifelike dioramas, which reveal how the building structures were incorporated into the lives of the Ancestral Puebloans.

Although there are many beautiful artifacts in the museum, it is sad to think that

Kivas of Spruce Tree House

many others have been removed from Mesa Verde. Some Mesa Verde relics can be found in the galleries of the Museum of New Mexico's Palace of the Governors in Santa Fe, while others are in the Colorado State Museum in Denver and at several other museums throughout the United States. Surprisingly one large group of artifacts resides in the National Museum in Helsinki, Finland, the legacy of a scientific study of the Mesa Verde ruins in the 1890s by the Swedish scientist Nordenskiold. Never displayed in Sweden, these well-traveled artifacts were stored there until 1938, when they became the property of the Helsinki Museum. Though this Swedish scientist, who was of Finnish descent, may have taken Mesa Verde artifacts to distant lands, he was not the first nor the last to disperse Mesa Verde's pottery and other treasures to far-flung repositories. In spite of laws placed on the books from 1906 on, both Americans living in the Southwest and visiting treasure hunters have for decades dug relics from ancient American Indian sites like they were potatoes and sold them both here and abroad. It is hoped that the recent tough enforcement of the antiquities laws will bring these illegal practices to an end.

From the Chapin Mesa Museum you can take a self-guided walk to **Spruce Tree House,** a cliff dwelling built in the giant alcove of a sandstone wall. One of the best-preserved dwellings in Mesa Verde, it is also the third largest, with more than 114 living rooms. Probably 100 to 150 people once lived there. Spruce Tree was one of the earliest cliff dwellings to be discovered by Richard Wetherill, who found it in December 1888, shortly after finding Cliff Palace. He named it for a large tree in front of the dwelling that in his time was thought to be a Douglas spruce. Today we know trees like that as Douglas firs. He must have wondered why these early people chose to live in such remote, inaccessible locations. For reasons not well understood, some of the mesatop dwellings were deserted in the early 1200s for these alcoves.

Echoing their lifestyle on top of the mesa, they built the same type of pueblo buildings within the caves. Ironically, the craftsmanship was not nearly as good in these later efforts. But since the stone walls were plastered over with a thin wall of mud, perhaps it made little difference. Some say the reduced quality in workmanship may have been due to the fact that in the great caves the buildings were less exposed to weather and did not need to be so carefully constructed. Others think the buildings were constructed hastily to avoid potential enemies. This view is, however, debunked by most archaeologists, who point out that Spruce Tree House would have been hard to defend and might even have led to entrapment.

Ancestral Puebloan doorway, Spruce Tree House

Note the circular kivas at Spruce Tree House. They are a dramatic sight, with their ladders protruding out of the ground. And the roofs of the kivas served as the floor of the plaza. What reverberations there must have been in the kiva below, with the dancers pounding their feet in rhythm above!

You may note that the stonework of some of these former three-story structures is not as fine as at Far View House. Nonetheless it is impressive. The small, T-shaped doorways indicate that the Ancestral Puebloans may have carried wide loads on their backs, the wider aperture at the top allowing the burden to pass through. Although these openings appear small, you must remember that the average Ancestral Puebloan male is thought to have been only 5 feet 4 inches tall, while the average female was around 5 feet tall.

After completing your tour of Spruce Tree House, return to the museum parking lot. If you want to visit more cliff dwellings, return to the four-way stop and continue straight ahead onto **Mesa Top Loop Drive.** Continue south until you come to the first intersection. There you can either continue straight on to the mesatop dwellings and to turnouts offering views of cliff dwellings, or turn left at that intersection to reach Cliff Palace and Balcony House. **Cliff Palace** is a ten-minute drive from the museum. The approximately hour-long ranger-guided tour is about 0.25 mile in length. The tour includes a 75-foot ascent via steps and several short ladders. Picnic tables and rest rooms are near the parking lot.

Many of the pictures you have seen depicting the cliff dwellings are of this dramatic site. Not only was it the first dwelling to be found by the Wetherill brothers in December 1888, but it is also the largest cliff dwelling in the Southwest. Because of its many rooms and dramatic honey-colored, golden-hued stone towers, it was dubbed Cliff Palace. It was not a palace to the Ancestral Puebloan. It was just the site of another agrarian Pueblo community built along fairly standard lines during the Classic Pueblo Period. Its cave is 325 feet long and 90 feet deep. The

Cliff Palace

cave entrance is more than 60 feet tall at its highest point, allowing for structures that were four stories high in places. It contained twenty-three kivas and nearly 200 rooms, but typically the living spaces were very small and some rooms probably were used for storage. Note the high ledge up and to the back of the cave. An ingenious attic space squeezed out of the cave's dimensions—it contained fourteen storage rooms. Approximately 200 to 250 people lived there.

Under the alcove roof several of the masonry structures rise from the earth and extend to the earth, reaching for the cave ceiling, not the sky. Some have speculated that this intense recontact with the earth had religious or ritual significance. Look for the window in the base of the tallest masonry remnant that looks like a tower. Peek in that window and you will get some idea of the room size. While peering in, note high up on one of the original plastered walls the fine Ancestral Puebloan painting. After almost 800 years this superbly designed painting is still mostly intact. On finishing your tour of Cliff Palace, retrieve your car and continue in a southerly direction toward Balcony House. There are several places to park along this road to view cliff structures from the mesa rim across the canyon. You will round the very southern tip of Chapin Mesa before heading north along the east face of the mesa finger above **Soda Canyon.** Balcony House parking lot is about a ten-minute drive from Cliff Palace.

Balcony House, open generally only in the summer, is perhaps the most interesting dwelling site on the mesa. The remarkably intact second-story walkway, which looks like a balcony, gives the structure its name. There may be fewer crowds at Balcony House, since touring it requires a 32-foot climb up a sturdy, wide Puebloan-style ladder and a hands-and-knees scramble through a 12-foot-long tunnel. Skirts and high-heeled shoes are not compatible with either of these activities. Neither are people who have fears of heights, tunnels, or climbing lad-

Balcony House

ders. But if none of these apply and you have a ticket, join the ranger-guided tour to take your turn as a modern-day Puebloan. Children delight in the exciting aspects of Balcony House, and adults are usually intrigued with the entry and exit routes. The entry ladder is provided compliments of the park service, since experts believe that today's exit route was the only access path to and from the dwellings. The exit is through a narrow cleft in the rocks, with improved toeholds for the modern visitor.

In spite of its inaccessibility, Balcony House, unlike many of the other cliff dwellings, seems to have been built with care and without haste. You will notice that the early Pueblo stonemasons demonstrated a very high quality of workmanship there. Also notice the ancient timbers projecting from the stone walls. Core samples drilled from those Douglas fir timbers were used to date the dwelling by means of comparative tree ring growth patterns. While the men cut and hauled the timbers, the women in this village processed the corn, using a *mano,* or grinding stone, and a *metate,* or grinding basin, (on display at Balcony House).

From the parking area continue north to the junction with the **Mesa Top Loop Road.** At this junction you can turn left and take the 6-mile loop trip, which includes numerous modified Basketmaker pit house sites on the mesatop, dating from A.D. 575 to 750, that precede the cliff dwellings by many centuries. If you take this road, you may want to turn off at the Square Tower House turnout. After a short walk you will see **Square Tower House,** the tallest cliff structure in the park. Going back to your car, wind your way through numerous other dwelling sites, eventually reaching the **Sun Point view** area. From that location, thought to be the spot from which the Wetherill brothers first glimpsed Cliff Palace, you will catch your first view of the **Sun Temple,** a later stop along the Loop Road. This haunting mesatop structure probably served a religious function

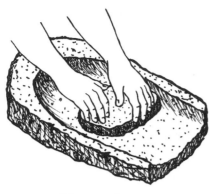

Metate and mano

for many of the Ancestral Puebloan communities. From the Sun Temple return along the Mesa Top Loop Road to the four-way stop at the Main Junction. Turn right toward the visitor center and in approximately 24 miles, exit the park.

Provided that you have time and are not too saturated with early Pueblo dwellings, you may want to spend a few hours seeing another early Indian gem, well off the tourist track. The Lowry Pueblo at Pleasant View, Colorado, approximately 35 miles northwest of Mesa Verde, should not be missed. It can be seen as part of a Mesa Verde circle tour or as you enter or exit southwestern Colorado going to or from southeastern Utah.

Lowry Pueblo National Historic Landmark–Canyons of the Ancients National Monument: A Narrative Account

From the Mesa Verde spur road, we turn left and head west on National Forest Scenic Byway U.S. Highway 160, through the **Montezuma Valley** toward Cortez, Colorado. We are tired and hot. It has been an exhausting day. We arrived at the Chapin Mesa Museum and Spruce Tree House at 9:30 A.M. Except for a quick picnic lunch, we have been viewing ruins and hassling with crowds for five hours. Yet the experience was exceptionally worthwhile. We gained a much better understanding of the people who once inhabited this land. But we all agree that the experience was more educational than inspirational. Now we yearn for some solitude and peace and quiet to reflect about what we have learned. The isolated Lowry Pueblo will help us do just that.

We relax as the car's air conditioner takes over. There's a storm building to the west, and every few minutes we drive under the welcome umbrella of a cloud and then back out again into the hot, bright afternoon sun. Passing through the outskirts of **Cortez,** we see several of the trading posts and shops where we have purchased Indian crafts. These posts cater mostly to the Navajo farther south, but occasionally Jicarilla Apaches from New Mexico or Utes from the area immediately south will trade here. As we pass pleasant **Cortez Park** with its shade trees and picnic tables and the **Colorado Welcome Center** (Cortez Chamber of Commerce, Mildred and Main Streets, P.O. Box HH; Cortez, Colorado 81321; 970–565–3414 or 800–253–1616), we notice the slower pace in Cortez and the lack of traffic this afternoon. Although it is an active farming and ranching community and a former center for oil and gas production, it is a sleepier town than Durango and smaller with a population of 7,900.

There is a good mix of Anglos, Mexican Americans, Navajo, and Utes here today. Tourism is booming—Cortez is well situated to serve as a base for many of

Lowry Pueblo National Historic Landmark–
Canyons of the Ancients National Monument

the attractions in southwestern Colorado. At an altitude of 6,198 feet, it is lower (consequently hotter) and not as picturesquely situated as Durango. The chamber of commerce, promoting Cortez as a place where the mountains meet the desert, emphasizes the sun when it points out that you need sunglasses in the winter as well as the summer. Those claims are not exaggerated. It is dry here, with an annual rainfall of only 12 inches.

We drive through town, following the signs to U.S. Highway 666 North, Pleasant View, and Dove Creek, Colorado. About 2 miles from Cortez, we pass the sign and junction road on the left leading to the outstanding **Crow Canyon Archaeological Center.** We recall that just a few days ago we met and visited with one of the Southwest's leading archaeologists who helped develop the center. He told us about various daylong and weeklong programs (see "Staying There: Tours, Events, and Activities" this section) for travelers who want to dig a little deeper into the Southwest's early history. Visitors who are willing to spend a week there can actually participate working side by side with skilled professionals in the ongoing excavation and analysis of artifacts. No previous archaeological experience or knowledge is required. We decide that it would be fun to follow up some summer.

Now heading northwest we drive across the high plains approximately 21 miles to **Pleasant View.** On the way we have more good views to our left of the **Sleeping Ute Mountains.** Its rounded outcroppings are well named, for their pleasing shapes combine to form an image of a giant man lying on his back, with emphasis on his arms folded and resting on his chest.

At Pleasant View we see the sign to the **Lowry Pueblo,** turn left onto road CC, and drive west 9 miles to the site. The flat, relatively straight road (paved partway and gravel the rest of the way) is in good shape as it cuts through the farm and scrub desert country to the site. Dust swirls around us as we pull into the parking area. Although it is hot this afternoon, the wind that has been kicking up

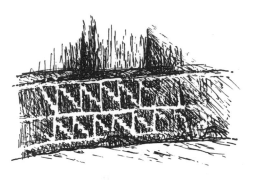

Lowry Pueblo—
painted kiva wall, before removal

the dust also makes the temperature tolerable. The breeze feels good on our backs as we get out of the car.

Luckily we are the only people here. In fact the only other living creature in sight as we walk to the ancient pueblo is a western red-tailed hawk circling lazily above us. Our tour will be self-guided, with several smaller Bureau of Land Management reader boards telling us about the pueblo. The ancient dwelling appears like a diminutive pile of rubble compared with some of the grand reconstructions at Mesa Verde. But we are drawn to it. Its scale is more human in size than the larger dwelling sites we saw this morning. It speaks to us as no signs, brochures, or rangers can in this spectacularly understated setting here on the lonely high plain.

It is eerily quiet this afternoon. Away from the earlier crowds, we now get a keen sense of what it must have been like to live in one of these remote Ancestral Puebloan villages. We walk through some of the forty rooms that have been excavated, their thick, 800- to 900-year-old walls casting cool, refreshing shadows under the hot afternoon sun. Although the Ancestral Puebloan farmers who lived here probably appreciated the shade these walls provided in the summer, they were doubtless even more grateful for the protection they provided in the winter as blinding snowstorms howled outside.

From the highest point on the site, vistas of the wide agricultural plain open up before us, with the mountains looming up in the distance. For more than fifty years the Puebloan farmers who occupied this village must have been able to scan the horizon as we are doing now, perhaps spotting their neighbors and friends in the distance as they traveled on pilgrimages to one of the eight kivas plus the Great Kiva here.

This afternoon we walk the path through the pueblo to kiva B, the original site of an unusual painted kiva wall fragment we saw earlier at the Anasazi Heritage Center. We thought that the painted design on the fragment resembled either lightning, a snake, or possibly the steps of a pyramid. But no. We learned at the center that that intriguing steplike design was an abstract symbol for cloud formations—and possibly of Chacoan origin, because it is thought that this site may have been an outlier of Chaco Pueblo to the south. Walking beyond the kiva, alongside the remains of more pueblo walls, we recall that for unknown reasons these dwellings were abandoned by the middle of the twelfth century, long before the great drought of the thirteenth century that some think may have contributed to the mass abandonment of Mesa Verde.

Now we walk in a wide circle on the somewhat sloping ground above the pueblo. The only noise is the wind. A cottontail rabbit scurries into the brush. The dusty ground below our feet is honey-colored like the sandstone building blocks. We find an old tree, long dead, its stiff branches still reaching to the blue sky.

Behind it are the stone remains of an ancient pueblo, its ladders pointing upward, its kivas firmly anchored in the ground. We sit down for a few minutes, in the warm, loose sand at the base of the old walls.

We can imagine these people of the earth and the sky, climbing ladders to their second- and third-story dwellings. Perhaps they stood on the high walls, assessing the meaning of the clouds over the mountains. Or perhaps, just as we are doing this afternoon, they sat here in the open to catch a cool breeze, soaking in the pleasant view and gazing out over the horizon where the brown plain meets the intensely blue sky. Our son digs his feet into the warm sand. When he kicks the sand away, a small potsherd surfaces. There is just a trace of a design on it. Indeed, someone did use this barren ground we are sitting on. Maybe 800 or 900 years ago another small boy broke his mother's best bowl here. We wonder about that as we rebury the potsherd, laying it to rest where it has been for more than eight centuries.

Returning to the car, we drive back toward the highway. After a few miles we see the junction road heading off to the south, which would take us over 21 miles of gravel road to **Hovenweep National Monument** (970–562–4282; www.nps.gov.hove), which straddles the Colorado-Utah border. That Ancestral Puebloan area is known for its many varied-shaped tower structures. But with rain threatening and the possibility that the road might be difficult to negotiate when wet, we drive back to the highway. Retracing our route for about 10 miles toward Cortez, we then turn left and head southeast on Colorado Highway 184 toward Dolores and Mancos. On our left about 5 miles from the junction with U.S. Highway 666, we see the **Anasazi Heritage Center** set into the hillside near the **Domínguez and Escalante Pueblo Ruins.** We have taken the short walk through these dwellings many times before, giving them a special priority, since they were the first Ancestral Puebloan ruins in southwestern Colorado to be discovered by non-Indians when the Domínguez-Escalante expedition came upon them in 1776. And we all remember the wonderful vistas from this site out over the **Dolores River Valley,** now the **McPhee Reservoir.** We have just enough time this afternoon to make a reconnaissance of the Anasazi Heritage Center (27501 Highway 184, Dolores; 970–882–4811; TTY 970–882–4825; www.co.blm.gov/ahchmepge.htm). We enter the large, handsome, modern, pueblo-style building and soon discover that it is not a part of the National Park Service. Rather it was built by the Bureau of Reclamation (but operated by the Bureau of Land Management) as part of the McPhee Dam Reservoir Project mitigation. We learn that McPhee Reservoir, located just outside of Dolores, Colorado (created by damming the Dolores River), is the second-largest freshwater lake in Colorado, and it is fully stocked for fishing.

The Anasazi Heritage Center, which also serves as headquarters for Canyons of the Ancients National Monument, is divided into public exhibit areas and collection, storage, laboratory, and administrative areas. Many of the materials in the permanent exhibit were recovered from the McPhee Dam and Reservoir site, and some of the materials on exhibit here are from the Domínguez and Escalante sites. Other materials are from a variety of public lands in southwestern Colorado and the Four Corners area, representing the San Juan Puebloan tradition. We quickly discover that it is a museum not to be missed. In addition to the superb exhibits of

Ancestral Pueblo Culture pottery, other artifacts are highlighted using a time line to fit them into the context of the early historical period. Besides these displays there are a full-size replica of a pit house and a full-scale replica of an archaeological test trench, backed up with video and earphones for a very instructive interpretation. But visitor participation doesn't end there. A hands-on approach is encouraged through the use of interactive computers and microscopes highlighting a variety of archaeological and environmental subjects. And there are numerous "touch-me" drawers filled with Southwest artifacts. There's also a do-it-yourself Indian weaving loom, as well as several manos and metates that invite you to try them. After one of the most fascinating hours we have spent in southwestern Colorado, we conclude that this museum is without question the best in the region— worth a stop at almost any cost. We hope to return another day for the instructive slide programs in the auditorium. On the way out we quickly peruse the bookstore with its extensive collection of well-selected books on the Southwest's exciting early history. We are pleased that there is now a showplace and center for archaeological artifacts from the varied public sites in this part of the Four Corners region, including those from one of our favorite sites, the Lowry Pueblo. We drive on toward Mancos, Colorado, on a course that roughly approximates the trail blazed by those brave Spaniards from Santa Fe, New Mexico, who trudged across this land searching for a route to California. Glad that we are tourists headed for grub at Durango and not Spanish explorers riding into the unknown, we rush through Mancos, connect with U.S. Highway 160, and arrive back in Durango at dusk.

South of Durango: A Brief Visit to the "Fourth" Corner, Northwestern New Mexico

To view some other interesting Indian dwellings and visit a town that serves as a market center for part of the Navajo reservation, you may want to visit northwestern New Mexico.

Leave Durango to the south via busy U.S. Highway 550, which leads to the largest town in the Four Corners area, Farmington, New Mexico. It is approximately 37 miles to **Aztec Ruins National Monument** from Durango. You will travel through the Southern Ute reservation the highway bisects it as you travel south. East of the highway is **Ignacio,** Colorado, the home of the **Southern Ute Tribal Headquarters,** where a visitor center and tribally owned motel and restaurant are open to the public. For most of the way, the road runs parallel to the Animas River. Pass through the small town of **Aztec** (off the highway—a delightful town to explore if you have the time) and follow the signs to the monument west of town where the large tree-shaded parking lot is always a welcome sight on a hot day. There is a small entry fee to be paid at the desk in the visitor center.

Declared a National Monument in 1923, this site has coughed up some exceptionally fine ceramic artifacts that you should take time to see in the small museum just off the lobby. The dwelling structures resemble those at Lowry Pueblo and the three- and four-story surface ruins at Mesa Verde. The Chacoan influence is strong here, from the careful planning of the architecture to the open plaza and the fine-banded stonework. But there also is evidence that people from

Great Kiva, Aztec Ruins National Monument

Mesa Verde lived here later in time, rebuilding some of the walls in their style and leaving much of their distinctive pottery behind.

Yet it is the **Great Kiva** here at Aztec that catches your attention and holds it. Entering its chambers is a sacred experience not dissimilar from walking through the doors at Chartres or Notre Dame. With a diameter of nearly 50 feet, the main floor is 8 feet below the surface of the ground. Do take time to visit this wonderfully reconstructed kiva and experience some of the grandeur that was a part of this ancient high-desert civilization. Early settlers to the area thought these and other structures were built by the ancient Indian civilizations from Mexico, so they named them after the Aztecs. Average touring time at Aztec Monument is less than one hour. Information: Superintendent, Aztec Ruins National Monument, P.O. Box 640, Aztec, New Mexico 87410; (505) 334–6174; www.nps.gov/azru.

Now continue down U.S. Highway 550 to **Farmington,** New Mexico, at 5,390 feet elevation, population 37,800 (Farmington Visitor Center, 3041 East Main, Farmington, New Mexico 87402; 505–326–7602 or 800–448–1240). This oil, gas, coal, and power-generating corner of New Mexico centers on this farming and ranching community. Although Farmington is situated in a well-watered spot near where the La Plata, Animas, and San Juan Rivers come together, it is often dusty and dry, receiving less than 8 inches of rain annually. In the 1950s, when I first passed through Farmington, New Mexico, the oil and gas boom was just beginning. Much of the town was a trailer city, ugly and sprawling in the hot sun. I swore at that time I would never go back there. But in the early 1970s, after visiting Aztec Ruins National Monument, we drove to Farmington for lunch. What we found then and since that time is a modern, progressive town, showing its best side. It is also one of the leading trade centers for the eastern half of the Navajo reservation. Consequently this is a good place to see some genuine trading posts and to purchase Navajo as well as Hopi crafts.

In spite of the scarred, rough-looking edges coming into town, Farmington is

Interior of Great Kiva, Aztec Ruins National Monument

a friendly western town, and you will feel welcome there. Perhaps you will want to have lunch at one of the air-conditioned restaurants or one of the many fast-food outlets. By all means visit one of the Indian arts and crafts shops or trading posts. Browse the streets. Most likely you will see many Navajo in traditional dress doing their shopping and trading in this up-and-coming boom 'n' bust town bordering the northwest corner of the Navajo reservation. And you'll see a lot of travelers on the way to some of the nearby sights, such as the **Bisti Badlands,** 32 miles south along New Mexico Highway 371. There in a paleontological paradise of 30,000 acres of geologic whimsy your explorations may turn up unusual varieties of rocks, fossils, and petrified logs. There are no facilities, so carry plenty of water.

Leave the traffic of modern Farmington and head east toward **Bloomfield** on U.S. Highway 64 to the well-marked **Salmon Ruins and Heritage Park.** This is also the site of the **San Juan County Archaeological Research Center and Library.** The museum's spacious lobby has a very helpful information desk, and gift shop. The museum is well worth visiting. In it you can see the best of the 1.5 million artifacts removed from this ancient pueblo. The pottery on display repeatedly reveals the outstanding handwork of the Chaco Ancient Puebloans. In addition to interesting time-line displays, there are also hands-on, pull-out drawers and other innovative features both children and adults can enjoy. It is worthwhile to note that this is one of the only archaeological sites in the Southwest where most or all of the artifacts have remained permanently on site. Sensing the cultural value of the ruins he found on this land he homesteaded in the late 1880s, George Salmon and later his family protected them from pilferers and fortune hunters. The ruins were kept intact until they could be purchased by the San Juan County Museum Association in 1967. But it was not until 1971 that

Salmon Ruins

the voters of San Juan County passed a bond issue to investigate, excavate, and improve the site. Full-scale excavation began in 1972 and continues intermittently to this day. Exit the lobby on the back side to visit Salmon Ruins and Heritage Park. From the visitor center the walk through the dwelling site and back is about 1 mile. There is a steep section at the beginning of the trail. The distance can be shortened somewhat by driving around the west side of the building down to a parking lot closer to Heritage Park and the ruin.

The flat, arid dwelling site is just a few hundred yards from the fabled **San Juan River** that spawned many of the ancient pueblos. Although only about 40 percent of the original pueblo—one of the largest built by the people of Chaco Canyon in the eleventh century—has been excavated, that's enough for you to see good examples of Chacoan masonry, with its wide layers of large rectangular blocks alternating with narrow bands of smaller and thinner, finely spalled pieces of sandstone. Note how this differs from Mesa Verde masonry, which uses little mortar and consists of large sandstone blocks almost exclusively.

You may marvel that the stone for this 600- to 750-room mud-and-stone pueblo was brought by the Ancestral Puebloans from 30 to 40 miles away. The timbers may even have been carried from as far as today's southwestern Colorado. The early Pueblo People had not developed the wheel, so for a moment contemplate what their options must have been. One theory supports the idea that all these materials were probably hand-carried over a network of specially constructed roads.

Heritage Park is on the east side of the museum building. Here reconstructed dwell-ings representing most of the San Juan Basin Indian cultures serve as part of the "time line" through the museum's outdoors exhibits, which include petroglyphs. Both children and adults will enjoy exploring the life-size structures, which include a subterranean pit house, a furnished Navajo hogan, tipis, and wick-iups, all authentically replicated. The Salmon family homestead can also be visited. Nearby is a tree-shaded picnic area. Full-day professionally guided tours (fee; lunch included) are conducted from Salmon Ruins to *Chaco Culture National Historical Park*. Advance reservation (preferably a week or two) is required for the Chaco Canyon tours. Information: Salmon Ruin and Heritage Park, P.O. Box 125, Bloomfield, New Mexico 87413; (505) 632–2013.

Leaving Salmon Ruins, proceed 2.5 miles to Bloomfield, New Mexico. From Bloomfield take New Mexico Highway 554 to Aztec, where you can reconnect with U.S. Highway 550 to Durango. This round-trip circle trip from Durango, with stops and lunch, takes approximately six hours. The total round-trip distance is 112 miles.

But if you are not returning to Durango, and Santa Fe or Albuquerque, New Mexico, is your destination, take U.S. Highway 64 from Bloomfield east through the picturesque Jicarilla Apache Reservation to Dulce, Chama, Abiquiu, and Espanola on your way there. Or take the southern route to I–25, Albuquerque and Santa Fe via Bernalillo by following U.S. Highway 550/New Mexico 44. On the way, about 3 miles south of Nageezi, New Mexico (41 miles from Bloomfield), is the turnoff to Chaco Culture National Historical Park. Get the details on this problematic route before setting out (see Northeastern Arizona: Indian Country, the last paragraph in the "Seeing Indian Country"). Continuing south on U.S. Highway 550/New Mexico 44, you will eventually pass through the Jemez and Zia Pueblo Indian reservations and Coronado State Monument (see Section 4, "Seeing the Spanish Rio Grande Country—Tours around Albuquerque") before reaching I–25.

STAYING THERE

Durango

The logical touring base for this area is Durango, Colorado. Numerous modern and well-run motels, inns, and hotels are there. During summer tourist season, it's wise to book early to tie down the type of accommodation you want.

Listings for lodging (some of the places date back to the turn of the twentieth century), food, and a few of the more popular events in Silverton, Ouray, Telluride, Mesa Verde, and Cortez are included as well. These other towns are also interesting places to stay, especially if you desire an even smaller and more remote location than Durango. In addition, one or two of the area's better-known dude ranches are mentioned. Usually the rates are based on a week's stay, which includes three meals a day and may include a variety of activities.

If you exhaust the entries in this section searching for lodging and need more hotel, motel, bed-and-breakfast, condominium, and dude ranch listings (with prices), or if you need reservation services or current information about events in the area, contact the **Durango Area Chamber Resort Association.** Information: P.O. Box 2587 VG, 111 South Camino del Rio, Durango, Colorado 81302; (970) 247–0312 or (800) 525–8855 or for reservations (866) 294–5187; www.durango.org. The Public Lands Center at 18 Burnett Court (970–247–4874) offers outdoor hiking and camping information.

Durango has a budget-priced hostel (see Lodging), and international visitors can exchange traveler's checks

View of the Rockies

Strater Hotel, Durango

or currency at the First National Bank of Durango, 259 Ninth Street; (970) 247–3020.

As Durango has become a more and more popular destination for travelers, some of the action has moved off Main Avenue and one block up the hill to **East Second Avenue.** This interesting corridor is well worth exploring. It boasts the **Durango Arts Center,** the **Durango Children's Museum,** a photography gallery, two historic places to stay, and a variety of venues to eat and drink.

Lodging

Strater Hotel. Anchoring the oldest restored section of downtown Durango at the corner of Seventh and Main Avenues, just 2 blocks from the rail depot, is the impressive four-story Strater Hotel. It was built in 1887 as a showplace hotel during Durango's boom years. It has been a hotel continuously since that time. But you no longer have to go outside to reach the bathroom as you did at the turn of the twentieth century. All 94 air-

conditioned rooms have private baths and are beautifully restored and furnished with turn-of-the-twentieth-century antiques. This decorating has obviously been a labor of love. The Strater offers Henry's restaurant as well as the Diamond Belle Saloon. Some parking. Information: Strater Hotel, 699 Main Avenue, P.O. Drawer E, Durango, Colorado 81301; (970) 247–4431 or (800) 247–4431; fax (970) 259–2208; www.strater.com. Expensive.

General Palmer Hotel. This hotel sits in an enviable location almost adjacent to the Denver and Rio Grande rail depot and in the midst of numerous restaurants and shops. Originally there was a hotel on this site, which was built in 1890, but it was not until 1964 that the building was converted from other uses back to hotel status and an annex added to give more space. The small lobby gives a strong turn-of-the-twentieth-century flavor. The hotel's thirty-nine air-conditioned rooms with private baths are restored to late-1800s elegance. Parking lot. Continental breakfast included in room rate. Advance reservation deposit required. Information: General Palmer Hotel, 567 Main Avenue, Durango, Colorado 81301; (970) 247–4747 or (800) 523–3358; fax (970) 247–1332. Moderate to very expensive.

The Rochester Hotel. Up on East Second Avenue, just a block from Main Avenue and within easy walking distance to the train, is this historic 1892 hotel, a bed-and-breakfast accommodation in the spirit of the Old West. Although smaller than the better-known Victorian hotels in town, its quiet location, intimate atmosphere, and excellent service make it a standout. The fifteen spacious and comfortable rooms are handsomely furnished (the decor often inspired by the Western movies filmed in the area) and come with all the amenities. A full breakfast is served each morning. A patio and garden welcome you outdoors. Information: Rochester Hotel, 721 East Second Avenue, Durango, Colorado 81301; (970) 385–1920 or (800) 664–1920; fax (970) 385–1967; www.rochester hotel.com. Moderate to expensive.

The Leland House. This historic bed-and-breakfast suite inn is across East Second Avenue from the Rochester Hotel. Its ten rooms are tastefully decorated and vary in size. Some are small studio efficiencies while six of the rooms are three-room suites with kitchen facilities and private baths. A full breakfast is served every morning. Information: Leland House Bed and Breakfast Suites, 721 East Second Avenue, Durango, Colorado 81301; (970) 385–1920 or (800) 664–1920; fax (970) 385–1967. Moderate.

The Gable House Bed and Breakfast. In a quiet residential area five blocks from the train station is this very nice historic 1892 Victorian home-turned-inn. The rooms in this two-story house are elegantly appointed with antique furnishings. From the public room, a Victorian parlor, and the delicious full breakfast, the Gable House pleases. Information: The Gable House Bed and Breakfast, 805 East Fifth Avenue, Durango, Colorado 81303; (970) 247–4982; www.creativelinks.com/ Gablehouse. Moderate.

Durango Lodge. In a good position just 2 blocks from town center. There are thirty-eight air-conditioned rooms with private baths, TVs, and phones. Cafes and restaurants nearby. Heated swimming pool. Information: Durango Lodge, 150 East Fifth Street, Durango, Colorado 81301; (970) 247–0955. Inexpensive to moderate.

Best Western Rio Grande Inn and Suites. In an enviable location close to the railway station, this modern four-story structure with 102 air-conditioned rooms is built around a central enclosed atrium with a heated swimming pool. Amenities include hot tubs (as well as rooms with whirlpool baths) and saunas. Continental breakfast included. Information: Best Western Rio Grande Inn and Suites, 400 East Second Avenue, Durango, Colorado 81301; (970) 385–4980 or (800) 245–4466; fax (970) 385–4980. Expensive.

Jarvis Suite Hotel. Conveniently located right in the heart of downtown Durango. The twenty-two air-conditioned suites in this historic downtown building offer the comfort and luxury of a small European hotel, and in addition, each has a kitchen. The handsomely appointed accommodations—one-bedroom, two-bedroom, and studio suites—all have private baths and offer a quiet, restful place to stay, with restaurants and shops a few steps out the door. Parking lot. Information: Jarvis Suite Hotel, 125 West Tenth Street, Durango, Colorado 81301; (970) 259–6190 or (800) 824–1024; fax (970) 259–6190. Moderate to expensive.

Doubletree Hotel Durango.
Located on the banks of the Animas River, 2 blocks west of the downtown historic railroad station, is this chic, elegant, ultramodern hotel with 159 air-conditioned rooms. The rooms are attractively decorated, and most have small balconies. The rooms on the quiet, north side overlook the river. The public rooms are handsome and in the summertime are bustling with activity just like a big-city hotel. Heated indoor swimming pool, sauna, exercise room, and dining room with river view. Parking. Pets. Information: Doubletree Hotel Durango, 501 Camino Del Rio, Durango, Colorado 81301; (970) 259–6580 or (800) 222–8733; fax (970) 259–4398; www.doubletreehotels.com. Expensive.

Holiday Inn—Durango. Nothing nostalgic or western here. A fairly typical Holiday Inn, but only a stone's throw from the Animas River and just a few blocks from town center and the railway depot. The larger inner courtyard contains a very nice swimming pool and wading pool, welcome amenities on a warm day. Ideally situated for families with children, it generally offers some kind of family rate. There are 139 air-conditioned units with private baths, TVs, and phones. It has a dining room that offers three meals a day. The property is located between Eighth and Ninth Streets on Camino Del Rio, which is 2 blocks west of Main Avenue. Information: Holiday Inn—Durango, 800 Camino Del Rio, Durango, Colorado 81301; (970) 247–5393 or (800) 465–4329; fax (970) 259–4201. Moderate.

Durango Youth Hostel. Located downtown, this AYH hostelry provides dormitories, family rooms, and some private rooms at bargain prices. Information: Durango Youth Hostel, 543 East Second Avenue, Durango, Colorado 81301; (970) 247–9905 or (970) 247–5477. Inexpensive.

Best Western Durango Inn and Suites. Pleasantly located just off U.S. Highway 160 (the Mesa Verde–Cortez Highway) about 1 mile west of the center of town. Seventy-two spacious rooms. Large open grounds with plenty of room to roam and a heated swimming pool. A good place for families. Restaurant. Information: Best Western Durango Inn, Box 3099, Durango, Colorado 81302; (970) 247–3251 or (800) 547–9090; fax (970) 385–4835. Moderate to expensive.

Comfort Inn. Also north of downtown, this motel near the Animas River has forty-eight air-conditioned rooms with TVs. Advance reservation deposit required. Information: Comfort Inn, 2930 North Main Avenue, Durango, Colorado 81301; (970) 259–5373 or (800) 532–7112; fax (970) 259–1546. Moderate.

Spanish Trails Motel. Also located along U.S. Highway 550 north of downtown, this basic motel has forty-one air-conditioned or air-cooled rooms with TVs. Some kitchenettes. Swimming pool and playground. Family motel. Information: Spanish Trails Motel, 3141 Main Avenue, Durango, Colorado 81301; (970) 247–4173. Inexpensive.

Siesta Motel. Also located along U.S. Highway 550 north of downtown is this twenty-two-room basic motel with some kitchen units. Picnic area with cookout facilities. Information: Siesta Motel, 3475 North Main Avenue, Durango, Colorado 81301; (970) 247–0741; fax (970) 247–0971. Inexpensive.

Hampton Inn. Located about 3 miles north of downtown on U.S. Highway 550 is this seventy-six-unit family-friendly motel with a heated indoor swimming pool and guest laundry. An extended continental breakfast comes with the territory. Information: Hampton Inn, 3777 Main Avenue; (970) 247–2600 or (877) 675–0586; fax (970) 259–8012; www.durangohotel.com. Moderate.

Iron Horse Inn. Located about 4 miles north of the town's center in a picturesque western Colorado setting along the Animas River is this 140-unit, air-conditioned inn. It boasts an indoor swimming pool, restaurant, saunas, and a hot tub. Many of the nice bilevel rooms have fireplaces. Information: Iron Horse Inn, 5800 North Main, Durango, Colorado 81301; (970) 259–1010 or (800) 748–2990; fax (970) 385–4791; www.ironhorseinn. Moderate.

Days Inn Durango. Nicely situated along U.S. Highway 550, about 4.5 miles north from the center of town, with vistas over the Animas Valley and San Juan Mountains. Ninety-five air-conditioned rooms in a multistory building with a heated, Olympic-size indoor swimming pool and restaurant. Advance reservation deposit required. Information: Days Inn Durango, 1700 CR 203, Durango, Colorado 81301; (970) 259–1430 or (800) 325–2525; fax (970) 259–5741. Moderate.

Apple Orchard Inn. Located 8 miles north of Durango off U.S. Highway 550 (take Trimble Lane west to County Road 203, then turn north again) on 4 acres are this large farm-style home and six cottages spaced around a pond. There are apple trees, flower gardens, a patio, and a hot tub. And there are nine very attractively decorated rooms, four with fireplaces. The property offers good views of the surrounding red rock cliffs and the mountains. Children welcome. Full gourmet breakfast. Information: Apple Orchard Inn, 7758 County Road 203, Durango, Colorado 81301; (970) 247–0751 or (800) 426–0751; fax (970) 385–6976; www.appleorchard. com. Moderate to expensive.

Logwood Bed and Breakfast. Located 12 miles north of Durango just off U.S. Highway 550, this delightful, contemporary, and western red-cedar-log mountain inn offers the river flowing close by and mountain and forest views from its eight handsomely decorated, comfortable rooms and one suite, all with private baths. After fishing, hiking, or golfing, you can relax on the spacious verandah or in the living room and enjoy afternoon tea or coffee with desserts. Full country breakfast. Information: Logwood Bed and Breakfast, 35060 U.S. Highway 550 North, Durango, Colorado 81301; (970) 259–4396 or (800) 369–4082; fax (970) 259–7812. Inexpensive to moderate.

Tamarron Resort. Located 18 miles north of Durango on U.S. Highway 550 in a beautiful, forested, high-elevation mountain setting is this full-service ski (close to nearby Purgatory ski area) and summer resort. There are more than 300 luxury units in multi-story lodges and townhouses with kitchens. Large heated indoor/outdoor pool, saunas, whirlpools, recreational program, and children's program. For a fee you can play eighteen holes of golf on the championship Cliffs golf course, fish, river-raft, play tennis, go horseback riding, take jeep tours of the region, or work out in the health club. Picnic lunches packed for walks on the expansive property or nearby hiking trails. There are two dining rooms. Information: Tamarron Resort, P.O. Drawer 3131, Durango, Colorado 81302; (970) 259–2000 or (800) 678–1000; www.tamarron.com. Expensive to very expensive.

Wilderness Trails Ranch (dude ranch). Twenty-eight miles northeast of Bayfield, Colorado, and 35 miles northeast of Durango. Horseback riding, lake fishing, sailboating. American Plan with weekly rates during the summer season. Information: Wilderness Trails Ranch, 23486 County Road 501, Bayfield, Colorado 81122; (970) 247–0722 or (800) 527–2624; fax (970) 247–1066; www.wilder nesstrails.com.

Blue Lake Ranch. Located approximately 16 miles southwest of Durango, south of Hesperus, Colorado, is this nicely secluded B&B situated on a large piece of property overlooking a pretty lake and surrounded by beautiful gardens. There are fish in the lake, nice walks to take through the meadow and along the lake, and a very comfortable feeling overall. The four rooms in the main, old homestead house are all individually and attractively furnished. There are fully equipped cabins that can be rented as well. A breakfast buffet awaits you inside or out on one of the garden patios. Hot tub and sauna. Some units with fireplaces. Information: Blue Lake Ranch, 16000 Highway 140, Hesperus, Colorado 81362; (970) 385–4537; fax (970) 385–4088; www.frontier.net/~bluelake. Moderate to expensive.

Colorado Trails Ranch. Located east of Durango off U.S. Highway 160 on County Road 240 is this 500-acre ranch that backs up to the San Juan National Forest. A premier fly-fishing destination with 4 miles of private water on two rivers, this ranch also has a full recreational horse program, archery, swimming, hiking, and water skiing. Information: Colorado Trails Ranch, 12161 County Road 240, Durango, Colorado 81301–6306; (970) 247–5055; (800) 323–3833; fax (970) 385–7372; www.coloradotrails flyfish.com or www.colotrails.com.

Campgrounds

Cottonwood Camper Park. About 0.33 mile west of Durango at 21636 U.S. Highway 160 West; (970) 247–1977.

United Campground. Just off U.S. Highway 500, 4 miles north of Durango, at 1322 Animas View Drive. Pool. Close to river; (970) 247–3853.

Lightner Creek Campground. Some 2.5 miles west of Durango on U.S. Highway 160 and then about 2 more miles up Lightner Creek Road (Country Road 207). Stream fishing. Camp or cabins; (970) 247–5406.

Alpen-Rose RV Park. Two miles north of Durango at 27847 U.S. Highway 550 North; (970) 247–5540 or (800) 259–5791.

Junction Creek Campground. Approximately 5 miles northwest of Durango on Junction Creek Road or Twenty-fifth Street. Eighteen sites. San Juan National Forest; (970) 247–4874.

K.O.A. Durango East. Seven miles east of Durango on U.S. Highway 160 to Pagosa Springs, Colorado; (970) 247–0783 or (800) 562–0793.

Hermosa Meadows Camper Park. Nine miles north of Durango on U.S. Highway 550. Stocked fishing pond, open to the public; (970) 247–3055 or (800) 748–2853.

Ponderosa K.O.A. Ten miles north of Durango on U.S. Highway 550. Stream. (970) 247–4499.

Food

The Palace Restaurant/Quiet Lady Tavern. 501 B Main Avenue; (970) 247–2018. The Palace is located adjacent to the Durango and Silverton Narrow-Gauge Railway depot. Its turn-of-the-twentieth-century decor makes it a fun place to dine. The menu includes delicious stuffed pork chops, fish (always trout), and fowl, continental specialties, and some additional down-home western dishes such as chicken and dumplings. Open for lunch and dinner. Moderate.

636 Main—Ken and Sue's East. 636 Main Avenue; (970) 385–1810. In the middle of downtown is an eclectic upscale restaurant with an Asian flair open for lunch and dinner inside or out on the spacious patio. Start with ginger-chicken potstickers glazed with hoisin sauce and orange-honey dipping sauce, and move on to basil-marinated chicken atop fazzoletti, kalamata olives, capers, feta cheese, and tomatoes. Wine and beer list. Desserts. Moderate.

Gazpacho. 431 East Second Avenue; (970) 259–9494. Didn't get enough northern New Mexican fare while you were in Spanish Rio Grande Country? Here's your chance to catch up. Well-prepared carne *adovado,* tortilla soup, green chili cheeseburgers, sopaipillas, blue corn chips, and salsa are served up in this pleasing restaurant specializing in the native foods of the state just south of the Colorado border. Vegetarian specialties. Lunch and dinners. Inexpensive to moderate.

Ariano's. 150 East College Drive (East Sixth Street); (970) 247–8146. This northern Italian dinner restaurant specializes in homemade pasta, veal, seafood, and steaks. Top it all off with tempting desserts and the espresso coffee drink of your choice, and you will think you're back in Florence again. Good wine list. Dinner only. Moderate.

Ore House. 147 East College Drive (East Sixth Street); (970) 247–5707. This well-deserved old-time Durango favorite continues to serve a variety of steaks and seafood in an atmosphere evoking the area's mining heyday. Full wine list. Dinner only. Moderate.

Randy's. 152 East College Drive; (970) 247–9083. Open nightly for dinner, this restaurant is popular with Durango families who want to celebrate special occasions. Slow-roasted prime rib is a specialty, but poultry, pasta, and fresh seafood are also offered. Good children's menu. Espresso coffees and homemade deserts. Wine bar. Moderate.

Lady Falconburgh's Barley Exchange. 640 Main Avenue; (970) 382–9664. Located downstairs in the Century Mall is a short-order establishment with a long list of brews— seventy in the bottle and twenty on tap. Foreign, domestic, and micro-brewery beers. Open from lunchtime on, with a wide variety of appetizers, soups, salads, sandwiches, and desserts.

Henry's (Strater Hotel). Seventh and Main Avenues; (970) 247–4431. A pleasant restaurant evoking a turn-of-the-twentieth-century ambience. A casual, fun place to dine, offering breakfast, Sunday brunch, and dinner. The extensive breakfast menu features full breakfasts or a simple continental breakfast. Inexpensive to moderate.

Durango Coffee Co. 730 Main Avenue; (970) 259–2059. Drop in at this espresso coffee bar and emporium (espresso makers and other kitchen supplies) anytime from breakfast on (certainly in the evening after a movie

or play). Scrumptious homemade pastries as well, along with a wide variety of *biscotti*. Oh, hot chocolate too.

Seasons—Rotisserie and Grill. 764 Main Avenue; (970) 382–9790. This restaurant brings Durango into the fold of increasingly culinary-conscious towns like Flagstaff and Moab. Don't miss this one. Start with pan-seared crab cakes with spring greens and chipotle aioli or a hearts of romaine salad with applewood smoked bacon, chopped eggs, and herb buttermilk dressing. Then from the rotisserie, spit-roasted chicken with garlic mashed potatoes or a grilled double-cut pork rib chop with asparagus and caramelized shallot-sage sauce. Wine and beer list. Espresso drinks. Desserts. Patio. Moderate.

Le Rendezvous Swiss Bakery and Restaurant. 750 Main Avenue; (970) 385–5685. Breakfast at this early-to-open establishment can start with a tantalizing array of freshly baked pastries, breads, and other baked goods, pancakes, omelettes, a fruit boat, or a special Swiss breakfast. Salad Niçoise, quiches, soups, and sandwiches top the tables at lunch—with dessert, of course. Light dinners also served. Also available: French sodas, shakes, malts, espresso drinks, beer, and wine. Breakfast, lunch, and dinner. Box lunches prepared for the train. Inexpensive.

Cyprus Cafe. 725 East Second Avenue; (970) 385–6884. Up on quieter and more pleasant Second Avenue is this bastion of Mediterranean food, where either indoors or out on the pleasant patio you can start with assorted olives with fresh oregano or a combo meze. Then you can get your teeth into lamb souvlakia, grilled eggplant sandwich, or free-range Moroccan chicken tagine. Inexpensive to moderate.

Steamworks Brewing Company. 801 East Second Avenue; (970) 259–9200. Just across from the Durango Art Center is this brew pub that serves lunch and dinner. Soups, salads, sandwiches, and a few Southwest specialties like Anasazi enchiladas, Chimney Rock chimichangas, Southwest chili burgers, and steak are on the menu. Pizza. Sodas. Desserts. Kids menu. Beer. View deck.

Red Snapper. 144 East Ninth Street; (970) 259–3417. Entering this restaurant with its 200 gallons of fish-filled aquariums is like visiting the waterfront. With a fresh fish menu featuring a "today's catch" section, you'll begin to believe you're seaside instead of mountainbound. Enjoy the wide selection of items, from rainbow trout to Boston bluefish. Prime rib and steaks as well. Extensive wine list. Dinner only. Moderate.

937 Main—Ken and Sue's Place. 937 Main Avenue; (970) 259–2616. Either inside or out on the pleasant enclosed patio in the back, you can start lunch at this very smart and good restaurant with tomato-bisque soup followed by a vine-ripened tomato and arugula salad with Maytag Blue Cheese or a specialty sandwich, a pasta, or an oriental stir-fry dish. For dinner you can choose a chicken quesadilla starter and for an entree Aunt Lydia's meatloaf with red wine gravy and mashed potatoes or grilled tuna steak in tomato-ginger coulis. Dessert. Wine and beer. Moderate.

Olde Tymer's Cafe. 1000 Main Avenue; (970) 259–2990. Located in a restored nineteenth-century building, this cafe, with its high ceilings and interesting, very pleasant outdoor patio, evokes much of Durango's past. Serving excellent hamburgers, sandwiches, soups, salads, and daily specials, it is open daily for late lunch and dinner. Patio dining in summer. Inexpensive.

Carver's Restaurant and Brewpub. 1022 Main Avenue; (970) 259–2545. Serving three meals a day this casual establishment offers for breakfast buttermilk pancakes, oversized muffins, or fresh vegetable bread grilled and topped with powdered sugar. Soups, stews, sandwiches, and salads for lunch. At dinner Greek pizzas to start, followed by salmon with roasted pepper salad or a fiesta burrito grande. Beer, of course, and wine. Inexpensive to moderate.

Serious Texas Bar-B-Q. 3535 North Main; (970) 247–2240. Located north of downtown is this funky but fun eatery where you can drown yourself in a tasty barbecue sauce atop oak-smoked pork spare ribs, beef briskets, or pork loins. Pinto beans and cole slaw mellow you out. Iced tea and soft drinks. Beer. Inexpensive.

Sweeney's Grubsteak. Four miles north on U.S. Highway 550 across the highway from the Iron Horse Resort; (970) 247–5236. The owners call this interesting contemporary wooden building and its pleasant atmosphere "contemporary Durango." The steaks are excellent, and the salad, which not even a hutch of rabbits could finish off, is equally good. Also prime rib, seafood, lamb, and fresh local rainbow trout. Dinner. Moderate.

Cascade Grill. In the lodge at Cascade Village, approximately 25 miles north of Durango on U.S. Highway 550 (1.5 miles north of Purgatory Ski Resort entrance), is this well-known gourmet restaurant; (970) 259–3500, ext. 250. The menu reads like a fusion of Southwestern, Asian, and Cajun cuisine. Start with Cajun barbecued rock shrimp, and then choose the grilled elk tenderloin with four-peppercorn demiglace or the grilled prawns with red chili pesto and pasta or the marinated ahi tuna with ginger butter. Special children's menu. Well-chosen wine list. Moderate to expensive.

Bar-D Chuckwagon Suppers. Nine miles north of town on County Road 250 just off U.S. Highway 550; (970) 247–5753. This listing might well be called an "event" rather than a restaurant. The proprietors have done all they can to conjure up the western atmosphere. Although at times you feel you are part of a Hollywood western movie set, it is all good fun and does create some of that Old West feeling. Of course, there is nothing but "ranch" food available. Chuckwagon meals, including barbecued beef, baked beans, and homemade biscuits, are served. There are small shops on the premises that recreate aspects of early Durango life. And to top it off, there is a real western band, complete with fiddles, guitars, and trail songs. Dinner only. Closed early September to late May. Reservations required.

Tours, Museums, and Activities

Durango and Silverton Narrow-Gauge Railroad and Museums.

From early May through October, several trains leave Durango daily for a three-and-one-half-hour trip to Silverton, Colorado, high in the San Juan Mountains, 45 miles away. The train stops at Silverton for about two hours before returning. During the peak season, mid-June to early August, more trains are added to the schedule, with trains leaving at 7:30, 8:15, 9:00, and 9:45 A.M. From early September to early October, the High Noon Cascade Train runs to the halfway point, Cascade Canyon. This is followed by the High Noon Cascade Canyon Winter Train to Cascade Station at the Cascade Canyon Wye from late November to early May. In addition, during the summer season, there are "Day Out with Thomas" event trips for kids behind a life-size Thomas the Tank Engine.

You may purchase a round-trip ticket for use the same day (or by prearrangement, use the return portion on another day); a one way ticket (call to get the details); or a rail one way with a bus return ticket (the bus takes a different scenic route). If you reserve and purchase tickets two weeks or more ahead, they will be mailed to you; less than two weeks they will be held at the will-call desk at the station. Reserved, unpaid tickets can be held similarly. Either way, be certain to ask about the deadline for picking up your tickets. Those who want on-the-spot tickets should check with the station after 6:00 P.M. the night before for cancellations (cancellation fee imposed), or check the day of to see if there are any no-shows before the train departs.

Passengers must be in their seats on their designated train at least thirty minutes before the train departs. Ticket holders may also visit the Durango Railroad Museum and the Silverton Freight Yard Museum. Inquire about open gondola trains and special trains with lift facilities. Information: Durango and Silverton Narrow-Gauge Railroad, 479 Main Avenue, Durango, Colorado 81301; (970) 247–2733 or (888) 872–4607; www. durangotrain.com.

Horse-Drawn Carriages for Hire. Located across the street from the Strater Hotel. Tour historic Durango in a horse-drawn carriage anytime between noon and dusk during the summer tourist season. Just show up. First come, first served.

Durango LIFT. This in-town bus service provides service to most of the Durango area, and the **Main Avenue Trolley Service** serves all of Main Avenue. (970) 259–5438.

Durango Transportation Company. Whether you need a taxi, shuttle service to or from the airport, or a tour of surrounding old mining towns, Mesa Verde, or Chaco Canyon, this company has it; (970) 259–4818 or (800) 626–2066.

Durango Fish Hatchery, Visitors' Center, and Wildlife Museum. 151 East Sixteenth Street (take Main Avenue north across the Animas River Bridge and then make the first right); (970) 259–3009 or (970) 247–4755. Tour one of the oldest fish hatcheries in the state of Colorado that is still stocking southwestern Colorado's streams. See the largest trout you've ever laid eyes on and tour the wildlife center.

Durango Arts Center. Located at 802 East Second Avenue, this center for the arts showcases a wide range of artists and media, often focusing on the works of local and regional artists. Well worth seeing; (970) 259–2606; www.durangoarts.org.

Durango Children's Museum. Up the stairs at the Durango Arts Center, 802 East Second Avenue, (970) 259–9234, is the children's museum. Explore some hands-on exhibits. Featuring a variety of themes; native cultures loom large here.

Center for Southwest Studies Museum. Located on the Fort Lewis college campus, this museum is worth a visit. Exhibits encompass all aspects of the history of the Southwest. There is also a special collections library. Call for hours; (970) 247–7456; www.fortlewis.edu.

Durango and Silverton Narrow-Gauge Railroad Museum. Located at the train station. Besides all the railroad memorabilia for sale in the train depot gift shop, this museum opens the doors on two full-size, turn-of-the-twentieth-century locomotives and other rolling stock, a railroad library, and much more. Free with your train ticket. Fee otherwise; (970) 247–2733; www.durangotrain.com.

Mesa Verde. If you've arrived in Durango or Cortez without a car and want to tour Mesa Verde National Park, call Durango Transportation at (970) 259–4818 or (800) 626–2066. Durango Transportation also offers tours to Chaco Canyon, Ute Mountain Tribal Park, and the San Juan Skyway. But if you want a tour from Morefield Campground or Far View Lodge at the park, then call ARAMARK Mesa Verde National Park Concessioner at (970) 533–1944 or (800) 499–2288; www.visitmesa verde.com.

Hassle Free Sports. 2615 Main Avenue. Rent mountain or road bikes, bicycle clothing, and accessories to tour the area; (970) 259–3874 or (800) 835–3800; www.hasslefree sports.com.

Mountain Bike Specialists. 949 Main Avenue. This outfit sells, repairs, and rents bikes; (970) 247–4066. They're got it all.

Flexible Flyers—Rapid Thrills. Conveniently located across the river from the Holiday Inn is this river-raft company that offers one- and two-hour raft trips of the Animas River rapids. Information: 2344 County Road 225, Durango, Colorado 81301; (970) 247–4628 or (800) 346–7741.

Durango River Trippers. Half-day or shorter raft trips on the Animas River. Inflatable kayak trips as well. Information: 720 Main Avenue, Durango, Colorado 81301; (970) 259–0289 or (800) 292–2885; www.durangorivertrips.com.

Mountain Waters Rafting. Economy half- and full-day river-raft trips on the Animas River. Specially arranged longer trips to raft the upper Animas River, the nearby Dolores River, and the Colorado River. Also inflatable kayaks, rentals, and training. Information: 108 West College Drive, Durango, Colorado 81320; (970)

259–4191 or (800) 748–2507; www.durangorafting.com.

Outlaw Rivers And Jeep Tours. This outfit offers mountain biking and white-water tours; they also give jeep tours to forgotten ghost towns, old gold and silver mines, wildflower displays, and other Southwestern sights. Information: Outlaw River and Trails, 690 Main Avenue, Durango, Colorado 81301; (970) 259–1800 or (877) 259–1800; www.outlaw tours.com.

Horseback Riding

Rapp Guides and Packers. Hourly, half-day, and full-day rides cover some of the beautiful high San Juan Mountain country. Pack trips and extended trips also available from this reliable outfitter who wants to take you for a ride on one of his "all-terrain vehicles"; (970) 247–8454; www.rapp guides.com.

South Fork Riding Stables. Hayrides. Breakfast, lunch, and evening chuckwagon supper rides as well as moonlight champagne rides and hourly or daily rides. Overnight regional safaris arranged. Located 6 miles southeast of Durango. Information: 28481 U.S. Highway 160 East, Durango, Colorado 81301; (970) 259–4871.

Adventures Beyond, Inc./Over the Hill Outfitters. Hayrides. Breakfast rides, hourly and daily rides, family pack trips, summer fishing trips, and elk and deer hunts. Located 12 miles north of Durango just off U.S. Highway 550 on County Road 234. Information: 3624 County Road 234, Durango, Colorado 81301; (970)

247–1694 or (970) 385–7656; www.overthehilloutfitters.com.

Fishing

If you are an avid trout fisher, you will want to seek information from one of the tackle shops (see "Shopping") or from the Public Lands Center in Durango (970–247–4874) or the Colorado Division of Wildlife (970–247–0855) for Southwest regional fishing conditions.

Other Activities

Backpacking and Hiking. If you are interested in hiking the trails of the San Juan National Forest and Weminuche Wilderness Area, contact the Public Lands Center office in Durango for information, trail guides, and maps. It is located in the federal building across from the Holiday Inn. Information: Public Lands Center, 15 Burnett Court, Durango, Colorado 81301; (970) 247–4874.

Jogging. Opie-Reams Nature and Jogging Trail (see "Seeing Rocky Mountain Frontier Country: "Durango" for description).

Golf. There is an eighteen-hole golf course at the **Hillcrest Golf Club** next to Fort Lewis College on College Hill. Follow Eighth Street to Eighth Avenue, turn left, and follow the signs past the college to Hillcrest Municipal Golf Course; (970) 247–1499. Another eighteen-hole course is 6 miles north of Durango on U.S. Highway 550: **Dalton Ranch Golf Course;** (970) 247–8774. Still another course is 18 miles north of Durango on U.S.

Highway 550 at **Tamarron Resort;** (970) 259–2000.

Trimble Hot Springs Park and Gardens. Drive 7 miles north on U.S. Highway 550 to this watery oasis and rest your weary bones in the Olympic-size natural hot springs pool. Also private indoor tubs, lap swimming, massage, women's fitness studio, and water aerobics. RV hookups by reservation. Information: Trimble Hot Springs Park and Gardens, 6475 County Road 203, Durango, Colorado 81301; (970) 247–0111; fax (970) 247–4493.

Swimming. Municipal Swimming Pool. Twenty-fourth and Main; (970) 259–9988.

Fairs, Festivals, and Events

Durango has many fun-filled events. For a complete list and more details, call (800) 525–8855 or visit www.durango.org. In March there's the **Durango Film Festival** and **Hozhoni Days,** followed by the **Durango Wine Festival** in late April. In early May comes **Narrow-Gauge Days** (the Silverton-Durango train makes its first run), followed by the **Animas Music Festival** and the **Iron Horse Bicycle Classic.** June sees **Animas River Days** and **Mountains by Moonlight** tours aboard the narrow-gauge train. Of course, there's a **Fourth of July** celebration and **Music in the Mountains** events from mid-July to early August. August is a busy month, with the **La Plata County Fair,** the **Main Avenue Juried Arts Festival,** the **Narrow-Gauge Railfest,** and the twice-weekly **Durango Pro**

Rodeo events. Early September sees the **Four Corners Iron Horse Motorcycle Rally** followed late in the month by a **Gallery Walk** and the **Cinders, Song and Sauvignon** festival. October brings the highly touted **Durango Cowboy Poetry Gathering** and the **Durango Marathon.** The ski season and Christmas events follow shortly.

Theater

Diamond Circle Melodrama. Located in the Strater Hotel, this theater is open only in the summer. It specializes in melodramas and turn-of-the-twentieth-century entertainment; (970) 247-3400.

Gallery Theatre. Fort Lewis College hosts the Repertory Theatre Company del Rio de Las Animas Perdidas, which features a wide selection of historic and contemporary plays in repertory during the fall and winter months; (970) 247-7010.

Parking

A parking garage is available 1 block west of Main Avenue on Narrow Gauge Avenue between Eighth and Ninth Streets. No charge if you purchase something in the adjacent shopping mall.

There is also a large parking lot (fee) operated by the railway near McDonald's, between Main and Narrow Gauge Avenues, just off Sixth Street (College Drive). In addition, several more pay public lots are available. There are three more up on East Second Avenue at Fifth, Seventh, and Eighth Streets, respectively.

Shopping

Waldenbooks. 104 East Fifth Street; (970) 259-3728. Not only a good general bookstore, but one with a fine selection of regional books about mining ghost towns and the historical development of the area. Conveniently located near the rail depot.

Appaloosa Trading Co. 501 Main Avenue; (970) 259-1994. An outstanding selection of leather goods made on the premises (everything from belts and briefcases to flight jackets), plus a fine selection of belt buckles and silver and antler jewelry, as well as wooden steam locomotive whistles.

O'Farrell Hat Company. 563 Main Avenue; (970) 259-5900 or (800) 895-7098. If you are looking for a bronc or bull rider felt hat or, for that matter, a "Bogart" fedora or almost any other kind of fur felt hat, this custom hat maker and retailer will probably have it.

Martin and Roll Gallery. 635 East Second Avenue; (970) 247-2211; www.martinrollgallery.com. Saunter up to East Second Avenue one block off Main Avenue to see this native and cultural arts gallery and sculpture garden. With a fine selection of folk art, from Navajo crafts and Bolivian textiles to Mexican and Spanish antiques, this gallery pleases. Also whimsical Navajo wood sculpture, Edward Curtis photogravures, a selection of santos, retablos, and bultos, as well as Mayo and Yaqui masks from Mexico and a large selection of jewelry. Unusual items not found elsewhere.

Open Shutter Contemporary Fine Art Photography. 755 East Second Avenue; (970) 382–8355. The name alone pretty well describes this sophisticated gallery up on East Second Avenue. Well worth a visit.

Duranglers. Located at 923 Main Avenue; (970) 385–4081 or (888) 347–4346; www.duranglers.com. Claiming to be the most complete fly shop in the Southwest, this store for devoted fly fisherfolk can do everything from custom-building a fly rod to making custom flies (the largest collection of hand-tied flies in the Southwest). Also up-to-date stream reports and custom-guided fishing trips on the fabled San Juan River. And if you don't know how to fly-fish, the staff will teach you.

Toh-Atin Gallery. 145 West Ninth Street; (970) 247–8277 or (800) 525–0384; www.Toh-Atin.com. This gallery puts Durango on the map as a center for southwestern Indian arts and crafts. Here you will find a wide selection of carefully selected Navajo rugs, kachina dolls, and Pueblo Indian pottery, as well as an outstanding selection of southwestern Indian paintings and prints, all beautifully displayed. If you are a collector or interested in seeing high-quality Native American arts and crafts, you should not miss this gallery.

Maria's Book Shop. 960 Main Avenue; (970) 247–1438. This large shop has an excellent supply of books relating to the cultural and natural history of the Southwest. General books also.

Gallery Ultima. 1018 Main Avenue; (970) 247–1812; www.gallery ultima.com. This gallery focuses on watercolors and pottery mainly, but there are serigraphs, oils, bronzes, jewelry, and weavings as well.

Honeyville. On U.S. Highway 550, 10 miles north of Durango. Shopping is a pleasure at Honeyville, where you can browse the shelves of Colorado high-altitude wildflower honey, combed honey, mead (honey wine), wild chokecherry jelly, watermelon pickles, and chili sauce. In addition, the kids can watch the bees make the honey. Mail-order catalog and service. Information: Honeyville, 33633 Highway 550 North, Durango, Colorado 81301; (970) 247–1474 or (800) 676–7690.

Telephone Numbers

Durango Area Chamber Resort Association. (970) 247–0312 or (800) 525–8855.

Durango La Plata (DRO) Airport. (970) 247–8143.

San Juan National Forest, U.S. Forest Service. (970) 247–4874.

Mesa Verde National Park. (970) 529–4465 or (970) 529–4461; www.nps.gov/meve/.

Road and weather conditions. (877) 315–7623.

Durango and Silverton Narrow-Gauge Depot. (970) 247–2733.

Taxi or shuttle. (970) 259–4818.

Bus. (970) 259–5438.

Avis Car Rental. (970) 247–9761.

Enterprise Rent-a-Car. (970) 385–6860.

America West Express Airline.
(800) 235–9292.

United Express. (970) 247–9735 or
(800) 241–6522.

**American Airlines American
Eagle.** (800) 433–7300.

Rio Grande Air. (877) 435–9742.

Silverton

Lodging

Wyman Hotel and Inn. As Silverton's premier inn, this bed-and-breakfast establishment occupies the second
story of a downtown circa 1902 building. The nineteen comfortable, upscale
spacious rooms with private baths have
been brought up to modern standards.
Some rooms have whirlpool baths.
Almost all have mountain views. Free
videos. Full breakfast. Information:
Wyman Hotel, 1371 Greene Street,
P.O. Box 780, Silverton, Colorado
81433; (970) 387–5372 or (800)
609–7845; fax (970) 387–5745;
www.silverton.org/wymanhotel.
Moderate.

**Silverton's Inn of the Rockies at
the Historic Alma House.** This
handsome, historic building (circa
1898) is now a comfortable hotel
with nine rooms that have turn-of-
the-twentieth-century ambience.
Gourmet breakfast and afternoon tea.
Mountain views. Information: Silverton's Inn of the Rockies at the Historic Alma House, 220 East Tenth
Street, P.O. Box 359, Silverton, Colorado 81433; (970) 387–5336 or
(800) 267–5336; fax (970) 387–5974.
Inexpensive to moderate.

Villa Dallavalle Inn. Located in yet
another turn-of-the-twentieth-century building, this B&B has seven
rooms with private baths, all nicely
decorated Silverton style. Full breakfast. Closest to the rail station. Information: Villa Dallavalle Inn, 1257 Blair
Street, Silverton, Colorado 81433;
(970) 387–5555; fax (970) 387–5965.
Inexpensive.

Grand Imperial Victorian Hotel.
Built in 1882, this hotel has been
restored to some of its past grandeur.
Forty rooms (double or twin beds)
with private baths are available, many
of them decorated with antiques. The
lounge and dining room, which serves
three meals a day, offer the same turn-
of-the-twentieth-century ambience.
Information: Grand Imperial Hotel,
1219 Greene Street, P.O. Box 57, Silverton, Colorado 81433; (970)
387–5527 or (800) 341–3340. Inexpensive.

Teller House Hotel and Inn. This
hotel offers modest accommodations
in a building built around the turn of
the twentieth century. The eight
rooms and two hostel dormitories are
on the second floor above the French
Bakery Restaurant. Some rooms with
the bathroom down the hall. Breakfast
included. Information: Teller House
Hotel, 1250 Greene Street, Silverton,
Colorado 81433; (970) 387–5423 or
(800) 342–4338. Inexpensive.

Smedley's Suites. These three one-
bedroom units on the second floor,
each with a living room, kitchen,
color TV, and private bath, are located
downtown above Smedley's Ice
Cream Parlor. Rates include breakfast
at the Pickle Barrel restaurant. Infor-

Grand Imperial Victorian Hotel, Silverton

mation: Smedley's Suites, 1314 Greene Street, Silverton, Colorado 81433; (970) 387–5713. Inexpensive.

Silverton Hostel. Located right in town is this convenient budget hostelry. Information: Silverton Hostel, 1025 Blair Street, Silverton, Colorado 81433; (970) 387–0115.

Campgrounds

Silver Summit RV Park. Located at the base of Kendall Mountain; an easy walk to town. Complete with hookups for RVs and grassy lawns for tents. Hot tub. Also jeep rentals and tours. Information: Silver Summit RV Park, 640 Mineral Street, Silverton, Colorado 81433; (970) 387–0240 or (800) 352–1637; www.silverton.org/silversummit.

Silverton Lakes RV Park and Campground. About 0.5 mile northeast of Silverton on 10 acres along Colorado Highway 110. One hundred RV and tent sites. Jeep rentals available. Lake and stream fishing. Information: Silverton Lakes Campground, P.O. Box 126, Silverton, Colorado 81433; (970) 387–5721.

Food

Chattanooga Cafe. 116 East Twelfth Street; (970) 387–5892. Conveniently located just half a block from the train station, the Chattanooga serves breakfast and lunch featuring fruit plates, hamburgers, beef stew, sandwich specials, and pies.

Brown Bear Cafe. 1129 Greene Street; (970) 387–5630. Visit this historic building (circa 1893) in the center of town and you can munch your way through either lunch or dinner. Order homemade soups and chili, a variety of salads from the salad bar, sandwiches, or stick-to-your-ribs dishes like lasagna or chicken fried steak with mashed potatoes. Homemade pies. Inexpensive.

Pickle Barrel Food and Spirits. 1304 Greene Street; (970) 387–5713. Open for lunch until late afternoon. Hamburgers and sandwiches, imported beers and cheeses, and a salad bar, as well as daily hot meal specials.

Handlebars Restaurant and Saloon. 117 Thirteenth Street; (970) 387–5395. Sort of an Old West, fun, cozy (a fireplace blazes on cooler evenings) kind of a place where you can dine for a late breakfast, lunch, or dinner. Great hamburgers, and then there are soups, barbecued pork ribs, and steaks. Or treat the place like a pub and eat at the bar. Inexpensive.

Tours, Festivals, and Events

Silverton is the northern terminus of the Durango and Silverton Narrow-Gauge Railroad. Visitors coming on the train from Durango with round-trip tickets may get off in Silverton and spend a night or two (or longer) and return to Durango at a later time. They must, however, prearrange this when they buy their tickets. Round-trip tickets that allow a layover in Durango may also be purchased in Silverton. It is also possible to take a bus to Durango and return the same day to Silverton by train. The bus and train follow separate routes to and from Durango, allowing the traveler to see different scenery both ways.

From June through August you may want to take in the daily **western–style gunfight** (free) staged by local businesspeople at Twelfth and Blair Streets each summer afternoon about 5:30 P.M.

San Juan County Museum and Mayflower Gold Mill. There's the museum in the old San Juan County jail next to the courthouse with its mineral collections, mining equipment, and gift and book shop. And then there's the museum's **Mayflower Gold Mill** 2 miles northeast of Silverton on Highway 110. There are one-hour professional guided tours of the old mill that show how gold and silver were processed. Rock shop. Gift

shop. Information: San Juan County Historical Society, P.O. Box 154, Silverton, Colorado 81433; (970) 387–0294.

Old Hundred Gold Mine Tour. Five miles east of town on Highway 110 (turn right at Howardsville) and County Road 4A is this historic mine where visitors can take a narrow-gauge electric mine train (fee) deep into Galena Mountain to see mining equipment demonstrations and learn about the history of gold mining. Pan for gold. Tours last about one hour and begin every half hour from May to early October; (970) 387–5444 or (800) 872–3009.

A Theatre Group. Partly funded by the Colorado Council of the Arts, this thespian troupe, made up of local, university, and professional talent, is one of less than a half-dozen year-round Colorado mountain town theater companies. All performances are staged in the old Miner's Union Theatre at 1069 Greene Street; www. silverton.org.

Throughout the year Silverton stages a number of interesting events, some of which are listed here. The summer season starts off in late May with the **Iron Horse Bicycle Classic,** followed by the **Silverton Jubilee Folk Music Festival** the end of June. Of course, there's the Fourth of July parade and celebration, followed two weeks later by the **Kendall Mountain Run.** Then comes one of the nation's most original festivals, **Hardrocker's Holidays,** in early August. This is not a "rock" festival but a mining celebration, featuring unique competitive events such as hand- and machine-mucking, machine drilling, and wheelbarrow racing. Close on the heels of that stellar event is the **Great Rocky Mountain Brass Band Festival** in mid-August, which in turn is followed by the annual **Silverton Colorfest Quilting Show** and sale in late September. A complete listing of year-round events and their precise dates, as well as hiking and fishing information, are available. **Silverton Chamber of Commerce,** P.O. Box 565, Silverton, Colorado 81433; (970) 387–5654 or (800) 752–4494; www.silverton.org.

Shopping

Silverton has many shops (with numerous rock and mineral and Colorado souvenir shops) greeting the hundreds of rail passengers who land there for a short time each day. Several shops of particular interest are listed here.

Silverton Standard and the Miner. 1139 Greene Street; (970) 387–5477. An interesting bookstore with a good selection of railroad, local, regional, and natural history books, as well as hiking books and maps of the area. Silverton walking-tour guides available.

The Crewel Elephant. Located on Thirteenth Street between Greene and Blair Streets; (970) 387–5714. This very nice gift shop features well-selected, handmade, one-of-a-kind items, including jewelry and clothing from the local area and around the world.

Silverton Artworks. 1028 Blair Street; (970) 387–5823. Located just 1½ blocks from the train station in a charming old home is this very nice

gallery and studio representing the works of local and regional artists. Pottery, weaving, baskets, watercolors, and sculpture are all for sale here.

Outdoor World. 1234 Greene Street; (970) 387–5628. This is a multifaceted emporium where you can, if you're struck with gold fever, pick up a gold pan and other prospecting supplies. Also USGS and other maps, as well as an excellent selection of regional books. And you can shop here for walking sticks, fishing supplies, and hiking and camping equipment as well.

Ouray

Lodging

For any additional information you may need either about Ouray or neighboring Ridgway, Colorado, contact the **Ouray Chamber Resort Association,** 1222 Main Street (U.S. Highway 550), P.O. Box 145, Ouray, Colorado 81427; (970) 325–4746 or (800) 228–1876; www.ouray colorado.com. Citizens State Bank at 600 Main has an ATM.

The Beaumont Hotel. The restoration of this historic landmark building in the heart of downtown gives the Ouray lodging scene a sophisticated boost. The fifteen spacious, thoroughly updated, and beautifully furnished rooms provide a peaceful haven for travelers. There are handsome public rooms, a conference area, a full-service spa, and much more. Also on board is **Bulow's at the Beaumont,** a coffee, food, and wine bar, and the full-service **Tundra Restaurant and Lounge.** Informa-

St. Elmo Hotel, Ouray

tion: The Beaumont Hotel, Main
Street and Fifth Avenue, Ouray, Colorado 81427; (970) 325–7000.
Expensive to very expensive.

St. Elmo Hotel (Bed-and-Breakfast Inn). This handsomely restored,
historic, two story brick hotel has
been in continuous service since
1899. Many of the original Victorian
and art nouveau furnishings remain.
All of the nine units have private
baths. The hotel is conveniently
located on Main Street right near the
middle of town. The Bon Ton
Restaurant is on the premises. Information: St. Elmo Hotel, 426 Main
Street, P.O. Box 667, Ouray, Colorado
81427; (970) 325–4951; www.stelmo
hotel.com. Moderate.

Manor Bed and Breakfast. This
historic house (circa 1881) has been
updated to accommodate guests.
There are seven upstairs guest rooms,
with private baths and views. Rates
include continental breakfast. Infor-

mation: Manor Bed and Breakfast,
317 Second Street, Ouray, Colorado
81427; (970) 325–4574 or (800)
628–6946; www.ouraymanor.com.
Inexpensive to moderate.

**China Clipper Inn Bed and
Breakfast.** One of the more luxurious lodgings in Ouray, with fine
mountain views from most rooms,
this European-style hostelry is only a
few minutes' walk from Ouray's center, just off Sixth Avenue on Second
Street. Eleven handsomely decorated
and furnished rooms (some with fireplaces, decks, balconies, or individual
hot tubs or Jacuzzis) are very appealing. Full breakfast. Information: China
Clipper Inn Bed and Breakfast, 525
Second Street, Ouray, Colorado
81427; (970) 325–0565 or (800)
315–0565; www.chinaclipper.com.
Moderate to expensive.

River's Edge Motel. In an enviable
location next to the lovely Uncompahgre River and only a short walk to

Main Street, Ouray, Colorado

Main Street. Many of the twelve rooms here also have mountain views. Some rooms are standard motel rooms while others have kitchenettes. All have queen-size beds. Picnic tables and cookout facilities along the river. Information: River's Edge Motel, 110 Seventh Avenue, Ouray, Colorado 81427; (970) 325–4621; fax (970) 325–7307; www.riversedge.com. Inexpensive.

Historic Western Hotel. This historic hotel, dating from 1891 and located just off Main Street, is full of charm—from the restored lobby and dining room to the large, old-time bar-saloon (there's even a face on the barroom floor). Twelve rooms on the second floor share several baths. Two large suites are up there too, each with its own private bath. All blessedly free of telephones and televisions. Information: Historic Western Hotel, P.O. Box 25, 210 Seventh Avenue, Ouray, Colorado 81427; (970) 325–4645 or (888) 624–8403; www.historicwestern.com. Inexpensive.

Damn Yankee Country Inn. This handsome bed-and-breakfast is down close to the river. The Victorian-style modern inn has ten rooms, all with private bath, televisions, and telephones. A full breakfast is served in a fine dining room downstairs. Complimentary afternoon snacks. Hot tub. Information: Damn Yankee Country Inn, P.O. Box 410, 100 Sixth Avenue, Ouray, Colorado 81427; (970) 325–4219 or (800) 845–7512; www.damnyankee.com. Moderate to expensive.

Alpenglow. These sixteen condominium units, nicely designed to reflect the "Colorado modern" look, have kitchens and fireplaces. Although close to restaurants and shops, the units are in a quiet location 1 block off Main Street. They can be rented by the day, week, or month. In addition, a hot tub spa is on the premises. Information: Alpenglow, 215 Fifth Avenue, P.O. Box 1955, Ouray, Colorado 81427; (970) 325–4664; www.alpenglow-properties.com. Moderate.

Ouray Hotel. Located right downtown. You'll find this historic late-1800s hotel at the end of a long flight of stairs up on a second floor. It has economy and regular rooms as well as suites with private baths. The rooms have been redone with turn-of-the-twentieth-century decor. The skylighted lobby is a pleasant touch. Information: Ouray Hotel, 303 Sixth Avenue and Main, P. O. Box 1862, Ouray, Colorado 81427; (970) 325–0500; (800) 216–8729; www. ourayhotel.com. Inexpensive.

Cascade Falls Lodge. A rather basic motel but one with a decidedly western flavor, a few blocks off Main Street and close to the river. This motel, with its nineteen ranch-style rooms, is good for families with small children because it has a playground area as well as an expanse of grass for picnics. Information: Circle M Motel, 120 Sixth Avenue, P.O. Box 126, Ouray, Colorado 81427; (970) 325–4394 or (888) 466–8729. Inexpensive.

Best Western Twin Peaks. Pleasant, modern motel with western flavor, not far from the river. Offers a natural hot springs whirlpool bath. Good location just 4 blocks from Box Canyon Falls. Forty-eight rooms with private baths. Advance reservation deposit required. Information: Best Western Twin Peaks, 125 Third Avenue, Ouray, Colorado 81427; (970) 325–4427 or (800) 207–2700; www.bestwestern.com/twinpeaks motel. Inexpensive to moderate.

Box Canyon Lodge and Hot Springs. Thirty-eight motel units with TVs, near the river and close to Box Canyon. Mineral springs hot tub. No pets. Advance reservation deposit required. Information: Box Canyon Lodge and Hot Springs, 45 Third Avenue, P.O. Box 439, Ouray, Colorado 81427; (970) 325–4981 or (800) 327–5080; www.box canyonouray.com. Moderate.

Wiesbaden Spa and Lodgings. This interesting motel-lodge is situated up on the hillside. Below its lobby, deep in the ground, are a hot mineral water vapor cave and exercise room. Outdoor hot mineral water pool. Massage. Twenty very pleasant rooms with TVs and some with fireplaces. Some kitchens. Cottage and detached house. Unlimited use of most facilities for guests. Located on the corner of Sixth Avenue and Fifth Street. Information: Wiesbaden Spa and Lodgings, 625 Fifth Street, P.O. Box 349, Ouray, Colorado 81427; (970) 325–4347; fax (970) 325–4358; www.wiesbadenhotsprings.com. Moderate to expensive.

Campgrounds

4J + 1 + 1 Trailer Park–RV Park and Campground. In town, 2 blocks west of U.S. Highway 550, or Main Street at 790 Oak Street. Some of the fifty-five sites are on the river; (970) 325–4418.

Ouray K.O.A. Drive 4 miles north on U.S. Highway 550, then turn west on County Road 23 for 0.25 mile. One hundred and twenty-five sites, some on the river. Jeep rentals; (970) 325–4736.

Amphitheater Campground. Located in the Uncompaghre

National Forest 1 mile southeast of town off U.S. Highway 550; (877) 444–6777.

Food

Bon Ton Restaurant. 426 Main Street, in the old St. Elmo Hotel; (970) 325–4951. This attractive dinner restaurant serves a fine array of tantalizing northern Italian and continental specialties, plus steaks and fresh seafood. Sunday brunches are served on the outdoor patio in the summer. Children's menu. Nice Italian wine selection. Reservations are recommended. Moderate.

Buen Tiempo Restaurant at the Beaumont. 515 Main; (970) 325–4544. Try this festive Mexican breakfast, lunch, and dinner restaurant in a historic setting for blue corn or spinach enchiladas, carne adovado, soft tacos, and tasty chili rellenos and sopaipillos. Historic bar. Dinner. Inexpensive to moderate.

Piñon Restaurant and Piñon Tavern. 737 Main Street; (970) 325–4334. This not only is a very attractive lunch and dinner restaurant, but the place has a knack for preparing excellent meals from fresh ingredients. The menu has considerable variety, and a light touch prevails, whether for beef, elk, duck, chicken, or seafood dishes. Wine selection. Homemade and flambé desserts. Children's menu. The tavern upstairs offers fine views, both inside and out. Reservations recommended. Moderate.

Outlaw Restaurant. 610 Main Street; (970) 325–4366. Located in the heart of downtown, this steak house serves choice aged Colorado beef. Also seafood, chicken, and pasta. Popular summer cookout high in the mountains—by reservation only—includes steak and Outlaw pan-fried potatoes. Reservations recommended. Moderate.

Le Papillon Bakery and Dog and Burger Bar. 219 Seventh Avenue; (970) 325–0644. This good bakery-cafe with inside tables and a few outdoor benches is a fine spot for breakfast or lunch, just ½ block off Main Street. Home-style hamburgers and hot dogs as well as New Orleans–style po'boys can be followed by homemade doughnuts, pastries, and cakes.

Pricco's. 736 Main Street; (970) 325–4040. A good spot for lunch. Features light fare such as salads, homemade soups, and a wide variety of popular sandwiches. Homemade desserts. Inexpensive to moderate.

Silver Nugget Cafe. 746 Main Street; (970) 325–4100. Breakfast, lunch, and dinner are served in this family-oriented restaurant, which offers fine views of Cascade Falls in the distance. Soups and sandwiches and other light fare for lunch and chicken-fried steak and rainbow trout for dinner. Homemade pastries. Inexpensive.

Timberline Delicatessen. 803 Main Street; (970) 325–4958. Just what it says it is, this full delicatessen offers a variety of sandwiches, soups, fresh pastries, and drinks. Inside or outside dining or, if you prefer, a box lunch for a picnic. Espresso and desserts.

Tours

San Juan Adventure Jeep Rentals/Tours. What could be a more southwestern Colorado thing to do than to take a jeep trip into the high mountains to see ghost towns and old mines? There are a variety of half- to full-day trips. Cookouts as well. Information: San Juan Adventure Jeep Rentals/Tours, 450 Main Street, P.O. Box 1154, Ouray, Colorado 81427; (970) 325–0120 or (877) SJA–TOUR; www.sanjuan-adventure.com.

Switzerland of America Jeep Tours and Rentals. See the wonders on a jeep tour or on your own by renting a jeep. Information: Switzerland of America Jeep Tours and Rentals, 226 Seventh Avenue, Box 780, Ouray, Colorado 81427; (970) 325–4484 or (800) 432–5337; www.soajeep.com.

Activities

Backpacking and Hiking. Ouray is a hub for getting into the wilderness. The chamber of commerce and sports stores can give you the details.

Swimming. You should not miss Ouray's famous outdoor Hot Springs Pool in an absolutely breathtaking setting at the north edge of town. Heated to between 85 and 95 degrees by diluting the natural springwater at 156 degrees with cold water, this giant pool (250 feet long by 150 feet wide and varying from 2 to 9 feet in depth) is well worth a stop. The Swim Shop at the pool rents anything you'll need to have fun, including bathing suits. For a fee there are changing rooms, lockers, and showers. Water aerobics classes. Massage. Open daily summer and winter; (970) 325–4638.

Bachelor-Syracuse Mine Tour. Located 2 miles east of Ouray on County Road 14. This tour, which has been mentioned in several national magazines, allows you to ride a mine train 3,350 feet, horizontally, into Gold Hill, the site of an authentic gold and silver mine. There you will see silver veins and other mineral deposits, as well as have the opportunity to visit some of the miners' work areas and pan for gold. The Treasure Chest, a jewelry store there, features gold and silver jewelry. The **Outdoor Cafe** there serves breakfast and lunch with barbecue specialties. Hourly tours every day from mid-May to mid-September. Information: Bachelor-Syracuse Mine Tour, County Road 14, P.O. Box 380W, Ouray, Colorado 81427; (970) 325–0220; fax (970) 325–4500.

Fairs, Festivals, and Events

May brings the **Art Gallery Walk,** followed early in June by the **Music in Ouray Chamber Music Festival** and late in June by the **Annual Hardrock 100 Run.** August introduces the national juried art show, the **Annual Artists Alpine Holiday,** which is followed later in the month by the traditional miner's festival, **Ouray High Graders Holiday.** Then in September there's the **Ouray County Fair and Rodeo** over Labor Day weekend and the **Annual Imogene Pass Run** to Telluride a little later. The **Annual Jeep Jamboree** comes next just in time for Mother Nature's celebration, the annual **Fall Color Spectacular and Octoberfest.** Soon the snow is

Mineral Hot Springs swimming pool

falling, and it's time to bring out the cross-country skis.

A complete and updated list of events is available. Information: Ouray Chamber Resort Association, 1222 Main Street, P.O. Box 145, Ouray, Colorado 81427; (970) 325–4746 or (800) 228–1876; www.ouraycolorado.com.

Shopping

Ouray has a variety of good shops, all within easy walking distance from each other. A few of special interest are listed here.

Meerdink Gallery. 512 Main Street; (970) 325–4818. This large and interesting fine art gallery runs the gamut, from traditional and contemporary painting to regional graphics, sculpture, and weaving. Well worth a visit.

Buckskin Booksellers. 505 Main Street; (970) 325–4044. Aside from a nice selection of Native American arts and crafts, the shop focuses on original western collectibles from the Frontier West as well. Extensive book and magazine section, with Native

American, cowboy, and Colorado mining and railroading titles, is well worth browsing.

North Moon Gallery. There are two locations: 505 Main Street (at the Beaumont Hotel), (970) 325–4885 and 801 Main Street, (970) 325–4808. The Beaumont Hotel location, with its Victorian emphasis, features fabulous contemporary one-of-a-kind jewelry, clocks, boxes, and mixed-media fine art, including photography. At 801 Main Street you'll find more great jewelry, as well as American Indian and contemporary arts and crafts.

Swiss Store Fine Arts and Crafts. 514 Main Street; (970) 325–4327. Why shouldn't the "Switzerland of America" have a genuine Swiss store to help it live up to its slogan? Enjoy shopping to see many Swiss-made items including jewelry, clothing, and not-to-be-missed children's toy items.

The Sandman. 640-B Main Street; (970) 325–4071. This unique store features bottles and lamps filled with an unbelievable array of colored sands from the Southwest, which are layered to make designs and pictures. Other unusual gift items as well.

Diversions Bookstore/Coffeehouse. 333 Sixth Avenue; (970) 325–4333. This cozy establishment serves the best specialty coffees in town, as well as quiches and pastries. The new and used book selection is large, including many regional titles. Cards by local artists as well.

Telephone Numbers

Road and weather report. (877) 315–7623.

Telluride and Mountain Village near Telluride

The lodging price categories listed here are based on the more reasonable "regular" summer rates rather than the pricier ski season rates. But these rates may increase steeply during some of the more popular summer festivals, when there may also be required minimum night stays. During the ski season and some of the more popular summer festivals, be certain to make lodging reservations far in advance, for there is a lot of competition for the rooms here. During those times expect a busy, crowded Telluride. But if you plan to visit in the summer between major festivals, when lodging rates are more reasonable, there is often plenty of room in either Telluride or in Mountain Village 5 miles away. Mountain Village is accessible by a free, thirteen-minute gondola ride; (970) 728–2710 (closed approximately one month in early spring and in the fall) or by car (park at the Mountain Village parking sta-

tion and ride the free shuttle to the village's pedestrian core).

Telluride has a regional airport about 5 miles from town. Shuttle service and rental cars are available there as well as at the airport in Montrose, Colorado (60 miles away), where the planes land if the Telluride airport is closed due to bad weather.

For further information on lodging, festival dates, and for other general information, contact **Telluride and Mountain Village Visitor Services and Central Reservations,** 700 West Colorado Avenue, P.O. Box 1009, Telluride, Colorado 81435; (970) 728–4431 or (888) 355–8743; fax (970) 728–6475; www.visit telluride.com or www.telluride.com.

Foreign traveler's checks and currency can be exchanged at the Bank of Telluride (970–728–2000).

Lodging

New Sheridan Hotel. This is a fine place to stay if you want to soak up some of Telluride's past in a very comfortable, centrally located hostelry. Sarah Bernhardt and William Jennings Bryan stayed here. So can you. Built in 1895, this historic three-story hotel has been tastefully refurbished. In the hotel proper there are twenty-six handsomely restored rooms and suites, all but six having private baths. Located down the street are the Colorado suites, six deluxe condominium units with kitchens. A hearty buffet breakfast is included in the rate and is served in one of the very comfortable public rooms off the lobby. Small fitness center. Bicycles. Library. Street parking. The New Sheridan Chop House is on the premises. Information: New Sheridan Hotel, 231 West

The New Sheridan Hotel, Telluride

Colorado Avenue, P.O. Box 980, Telluride, Colorado 81435; (970) 728–4351 or (800) 200–1891; fax (970) 728–5024; www.newsheridan. com or www.telluride.mm.com. Moderate to expensive.

The San Sophia Inn and Condominiums. In sight of Ingram Falls in the distance, set on a corner location about 1 block from Telluride's main street, Colorado Avenue, and a short distance from the San Miguel River and forest trails. Each of the sixteen rooms with a private bath is handsomely and individually decorated. The Cafe San Sophia (open to the public), where a full breakfast (included) is served, is a large, airy, pleasant space, with views. This luxury B&B is well run and exudes a sense of warmth and graciousness. Library and lounge. Sunken Jacuzzi. Below-level parking. No smoking. Information: San Sophia Inn and Condominiums, P.O. Box 1825, Telluride, Colorado 81435; (970) 728–3001 or (800) 537–4781; fax (970) 728–6226; www.sansophia.com. Expensive.

Johnstone Inn (Bed and Breakfast). A B&B in a centrally located, restored Victorian home. Rooms are tastefully appointed and furnished with turn-of-the-twentieth-century furniture. Eight rooms with private baths. Hot tub. Afternoon refreshments. Full breakfast. Information: Johnstone Inn, 403 West Colorado Avenue, Box 546, Telluride, Colorado 81435; (970) 728–3316 or (800) 752–1901; www.johnstoneinn.com. Inexpensive.

Victorian Inn. Centrally located yet off the main street is this twenty-nine unit inn. It offers standard motel accommodations with private baths and TVs on the two upper floors and less expensive lodging with shared baths on the lowest floor. Sauna, hot tub, and continental breakfast. No pets. Information: Victorian Inn, 401 West Pacific Avenue, P.O. Box 217, Telluride, Colorado 81435; (970) 728–6601 or (800) 611–9893; fax (970) 728–3233; www.telluride mtnlodging.com. Inexpensive.

Hotel Columbia. Located on the riverbank and right at the foot of the gondola that connects to Mountain Village is this four-story neo-Victorian–style hotel. The twenty-one luxury rooms all have fireplaces. Views. Some with balconies and some penthouse units. Exercise room. Hot tub. The Cosmopolitan Restaurant is on the premises. Information: Hotel Columbia, 300 West San Juan Avenue, P.O. Box 800, Telluride, Colorado 81435; (970) 728–0660 or (800) 201–9505; fax (970) 728–9249; www.columbiatelluride. Expensive to very expensive.

The Ice House. Just a short walk to town or the gondola, overlooking the river and adjacent to the old ice house. This is a luxury lodge with a sunlit central atrium on the mezzanine and forty-two spacious rooms and suites with balconies. Heated pool. Steam room. Whirlpool. Continental breakfast included. Information: The Ice House, 310 South Fir, Telluride, Colorado 81435; (970) 728–6300; (800) 544–3436; fax (970) 728–6358; www.icehouselodge.com. Expensive to very expensive.

Camel's Garden Hotel. Located right at the Gondola Plaza are these thirty-one luxurious and spacious rooms and suites with balconies, gas fireplaces, and CD players. Steam room and oversized outdoor hot tub. Continental breakfast included. Information: Camel's Garden, 250 West San Juan, Telluride, Colorado 81435; (970) 728–9300 or (888) 772–2635; fax (970) 728–0433; www.camelsgarden. com. Expensive to very expensive.

Bear Creek Bed and Breakfast. Walk upstairs from the storefront street level to this upscale hostelry at 221 East Colorado Avenue. Its ten well-appointed and comfortable rooms have private baths. Deluxe rooms have sitting areas and good views of the mountains. Several condominium units with kitchens available nearby. Full breakfast. Fireplace in the common area. Steam room and sauna. Rooftop deck with panoramic views. Information: Bear Creek Bed and Breakfast, 221 East Colorado Avenue, P.O. Box 2369, Telluride, Colorado 81435; (970) 728–6681 or (800) 338–7064; fax (970) 728–3636; www.bearcreektelluride.com. Moderate to expensive.

Oak Street Inn. Behind the New Sheridan Hotel in a convenient central location is this homey, twenty-two-unit, somewhat inexpensive hostelry offering a variety of nice but simply decorated rooms, mostly with shared bath. Information: Oak Street Inn, 134 North Oak Street, P.O. Box 176, Telluride, Colorado 81435; (970) 728–3383. Inexpensive.

Manitou Lodge Bed and Breakfast. This nicely designed, three-story frame building with a shed roof is located right on the banks of the San Miguel River at 333 South Fir, just 3 blocks from Colorado Avenue. There are eleven comfortable rooms with private baths and refrigerators; some have nice balconies with superb views. Nice public room with a TV and a large fireplace. Grassy play area alongside riverbank. Continental breakfast. Information: Manitou Lodge Bed and Breakfast, P.O. Box 100, Telluride, Colorado 81435; (970) 728–6621 or (800) 538–7754; fax (970) 728–6160; www.telluride lodging.com. Moderate.

Riverside Condominiums. These multistory condominium units (115) line the south bank of the San Miguel River only 2 to 3 blocks from downtown at the foot of South Pine Street. These nicely furnished, one-, two-, and three-bedroom luxury units have gas fireplaces, washers/dryers, color TVs, and kitchens. Most have outstanding views of the river, town, and mountains. Outdoor hot tub. Information: Riverside Condominiums, c/o Telluride Resort Accommodations, P.O. Box 666, Telluride, Colorado 81435; (970) 728–6621 or (800) 538–7754. Expensive.

Mountainside Inn. Along the south side of the river at the foot of South Davis Street is this basic two-story inn. Eighty-eight of the units are basic motel rooms with private baths, queen beds, and TVs, while eight units have kitchenettes. Hot tub; laundry. Information: Mountainside Inn, 333 South Davis, P.O. Box 2288, Telluride, Colorado 81435; (970) 728–1950 or (888) 728–1950; fax (970) 728–1957; www.telluridemtnlodging.com. Moderate.

Wyndham Resort and Golden Door Spa. Over in Telluride Mountain Village, just about everything revolves around this extraordinary, multistory, 212-room luxury hotel that looks like a transplant from St. Moritz. Within a chip shot of the first tee of the championship Mountain Village Golf Course, it also provides easy access to the ski lifts. The public rooms are spacious and beautifully appointed, as are the guest rooms. The facilities seem endless, with a 42,000-square-foot spa and a 25-meter Junior Olympic lap and aerobics pool, connected by a water slide to an indoor/outdoor pool. Private and public Jacuzzis, saunas, and steam rooms. Massage and personal treatment rooms. Squash and racquetball facilities. Meeting rooms and restaurants. Information: The Peaks Resort and Spa, Box 2702, Telluride, Colorado 81435; (970) 728–6800 or (800) 996–3426; fax (970) 728–6175; www.wyndham.com. Very expensive.

Skyline Guest Ranch. In an absolutely magnificent high-mountain setting at 9,600 feet elevation surrounded by grassy hillsides, wildflower meadows, several small lakes, and groves of aspen and pine. Just 8 miles south of Telluride. The large, inviting log lodge with its ten smallish bedrooms (all with private baths) and large, comfortable living room and dining room is only part of the scene. Near the lodge on this multiacre property are five very comfortable two- and three-bedroom view cabins with full kitchens. The lodge dining room serves three meals a day for its American Plan lodge guests. The rates also include a variety of activities, such as horseback riding and instruction; pack trips, van trips, and jeep trips to Mesa Verde, old mining towns, and other nearby sights; guided hiking or mountaineering trips; and fishing on the premises. Of course, there's picnicking and hiking on the ranch and into the national forest that surrounds it. Sauna. Hot tub. Reservations for summer must be made many months in advance. Winter stays also available. Information: Skyline Guest Ranch, Box 67, Telluride, Colorado 81435; (970) 728–3757 or (888) 754–1126; fax (970) 728–6728; www.skylineexperience.com.

Campgrounds

Telluride Town Park and Campground. Just 2 blocks east of Telluride. Forty-two sites, five primitive. Often crowded. No reservations; first come, first served (fee); (970) 728–2173.

Sunshine Campground. Located 7 miles southwest of Telluride on Colorado Highway 145. Eighteen sites. Fee. For advance reservations call the U.S. Forest Service; (970) 327–4261 or (970) 728–4211.

Matterhorn Campground. Ten miles southwest of Telluride on Colorado Highway 145. Camping and RV sites. Fee. Contact the Matterhorn Station for information about the area's trails, camping, and forest access; (970) 327–4261 or (970) 728–4211.

Food

New Sheridan Chop House. 233 West Colorado; (970) 728–9100. This excellent dinner restaurant located in a bright, cheery corner of the New Sheridan Hotel shines in more ways than one. There are mountain views out the large windows, the waitstaff seem to know what they're doing, and the culinary experience is often memorable—especially if you partake of some of the delicately prepared wild game entrees. More familiar dishes are simply but deliciously served up as well: double rack of lamb, steak, veal chops, fresh seafood. The accompaniments are equally tantalizing. Desserts are often innovative and satisfying. A very well-selected wine list; also microbrews. Moderate to expensive.

La Marmotte. 150 West San Juan; (970) 728–6232. This is an excellent country French dinner restaurant, located in the old icehouse 2 blocks south of Colorado Avenue. The restaurant has established a highly varied menu that borrows from the provinces of France. Rabbit confit, duck foie gras, and a variety of beef, veal, and fresh daily seafood entrees are prepared in a number of tantalizing ways. Excellent wine list and outstanding pastries. Outdoor patio-garden seating at lunch, weather permitting. Expensive.

Wildflower Cooking Company. 250 West San Juan Avenue (The Camel's Garden Hotel); (970) 728–8887. For scrumptious pastries or cooked-to-order breakfast and soups, salads, and sandwiches for lunch, this is a good bet. Also, dinners to go, selection of specialty cheeses, box lunches.

Allred's Top of the Gondola. Located at the top of the gondola, (970) 728–7474. This year round dinner restaurant features a wide range of fish and meat dishes and a long, delectable list of desserts. If you're not already high enough at 10,500 feet, there's a long wine list to push you along. Moderate to expensive.

Jody's Kitchen: A Mexican Eatery. 200 South Davis; (970) 728–5114. Not far from the gondola is this simple but good lunch and dinner restaurant with a Mexican flair offering many of your favorites. Inexpensive to moderate.

Campagna. 435 West Pacific Avenue; (970) 728–6190. A historic Telluride home is the scene of this award-winning dinner restaurant where you'll feel transported to the hills of Tuscany in northern Italy. Special touches with fresh ingredients make for good dining. On this mainly a la carte menu are three different homemade pasta dishes daily, a half-dozen entrees (try Sonoma quail roasted with fresh juniper berries and sage on grilled polenta), several vegetable dishes, and simple but memorable desserts like *vin santo* with homemade *biscotti,* homemade *gelati,* and Italian fruit tarts. Fine wine list. Espresso. Dinner only. Reservations. Expensive.

The Cosmopolitan and Tasting Cellar. 300 West San Juan; (970) 728–1292. Located in the Hotel Columbia at the foot of the gondola is this classy dinner restaurant. Dine on local baby beet salad, seared duck breast, and sea scallops or one of the many fine fish or meat entrees. The Tasting Cellar offers a fixed price menu (only for groups of ten or more) of six courses and five wines. Expensive.

Rustico Ristorante. 114 East Colorado; (970) 728–4046. The owner's frequent travels to Italy are reflected in the very Italian lunch and dinner menu. Start dinner with wild mushrooms sautéed with marsala over polenta and fontina cheese, followed by a pasta dish (maybe tube pasta in a spicy crushed red pepper and marinara sauce), risotto, or rack of lamb grilled with rosemary and thyme. Wine and beer. Delicious desserts and specialty coffees. Lunch and dinner. Moderate to expensive.

221 South Oak. 221 South Oak Street; (970) 728–9507. This cozy dinner bistro close to the gondola serves up fresh, inventive food. Begin with oyster and olathe/corn chowder with smoked bacon, then dig in to the herb roasted chicken with butternut squash risotto and haricot vert or pecan-crusted trout with kale and rock shrimp sauce. Expensive.

Eagles Bar and Grill. 100 West Colorado; (970) 728–0886. This attractive breakfast, lunch, and dinner restaurant on a busy Colorado Avenue corner has a nice general menu of light foods, from appetizers like pozole verde to fresh soups and salads, specialty pizzas, and tamerind plum barbecue pork ribs. Desserts. Wine and beer. Lunch and dinner. Moderate.

Leimgruber's Bierstube and Restaurant. 573 West Pacific Avenue; (970) 728–4663. No ski area winter or summer can be without one of these German imports. Paulaner imported beer is served on the view deck in the summer, and the American-Alpine/European dinner menu prevails all year. Outstanding *apfel strudel.* Moderate.

Between the Covers Bookstore and Espresso Bar. 224 West Colorado Avenue; (970) 728–4504. Located in the back of a bookstore is this cozy coffeehouse with a fully equipped espresso bar. But that's not all—excellent pastries and desserts are served, as are Italian cream sodas, fine teas, and chocolates. Open throughout the day until late.

Excelsior Cafe. 200 West Colorado Avenue; (970) 728–4250. There can't be a better place for breakfast or dinner, serving up many Italian dishes, than this interesting, casual, yet cosmopolitan trattoria-style cafe. Try bruschetta or crisp parmesan potato cakes or pesto-seared chicken breasts. Vegetarian dishes. Espresso. Outstanding desserts. Dining outdoors on the patio, weather permitting. Excellent wine list. Moderate to expensive.

Baked in Telluride. 127 South Fir Street; (970) 728–4775. This old Telluride fixture serves up home-baked goods and espresso for breakfast. Sit-down, continental breakfast in the morning, and at lunch and dinner there's pizza, calzone, and a host of other interesting tidbits. Open 5:30 A.M. to 10:00 P.M. Carryout.

Sofio's Mexican Cafe. 110 East Colorado Avenue; (970) 728–4882. This interesting restaurant serves good Mexican-style food daily for breakfast and dinner. And the very good breakfast menu includes many standard American favorites. Pleasant atmosphere. Moderate.

La Piazza del Villagio Ristorante. 117 Lost Creek Lane, **Mountain Village;** (970) 728–8283. If you're looking for Italian in the village, the menu here offers up a wide variety of very good northern Italian antipasto, salad, pasta, and meat and fish dishes. Excellent specialty coffees and desserts. Lunch and dinner. Expensive

Tours and Equipment

Galloping Goose Transit Service. From late May through mid-September, Telluride provides free in-town transportation; (970) 728–5700. In

Mountain village a similar service is offered; **Dial-A-Ride;** (970) 728–8888.

Telluride Historical Museum. At the head of North Fir Street in the old hospital. Take a self-guided tour of this museum at 317 North Fir Street (970–728–3344) with its interesting displays relating to the area's western mining past. Helpful museum staff members can give you directions for touring Telluride's historic area.

Historic Walks of Telluride. Beneath today's glitter see the Telluride of a century ago; (970) 728–6639.

John Sir Jesse Herb Walker Tours. Plant and mushroom discovery walks; (970) 728–0639.

Telluride Express. Airport limousine service to and from Grand Junction, Montrose, Cortez, and Durango. Free in-town shuttle; (970) 728–6000 or (888) 212–8294.

Telluride Outside/Telluride Angler. This organization can arrange just about anything your heart (and body) desires. Fly-fishing, four-by-four scenic tours (and rentals), mountain bike tours, hot air balloon tours, pack trips, jeep trips, horseback trail rides, and sleigh rides top but do not complete the list. Information: Telluride Outside/Telluride Angler, 121 West Colorado Avenue, Telluride, Colorado 81435; (970) 728–3895 or (800) 831–6230.

Paragon Ski and Sport. This all-round ski and sports shop offers everything from bicycle rentals to camping supplies. Information: Paragon Ski and

Sports, 213 West Colorado Avenue, Telluride, Colorado 81435; (970) 728–4525 or (800) 903–4525.

Telluride Sports. Headquarters for mountain biking where you can either buy or rent one. Camping and climbing equipment, hiking boots, maps, and books. Information: Telluride Sports, 150 West Colorado Avenue, Telluride, Colorado 81435; (970) 728–4477 or (800) 828–7547.

San Juan Hut Systems. Ski 56 miles over backcountry trails from Telluride to Ridgway and Ouray using well-placed huts to warm up and spend the night. Or bike 215 miles from Telluride to Moab, Utah, in a seven-day journey in which you will spend six nights in well-placed huts. Equipment can be rented. For the less hardy this outfitter provides shorter ski and bike trips in the San Juans. All levels of skiers and children welcome. Information: San Juan Hut Systems, P.O. Box 1663, Telluride, Colorado 81435; (970) 626–3033.

Fantasy Ridge Alpinism. This year-round rock-and-snow climbing school and guide service offers instruction by the hour, half day, or full day and can arrange multiday guided trips; (970) 728–3546.

Activities

Golf. Telluride Golf Club. For reservation and tee times at the championship Telluride Golf Course in Mountain Village, call (970) 728–6157.

Schools and Academies. Telluride is home to the **Telluride Academy,** which offers day and week camps for kids (natural science series, a junior fly-fishing camp, theater arts programs, a reading camp, and a baseball camp). And there is a program for adults, "Women in the Wilderness." Information: Telluride Academy, P.O. Box 2255, Telluride, Colorado 81435; (970) 728–5311; tellurideacademy.com. And there's the Ah Haa School for the Arts, offering summer art classes and workshops for children and adults. Information: Ah Haa School for the Arts, 135 South Spruce Street, Telluride, Colorado 81435; (970) 728–3886; www.ahhaa.org.

Fairs, Festivals, and Events

Besides the booming ski industry in the winter, Telluride is a major summer festival town. There are more than forty major events scheduled in Telluride each summer and fall. Some of the better-known festivals and events are listed here.

Telluride Bluegrass Festival. Held the third week in June. Four days of concerts and contests preceded by a week of workshops.

Telluride Jazz Celebration. Three days of concerts in Town Park, the first weekend in August.

Telluride Chamber Music Festival. Chamber music over two weekends in mid-August.

TAF Airman's Rendezvous—A Hanggliding Festival. This renowned event is held for five days in mid-September and attracts more than 250 of the world's most skilled hang-gliding pilots.

Telluride Film Festival. Held late August or early September through Labor Day weekend. Small, prestigious international festivals like this have helped put Telluride on the map.

Imogene Pass Run. This popular but grueling running event is held early in September. Runners traverse the steep, rocky mountain terrain between Telluride and Ouray for a distance of 18 miles.

There are many other events such as **Mountainfilm,** over Memorial Day, a film festival focused on mountain environment and sports. Early June brings the **Invitational Balloon Festival** with the **Telluride Wine Festival** following in late June. **Fireman's Picnic and Parade** marks the Fourth of July, and later in the month and into August **Dance in Telluride Presents** stages ballet dance performances. August sees the **Rotary 4x4 Rally** and, near the end of the month, the **Mushroom Festival.** Telluride Octoberfest is held early in October, while **Writers in the Sky,** a regional writer's roundtable, nearly finishes off the season.

(For additional information on these and other festivals and their precise dates, contact the Telluride Visitor Services listed at the beginning of the Telluride portion of this "Staying There" section or see www.telluride. com or www.visittelluride.com.)

Telluride Repertory Theatre Company. Starting in March and running through early August, this community theater group performs an eclectic array of plays. Information: Telluride Repertory Theatre Company, P.O. Box 2469, Telluride, Col-

orado 81435; (970) 728–4539; www.telluridetheatre.com.

Shopping

Just as in any booming ski town, shops come and go, becoming more upscale with each new rise in rent. There are a number of unique shops and galleries in Telluride. A few of them are listed here.

Between the Covers Books and Espresso Bar. 224 West Colorado Avenue; (970) 728–4504. This full-service bookstore has a fine selection of Southwest, Four Corners, and Colorado–related books. Its stock of general books has been selected as carefully as the regional books. Also CDs, tapes, and magazines from the United States and around the world. Large children's book section in the back, where there is an excellent espresso and pastry bar.

Telluride Gallery of Fine Art. 130 East Colorado Avenue; (970) 728–4242. This gallery is one of the finest in the Four Corners region. Although it has a good selection of Southwest regional and Colorado art, including limited edition prints, paintings, ceramics, and jewelry, it also displays the works of contemporary national and international artists. Well worth a stop.

East End Gallery. 215 East Colorado Avenue; (970) 728–3617. Walk down the steps to this gallery where you will see some of the most interesting contemporary paintings, ceramics, and mixed media on exhibit in Telluride.

Potter's Wheel. 221 East Colorado Avenue; (970) 728–4912. Visit this gallery for fine functional and decorative pottery from area artisans.

Bookworks. 191 South Pine Street; (970) 728–0700. This large bookstore has a wide selection of adult and children's books, including many regional titles, guides, and maps.

Telephone Numbers

Road conditions. (877) 315–7623 (dialed from Colorado only).

Ski conditions. (970) 728–7425.

Weather conditions. (970) 240–4900 or (303) 494–4221.

Telluride Express Taxi-Shuttle. (970) 728–6000 or (888) 212–8294.

Telluride Airport. (970) 728–5051.

United Airlines/Great Lakes Airlines. (800) 241–6522 or (970) 728–1262.

America West Express. (800) 235–9292 or (970) 728–4868.

Budget Rent-a-Car. (970) 728–4642.

Thrifty Rent-a-Car. (970) 249–8741.

National Rent-a-Car. (970) 252–8898.

Mesa Verde National Park

Lodging and Food

Far View Lodge. Located at the summit of Navajo Hill near the visitor center. The lodge is 15 miles from the park entrance and only 5 miles from most of the major sights. The ranger at the park entrance, just off U.S. Highway 160, has information about room availability at the lodge. There are 150 rooms with private baths. The accommodations are scattered over the hillside in units containing a variable number of rooms. The restaurant at the lodge serves only dinner. The Far View Cafeteria, not far away, serves three meals a day. Information: Far View Lodge, Box 277, Mancos, Colorado 81328; (970) 529–4421 or (877) 264–4916; fax (970) 533–7831; www.visitmesaverde.com. Moderate.

Campgrounds

Morefield Campground. With 450 sites, this large campground is the only one in Mesa Verde National Park (there are several private campgrounds just outside the park). It is located below the mesa just 4 miles from the entry station and U.S. Highway 160. All sites are designed for both tent and trailer camping and have picnic tables and fireplaces or charcoal burners. Can be open mid-April through October, but call to check. Some RV hookups (higher fee). Comfort stations. Morefield Campground general store has gas, groceries, camping supplies. On summer evenings rangers give talks about the archaeology, history, and natural history of the area. Reservations can be made but are typically not necessary. Fee; (970) 565–2133 or (800) 449–2288.

Tours and Events

Guided Bus Tours. These half-day bus tours leave twice daily from Far View Lodge (morning and afternoon) and Morefield Campground (morning). The three-hour tour is comprehensive and includes the major

Chapin Mesa sights. Also full-day tours; (970) 529–4421 or (800) 449–2288.

Annual Mesa Verde Country Indian Arts and Culture Festival. This week-long history, music, drama, and art celebration, the end of May through early June, is held at several venues including Chapin Mesa Amphitheatre, Mesa Verde National Park; Anasazi Heritage Center; Cortez Cultural Center; and Boyle Park, Mancos. In conjunction with this celebration is the **Mesa Verde Country Indian Market** held at Morefield Campground, Mesa Verde National Park; (970) 565–8227 or (800) 253–1616; www.mesaverde country.com.

Cortez, Colorado

For more information on this town near Mesa Verde National Park, contact the **Cortez Chamber of Commerce** and the **Mesa Verde Country Visitor Information Bureau,** P.O. Box HH, Cortez, Colorado 81321; (970) 565–3414 or (800) 253–1616; www.mesaverdecountry.com; www.cortezchamber.org.

Lodging

Holiday Inn Express. Located near the center of town on Main Street, this attractive, multistory, one-hundred-unit air-conditioned motel offers all the amenities. The rooms are nicely furnished and comfortable. There is a nice, large public room with a fireplace. Indoor pool with hot tub, spa, and sauna. Information: Holiday Inn Express, 2121 East Main Street, Cortez, Colorado 81321; (970)

565–6000 or (800) 626–5652; fax (970) 565–3438. Moderate.

Western Turquoise Motor Inn. Located near the center of town on U.S. Highway 160. There are forty-six air-conditioned units with private baths. Heated pool. Information: Best Western Turquoise Motor Inn, 535 East Main, Cortez, Colorado 81231; (970) 565–3778 or (800) 528–1234; fax (970) 565–3439. Moderate.

Travelodge. Located 0.75 mile south on U.S. Highway 666. This motel has thirty air-conditioned units with private baths. Heated swimming pool. Whirlpool bath. Information: Travelodge, 440 South Broadway, Cortez, Colorado 81321; (970) 565–7778; fax (970) 565–7214. Inexpensive.

Kelly Place (Bed and Breakfast). Located just a few miles west of Cortez on a 100-acre farm in McElmo Canyon is this unique, remote southwestern-style B&B with seven lodge rooms and two cabins, each with private bath. The owners call the place "a living history and archaeology preserve." They introduce visitors to a hands-on approach to archaeology through an exploration of the ruins on this "living history farm." Horseback rides. American Indian Craft seminars. Covered wagon campouts. Information: Kelly Place, 14663 County Road G, Cortez, Colorado 81321; (970) 565–3125 or (800) 745–4885; fax (970) 565–3450; www.kellyplace.com. Inexpensive.

Food

Homesteaders. 45 East Main; (970) 565–6253. This excellent western-style restaurant is open for breakfast, lunch, and dinner. Western breakfast favorites include biscuits and gravy and buttermilk hotcakes; lunch and dinner feature many Mexican-style specialties. Good hamburgers. Children's menu. Inexpensive.

Earth Song Haven Tea Room. 34 West Main; (970) 565–9125. This tearoom located in the Quality Bookstore offers some alternatives to the usual local fare, including excellent light breakfasts and lunches. Espresso all day until early evening. Inexpensive.

Main Street Brewery. 21 East Main Street; (970) 564–9112. Besides their very own beers, this pleasant establishment offers lunch and light dinner including shakes and malts, soups, salads, and sandwiches. Also gourmet pizzas and pasta dishes as well as other specialties for dinner. Inexpensive.

Nero's Italian Restaurant. 303 West Main Street; (970) 565–7366. This popular local Italian restaurant does a decent job. Try the minestrone soup or the antipasto for starters. Then dig into a hearty meatball sandwich or savor angel hair pasta with clam sauce or sautéed scampi. Steaks too. Wine and beer. Inexpensive to moderate.

Tours, Events, and Activities

Crow Canyon Archaeological Center. Located a few miles northwest of Cortez off U.S. Highway 666 North. (About 2 miles north of Cortez, look for a sign marking the turnoff to the left, and follow the signs for approximately 0.8 mile to the center.) Under the direction of some of the Southwest's best-known archaeologists, the programs at this dynamic center make the region come alive. There are daylong, weeklong, and even customized archaeological learning and research experiences for adults, children, and families. Also offered are weeklong cultural expeditions to important sites in the Four Corners area and beyond. And there are programs tailored just for educators and student groups. See their Web site for all of the enticing possibilities available. No experience is required for any of these programs, but all (including the Day Program) must be prearranged and are available by reservation only. Anyone, though, is welcome to visit the center. Information: Crow Canyon Archaeological Center, 23390 County Road K, Cortez, Colorado 81321; (970) 565–8975 or (800) 422–8975; www.crowcanyon.org.

Ute Mountain Tribal Tours. If you want to see some remote Anasazi ruins that few people have visited, Ute Mountain and Mancos Canyon Indian Park await you. Here is a good chance to meet the Utes and see their pottery, plants, and beadwork at Towaoc, Colorado, where the tours begin (15 miles south of Cortez on U.S. Highway 666). Reservations must be made in advance. Information: Ute Mountain Tribal Park, P.O. Box 109, Towaoc, Colorado 81334; (970) 565–3751, ext. 330, or (800) 847–5485.

Cortez Cultural Center. 25 North Market Street; (970) 565–1151; www.cortezculturalcenter.org. Located in one of Cortez's historic buildings, this museum and interpretive center offers permanent exhibits of the Ancestral Puebloan civilization, displays from the Ute Mountain tribe, and, during the summer, demonstrations of native craft techniques. Also Native American storytellers and dances on summer evenings.

Indian Dances. On summer evenings visitors can see Indian dances at Cortez City Park, next to the Welcome Center. And not to leave anybody out, gunfights are staged in the park one night weekly.

Shopping

City Market. 508 East Main; (970) 565–6504. This large, egalitarian grocery store often stocks a good supply of the native pinto beans grown on nearby farms. They come in small, gift-size burlap bags, and some bags contain a speckled "Anasazi" bean. This store also has a good supply of Colorado's delicious and famous high-altitude honey.

Quality Bookstore. 34 West Main; (970) 565–9125. This is a good general bookstore, but as you would imagine, it has an extra-good selection of hiking, camping, Colorado-focus, and archaeological books. It also stocks topographical maps of Colorado and the three adjacent "Four Corners" states. Espresso.

Farmers' Market. This lively affair is held on Saturday mornings, June through October, in the courthouse parking lot.

There are several regional craft and gift stores, plus some reliable places to buy Indian arts and crafts, including **Don Woodard's Indian Trading**

Post and Museum (U.S. Highway 160, 1 mile east of town, 970–565–3986) and **Notah-Dineh** at 345 West Main Street (970–565–9607).

Mancos, Colorado

For further information on this town near Mesa Verde National Park, contact Mancos Visitors Center, 171 Railroad Avenue, P.O. Box 494, Mancos, Colorado 81328; (970) 533–7434; www.mancosvalley.com

Lodging

Bauer House Bed and Breakfast. Located in the center of Mancos, this historic mansion offers three handsomely furnished Victorian-style bedrooms with private baths and a penthouse suite, all with mountain views. Spacious lawn area. Full breakfast. Information: Bauer House B&B, 100 Bauer Avenue, P.O. Box 1049, Mancos, Colorado 81328; (970) 533–9707 or (800) 733–9707; www.bauer-house.com. Moderate.

Willowtail Springs Lodge and Cabins. Located outside Mancos on San Juan Skyway Loop on 40 acres by a lake, pasture, and stream are these pleasant accommodations, a 10-minute drive from the Mesa Verde National Park entrance. The three units are furnished with antiques and have fireplaces and kitchens. Gardens, hiking trails, views. Information: Willowtail Springs, P.O. Box 89, Mancos, Colorado 81328; (970) 533–7592 or (800) 698–0603; fax (970) 533–7641; www.subee.com/willowtail/home.html. Moderate.

Echo Basin Resort and RV Park. Located just east of Mancos, 3 miles north off U. S. Highway 160 is this several-hundred-acre spread on the Mancos River with mountain lakes and lush meadows. There are eighteen rustic A-frame cabins and deluxe cabins with kitchens, some with fireplaces. Fishing, horseback riding, hiking, hayrides, cookouts, and a heated swimming pool are part of the scene. Also shaded tent sites and RV sites with full hookups and a restaurant and bar. Information: Echo Basin Resort, 43747 County Road 44, Mancos, Colorado, 81328; (970) 533–7000, (800) 426–1890, or (800) 426–1890; fax (970) 533–7000; www.echobasin.com.

Lake Mancos Ranch. This genuine dude ranch is located at 8,000 feet elevation about 6 miles from Mancos. Horseback riding, lake and stream fishing, a swimming pool, pleasant lodging, and three meals a day complete this sylvan scene. Weekly reservations only during summer season. Information: Lake Mancos Ranch, 42688 County Road N, Mancos, Colorado 81328; (970) 533–1190 or (800) 325–9462; www.subee.com/lake-mancos-ranch/home.html or www.lakemancosranch.com.

Food

Dusty Rose Cafe. 200 West Grand Avenue; (970) 533–9042. This friendly cafe offers a varied selection of breakfast and lunch dishes with a Mancos twist, then for dinner puts on the dog with Northern Italian veal and seafood specialties. Inexpensive.

Millwood Junction. At the junction of U.S. Highway 160 and Main Street; (970) 533–7338. They come from miles around for the Friday night seafood buffet here, and the rest of the time for the daily seafood specials, barbecued pork ribs, steaks, sandwiches, and the bountiful salad bar. Homemade desserts. Beer, wine, lounge. Dinner only. Inexpensive to moderate.

Absolute Baking and Catering. 110 South Main Street; (970) 533–1200. For breakfast or lunch or your favorite espresso drink in a casual, cozy atmosphere.

Farmington, New Mexico

You will have little trouble finding a fast-food concession for lunch in Farmington. If you are looking for American Indian arts and crafts, do not fail to visit the Foutz Indian Room at 3041 East Main, where you will find an excellent selection of Navajo jewelry, kachina dolls, and Navajo rugs. To see the rugs, you must ask to visit the rug room in the back of the store. Information: Farmington Convention and Visitors Bureau, 3041 East Main, Suite 101, Farmington, New Mexico 87401; (505) 326–7602 or (800) 448–1240; www.farmington.org.

The Spanish Rio Grande Country

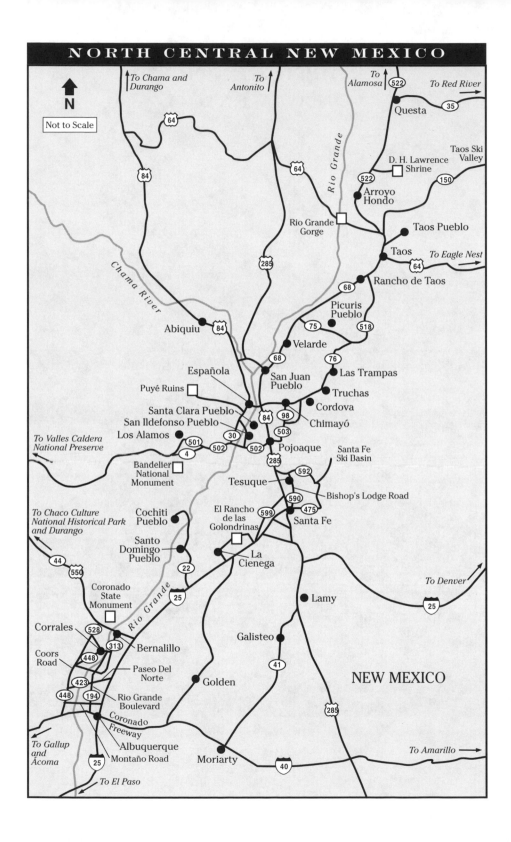

NORTH CENTRAL NEW MEXICO

N
Not to Scale

To Chama and Durango
To Antonito
To Alamosa
To Red River

64
522
35
Questa

84

64
Rio Grande

522
D. H. Lawrence Shrine
Taos Ski Valley
150

Arroyo Hondo

Chama River

Rio Grande Gorge
Taos Pueblo

Taos
To Eagle Nest
64

68
Rancho de Taos

285
Picuris Pueblo

75
518

Abiquiu
84

68
Velarde

76
Las Trampas

Española
San Juan Pueblo
Truchas

Puyé Ruins
Cordova

Santa Clara Pueblo
84
98
Chimayó

San Ildefonso Pueblo
503

Los Alamos
30

To Valles Caldera National Preserve
501
502
502
Pojoaque
Santa Fe Ski Basin

4

Bandelier National Monument
285

Tesuque
592

To Chaco Culture National Historical Park and Durango
Cochiti Pueblo
El Rancho de las Golondrinas
590
475
Bishop's Lodge Road

Santo Domingo Pueblo
599
Santa Fe

44
22

550
La Cienega

Coronado State Monument
To Denver

25
Lamy
25

Corrales
528

313
Bernalillo
Galisteo

Coors Road
448

Paseo Del Norte
41
NEW MEXICO

423

448
194
Rio Grande Boulevard

Coronado Freeway
Golden

To Gallup and Ácoma
Albuquerque
To Amarillo

25
Montaño Road
Moriarty
40

To El Paso

INTRODUCTION

If you want to savor the Spanish colonial atmosphere of Old Mexico without leaving the United States, visit northern New Mexico. There in a broad valley between high mountains whose snowmelt waters feed the Rio Grande that flows through it, you will find the Spanish spirit very much alive. As you drive over highways and walk along streets and roads there, you will be separated by just a few inches of pavement from some of this continent's oldest and most famous western trails. Some were used by the first European settlers to make their homes deep in the interior of the United States, whereas others were used by Americans who opened up and settled the West. You will pass by graceful, tan adobe buildings, rising easily from the earth they are made of, some built in the name of the king of Spain less than twenty-five years after the Spanish Armada. You will see ruins of seventeenth-century missions, as well as intact missions and churches from the early eighteenth century and later, that were built by Spain's Franciscan Brothers on orders from the pope in Rome. And you will see modest adobe homes with tin roofs whose only ornamentation is a trim of blue around the windows and doors. In Spanish New Mexico, just as in Moorish Spain, blue paint is applied to keep the devil away. And setting off the blue trim will be five-pound strings of bright red chili peppers, called *ristras,* hanging from the adobe walls as they dry in the bright sun.

The Anglo population is the minority population in most of this high valley north of Albuquerque. The Anglos who reside there have made adjustments in their lives to adapt to the dominant Spanish culture, rather than the other way around. Much of the Spanish tradition lives on. In the cities, towns, and villages of the region, you will sometimes hear English spoken with a Spanish accent by Americans of Spanish descent whose heritage in this country goes back more than three centuries. In some of the villages, you may also rub shoulders with older people who speak very little English and whose archaic Spanish expressions date from the time of Cervantes. It is no wonder, then, that most of the Spanish descendants living in northern New Mexico prefer to be called *Hispanic,* the Latin term pertaining to the people, speech, or culture of Spain.

You will detect soon enough that this is a land of *poco tiempo,* where everything is done "in a little while." In this high country there is a more relaxed approach to living, similar to that found south of the border in Mexico. Even Anglo residents talk about being more "laid-back" than their contemporaries in the East and West. As a visitor you may find yourself tiring easily, perhaps even wanting to take a siesta in the afternoons. You should probably give in to this urge. For as you sightsee in Santa Fe, New Mexico's capital, you will be walking in an atmosphere almost as rarefied as that of the *alto plano* or "high plain" where Mexico City rests. Santa Fe's

7,000-foot elevation is more than a quarter mile higher than the much-touted "mile-high city" of Denver, the capital city of Colorado. Thus it is the highest capital city, as well as the largest city at such a high altitude, in the United States. So slow your pace a little and try to absorb some of the centuries-old ambience. Museums and historical monuments abound. Walk and mix with the people. Slow down, look, listen, observe. For more than anything else, it's the people and how they live that make the real difference in northern New Mexico.

The Spanish heritage is so rich and so deep that you will not have to strain to detect it. First there are the names on the land. Spanish names are everywhere. *Rio Grande* is Spanish for "great river." The high mountains to the east were named *Sangre de Cristo,* a Spanish term meaning "blood of Christ." And Saint John the Baptist was remembered in the mountains and pueblo that carry his Spanish name, *San Juan.* Many towns, cities, and hamlets have names that can be matched with the names of older towns by the same name in the mother country. Valencia, San Miguel, and Guadalupe counties, as well as Madrid, Santa Cruz, Albuquerque, and Santa Fe, were all named for towns and cities in either Spain or Mexico. Where that is not the case, towns often were named for the Spanish or Mexican families who founded them. Even many of the Indian pueblos lost their ancient Indian names long ago and are best known by Spanish place-names. San Juan, Santa Clara, and San Ildefonso all carry Spanish names, and many of their Indian residents speak Spanish as a second or third language.

Telephone books in this area of New Mexico, like those in Mexico and Spain, list just about every variety of Spanish surname imaginable. In Spanish New Mexico midwives have always been part of the scene, along with *curanderas,* or "good witches," whose healing powers can break the spell of an *infermedad puesta,* or "hex," placed on someone by a *brujo,* or "bad witch." The topography of the land is sprinkled liberally with Spanish terms such as *arroyo* and *rio,* Spanish names for "canyon" and "river." Restaurant menus are studded with Spanish-language words—*frijoles, guacamole,* and *tortillas* are just a few of the tempting items. The majority of the people are Catholic, so the names of the churches and missions read like a who's who of the Spanish and Mexican list of saints and religious figures. San Miguel Mission Church, Santuario de Guadalupe, and Saint Francis Cathedral are just a few of the many you will encounter.

The architecture is one of the distinctive features you will see. Variously called Spanish Pueblo, Pueblo Territorial, and Pueblo Colonial, it will catch your eye and add to the sense of disbelief that you are still in the United States. Adobe houses and buildings rise discreetly from the brown earth, their square and rectangular shapes gracefully rounded by time and weather, blending with the high desert, just as their mud-brick counterparts do in Spain and Mexico. The Indians also built great houses out of mud before the Spanish arrived. But it was the Spanish who taught the Indians how to make durable adobes of mud bricks, a skill they in turn had learned from generations of living with the Moors.

So today you will see old Spanish colonial buildings built for the Spanish by their Indian subjects, buildings that are still standing almost 400 years later. The Palace of the Governors is the oldest public building in the United States, dating to 1610. Still standing and still in use by the public as a museum and educational center, its 3-foot-thick adobe walls have aged gracefully. But there are not many other seventeenth-century buildings so intact. Most of what the Spanish built was destroyed by their Pueblo Indian subjects in 1680 when, after nearly one hundred years of servitude and oppression, they rose to lay waste to every existing memory of their Spanish conquerors. But you will find great delight in rambling through thoroughly intact eighteenth- and nineteenth-century buildings, churches, and homes that have been well preserved in the high arid environment.

If you are in northern New Mexico at the right time, you may hear the rich, mellow sounds of old bells in adobe churches, calling the faithful to their duty or ringing out in joyous celebration of some special occasion. Although this is a land of great hardship and poverty, lively fiestas with a Latin flair and wonderfully happy celebrations older than the Fourth of July are carried out regularly each year. The preservation of these customs by New Mexico's Spanish population reflects the seriousness of purpose and great sense of duty shown to their long and rich cultural past. This devotion has allowed the Spanish influence to remain amazingly intact in the mountain fastness of northern New Mexico.

But preceding the Spanish were the Indians. They inhabited this area for hundreds of years before the Spanish arrived. It is thought that most of today's Pueblo Indian ancestors came from the Four Corners area, migrating to the Rio Grande region around 1300. They came from the great Ancestral Puebloan (or Anasazi) tradition (see Section 2, "A Prehistory of Indian Country") and knew how to build multistoried houses from hand-shaped, stone building blocks. At first they settled in areas like Frijoles Canyon (Bandelier National Monument) and Puyé, where they built villages resembling the ones they had left at Mesa Verde and Chaco Canyon. Then several hundred years later, for reasons not yet fully understood, they moved down from the canyons onto the high, flat plain next to the Rio Grande.

Adobe church, Saint Francis of Assisi, Ranchos de Taos

It was there that the Spanish explorer Francisco Vásquez de Coronado's men found them. By then the Indians had learned to make houses from mud laid up in courses and from rounded, hand-shaped mud loaves known as turtlebacks. They farmed an estimated 25,000 irrigated acres, made beautiful pots, and wove clothing from cotton. At that time there were thirty to possibly seventy or one hundred villages thought to have 30,000 or more inhabitants. Tanoan was their language. Then as now, each village spoke one of the three Tanoan dialects—Tewa, Tiwa, or Towa—or the Keresan language. Today all up and down the banks of the Rio Grande, you will see the ancestors of those very first colonizers. They are called Pueblo Indians, *pueblo* being a Spanish word for "village." You may wish to visit several of the pueblos, where you will be met with warmth and friendliness. Try to time your visit to see one of the many Pueblo ceremonies or dances open to the public.

The Johnny-come-latelies on the scene have been the Americans and other assorted Anglos. They arrived in the 1800s and have been settling there ever since. It was the Anglo who romanticized and popularized north central New Mexico. The Spanish did little to spread the reputation of this region. In fact they did all they could to keep non-Spanish people out. In addition, they did not find anything very special about the area. After all, the mountains were not grander than the Spanish Sierras, and the plains were not browner or hotter than those of La Mancha and Estremadura. Living with the Indians seemed little different from coexisting with the Moors and the Jews in their native Spain.

It was the Anglo who came to northern New Mexico and was awed by what he saw and felt. For he encountered two unique cultures, the Spanish and the Pueblo Indian, living together but separately in this dramatic, remote land of high mountains and dry plains. It was Kit Carson, D. H. Lawrence, Willa Cather, Mary Austin, and many other well-known Anglos who put northern New Mexico on the map. They gave it unprecedented worldwide publicity. Georgia O'Keeffe's paintings of Spanish crosses, old adobes, and bleached cow bones had much the same impact. Partially because of this romanticizing, New Mexico is variously known as the Land of Enchantment and the Land of Contrasts. People talk of the "mystery" of its mountains and the "spell" of its land. For some who rush through it on two- or three-day tours, the buildup seems out of proportion to what they see. To others who stay long enough to savor it, not enough can be said to describe this unique area. For many the spell of New Mexico takes hold and will not let loose. In spite of changing times and increasing modernization, the area still exerts its magnetic pull. Some years 1.5 million visitors are drawn to Santa Fe alone. You may be next.

If you travel there, keep your ears open as you go from place to place. You may hear something that will be so exciting and mysterious that it will stay with you for a lifetime. On several occasions over the years, while browsing in the Taos Book Store, I have overheard hushed conversations between the proprietors and some of their customers. The spicy topics have ranged from the secret rites of the Indians to rumors about the Penitentes. Once the conversation centered on alleged threats of a few Taos Indians toward an Anglo writer who had overstepped his bounds and become too intrusive. And, of course, almost everywhere you go, you may hear tidbits of information about the famous and near famous. Over the years a host of movie stars and television personalities have either lived in or vacationed frequently in Santa Fe. So not all the excitement of New Mexico is in the landscape!

Today north central New Mexico is truly one of the cultural heartlands of the Southwest's high-desert country. In wide-open spaces ringed by mountains whose tall peaks reach up to the bluest skies you will ever see, three visions have developed into a human mosaic unlike any other known in the United States. The Pueblo Indian, the Spanish, and the Anglo all live out their lives together yet separately. They share in community living but retreat, daily, to homes of different values and traditions. Their shared life is called "New Mexican." New Mexicans, regardless of extraction, often prefer pinto beans to green beans, consume tons of chili each year, and dote on the sopaipilla, a cousin to Indian fry bread developed by the Spanish and devoured by thousands of both residents and tourists.

The region's isolation has led to a gentle, mellow entry into the modern world. But not all is as tranquil or content as it would seem. Part of the quaintness and charm you may see in certain areas is as much the product of poverty as it is of isolation and cultural difference. Per capita incomes and educational levels in certain northern New Mexico's counties are some of the lowest in the country. Unemployment is endemic in many areas. There is a multitude of tensions, prejudices, and biases as the people of this area struggle with their future development (see "History"). For the most part differences are worked out cooperatively. In the 1960s and early 1970s, many of America's young people became wrapped up in the romantic idealism of the area without recognizing the realities. In seeking an alternative lifestyle, they sought a haven in what they thought would be a tolerant, multiethnic, trilingual society. But what they found was similar to what they discovered elsewhere. No one embraced them with open arms. There was some violence. Northern New Mexico could not at that time easily absorb such a provocative culture. But since then the more recent immigrants to the Santa Fe area, particularly—yuppies, yoga gurus, holistic and natural healers, New Age crystal devotees, and people pursuing other alternative lifestyles—have all been absorbed without a fuss, making Santa Fe one of the trendiest places in the country.

THE SETTING

New Mexico's three cultures have developed in a splendid setting. For it is in north central New Mexico that the Rockies rise in a maze of parallel and conflicting ridges from the Chihuahuan Desert to the south, the great Staked Plains to the east, and the Colorado Plateau to the west. It is at this meeting of desert, plain, plateau, and mountains that the Gulf Stream, Pacific Westerlies, and Canadian Northerlies all converge to produce a fascinating scenario of ever-changing weather. These conditions lend to the sense of mystery that prevails in New Mexico. You may experience a part of this when on a warm, sunny August day the peaceful morning calm is broken by the sound of thunder as it reverberates through the canyons and bounces off steep mountain faces. Then in a wink the bright clear air becomes dark and ominous. The dust begins to blow. The mountains become dark, purple, and foreboding. Animals scurry for cover. Then it comes. A few large drops at first, falling "splat" on the dry ground. Then more drops until finally you are pummeled by a torrential downpour so forceful that in moments thousands of gullies are washed out and flooded. Soon it's all over. You are left wondering about the magic chemistry of high mountains and rising hot air. Yet in spite of the dramatic summer thunderstorms, howling snowstorms in the winter, and windy, dusty spring days, the sun shines more than 300 days each year, making this one of the most sun-drenched regions in America.

Sunny? Yes, and bright too, for the high elevation tends to make the air less dense. Scientists say that for every 900 feet elevation gain, the atmosphere loses one-thirtieth of its density. By the time you reach Santa Fe at 7,000 feet elevation, the air has lost one-fourth of its density. Since the rainfall in some areas is less than 10 to 12 inches per year, the air is free of light-distorting moisture particles. In that crystal-clear air that some have described as being "transparent," distant objects seem closer and more sharply outlined, creating a sense of space and openness rarely experienced elsewhere. It is possible on some very clear days to see more than 100 miles distant. The unfiltered light has a pure quality and a clarity that artists notice immediately when they arrive in the area. So seeing things in a "different light" is not just an abstract expression in New Mexico's high country; it is a reality. You will literally see things differently. That dry, rarefied air often carries the pungent aromas of piñon, sage, and juniper, waking yet another of the senses. These sensual changes, plus your body's adjustment to the high elevation, will alter your perceptions considerably. Pretty soon even the doubting Thomases begin to believe in the legendary "mystique" of New Mexico's high country.

Most authorities talk about the Rockies petering out in north central New Mexico. But whether the Rockies begin or end in New Mexico depends on which way you are traveling. When I first approached Albuquerque and Santa Fe from the southeast decades ago, I had the same impression the first Spaniards to the area must have had. New Mexico is where the mountains begin. The low eastern plains and southern deserts give way to rolling land, leading to undulating hills. Those hills fade as higher foothills take their place, eventually rising to 12,000- and 13,000- foot peaks. Coming from the west a similar impression is gained. The Continental Divide is but an imaginary line across a level, high desert. From that desert the high, purple peaks of the Rockies rise to the north.

Piñon pine

The Rockies descend from Colorado into New Mexico like a forked stick, with space between the prongs for the Rio Grande and its wide valley. The western range thrusting down is a continuation of Colorado's San Juan Mountains. The Spanish first called this range the *Sierra de las Grullas,* or the "Sierra of the Cranes." Today throughout most of northern New Mexico, these mountains are referred to as the Jemez Mountains. They are cut and watered by the Chama River, one of the Rio Grande's major tributaries. The Jemez Mountains embrace a giant *caldera,* the term for large craters measuring from 3 to 18 miles in diameter. Stretching 14 miles across, the Jemez Caldera, or Valle Grande (the centerpiece of Valles Caldera National Preserve), is at the upper end of the scale. Before it had spent all of its explosive forces, the Jemez volcano blasted and forged much of the country you will see west of the Rio Grande. Ash from its eruptions accumulated in depths measured in hundreds of feet and spread as far as today's Oklahoma and Kansas. Over time the ash hardened to become a honeycombed rock form called *tuff.* Out of this soft rock, nature chiseled caves that became home to some of the first Ancestral Puebloan settlers of the region. Today sheep graze and wildflowers grow in peaceful meadows that cover that ancient caldera's scarred surface.

To the east another great mountain mass comes down into New Mexico from Colorado. These mountains were first named the Sierra Madres, because they reminded the Spanish of peaks in their homeland. Later the name was changed to the Sangre de Cristo Mountains. There are many stories about how this name came to be used. One relates to a natural phenomenon. At sunset these mountains take on a red glow that reminded the Spanish of the blood of Christ, thus the Spanish translation, *Sangre de Cristo.* This range includes New Mexico's highest peak, Mount Wheeler, topping out at 13,151 feet. The Sangre de Cristo range fades north of Albuquerque, where the Sandia Mountains drop down to the lower, flatter deserts and plains to the south and east.

But the soaring mountains and their high deserts are not sufficient to make the land livable. In this arid country there has to be water or human beings cannot survive. When faced with prolonged drought and depleted soil conditions, the Ancestral Pueblo People left their Mesa Verde, Aztec, Salmon, and Chaco Canyon sites in the Four Corners area (see Section 2, "A Prehistory of Indian Country," and Section 3, "Indian Past: The Ancestral Puebloan Circle Tour"). Many of them drifted southeast, looking for a well-watered place to farm, leaving the Colorado Plateau and the lands of the San Juan drainage area behind them. Soon they found a welcome river and its tributaries. Cottonwood trees grew along its banks. Its soil was rich in volcanic ash.

So it was the Rio Grande and its tributary rivers, like the Euphrates in Mesopotomia, that gave birth to the great Pueblo civilization that bloomed in the southern Rockies while Europe was slumbering in the Middle Ages. When the dream of discovering easy riches had eluded the Spanish, it was this river and its valleys that, in the end, attracted them and cradled the first European civilization in the interior of the United States.

The Spanish first discovered this river in 1519 at its terminus. There in the midst of palm trees and a semitropical setting, it empties into the Atlantic Ocean's Gulf of Mexico. They called it the *Rio de las Palmas,* "the River of the Palms." Little did the Spanish know at that time, only twenty-seven years after the first voyage of Columbus to America, that the river extended nearly 2,000 miles northwest to its source. Later in the sixteenth century, when the river was discovered by the Spanish in New Mexico, they gave it several different names. It was known variously as the *Rio del Norte,* the "River of the North," and the *Rio Bravo del Norte,* the "Bold River of the North." Eventually the Spanish in New Mexico would call it the "Great River," the *Rio Grande.*

It is a "great river." It stretches more than 1,800 miles in length and is either America's second or third longest river, depending on which "fact" you choose to believe. If the Missouri River, a tributary of the Mississippi, is considered just a segment of the "Father of Rivers," then the Rio Grande earns the distinction of being the second-longest river. But local tradition and regional interest frequently overrule the geographers. The Missouri is often considered a river unto itself. In that instance the Rio Grande slides into third position. The Spanish followed the Rio Grande north from El Paso del Norte, Mexico, where today it serves as the international border between the United States and Mexico. The early Spanish settlers established El Camino Real ("the Royal Road") alongside it, and farther north they settled along its banks in the Española Valley.

But the Spanish were never inclined to follow the river much farther north. Their maps told them that the Rio Grande originated near the North Pole. No hot-blooded, gold-seeking Spanish conquistador would waste his time going there. They searched for gold and silver to the west and as far east as Kansas, but they never went north. If they had followed the Rio Grande just 100 miles north to its source in the San Juan range of the Colorado Rockies, they might have found the fortune they were seeking. In the 1800s American prospectors ascending the Rockies near the headwaters of the Rio Grande, just below the 13,888-foot massif known as the Rio Grande Pyramid, found their way through Rio Grande Pass (today's Stony Pass) across the Continental Divide. There on the western slope, near today's Silverton, Colorado, they found the fabulously rich deposits of silver and gold that had eluded the Spanish. Whether the Spanish could have fully exploited these riches we will never know. Some say that the Spanish were looking for easy riches and that unless, as in Mexico and Peru, they had had thousands of slaves to do the mining for them, they would not have gone after the plum. Today much of the crystal-clear Rio Grande water is trapped in several reservoirs just below its source, allowing better control of the river's flow and providing water for Colorado's irrigated farms. From there the river cascades in pristine pureness down to Creede, Colorado, another fabulously rich mining area in the early days.

From Del Norte, Colorado, the Rio Grande winds ever eastward to hit the high plains at Alamosa. There it begins to make close to a ninety-degree turn to the south. Near this location in 1779, the explorer Juan Bautista de Anza led a Spanish expedition up from the south to conquer the Comanches. He was the first Spaniard known to have followed the Rio Grande that far north. He discovered to his surprise that the Rio Grande took off to the west at a sharp angle rather than continuing northward to the pole as the Spanish maps had suggested for two centuries. But de Anza never had a chance to explore the western Rockies. He went on to defeat the Comanches and opened the way for more accessible trade routes to Santa Fe.

Before heading south, just east of Alamosa, the river passes near Blanca Peak, that 14,363-foot mass of stone just north of Fort Garland, Colorado. It is a peak sacred both to the Navajo and to certain Pueblo groups. Reportedly it can be seen from as far distant as Taos, New Mexico, 80 miles to the south. Now flowing southward, the river passes the place where Lieutenant Zebulon Pike was captured by the Spanish in 1805 and transported to Santa Fe. The site is now marked as the Pike Historical Monument. From there the river cuts through the wide San Luis Valley. Migration of the Spanish from northern New Mexico to that area in the 1800s established the final northern extension of the Spanish culture. The quiet Spanish farming towns along the valley point to the fact that by the 1800s the settlers of Iberian ancestry were looking not for gold but for better farmland to help them survive in that rough country.

The river then passes over the Colorado border into northern New Mexico. From the border south, for a distance of 48 miles, it flows deep in the shadowy recesses of a gorge where it becomes frenetic in its push southward. There the raging white water with drops of 10 to 15 feet won for this segment of the river its designation as the Rio Grande Wild River Area, becoming the first river in America to receive that label. Many a kayaker and rafter knows that the rapids are as challenging there as any place in the country. Near Arroyo Hondo, north of Taos, the crystal-clear waters give up numerous brown trout to the delight of both visiting and local anglers.

Near Taos the river is deep in a gorge, 650 feet below the surface of the rim of the high sagebrush plain. The tan basalt and sandstone walls are so steep and narrow that sunshine penetrates to the bottom only in the summer at midday. There on the second-highest bridge in the national highway system, you can see the narrow flash of river below. Standing there you will understand why the Taos and Picuris pueblos, unlike their neighbors to the south, are not situated along the

Rio Grande Gorge and Bridge

Rio Grande. The river is most inaccessible along this stretch. So Taos and Picuris are situated closer to the mountains, along accesible streams that eventually feed the Rio Grande.

Below the junction of "trouty" Taos Creek, the clear water rushes through ever-widening rock walls as the gorge gives way to a broader canyon. Above Pilar the wild river gasps its last breath over moderate rapids. These rapids are a favorite of local rafting devotees. Then the river faces the first impediment in its long course down from Colorado. A series of small diversion dams takes the water to the surrounding orchards. There apples, peaches, apricots, and cherries flourish in this otherwise dry land. Corn and chilies receive the moisture required to ripen in time for the fall harvest. The Spanish villages of Pilar, Embudo, and Velarde are garden oases. Their green is particularly inviting in this otherwise brown country. At Velarde, 30 miles south of Taos, the canyon ends. Leaving black lava walls behind, the river enters the broad Española Valley. There it is wider, calmer, and very accessible. Continuing south the river lays claim to a broad, fertile valley where it cradled and nurtured three cultures. In ancient times there were thirty to seventy towns along this central and northern segment of the Rio Grande. With irrigation water from the river and its tributaries, it is estimated that 25,000 acres were under cultivation at that time. The Indians grew corn, beans, pumpkins, gourds, and in certain dry areas, cotton.

When the Spanish came, they improved on the ancient Indian irrigation system, providing rules to govern the use of the canals. In cities like Valencia, Spain, the Water Tribunal meets every Thursday morning at 10:00 A.M., just as it has done since the Middle Ages, to settle disputes arising from the management of eight great irrigation canals along the Turia River. These were first established by the Romans and later improved by the Arabs. Similarly today in numerous Spanish villages along the Rio Grande watershed, ancient Spanish rules regulate a hefty bureaucracy that governs the maze of *acequias,* or water ditches, on which life in the valley depends. The wooden gates and the ditches are blessed in elaborate ceremonies each spring. Everyone whose land is irrigated by the ditches must provide labor to clear them and ready them for another fruitful season. Just about all the green you see along the Rio Grande is due to the watering of the high, dry land by the irrigation ditches. After its annual rainfall of between 8 and 12 inches per year, the land is still 20 inches short of sufficient moisture to be productive. Yet in spite of providing enough water for irrigation most years, the Rio Grande has been dubbed "forever undependable." In drought years it fails to supply what is needed, while in other years it has flooded uncontrollably.

Just north of Española the Rio Grande meets its best but dirtiest contributor, the Chama River. The Chama is one of the few perennial streams that does not die in the summertime. It cuts a mighty swath through the San Juan mountain range. In fact it divides that range so completely that different names have arisen for the different segments. The mountains north of the river are often called the San Juan Mountains, and the part south of the river is generally known as the Jemez Mountains. The Chama cuts through many red sedimentary layers so that by the time it reaches its confluence with the Rio Grande, the waters are muddy and red, despoiling the crystal-clear waters that come surging out of the gorge below Taos. A large dam has been built on the Chama at Abiquiu to minimize this problem. From the confluence on, the Rio Grande takes on a much more muddy, silty, even sluggish appearance as it proceeds southward. But it was there at the confluence of the two rivers that the Spanish established the first European town in America's interior and the first capital in what would later be called New Mexico. They called the first permanent capital San Gabriel del Yunque. Today you can see the location of the site just across the river from San Juan Pueblo.

After passing by Santa Clara Pueblo, the river passes through San Ildefonso Pueblo lands, below Black Mesa. Then it enters White Rock Canyon. There it waters the border of the Pajarito Plateau, which is cut by one of its tributaries, the Rio de los Frijoles. This river drains a region, preserved today as Bandelier National Monument, that sustained a variety of Ancestral Puebloan groups. In White Rock Canyon the Rio Grande's muddy waters froth over the last rapids it will meet for hundreds of miles. In the canyon the river is 15 to 20 miles west of Santa Fe and farther south receives the waters of the Santa Fe River.

Now in its southwestern course, the river comes to its first major impediment since the reservoir at its source, Cochiti Dam. It is touted as one of the world's twenty largest earthen dams. Cochiti Lake is too big for the Rio Grande to fill by itself. Water from the San Juan River drainage system is diverted from the other side of the Continental Divide to help fill this massive reservoir. Below the dam the river passes near Cochiti Pueblo not far from Santo Domingo Pueblo on Galisteo Creek. As it enters more open country, it passes near Bernalillo, where it is thought Coronado made his first crossing of the river. A little farther south at Albuquerque, you will sometimes see a mostly dry riverbed. There you may wonder why the river is so "great," especially if that is where you see it for the first time. Much of the Rio Grande water north of Albuquerque is drawn off in a series of canals built for flood and irrigation control. So its greatness is best seen in the benefits it produces. Those are many and include the verdant alfalfa fields and orchards in that rich midsection of the Rio Grande Valley that Albuquerque's citizens call North Valley. Looking at the windswept, arid country around Albuquerque, one finds it difficult to imagine that finally this river, after serving as the border between the United States and Mexico, will enter the Gulf of Mexico in a semitropical environment of palm trees and citrus orchards where it is better known as the Rio Bravo del Norte.

HISTORY

far removed in place and time from today's Santa Fe, New Mexico, yet in a similar environment of arid land and high mountains, the Spanish monarchs Ferdinand and Isabella gathered their considerable forces at Santa Fe de Granada in 1492 to push the Moors, once and for all, out of their Alhambra fortress and back into North Africa. The conquest was successful, and Spain was purged of the Arabs, who had occupied Spanish lands for more than 300 years. But the influence of those many centuries of Arabic-Moorish culture on the lifestyle and ways of the Spanish was to remain. In fact this influence would be spread to the New World. For while still camped at Santa Fe, Isabella and Ferdinand signed papers giving approval to Christopher Columbus's first voyage to the Americas. This action set in motion a series of expeditions that would, in just a little more than a hundred years, bring settlers to the area known today as northern New Mexico. That in turn would lead to the establishment in 1610 of another town named Santa Fe. It would become the political capital of the northernmost province of New Spain and later the political and cultural capital of New Mexico, USA.

Today in Santa Fe, New Mexico, there is ample evidence that Ferdinand and Isabella purged the Moors from their land but not from their culture. The Spanish explorers who came to the New World brought with them many traditions borrowed from the Moors, who had lived on Spanish soil for so many generations. Perhaps the most important one you will see in your travels is the use of clay or mud bricks for constructing buildings. *Af-fub* is an Arab word meaning "brick of clay or mud." The Spanish corruption of that word is *adobe*. And for centuries Spanish women in New Mexico have adorned themselves with beautiful scarves wrapped around their necks and shoulders. The scarf, or *rebozo*, is also Arabic in origin. In addition, the Moors brought to the Spanish their centuries-old tradition of irrigated farming. The Spanish who came to New Mexico carried this knowledge with them and built irrigation canals that are still being used today in modern Santa Fe.

After Columbus "discovered" the Americas, he made additional voyages, as did Spanish explorers. Where the Spanish explored they often set up colonies. Some of the earliest colonies were established in today's Puerto Rico and Cuba. From Puerto Rico Ponce de León sailed to the Florida coast in 1513. In just a little more than fifty years, the Spanish would establish America's first city, St. Augustine, in 1565, near the site where Ponce de León landed. In 1518 a Cuban plantation owner who was eager to seek the kinds of riches found later by Francisco Pizarro in Peru left Cuba to explore the western curvature of the Gulf of Mexico. Hernando Cortez landed in Mexico that year and by 1521 had conquered the great

Aztec Indian Empire. Within a few years most of that great civilization had been plundered and destroyed as the Spanish began building a new city on the site of the Aztec ruins. By making slaves of the Aztecs, Cortez was able to accomplish much in a short period of time. New Spain, as the newly conquered land was called, grew by leaps and bounds. Within twenty years the restless Spanish were looking for more riches.

After all, the Spanish monarchy did have riches in mind when it launched Columbus's first expedition. One of Columbus's missions was to keep an eye out for the legendary Antilla, a mysterious island that rose from the sea, far out in the Atlantic. There, it was said, sea mists hid seven rich cities, the seven cities of Antilla. Legend had it that they were founded by either seven Christian brothers or bishops who had fled with their people from Portugal when it was invaded by the Moors. The seven cities were a refuge provided by the Divine Providence in the west. Columbus did land in the West Indies, or the "Antilles," but there were not seven rich cities there. The myth persisted anyway. Ponce de León found no such cities in his travels either, but he did find gold on the island of Puerto Rico. Neither did Cortez find the seven fabulously wealthy cities, but he did find the Aztecs, whose rich civilization should have sated even the greediest explorers.

The Aztecs told the Spanish that their ancestors had lived in seven remote cities to the north of their immediate homeland. A seed was planted! Then in 1532 to 1533, the stunning news of Pizarro's conquest of Peru and his rich discoveries there reached New Spain. They seemed to give credence to another legend, the legend of El Dorado. *El Dorado* is a Spanish term meaning "Golden Man." Somewhere in the New World, the legend stated, there was a land of great riches where each year the chief of the mythical land was rolled in gold and then placed in a sacred pond where the gold was rinsed from his body. What a find that pond would be, filled with the accumulation of hundreds of years of gold silt! The atmosphere was now ripe in New Spain for an event that would trigger new expeditions to the unexplored lands north of Mexico City.

That event came in 1536 when the Spanish explorer Alvar Nuñéz Cabeza de Vaca, along with a Moorish slave by the name of Estévan and two other Spaniards, reached Culiacán, Mexico, after several years of rugged cross-country travel. They had been part of a Spanish expeditionary and settlement party landing in Florida in 1528. They scrapped their expedition and fled when Indian hostilities intensified. Traveling in crude, handmade boats, they shipwrecked on either Mustang or Galveston Island, just off the coast of today's Texas. Taken captive there by the Indians, Cabeza de Vaca and his group were able to escape after five or six years. They made their way across today's Texas, New Mexico, and Arizona before turning south to Mexico. It is believed they were the first white men to see the buffalo and were probably the first to see the Rio Grande in New Mexico. But more importantly they learned from Indians they encountered about other Indians to the north who lived in permanent multistoried houses and who wore cotton garments as well as jewelry of coral and turquoise.

When they reached Mexico and related their fantastic story, the oft-reported tendency of the Spanish to blur illusion with fact took hold. The seven cities must be to the north! An expedition was organized pressing Estévan, de Vaca's black

Spanish conquistador

slave, into service as a guide under the leadership of a Franciscan Catholic friar, Marcos de Niza. After a number of months of travel, Estévan did in fact find a cluster of six Zuni villages spaced over a distance of 15 miles. Each had multistoried homes, but the streets were of dust, not gold. The people were rich in history and culture but not in gold or jewels.

Estévan apparently stayed awhile in the villages but for unknown reasons was murdered by the Indians shortly thereafter. Some of his companions escaped and retraced their route back to Fray Marcos, who had been trailing woefully behind. No one is quite sure what happened at this point, but Marcos returned to Mexico, where he told of viewing seven cities from a distance. He described them as a wonder larger than the city of Mexico, and he detailed one city in particular called Cibola. It was the smallest of the cities but very beautiful, having terraced houses made of stone. But Fray Marcos did not stop there. He embellished his story by saying there were "emeralds and other jewels—vessels of gold and silver—whereof there is greater and more abundance than in Peru." No one knows how his imagination led him to stray so far from reality. What he had seen was a Zuni village of stone and mud. If he had seen it at sunset when the tan sandstone building blocks and the yellow straw in the mud mortar had reflected a golden glow, perhaps he could have concluded that this was a city of gold.

No one questioned Marcos any further. In the minds of the opportunistic Spaniards, the myth was complete—the seven cities had been found. They would be known as the Seven Cities of Cibola, because Fray Marcos used the term *Cibola* in his report. *Cibola* is possibly a Spanish corruption of the Pima Indian word for the Zuni's sacred mountain range, the *Shiwina*. Later the Spanish used the same word to name the buffalo. The Kingdom of Cibola, as it came to be called, had to be explored and, if necessary, conquered. Mounting an expedition of this kind was entirely possible for the powerful Spanish nation. After all, Charles V, the Spanish king, was also the Holy Roman Emperor, and he ruled much of Europe from Holland almost down to the boot of Italy.

Thirty-year-old Vàsquez de Coronado, the son of a prosperous family from Spain and the governor of New Galicia in New Spain, was chosen to lead the expedition. By this time King Charles V, grandson of Isabella and Ferdinand, had received reports about the mistreatment of the Indians by Cortez in New Spain and by other Spaniards elsewhere in the colonies. Influenced by Spanish missionaries such as Bartolomé de las Casas, he implored that the Indians be treated well so their souls could be saved for Christianity. According to his wishes the "New

Law of the Indies," a humanitarian conduct code, was drawn up several years later and was adopted by 1542. Although difficult to enforce and often totally disregarded, it nonetheless may have had a moderating influence on the way the Spanish conquistadors treated the Indians.

In 1540 Coronado amassed a large expeditionary force at Compostela (not far from today's Guadalajara) containing 336 Europeans, of which 275 were cavalrymen. Many were from Charles V's wide-ranging empire. It has been reported that the group included two Italians, five Portuguese, and one German. In addition, Coronado enlisted the aid of four friars, including the redoubtable Marcos de Niza. He also recruited 800 Indians to help with the expedition. A total of ten European and Indian women went along. It is thought that he took more than 1,000 horses, plus hundreds of other animals, including many sheep, goats, and cattle. These would be the first horses and sheep the American Indians had ever seen, and they would be the first horses to roam the high deserts since the horse became extinct on the North American continent sometime after the last Ice Age (see Section 2, "A Prehistory of Indian Country").

In gilded armor and a steel helmet decorated with plumes, Coronado led the expeditionary force, traveling several hundred miles north to Culiacán near the west coast of Mexico. From there it was an arduous 1,000 miles to Cibola, in La Tierra Nueva, as the northern frontier was called. His route somewhat paralleled today's Guadalajara-Nogales Highway. Then it ascended the higher country near today's New Mexico–Arizona border. From there the group went north to the Zuni villages, de Niza's Cibola, just south of today's Gallup, New Mexico. The Zunis put up a heavy resistance. Their accurate throwing arms unleashed such a damaging barrage of stones that Coronado was nearly pummeled to death. The Spanish, with their superior weaponry, forced surrender of the pueblo after an hour of fighting. Upon entering the Zuni farming village of Háwikuh, the Spanish saw no evidence of the wealth of El Dorado. There was nothing to resemble the splendors they had heard about in Peru. In fact the people seemed to be barely eking out a living in the high, dry desert. Marcos de Niza was discredited and sent back to Mexico in shame.

Coronado made Zuni his headquarters. From there he sent various expeditions into the surrounding countryside, still looking for the elusive riches that had thus far evaded him. He sent Pedro de Tovar and Fray Juan de Padilla north to the Kingdom of Tusayan (today's Hopi villages) on the hunch that they might be the fabled seven cities (see Section 2, "The Hopi: A Long and Continuous Past"). He sent Garcia López Cárdenas to explore reports of a large canyon (the Grand Canyon) with a river running through it. Hernando de Alvarado was sent east to explore the village areas around the Rio Grande and Pecos Rivers, in the area of today's New Mexico. These men became famous in time as the first white discoverers of some of the richest scenic and cultural wonders in America. But the wealth of these rich lodes would not be mined for another 350 years, when they would be discovered by twentieth-century tourists.

Alvarado explored the Rio Grande Valley north to the Taos Pueblo. But he was most impressed with the area called Tigeux. He sent word that the latter area would be a good place to make winter camp. So Coronado and his party traveled east to a point near today's Isleta Pueblo, then north up the Rio Grande to Tigeux, near today's Bernalillo, close to the site of the Coronado State Monument. From there they explored north to Taos and east of Santo Domingo Pueblo to the Cerrillos Hills, where they saw the turquoise deposits that had been mined by the Indians for hundreds of years. During that winter Coronado and his men came upon a Plains Indian living in the Pueblo at Pecos. He told the Spanish about a land to the east called Quivira where there were villages in which the people made gold jewelry. In fact, he said, a gold bracelet had been taken from him by the Pueblo chiefs.

Gold fever rose again. The chiefs were interrogated. They knew nothing about a gold bracelet. The revered chiefs were placed in chains, and dogs were set upon them in an attempt to force them to reveal the hiding place of the gold bracelet. Still they insisted they did not know anything about a gold bracelet. Nonetheless Coronado and his men, smitten with desire, decided that in the spring they would follow the Plains Indian, whom they called the Turk, to the eastern plains to search for those elusive riches. But before spring came, winter had to be conquered. The cold weather and snows were so severe that the Spanish made some of the Pueblo people abandon their villages so they could live there. That act, plus the insults heaped upon their chiefs, as well as the confiscation of their winter food supply, made the Indians angry. Soon they began to retaliate.

But the Spanish, tiring of the insolent Indians, decided to put an end to the revolt. They destroyed one village and burned several hundred Pueblo Indians at the stake. Coronado and his men were later put on trial for these and other atrocities committed against the Indians. Coronado was cleared at the trial, but his compatriot, Cárdenas, was found guilty. It seemed that the Spanish government did wish fair treatment of the Indians after all, but La Tierra Nueva was so far from the Spanish seat of government that the law of the frontier took precedence over the humanitarian "New Law of the Indies." This scene was to be repeated over and over again for the next 200 years. Atrocities would be committed. Later, usually years later, the Spanish official in charge would be recalled to Mexico City or Spain and placed on trial.

Coronado and his men did set out with the Turk to the eastern plains. They passed into what is now part of the Texas Panhandle near Palo Duro Canyon, thence north through part of present-day Oklahoma until they reached some Indian villages near today's Lyons and Salina, Kansas. The Turk had lied. There was no gold in these poor villages. He was summarily executed. Coronado marched the long way back to Tigeux, where he spent another disconsolate winter. He was injured for the second time when he fell from his horse during some recreational horse racing and was nearly trampled to death. With the coming of spring, the first European expedition to penetrate the continent packed up. With their injured leader, who had to be carried most of the way, they started the long trek, empty-handed, back to Mexico City in 1542. If riches could not be found, perhaps souls could be saved. Three friars were left behind for that purpose. It is believed that all three were later killed by the Indians.

With the myth of easy riches put to rest in the remote northern hinterlands of New Spain, forty years passed before any major expeditions were dispatched to the north. In that period of time, the old Spanish empire in Europe began to fade and its power to diminish. But exciting things were happening in New Spain. The first great silver strike was made at Zacatecas, Mexico, in 1546, leading to the founding of the city of Durango (see Section 3, "Durango"). By 1567 another great silver strike had been made in the northernmost province of Chihuahua, centering on the town of Santa Barbara. There were high hopes that more silver might be found farther north. Obviously the disappointing reports of Coronado's expedition had long been forgotten in the intervening forty years.

Fray Augustine Rodríguez and Captain Francisco Chamuscado set forth in 1581 for Tigeux, the region of Coronado's former base camp. They entered New Mexico from Chihuahua, Mexico, and followed the Rio Grande to Tigeux. They established the route that would later be known as *El Camino Real,* or "the Royal Road." They were the first white men to pass through the desolate, extremely parched 90-mile-long piece of land called the *Jornado del Muerto* (Spanish for "Journey of the Dead Man") near where, more than 300 years later, the first atomic bomb would be exploded. From Tigeux they explored in all directions. They finally returned to Mexico, having found neither gold nor silver. But their commercial instincts told them that the cotton goods made by the Pueblo Indians might be useful trade items for the mines in New Spain. Three more friars stayed behind to save the souls of the many Indians encountered along the Rio Grande.

A year later Antonio de Espejo and Fray Bernaldino Beltrán led another expedition to learn what had happened to the trio of priests, since they had not sent any messages south. Of course, Espejo also planned to search for gold and silver. Upon reaching La Tierra Nueva, they discovered that the three friars had been martyred by the Indians. Espejo then traveled west among the Hopi villages in search of gold and silver. He later reported finding some rocks that looked promising. But his report is better known for the new name he gave to this, the most remote of the Spanish colonial outposts. He called it *Nuevo Mexico,* or "New Mexico." Before Espejo's visit it had variously been called La Tierra Nueva and Cibola. Although a provincial governor of Mexico had called it *Nuevo Mexico* in 1562, Espejo's use of the term began to catch hold. The term Nuevo Mexico implied that this land might be as rich as its namesake to the south, where silver mines had made many a Spaniard wealthy.

But Espejo's PR was not enough. Once again, except for an abortive, unauthorized expedition by Don Gaspar Castaño de Sosa in 1590, Nuevo Mexico slid into obscurity, receiving little attention from Mexico City or Madrid. After a number of years, when the church in Spain finally began to hear about the thousands of Indians along the Rio Grande whose souls needed saving and the shocking stories of the martyred priests, Spanish interest was once again renewed. But another event also placed the Spanish spotlight on New Mexico. In 1579 Sir Francis Drake raided some Spanish ships off the Pacific coast of South America. He made such a quick retreat that the Spanish thought he had found a new, secret passage from the Pacific to the Atlantic. Although Drake had taken the conventional route back to England, the Spanish believed he took a quick sea route back to the Atlantic. They imagined this sea passage to be just north of New Spain. They called it the Strait of Anian and placed it on their maps, where it appeared just north of

New Mexico. Eager to find evidence of this new sea route and always eager to save souls and to explore for riches, the Spanish decided to establish a permanent settlement in northern New Mexico in 1598.

By then Spain, under Philip II, had been badly defeated by England when the Spanish Armada was destroyed in 1588. Philip himself was dying the summer of 1598. But New Spain was vigorous and, by now, producing its own sons born in the New World. So it is no surprise that Juan de Oñate, the son of a wealthy miner from Zacatecas and a native of New Spain, was chosen to lead the settlement expedition. Although many of these New World Spaniards were of Spanish stock, some historians have pointed out that others were apparently of Spanish-Indian descent. Oñate's wife was one of these, being a descendant of both Cortez and Montezuma, the Aztec chief.

Oñate's expedition stretched the length of 4 miles as it traveled the route of the Camino Real. There were 400 men. About 130 of the men were accompanied by their wives and families. They carried all of their earthly belongings in eighty-three *carretas,* or oxcarts, which were followed by 7,000 head of livestock. The expedition marched under two flags, the royal flag of the Spanish crown and the banner of the Catholic church. The latter was held high by eleven members of the order of Friars Minor, followers of Saint Francis of Assisi, who preached the brotherhood of man and the joys of poverty.

One of the first stops the group made was at a mountain pass named El Paso del Norte, near the site of today's El Paso, Texas. There on Holy Thursday of 1598, the expedition stopped for religious observances. Part of the ritual of the Third Order of Saint Francis included the custom of scourging or beating oneself. Don Juan and his soldiers beat their backs until they drew blood. Arriving in northern New Mexico, Oñate established the religious center for the new Spanish kingdom at Santo Domingo Pueblo. Moving north he established the first political capital and European settlement deep in America's interior on July 11, 1598.

There near the confluence of the Rio Grande and the Chama River in a wide, fertile valley surrounded by the Sangre de Cristo Mountains to the east and with rugged lava cliffs and the Jemez Mountains to the west, he took over an Indian village, O'ke or Ohke. He called the new town San Juan de los Caballeros. In naming it he honored Saint John the Baptist and his own Saint's Day and noted the virtues of the *caballeros,* or gentlemen like himself and his followers. Soon Oñate moved the settlement to the west side of the Rio Grande to the Indian pueblo of Yuqueyunque, leaving the name of San Juan behind. Oñate named the new permanent settlement San Gabriel del Yunque.

Almost immediately he ordered a chapel constructed. The colonists set to work to make a new life for themselves. By September they were sufficiently settled that they could stage the popular play *Los Moros y Los Christianos,* commemorating the expulsion of the Moors from Granada, Spain. This celebration was revived a number of years ago and is celebrated at Chimayó, New Mexico, on the feast day of Santiago, near the end of July. Only partially excavated ruins attest to the presence of this first Spanish capital in North America and the town that would later gain for New Mexico the title of the oldest of the fifty states in terms of having the first organized government.

Oxcart

Life was very difficult for the first settlers. Although they were allowed to exact a certain amount of free labor from the Indians, there were not enough Indians available to do all the work. So the early Spanish settlers did much of their own farming.

Oñate and his group made several expeditions from the new settlement. On one he sent his nephew Juan de Zaldivar to take food from the Ácoma Pueblo for the Spanish settlers. The Ácoma Pueblo Indians, not warming to the idea, attacked Zaldivar. They killed him and twelve others. Oñate, seeking revenge, led an expedition of seventy men and assaulted the pueblo. With considerable violence he conquered it, leaving in his wake from 600 to 800 dead Ácoma Indians. He then rounded up all of the other villagers and took them to the mission capital of Santo Domingo. There all males over the age of twenty-five had one foot cut off, and sixty girls were carted away to convents in New Spain. By 1601 more Pueblo unrest was met by the Spanish with the burning of three pueblos, killing 900 people and taking 400 more captive. These actions and others like them would eventually come back to haunt the Spanish. One day the Pueblo Indians would avenge themselves.

By 1607, the year Jamestown was established by the British on America's East Coast and the year before Samuel de Champlain established the French city of Quebec, Oñate was having difficulty with the leadership of the new Spanish settlement. He was not well respected, and he was frequently absent, spending much of his time on exploratory missions. Twice he went to the Sea of Cortez, or the Gulf of California. Once upon returning from there, he carved a message on a sandstone rock not far from the Ácoma Pueblo. Roughly translated, it reads: "There passed by here Don Juan de Oñate, from the discovery of the South Sea in 1605." That ancient message carved in sandstone is preserved today as a tourist attraction known as Inscription Rock at El Morro National Monument. While Oñate was exploring and writing on rocks, Miguel de Cervantes in Spain was writing the last pages of his first volume of *Don Quixote*.

In Oñate's absence there was much unrest. The settlers were unable to produce much from the land. The difficult living conditions prompted such a high desertion rate at one point that there were only forty Spanish adult males and their families remaining. By 1608, the year Cervantes's first volume of *Don Quixote* was published, Oñate was recalled to Mexico City, where he was eventually placed under investigation, tried, and found guilty of a number of charges, including misconduct in office.

The viceroy of Mexico appointed Pedro de Peralta to replace Oñate. He was given the mandate to move the provincial capital of the kingdom of New Mexico to a militarily defensible location where there would be good grazing for the settlers' livestock and where there would be no conflict with the Indians over water.

Peralta did move the capital to a well-watered, higher location along the Santa Fe River, near the site of an old abandoned Pueblo village. The town was laid out in 1609–10 and occupied in 1610. It was called Villa de Santa Fe but later became known as La Villa Real de Santa Fe. Still later it was known as La Villa Real de Santa Fe de San Francisco. Since that time, regardless of which nation controlled it, Santa Fe has continuously been the capital city of the area. This makes it the oldest capital city in the United States. The capitol buildings, or *casas reales,* were built in 1610. One of those buildings, El Palacio Real, better known as the Palace of the Governors, is the oldest continuously occupied public building in the United States.

Mission churches were built at an astounding pace all over the Rio Grande Valley. By 1625 the busy Franciscans had fifty churches in place and were claiming to have saved thousands of souls among the Pueblo Indian population. By 1680 the number of mission churches had increased to eighty. Today two of these early-seventeenth-century mission churches are still intact and in use. They are without doubt the two oldest churches in the United States. The mission church at Isleta Pueblo was built between 1613 and 1630, while the mission church at Ácoma, to the west, was built in 1629.

Although the Indians already knew how to construct multistoried houses out of mud, the Franciscan missionaries taught the Indians how to build, using techniques their culture had borrowed from the Moors. They taught the Indians to make sun-dried rectangular building bricks called *adobes* and showed them how to construct a building from those bricks. The Franciscans saw to it that their churches would last a long time. Using Indian labor they had 40-foot beams hand-carried to the building sites from many miles away. They made sure that the adobe walls, often rising 35 feet in height, were 5 to 8 feet thick. Twin towers were often 25 feet taller than the buildings.

The law allowed a certain amount of Indian labor to be donated each year. But the governors of Nuevo Mexico, in their eagerness for profit, often made the Indians perform more gratis work than they were supposed to. From tilling fields, to building adobe missions, to weaving garments in sweatshops for trade in Mexico, the Indians came to be overworked and abused. By the middle of the seventeenth century, the Indians, for all practical purposes, were slaves. Apparently both the priests and the government officials were guilty of this offense, each bitterly accusing the other of mistreating the Indians. As the mission churches went up around the countryside and the Indians were subjected to more and more bondage, the ninety or so Pueblo villages that Oñate observed in 1598 had shrunk to half that number by 1650. By 1630–40 the Indians had had enough. Rebels at Jemez and Taos pueblos killed their Spanish priests. After that the Pueblos were so

Palace of the Governors, Santa Fe

savagely subdued that no further resistance was offered for a while.

But things were not going well for the Spanish colonists and their charges either. The rugged land was exacting its toll. Persistent drought, epidemics of one sort or another, and marauding Apaches made living conditions there barely tolerable. Being 800 miles from civilization in Mexico, they were isolated. Supplies from the south came only every three years. By 1675 the Franciscans were upset that many of the Pueblo Indians were still practicing their old rituals. In concert with the governor of Nuevo Mexico, the decision was made to suppress these practices. Systematically all *estufas,* or kivas, were burned and destroyed. Later all the religious leaders or shamans of the Pueblos, whom the Spanish termed "wizards," were rounded up and tried for sorcery and witchcraft. Three were hanged, and more would have met the same fate but for the seventy Pueblo warriors who stormed the Palace of the Governors demanding release of their brothers. They threatened that if the shamans were not released, they would not help the Spanish fight the Apaches, a group that had acquired Spanish horses and was increasingly a menace.

One of the Indians released, called Popé, fled to Taos Pueblo, farther away from watchful Spanish eyes than his own San Juan Pueblo. There with a half-Spanish, half-Indian Taos resident named Naranjo, an Indian revolt was planned. At the time of the revolt, there were from 16,000 to 30,000 Pueblo Indian people and about 2,400 Spanish, including many Spanish sympathizers who were of mixed descent. Popé and Naranjo, in concert with other Pueblo leaders, set a date for the rebellion. Runners were to carry knotted cords to each pueblo. Each day a knot was to be untied. When all the knots had been removed, it was time to strike. On August 11, 1860, all the Pueblos were to rise up and kill every Spanish sympathizer, including men, women, and children.

The Spanish governor got wind of the plot. Knowing of this, the Indian leaders again dispatched runners to tell the Pueblos to rise up on the tenth rather than the eleventh. In the first few days, 400 Spanish in the outlying areas were killed, as were 21 of the 32 priests who were in New Mexico at the time. Those who survived took refuge in the Palace of the Governors in Santa Fe. That great, fortified building, with its impenetrable walls, allowed the Spanish to hold out for ten days, during which they killed 300 Indians and captured and shot 47 more. The

Indians, tiring of the battle, cut the water ditch to the palace. With this act Governor Otermín realized he was beaten. He led the 1,000 Spanish refugees in a retreat and headed south to friendly Isleta Pueblo. In their hasty retreat, it is said, the Spanish people took time to gather up a 3-foot-tall, crowned, wooden statue of the Virgin Mary that had stood in the parish church since it had been brought to Santa Fe from Mexico in 1625. The defeated Spanish left with their beloved Madonna on August 21, 1680. At Isleta they met up with other refugees and eventually evacuated all the way to the state of Chihuahua in Mexico. There they began plotting a reconquest.

Meanwhile the Indians took over the Palace of the Governors and redesigned its interior to their liking. They then set about to destroy all material evidence of the Spanish occupation. Santa Fe became the center for a loose federation of Pueblo tribes. The Isleta Mission Church and the Ácoma Mission Church were the only two churches of the eighty or so built before 1680 that were not completely destroyed in that revengeful spree. These two ancient churches are still in use today. Governor Otermín attempted a reconquest in November 1680 but, upon arriving at Isleta, found that the Indians were ready to entrap him to the north. He abandoned the plan and returned to Mexico with close to 400 Isleta Indians for whom he feared reprisals. They eventually settled at a site near today's El Paso, Texas, known as Ysleta.

Perhaps losing New Mexico to the Pueblo Indians was just another example of what was happening to declining Spain. Between 1621 and 1665 under Philip III and Philip IV, the Spanish had lost the Thirty Years War and had lost Portugal as well. By 1680 Spain was truly a lesser nation headed for the doldrums, led by Charles II, who was apparently mentally incompetent.

It would be twelve years before another reconquest of New Mexico would be attempted. The indomitable Spanish would not give up, especially since La Salle and the French landed on the Texas coast of the Gulf of Mexico in 1684. It was thought the French might threaten Spanish holdings in New Mexico or their silver mines in New Spain. La Salle had arrived on the gulf largely due to information given to France by a Spanish traitor, Don Diego de Peñalosa, who ironically had been governor of New Mexico from 1650 to 1655. Like most Spanish governors of New Mexico, he was accused of misconduct in office, tried, and stripped of his wealth. But instead of retiring to lick his wounds, he became a turncoat and aided France in its New World interests.

In 1692 Captain General Diego de Vargas Zapata Lujan Ponce de León y Contreras marched resolutely back into New Mexico. He found little resistance to his expeditionary force. He went peaceably up and down the Rio Grande and even traveled to the Hopi mesas without event. In his report he used the word *moqui,* derived from a Zuni word to describe the Hopi. He also stopped by Inscription Rock. There, not to be outdone by Juan Oñate, he inscribed the following: "Here was General Don Diego de Vargas who conquered for our Holy Faith and the Royal Crown all New Mexico at his own expense in 1692." After four months traveling around as the "reconquistador," he returned victorious to Mexico.

In 1693 he led a resettlement expedition back up the Camino Real to Santa Fe with 100 soldiers, 73 families, 18 Franciscan priests, some Pueblo Indians, and

4,000 animals. This resettlement party returned to Santa Fe with the little wooden statue of the Virgin they had taken with them in 1680. They took solace from the Virgin as they camped outside Villa de Santa Fe that winter. As the weather became colder and the Spanish food supplies dwindled, the Spaniards suggested that the Indians give them the Palace of the Governors and also find food for them. In this request the Indians saw in these "new Spaniards" the same traits present in the Spanish twelve years before. They resisted and a battle ensued. The Spanish immediately cut the water ditches to the palace, forcing the Indians to surrender. The Spanish executed 70 of the resisters and took 400 others as captives to be used as servants.

It was not a peaceful reconquest. Over the next few years, some of the bloodiest battles in the history of the region were fought at San Ildefonso, Jemez, and Ácoma pueblos. Many Rio Grande Pueblo people, fearing reprisals, fled west to live with the Navajo and the Hopi (see Section 2, "The Hopi: A Long and Continuous Past"). By 1696 most of the villages had been subdued by de Vargas's heavy hand. But the Hopi remained adamant, slaughtering some of their own people who were about to invite a Franciscan priest to live in their village rather than submit to Spanish control. The resolute Hopi offered a home to Rio Grande Indian refugees who feared Spanish reprisals. Spain finally regained some lost territory in this far distant colonial empire. The little wooden statue of the Virgin became known as *La Conquistadora,* since it was to her that the Spanish colonists attributed their victory. *La Conquistadora* became the focus of a

La Conquistadora or Nuestra Señora de la Paz

procession and festival of thanksgiving that began in 1716 and has continued to this day. The statue of the Virgin was carried from the church to the place where the Spanish colonists waited while the battle for the Palace of the Governors ensued. This venerated figure now known by the additional name of Nuestra Señora de la Paz, or Our Lady of Peace, can still be seen today in Saint Francis Cathedral in Santa Fe. Divine intervention aside, de Vargas was tried for misconduct, imprisoned, and dishonored. But as was usually the case, his name was eventually cleared and he even returned to New Mexico to serve a second term as governor.

By 1695, 1,500 more colonists had arrived from Mexico. Often on the last night before entering Santa Fe, the weary travelers would spend the night near today's La Cienaga at El Rancho de las Golondrinas. This ancient ranch with its *torreons,* or towers, dating back to the 1650s has been restored and is open to the public on a limited basis. Now firmly in control, the Spanish set about seriously to colonize this area. A second villa, Santa Cruz de Cañada, was established as de Vargas issued the first recorded settler grant in New Mexico. The third villa to be established was Villa de Albuquerque in 1706.

The greatest threat to the newly resettled colony in the early part of the 1700s came from the Apaches. They threatened the lives and livelihood of both the Pueblo Indians and the Spanish. Consequently the Spanish and Pueblo peoples found some common ground as they both fought a hated enemy. The other common denominator uniting the two was survival in this rugged country. Each learned from the other a variety of lifeways that made living not just possible but a little easier. Learning from the land's native inhabitants was critical for the Spanish New Mexicans, because Spain gave them very little attention during this time and they had to rely more and more on themselves. It has been said that while the rest of the world flourished and technology grew by leaps and bounds in the 1700s, the Spanish in New Mexico were defeated by distance and time, finally having to live much like their former enemies the Pueblo Indians, in a static state where survival was the name of the game.

The Apache threats lessened after 1720, when the Comanches became more of a problem. Within time the Utes were also threatening the Rio Grande settlements. To cope with the problem, the Spanish established settlement grants at Abiquiu, Belen, Tomé, and San Miguel, which were to be settled predominantly with Indians of obscure identity, known as *genizaros*. They were usually captured Ute, Apache, and Comanche slaves. With these people serving as the first line of defense against Indian raids, it was thought that the Spanish settlers would not be bothered quite so much. The vanguard of most Spanish expeditions in pursuing the marauding Apaches and Comanches were the Pueblo Indians.

The years 1739–40 saw the beginning of French explorers making their way across the plains to the Rockies. Within a few years they were trading at the Taos summer fair, a wild event in which Indians, both friendly and hostile, traded with the Spanish. Upon leaving the fair the Utes or Comanches would often raid the countryside. Fearful of further French encroachment from the east, the Taos trade fair was closed to the French in 1752. In 1763 the French were driven from the North American continent when England took Canada. Shortly after that, to keep England from grabbing up Louisiana, France ceded that territory to Spain. Spain could breathe a sigh of relief, at least for a while. The French were no longer a threat. Later Spain, supporting the American Revolution, declared war on England. Years later Spain would come to distrust the new American government.

In the last quarter of the 1700s, an amazing man entered the scene. It was said that by the time he died, he had ridden more than 20,000 miles on horseback. In 1774 Juan Bautista de Anza helped settle California in an effort to ward off the threat of the Russians along the Pacific Coast. In 1776, the year the American colonists declared independence from Great Britain, he founded the city of San Francisco. That same year the Spanish crown took the northern Spanish provinces out from under the control of the viceroy of Mexico and created *provincias internas,* or internal provinces, to be directed by a military officer known as the commandante general, who was to be stationed in Chihuahua, the Mexican state that borders New Mexico today.

The tireless de Anza was appointed the first governor of New Mexico under the new system. In 1779 he launched an entirely innovative and very clever attack on the great Comanche leader Cuerno Verde. On this punitive expedition he

Historical trails

became the first Spaniard to follow the Rio Grande north to today's Colorado. There doing battle with the Comanches, he discovered that the river took a sharp turn to the west, rather than going on to the North Pole as the Spanish maps had shown for years. With his defeat of the main Comanche elements, he was able to temporarily enlist their support in fighting the Apache, who had once again become a menace. More amazingly he was able to pacify the Moqui or Hopi in 1780, the last defiant pueblo to make peace.

By that time the Hopi had been through a series of severe droughts and numerous devastating epidemics of smallpox, a disease unknown in the New World until the Spanish came. By 1786, one year before the United States Constitution was completed, de Anza was able to strike a lasting peace with the Comanches, opening up trade to the east. Soon Pedro Vial, a French explorer hired by Spain, blazed a trail from Santa Fe to the Spanish Presidio at San Antonio. He also explored a route to St. Louis that eventually would lead to the development of the Santa Fe Trail. In 1776 the Domínguez-Escalante expedition left Santa Fe to explore trade routes to California. In spite of the discovery of these new routes, northern New Mexico was still isolated except for the regular trading up and down the Camino Real, a distance of more than 500 miles from Taos to the trade centers in Chihuahua, taking six months for a pack train to leave and return.

In 1800 the victorious Napoleon forced Spain to give Louisiana back to France. To Spain's dismay and Thomas Jefferson's delight, Napoleon sold the whole Louisiana Territory to the United States three years later, in 1803. Now New Spain

Burros

would have to be wary of its former ally, the United States. In fact it was just two years later that those fears would be heightened. For in 1805 twenty-seven-year-old Lieutenant Zebulon Pike set out on an exploratory expedition to determine the extent of the lands the United States had acquired in the Louisiana Purchase. His travels led him to the Rockies. There, thinking he was near the Red River, he built a stockade just a few miles from the Rio Grande as it courses through the San Luis Valley. For reasons not entirely clear, one member of his group headed for Santa Fe. There in the New Mexico capital, he was questioned. He told the Spanish about Pike's stockade in the San Luis Valley. Spanish forces headed north, picking up Pike and his men. They were taken to Santa Fe, questioned, and then sent back to the United States via a circuitous route to the south. No doubt Pike was able to observe the Spanish lands and their defenses.

But Pike and his men were not the first Americans to be seen by Santa Feans. A few months earlier several American-based trappers had made their way to Santa Fe. From this point on more and more American traders and trappers would find their way to New Mexico, especially to Taos, which became a prime trading and commercial center. Soon the unrest that was spreading through New Spain like wildfire and that was manifested in the revolutionary acts of the inspired Mexican priest Hidalgo crept northward into New Mexico. The Mexican revolution of 1810–15 finally led to establishing Mexico's independence from Spain in 1821. Under the new Mexican law, the Pueblo Indians were granted full citizenship. Restrictive trade laws that had been adopted by the paranoid Spanish were abandoned, and Taos, a local trade center for the Spanish and Indians for many years, now became a major trade center.

In 1812 St. Louis merchants were sending good-size trade expeditions to Taos. By 1821 William Becknell brought the first major trade caravan over part of the same route Pedro Vial had traveled earlier. This route, called the Santa Fe Trail, originated at Independence, Missouri, near America's westernmost river port along the Missouri River. It ended 800 jarring miles later in Santa Fe. But it became a beehive of activity when both New Mexican and American traders began to realize that it was 1,000 miles shorter than the Camino Real or Chihuahua Trail route to Veracruz, the closest Mexican water port. Soon more goods were rolling into Santa Fe at cheaper prices. Over the years the Santa Fe Trail carried so much traffic that even today you will be able to see traces of wagon ruts near Fort Union National Monument, northeast of Santa Fe. Huge, red-wheeled freight wagons, pulled by spans of mules or yokes of oxen, brought hardware and calico to Santa Fe and hauled furs, hides, and Mexican mules and burros to Missouri. Yes, the legendary Missouri mules originally came from Mexico!

Within a short time Santa Fe and Taos became major way stations as American traders pushed south along the Camino Real into northern Mexico, returning all the way home with pesos jingling in their pockets. All this activity in northern New Mexico attracted the likes of Kit Carson, Peg-leg Smith, Antoine Robidoux, and other well-known American mountain men. Kit Carson was so enthusiastic about Taos that he was reported to have said, "No man who has seen the women, heard the bells, or smelled the piñon smoke of Taos will ever be able to leave." Needless to say, Carson married a Spanish woman and settled in Taos. His home there is still standing and has become an excellent museum accurately portraying early-nineteenth-century life in northern New Mexico. Possibly because of new information brought back to New Mexico by the American mountain men, who had explored the west, the Old Spanish Trail was developed within a few years (see Section 1, "History"). Pack trains traveled its route from Santa Fe to Los Angeles, making Santa Fe an important commercial hub.

In the late 1820s gold was discovered south of Santa Fe near Mount Chalchihuitl, not far from the ancient site of the Indian turquoise mines. By 1830 another strike was made at Tuerto. These were the first gold strikes west of the Mississippi and preceded the discovery of gold in California by twenty years. Now for the first time, northern New Mexico, the distant cousin of Spain and the ignored half-brother of Mexico, began to flourish on its own.

But not all was well with the New Mexican people. In the late 1700s and early 1800s, the Spanish decided that if the Indians weren't converted to Christianity after 162 years, they never would be. The expense of maintaining missions in that remote country was more than Spain could afford. Consequently the Franciscan priests were gradually withdrawn from the Indian pueblos. The removal of the Franciscans became even more widespread after the takeover by Mexico. The Mexicans, having just freed themselves from oppressive Mother Spain, were eager to rid their country of all Spanish influence, including religious influence. They ordered all Spanish-born Franciscans out of New Mexico in 1828.

Needless to say, the Spanish villagers of New Mexico were unhappy about the loss of contact with the mother church. From that point on religious duties came more and more into the hands of secular clergymen and laymen. Over the years they developed a unique form of Catholicism that continues to influence the area to this day. Carrying the belief of salvation through penance to its limits, the "Penitente" movement became more radical in its practices. Some of the rites of self-flagellation and punishment became so abhorrent to the mother church that the Penitentes were not allowed in traditional churches and were forced to build their own chapels. These they called "Moradas." Of course, the chapels had to be decorated without help from the organized church, so villagers began decorating the chapels themselves.

From this beginning sprang the fine tradition of New Mexican Spanish wood carvers and craftsmen who continue to turn out some of the most beautiful and unique pieces of religious and secular art in the United States today. The *santeros,* as the craftsmen were called, became revered figures who often went from house to house carving from wood and painting three-dimensional statues called *bultos* and painting religious figures on wood or tin, called *retablos.* In the early 1800s almost all non-Indian Catholics belonged to the Penitente sect. It has been said that the Indians viewed the severe practices of this sect as a form of Spanish dementia.

In addition to resenting the loss of their beloved Franciscan priests, the New Mexicans bitterly resented the high taxes imposed on them from a distant, impersonal capital. This resentment came to a head in 1836, when Mexico reorganized the country, changing New Mexico's political status and installing a Mexican, rather than a native-born New Mexican, as governor. The atmosphere was once again ripe for revolt.

For the first time in New Mexico's long history, Spanish Mexican villagers united with Pueblo Indians in an alliance that would spearhead two revolts in the following ten years. In 1837 some Taos residents, led by a General Chopón, established revolutionary headquarters at Santa Cruz. There in a clash with government troops, the Mexican governor was forced to retreat. In anticipation of this, however, his escape route was cut off, and he was captured at Santo Domingo Pueblo, where he was summarily killed and decapitated.

The insurgents took over the capital. The General Assembly of New Mexico joined the revolt by electing Jose Gonzáles, an Indian living at Taos Pueblo, as governor. For the second time in history, the Palace of the Governors was occupied by a revolutionary leader from Taos Pueblo. But his rule was short-lived. A little more than a month later, General Manuel Armijo, representing the Mexican government, was appointed chief of a liberating army by that government. Reinforced with troops from Mexico, he marched from Albuquerque to Santa Fe. González and his followers, seeing the handwriting on the wall, retreated to Santa Cruz, where they were finally overwhelmed. Armijo had González shot on the spot.

But the atmosphere was ripe for rebellion in other parts of Mexico as well. In 1835 settlers in Texas revolted and ran the Mexican citizens out of that part of Mexico, declaring their independence from Mexico in 1836. After being defeated by the Mexicans at the Alamo, the Texans came back to win the day at the Battle of San Jacinto. Texas became an independent nation. But the Republic of Texas was not to be annexed into the United States for another ten years. In 1841 the president of the newly independent Republic of Texas sent expeditionary forces to take the New Mexican capital at Santa Fe. Armijo, fresh from quelling rebellion there, got wind of the expedition and captured the Texas troops. Some were killed. Others were sent to Mexico in chains.

In 1845 the Republic of Texas was annexed into the United States. This action brought an immediate break in diplomatic relations between Mexico and the United States. In spite of this break in relations, the United States government continued to seek control of California and New Mexico. The United States placed special emphasis on the notion that all the land claimed by the Republic of Texas east of the Rio Grande should be transferred to the United States because of the annexation of Texas. Mexico was unwilling to negotiate such a transfer. Consequently in 1846 President James Polk declared war on Mexico. Gen.

Freight wagon

Bulto

Stephen Watts Kearny, leader of the "Army of the West," led his troops first into New Mexico and then on to California. His arrival in New Mexico was a fateful day for General Armijo. First he took his troops over Apache Pass near Pecos to fend off the American army. But then, for reasons not quite clear, he withdrew his resistance and retreated to Mexico. Kearny entered Santa Fe without a bullet being fired. The Americans called this takeover an occupation rather than a conquest. A third national flag now flew over Santa Fe, marking the end of 248 years of Spanish and Mexican rule.

Within a few weeks Kearny ordered the building of Fort Marcy. This massive, star-shaped, adobe fort, located north of the plaza, was the first American military post in the Southwest. It is no longer standing today. Having completed only part of his mission, Kearny appointed Charles Bent of Taos as first governor of the New Mexico area. Leaving Santa Fe in the hands of a subordinate, Kearny headed west to California. A few months later in January 1847, intrigue was brewing once again at Taos. The Spanish were fearful the United States would interfere with their land rights. A plot originating among the Spanish and enlisting the aid of the Taos Pueblo Indians was devised.

In January 1847 the Spanish and Pueblo Indians struck at Taos, killing the Catholic prefect, the prosecuting attorney, and the sheriff. But the final prize was finding Governor Bent in Taos. He had come there to celebrate Christmas with members of his family. The marauders stormed his home, scalped Bent alive, and then riddled him with bullets. U.S. troops from Santa Fe immediately came to the rescue. With the help of several veteran American mountain men like Dick Woottan and Jim Beckworth and able American soldiers like Colonel Sterling Price and Captain John Burgwin, the insurgents were defeated at Santa Cruz and Embudo. In the final battle the Americans stormed the mission church at Taos Pueblo, where the last renegades had taken cover. With cannons blazing they blew holes in the thick adobe walls. They routed the Indians from the demolished church. Two hundred Indians were killed. Those who lived were tried and executed on the spot.

But it wasn't until the signing of the Treaty of Guadalupe Hidalgo in 1848 that New Mexico was officially transferred to the United States. In 1850 Congress paid the state of Texas for its claims to the land east of the Rio Grande and established the territory of New Mexico. By 1853 the western borders of New Mexico were established after purchasing land from Mexico in the Gadsden Purchase. Northern New Mexico, now a territory of the United States, continued to suffer from Apache, Navajo, and Comanche raids. The U.S. government built several protective forts. Fort Union, the first one to be constructed in 1851, stood 90 miles east of Santa Fe.

Wagon trains or stagecoaches found the fort a welcome oasis in a desert filled with marauding Comanche and Kiowa Indians. Today you can visit the ruins of the fort; they are highlighted by an interpretive trail through them. Most of the American forts remained active until about 1886, when the Apache Indians were finally subdued. Another fort to be established was Cantonment Burgwin, which was built in 1852 to help ward off Comanche attacks from the east. With Comanche raids drying up, the fort was closed, and its detachment of troops of the First Dragoons left in 1860. You will be able to see parts of this reconstructed log fort today on the outskirts of Taos (see "A Day Traveling through Spanish New Mexico: A Narrative Account" later in this section).

Aside from the political and military intrigue of the mid-1800s, life in the villages went on much as before. Nonetheless the takeover by the United States brought two major changes directly to the people, changes that established the tone for many of the cultural nuances you will see today. The 1848 Treaty of Guadalupe Hidalgo stated that property rights legally held under Mexican law would be respected by the United States. But the concept of land ownership held by the newly arrived Americans was entirely different from the concepts practiced by the Spanish and Mexicans. Conflict arose on several points that, over the years, would create an atmosphere of rancor and bitterness.

Many of the native New Mexicans lost land in the attempt to translate their holdings into the rigid system of surveys and measurements taken by the Americans. The Spanish had used natural objects like trees and rocks to define the boundaries of their property. Strict surveys employed by the Americans often diminished the size of certain parcels of land. Under Spanish and Mexican law, land grants had been made not only to Spanish families for plots of land around their homes and adjacent to the *acequias,* or irrigation ditches, but to each village as well. This large, community-owned parcel of land outside the village was called the *ejido,* or the commons. All families in the village shared in its use. Over time the Spanish lost much of this *ejido* land because the concept of community-held land was foreign to the American system of land ownership and was therefore subject to question and could easily be challenged. The Spanish and Mexicans did not impose taxes on land. The U.S. government did. Not only taxes but also assessments of one sort or another were placed on property.

Probably the bulk of the land was lost through foreclosure when the Spanish landowners could not afford to pay the taxes or just did not understand what taxes were all about. After all, the Americans in power did not issue tax statements in the Spanish language. Those foreclosed lands were eventually sold to speculating Anglos. Of the original 35 million acres of land held by native New Mexicans before the United States took over, those early Spanish families now own very little. That

Cantonment Burgwin

which was not wrested away from them by United States law the Spanish people have held onto faithfully.

This devotion to the land has given rise to the phrase still heard today that "he who sells his land sells his mother." This strict retention of small family plots has led to so much subdivision of the land that some pieces of property have taken on strange proportions. Some have cited parcels of property that are 26 inches wide by 1.5 miles long and that are owned by seven or eight heirs. You will notice, as you travel around the Spanish villages, that the land takes on the appearance of a postage stamp album, with each little square or oblong *rancho* fenced and farmed separately from the adjacent properties.

The U.S. occupation also had an effect on the vital religious life of the original Spanish and Mexican residents. Over the years they had known many changes in their religious leadership. First there were the Franciscans, provided by the Spanish, and then came the secular leadership of the very devout laity. Finally the people came under the leadership of a few native priests—like José Martinez of Taos—who were born in New Mexico but trained in the churches of Mother Mexico.

The U.S. ecclesiastical authorities made yet another change. They appointed a dynamic Frenchman, Jean Baptiste Lamy, as bishop of the new diocese. Although he had been working in Cincinnati, his heart was still in France. He began a crash program of bringing European Catholicism back to New Mexico. He filled vacant missions and parishes with priests imported from France and other locations in Europe. In 1852 he brought the Sisters of Loretto from Kentucky to establish a girls' academy at Santa Fe. Shortly thereafter he brought an order of the Christian Brothers from France to found St. Michael's College. He imported French architects and Italian stonemasons to begin construction of the Romanesque Cathedral of Saint Francis in Santa Fe in 1869. He also ordered the construction of the Gothic chapel of Our Lady of Light, the Loretto Chapel. But it was not long after the American takeover that the first Protestants would also enter the scene. The first Protestant church, built by the Baptists, was constructed in 1854. That building is no longer standing, but today you can see a lovely old adobe built in the early 1900s by the Presbyterians, who have occupied that site since 1866 (see "Half-Day Tour of Santa Fe, North of the River" later in this section).

Lamy immediately came into conflict with the Penitentes, the sect that had grown out of the Third Order of Saint Francis and that had flourished in its own peculiar way in the absence of the Franciscan priests. Los Hermanos de Luz, or the Brothers of the Light, as these Penitentes were known, had continued the development and perpetuation of severe religious practices in the fifty-year hiatus when there were so few priests. Flagellations had become so severe that often people were thrashed until the flesh was torn away to the bone. Others were allegedly crucified on the cross at Eastertime.

In spite of these excesses, the Penitentes engaged in many good works. They ministered to village people at times of sickness and death. In difficult times their unfailing belief in their religious practices helped keep their faith alive. One of the lasting legacies of the Penitente movement was the development of the great *santero* tradition wherein artisans traveled from village to village creating the religious figures called *bultos* and *retablos*. But in 1856 Lamy took a strong stand to limit some of the Penitente practices. In 1947 the Catholic Church agreed to recognize the Penitentes as long as they agreed to restrain their practices. Since that time there has been gradual moderation of the Penitente rituals. Today, active Penitentes in northern New Mexico contribute to the rich cultural mix you will see in your travels.

By the 1860s another lode of gold had been discovered in New Mexico, leading to a minor boom that brought more American settlers. The American influence on the area was growing and even becoming visible in the architecture. The previous architecture, variously called Spanish Colonial, Franciscan, or Pueblo, gave way to Territorial Pueblo, showing traces of the neo-Grecian and Victorian influences that were sweeping the middle part of the United States at that time. You will see many examples of this style of architecture. One of the best is the Pinckney R. Tully House in Santa Fe. American technological advances replaced dirt floors with wood, introduced kiln-fired bricks to cap adobe sidewalls, and brought in glass for windows. The Americans also brought with them the design for pitched roofs, which slowly began to show up among the flat-roofed adobe homes.

During this period of increased settlement, the gold strikes in Colorado were under way and the Civil War broke out. Shortly after the war started, there was another invasion of New Mexico from Texas. This time it was under the Confederate flag. The invasion force streamed north out of El Paso, hoping to conquer New Mexico and thereby gain control of the rich Colorado gold mines and interrupt the flow of gold and trade goods from California to the north. In 1862 the upstart Confederate troops marched through Albuquerque and on to Santa Fe without contest. They raised the fourth flag over the Palace of the Governors. Their rule was short-lived, for a few weeks later the Confederates were defeated at the "Gettysburg of the West" en route to attempt the takeover of the Union stronghold, Fort Union. Confederate troops, misjudging the strength and position of the Union forces, retreated back to Texas, and once again the United States flag was raised over Santa Fe and New Mexico. A third invasion by Texas would not occur until later in the twentieth century, when Texas tourists "discovered" northern New Mexico and began to flock there in unprecedented numbers.

In 1866 gold was discovered near Elizabethtown north of Taos. But by 1879 more significant strikes were made near the location of the earlier gold strikes in New Mexico, south of Santa Fe. Cerrillos, Madrid, and Golden became boomtowns. By the 1880s Albuquerque had become a railroad town, even boasting a large number of Irish railroad workers, and soon Santa Fe, previously neglected by the major lines, would have its own railroad. The Denver and Rio Grande pushed down from Chama to Española, finally reaching Santa Fe. The line was dubbed the "Chili Line," as it transported carload after carload of famous New Mexican Rio Grande Valley peppers out of the state. By 1890 most of the mineral boom days in northern New Mexico were over, and the territory concentrated on moving toward statehood, finally reaching that goal in 1912, as the forty-seventh state.

With the excitement of the gold rush gone, northern New Mexico settled down to become the agriculturally based, sheep-raising culture it had been under Spanish rule, when the first churro and merino sheep were brought to New Mexico in the livestock herds of Coronado, Oñate, and others. It was from these animals that the sheep industry got its start. Both the Indians and the Spanish grazed sheep in the pastoral mountain valleys of northern New Mexico and on the community lands, mentioned earlier, that were granted by the Spanish and Mexican governments. Eventually, though, overgrazing of the grass and excessive cutting of the timber led to such severe erosion that, by the end of the nineteenth century, the grazing lands were not productive.

In 1906 the United States government, in its zeal to put more forested and natural land into the public domain, grabbed up much of this *ejido,* or community property. In Taos County the U.S. Forest Service came to own 44 percent of the county. Although the people were able to obtain grazing permits from the government, it was easier for some than for others because of the politics involved. Too often favoritism was the name of the game. Within time the U.S. government felt the land was being overgrazed, and the number of grazing permits was reduced, hitting at the lifeblood of many of the people. Land around Indian reservations was also taken by the government about the same time. In one of these land grabs, 12 miles from Taos Pueblo, the government gobbled up, without compensation, Taos Pueblo's sacred Blue Lake, site of religious rites and ceremonies since A.D. 1200. After years and years of politicking, debate, and bitterness, the Taos Indians in 1971 won their long-fought battle, and the U.S. government returned this hallowed ground to them.

The Spanish people were not so fortunate. Less organized and unable to wield the clout at the federal level that the Pueblo Indians did, some sat in smoldering anger until 1967, when all hell broke loose. Led by a Texas-born Hispanic who had formed an alliance called Alianza Federal de Mercedes (Federal Alliance of Land Grants), which sought to regain the *ejido* land for New Mexico's Spanish descendants, a violent revolt once more hit New Mexico in the summer of 1967. Occasionally you will still hear mention of the courthouse raid in Tierra Amarilla wherein three law officers were wounded and a deputy sheriff and newspaper reporter were abducted. That was the highwater mark for the Alianza. After that several factions developed among its members, and the movement lost much of its impetus. Although the "raid" focused national attention on the issue, the ownership of the lands in question remains unchanged.

But these days you are apt to read and hear more about the explosion of the arts in Santa Fe than anything else. Perhaps the first intimation that northern New Mexico was to become an inspirational haven for writers and artists came during the term of Governor Lew Wallace (1878–81) who, while occupying the Palace of the Governors in Santa Fe, wrote the famous epic *Ben-Hur,* the first biblical novel in United States history. He was certainly a cut above the rowdy frontier types who had prevailed until then. His predecessors were known to have thrown valuable state documents helter-skelter into back rooms under leaky roofs. At other times, when no one knew what to do with the increasing mounds of public records, the problem of storing them was allegedly solved by stuffing them down the outhouse "two holer." Governor William A. Pile is most often accused of these acts.

Into this colorful, stranger-than-fiction atmosphere came two well-known American artists in 1898. Bert Phillips was one of the first. He had heard about northern New Mexico from one of his teachers in Paris, Joseph Henry Sharp, who had come through the area earlier. With his fellow artist Ernest L. Blumenschein, he set out from Colorado on a sketching trip to Mexico. Their wagon broke down north of Taos. Phillips left Blumenschein and went into Taos to have the wheel repaired. While riding along he was inspired and overwhelmed by the scenery and the people. These two men settled in Taos and were later joined by Sharp, who, with his earlier visit in the 1880s, is credited as the first artist to come to New Mexico. Then came Berninghaus, Higgins, Ufer, and Dunton.

But it was not until Mabel Dodge arrived from New York with her painter husband Maurice Sterne, in 1916, that the town began to buzz. Mabel had previously been married to architect Edwin Dodge. She had established herself as a wealthy socialite and arts patron when she and her husband renovated the Villa Curoni in Florence, Italy. There, for ten years they held court, hosting the likes of Gertrude Stein and Alice B. Toklas. Wherever Mabel went she made a big splash, and her career was carefully watched by writers and artists alike early in the twentieth century. She began extending invitations to her friends to come to Taos.

Mabel called, and the famous and famous-to-be came. Before she died her guest list read like a who's who of American arts and literature. John Marin, Georgia O'Keeffe, Robert Henri, Marsden Hartley, E. A. Robinson, Edward Weston, Willa Cather, and D. H. Lawrence were but a few who visited Taos at her invitation. Some of these people returned to New Mexico and set up residence there. So it is not by happenstance that Taos, a town of around 6,000 inhabitants, has nearly ninety arts and crafts galleries. More than a thousand visual artists live in the area. Stemming from a small nucleus of five painters in the 1920s who became known as Los Cincos Pintores, Santa Fe has become equally blessed with an even larger component of painters and writers, as well as an unprecedented number of arts and crafts galleries for a city of its size.

The tourist industry began in earnest in the 1920s and 1930s. The relative isolation of the area, especially after abandonment of the "Chili Line," meant that Santa Fe, Taos, and all that was between would not be hit as hard by the variety of technological changes sweeping the country. The growth of the area remained fairly steady until World War II. In 1943 the Los Alamos Ranch School on the Pajarito Plateau was taken over by the United States government as a secret hideaway for Robert J. Oppenheimer and his compatriots to work on developing the atom bomb. The population and economy of the state have been greatly influenced by a variety of federal projects since that time.

Today the three linked but never-to-be-united cultures go about their separate ways. Things are peaceful in northern New Mexico, but economic problems remain. In many areas poverty is on a level with that of Appalachia. For years the mean level of education has been below high school for the Hispanics. Unemployment is high. Nonetheless the richness of the three cultures that you will see as a tourist still sustains the people. Modern technology is finally making life easier, but the old ways often persist.

In your visit to New Mexico, you may see Hispanic women from distant villages give each other a warm kiss and embrace, European-style, at one of the colorful religious feast days. Or you may see people from a Spanish village follow their Spanish-born priest to the *acequias,* or water ditches, in May in a centuries-old procession that honors San Ysidro de Labrador, the patron saint of the fields, to pray for the fertility and productivity of the land. And you may also see in the pueblos the village chief, the cacique or religious priest, announce on a fine spring day that it is time to plant the field because the sun has reached the right spot along the mountain's ridgeline. Then that hooded, mysterious figure, the *pregonero,* will climb to the top of the pueblo and, like the town criers of old, announce to all that it is time to plant. Nowhere else but in northern New Mexico will you discover such a unique center of foreign culture smack-dab in the heart of "Apple Pie America."

SEEING THE SPANISH RIO GRANDE COUNTRY

Albuquerque, a vibrant, expanding area, rapidly approaching 700,000 citizens, is a popular destination for many travelers. But it wasn't always so. Situated out of the mountains above the northern edge of the high, yet flat, sunbaked **Chihuahuan Desert,** at 5,300 feet elevation, Albuquerque was long seen as too hot, too windy, too dusty, too cold, or too barren for most travelers' tastes. Years ago, cars on old U.S. Highway 66 used to roar through the town, their occupants looking neither right nor left as they sped toward far-flung destinations to the east and west or sought the cooler elevations of the mountains to the north and south. The Santa Fe train stopped there back then, just as Amtrak does now. There was always a brief stop to see the Pueblo Indians selling their wares on the station platform before speeding on to Chicago or Los Angeles. But in the last decade, increasing numbers of travelers disembarking at the Albuquerque airport have come to savor the attractions in New Mexico's largest city.

Disjointed, sprawling Albuquerque may be hard to love, but it is easy to like—and it is an interesting, pleasant place to spend some time. Modern Albuquerque, the hot air balloon capital of the world, is also the educational, industrial, medical, and commercial jet air capital of New Mexico. The growing **University of New Mexico,** with 25,000 students, has brought considerable life to this desert city. Once thought of as a cultural dustbin, Albuquerque has dramatically changed its image as new galleries, museums, and upscale stores and shops reflect a level of sophistication previously unknown there. Today Albuquerque is filled with new, vibrant young residents from Maine to California who have joined this city's progressive New Mexicans in their efforts to create a better place to live.

More and more Albuquerque has realized its potential as host city to thousands of jet travelers who rely on the only commercial jet airport for miles around. There in the comfortable surroundings of the modern airport, whose architecture reflects the ambience of the region, you will catch a glimpse of New Mexico's three cultures. Pueblo Indians in traditional dress prepare to board a plane to Seattle, Washington, where they will give seminars about the way they dig their clay and make their pottery. From New Mexico's eastern plains, Anglo cowboys dressed like they were born that way discuss an upcoming helicopter trip to look after their oil and gas holdings. Meanwhile a group of Spanish New Mexicans who hold government jobs in Santa Fe buzz excitedly in Spanish about their upcoming trip to Washington, D.C.

San Felipe de Neri Church, Albuquerque

Some Albuquerque Tour Sites

A more in-depth introduction to north central New Mexico's diverse cultures has been arranged by Albuquerque's city founders. **"Old Town"** Albuquerque has been beautifully preserved to capture the essence of the Spanish tradition of this city that proudly boasts a large Hispanic population. Old Town is one of the most interesting and charming sections of this 276-year-old settlement. In fact the city got its start there when about a dozen families from the Bernalillo area created a new community in 1706, the third major "villa" to be developed in New Mexico. In the center of this approximately 5-square-block area located between Rio Grande Boulevard on the west, Mountain Road on the north, and Central Avenue on the south is a grassy, **tree-shaded plaza** from which all activity stems. There Texans and New Yorkers mingle near two old Confederate cannons, reminders that the Confederate government ruled Albuquerque for a short time in 1862. Anchoring the north side of the plaza is **San Felipe de Neri Church.** Although that lovely old adobe building is not the original structure, having been enlarged and remodeled many times, church services have been held at this location every Sunday without fail since 1706, when the original church was first constructed on this site.

Across Romero street from Old Town Plaza, tucked in the back of a shopping area called **Plaza San Luis,** is the **Old Town Visitor Center and Public Restroom** facility. There you can pick up useful information about Albuquerque and the surrounding area. From the plaza, spreading in all directions for several blocks, the adobe and territorial-style buildings, many the former homes of Spanish families, line the streets, offering the traveler a variety of shops and restaurants. There are several fine American Indian arts and crafts shops, as well as one of the finest contemporary craft shops in the region. Within walking distance, on the northwest corner of Old Town, is the **Albuquerque Museum** on Mountain Road. The rotating art exhibits and the museum shop are worth a visit. The shop carries some regional crafts, as well as an excellent supply of books about the area. **Walking tours of Old Town** depart from the museum several days a week from mid-April through mid-November. For tour inquiries call (505) 243–7255 or, for information on current exhibits, (505) 242–4600.

But don't stop there. Walk from the museum across the street to 1801 Mountain Road where a large, sand-colored modernistic building houses the **New Mexico Museum of Natural History and Science.** The first state-sponsored museum of its kind to be built in the United States in this century, it is well worth a visit (fee). Its attractions are many. The most modern technological advances in digital sound systems, edge-lit fiber optics, and polarizing filters are used to re-create a variety of ancient prehistoric phenomena, making this museum an experience not to be missed. The museum's well-conceived, almost magical exhibits, plus regular showings in its almost more-real-than-life **Dynamax Theatre,** transform you into a time traveler by taking you on a journey spanning 4.5 billion years of this region's natural history. As you go sleuthing through the museum following the well-laid-out "Timetracks: A Journey through Time," you will learn about the forces that helped create the earth as it is today, including the development of the phenomenon known as the Continental Divide, which splits our continent into two distinct watersheds. Along the way you will have a chance to walk into the heated inferno of a simulated volcano (complete with a realistic illusion of flowing magma) and view unique three-dimensional kinetic light collages that depict prehistoric scenes with a lot of emphasis on dinosaurs and other extinct creatures in the **Age of Giants** exhibit. Stroll through the cool, damp interior of an Ice Age cave complete with incredibly realistic stalagmites and stalactites, or ride the one and only "Evolator" time machine. The **Naturalist Center** where "kids as curators" is the theme allows visitors a hands-on natural history experience, while **Fossilworks,** where fossils are cleaned and prepared for exhibit and preservation, is an exciting public display and viewing area. And the not to be missed **Lodestar Astronomy Center and Star Theatre** provides every child with an otherworldly experience.

The museum's **Natureworks Store** is an event in itself, containing a wide selection of books, replicas, models, and toys that echo the biological, geologic, and paleontological exhibits of the museum. This museum is the sort of place that will have a lasting educational effect on young and old learners alike. A soft drink and snack bar is on the mezzanine. Open daily except nonholiday Mondays in September and January. Information: New Mexico Museum of Natural History and Science, 1801 Mountain Road Northwest, Albuquerque, New Mexico 87104; (505) 841–2800; www.nmnh.abq.mus.nm.us.

But there are four other natural history and science sites you may want to visit that are just a few minutes drive away from the New Mexico Natural History and Science Museum. At 1905 Mountain Road Northwest is the **National Atomic Museum;** (505) 284–6083; www.atomicmuseum.com. Exhibits there reveal all aspects of atomic power, from wartime to domestic energy production (fee). Also on Mountain Road Northwest is **¡Explora! Science Center and Children's Museum.** Here the many hands-on exhibits and rotating shows will make your children feel right at home as they learn still more about science and nature. Information: ¡Explora! Science Center and Children's Museum, 1701 Mountain Road; (505) 842–1537; www.explora.mus.nm.us. And also just a few minutes drive away is **Albuquerque Biological Park** near the banks of the Rio Grande. Here you will find the **Albuquerque Aquarium** and the **Rio Grande Botanic Garden.** The aquarium highlights the river life of New Mexico, as well as the sea life of the Gulf of Mexico, where the Rio Grande meets the Atlantic Ocean. This stellar aquarium includes a shark tank and an eel cave for viewing. The Rio Grande Botanic Garden exhibits a variety of desert gardens along with the Spanish-Moorish Garden, the Curandera Garden, and other garden habitats. Nature shops, fast food, and cafeteria service available. Take Rio Grande Boulevard south to Central Avenue then turn right onto New York Avenue to access the park at 2601 Central Avenue Northwest; (505) 764–6200. The third natural history site is **Rio Grande Nature Center New Mexico State Park** (fee) in a *bosque* alongside the Rio Grande.

Although located in the city limits, the center seems far removed from the urban environment. The bunkerlike, glass-enclosed, low-slung concrete building that serves as a visitor center rests in the middle of a bosque. Bosque is the Spanish word for "forest" or "grove of trees." And how well it applies to the 270 acres of century-old cottonwood groves, salt cedar and tamarisk thickets, and mature Russian olive trees that compose this narrow verdant strip along the river's edge. Bosques occur many places along the course of the Rio Grande, and where they do they serve as a refuge for all sorts of wildlife, giving them sanctuary from the harshness of the adjoining desertlands. Coyote, fox, muskrat, and beaver share these verdant living spaces with turtles, roadrunners, and owls, while all seem to tolerate the temporary visitation of migrating Canada geese and sandhill cranes.

Visitor center (open daily) exhibits pertain to such river-related topics as ecology and geology. The glass-enclosed library and observation room focuses on the brimming bird life around a 3-acre pond and marsh area where you may see some of the more than 260 species of resident and migrating birds that inhabit the Rio Grande bosques throughout the year. There you are just as apt to see a pied-billed grebe as a black phoebe. More than 2 miles of trails through the Rio Grande bosque and along the riverbank reveal even more of the natural flora and fauna as they wind through forests, grasslands, and sand flats. At certain times of the year, you can catch glimpses of many species, including ash-throated flycatchers, blue grosbeaks, and black-capped chickadees. There are naturalist-led walks on the weekend. The small bookstore and gift shop have a nice selection of titles on Southwest ecology, birds, wildflowers, and other natural history subjects. Open daily except for major holidays. To find the Rio Grande Nature Center, drive from the New Mexico Museum of Natural History and Science to Rio Grande Boulevard and turn right, or north. Travel about 1.5 miles to Candelaria Road. Turn left or west onto Candelaria, and follow it a little more than 0.5 mile to the visitor center; (505) 344–7240.

Although Albuquerque has a very small Native American population, it is the home of the **Museum of the Indian Pueblo Cultural Center,** 1 block north of U.S. I–40 West at 2401 Twelfth Street Northwest (505–843–7270; 800–766–4405; www.indianpueblo.org and www.indianpueblo.com). Opened to the public (fee) in

1976, it is jointly owned by the nineteen Indian pueblos of New Mexico, some of which are but a few miles out of Albuquerque. It provides a fine introduction to the Pueblo Indian life you will see later as you drive north along the Rio Grande. Try to see it if you can. The museum is in a contemporary structure that echoes the graceful architectural lines of prehistoric Pueblo Bonito at Chaco Canyon. The excellent permanent exhibits detail early Pueblo Indian life to modern times. The favorite of many visitors is the exhibit of contemporary Pueblo life, which gives a preview of each pueblo, including the handicrafts made in each village.

The **Pueblo House Children's Museum** (by appointment only), a hands-on facility for children, is a must. On weekends **Indian dances** are held at the center; call for a precise schedule. The cultural center also has a large shop selling Indian crafts. The Pueblo Harvest Cafe offers typical Pueblo and Indian foods. (See "Staying There: Albuquerque," this section.)

If the exhibits at the Pueblo Cultural Center inspire you, take another hour or two to walk the trails at **Petroglyph National Monument,** approximately 8 miles from the Indian Pueblo Cultural Center. There on Albuquerque's West Mesa, where more than a half-dozen volcanic cinder cones dominate the park's 7,100-acre preserve, you'll find some of the Southwest's finest examples of prehistoric rock art. Most were carved by the resourceful ancestors of the Pueblo Indians sometime between A.D. 1100 and 1600. And they must have kept busy. For packed into the boulders and other lava formations along a serpentine, 17-mile-long, 3-block-wide volcanic escarpment are more than **15,000 images.** The incised lines appear gray or white against the dark surfaces of the porous lava rock.

Petroglyph National Monument

There is plenty to see along the monument's major walking trails. At the popular and easily accessible **Boca Negra Canyon** unit of the monument (fee)—formerly Petroglyph State Park—at 6900 Unser Boulevard, several short self-guided trails bring you face-to-face with ancient Pueblo Indian art in this huge outdoor gallery. Paved **Mesa Point Trail** (rated strenuous and the longest of the trails, taking about thirty minutes round-trip) winds to the top of the lava heap. Along the way you will encounter rock art images reflecting the artist's view of himself—including hand prints—the sun, four-pointed stars, and, of course, southwestern clouds. The images of the flute player *kokopelli* as well as a whole menagerie of plant, insect, bird, and animal likenesses can also be seen. And if that isn't enough, atop the ridge of these volcanic cliffs you can see forever, as your gaze stretches from the Rio Grande and its valley eastward toward the Sandia Mountains. Picnic shelters and water are available in the monument's Boca Negra Canyon unit, which has extended hours in the summer. To reach Petroglyph National Monument, turn west off I–25 (north of I–40, exit 228) onto Montaño

Road, and follow it west until you reach Unser Boulevard. Or take I–40 West across the Rio Grande bridge to the second exit, the Unser Boulevard exit. Follow Unser Boulevard north for about 3 miles, where signs will direct you to Petroglyph National Monument's **Visitor Center,** 6001 Unser Boulevard Northwest; (505) 899–0205; www.nps.gov/petr.

The University of New Mexico contributes greatly to the culture of Albuquerque. It is unique in the world, as all of its architecture is in the Spanish Pueblo style. It is a pleasant campus with tree-shaded walkways and refreshing fountains. The **Maxwell Museum of Anthropology** is located on the west end of the campus. Its permanent exhibits, "People of the Southwest" and "Ancestors," trace the history of earliest human habitation in the area to modern times. Its superbly mounted rotating exhibits feature both regional and world cultures in depth. The **museum store** offers a wide array of Pueblo, Navajo, Mexican, and South American crafts. The museum is located on University Boulevard just north of Martin Luther King Jr. Avenue, which is 3 blocks north of Central Avenue. No fee is required; (505) 277–4404 for a recorded message or (505) 277–4405; www.unm.edu/~maxwell. Also free and on the campus are the outstanding **Geology Museum; the Jonson Gallery,** featuring contemporary art (505–277–4967); the **Meterorites Institute Museum** (505–277–2747); and the **University Art Museum** (north of Cornell and Central, 505–277–4001). Call the University of New Mexico's Information Office at (505) 277–0111.

And if you have more time while in this area, don't miss the outstanding **National Hispanic Cultural Center** southwest of the University of New Mexico off Avenida Caesar Chavez. It is well placed because New Mexico has the highest percentage (approximately 30 percent) of residents who speak Spanish nationwide. This monumental Hispanic culture complex with its striking architecture, open plazas and patios, superb museum (fee), performing arts spaces, geneology center, library and Spanish resource center, gift shop, and restaurant is unparalleled in the United States. You could easily spend several hours here absorbing information about the roots as well the contemporary aspects of this important part of American cultural life. Information: National Hispanic Culltural Center, 1701 Fourth Street Southwest, Albuquerque, New Mexico 87102; (505) 246–2261; www.nhccnm.org.

Tours around Albuquerque

Coronado State Monument and Park by Way of Corrales, New Mexico

The monument is located just outside of Bernalillo, a small community just north of Albuquerque. To reach Coronado State Monument by way of a scenic route from Albuquerque, take the Rio Grande Boulevard exit from I–40 and follow Rio Grande Boulevard through the very nice **Los Ranchos de Albuquerque** residential district approximately 6.5 miles to Alameda Road (New Mexico Highway 528). Turn left or west onto Alameda Road, cross the bridge over the Rio Grande, and in slightly less than 1 mile, at the corner of the Las Tiendas de Corrales

Kiva mural, Coronado State Monument

Shopping Center, turn right onto Corrales Road (New Mexico Highway 448). Follow it north as it leads you into the historic, rural settlement of **Corrales.** Watch your speed. A sign once posted on the outskirts of town admonishes DRIVE SLOW AND SEE THE TOWN, DRIVE FAST AND SEE THE JUDGE. Corrales is a picturesque rural community, with its many lovely old adobes and *ranchitos* scattered along the lush Rio Grande bosque, where the fertile soil yields up an abundance of corn, chilies, grapes, and apples. For such a small community, it has an abundance of good luncheon and dinner restaurants, several wineries, and a few small, charming B&Bs (see "Staying There: Albuquerque, Lodging"). Continue onto the north side of Corrales and turn left onto Old Church Road following the signs to the old San Ysidro Church. **Iglesia de San Ysidro** was constructed in 1868. It is one of the best surviving examples of mid-nineteenth-century New Mexico religious architecture. Across the road from the church is the Albuquerque Museum's historic **Casa San Ysidro** (the Gutierrez/Ming House), an authentically restored nineteenth-century "rancho," which contains a fine collection of eighteenth-century and later New Mexican furnishings and decor. Living history demonstrations are given on Heritage Day on a weekend in early May when the house is open to the public. But one-hour tours of the house are given by reservation only, four times a day, Wednesday through Friday and once daily on Sunday from February through November (fee); (505) 898–3915. Return to Corrales Road continuing north to the junction with New Mexico Highway 528. Turn right and drive 4.5 miles to the junction with U.S. Highway 550/New Mexico Highway 44. Take a right and watch for the signed spur road—taking off to the left in less than 1 mile—to Coronado State Monument.

Although dedicated to the Spanish explorer Francisco Vásquez de Coronado, this excellent museum and the ruins around it focus mostly on the Indian culture that Coronado found at this location, rather than on the early Spanish culture that archaeologists had hoped to find at this site. Little evidence has been found to support the notion that Coronado stayed at this village called Kuaua, one of the Tigeux Pueblos. But scientists did find an astonishing number of kiva murals, painted one on top of another, that span the years between A.D. 1350 and 1600. The original murals were removed from the kiva walls and are displayed in the museum. Please note that this is one of the most outstanding exhibits of its kind in the Southwest. These murals rival the intricacy and beauty of the Hopi art found in the ruins of ancient Awat'ovi (see Section 2, "The Hopi: A Long and Continuous Past").

In addition to seeing the display inside, you can tour the ruins outside on well-marked trails around the museum. There you can descend a ladder into a reconstructed kiva where the original murals were found. You will see replicas of some of the murals that have been reproduced on the walls. Most of the partial mud walls of the ruins are twentieth-century reconstructions. They were rebuilt using Spanish-style adobe bricks rather than the original Pueblo Indian construction of mud turtlebacks or mud laid up in courses. A small gift shop sells some crafts from the pueblos and a few books related to the Pueblo culture. A picnic area and campground are nearby. Almost all of the monument lands offer good views of the Rio Grande. Open daily except major holidays. Fee; (505) 867–5351.

After leaving the monument, travel U.S. Highway 550/New Mexico Highway 44 east back across the Rio Grande. You can then return to Albuquerque by turning right or south on New Mexico Highway 313 through **Bernalillo.** This is a slower, scenic route roughly paralleling the old Camino Real. Or you can travel a little farther east to I–25, where you can either turn north to Santa Fe or return to Albuquerque. The round-trip driving distance from Albuquerque is a little less than 40 miles.

Sandia Peak and Sandia Tramway

For panoramas out over the desert, either drive to Sandia Peak or take the tramway up to the top, elevation 10,678 feet. The views up there will knock your socks off, daytime or nighttime, as 11,000 square miles of desert, mountains, and plateaus unfold before you. Some have called the **Sandia Mountains** an "afterthought" of the Rockies. *Sandia* means "watermelon" in Spanish. That place-name was given to the mountain, as well as the pueblo of the same name, by the Spanish. No one is certain why. Some say it was because of the watermelons that grew in the valley near the pueblo. A more popular notion has it that the Spanish thought the Sandia Mountains resembled a watermelon, either because of the striped appearance of the rocks along the west face or because of the pink reflection of the mountain's rocks at sunset.

To reach **Sandia Crest** by car, drive east 16 miles on U.S. I–40. Take exit 175 north on New Mexico Highway 14 through Cedar Crest. Turn left onto New Mexico Highway 536 **(Sandia Crest National Scenic Byway),** and follow the signs to the top. One-way driving time is about forty-five minutes. Alternatively you can take the **Sandia Aerial Tramway** up the west side of the mountain. That 2.7-mile, fifteen-minute-long ride is the longest tramway ride in the United States. The tram terminal can be reached by driving 5 miles north of Albuquerque on U.S. I–25 to the Tramway Boulevard exit (234), then 4.5 miles east to the station. There is a fee for parking as well as a tram fee; (505) 856–6419 or 856–7325. A restaurant and complete facilities are available on top.

Continue north on New Mexico Highway 14 for an interesting alternative route to Santa Fe. This excellent two-lane paved road, dubbed the **Turquoise Trail,** winds through the scenic high desert to the old mining towns of **Golden, Madrid,** and **Cerrillos**. Mining relics of a bygone era dot the countryside. The old mining towns are not ghost towns any longer. Some of New Mexico's finest artists

and craftspeople now inhabit these isolated towns, finding them a haven for their creative work. All along the route you will see old buildings that have been converted into shops and galleries that market the visual arts produced there.

A Three-Quarters-of-a-Day Auto Tour West of Albuquerque to Ácoma Pueblo

Sixty-five miles west of Albuquerque at a cloud-scraping elevation of 7,000 feet is the oldest and most dramatically situated Indian pueblo in New Mexico. Sometimes called the **Sky City, Ácoma Pueblo** spreads out across 70 acres of a flat mesatop, which caps a huge, malformed hunk of sandstone jutting like an island in the sky 367 feet above the surrounding desert. Blending with the tan rock from which it rises, this exposed yet almost completely camouflaged sentinel village overlooks 344,000 acres of arid Ácoma farming and grazing land where cornfields are patiently nurtured and cattle and sheep graze. It is a scene of splendid isolation and solitude that has been on hand since the village was first inhabited in the twelfth century. The Ácoma people, who speak the ancient western Keresan language, proudly assert that theirs is the **oldest continually inhabited city in the United States.** And who is to quibble, except, of course, their western pueblo neighbors at Old Oraibi village on the Hopi reservation who make a similar claim.

Atop the mesa, you know you have stepped far back into time as you walk the dusty streets, for you will see weathered kiva ladders stretching skyward, reminding you that an ancient religion is still being practiced there. And you will see one of the oldest, largest, and noblest Spanish mission churches ever to be built in the Southwest, with its two bell towers reaching to the heavens—a symbol of the first white contact in 1540 and a reminder of the bitter struggles with the Spanish that subsequently ensued. (See this section, "History.")

There are not many people who continue to live on the mesa nowadays. Ácoma's three thousand citizens began drifting away several decades ago when it became evident that parents and their children living in this mesatop village would have to be separated in order for the children to receive an education. In addition, the lack of an adequate water supply and modern energy sources there made the subzero winter temperatures and the one-hundred-degrees-and-above summer temper-atures intolerable for most of Ácoma's citizens. Over the past few decades, almost all have moved closer to the schools in the nearby well-watered modern villages of Ácomita, McCarty's, and Anzac along the Rio San José. Nonetheless they return regularly to their ancestral homes and kivas, staying on the mesa several days and even weeks at a time during certain important ceremonial occasions.

When you arrive at the base of the mesa, follow all signs and instructions with respect. You will be asked to enter the **visitor center** to purchase an entry and tour permit. You will also need a camera permit if you want to take pictures. The visitor center has several good permanent exhibits detailing Ácoma's history and culture. There is also a snack bar with sandwiches and cold drinks and a full-service restaurant open from 8:00 A.M. until 4:00 P.M., in season. The gift shop stocks a good supply of Ácoma pottery, the art form that has brought fame and fortune to some of the better Pueblo artists. Many of the artists also sell from their

Ceramic owl, Ácoma Indian Pueblo   *Pottery vessel, Ácoma Indian Pueblo*

homes, a few on the mesa but mostly elsewhere on the reservation. Look for signs in windows and yards or on fences that say POTTERY. The strong, thin-walled vessels produced at Ácoma are an attribute of the special, fine, light gray clay that is dug on the reservation.

For the mesa-top tour you will join about fifteen others in a small bus that travels the short but steep road to the top of the mesa. The half-hour- to one-hour-long guided tour by a tribal member is informative and interesting. You will see the natural cisterns on the mesa top that catch rainwater and provide the only source of water there. You will see the entrances to the square kivas that are typical of the western pueblos of Zuni, Hopi, and Ácoma. You will walk the timeless, treeless streets between the three long rows of historic two-story and terraced three-story adobe apartment dwellings. And you will soak in views, views, views! Everywhere views: east to Mesa Encantada, or the **Enchanted Mesa,** where Ácoma legend has it that the pueblo first began; north to 11,301-foot-high Mount Taylor, a mountain sacred to many southwestern Indians; and south and west as far as your eye will take you. Some of the permanent residents will invite you to look over their pottery wares, which are displayed for sale on small tables outside their apartments.

Finally, after passing by the picturesque cemetery at the mesa's edge, you will tour the interior of the large **San Esteban Rey Mission Church,** where the insulating effects of its 10-foot-thick adobe walls, constructed between 1629 and 1640, provide instant relief from the heat. You will hear about the tragic conflict with the early Spanish. You will learn how the original 40-foot-long heavy wooden beams were carried on the shoulders of Ácoma men from the Cebelleto forest near Mount Taylor, a distance of more than 30 miles. And you may begin to wonder why the Spanish decided to build such a large church in this remote, inaccessible location when you discover that each adobe brick, as well as the dirt for the church floor and cemetery, had to be laboriously carried up the sides of the steep escarpment from the desert below. In this church without pews, you will walk over the smooth, hard-packed clay floor to view ornate Spanish altarpieces, *reredos,* and the venerated *bulto* (carved statue) of Ácoma's patron saint, Saint Stephen, all of which date back as far as the seventeenth century. You will hear the remarkable story about the miracle-giving painting of Saint Joseph that was presented to the Ácoma Pueblo by the king of Spain in the seventeenth century. Stolen by Laguna Pueblo, it was later regained by Ácoma only through legal action.

Indeed, before the walking tour ends, you will enjoy these and other interesting facts and anecdotes told by your Ácoma guide atop this rocky mesa far removed from the Blarney Stone. Allow two hours for the visitor center and tour. At the conclusion of the tour, you can ride the bus back to the visitor center or return by walking down the mesa via the narrow path called the **Padre's Trail.** If you choose to walk down the steep hillside of eroded, malformed rocks, you will know why the Spanish thought that Ácoma Pueblo was an impregnable fortress.

To reach the pueblo drive west from Albuquerque on I–40 for approximately 50 miles until you reach the junction with Indian Route 23 at the Ácoma exit 108. Then travel approximately 13 miles south on Highway 23 to the visitor center. Along the way you will pass by the legendary home of the Ácoma people, Katzimo, better known today as the **Enchanted Mesa,** as it rises 400 feet from the desert floor. If you wish to shop further for crafts, return to Albuquerque by way of the modern Ácoma villages. Go back to I–40 by way of Indian Route 38 and take one of the several side roads near the interstate to **Anzac** or **McCarthy.** Look for signs in the windows of homes and for small shops or stands that advertise pottery and other crafts.

In the summer it may be best to tour Ácoma Pueblo in the cool of the early morning or in the early evening. Hours are variable, but spring and summer hours are usually from 8:30 A.M. until 6:00 P.M. Visitors are welcome on certain special festival and dance days but are not allowed on the mesa for others. It is best to check ahead of time. Closed July 10–13 and the first or second weekend in October. One of the several festivals that is open to the public is **San Esteban Feast Day,** held in early September and celebrated with a **Corn Dance** and an arts and crafts fair. Information: Pueblo of Ácoma, Tourist Visitor Center, P.O. Box 309, Pueblo of Ácoma, New Mexico 87034; (505) 469–1054 or (800) 747–0181; www.skycitytourism.com.

For side trips north of Albuquerque to Santo Domingo and Cochiti pueblos and El Rancho de las Golondrinas Spanish Museum at La Cienega, see the Santa Fe section. Information: **Albuquerque Convention and Visitors Bureau,** 20 First Plaza, Galleria Level, Albuquerque, New Mexico 87102; (505) 842–9918 or (800) 284–2282; www.itsatrip.org.

Santa Fe

Santa Fe makes an excellent base for touring northern New Mexico. It offers the traveler a harmonious blend of the old and the new. Its 7,000-foot altitude (first frost in early October, year's snowfall 32 inches), its small size (around 65,000 people), its ethnic mix (somewhat less than half Hispanic), and its tendency to attract visitors and residents who are interested in art (Sante Fe is said to be the third largest art market in the country) and music make Santa Fe a unique city. That nearly 1.5 million people vacation in the city each year attests to the fact that Santa

A casita in Santa Fe

Fe is a major attraction. But it is also a real city, a working, capital city. It has evolved into its present unique form over a period of 370 years. Santa Fe was never shut down and later rebuilt as a tourist attraction, so do not expect the fantasy-perfect world of a Williamsburg or a Sturbridge Village. Yet Santa Fe does have a large number of homes and buildings on the National Historic Register and many others that are plaqued by state and local historical societies. It preserves the past gracefully, yet it is definitely a part of the modern world.

The only major attempt to control Santa Fe's outward appearance came in 1957, when an ordinance was passed requiring all new construction in the older area, composing about one-third of the city, to be in character with Old Santa Fe architecture. Most of the newer buildings in these areas are in good taste, but some look like a developer's attempt to push the ordinance to its limits. Nonetheless the city has a warm, friendly atmosphere that I think comes in part from the rounded, earth-tone adobes that meet your eye everywhere.

The ancient El Palacio Real, or **Palace of the Governors,** sits regally on the north side of the plaza, and traffic sometimes gets snarled just a few hundred feet away from that seventeenth-century structure. Meanwhile, on any warm evening, young and old alike jam into the ice-cream parlor on the south side of the plaza, not far from the terminus of the old Camino Real, to slake their thirst and feed their appetites like modern Americans everywhere.

Lying deep in the heart of America's high desert, Santa Fe evolved from a different set of circumstances from that of the rest of America (see this section, "History"). It has retained much of its differentness because of the strong character of its people and because it still remains somewhat out of the way. Although it was the hub of commerce for wagon trains and pack mules going every which way in the 1800s, the twentieth century left it relatively isolated. There is no major airport in New Mexico's capital city, and there is not even a major passenger railroad through the city. The former Santa Fe Chief (now Amtrak) stops at Lamy, 20 miles from Santa Fe. Even the interstate highways just about missed Santa Fe until U.S.

I–25 was built, connecting Denver and Albuquerque. It skirts the periphery of Santa Fe but without question has made Santa Fe much more accessible. Santa Fe's sometimes choked arterials now get some relief provided by the Northwest Santa Fe relief route, New Mexico Highway 599, a bypass from I–25 south of town (just north of Santa Fe Downs racetrack) around Santa Fe's west side to northbound U.S. Highways 84 and 285, for those not wishing to stop in Santa Fe.

If you drive to Santa Fe from Albuquerque, you will travel on U.S. I–25. On approaching Santa Fe do not be tempted to take the first Santa Fe exits. Instead, travel a little farther on to Santa Fe exit 284 to Santa Fe's Plaza and Downtown Historic District. From I–25 exit 284, turn left onto New Mexico Highway 466 and follow it, keeping to the right, to merge with **Old Pecos Trail.** Follow Old Pecos Trail as it merges with **Old Santa Fe Trail.** This picturesque entry into old Santa Fe winds through narrow streets between time-worn adobe buildings until it reaches the Santa Fe River and the old part of the city centered on the plaza. On the way in, after you pass the junction with **Paseo de Peralta,** (the state Capitol building to the left), look to your right for a sign at 491 Old Santa Fe Trail that directs you to the **New Mexico Department of Tourism/ Santa Fe Welcome Center** (505–827–7400 or 800–545–2040), where you'll find a large parking lot, visitor center, and rest rooms. The welcome center is just several blocks from the heart of historic Santa Fe.

Resting on a high plain 20 miles east of the Rio Grande, Santa Fe is surrounded by pine-clad foothills and the towering peaks of the Sangre de Cristo Mountains. Far to the west are the Jemez Mountains. To the south are the Ortiz and Sandia mountains. Nestled next to the Santa Fe River, which cuts through the center of town, the city commands beautiful views in all directions. Approaching Santa Fe from any direction is like finding an oasis in the desert. Its tree-lined, shady, sometimes narrow, winding streets offer relief from the frequently relentless New Mexico sun. With the **Santa Fe Opera, the Santa Fe Chamber Music Festival,** and more than 250 **art galleries,** Santa Fe bills itself as a cultural mecca for this sparsely populated region of the country, a place the media have dubbed an American Salzburg. So allow enough time to see the "city different," as the chamber of commerce likes to call it. Take off your boots, put up your feet, and rest for a few days in Santa Fe. You will not be bored. In fact you will discover so much to see and do that you may find yourself soaking your feet, swollen from long days of walking and sight-seeing.

It is often said that Santa Fe is a walking city. And it is. The **Downtown Historic District, Canyon Road,** and the **Guadalupe-Sanbusco District** are excellent walking areas. But to visit the four major museums 2.5 miles south of downtown on Museum Hill (Museum Milner Plaza Complex), just off Camino Lejo, you will probably want to travel by car, a city bus, a tour bus, trolley, or a taxi cab (see Other Telephone Numbers at the end of the Staying There: Santa Fe section).

Driving in Santa Fe is a bit tricky. The street names read like an extended history of northern New Mexico. Streets that have evolved in chronological order over 320 years are no substitute for lettered or numbered streets in some kind of logical sequence. The original layout of the city in 1609, ordered by the king of Spain, must have made sense to its creator, **Governor Pedro de Peralta.** But as the city grew, new streets were added in a wandering, random fashion, without much concern for what went on before. Imposed on this hodgepodge of streets are a few obstacles such as one-way streets in unlikely locations and unexpected diagonal access routes to major arterials. **Will Rogers** reportedly once said after visiting Santa Fe, "Whoever designed this town did so while riding on a jackass backwards and drunk." The traffic is not particularly bad, except during rush hours; it is the pathfinding that can get you down. You may even want to augment the accompanying map with a more detailed version from the tourist information office summer satellite (located in the shopping arcade just across from the west side of the plaza) and mark your route before setting out. Doing this will save you a lot of headaches.

You may just want to spend the first day in Santa Fe adjusting to the dry air and altitude by resting and drinking plenty of water. If you are an early riser, you will find you may have the city to yourself, as Santa Fe seems to take its waking slow. In the early morning and late evening, the streets are practically abandoned. Those are good times to see and appreciate the beautiful lines of the old adobe buildings, without scads of cars and people to block your view. The very historic plaza is a particularly nice place to visit before the hustle-bustle of the day's activities begins (see "Revisiting the Plaza and a Day with the Pueblo Indians North of Santa Fe: A Narrative Account" later in this section). But despite the throngs of visitors crowding the sidewalks and roadways and the difficulty at times of finding a parking space, Santa Fe still feels like the relatively small city it is, and that is one of its charms.

The main old portion of the city is divided by the **Santa Fe River.** This is not a river like the Thames or the Seine. It is small, even inconspicuous during the dry summer as it trickles through the city. But you know it is there because of its very visible, moisture-laden banks, which are verdant with shade trees and other vegetation. Sidewalks, walking paths, and picnic tables abound in the plentiful shade. It is no wonder that the Spanish dubbed this greenbelt the *Alameda,* the Spanish word for "a park with a grove of trees," and carried the name over to the street that parallels the river where teenagers in souped-up "lowriders" often drag on weekend evenings. One half-day walking tour can include the sights north of the river, and in another half day you can cover the sights south of the river.

Half-Day Tour of Santa Fe, North of the River

The best place to start a walking tour of Santa Fe is **the plaza,** north of the river. The amount of history the plaza has seen is enough to fill at least one good-size history text. Some of the most famous events that occurred there are marked by monuments. Walk over to the **obelisk**. It commemorates some of the turbulent history of the 1800s. The plaque tells about the difficult times faced by white settlers in northern New Mexico because of marauding Apache and Comanche Indians. And it tells about the Confederate occupation of Santa Fe. Later in the nineteenth century, Billy the Kid was allegedly kept in chains in the plaza until he could be removed to a sturdy jail. Prior to these events and under Mexican rule, the plaza contained a bullring.

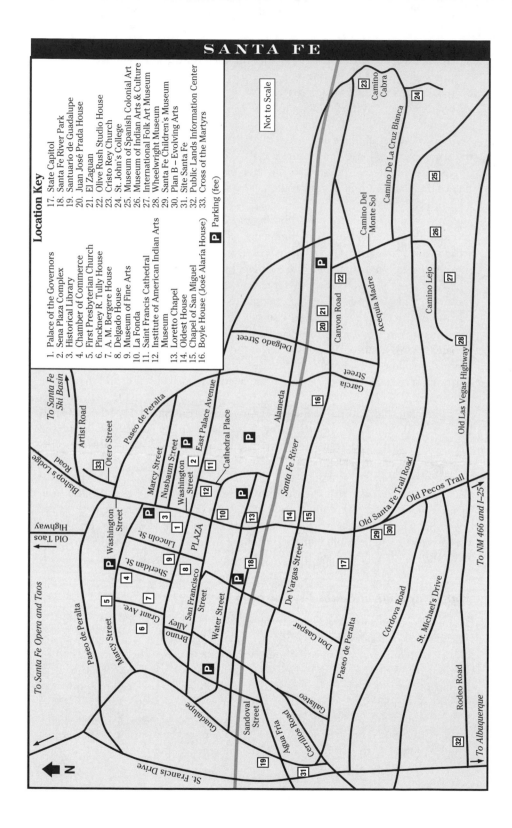

SANTA FE

Location Key

1. Palace of the Governors
2. Sena Plaza Complex
3. Historical Library
4. Chamber of Commerce
5. First Presbyterian Church
6. Pinckney R. Tully House
7. A. M. Bergere House
8. Delgado House
9. Museum of Fine Arts
10. La Fonda
11. Saint Francis Cathedral
12. Institute of American Indian Arts Museum
13. Loretto Chapel
14. Oldest House
15. Chapel of San Miguel
16. Boyle House (José Alaría House)
17. State Capitol
18. Santa Fe River Park
19. Santuario de Guadalupe
20. Juan José Prada House
21. El Zaguan
22. Olive Rush Studio House
23. Cristo Rey Church
24. St. John's College
25. Museum of Spanish Colonial Art
26. Museum of Indian Arts & Culture
27. International Folk Art Museum
28. Wheelwright Museum
29. Santa Fe Children's Museum
30. Plan B – Evolving Arts
31. Site Santa Fe
32. Public Lands Information Center
33. Cross of the Martyrs

P Parking (fee)

Not to Scale

To Santa Fe Ski Basin

To Santa Fe Opera and Taos

Old Taos Highway

To NM 466 and I-25

To Albuquerque

N

At the southeast corner of the plaza, diagonally across from La Fonda Hotel, is a **plaque** on a rock commemorating an even older historical landmark. It is a reminder that the 800-mile-long **Santa Fe Trail,** starting first in Franklin and then later in Independence, Missouri, ended right there after six arduous weeks of travel across the plains. All goods coming in from the United States had to be taxed and cleared at the customs building, formerly on the east side of the plaza.

Although the plaza has shrunk over the years, it is still the pulsating heart of the city, a place where fiestas and fairs are held annually. But to visualize the plaza as it was in Spanish times requires some imagination. Then it was longer and extended without obstacles to the *parroquia,* or parish church, on the site of today's **Saint Francis Cathedral.** The church, the Palace of the Governors, and the houses around the plaza were enclosed by a thick adobe wall. For all intents and purposes, Santa Fe was a seventeenth-century European walled city.

But probably the main reason to visit the plaza is to lay your eyes on the oldest continually occupied public building in the United States, the **Palace of the Governors.** It covers the entire north side of the plaza. Up and down its long *portico,* or porch, Pueblo Indian artisans, some in traditional garb and some in contemporary dress, display and sell their goods. After browsing along the portico, go inside the Palace of the Governors, for it contains an excellent **regional historical museum** (fee); (505) 476–5100; www.palaceofthegovernors.org. There you will see some of the most interesting historical artifacts in America and gain an appreciation for much that you will see later as you explore more of New Mexico. A considerable amount of New Mexico's eventful history took place within these walls, which were constructed about 1610. In addition, the museum maintains a superb shop, where some of the finest Southwest American Indian and Spanish crafts can be purchased. This shop offers an excellent supply of regional books and magazines, ranging from cookbooks to monographs by local artists and writers. Note the sturdy construction of this building, which was originally known as the Casa Real. Inside walk around the grassy courtyard or plaza and note how the thick adobe walls create a quiet haven from the noise outside.

After touring the Palace of the Governors, return to the street that fronts it, Palace Avenue, and turn left. Cross Washington Avenue, and in a short distance you will enter a *portal,* or long porch, fronting numerous small stores trimmed in white. This is the Arias de Quiros site. De Quiros, from Asturias, Spain, was given this site by General de Vargas, the reconquistador, for his services in helping regain New Mexico from the Indians in 1693. The original structure probably deteriorated. Many of the early adobes have simply "melted" through the years. Adobe brick walls will succumb to moisture over time, eroding much the way sandstone does. This is especially true of the early adobes. Those sun-dried adobe brick walls were not capped by the harder, more resilient surfaces commonly used today, so the water from torrential thunderstorms easily could get a foothold in the soft brick. In addition, many of the earlier adobes were not plastered on the outside, thus opening the full length of the walls to weathering from rain and freezing conditions.

The structures you see on this site were probably built in the nineteenth century, although it is thought that part of one of the structures may date back to the eighteenth century. The most famous unit is 109 East Palace, which served as the

Sena Plaza Building, Santa Fe

first office for the Manhattan (atom bomb) Project in 1943. The citizens of Santa Fe were kept in the dark about this project until several years after the clandestine office was set up. The small plaza just west of the 109 address is Trujillo Plaza. The 113½ East Palace location is well known for another reason. Its *zaguan,* or covered entry, leads into a small courtyard, Prince Plaza, and a popular lunchtime restaurant.

At 125–127 East Palace Avenue, the doors are trimmed in blue. This is the Sena Building. Turn into the courtyard where the sign above the door says SENA PLAZA. You will now find yourself in the secluded, flower-filled patio that once belonged to José Desiderio Sena. He lived at this location with his family, which included eleven children. His grand Spanish colonial home with its interior placita, or plaza, was built in the mid-1800s. It is a classic example of the "Mexican Surprise." For even today in Spanish colonial Old Mexico, doorways along dusty busy streets like Palace Avenue, flanked by cracked and peeling plaster walls, open into the most exquisite and lush interior plazas imaginable. Many homes in Santa Fe are arranged in a similar way to give relief from the commotion outside the walls. The **Sena Plaza garden** is in constant bloom most of the summer, but it is especially beautiful in May when the redbud trees and lilacs are in bloom. It is one of Santa Fe's best sights. Shops and small businesses line the courtyard, and located on the backside of the garden is one of Santa Fe's most atmospheric restaurants.

Return toward the plaza. Cross Washington Avenue and turn right or north. You will immediately notice the entrance to the **Palace of the Governors' Museum Shop,** and at110 Washington is the Museum of New Mexico's Research Library. There are many local historical artifacts on display in this research library, which is open to the public. Across the street is the public library. Continue walking along Washington Avenue until it intersects tree-lined Marcy Street. (For great views overlooking Santa Fe and environs, follow Washington Avenue north past Marcy Street and alongside the historic stone block federal building to Paseo del Peralta. Cross to the east side of Washington Avenue and then to the north side of Paseo del Peralta. Walk east along Peralta past Otero Street to the stairway signed the CROSS OF THE MARTYRS ascending to the left. There are also interesting historical plaques at this prime viewing location. Follow the steps

Detail of painting false bricks at Tully House

Pinckney R. Tully House, Santa Fe

from the cross farther up to Fort Marcy Park for even broader vistas.) Turn left or west onto Marcy. In this block are several luncheon cafes, as well as apparel and gift shops. As you continue west along Marcy, you will notice a small shop—set back a short distance from the southeastern corner of Lincoln and Marcy—handling regional and Mexican folk art pieces. The owner's fine sense of the Santa Fe style provides unique and interesting window displays. Continue on Marcy to Sheridan, where you will notice across the street the **Sweeney Convention Center.** Located inside is the **Santa Fe Convention and Visitors Bureau,** which, along with the chamber of commerce across town at 510 North Guadalupe, offers up-to-date, useful information to travelers and would-be residents. Continue walking west on Marcy to Grant Street. Cross Grant to the attractive, large adobe structure on the corner, the **First Presbyterian Church,** designed by well-known Santa Fe restoration architect John Gaw Meem (see "History," first Protestant church site).

Now walk south, cross Griffin Street, and turn left. Almost immediately to your right, you will see a red brick structure with white trim. This is the **Pinckney R. Tully House** at 136 Grant Avenue. Built in 1851 by one of Santa Fe's prosperous traders, it is a fine example of territorial-style architecture. Note that the brickwork is fake. The outline of rectangles, simulating the shape of brick, has been applied with white paint over red plaster, giving the appearance of a brick surface. Over the years there have been no major structural changes affecting the appearance of this building, a rarity in Santa Fe. The house, used for business purposes, is open to the public during business hours. For more information on this or other historic homes, call the **Historic Santa Fe Foundation** at (505) 983–2567.

Across the street at 135 Grant Avenue is the **A. M. Bergere House.** This house was built in the 1870s as officers' quarters for the Fort Marcy reservation located on that site. The apricot and other fruit trees planted by the home's Italian immigrant owner in the early 1900s still blossom and fruit each year (not open to the public). And notice at 122 Grant Avenue the Grant Corner Inn on your right. Housed in a historic older home built in the early 1900s, this inn is typical of the numerous charming B&Bs in Santa Fe.

Continue on down Grant Avenue and turn onto Johnson Street. At 217 Johnson Street is the **Georgia O'Keeffe Museum** (505) 995–0785; www.okeeffe museum.org. Plan to spend some time in this bright, airy museum with its welcoming sculpture courtyard. An excellent collection of works by the region's most celebrated artist are on display here. Oil paintings, watercolors, works on paper, and sculpture reveal the talent of this revered artist whose works can be found in the National Gallery of Art in Washington, D.C., the Museum of Modern Art in New York, the Georges Pompidou Center in Paris, and the Museum of Modern Art in Tokyo. Return to Grant Avenue, turning right past the courthouse to Palace Avenue.

Across the street on the northeast corner of Grant and Palace Avenues is the Palace Court Building with its specialty retail stores and restaurants. Cross Palace. Immediately facing you is **Burro Alley** on the west side of the Palace Restaurant property. Walk down the alley and see the large mural high up on the wall to the right depicting the alley's historical use. This narrow street, connecting Palace Avenue and San Francisco Street was for many years a donkey parking lot. Firewood was brought from the mountains by being piled high on the backs of burros that plodded down Canyon Road and then finally came to rest at this point while their owners hawked firewood in town.

To catch a glimpse of Santa Fe's pride and joy—the exotic 1930s art deco, restored, and renovated Lensic Performing Arts Center—walk down Burro Road and turn the corner to 211 West San Francisco Street. Otherwise continue walking east on Palace Avenue past the Palace Restaurant building until you come to a doorway sign marked 130–136 PALACE. Enter and take the corridor past interesting shops, studios, and a patio and cafe to reach San Francisco Street or retrace your steps to Palace Avenue. Continuing east up Palace toward the plaza will bring

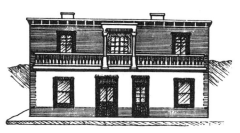

Delgado House, Santa Fe

you to the lovely old **Delgado House,** built of adobe in the 1890s and later modified to fit the trends of the time, including the interesting Victorian additions on the second level. Its original owner was also a prosperous trader, because Santa Fe was a hub of commerce during much of the nineteenth century. Before the house was built, the site was used by traders to store their wagons, as it was near the end of the Santa Fe Trail. This home has been converted to business use.

St. Francis Cathedral, Santa Fe

Now cross Palace Avenue to the large adobe building in the direction of the plaza. This is the **Museum of Fine Arts** (505–476–5072; www.museumofnew mexico.org), part of the Museum of New Mexico's network. This lovely adobe was built in 1917 on ground that was previously occupied by part of the first United States fort in the area, Fort Marcy. This museum, constructed in Pueblo Mission or Spanish Pueblo style, sparked a rebirth of that type of native architecture, thus leading to the construction of many more buildings in that mode. The Museum of Fine Arts houses a permanent collection of paintings, photographs, and statues. In addition, it has a rotating display of contemporary artwork. The museum's St. Francis Auditorium, built to resemble the interior of a Spanish church, is often host to such prestigious music events as the Santa Fe Chamber Music Festival. There is an excellent fine arts bookstore on the first floor. And, of course, the museum's permanent art collections, as well as the special exhibits and traveling shows often displayed there, are well worth a visit. Leaving the Museum of Fine Arts, continue east on Palace Avenue to the west side of the Palace of the Governors.

Now cross Palace Avenue to the plaza. Walk across the plaza at a diagonal to its southeast side. There fight your way through the crowds (this is probably the most crowded corner in Santa Fe) to **La Fonda,** the large, multistoried adobe building, across the street. Built in 1920 on the site of several previous *fondas,* or inns, it is an imposing sight. Its public rooms are well worth a visit, even if you are not staying there. Its spacious, cool, shop-lined lobby and covered court offer welcome relief on a warm day. Paintings by some of Santa Fe's historic artists hang from the lobby's walls.

From La Fonda, cross San Francisco Street and walk to the right up to the **St. Francis Cathedral.** Both the cathedral and the street honor Santa Fe's venerable patron saint, Saint Francis. You cannot miss the cathedral, with its stubby European Romanesque double towers that, because of lack of funds and other complexities,

Detail of keystone in St. Francis Cathedral

were never finished off with the proposed 160-foot-tall steeples. On Sunday and on special occasions, the bells from the cathedral ring out for all Santa Fe to hear. The construction of today's church was started in 1869, more than twenty years after the American occupation. The site had been the location of several previous churches, or *parroquias*. During the twenty years it took to construct the building, services in the old church continued without interruption as the new building was built around it.

The old building was finally taken down section by section as the new building was being completed. Many of its adobe bricks were used in constructing the north walls of the new church. One small chapel of the early church, dating to 1714, remains intact. There you may see America's oldest Christian religious statue, the famous figure carved from willow wood, *La Conquistadora* (see "History"), which is also known as Nuestra Señora de la Paz, or Our Lady of Peace. Every year the statue is carefully lifted from its age-old resting place in St. Francis Cathedral and taken to the Rosario Cemetery, northwest of the city, to commemorate the difficult winter of 1692, resulting in the final reconquest of New Mexico. The paintings surrounding the statue are part of a *reredos* or a Spanish mural. Two of the early priests are buried in the wall of the chapel. This beautiful cathedral is definitely worth seeing, especially its nineteenth-century stained-glass windows from Clermont-Ferrand, France. Of interest too is the Hebrew religious symbol on the keystone over the main entrance to the cathedral. The symbol was allegedly placed there in appreciation of Santa Fe's Jewish citizens who contributed funds to help build this edifice. Archbishop Lamy, made famous in Willa Cather's novel *Death Comes for the Archbishop*, is buried in the crypt behind the altar (see "History"). Adjacent to the cathedral in a detached building is the Archdiocese of Santa Fe Museum. Now for a change of pace, cross the street to 108 Cathedral Place, home to the **Institute of American Indian Arts Museum** (505–983–8900; www. iaiancad.org), where the National Collection of Contemporary American Indian Art (Indian art through Indian eyes) and the outdoor Allan Houser Art Park are featured.

At this point you may be fully saturated after seeing the sights. If so, it is time either for lunch at one of the many good restaurants north of the river or for a siesta. Another pleasant alternative is to have a picnic lunch at the shady **Santa Fe River Park** just 2 blocks south of the plaza. (See the Santa Fe "Food" section for restaurant-delis that have fixings for picnics.)

Half-Day Tour of Santa Fe, South of the River

For another half-day of walking in the plaza area, go to the southeast corner of the plaza, cross the street, and walk down **Old Santa Fe Trail** alongside La Fonda.

Loretto Chapel, Santa Fe

Cross East Water Street and you will be facing the **Loretto Chapel,** or "The Chapel of Our Lady of Light," at 219 Old Santa Fe Trail. This lovely little chapel was just about squeezed out of existence when the Sisters of Loretto sold most of the grounds for the construction of the Hotel Loretto. Another of Bishop Lamy's enterprises, the chapel was modeled after the Sainte-Chapelle in Paris, France.

One story has it that the French architect for the chapel became enamored with the wife of Bishop Lamy's nephew. The nephew discovered the tryst and did the architect in, so plans for the chapel were never completed. One of the essential features that did not make it onto the design boards was a stairway from the chapel floor to the choir loft. By all indications there was not enough room for a conventional stairway. So the Sisters of Loretto prayed for a solution. In answer to their prayers, so the legend goes, a carpenter (whom the nuns believed to be St. Joseph) appeared one day. In no time he constructed from wood a 23-foot-high spiral staircase that made two complete turns and had thirty-three steps, using only wooden pegs to secure it. He then disappeared as mysteriously as he had come. Local historians now believe that the "miraculous staircase" was built by a master French woodworker named Francois-Jean "Frenchy" Rochas, a reclusive rancher who lived in a remote New Mexican canyon. A small entry fee is charged.

Now continue your walk south past the handsome Hotel Loretto and cross East Alameda and the **Santa Fe River Bridge.** The river is often dry in the summer, pointing up the fact that water is a scarce commodity in this part of the high desert. As you cross the river, note the sidewalk paralleling it. The **"river walk"** is a pleasant excursion you may want to take advantage of some evening. It is also a good jogging trail.

Continue south on **Old Santa Fe Trail.** Underneath the pavement lies the dusty Santa Fe Trail as it came winding down the hill toward the plaza and the inn at the end of the trail, 800 miles from the starting point in Missouri. Next you will come to De Vargas Street. Turn left to view what is purported to be the **oldest house in the United States** (for hours call 505–983–3974 or inquire at San Miguel Mission). It most certainly could win honors as being the **oldest house**

"Oldest house," Santa Fe

in Santa Fe, but it has not been officially recognized as the oldest house in the United States. A Spanish house was built around an earlier Indian dwelling on this site that dates back more than 800 years.

But this is not the oldest Indian house in the United States either. Pueblo houses at Ácoma Pueblo and at Old Oraibi in Hopiland are older. The Spanish portion is thought by some to have been added before 1628. Yet tree ring specimens taken from the oldest Spanish section date back only to 1740–67. So it is not the oldest European-built house still standing in America, since one house in St. Augustine, Florida, has been reliably dated to 1727 and may date back to the late sixteenth century. When I visited this house at age ten, I was greatly impressed, and it somehow altered my sense of historical perspective.

Regardless of all the hokiness and unsubstantiated claims, this is truly one of the oldest buildings in the United States and should not be missed. Its value is to reveal how circumstances and environment reduced the Spanish to living much like the Indians. Any notion that the very early Spanish lived in great haciendas will be quickly and realistically dispelled by your visit to this house. Survival took precedence over aesthetics in those days, and the Spaniards lived no more regally than did the American pioneers on the prairie in their dark sod houses. Some of the walls of the oldest house were made by the Indians of puddled adobe and taper toward the ceiling. Other walls were made during the Spanish period of adobe brick. The Spaniards also added entryways to this Indian house from the side rather than from the roof and contributed a fireplace with a chimney, rather than fire pits whose only outlet for the smoke was the entry hole in the roof. Of course, the Spanish added furniture made out of wood and utensils out of metal, but these improvements did not alter the fact that the early Spanish, like the Indians, lived in dark spaces behind mud walls.

Leave the oldest house and cross De Vargas Street to the south. There on the corner is the old **San Miguel Mission** church. The Christian Brothers who own it claim that it is the oldest church in the United States. Again, this claim has not been made official by any certifying historical society. The original chapel was

San Miguel Mission church, Santa Fe

built before 1626, perhaps as early as 1610 to 1615, as a house of worship for the Tlaxcalan Indians whom the Spanish brought with them from Mexico. That first church was destroyed in the Pueblo Rebellion of 1680 and was not reconstructed until 1710. It was completely rebuilt then, using a different foundation. But the new chapel was built over the remains of the old seventeenth-century chapel. Those remains can be viewed through peepholes in front of the altar.

It is on the basis of these remains, which have been dated back to the early 1600s, that the claims of being the oldest church have been made. But many would claim that the oldest of the Spanish churches still standing in the United States are the mission churches located at Ácoma and Isleta Pueblos. These churches were also built in the early 1600s, and although parts of them have been rebuilt from time to time, they are essentially still standing as they were then. So here again the controversy of what is the "oldest" in the United States rages on. The issue may never be settled. But just for the record, the oldest Christian church is one of these three; one of the oldest most continually inhabited villages is Ácoma; and the oldest public buildings still in use in America reside in New Mexico, whereas the oldest wooden school building and the oldest masonry fort still standing in the United States are in our oldest city, St. Augustine, Florida.

Whether San Miguel's is the oldest church or not is a moot point. Be sure to visit it, for inside are some precious religious art objects. Upon entering the chapel, your eye will be drawn immediately to the painted, wooden altarpiece or altar screen that the Spanish call a *reredos*. This one was constructed in 1798 and is the oldest dated wooden altarpiece remaining in New Mexico. Note particularly the *salomónicas,* or spiraled columns, a design used frequently in both Spain and New Spain. Also note how a beautifully designed, elegant screen like this enhances the stark plainness of the white plastered walls of an adobe church.

Altar screen, San Miguel Chapel

Also note the largest of the several paintings of Saint Michael. It was executed by Captain Bernardo Miera y Pacheco, who served the Spanish as mapmaker for the region in the eighteenth century. Some of his maps of New Spain, which became famous over time, are now in the British Museum in London. Of interest too are the religious paintings on deerskin and buffalo hide that the early Franciscan priests used in teaching the Indians about Christianity. Another highlight is the gilded statue of Saint Michael. This statue was taken around the countryside in 1709 to aid in solicitation of funds for rebuilding the church. The old bell in the gift shop is alleged both to be from Spain and to date back to 1356. But more objective data would suggest that the bell was cast in 1856 in New Mexico. Both the oldest house and the San Miguel Mission Church were in a part of Santa Fe known as **Barrio de Analco.** *Analco* is a term derived from an Indian word meaning "the other side of the water." That was where the Tlaxcalan Indian slaves who had been brought up from Mexico by the Spanish lived. Note the old building south of San Miguel Mission, built in 1878 by the Christian Brothers. It is the former home of Santa Fe College and served as a dormitory for St. Michael's School. It now houses state offices.

Continue 1 more block south on Old Santa Fe Trail to the unusual territorial-style **New Mexico State Capitol,** whose shape was inspired by the Zia Pueblo Indian sun symbol. You may want to visit several of the public rooms or the art gallery there. Or from San Miguel Mission, you can walk east on De Vargas Street past several interesting old adobe homes, including the historic Boyle House, a late-eighteenth-century home with adobe walls 4 feet thick. Boyle, one of its later owners, was a New Mexican agent for an English land speculator in the late 1800s. Continue walking east to the intersection of De Vargas and Paseo de Peralta, where you will be in easy reach of Canyon Road as it intersects Paseo de Peralta just 1 block to the north.

Still another interesting alternative from San Miguel Mission is to retrace your steps back across the Santa Fe River and turn to the left or west onto East Alameda, taking the tree-lined river walk on the sidewalk paralleling the river. Follow the river west, past numerous picnic sites. Soon you will see, approximately 4 blocks to the west, directly in front of you, the **Santuario de Nuestra Señora de Guadalupe** (popularly known as the Santuario de Guadalupe), on the corner of Guadalupe and Agua Fria Streets on the west side of Guadalupe. The *santuario,* with its simple lines and beautiful grounds, is one of the most attractive churches in New Mexico. Its light, uncluttered interior allows you to focus on some of the building's more interesting features.

Note the choir loft, where you will see some handsome carved *vigas,* or ceiling beams, and their supporting vertical *corbels,* or posts. Perhaps it is the removal

Santuario de Guadalupe, Santa Fe

of the pews from the chapel that has given the interior a sense of spaciousness that enhances its simple elegance. The chapel, built around 1765 alongside New Mexico's historic lifeline, El Camino Real, was dedicated to the Virgin of Guadalupe, a venerated figure in the section of New Spain that would become Mexico. The chapel is now used as a museum and performance hall. Arts and crafts exhibits relating to New Mexico's Spanish tradition are the primary focus. In addition, the chapel contains some very old religious objects taken from the military chapel on the plaza, La Castrense, after it was dismantled in the 1800s. Notice the deep red altar wall. The color comes from mixing ox blood with plaster. Closed Sunday; (505) 988–2027.

From the Santuario you may want to continue south on **South Guadalupe** Street to explore the **Guadalupe Sanbusco** and the **Guadalupe/Railyard Districts.** This five- to six-block-long stretch of small shops, cafes, restaurants, galleries, and specialty stores rivals Canyon Road in popularity. Before going too much farther, you may want to catch your breath at one of the small cafes along the way. Refreshed, continue down South Guadalupe to Montezuma Avenue, where you will want to explore (west on Montezuma) the upscale shopping and dining along the route to and inside of the **Sanbusco Market Center** at 500 Montezuma Avenue. Walking several blocks west along Montezuma and then south on Sandoval, you will find yet another collection of shops and restaurants, the **Design Centre of Santa Fe.**

Continuing south on Montezuma, take time to visit the shops and galleries lining the intersecting streets of Garfield and Read, known as the Guadalupe Railyard District. Keep your eyes open for interesting large-scale murals painted on the sides of buildings. And especially on the route south from Montezuma you will see many of the buildings that served the terminus of Santa Fe's historic Chili Line Railway. Most of these buildings have been renovated and now serve as shops, galleries, and restaurants. But the old railyard alone is worth a visit, with its collection of vintage railway cars and an active passenger station serving the **Santa Fe Southern Railway's excursion train** that takes visitors 20 miles from Santa Fe to Lamy, a stop on the Amtrak route between Los Angeles and Chicago.

If you are in Santa Fe from late April through October, you may want to visit the **Railyard District** on a Tuesday or Saturday morning to attend the busy **Santa Fe Area Farmers' Market** (505–983–4098) in the parking lot behind the Santa Fe Railroad Depot. The winter farmers' market is held nearby at the **El Museo de Cultural de Santa Fe** at 1615-B Paseo de Peralta (505–922–0591), which is devoted to the Hispano Culture of Northern New Mexico.

A Three-Quarters-of-a-Day Auto Tour of Southeastern Santa Fe

If you are hardy and young, without children, and are looking for a challenging high-altitude walk, you might want to leave your car downtown and walk this one. But if you are the average traveler, swallow your pride and hop into the American version of the Spanish horse and drive east on Alameda to the Paseo de Peralta. Turn right onto Peralta, where you'll cross the Santa Fe River. Then turn off Peralta to the left or east at the sign designating **Canyon Road.** Canyon Road is a paved-over version of an ancient Indian trail that went from the Pueblo villages near today's Santa Fe to Pecos Pueblo to the east. In the early days of Santa Fe, this route to and from the Sangre de Cristo Mountains was the entry point for wood vendors, who brought their products heaped high on the backs of sturdy burros. There is still a dusty, rural feeling to this street, but it has mostly become a shopping street with numerous high-end galleries. Many artists have their studios on or around Canyon Road. Canyon Road is a one-way street for approximately 4 or 5 blocks up to Camino del Monte Sol. Try to find a parking place in the shade, if possible, as close to Peralta or Garcia as you can, then walk up Canyon Road. If parking is tight at the entrance to Canyon Road, drive up to the parking lot (fee) just beyond Camino del Monte Sol and do the following tour in reverse. This venture can take several hours. Hardened, veteran shoppers might even spend a half-day there.

You will find Canyon Road an interesting if not exhausting experience. There are many galleries and shops to see and numerous little back alleys and *placitas* to explore. You will have to sort the wheat from the chaff, as some curio-type stores are also part of the scene. (For some of the galleries and shops of particular note in this area, see the shopping section under Santa Fe in "Staying There.") While shopping on Canyon Road, you may wish to note several of Santa Fe's historic homes. On the left at 519 is the **Juan José Prada House,** a private residence built perhaps as early as 1768. At 545 is **El Zaguan.** These private apartments are in the original residence, which was built before 1849. One of the units houses the **Historic Santa Fe Foundation** (505–983–2567). This helpful organization has a wealth of important information about historic Santa Fe and can answer many of the questions you might have. The Victorian flower garden to the west side, contains several large, old horse chestnut trees and is open to the public for viewing. Farther down the road on the right is the **Olive Rush Studio Home** at 630 Canyon Road. Olive Rush, a Quaker artist, purchased this nineteenth-century adobe home in the early 1900s. It is now a meetinghouse for the Santa Fe Religious Society of Friends. At 724 Canyon Road is the **Borrego House.** Parts of the house date to 1753, while the more modern sections were built in the late

1800s. A popular restaurant is there now.

After you are shopped out, your pocketbook is flat, and your eyes are bulging from fatigue, return to your car and drive east on Canyon Road, retracing the route you have just walked. At the T intersection, make a right turn on Camino Cabra, leading to Upper Canyon Road. To your right note the **Church of Cristo Rey.** This is the largest adobe church in America, containing nearly 200,000 adobe bricks. Even though this church was not constructed until 1939–41, the old Spanish

Stone reredos, *Cristo Rey Church, Santa Fe*

custom of making adobe bricks by hand from the dirt at the building site was followed. The church was built to commemorate the four hundredth anniversary of Coronado's expedition to the Southwest. The walls vary from 2 to 7 feet in thickness to guarantee that this building will be intact on the eight hundredth anniversary! Inside the church is one of the most famous pieces of church art in New Mexico, a carved, stone altar screen or *reredos* that was executed by craftsmen from Mexico in 1760. Cut from local stone, this rendering is thought to have been the model for many of the altar screens produced later by native New Mexican *santeros.*

From the Cristo Rey Church, travel to the end of Upper Canyon Road to the **Randall Davey Audubon Center.** The distance is less than 2 miles, and all but the last 0.5 mile is paved. Be certain to bear right when you come to the Y in the road, and continue on to the parking lot adjacent to the visitor center. A few steps away amid grassy lawns, large cottonwoods, aspen and pine forests, and beautiful vistas, you will find the Randall Davey home. The home rests on 6 developed acres of grassy lawns, orchards, and gardens, amid 135 acres of undeveloped meadow and forest land, now a wildlife sanctuary owned by the National Audubon Society. Trails branch out in several directions, taking you into the heart of this peaceful place. Once there it seems incredible that you are only a few miles from the busy, congested downtown area. One hundred species of birds call this oasis their home during various times of the year, and they don't seem to mind sharing it with the 120 plant and wildflower species that grow so abundantly there. Migrating osprey, blue heron, and egrets may be seen, along with brown creepers, yellow-bellied sapsuckers, and lazuli buntings. Bears periodically pay visits to the old orchards on the property, and raccoons and coyotes are sometimes spotted at night, along with an occasional mountain lion or bobcat that has found its way into this pocket of civilization on the border of the **Santa Fe National Forest.** The old adobe home, formerly a sawmill built in 1847, was refurbished and occupied by its internationally known artist and bon vivant owner Randall Davey from the early 1920s until his death in 1964. The National Audubon Society received the historic property in 1983 and now uses it as a wildlife refuge and educational center. The property is open daily for exploring the nature trail, El Temporal (a comprehensive self-guiding trail booklet is available at the visitor center), which meanders uphill into forest and down dale into meadows and across the Acequia del Llano. The tastefully decorated home, with its New Mexican and European accents and its flamboyant wall murals painted by Davey, can be toured (fee) one afternoon a week (call ahead) from Memorial Day to Labor Day. Lecture programs and workshops for adults are sometimes held on Saturdays. Do take time to see the orientation exhibits in the **visitor center;** (505) 983–4609.

Return to the Cristo Rey Church and retrace your route back down the two-way stretch of Canyon Road to Camino del Monte Sol. Turn left onto Camino del Monte Sol and drive south for several miles. Many of Santa Fe's picturesque adobe residential sections are in this area on little dirt roads along the **Acequia Madre** or in the foothills. At the junction with Camino Cruz Blanca, note the building to the left on the north side of the road. This is the **Santa Fe Preparatory Academy.** Farther up the same road on the south side is the stringently academic **St. John's College,** a twin to the college of the same name in Annapolis, Maryland. Soon Monte del Sol intersects with Old Santa Fe Trail Road. Turn right onto that road and travel for a short distance to Camino Lejo Street and the sign directing you to the Camino Lejo **Museum–Milner Plaza Complex,** which includes the Museum of Indian Arts and Culture/Laboratory of Anthropology (505–476–1250; www.nmculture.org), the Museum of International Folk Art (505–476–1200; www.moita.org) next door the Wheelwright Museum of American Indian (505–982–4636; www.wheelwright.org) and the Museum of Spanish Colonial Art (505–982–2226; www.spanishcolonial.org). The Museum of New Mexico's **Museum–Milner Plaza** with the convenient **Museum Hill Cafe** offers broad vistas of the foothills and mountains.

Before reaching Museum Plaza you will see signs to the Spanish Colonial Arts Society's **Museum of Spanish Colonial Art,** where there is an extensive collection of historic and contemporary art from Spain, Latin America, and New Mexico in a handsome 1930s John Gaw Meem Spanish pueblo-revival structure.

Occupying one end of Museum Milner Plaza is the **Museum of Indian Arts and Culture.** It is an offshoot of the Laboratory of Anthropology, whose spectacular collection of thousands of Southwest Indian artifacts has never had a proper showroom. Now it is possible for many of those artifacts to be displayed in the permanent exhibit "Here, Now and Always" in the spacious 40,000-square-foot passive solar building, with its permanent exhibits wing located to the left as you drive up Camino Lejo. In addition to many rarely seen artifacts and an outstanding Pueblo pottery collection, the museum focuses on the Indian people of the Southwest, with interesting displays that poignantly tell the story of individuals, pueblos, and tribes as they were in the past and as they are today. These exhibits also focus on the beautiful art and many crafts that are such an important part of Indian cultural life. The museum devotes space to craft exhibits and demonstrations. The museum's shop features authentic Indian crafts, books, and gift items. Next door the renowned Laboratory of Anthropology continues to offer the services of its outstanding research library to scholars and others wanting to know more about the history and culture of the Southwest Indian people. The laboratory is part of the Museum of New Mexico and was given to the state by John D. Rockefeller Jr., in 1949. At the other end of the plaza is another branch of the

New Mexico Museum system, the **International Folk Art Museum,** which contains the Alexander Girard and the Neutrogena collections of folk art. This is without doubt the largest museum dedicated exclusively to the folk art of the world. It is appropriate that northern New Mexico, with its intense concentration of folk artists, should host such a fine museum. Of course, the museum's collection of local Spanish colonial craftwork is superb. If folk art and folk costumes interest you, do not miss this museum. A small shop in the lobby is the source of folk art crafted by local Spanish carvers and other artisans.

The twenty-four-hour number for recorded information on this museum and all of the other Museum of New Mexico's museums in Santa Fe is (505) 827–6463; www.museumofnewmexico.org.

Farther along Camino Lejo is the **Wheelwright Museum of the American Indian** (505–982–4636), a private museum. It was formerly known as the Museum of Navajo Ceremonial Art, even though there are no Navajo towns in the Rio Grande Valley. For a long time this was the only museum in the Southwest dedicated to preserving the best of that Four Corners culture. The Navajo tribe is preserving its heritage on its own reservation now (see Section 2, "Back to Navajoland: Keams Canyon to Ganado via Hubbell Trading Post and on to Window Rock . . ."), so the Wheelwright Museum has expanded its interest to all southwestern Indians. The exhibits at the Wheelwright are of the highest quality and are nicely displayed in a large building shaped like a Navajo hogan. In the basement of this unique building is the **Case Trading Post,** done up in Navajo-trading-post style. Specializing in quality Indian crafts, it serves as the shop for the gallery upstairs.

Now drive back down the hill to the Old Santa Fe Trail Road. Turn left onto that road, and follow it approximately 2 miles back to the plaza in downtown Santa Fe. If you just want to take a trip to the museums and not visit Canyon Road, get on the Old Santa Fe Trail Road downtown and follow it all the way to the museums, being certain to take the left fork at the signed intersection with Old Pecos Trail.

Tours around Santa Fe

Revisiting the Plaza and a Day with the Pueblo Indians North of Santa Fe: A Narrative Account

The sun is already bright this morning. It is comfortable in the sun, but in the shade it is still cool. I am up early; the rest of the family is still sleeping. (We were up late last evening, not returning to our room until after midnight.) I walk out of the inn and stroll south to the plaza. I have walked this tree-lined street many times over the years. Particularly I remember the profusion of lilacs in bloom along this street in May. The sun's warmth will not penetrate the canopy of these trees for another few hours, but looking up I can see the sunlight beginning to come through as it reflects off the shiny green leaves.

All the shops along the front of **Sena Plaza** are quiet this morning. They will not open for another hour or so. As I round the east corner of the **Palace of the Governors** and look down the long, empty portal, I realize I have arrived before the Southwest American Indian vendors who will take their places along the portico later in the day to sell their crafts. Anglo vendors are not allowed here, just the Indians of this region. I think to myself that is the way it should be. After all, the Pueblo Indians had the first villages along the Santa Fe River long before the Spanish came. And later, in historical times, when they were subjected to the "civilizing influences" of the Spanish, Mexicans, and Americans, they revolted several times, capturing and occupying the very same building they will sit in front of today.

I find a bench in the plaza and sit down across from the Palace of the Governors. My gaze fixes on that old adobe that the Spanish called El Palacio Real. Built in 1610, it is the oldest public building in the United States and has always symbolized to me the enduring strength of this region. It was built to last, with adobe walls up to 5 feet thick in places. Someone has said that two or three workers can turn out 500 to 600 adobe bricks each day. The bricks for this building were probably obtained from the mud taken from the building site. The mud, mixed with straw to give it strength, was then poured into wooden molds to make bricks approximately 56-by-30-by-10 centimeters or 22-by-12-by-4 inches. After drying in the sun, these rectangular bricks were most often laid end to end, forming a wall approximately 4 feet thick. Mud mortar was used between the bricks, and after the walls were laid up they were then plastered to a warm smoothness. Yesterday in spite of the intense midday heat, the Palace of the Governors was a cool haven due to the insulating qualities of those old adobe walls.

A few more people are out now. The town is waking up. I reflect that I first sat in this plaza decades ago. The plaza has not changed much. But I do recall my astonishment some years ago when I realized how much Santa Fe had changed when I returned more than a decade ago after a four-year hiatus. Houses were being built on the hills north of town, fast-food places had cropped up all over the place, and the world's most splendid hole-in-the-wall steak house, Tony's U and I Cafe, had disappeared. The Hotel Loretto was under construction. La Fonda was undergoing a variety of changes, and the traffic was heavier and seemed uglier. A jillion little shops had cropped up.

For a while I thought all my pleasant memories of Santa Fe had been destroyed. Then I came and sat here in the plaza on a morning like this. I sat and looked around. It was quiet and peaceful. The old landmarks were still here—La Fonda anchoring the southeast corner, the **St. Francis Cathedral** looming up to the east, and the Palace of the Governors buttressing the north side. The center had held! Today as I look at the downtown storefronts it's apparent that the utilitarian retail core has been replaced by a sea of tony galleries, specialty shops, boutiques, and more fine restaurants and luxury hotels than you might find in many cities ten times the size of Santa Fe. It's apparent that it takes a lot of out-of-town visitors to fuel all this upscale retail activity. And when they periodically fill the city, their presence results in crowded sidewalks, traffic congestion, and a critical shortage of parking places. It's hard to see how many more visitors can easily be absorbed here without major changes regarding the use of the automobile. Yet even with the hassles, I come here every chance I get. It's still a wonderful city to visit. And in spite of all the trendiness, it remains a very real city—make no mistake about that. Last evening we sat here and watched a continuous stream of Santa Fe's teenagers congregate around the ice-cream shops, squeeze down the crowded corridors of a fancy minimall, and use the plaza, noisily, just like they knew what it was for. It was reassuring to see that the old plaza is still an integral part of people's lives here even though the downtown historic district seems worlds apart from the strip malls, barrios, and housing developments of the real Santa Fe. The center of Santa Fe's soul still holds. No one would dare screw up this centuries-old historic plaza. The people wouldn't stand for it.

The warm sun is breaking through the trees. I shed my sweater and start walking back to the inn from this plaza that has seen so much. I decide to walk around the east side of the Palace of the Governors to see my favorite Santa Fe antique. It is a set of ancient doors, painted blue, framed by lovely old beams that blend naturally into the old adobe wall supporting them. Formerly a wooden plaque on the adobe wall stated that "from 1610 to 1910" this building, originally known as El Palacio Real, was "the residence of over a hundred Governors and Captains General."

Perhaps through these very doors rode messengers from the king of Spain in Madrid and the viceroy of New Spain in Mexico City. Near these walls both Spanish and Indians were killed as battles took shape around this building. Perhaps Popé, the San Juan Pueblo Indian leader, entered these doors after conquering the Spanish in 1610. Or perhaps it was through these portals that the venerable Spanish Madonna *La Conquistadora* was lovingly carried in 1692 when the Spanish regained control of this, the Casa Real, their Royal House. And quite possibly secret messages were slipped under the doors, telling of the impending revolution in New Spain that would eventually place this royal seat of government under Mexican rule rather than Spanish domination. It may have been through

Blue doors, Palace of the Governors, Santa Fe

these doors that captured trespassers onto Spanish lands, like America's Lieutenant Zebulon Pike were brought to face their Spanish inquisitors. And Pike presaged the entrance through these portals forty-one years later of United States General Stephen Watts Kearny and his victorious American Army of the West.

But before that some mules no doubt left this passageway heading for St. Louis along the Santa Fe Trail and to Los Angeles along the Old Spanish Trail. In addition, my active imagination has pictured Governor Lew Wallace slipping quietly out of these side doors, away from the clamor and din of the seat of New Mexican territorial government, to walk the quiet side streets while he pulled his thoughts together to write another series of lines for his best-seller *Ben Hur*. And I am sure that some of Santa Fe's Los Cincos Pintores ("The Five Painters") must have looked at this historic wall and doors as I am doing now and seen the beauty of it all as the morning sunlight illuminates the vibrant blue of the old doors framed by smooth, rounded, sand-colored walls.

When I see these **blue doors,** I am reminded that the Spanish brought with them from the Old Country a superstition borrowed from their Moorish-Arabic enemies. It is said the color blue helps keep the devil away. Blue doors, blue window frames, even blue roofs help protect homes as well as public buildings. Ironically the Indians, long before the Spanish came, believed that turquoise would keep the evil spirits away. So another shade of blue, used for the same reason, adorns many a Pueblo Indian home.

Now I rapidly return to the inn, realizing that I have spent more time here wrapped in reverie than I should have. Sure enough, my family is up and raring to go. We find the Paseo de Peralta and follow it until we see signs to U.S. Highway 84–285 to Española. We quickly leave the city behind as we pass the Rosario Cemetery, the home of the **Rosario Chapel,** and head into the sagebrush hills. In 7 miles we see the modern structure of the **Santa Fe Opera Building** on the left in the Tesuque hills and many modern adobe homes in the hills to the right. As we continue north, we notice on the left the several weirdly eroded sandstone formations, including **Camel's Rock,** that have delighted us for years. From Santa Fe we drive approximately 15 miles to the junction marked LOS ALAMOS. This is New Mexico Highway 502; it is also the road to **San Ildefonso Pueblo.** We turn left or west onto Highway 502. Now the road goes up and down but mostly down, as we drive the approximately 5.5 miles to the pueblo access road near the Rio Grande.

San Ildefonso clay vessel

We spot the pueblo in the distance to the right. At the marker sign we turn to drive the approximately 1 mile into the pueblo. As the sign suggests, we stop at the visitor center (505–455–3549), check in, and pay an entry fee. The physical aspects of the village are little changed since my first visit here many years ago, especially the extra large, bare, dusty plaza, with its fine sense of openness. In the plaza I show my children, as my parents showed me, the solitary, lone old cottonwood tree that provides cool relief from the midday sun.

Years ago the plaza was full of people, especially children. Today the plaza is quiet, attesting to the fact that many Pueblo men and women work at jobs away from the village in towns like Los Alamos and that others have moved away, leaving a stable population of around 500. Farming the land here no longer provides enough income for all the people. Often in coming here we have seen smoke curling up to the sky from the pottery fires. Today no one is firing pottery, although we notice that a few of the homes still have signs up, indicating that their occupants will sell craftwork from their doors.

This was the pueblo home of the famous potter **Maria Martinez.** Maria possibly made the finest pots ever constructed, using the coil method. Only a few have even come close to duplicating the thin walls and lifelike forms of her pots. Her talented hands had a delicate touch, the sure touch of a master. Her sister hand-rubbed the pots patiently with a smooth stone, burnishing them to a high, rich gloss. Then her husband, Julian—and later her son Popovi Da, and later other relatives—put designs on her pots. I recall the first black-on-black San Ildefonso pot I ever saw. I was fascinated by its utter smoothness, as I traced the beautifully executed serpent design all the way around the pot.

My father had purchased the pot for a few dollars and some jelly beans. Both the seller and the buyer felt they had completed a good deal. That was in the late 1920s when the Pueblos were just reviving their pottery craft after having been exposed to some of the fine pottery produced by their ancestors, which had turned up in the archaeological digs of the time. I tell my children about my first visit here in the 1940s, when the plaza was filled with activity and the smoke trailed up from the beehive ovens, those remnants of Moorish Spain, as they slowly baked some of the best bread I have ever tasted in my life.

We walk around the empty plaza. One of the large kivas here is built into the adobe house block on the north. It is from this ceremonial kiva that many of the dancers will emerge on festival days. To our right is the large, handsome circular ceremonial chamber that we passed as we drove in. It is harmoniously designed to fit in beautifully with the **Pajarito Plateau** that rises behind it in the distance. My daughter asks why the stair rails are notched. That one stumps me. But as we look at those notches and see rising behind them a billowy thunderhead cloud with terraced edges forming over the

Ceremonial chamber, San Ildefonso Pueblo

mountain, we wonder if we have not found the answer.

We have read that this plaza is lined up with *toonyopeeng/ya* or **Black Mesa,** a sentinel, fortresslike rock structure exactly to the north. Black Mesa is a sacred structure, and its flat top holds several ancient ruins. It was also used as a fortress. When the Spanish returned to New Mexico in the 1690s, San Ildefonso was one of the last Pueblo strongholds to be reconquered. To strengthen their position the village residents moved to the top of Black Mesa. From its craggy heights, which they used as a fortress, they fended off the Spanish for several years before being subdued.

Looking toward the west end of the plaza, we see the Catholic church, newly constructed, outside the plaza. We have learned that most of the residents here are Catholic and that many have Spanish surnames. But the Indian religion and the Indian way supersede both of these influences. In spite of the great pressure the Spanish imposed on the Puebloans to give up their old religion, the Indians were able to keep their religion and culture intact. Spanish law stated that the Indians should be left on their own lands. So the Spanish, who had some experience in

Bandelier National Monument

coexisting with a second, alien culture on their native soil, the Moors, learned to live side by side with the Indians here. Unfortunately as much cannot be said for their European counterparts in the eastern part of the United States who displaced the Indians from their lands. Today in the East there are no Indian villages that have been continuously inhabited as long as those in the Southwest. The large wooden structure just east of the church catches our attention. It is called the "Hollywood Gate," for it is a relic from the Hollywood movie set for a movie made at the pueblo. Before leaving we visit the **Pueblo Museum** next to the church.

Returning to the car, we drive back to New Mexico Highway 502, turn right, and head for **Bandelier National Monument.** It is thought that the ancestors of today's San Ildefonso's residents as well as other Pueblo ancestors lived on the Pajarito Plateau. Bandelier National Monument is dedicated to the preservation of what remains of the dwelling sites and lifeways of those early Pueblo people in a 50-square-mile area of the plateau, including the easily accessible sites along Frijoles Canyon. After leaving San Ildefonso Pueblo we cross the Rio Grande. The river is brown and sluggish, quite a contrast with its appearance in Colorado, where we have seen its clear, fast-flowing waters sparkle in the sunlight. In Spanish times and even later, it flowed more freely. Today much of the water is diverted to the farms and ranches of southern Colorado before it ever reaches New Mexico. Nevertheless the river and its tributaries still provide much of the water required for farming in this region.

The road begins to climb fairly quickly now as we head west to Bandelier National Monument and ascend the Pajarito Plateau. We wind and weave through interesting rock formations. The rock with all the holes in it that looks like honeycomb is called *tuff*. Tuff is consolidated volcanic ash. Ash covered this region in great depth after the eruption of the Jemez Volcano just west of here during the Quaternary Period a million years ago. When that volcano blew its stack and collapsed into its magma chamber, it left an immense bowl, the **Jemez Caldera** or Valle Grande, measuring more than 14 miles across. Approximately 89,000 acres of the caldera's forest and meadowland have been protected with the establishment of the **Valles Caldera National Preserve** (505–438–7891 or 438–7892).

We note the signs to White Rock and follow New Mexico Highway 4 as it courses south, winding all the way to **Bandelier National Monument** (505–672–3861, ext. 517; www.nps.gov/band) 46 miles northwest of Santa Fe. The monument was established in 1916 and covers nearly 40,000 acres. It is named for Adolf Bandelier, a Swiss archaeologist who began studying this area in the late 1800s. We pay the admission fee and enter the tree-shaded parking area and visitor center near *El Rito de los Frijoles* ("The Little River of the Beans"). The shade is very welcome now as the sun hits high noon. We find a nice picnic area near the stream and enjoy the cool breeze at 6,100 feet above sea level. The cold drinks from the snack bar near the visitor center help soothe our parched throats.

We take a quick tour of the museum, which houses many of the artifacts from the ruins here. We purchase the inexpensive guide titled *The Trail to Frijoles Ruins* and take off on a self-guided tour of the area. We walk the dusty trail in the canyon bottom that was probably used by the inhabitants during the 300 years the canyon was occupied. Some of the first occupants probably trickled down from the great Ancestral Puebloan civilizations in the Four Corners area around 1250, when for unknown reasons they left their home there. This well-watered canyon must have looked good to them. We pass by the ruins of a circular kiva or ceremonial chamber (see Section 2, "A Prehistory of Indian Country") and are reminded of the kivas we have seen at Mesa Verde National Park and at Aztec National Ruins Monument, as well as the one we saw this morning at San Ildefonso.

Now we come across a small hill or mound next to the trail. This is the way an unexcavated site often appears. When archaeologists see mounds like this, they begin to look in the dirt around them for potsherds or other evidence of habitation. Such evidence frequently leads to the decision to excavate an area. We now reach the famous ruin of *Tyuonyi,* a word in the Keres language meaning "meeting place." Although practically leveled now, this complex once stood two stories high and contained 400 rooms. Perhaps one hundred people lived here. This large site was excavated in 1909–10. From artifacts found at sites like this and others on the Pajarito Plateau, the Pueblo Indians were able to discover much about their past early in the twentieth century. This rediscovery of early pottery and design motifs was thought to be instrumental in sparking the renaissance of fine Pueblo crafts near the beginning of this century.

We now continue on the trail to the cliff dwellings. Here we explore in some detail the caves carved out of the soft volcanic tuff. Some of the caves we see, though, are natural. Many of them look too small to be occupied. Our children climb several of the ladders to peek into the caves. I do the same and find several cave ceilings darkened with black soot from ancient cooking fires. Now we come to **Talus House,** resting on a talus or rock slope beneath the cliff. Here the viga timbers supporting the roof protrude dramatically from the rebuilt walls. The walls are of stone and to our eye look very similar to the buildings we have seen in the Four Corners area.

In the "cave kiva" we see long poles fastened to the ceiling; these served as supports for the upper portion of an ancient loom. The lower horizontal bar of the long, vertical loom was anchored to supports imbedded in the small holes we see in the floor. Like the Egyptians, the Pueblo people wove cotton, which they grew in selected areas along the Rio Grande. When the Spanish came and discovered that the Pueblo people manufactured cotton clothing, they began to see dollar signs. Profit could be made by shipping cotton garments to the increasingly populated mining regions of northern Mexico.

Yucca (New Mexico state flower)

We come to a fork in the trail. We have been walking and looking for about forty-five minutes. Instead of turning back to the center, we take the trail to the right, to **Long House Ruin.** We have heard that it abounds in petroglyphs and pictographs. Only a few intact stone walls of the Long House remain, but they are dramatically situated under the sheer cliff face that rises hundreds of feet above them. Here we see a pictograph outlining the same terraced stair-step design we saw this morning on the stairway of the round kiva at San Ildefonso. In subtle tones of terra cotta and cream, this beautiful design tells us that the Ancestral Puebloans, like their descendants, were superb artists.

At this point we cross the Little River of the Beans. Instead of turning right to the Ceremonial Cave, we choose to return to the visitor center. On our walk back along the river, we encounter an excellent self-guided nature trail that graphically tells about the high-desert vegetation. We are able to identify vegetation such as rabbitbrush, sage, box elder, and, of course, New Mexico's state flower, the yucca plant. We all agree that this unexpected natural history find is a nice bonus to our very pleasant two hours here at Bandelier. We return to the visitor center and refresh ourselves with a cool drink. As we walk back to the car, we discuss the fact that the Indians left here sometime in the 1500s. By the time the first Europeans arrived in 1540, the Frijoles Canyon area was practically abandoned.

Returning to New Mexico Highway 4, we can choose either to continue west to Valle Caldera National Preserve and Jemez State Monument or to retrace our steps. We choose to do the latter. When we come to the junction leading to **Los Alamos** we resist the temptation to stop there. On previous visits we have seen the excellent **Bradbury Science Museum** (505–667–4444), with its atomic bomb and nuclear science exhibit, as well as the instructive **Los Alamos Historical Museum** (505–662–4493). Los Alamos continues to be an interesting, scientific town, with more Ph.D.s in residence than you can shake a stick at. In the past many here were employed at the National Scientific Laboratory, but today Los Alamos hosts a growing number of privately held high-tech industries that in the future may be the largest employers. From previous experience we have learned that after 3:00 P.M. the traffic leaving Los Alamos and heading east on New Mexico Highway 502 toward the valley can be slow, as many commuting government workers return to their homes along the Rio Grande.

It is now 2:00 P.M., and we seem to be just ahead of the traffic. Instead of crossing the Rio Grande, we turn off Highway 502 to New Mexico Highway 30 at the junction just west of the river. We pass the spur road leading a few miles through beautifully forested land up to the ancestral home of the Santa Clara people, the **Puyé Cliff Dwellings.** (Call 505–753–7330 or 753–7326 to see if open.) I remember visiting both the cliff and the mesatop ruins there a few years ago and finding them more peaceful on a busy summer day than Bandelier. We also regret-

Buffalo Dance, San Juan Pueblo

fully bypass **Santa Clara Pueblo,** population 2,500, which appears shortly on our right. Santa Clara, like San Ildefonso, is one of the great Pueblo pottery villages. We reflect that our many visits there have been very enjoyable and that we have often seen some of the well-known Santa Clara potters firing their distinctive burnished black pottery. Now we enter **Española.** We find our way through a confusing array of streets to New Mexico Highway 68 North (Taos Highway), where in approximately 4.5 miles a sign marks the turnoff to the left or the west, 1 mile, to **San Juan Pueblo.** Just north several miles in Alcalde is the small **Oñate Monument Visitor Center** where you can explore Pueblo and Hispanic farming traditions in the northern Rio Grande Valley; (505) 852–4639.

We are excited to return to San Juan Pueblo as it is a very enjoyable pueblo to visit. It is not architecturally stunning like Taos, but it is laid out in a pleasant way near the Rio Grande, amid great old cottonwood and Chinese elm trees. We all agree as we drive along the shaded road that the Spanish chose well when they sited this spot for the first European settlement in the interior of America (see "History"). But the San Juan Indians knew this was a special place long before the Spanish came. They established their village Oke near here sometime in the 1300s. This is one of the largest Tewa-speaking villages, having a population of around 2,000. It is also the most northerly of the Tewa communities. It is surrounded on two sides by the Spanish-speaking community of Chamita.

Parking in front of the **Oke Oweenge Crafts Cooperative,** we notice that it is very quiet this afternoon in the outer plaza of the pueblo. We note the Catholic church to the west and the Pueblo chapel to the east, as we walk over to the Pueblo's craft cooperative. It is interesting that the San Juan residents have chosen their Tewa name Ohkay or Oke for their traditional crafts shop. We are greeted warmly by several of the San Juan women behind the counter. Our daughter strikes up a conversation with one of the women about a painted gourd she likes, while we admire a white cotton woven "rain" sash, a type of sash made here and on the Hopi reservation. We note excellent displays of finely crafted brown and red, plain black, and plain red pottery. Once again the Pueblo women eagerly tell us who made them and how they are used. We see several Pueblo women doing handiwork, and several San Juan wood-carvers also at work. We purchase a few items, return them to the car, and then walk across the plaza. The smaller church to the east is the church the Pueblo uses. The one across the plaza, larger and more formal, is the one built for residents of Chamita. We walk around the church and enter the main plaza of the pueblo.

It is very quiet and almost empty this afternoon. This is very different from what it was like on a June day two years ago. Then we visited the pueblo to attend the **San Juan Feast Days** festivities, which included a Buffalo Dance. The plaza was crowded that June day with not only many Pueblo Indians who had come for this important event but some Anglos as well. Circulating in the crowd were a number of San Juan men whose job it was to make certain that all cameras, sketching equipment, and so on were duly registered and fee permits issued to their owners. We had our camera along with us. After it was inspected and we were queried about the purpose of the pictures we were going to take, we paid a fee and were given a permit that we were asked to display. We jockeyed for position in the plaza for the best viewing spot. The drums began to beat as five men carrying large, handsomely handcrafted Pueblo drums entered the plaza. Over the course of the afternoon, we saw beautiful costumes, watched fine dancing, and enjoyed being a part of a happy, spirited crowd for whom the dances had more meaning than we would ever know.

But today in the plaza, it is so quiet that we can hear the cottonwood leaves rustle as we walk back to the car. The traffic is heavy in the opposite lane as we drive out. Many San Juan residents are returning from jobs elsewhere. We drive the short distance back to Española, which some have dubbed a Spanish island in a sea of pueblos, realizing that in many ways this Hispanic community is the cultural hub of northern New Mexico. There are six Pueblo villages within 20 miles of here, and there are more than a dozen Hispanic villages equally close. With much anticipation we find our way through busy, sprawling Española to the family-run Rio Grande Cafe. We are starved. We know from past experience that the owners of this cafe will fill our stomachs with delicious New Mexican food without depleting our pocketbook. Full and content, we should be back to Santa Fe by 9:00 P.M., just in time to join the evening crowd for ice cream on the plaza.

There are two interesting sights south of Santa Fe: El Rancho de las Golondrinas and Santo Domingo Pueblo. They can be seen either as part of a day trip out of the capital city or, because of their proximity to the freeway, as a stop on the drive to or from Albuquerque. Seeing both sites takes more than a half day.

El Rancho de las Golondrinas ("Ranch of the Swallows"): A Living History Museum near La Cienega

If you would like to learn more about the early Spanish settlers in New Mexico and capture the flavor of their lifestyle, this village museum fifteen minutes' drive south of Santa Fe is the place to go (fee). It has one of the best historical exhibits in New Mexico. Drop-in, self-guided tours are available Wednesday through Sunday from June through the end of September. Guided, prearranged group tours (parties of ten or more) are led from the first weekend in April through the last weekend in October (505–473–4169). The public is also invited on the first weekend in May, June, July, August, and October for a series of festivals and during certain "theme" weekends when this living Spanish museum comes alive. During the festivals as well as the living history weekends (call for schedule) held throughout the summer, El Rancho de las Golodrinas becomes the Sturbridge Village of New Mexico. On certain weekends you'll see Spanish wood-carvers, musicians, embroiderers, weavers, and tinsmiths show their stuff, while local cooks stoke the fires of ancient adobe fireplaces and ovens, turning the rancho's kitchens or *cocinas* into a frenzy of culinary activity.

El paisano, or roadrunner (New Mexico state bird)

What is all the fuss about anyway? It is about a 200-acre, authentic Spanish village developed in the twentieth century on the site of an old rancho, which in turn was built early in the eighteenth century on ground that contained a defensive *torreon* (tower) constructed around 1650 by orders of the king of Spain. This small valley was a well-watered place kept so moist by flowing springs that the Spanish named it *Cienega,* or "marshy place." Because of its location along the Camino Real and its close proximity to Santa Fe, it became a *paraje,* or stopping place, for travelers going to or coming from the capital city. Fifteen miles was a long distance in those days. But as time went on and the Camino Real was replaced with other trails and roads, La Cienega ceased to function as a *paraje* and became a typical Spanish rancho. The Spanish family who had owned the land for more than two hundred years eventually sold 400 acres of it to an Anglo family from out of state in 1932. Most of the buildings had weathered away or were otherwise in disrepair by then.

Shortly after that, in the 1940s, a Finnish diplomat met and married one of the owners. This couple took up residence on the old rancho and decided to reconstruct it. With great dedication and care, they bought up old Spanish buildings from all over New Mexico and carted them piece by piece to the site, where they were reconstructed. In addition, they collected a wealth of artifacts and furniture relating to the early culture of the Spanish. Besides the main house there are more than twenty other buildings, containing three fully equipped *cocinas* and their adobe fireplaces, several *capillas* (chapels) with many religious artifacts, a wide variety of handcrafted Spanish New Mexican furniture, and a rich selection of kitchen, craft, and farm tools.

You will see the typical New Mexican well houses called *norias,* as well as the outdoor beehive ovens called *hornos,* both of which are still being used in the Spanish villages to the north. While walking up hill and down dale of the village, look for the barn swallows, or *las golondrinas,* for which the ranch was named. Also keep an eye out for New Mexico's state bird, the spritely roadrunner, which the Spanish call *el paisano.* If you tour the whole rancho, you will have walked 1.75 miles round-trip. Allow at least two and a half hours for a guided tour visit. There is also a museum shop with books and information about the rancho and the Spanish in New Mexico. Information: Las Golodrinas, 334 Los Pinos Road, Santa Fe, New Mexico 87505; (505) 471–2261; www.golodrinas.org.

To reach Las Golodrinas leave Santa Fe via U.S. I–25 headed south. Take exit 276 and bear right onto New Mexico Highway 599. Turn left at the first intersection on the frontage road and right just before the racetrack on Los Pinos Road. Follow the signs 3 miles to the museum.

Santo Domingo Pueblo

The major jewelry-making village along the Rio Grande is Santo Domingo (505–465–2214). On any warm summer day, you may see expert craftspersons there working in the shade of hastily constructed ramadas adjacent to their homes, their electric grinders and polishers going at a clip. The quality of this pueblo's best artisans is very good, with much of the work still being done by hand. The Santo Domingo jewelers come by their trade honestly. Pueblo residents from this area have been making shell and turquoise jewelry for centuries. In fact the Santo Domingo Pueblo claims ownership of the ancient Indian turquoise mines at Mount Chalchihuitl in the **Cerrillos hills** just east of the pueblo. One of the specialties at Santo Domingo is the crafting of *heishi* necklaces. Shells are cut into rounds, hand-drilled, polished to an exquisite fineness, and then strung on a cord. Silver jewelry, especially the style called liquid silver, is also made at the pueblo. These items and others like them are for sale during the **Santo Domingo Arts and Crafts Market** over Labor Day weekend.

Storyteller clay figure, Cochiti Pueblo

The Keres-speaking Santo Domingoans are known as excellent traders and, like the Taos Indians, are extremely conservative. Intent on keeping their ancient ceremonies and rituals intact, they maintain a healthy suspicion of Anglo intentions. Although Oñate made his first stop at Santo Domingo and established ecclesiastical headquarters there for all the Indians of the region, the village is more of a mecca for traditional ways than it is a Christian Vatican

Church at Santo Domingo Pueblo

for the Pueblo world. Even the beautiful Catholic mission church dedicated to the thirteenth-century Spanish preacher and founder of the Dominican order, Saint Dominic, is outside the village proper, being separated from it by an irrigation ditch.

The mission church is as unique a building as you will see along the Rio Grande. Its single, terraced adobe bell tower caps a rectangular adobe structure with a bright, sky-blue balcony. The front facade is painted with the figure of two horses facing one another, signaling almost immediately that the pueblo is a farming community first and foremost. Its lands bordering the Rio Grande on both sides of the river are easily irrigated and productive. So the people chose well centuries ago when they moved off the Pajarito Plateau to the valley. But they did not foresee the ravishing Rio Grande floods that would finally destroy the old village in 1886. The pueblo and church you see have all been rebuilt since then.

See the beautiful altar screen in the church and walk for a while in this village of more than 2,000 inhabitants. Jewelry and pottery, as well as some willow and yucca baskets, can be bought here. If you are in the area the first weekend in August, do not miss **Santo Domingo Feast Day and Corn Dance,** a spectacle of more than 500 dancers that rivals the Santa Fe Opera in costuming and comes close to matching the drama of the dances on the Hopi mesas to the west. If you have more time upon leaving Santo Domingo Pueblo, you may want to continue on New Mexico Highway 22 approximately 9 miles to **Cochiti Pueblo,** where fine drums, clay storyteller figures, and *nacimientos* (nativity scenes) are made. If you would like to visit the nearby fanciful rock formations at **Kasha-Katuwe Tent Rocks**

National Monument, travel 5 miles northwest of the pueblo on a washboard dirt road (Tribal Road 92 and Forest Service Road 266) to the parking lot, which accesses a loop hiking trail. Before visiting check with Cochiti Pueblo (505–465–2244 or 465–0121).

To reach Santo Domingo Pueblo, leave Santa Fe via U.S. I–25 South in the direction of Albuquerque. In approximately 25 miles take the New Mexico Highway 22 exit, and head west on Highway 22 about 6 miles to the pueblo.

A Day Traveling through Spanish New Mexico: A Narrative Account

Today is one of those incredibly beautiful summer mornings in Santa Fe. The light is bright; the air, cool, dry, and invigorating. A few minutes ago the waitress seated us at this table in the sun here on the patio. My daughter is reading Willa Cather's *Death Comes for the Archbishop.* I reach over and borrow the book for a moment

Wooden statue of Saint Francis

and thumb through it to this passage: "In New Mexico, he always awoke a young man; not until he rose and began to shave did he realize he was growing older. His first consciousness was a sense of the light dry wind blowing in through the windows, with the fragrance of hot sun and sagebrush and sweet clover; a wind that made one's body feel light and one's heart cry 'To-day, to-day,' like a child's." My family chides me for my romanticism, but all agree that Cather caught the essence of mornings like this one in that passage. We have ordered *huevos rancheros,* a favorite dish in New Mexico. A fried egg is placed atop a corn tortilla, and over that is poured a fresh sauce of tomatoes, onions, chili peppers, and oregano. While we devour this mildly piquant dish, we make our plans for the day.

We are going to **Taos.** Instead of taking the major highway north from Española, New Mexico Highway 68, the **"low road"** that follows the Rio Grande, we will take the scenic, culturally rich 80-mile route by way of New Mexico Highway 76 through the mountains, the so-called **high road to Taos.** Besides being an excellent, paved, two-lane road, it winds through some of the more remote and interesting Spanish villages. We leave Santa Fe the "back way" to head northwest on **Bishop's Lodge Road,** an extension of Washington Avenue. At the confusing intersection of Washington Avenue and Paseo de Peralta, we continue straight across the intersection, staying on Washington as we follow the sign that says SKI BASIN ROAD. We are now on Bishop's Lodge Road (New Mexico Highway 590), and we continue straight ahead, disregarding the spur road, New Mexico Highway 475 (Artist Road and Hyde Park Road) that comes in a short distance leading to the **Santa Fe Ski Basin.** At approximately 3.5 miles we pass the entry road leading to **Bishop's Lodge,** which we see to our right. This

Santa Cruz Mission Church

famous Santa Fe resort was constructed on the grounds of Archbishop Lamy's home, where his chapel is still intact.

Continuing north on Bishop's Lodge Road or New Mexico Highway 590, we pass the **Tesuque** post office (bypassing a family favorite lunch stop, the Tesuque Village market) and follow New Mexico Highway 591, before entering U.S. Highway 84/285. For several miles we retrace the route we took two days ago to San Ildefonso. Today we pass by that exit and continue north to Española, where New Mexico Highway 76 intersects U.S. Highway 285, 25 miles north of Santa Fe. We see the sign to New Mexico 76, and **Chimayó** and **Penasco** to the right just before the intersection, and then we see our identifying landmark, McDonald's, across the highway from the U.S. Highway 285 and New Mexico Highway 76 junction. We turn right or east onto New Mexico Highway 76.

Even though we will stay down in the valley for the next 12 miles or so, we are now, for all practical purposes, on the high road to Taos, the heartland of Spanish New Mexico. In less than half a mile, we pass a lovely small adobe chapel dedicated to the local saint, **San Niño de Atocha.** In another half mile we see the large old **Santa Cruz Mission Church** off the road to the left, with its thick adobe walls and its tin roof shining in the morning sun. Built in 1733, it was one of New Mexico's leading churches in the eighteenth century, serving the village of Santa Cruz, which was founded in 1695, the second villa or city to be established by the Spanish government in New Mexico. Already we feel transported to another age, another time, and we are only 1 mile away from urban sprawl.

In a few more miles, we reach the outer barrios or sections of **Chimayó**. Originally a compact village, Chimayó is now spread out along the **Santa Cruz River.** We pass adobe houses with *ristras,* or strings of chili peppers, hanging from their walls, with flowering plants climbing their fenced courtyards, and with dusty yards scattered with stands of multicolored hollyhocks, their long flowering stems belligerently blooming out of the dry soil. We see the lilac hedges that were in bloom last May when we were here, and in front of several of these homes we see the quaint water well houses, or *norias.* Signs advertising peppers and fruit for sale dot the road. A small cafe advertises homemade tamales and enchiladas.

Chili ristra   *Chimayó weaving*

Many houses in Chimayó contain a handloom. For this is the home of the brightly colored, handsome, woven wool Chimayó blankets. Weaving has a long history in this region, and some believe the link between the famous Saltillo serapes in Mexico and the later development of Navajo weaving is right here in Chimayó (see Section 2, "The Navajo (Diné): Nomads and Survivalists"). In a few minutes we come to **Trujillo's Weaving Shop** on the left side of the road. We have often stopped here to see the weavers at work on the several different sizes of handcrafted looms (see "Shopping"). A short distance farther, just past the sign to Santuario de Chimayó, is the junction of New Mexico Highway 76 and Santa Fe County Road 98, approximately 8.5 miles from Española. We turn right onto Santa Fe County Road 98 and pass by Ortega's large weaving and Spanish craft shop to the right. We recall that the road in front of Ortega's entrance (County Road 94E) leads 0.25 mile to the old plaza and village center of Chimayó, the location of Rancho Manzano B&B, a favorite of ours. In 0.5 mile we pass the Rancho de Chimayó Restaurant on the left, as we drive several miles farther to the barrio of Potrero.

We park near the entrance to the **Santuario de Chimayó;** (505) 351–4889. Thirsty, we walk over to **Leona's** little outdoor restaurant in the shade of the cottonwoods for a cold drink and to share one of her delicious taquitos, a popular tamale, and several of her flavored tortillas. Refreshed, we walk over to the church. We are now facing one of the most venerated and charming adobe structures in New Mexico. We have visited this church three or four times and have taken many pictures of it. Yet today we are once again awed by its setting beneath the Sangre de Cristo Mountains and by its simple charm. We have been told that the spot where the church was built was also a sacred place to the early Indians of the area. Moreover, we have read that the lovely pyramid-shaped mountain rising behind the *santuario* is the sacred mountain of the east for San Juan Pueblo. So here is the sacred church lying in the shadow of the ancient sacred mountains of the Tewa Indians. No wonder, then, that this plaza is filled with both Hispanics and Indians several times a year.

Once again we find ourselves intrigued with the notion of the intermixing

Santuario de Chimayó

of Spanish Catholicism and Indian religion. Even the name Chimayó is a Spanish corruption for the name of the Tewa Indian village that once occupied this area, *Tsimayo*. That Tewa word means "good flaking stone," referring to the obsidian found in the area. During Holy Week, it is said that in some years as many as 30,000 to 50,000 mostly Hispanic and Indian pilgrims swarm to this tiny church, some hiking or hitchhiking distances of more than 300 miles, while some bear rough, hand-hewn crosses on their shoulders. The devout have called the *santuario* here at Chimayó the **Lourdes of America**. Perhaps it is the Fatima as well. We reflect that the plaza, so quiet this morning, must once again be jammed late in July on the feast day of Santiago, or Saint James, the patron saint of Spain. At that time there is a ceremonial enactment commemorating the Spanish victory in driving the Moors out of Spain. The festival is called Los Moros y Los Cristianos, "the Moors and the Christians." In costumes reminiscent of each faction, men on horseback stage a dramatic mock battle, resulting in a Christian victory.

We enter this small church that was built between 1814 and 1816. It was constructed as a public church but financed by one man and his family. Its purpose was to serve as an auxiliary to the larger church at Santa Cruz so that people in the new village of Chimayó would not have to travel so far to worship. It is said that this building was constructed entirely without nails. Our eyes seem to make a slow adjustment from the very bright light outside to the very dim interior in here. Even though the whitewashed walls help accentuate the light, it is still fairly dark. This is an exquisitely beautiful interior, splashed with color from the altar screen in front and from the various *reredos* and painted *bultos* on both sides of the nave. Our son immediately points out his favorite figure, the *bulto* known locally as Señor Santiago de Chimayó, on the right side of the altar. It is a local representation of Saint James. So revered was Saint James of Compostela that Spanish soldiers often shouted "Santiago" before they charged their enemies. The glass case

*Bulto, Señor Santiago de Chimayó
(San Juan)*

around the statue is to keep it safe from devout, loving hands, which at one time just about destroyed it. We note that this New Mexican version of Saint James depicts him in caballero dress with boots, long spurs, and a straw hat.

Our eyes now focus on the colorful altar screen made by New Mexico's greatest *santero*, Molleno, who is sometimes called the "Chili Painter." At the bottom of the large niche that holds the crucifix are painted representations of wheat and grapes. In the center is the 6-foot-tall crucifix of Our Lord of Esquipulas, a Guatemalan Christ figure. We wonder how it got here. Local legend has it that on a Good Friday early in the 1800s, the head of the family who finally built the church saw a burst of light centering somewhere in the area of today's *santuario.* He thought the light was coming from a particular spot in the ground, so to sate his curiosity he felt compelled to dig at that spot. When he did so, he unearthed a crucifix with a dark green cross and a darkened Christ figure. Some said it resembled crucifixes carved in Esquipulas, Guatemala, where the "Black Christ" is worshiped. At any rate the discovery caused quite a stir. In addition to helping its discoverer overcome an illness, it sped along his earlier request for a church to be built near this site.

When the church was built, it was constructed near the site of some springs that the Indians thought had healing properties. We walk into the small room to the left of the altar and then into a smaller room off that called *El Pozito,* "the little well room." We see a hole in the floor exposing the dirt underneath. For more than 150 years thousands upon thousands of the faithful have come to take small bits of this healing clay soil, either to ingest or to apply to various afflicted body parts. There is no mystery why the hole is not deeper. The priest and his assistants keep filling it up with more clay and sandy soil. Still they come.

In this same room we see a smaller crucifix of the Esquipulas Christ. We ask someone, who tells us that this is the crucifix discovered in the ground and that the one in the main sanctuary is an enlarged replica. We step back into the little prayer room, where we see an astonishing array of crutches, braces, and other testaments to the healing power of this shrine hanging from every wall surface. We also see a *bulto* of Santo Niño de Atocha, the venerated local saint. He also is credited with healing powers. The belief is that he does his good work by walking through the surrounding communities each night, keeping them safe and protecting them from harm. In accomplishing this task Santo Niño, the Holy Child, wears out his shoes nightly so that every day he must have a new pair.

We walk back to the entrance and step outside. We are all squinting in the bright sun as we get into the car and drive the short distance on Santa Fe County

Rancho de Chimayó

Road 98 back to **Rancho de Chimayó,** seeking the restorative powers of an early lunch. We turn off the road into the long driveway leading to the late-nineteenth-century territorial-style rancho, with its tin roof, adobe walls, and shaded, terraced patio. It is one of the most inviting restaurants to visit in the region.

We have a hard time deciding where we want to sit. We consider an open, lighter room near the bar with its authentic shepherd's bed or hooded fireplace. In the old days its adobe ledge right above the fire provided a warm place for some tired shepherd to sleep. But we decide instead to sit outdoors on the patio rather than inside. This delightful patio in the shade of the cottonwood trees is always pleasant on a warm day. While the kids go off exploring, we sit and sip a Chimayó cocktail, made from local apples and tequila.

Finished with lunch and a tour of the kitchen to see just how the sopaipillas are made, we return to Santa Fe County Road 98 and retrace our route to New Mexico Highway 76, where we turn right or east. Shortly we pass **Centinela Traditional Arts,** another good Hispanic weaving center. Now the road begins to live up to its name as we climb steadily in an easterly direction to **Cordova.** The brown, dry earth meets a bright blue sky this afternoon, but there are a few thunderheads building over Truchas Peak to the east. Now a little more than 3 miles from the New Mexico Highway 76 and Santa Fe County Road 98 junction, we look for a small sign that will direct us, rather suddenly, off New Mexico Highway 76, down a moderately steep dirt road to the village of Cordova.

At the bottom of the hill, we see a few small ranchos with signs out in front advertising wood carvings by the well-known Lopez family.

Now we descend farther into the village, keeping to the left as we negotiate the dusty streets. In a few minutes we pass the post office and the center of this small village. We park and walk up the narrow road to the Catholic chapel,

Church at Las Trampas

St. Anthony of Padua. It is not open today, but in the past we have seen the lovely altar screen in the back and the many carved *bultos* of various religious figures. Most of the carving done in this village is from white pine, red juniper, and aspen. These carvings are extremely handsome, and the lines are generally clean and simple. As we walk back over the dusty road through the narrow street, we have a mounting feeling that we are walking a village street somewhere in the high dry plains of Spain.

Returning to Highway 76, we continue to wind and ascend through the Sangre de Cristo foothills. We can see great distances from up here as the car rolls along this high ridge road. We feel like we are sitting on top of the world. Now 18 miles from Española and at an elevation of 8,600 feet, we reach the picturesque village of **Truchas,** perched on a high bench of the Sangre de Cristo Mountains. The village is situated across a deep valley from **Truchas Peak,** New Mexico's second highest mountain, at 13,102 feet. *Truchas* is the Spanish word for "trout," an abundant fish in these mountain streams.

Exiting from the highway to enter the village, we drive several blocks down the narrow street that follows the edge of the escarpment and then pull off the road to park. We get out and walk a few blocks, seeing some very old, weathered houses and noticing how the architecture differs up here close to the pine forests. Instead of flat roofs we predominantly see steeply pitched, corrugated tin roofs designed to help shed the large amount of winter snow this area receives. Although many homes have adobe walls, we also see quite a number of homes with walls made of logs and other materials.

As we wind our way back down the narrow street to New Mexico Highway 76, we pull over at times to allow cars to pass. Now we continue in a northeasterly direction to **Las Trampas.** There are few tourists up here today, so when we stop in the Spanish villages, we seem to be the only Anglos around. We notice that the older people especially speak Spanish among themselves, not English. The young people speak English but with a strong Spanish accent. Our daughter points out that some of the Spanish terms used by the older women are different from the Spanish she is learning in school.

And it may be, for I have read that in this part of New Mexico, partially because of isolation and partially because of resistance to change, some archaic Spanish terms dating back to the time of Cervantes in the early 1600s are still in use. Some of the priests in residence here from Spain are often astounded by this language phenomenon that is a direct result of the isolation of these small villages. The 12,000- to 13,000-foot peaks of the Sangre de Cristos loom large to our right, but they do not seem that overwhelming, since the roadbed we are on is well over 8,000 feet elevation. Large quantities of piñon wood are stacked near most of the farmhouses, and smoke curls up from the chimneys, as it is no longer hot. The weather is changing rapidly up here, becoming very cloudy and cool in the past fifteen to twenty minutes. We see the sheets of rain dancing over the Sangre de Cristos and know it will be here before long.

We pass through the small sleepy village of **Ojo Sarco**. The farmhouses come closer together now as we approach **Las Trampas**. Our son asks if there will be tramps in Las Trampas. I explain that *trampas* is a Spanish word for "traps" or "snares" and that the town is named for the river that flows through it, which was well known in Kit Carson's day as a fine place to trap beavers. As we enter Las Trampas, almost immediately our eyes are drawn to the church, **San José de Gracia.** The historical marker in front of the church tells us in Spanish that the town was founded in 1751 by families who came here from Santa Fe. Many have

Death cart with La Muerte, the death angel

likened Las Trampas to an eighteenth-century walled Spanish colonial village. Because of many of the old adobes remaining and because of the beauty and intactness of the Spanish colonial mission church, San José de Gracia, the area was declared a National Historic Landmark. The region itself was also once populated with numerous Penitentes (see "History").

We stand in the plaza admiring the church. Completed in 1776, it was dedicated to the Twelve Apostles. Legend has it that only twelve men were allowed to build it. Perhaps that is why it took twenty years to complete it. Money for building materials came from the villagers, who gave one-sixteenth of their crops each year until it was finished. This is one of the few adobe structures remaining that has genuine mud-plastered walls rather than the artificial commercial materials more commonly used these days to achieve the same effect. Rising gracefully above the heavy, 4-foot-thick adobe walls are two bell towers made of wood. We now notice that the portal to the plaza has the same terraced cloud pattern we saw on the stairway of the kiva at San Ildefonso. This is not an Indian village, yet the

Chamiza (rabbitbrush)

same imagery is used. The exterior choir loft is an unusual feature of the church, and we admire the fine carving of its vertical members. Here in the ceiling of the choir loft, we see an excellent example of *latillas,* the peeled juniper or aspen poles that are laid over the vigas—roof beams of pine and spruce, extending under the balcony. The door and lintel are beautifully carved.

In spite of efforts to raise the caretaker to unlock the door, we can find no one. The unattached structure on the east side of the church, bordering on the cemetery, catches our attention. This is a *morada,* a special place once used for Penitente services. Over the years it has contained many unique religious objects, including a Penitente death cart. These carts hold a carved wooden statue of the death angel Doña Sebastiana, better known as La Muerte. This unique piece of folk religious art was first developed by Nasario Lopez, the father of Jose Dolores Lopez of Cordova, who is the father of George Lopez, who lived in Cordova, the town we have just visited. We return to the car and then drive up a few of the village streets. Small gardens growing squash, corn, chilies, and apple trees abound. We now exit this Spanish village, reflecting that it was founded in 1751 as a distant outpost to protect the people of Santa Cruz from Comanche Indian raids.

Once again we enter New Mexico Highway 76, the road to Taos. We continue to lose altitude as we approach the village of **Chamisal,** named for the *chamiza* (rabbitbrush) that abounds in this area. We note the special visual treat of small, well-tended fields and recall the much-used phrase of "postage-stamp ranchitos." Much to our amazement we see an old horse-drawn wagon with large wooden wheels approaching us from the other direction. For a moment we doubt our senses, for we thought that carts like these disappeared from the highway many years ago. But as it comes closer, there is no doubt that it is a *carro de vestias.* One of our favorite New Mexican authors, Rudolf Anaya, has written about just this type of wagon that his grandfather used many years ago to drive into town to sell produce. We stop and wave as I point to my camera. The driver smiles and nods his head, so I take a picture. We say adios and are on our way again in this "Land of Enchantment." Midway between Chamisal and Peñasco, New Mexico Highway 76 intersects New Mexico Highway 75. The latter highway connects, via **Dixon,** New Mexico, with the other main route to Taos, the "low road," or river

Church at Talpa

road. Dixon has become a popular place for many of New Mexico's artists and craftspeople to live, and several galleries are there as well as in the nearby village of Embudo. Once we took an excursion to the **Indian pueblo of Picuris** from this junction by turning left and traveling a short distance on New Mexico Highway 75, following the signs to the pueblo with its 342 residents. We enjoyed the museum and admired one of the very durable micaceous clay bean pots made there. But today we turn right onto New Mexico Highway 75 and continue toward Taos. We pass other Spanish villages in their quiet settings along the road with names such as Peñasco, Vadita, and Placitas. Since leaving Chimayó we have seen few facilities with a tourist orientation. Once again we comment on the remoteness of these villages. Now that we have descended to an elevation of 7,000 feet, some of the mystery we felt in that higher country is gone.

Just beyond Placitas, New Mexico Highway 75 intersects New Mexico Highway 518. We turn north onto Highway 518. At the top of a long incline called U.S. Hill, we catch glimpses of New Mexico's highest peak, snowcapped **Mount Wheeler** at 13,161 feet. We are now in a pine-aspen forest. As we descend to **Fort Burgwin Research Center** (505–758–8322), we find ourselves back to scrub country, loaded with juniper, piñon, scrub oak, cottonwood, and sagebrush. A large historical marker on the left side of the road interests us, so we turn off the road to stop and read it. It tells us that a cantonment or fort was built here in 1852 and was occupied by a troop of the First Dragoons who had several skirmishes with hostile Indians. This fort was built after the Taos Revolt in 1847, and its name commemorates the death of Captain John Burgwin, who was killed in that clash (see "History").

The authentically restored log fort is an imposing site and the only restored fort of its kind in northern New Mexico. The fort and surrounding buildings serve as headquarters for a research unit from Southern Methodist University whose staff study the military and Indian history of the area. At the fort we see a few military relics. The parade grounds, now planted with grass and trees, offer quiet seclusion and some amount of cooling shade this afternoon. Archaeological work is being done in the hills nearby, where several hundred Indian dwellings are being studied.

We continue on toward Taos, still 10 miles north. To our left we see the skeletal remains of an old adobe house, beautifully framed under billowing white clouds in the blue, blue sky. Now a little farther at 6 miles from Taos, we see the sparse, quaint village of **Talpa,** formerly called Rio Chiquita, after the river of the same name that flows nearby. This little village was founded around 1823 during the restless years of Mexican rule of New Mexico. A small lane leads to the church of **San Juan de los Lagos,** St. John of the Lakes Church. We get out of the car and walk over to the church. Our children comment that there are not any lakes nearby, so how did it get its name? I explain that I had read that some of the early settlers were devotees of a small statue of Our Lady of the Immaculate Conception that had graced a church in Jalisco, Mexico, in a town called St. John of the Lakes. These New Mexican devotees named their church in honor of that shrine. We are disappointed that we are unable to arouse an attendant to enter the church, for inside is another fine altar screen by the old master **Molleno,** one of New Mexico's best nineteenth-century *santeros.* But the beauty of the little church with its simple, centrally located bell tower is sufficient reward. Framed by the blue sky and the surrounding adobes, it is a perfect camera subject. Driving on, there is an especially picturesque Hispanic cemetery on the right, framed by Taos Mountain in the background. Colorfully festooned with flowers and containing white crosses of all shapes, sizes, and materials, the cemetery evokes a certain aura of optimism and acceptance.

We now pass **Ranchos de Taos** to our left, 4 miles south of Taos. It is a small village on the outskirts of Taos proper that has retained much of its old charm. It is fully anchored by what is unquestionably the most picturesque Spanish church in New Mexico, **St. Francis of Assisi Mission Church,** popularly known as the Rancho de Taos Church. We turn left onto New Mexico Highway 68 to catch a glimpse of the church. Admiring its fine exterior features, we pass it by this afternoon, since we are tired and the heat is beginning to take its toll. We will come back here for a longer visit later this evening or tomorrow. Now we return to New Mexico Highway 68 and drive on to Taos, about 4 miles north. Taos has sprawled considerably in this direction in the past few years. This approach, which used to offer beautiful vistas to the north as we looked across the sagebrush plain to Taos, is now cluttered with many unattractive, view-blocking commercial establishments spread out alongside the road. But our enthusiasm returns as we enter town and find the plaza and several other familiar landmarks much the way we remember them. We pull into the narrow driveway that leads to the parking lot of the **Taos Inn,** a popular resting spot here. We get out of the car, walk into the historic old lobby, order some drinks, and sit down to rest. We can check in later!

Taos

Taos is a place-name used in the title of three separate and very different communities: Taos, Taos Pueblo, and Ranchos de Taos. Travelers are often confused by this.

The principal community by that name is, simply, **Taos,** formerly known as Fernando or Fernandez de Taos. Taos is predominantly a Hispanic community, with more than half of its full-time population of more than 6,000 persons belonging to that group. It is the touring base for the area around it. Three miles to the northeast is Taos Pueblo. This very conservative, traditional Indian village, with a population of more than 2,000, has carried the name Taos longer than either of the other two communities bearing that name. In fact the name *Taos* is probably a Spanish corruption of the Tewa Indian name for this Tiwa-speaking village, which means "down at the village." Ironically this name, of Indian origin, was used to later name the nearby Spanish community of Taos. This is unusual, because the Spanish usually hispanicized the names of the Indian pueblos to suit them and generally did not name their settlements after Indian villages. The other community that uses the word *Taos* in its name is Ranchos de Taos, a small Hispanic community 4 miles south of Taos, centered on the beautiful and historic St. Francis of Assisi Church.

You will enjoy your visit to Taos. Resting on a high plain like Santa Fe, it is in many ways more dramatically situated. The flat, undulating sagebrush plains roll right up to it from the west, while **Taos Mountain** and the Sangre de Cristo range snug close up and dominate it to the east. The immediacy of the mountains to the east with the wide-open spaces to the west lend an aura of mystery to Taos that I have found in only a few other places in northern New Mexico. Storms build up almost over your head, then let loose their barrage of rain pellets as they spread west over the dry sage plain, releasing the pungent aroma of sagebrush into the air. Otherworldly? It often seems so in Taos.

But Taos is very much a part of this world too, and it changes every year. In the late 1940s and early 1950s when I first visited there, I remember quiet, tree-shaded streets, little traffic, and many dusty, unpaved roads. There were some shops but not many, and the town seemed relaxed and laid-back. Today in midsummer, traffic snarls the main entrance to town. Pay parking lots are increasing as on-street parking becomes even more dear. Shops by the hundreds, so it seems, line the formerly sleepy old streets, and, heaven forbid, even shopping malls have made their way close to the heart of Taos. The plaza has been updated and refurbished, and a chamber of commerce booth has been placed there in the summer to help travelers. Additionally, the University of New Mexico branch, **UNM/Taos Education Center,** is experiencing remarkable growth.

Yet much of the Taos that captured my heart as a boy remains. The plaza and buildings that surround it are pretty much the same as they were, except for the modern development to the east. The low adobe buildings with their wide porches still attract and evoke nostalgic sighs of relief from me. The shady, grassy parks; the narrow passageways and alleyways between old adobes; and even some unpaved, dusty streets remain. Even the same slow, nonchalant, *poco tiempo* pace continues. The Taos Book Store anchors the east side of downtown; there it is still possible to linger in its cool interior on a hot day and overhear conversation by Anglo locals who talk in hushed tones about mysterious things going on out at the pueblo or about the *curanderas,* midwives, and *brujos* who are part of life in Taos County's large Hispanic population.

So in spite of modern change, the center holds. This town, founded in 1615 but not incorporated until 1934, offers the tourist much by way of its rich past (see "History"). Its cultural mix means that you will experience different foods and see different styles of living from what you are used to. Taos is not a rich town. From starving artists and struggling Hispanic subsistence farmers to aging hippies, the standard of living is low. At times almost half of the county's nearly 30,000 inhabitants have received financial assistance of one sort or another. The literacy rate is much lower than the national average. Taos County is an undeveloped country in the heart of the United States. As charming and beautiful as it is, these charms, as local author John Nichols has so poignantly written, are bittersweet in terms of the misfortunes that strike many of the families who live year-round in this beautiful but terribly harsh land.

A Three-Quarters-of-a-Day Walking Tour of Taos

Because the town is small and reasonably compact, many interesting sites can be seen in a short time. Taos is more conducive to walking than driving. A good starting point for a tour is **the plaza.** If you are staying in one of the motels or inns right in town, walk to the plaza. If you are staying outside of town, you may want to drive in, park your car, and then walk to the plaza. Unless you drive into town early in the morning, before 9:00 A.M. in the summer, on-street parking will be hard to find. In that event park in one of several municipal lots. These are close in yet sometimes well hidden from view. If traffic is backed up along South Pueblo Road and you are approaching from the south, turn left onto Camino de la Placita (Placitas Road), which intersects South Pueblo Road about 1 block below the plaza intersection. Follow Placitas Road, always keeping to the right as it doglegs around the town. It will take you to the marked municipal parking lot north of the plaza or all the way around to U.S. Highway 64, heading north.

In the plaza note the flagpole with the American flag flying. By tradition and special approval of the United States Congress, the flag flies day and night. This does not especially mean that the people there are superpatriotic. The tradition stems back to the Civil War, when Confederate citizens kept taking down the American flag from the plaza. A few Union sympathizers like Kit Carson did not like their antics, so they went into the mountains and brought back to Taos one of the tallest and sturdiest timbers they could find. Then they nailed the flag to it and planted the pole deeply, thereby raising a permanently installed flag high above the plaza. Just to make sure no one tried to remove the flag, they stationed sentries on the rooftops of the plaza. Then they patrolled the plaza day and night, armed with rifles, with orders to shoot anyone wanting to remove the flag. Rumors had it that Kit Carson and his cohorts were pretty good shots, so the flag flew without incident twenty-four hours a day until it finally wore out.

Since that time the flag has continued to fly day and night, and in a special ceremony each year in May, near Memorial Day, a new flag replaces the worn, tattered one. The plaza goes back to 1710 when the town was rebuilt after the Pueblo Revolt of 1680. The buildings faced the plaza. They completely encircled the plaza space, their rear walls offering fortresslike protection to the Spanish settlers from the marauding Plains Indians. Walk to the south side of the plaza, cross the street, and enter **La Fonda Hotel**, not to be mistaken for the large hotel by the same name in Santa Fe. At the desk toward the back of the beautiful old lobby, you can pay a small fee to view some of D. H. Lawrence's paintings. His paintings apparently caused as much of a stir in the early days as his books did, even though neither Lady Chatterley nor her lover are the subjects of his paintings!

Exit the front of the hotel, turn left, and soon turn left again onto the small side street (West Plaza) that leads to Camino de la Placita (Placitas Road). Cross Placitas and enter **Ledoux Street.** Now with the hustle and bustle of the plaza behind you, walk this narrow, quiet street bordered by some of the loveliest adobe homes and courtyards you will see in New Mexico. One of the restored adobes is the former home of **R. C. Gorman.** It is now a gallery open to the public (see "Taos: Shopping"). The modern treatment of its interior has only enhanced the beauty of this fine old adobe, where Gorman, a renowned Navajo painter, sculptor, and printmaker, exhibits his work.

Continue down Ledoux Street to the **Ernest L. Blumenschein Memorial Home** (505-758-0505), a registered National Historic Landmark. Blumenschein, one of the cofounders of the first art colony in Taos, purchased this old Spanish home, built in 1797, on returning from Paris to make Taos his permanent residence in 1919. The intact furnishings are representative of the years Blumenschein and his talented wife made their home and studio there. It is well worth a visit. Reenter Ledoux Street with its many walled, flower-filled patios on each side and proceed to the **Harwood Museum of Art** at 238 Ledoux Street (505-758-9826; www.harwood.unm.edu), another fine adobe owned and administered by the University of New Mexico. The large building and the adobes around it are some of the oldest in Taos. The art gallery displays representative pieces from the works of most of the artists who either lived for a while or settled in Taos since the 1890s as well as fine contemporary art of the region. You will also see some antique Spanish furniture, local Spanish handicrafts, and a collection of New Mexican *retablos* displayed there. There is also a gift shop.

Retrace your steps approximately 2 long blocks east, back to the plaza. Walk by the storefronts on the west end of the plaza, where most of the stores and shops still retain a local, small-town flavor. Then enter Teresina Lane, a pedestrian side street extending from the northwest corner of the plaza. Follow it, passing along the way several small shops and galleries. Then turn right to enter the municipal parking lot. Cross the parking lot and enter historic **Bent Street.** This street of shops and small restaurants (some with shaded outdoor dining areas) is one of Taos's best, as it retains some of the flavor of old Taos. It is especially noted for the **Governor Bent House, Museum, and Gallery,** 117A Bent Street; (505) 758-2376. Bent was massacred there by a Spanish and Indian coalition that was not pleased with the American takeover of the areas in 1846 (see "History").

Walk east along Bent Street to the very busy North Pueblo Drive (Paseo del Pueblo Norte). Cross the street, if you can, and enter the quiet lobby of the **Taos Inn,** secluded behind thick adobe walls. The lobby was formerly the open courtyard, or *placita*, of a Spanish home. The courtyards in those days were special places of beauty and peace. The home that the hotel now occupies was built in the early

1800s. Find your way from the hotel lobby through the restaurant to discover another Mexican surprise, a pool and a grassy outdoor patio surrounded by small casitas. Return to the Taos Inn lobby and exit on North Pueblo Road. Turn right and walk to the **Taos Center for the Arts** next door. This center, operated by the Taos Art Association, oversees an art gallery and the adjacent Taos Community Auditorium.

Return to North Pueblo Road, turn right, and walk north. In less than the distance of ½ block you will come to the sign marking one of the pedestrian entrances into the 20-acre **Kit Carson Memorial State Park,** with its tree-shaded picnic tables, cooking grills, and playgrounds. You may want to stroll to the back of the park to the **historic cemetery** to see the graves of Kit Carson and his family, as well as those of Padre Martinez, Mabel Dodge Luhan, and other historic Taos figures.

Now continue north 2 more blocks until you come to a sign indicating the **Fechin House.** For many years this beautiful adobe, set back some distance from the road yet visible from it, brought excited exclamations from vacationing flatlanders as they traveled up North Pueblo Road. Many travelers knew that someone special had to have built a home like that, but most never took time to find out who. Then in 1979 the home was listed on the National Register of Historic Places. Shortly after that, in 1981, the home became more visible to the public with the formation of the Fechin Institute, named after the longtime occupant of this historic Taos adobe. The institute was formed to commemorate the one hundredth anniversary of Nicolai Fechin's birth. Nicolai Fechin was born in 1881 in Kazan, Russia, a trading center along the Volga River. His artistic talents, which were recognized at an early age, led to a career as an artist and art teacher. In 1923 at the age of forty-two, Fechin, along with his wife and daughter, immigrated to the United States. In 1926 Fechin left New York to visit a friend in Taos. As with many other artists who visited Taos in the 1920s, Fechin was immediately taken with the region and within a year established residence there. He soon purchased an adobe house at this site and set about renovating it. The result, both inside and out, is nothing short of spectacular, for Fechin was an artist's artist. He was at home with wood carvings, ceramics, sculpture, and architecture, as well as the impressionistic oil paintings that brought him fame.

If you have time to see the interior of only one of Taos's many famous adobes that are open to the public, this is the one to see. It offers the rarest and most beautiful blend of two worlds that you are apt to find anywhere. For inside this twentieth-century New Mexican adobe rests the spirit of historic Russia. Pursuing his oil painting career during the best daylight hours, this complete artist put aside his brushes in the evening to wield adze, chisel, and mallet as he shaped wood and adobe to resurrect the spirit of his homeland in this remote American hinterland. There is a feeling of richness and warmth in these rooms that makes you want to linger. You wonder what artistic magic has created such nurturing, comfortable spaces. Is it the artist's profound use of light and proportion or is it his remarkable knowledge of the centuries-old techniques of wood carving and surface finishing that creates the wonder here? Beautifully carved wood panels, doors, mantels, and furniture will no doubt please your aesthetic senses, but it is the sculptured adobe

The Mabel Dodge Luhan House, Taos

fireplace that makes you feel like you have just entered the portals of aesthetic heaven. The institute hosts musical events and rotating art exhibits. Of course, Fechin's paintings are showcased several times during the year. The home, adjacent studio, and the handsome Fechin Inn are repositories of Fechin's work. Open year-round. Information: Fechin Institute, Box 832, Taos, New Mexico 87571; (505) 758–1710; www.fechin.com.

Now return to North Pueblo Road, turn left, and walk 3 long blocks back to Kit Carson Road. (You might choose to visit the **Kit Carson Memorial Park** now. If so, you can walk through the park to the cemetery and then to the south border of the cemetery, where you can enter Dragoon Lane. From there it is only 2 blocks to Kit Carson Road.) Turn left or east onto Kit Carson Road and walk up this street with its many shops and galleries.

Now about 1 block from the Kit Carson Road junction at the plaza, enter the narrow walkway to the **Kit Carson Home and Historical Museum** (505–758–0505). This is one of the most thoroughly delightful small museums in the area. Not only are the lives of the famous Indian scout and explorer Kit Carson and his Spanish wife detailed completely, but there are excellent regional historical and archaeological displays there too. In the museum you will learn about the Taos trappers, the American and French mountain men of the early 1800s who lived and worked using Taos as a base for their expeditions into the unknown mountain country to the west.

Farther up Kit Carson Road and across the street is the venerable **Taos Book Store,** a veritable mecca for books about D. H. Lawrence, New Mexico, and the Southwest. At this point if you have more time and are not too tired, you can continue to walk farther east on Kit Carson Road, past Dragoon Road, turning left at the second intersection. This is **Morada Road.** Now heading in a northerly direction, you will reach in about 0.5 mile **Las Palomas** or Los Gallos, the former twenty-two-room palatial adobe home of **Mabel Dodge Luhan,** on the edge of the Taos Pueblo property. By the time this house was built, Mabel Dodge had married for the fourth time to a traditional Taos Indian, Tony Luhan, a marriage that was to last forty years, until her death in 1962. It was through the efforts of this spirited woman that Taos became nationally and internationally known as a haven for artists and writers.

The Mabel Dodge Luhan House, the "big house" as locals call it, saw it all, including a period in the 1970s when it was owned and occupied by the movie star Dennis Hopper and his circle of friends. The big house at 240 Morada Lane is not just a B&B. It is also a conference center. Information: Mabel Dodge Luhan House, P.O. Box 558, Taos, New Mexico 87571; (505) 751–9686 or (800) 846–2235.

On the edge of the property is an old *morada,* or Penitente chapel. Adjacent to Las Palomas is another vintage adobe where the Taos artist Victor Higgins lived. From Las Palomas retrace your steps back to Kit Carson Road.

A One-Day Auto Tour around Taos: A Narrative Account

Last evening while it was still light, we drove south of town a short distance, turning off the highway onto a secondary road heading west. We got out of the car and walked along the road and through the sage for a while. The view from any of these open areas was splendid. As far as we could see, there was open space. In the distance the San Juan Mountains were visible to the west. Close at hand the pungent scent of sage permeated the air. We intensified the aroma by breaking off small pieces of sage and pinching them with our fingernails to release a double-distilled dose of that lovely incense. After about 1 mile we turned back to the car. Facing east, **Taos Mountain** loomed above us. The sunlight hitting this peak bathed it in a reddish glow. This reddish blush on the mountains so impressed the Spaniards that they named these mountains east of the Rio Grande the *Sangre de Cristos,* or the "Blood of Christ," Mountains. As the reddish glow faded, we saw the moon rising behind Taos Mountain, and we immediately felt a cool breeze. The warmth of the car felt good as we drove back to the inn. As we approached the inn in the purple of twilight, the aroma of sagebrush gave way to the delicious fragrance of piñon smoke drifting down from the chimneys of the adobe fireplaces in the casitas. After lighting our own piñon fire, we fell asleep in just minutes, exhausted from the day's activities.

Ranchos de Taos Church

But this morning we feel refreshed and ready to face another day of sightseeing as we walk into the inn's restaurant. We eat breakfast with gusto and prepare to leave for the day. It is chilly this morning, but we know that by midafternoon we will be sweating instead of shivering. We get in the car and drive south or left onto North Pueblo Road through the busy junction near the plaza and head south to Paseo del Pueblo Sur, or New Mexico Highway 68. On the way out of town we pass the handsome multiagency **Taos County Visitors Information Center** (505–758–3873 or 800–816–1516; www.taoschamber.com or www.taosguide.com)

on the left at the intersection with Paseo del Cañon, or New Mexico Highway 585 (U.S. Highway 64 Bypass).

Our first visit today will be the small Spanish village of **Ranchos de Taos,** approximately 4 miles south of Taos. We turn left or east at the scenic marker across the highway from the post office and park in the designated space near the **Mission Church of St. Francis of Assisi** (505–758–2754). Out of the car now, we stop and look at this old adobe church built sometime around 1776, the year of our Declaration of Independence. That event probably passed unnoticed here, for it would have meant very little to the colonists of Spanish descent who were struggling to survive in one of Spain's most remote colonies.

This lovely church commands our attention. We walk around to the back of it, for architecturally and aesthetically the back side is the most famous section of the church. The massive adobe buttresses seem to flow from the earth, supporting the walls like great hands. Although we have visited this church many times, our reaction today is just as intense as it was before. We stand for a few moments just taking it all in. This beautiful old church rises out of the ground on the flat plain, as if to echo the heights of the Sangre de Cristo Mountains behind it. We slowly walk around it until we find a view of the buttresses, reminding us of the painting of this church by Georgia O'Keeffe in 1929.

O'Keeffe used to point out that most artists must paint this church, just as sometime in their careers they feel compelled to paint a self-portrait. We are also reminded of the excellent photographs of this church done many years ago by Ruffin Cooper. Except for a few puffy white clouds, the sky is brilliantly blue this morning, just as it was in both of those well-known artistic efforts. The light-brown-colored church rises into that vastness of blue and white, providing a combination of shapes and colors that fixes our attention.

Now at the front of the church, we enter the sanctuary, finding it cool and dim. Our eyes have trouble adjusting. In a few minutes we can see better. What we see is a fine collection of Spanish art. In the east transept is one of the largest altar screens in New Mexico. Its 425 square feet of surface is beautifully painted and decorated, lending light and brilliance to the dim room. The *salomónicas* that we saw in the San Miguel Mission Church in Santa Fe are also part of the altar screen here. The image on the altar screen is that of Esquipulas, the Christ of Guatemala. We remember the wonderful legend behind that image from our visit to the Santuario de Chimayó the day before yesterday. This altarpiece is also the work of **Molleno,** one of New Mexico's great native *santeros.* Again we note the balance struck between the plain whitewashed walls of the church and the colorful religious artwork. We walk over to the rectory to see the painting of Christ done by Henry Ault in 1896. From June to September at 9:00 A.M. and 4:00 P.M. each day, a videotaped lecture about it is played. In complete darkness the painting changes form as a cross appears on the left shoulder of Jesus and a halo emerges above his head. More of the mystery of New Mexico!

We leave the church, return to New Mexico Highway 68, and head back to Taos. On the way we pass the junction of New Mexico Highway 240 (Lower Ranchitos Road) to the left. A few years ago we took that very scenic, rural route 4 miles west and north to tour (fee) the restored **Hacienda de Don Antonio**

Severino Martinez (505–758–0505), an early fortified Spanish colonial house that belonged to an important figure in the history of Taos. The living-history demonstrations we saw there added considerable interest to our visit. But today we pass it by and drive through town, thankful that the congestion near the plaza is minimal as we head north on North Pueblo Road, U.S. Highway 64. Before reaching the junction with New Mexico Highway 150, we see a sign on the right directing us to make a left turn onto Millicent Rogers Road. We follow the road less than 1 mile south to the parking lot of the Millicent Rogers Museum at 1504 Millicent Rogers Road (505–758–2462; www.millicentrogers.org). We walk into the reception area of this handsome building and pay a fee to enter what I call the Alhambra of New Mexico, a monument to the architecture, arts, and crafts of the region.

Millicent Rogers was an heiress to the Standard Oil fortune. She visited Taos in 1947 and decided, like Blumenschein, Dodge, and others before her, to stay. She became enamored with the local Spanish and Indian art. With the realization that this indigenous art might vanish someday, she wisely began collecting crafts of these cultures. She collected an incredibly rich cache of folk art. After her death her son established a museum to keep this valuable collection intact. For a long time this adobe hacienda-turned-museum retained many of the characteristics of the original residence and gave rise to the fantasy that we were visiting someone's beautiful home. And when I would look out the windows and see broad, unbroken vistas of sage plain and purple mountains through the adobe-encircled windows, I was always tempted to move to Taos—immediately if not sooner! We begin our tour of the museum's ten gallery spaces by spending some time in the textile gallery. We particularly like this gallery, where there are beautiful examples of both Indian and Hispanic weavings with an interesting commentary on the history of each and how to distinguish one type from the other. From there we go to the **Maria Poveka (Martinez) Family Collection.** We never seem to tire of looking at the museum's stunning collection of burnished black San Ildefonso pottery created by Maria and her family. We quickly move on to the **Hispanic Collection,** one of our favorites, which details the Hispanic settlement of the area by exhibiting their agricultural tools as well as their superb art. There is a fine collection of *santos, retablos,* and *bultos* here, along with a beautiful example of the death cart, with its defiant-looking skeletal occupant La Muerte. We then spend a few moments looking at the permanent jewelry collection, which has several extraordinary pieces of jewelry on display by the out-standing Hopi artist, now deceased, Charles Loloma. I anxiously glance at my watch and realize that our quick run through the museum has taken well more than an hour and comment that we must move on. The reply is that when the going gets tough, the tough go shopping, so we spend a few minutes in the excellent museum shop with its wide assortment of Southwest Indian and Hispanic arts and crafts for sale (see "Taos: Shopping").

We return to the car and drive back to the highway. We make a left onto U.S. Highway 64 to Tres Piedras, which will take us to the **Rio Grande Gorge Bridge** 7 miles away or approximately 15 miles from Taos. The wind is blowing some this morning, perhaps presaging an early afternoon thundershower. Since we plan to picnic near the gorge, we hope it holds off. Now several miles in the distance, as we look west across what seems to be the flattest stretch of land in the United States, we see many cars and people—specks in the distance—gathered at the edge of the gorge. We pull into the parking lot and join the other gorge watchers. This narrow, steep gorge, truly a deep slot into the bowels of the earth, is so long that it extends from north to south as far as we can see, giving us the impression that it is a huge fault that splits the continent. Of course, it is not a fault and it does not go on forever. It is a slot carved by the constantly flowing water of the Rio Grande as it cuts deeper and deeper into the hard basalt rock. If the rock here had been soft sandstone, the river would have carved a wide canyon rather than the narrow gorge we see.

We walk to the edge and look down. We are bathed in sunlight, but the Rio Grande is still in shade 650 feet below us. We begin to wonder how deep 650 feet really is. The gorge would easily contain the 555-foot-high Washington Monument. Then someone says that if you could place the Eiffel Tower in the gorge, 350 feet of the narrow top portion would protrude above the surface. Getting into this imaginary frame of mind, we look up to see just how high it would protrude. As we look up, we see a few thunderheads building above us, so we quickly cross the second highest bridge in the national highway system to the west side of the gorge. There we enjoy the protection of one of the picnic shelters, while the dark clouds are rapidly forming. The wind is blowing many miles away across the sage plain, where we see numerous dirt devils or whirlwinds, those small funnels that are set into motion by the action of the wind.

Lightning zigzags across the sky, its thunder reverberating across the plain. We see sheets of rain moving toward us. It starts—a few giant drops at a time— s-p-l-l-a-a-t! Suddenly more drops. And now we are grateful for the shelter as the rain pounds the ground around us. In about five minutes the storm is over. There is an incredibly sweet, fresh smell in the air. The aroma of sage is very intense now. Where else could air be so fresh, so clear, so fragrant? Refreshed by the cool breeze and a good lunch, we get back into our newly "washed" car.

D. H. Lawrence shrine, northeast of Arroyo Hondo

We retrace our route back across the bridge and along U.S. Highway 64 until we reach the junction with New Mexico Highway 522. Instead of going on into town, we make a left turn at the intersection with the light and follow New Mexico Highway 522 to the northwest, as though we were going to Questa. We follow this road about 6 miles to **Arroyo Hondo** and another 3.5 miles beyond that town until we see a sign to the **Lawrence Ranch,** directing us 6 miles up a road to the right. We follow the dirt road through rolling sage lands toward the mountains. This road can sometimes be difficult during very wet periods. Although a little water is still standing in the potholes, the road has been graded recently and is in good shape. D. H. Lawrence's modest house, really a small cabin in the pines, and his ranch now belong to the University of New Mexico. Frieda, Lawrence's wife, allegedly traded Mabel Dodge Luhan the author's manuscript of *Sons and Lovers* for this property, which Lawrence eventually named Kiowa.

As we drive up the road through the pines, our daughter recalls her favorite painting by Georgia O'Keeffe, *The Lawrence Tree*. It was done in 1929 and was based on the artist's experience at the Lawrence Ranch about a year before Lawrence died in France in 1930. It is a fanciful, imaginative painting of an old tree near the Lawrence cabin that reflects what I have so often experienced here. The ordinary takes on a different character in this remote mountain fastness of New Mexico. In her rendition of the tree, O'Keeffe painted the brown tree bark at night a deep shade of plum. There is in that evocative painting a wonderful sense of the mysterious and intense beauty to be found in this heartland of the Southwest.

We pull into the parking lot below the shrine. In spite of all the talk about D. H. Lawrence's Taos, Lawrence did not spend much time here. He visited Taos three times between 1922 and 1925, spending about six months each time. On the last visit in 1925, he was ill with the tuberculosis that would end his life five years later. In Europe, ill and yearning nostalgically to return to New Mexico, he wrote a piece, at Mabel's request, for the publication *Survey Graphic* (1 May 1931) that summed up his feelings about New Mexico. Of his arrival there in 1922 with Frieda and in 1924 with Frieda and Lady Dorothy Brett, he wrote, "I think New Mexico was the greatest experience from the outside world that I have ever had. It certainly changed me forever. Curious as it may sound, it was New Mexico that liberated me from the present era of civilization, the great era of material and mechanical development. . . . But the moment I saw the brilliant, proud morning shine high up over the deserts of Santa Fe, something stood still in my soul, and I started to attend. There was a certain magnificence in the high-up day, a certain eaglelike royalty. . . . In the magnificent fierce morning of New Mexico one sprang awake, a new part of the soul woke up suddenly, and the old world gave way to the new."

In the short time he was in New Mexico, Lawrence did a lot of work, completing, revising, or composing some of his best works. Lawrence was intrigued with the Indians, especially the Taos Pueblo Indians and the Hopi Indians to the west. He was fascinated by the closeness with which they lived to nature. Loving the rare beauty found in this cultural vortex of America, he wrote that from his viewpoint one of the first commandments of the Indian's religion was "Thou shalt acknowledge the wonder." For it seemed to him that the Indians were truly in touch with their magnificent surroundings in a way that Anglos rarely are. Even steeped in the traditions of Europe, he felt he had no permanent sense of religion until he came to New Mexico and attended many of the Indian ceremonies and religious dances. He wrote, "For the Red Indian seems to me much older than Greeks, or Hindus or any Europeans or even Egyptians. The Red Indian, as a civilized and truly religious man, . . . is a remnant of the most deeply religious race still living . . . [with] a tribal integrity and a living tradition going back far beyond the birth of Christ, beyond the pyramids, beyond Moses. A vast old religion which once swayed the earth lingers in unbroken practice there in New Mexico."

As we walk the steep trail up to the shrine, the incense of pine lingering in the air, we begin to understand why Lawrence loved this ranch. He and Frieda had not been happy down at Las Palomas in Taos, but it was here at this mountain retreat that he would find peace and would be moved to write that he had never experienced anything like New Mexico. As he walked, hoe in hand, along a ditch to the canyon at the ranch, he witnessed a beauty that inspired him to rhapsodize about mountains "blue as chalcedony, with the sage-brush desert sweeping grey-blue in between, dotted with tiny-cube crystals of houses, the vast amphitheatre of lofty, indomitable desert." So it was here at the ranch that Lawrence broke through the "shiny sterilized wrapping," as he called civilization, and "touched" the country. When you do this in New Mexico, he wrote, "you will never be the same again."

We see Frieda's grave in front of the handsome stone shrine and Lawrence's remains encased in concrete inside the shrine. Frieda brought his ashes from Europe to the ranch. Some say she was fearful that Mabel Dodge Luhan might try to get hold of the ashes, so she had them buried in concrete. Although she remarried, she spent the rest of her life loyally promoting Lawrence's image and his works. On the way down we are even more taken with the views from the ranch that range out over the Rio Grande Valley. Piñon jays flit from one pine to another. The small picnic table in the pines makes us wish we had brought our lunch up here today. It is quiet, and the light is as pure as Lawrence described it. It is as Lawrence wrote, "So beautiful. God! So beautiful!"

Piñon jay

The three talented women in Lawrence's life lived out the rest of their lives in the Taos area. It is said that they developed a sense of loyalty to one another over the years. Frieda occupied the ranch until her death in 1956. Mabel Dodge Luhan, who authored numerous books on the region, died in 1963, and Lady Dorothy Brett, who had become well known for her paintings of the Taos Indians, died in Taos in 1977.

Returning to the car, we drive back to the highway, turning left to drive to Taos. On the way back to town, we decide to visit **Taos Pueblo.** We turn left or east off U.S. Highway 64, at the Mobil station this side of the Best Western Kachina Lodge, just before entering Taos. In doing so we pass by the **Van Vechten-Lineberry Taos Art Museum,** at 501 Paseo del Pueblo Norte (505–758–2690), where in the past we have seen an outstanding collection of art by members of the historic Taos Society of Artists and some excellent contemporary rotating exhibits. We drive the little more than 2 miles through the lush, irrigated meadows watered by the Taos River, passing the Taos Pueblo Casino on the way. I recount for my family that although I first came here in the 1940s, I have been here many times since. In my mind there is hardly a more beautiful valley in the world. More than 500 years ago the Taos Indians were directed by their legends to settle here. In Lawrence's terms the Taos Indians have indeed "acknowledged the

Hornos, or beehive ovens, at Taos Pueblo

wonder" in choosing this location for their home. For here the sage plain gives way to lush green meadows watered by the Rio de Pueblo Taos, whose source is high in the mountains above us at Blue Lake, the sacred lake of the Taos people. We can see the pueblo in the distance as it rests peacefully below Taos Mountain, a wonderfully rounded, symmetrical, pine-clad hunk of massive rock that cradles beautiful jewel-like Blue Lake. If ever there was a central place where heaven and earth meet, it is here. No wonder Blumenschein was enthralled. No wonder world traveler Lawrence was stopped in his tracks, becoming a born-again New Mexican almost overnight.

Beyond the backdrop of the mountains in front of us is one of the few ancient passes to the eastern plains. Over the years the Taos Indians were greatly influenced by the Apaches, Kiowas, and Comanches to the east. Being near the portal to the east, the Taos Indians traded with these eastern Plains Indians and in doing so acquired some of their cultural traits, not found in the other Pueblo groups. We drive on past meadows with beautiful horses, sleek cattle, and even buffalo. Now we catch glimpses of everyday life surrounding the pueblo that is thought to have been occupied continuously from sometime between 1370 and 1450 until the present. Some say the Taos Indians, like the other Pueblo people, migrated west from the Four Corners area, while others point out that their language is related to the Kiowa language, a language used by a group of eastern Plains Indians who now reside in Oklahoma.

But whatever their origins the Taos people settled here. And today we catch glimpses of their everyday life as we pass near the ruin of the old mission church destroyed by Captain Burgwin and the other soldiers of the First Dragoons in 1847 (see "History"). We join the line of cars bottlenecked at the admission booth just outside the plaza. I get out and walk over to the booth. While I wait in line, I muse about this whole process. The Taos Indians have figured out a way to let tourists see a little of their pueblo and their lifestyle, without revealing all. Over the years the Taos Indians have survived drought conditions, cold wint[...] marauding Indian enemies. They have protected themselves from the onsla[...] the Spanish, the Mexicans, the Americans, and, since the early 1900s, the [...] They are aware of the powerful impact outsiders can have on their lives.

The **large plaza,** cut in the middle by the sparkling clear Rio Pueblo de Taos and surrounded by multistoried adobe buildings supporting long ladders jutting into the sky, is quite a sight and a photographer's dream. Yet Taos Pueblo (505–758–1028; www.taospueblo.com) keeps a tight reign on its domain. Besides an admission fee, a photographer's/artist's fee is also levied. (Call ahead for visiting hours, because they may fluctuate. The pueblo is closed February to April, late August/early September, and during unannounced religious observances.) While we wander through the historic plaza, we hear distant drumbeats, signifying that more meaningful village functions are being performed in other areas of the reservation not open to the public. Thus Taos Pueblo maintains a public front and a private side simultaneously. The Taos Indians are known as good traders. In their transaction with the tourist, I think a fair bargain has been struck.

The pueblo is bustling with activity this afternoon. We understand that many of these ancient "apartment houses" are occupied. One of the first things we see are the beehive ovens or *hornos,* which are believed to have been introduced to the Pueblo by the Spanish. They are in full operation. As we walk close to one, the aroma of freshly baked bread is more than we can resist. From a very friendly Pueblo woman, we buy two loaves. In a few seconds we have torn one loaf into pieces and devoured it. Now we take a walk along the river that courses through the middle of the plaza. It irrigates Pueblo lands before dumping into the Rio Grande. The water is clear and cool. Signs urge us not to despoil the water in any way, as it is used for

Taos drum maker

drinking by the villagers. Sitting along the grassy edge of the river, we finish the second loaf of bread.

We cross the small bridge to the other side of the village and walk among the adobe structures. Today one family and their friends are applying a mudlike plaster to a newly constructed adobe building. They are having a good time. They laugh and joke in a language we do not understand. They are talking in Tiwa, a dialect of the Tanoan language. The building they are plastering looks like a new building, but all the buildings around it look very old. It is thought that some of the sun-dried mud houses here are exactly as they were in 1540 when Hernando de Alvarado, one of Coronado's men, first saw them. He, like us today, was impressed with these multistoried buildings and irrigated fields. Now we look at the building blocks to the north and the south of the river. In places on the north side, the buildings rise to five stories. Their stepped-back or terraced appearance

Pregonero, Taos Pueblo

relieves the harshness of the line, giving these buildings a warm and inviting feeling. Ladders reach from one level to another. In the olden days the units had no doors as we know them. Entry was through a hole in the roof. We walk back over the log bridge toward the north building block. We see numerous open wooden structures in front of the adobe buildings; these, we learn, are *ramadas* serving as drying racks for corn, peppers, and the like. In the winter some of them are covered with bundles of hay, providing shelter for many of the domestic animals.

In some of the apartments fronting the plaza, there are shops and even one or two upscale Indian art galleries. We see a sign on one of the apartment doors. The sign just says CRAFTS and OPEN. When we knock on the side of the open door, an elderly Taos Indian greets us with a warm smile and asks us to come in. The apartment is immaculately clean. The dirt floor is packed so tight that it almost shines. The furniture is simple but comfortable. Our host shows us the bows and arrows he makes. He is very proud of them. We purchase a bow and arrow set and say good-bye. On the way out we notice that the apartment contains no plumbing and that water is still carried in. Although most of the homes elsewhere on the reservation are thoroughly modernized, the older part of Taos Pueblo that we visit today is being kept "traditional."

We walk across the plaza near the entryway and stand in front of the chapel of San Geronimo de Taos. *Geronimo* is the Spanish name for Saint Jerome. The terraced portal to its courtyard and the unobtrusive bell towers seem very much in harmony with the surroundings. We enter the courtyard of the small church. Its brightly colored interior seems to lend light to the room. We learn that this chapel was built after the 1847 revolt when the older chapel, which we passed on the way in, was destroyed. As we admire the building, we discuss the fact that this Christian chapel is visible and easy to find, while the six or more kivas on the Taos reservation are much less obvious. Often this afternoon we have heard drums beating in the distance. We are told that their source is one of the kivas outside the area where guests are allowed. So the people here continue to practice their ancient rituals as well as being active participants in their adopted religion, Catholicism.

The Taos Indians fought the Spanish tooth and nail and, aside from the Hopi

Church at Taos Pueblo

people to the west, were the most independent of the Pueblo people, being one of the last groups to submit to Anglo domination. Today their enemy is creeping urbanism, a formidable foe. Yet at Christmas Eve each year, this church is the site of one of the most interesting rituals performed anywhere in the world. It occurs during the period the Taos Indians call **"The Time for Staying Still,"** a forty-day period of quiet and rest beginning on December 10 and ending January 20, during the interval between the death and rebirth of Mother Earth. But the quiet is broken for a Christian ceremony on Christmas Eve, when after vespers in the mission church of San Geronimo, the pueblo's inhabitants burst into the moonlit plaza carrying the figure of the Madonna Mary, firing rifles, and chanting to the pulsating rhythms of drums that reverberate through the night air. Cracking piñon pitch bonfires called *luminarias* light the way.

Returning to the plaza, we notice that most of the tourists are gone. Tourists may be required to leave the pueblo some days as early as 4:30 P.M. Call for hours. We see several men with blankets over their heads and upper torsos, reminiscent of Arab burnooses. They round the corner, walking with a resoluteness in their moccasin boots. Now we look up and see several more men with striped pastel cotton blankets wrapped around their heads and upper bodies ascend to the top of the pueblo. They are silhouetted against the darkening blue sky as they stand next to the smooth, rounded corner of the mud walls. Watching this ritual, we feel the mystery of Taos Pueblo as a foreign sound emits from one man's lips. He is the *pregonero,* or the pueblo crier, and he is performing an ancient ceremony whose true meaning will always remain obscure to us Anglos. But we know it is near the end of the day and it is time for us to leave. As we drive back to Taos, I continue to think about the friendly Taos Indians we have met today. There are around 2,000 residents living in the pueblo. The community is intact, independent, and knows where it is going. We feel certain that Taos Pueblo will continue to be here to greet us in the future, just as it always has in the past.

STAYING THERE

Lodging

In north central New Mexico you will often have a choice between two different kinds of accommodations. There are motels that resemble modern motels in any part of the United States. But there are also inns, posadas, *fondas,* lodges, B&Bs, ranchos, and even motels that evoke the spirit of the region, either through their architecture and interior design or through their location. In most instances their prices will be higher than those of the standard motels down the road from them. Wherever possible, accommodations with a southwestern ambience will be listed. Some accommodations in the Santa Fe area do not have air-conditioning, since even most summer nights are generally cool in this very high country.

Food

In many of the restaurants of north central New Mexico, you will see menus that refer to native foods, regional cuisine, local foods, Spanish American foods, and Mexican foods. All these notations generally mean a type of food similar to what is called "Mexican food" in most parts of the United States. Chili, enchiladas, tamales, burritos, tacos, and many other similar dishes are all part of the scene. But there is a distinct New Mexican influence on most menus.

You are likely to be served a basket of sopaipillas—little pillows of bread made from flour, lard, sugar, and milk that is rolled very thin, cut into small triangles or squares, and deep-fried. Usually honey or a fruit syrup is served with the sopaipillas. The idea is to poke a hole in the fried puff bread and put the sweetener inside. Sopaipillas filled with honey are a fine antidote to some of the *picante* (hot) chili dishes. Sopaipillas resemble Indian fry bread, which you will see in the pueblos and at Indian dances and fairs. The fry bread is equally delicious but thicker and flatter.

Sometimes the tortillas you are served will be made from blue cornmeal. This is a product made from the bluish black, sometimes dark-slate-gray kernels of Indian corn that have been grown by the Pueblo Indians for centuries. Other colors of corn are also cultivated by the Indians, but it is the cob that contains all blue kernels that is prized by the Hopi for making delicate, flat *piki* bread and by other Pueblo Indians for making a hot cereal known as *atole*. Further hybridization of blue corn has led to a blue-corn popcorn. Instead of mashed refried beans, you will often be served delicious whole brown beans that have been simmered many hours with seasoning. Generally that is the way the Indians have cooked beans since they threw away the basket and replaced it with a clay cooking vessel more than one thousand years ago.

Bean pots of micaceous clay are still fashioned and sold at Nambe, Taos, and Picuris pueblos. But instead of beans you may be served *posole*. *Posole* is like hominy, and it too has been a staple in the region for many years. And then there is *carne adovada*. Pork or beef is marinated for about twenty-four hours in a tangy paste of ground chilies, herbs, and vinegar. The meat is then baked just prior to serving. In ordering New Mexican food in the regional restaurants, you can often choose between a red chili sauce and a green one. (Inquire which one is hotter.) If you are still unsure about how *picante* the sauce is, ask for the sauce to be served on the side. Then you can titrate your own gastronomic distress. Some Santa Feans say that the proper titration is reached when you begin to sweat. But there is no requirement that you turn your dinner into a sauna bath.

Tours, Fairs, Festivals, Fiestas, and Events

If you are planning to be in northern New Mexico for one of the area's major unique summer weekend fairs, festivals, or fiestas, reserve your lodging months ahead of time and prepare yourself for a crowded city. If you are not interested in the special events in the area, schedule your visit there so it does not correspond with those busy dates. Information: **New Mexico Department of Tourism,** P.O. Box 20002, Santa Fe, New Mexico 87504–2004; (800) 733–6396; www.newmexico.org.

The Indian pueblos around Santa Fe open their doors to the public during a number of their celebrations and dance days. These are well worth seeing if you are i... list of some of the m... Native American events... subsequent "Fairs, Festivals,... tas" sections. Contact the visi... mation services listed in the fol... pages for precise dates and additio... information, not only about Native American celebrations but also about other types of celebrations. Also see the individual listings under "Indian Pueblo Telephone Numbers" at the end of the Santa Fe section.)

Shopping

At best it is very difficult for the average traveler who has come to north central New Mexico for a few days or a week or two to make any sense out of the several hundred galleries and shops selling traditional regional and contemporary arts and crafts. Although the galleries and shops listed below are but a few of many, it is hoped that this preselection will help you gain a better perspective about the art market and aid you in finding what you want as quickly as possible. There are many other establishments on the scene not listed here that are worthy of your attention if you have the time to locate them. You may also want to check this book's bibliography for material related to the region's art scene.

Many northern New Mexican cities and towns, such as Santa Fe and Taos, are predominantly Hispanic in their population, yet they have gained much of their popularity and notoriety from the various groups of Pueblo Indians who live in small pueblos up and down the Rio Grande Valley. Only a very small percentage of Indians live in the major cities of the region, yet the cities are the major

...ce for Pueblo Indian arts and crafts. Without a doubt Albuquerque, Santa Fe, and Taos are excellent places to buy pottery, jewelry, woven goods, and drums from the Ácoma, Cochiti, Jemez, Picuris, San Ildefonso, San Juan, Santa Clara, Santo Domingo, Taos, Tesuque, and Zia pueblos. You will also find that these towns are the best places to buy Hispanic or Spanish crafts, including woven rugs, wood carvings, and tin and iron work. In addition, there are many shops that import handcrafted items from Mexico. Although Navajo rugs and Hopi kachina dolls are featured in many stores, they are brought in from the Navajo and Hopi reservations in the Four Corners area. Similarly Zuni handcrafted work is brought in from western New Mexico. So if you plan to include Indian Country (Section 2) or western New Mexico in your travels, you might want to wait and see what is available there. Sometimes better values, as well as a wider selection of crafts, can be found closer to the craft source. But no matter where you choose to purchase traditional southwestern Indian arts and crafts (Navajo rugs, Pueblo pottery, silver and turquoise jewelry), please read this book's buying guide found in Section 2, Indian Country, "Staying There: Shopping (Consumer Tips for Buying Indian Arts and Crafts)." The brief guide you will find there is designed to help you sort out and deal with some of the complexities in today's marketplace. Do read it if you are planning to purchase traditional southwestern Indian crafts.

Because Santa Fe is the home of the prestigious Institute of American Indian Art and has been associated for many years with the Indian arts and crafts revival movement, it has become the contemporary Indian art capital of the United States. You will see excellent paintings, prints, sculpted pieces, and ceramics representing this movement. Many of these pieces are outstanding in their design and execution. Northern New Mexico has also attracted many fine Anglo and Hispanic contemporary artists working in similar media. Artistically this is a rich area.

Albuquerque

As each year goes by, Albuquerque enhances its facilities and services for the traveler. The result is that more people are not only discovering Albuquerque but returning to soak up more of what it has to offer. No doubt as efforts continue to revitalize the downtown area this trend will continue, given Albuquerque's stunning natural setting, its multiethnic ambience, its delightful fairs and festivals, and its unique regional museums. And when visitors discover the increasing number of new and diverse accommodations and good restaurants available there, a return visit may just be inevitable.

The majority of the accommodations listed here center on some of the locations of the major sight-seeing areas this book emphasizes, particularly Old Town, the Indian Pueblo Cultural Center, and the sights west of the Rio Grande. One of the downtown listings, La Posada de Albuquerque, is worth seeing whether you stay there or not (see details pertaining to that hotel in this section). Where possible, small inns and B&Bs that convey the ambience of the region are included. Sometimes this type of accommodation is away from the core of the city but not so far that you cannot easily slide into town to see the sights. Albuquerque also has a hostel, Route 66 Hostel (AAIH), located at 1012 Central Avenue Southwest, Albuquerque, New Mexico 87102; (505) 247–1813. To exchange foreign currency (bills only), contact any of the Albuquerque walk-in branches of Bank of America, or inquire at the visitor information desk in the baggage claim area at the airport.

As with most growing sunbelt cities, Albuquerque has experienced a restaurant boom that is unparalleled in its history. (Although this book lists good restaurants that serve American, continental, and ethnic foods of all sorts, the "Food" section primarily emphasizes the food of the region.) You can eat native New Mexican fare in large, upscale, trendy restaurants or in small, modest, family-operated, "hole-in-the-wall" cafes. You will find the full range listed here.

The airport is located in the southeastern part of the city, not far from the University of New Mexico campus (Albuquerque is served by most of the major airlines). Many of the sights mentioned in this book are located in the west end of town near Old Town, not far from the Rio Grande. Many of the accommodations, restaurants, and shops listed are also centered on that area, the Nob Hill area, and in Corrales. You will not have trouble getting from one end of town to another, as Albuquerque has an excellent freeway system feeding all four quadrants of the city. It is well marked and easy to negotiate. Information: **Albuquerque Convention and Visitors' Bureau,** 401 Second Street, Albuquerque, New Mexico 87102; (505) 842–9918, (800)

284–2282, or (800) 733–9918; www.itsatrip.org. Information booths are downtown at the convention center; in Old Town at Plaza Don Luis (across from Old Town Plaza); at the Albuquerque International Airport (Sunport) near the baggage claim area; and at the Indian Pueblo Cultural Center (New Mexico State Visitor Center).

Lodging

Sheraton Old Town Inn. Located within easy walking distance of "Old Town" Albuquerque, this eleven-story New Mexico Heritage Hotel offers one of the most pleasant places to stay in Albuquerque. From its upper stories there are excellent territorial views of the city and environs. There is an inviting outdoor swimming pool and patio area. Tigeux Park, several blocks from the hotel's north entrance, is a nice place to jog. The interior of the inn is tastefully decorated with regional arts and crafts. The inn has a moderately priced coffee shop and Cristobal's, a dinner restaurant. The 188 rooms are spacious and comfortable. Some have private patios. Airport transportation available. Information: Sheraton Old Town Inn, 800 Rio Grande Boulevard Northwest, Albuquerque, New Mexico 87104; (505) 843–6300 or (800) 237–2133; fax (505) 842–9863; www.buynewmexico.com. Expensive.

Casas de Sueños Old Town Country Inn. Very conveniently located just 2 easy blocks from Old Town is this 1930s former artists' home and adobe compound, with lovely gardens in a 1-acre location that has been converted into a charming, comfortable inn with 15 suites and casitas, all with private bath. Some have fireplaces, some have patios, some have small gardens, and all are individually and handsomely decorated. Hot tubs. Full breakfast is served inside or on the adjacent garden patio. Gift shop and gallery. Information: Casas de Sueños Old Town Country Inn, 310 Rio Grande Southwest, Albuquerque, New Mexico 87104; (505) 247–4560; fax (505) 842–8493; www.casadesuenos.com. Moderate to expensive.

Böttger-Koch Mansion Bed and Breakfast. About 1 block from Old Town is this Victorian-style, two-story historic home that now accommodates seven large guest rooms and one suite. Private jet tubs in some rooms. The suite has an ornate, pressed and sculptured tin ceiling and a carved marble fireplace. Continental breakfast inside or out on the patio. Information: Böttger-Koch Bed and Breakfast, 110 San Felipe Northwest, Albuquerque, New Mexico 87104; (505) 243–3639 or (800) 758–3639; fax (505) 243–4378; www.bottger.com. Moderate to expensive.

Old Town Bed and Breakfast. This conveniently located, adobe-style B&B is just a few blocks from historic Old Town Plaza and museums in a very nice, quiet, tree-shaded residential area. Its first- and second-story guest rooms are air-cooled; one room has a private bath, while the other (suite) shares a Jacuzzi with owner. Leave your car at the house and take the pleasant ten-minute walk through Tigeux Park to Old Town and the museums. Breakfast served on the patio or in the dining room. Call for directions. Information: Old Town Bed and Breakfast, 707 Seventeenth

Street Northwest, Albuquerque, New Mexico 87104; (505) 764–9144 or (888) 900–9144; www.inn-new-mexico.com. Inexpensive.

The Casitas at Old Town. Located just off Mountain Road Northwest with its many museums and just a few blocks from Old Town is this nineteenth-century adobe compound, converted and updated into two casitas, each with private bath, kitchen, and corner fireplace. Information: The Casitas at Old Town, 1604 Old Town Road Northwest, Albuquerque, New Mexico 87104; (505) 843–7479. Inexpensive.

Best Western Rio Grande Inn. Adjacent to I–40 but conveniently located near Old Town is this 170-room, four-story motel with southwestern ambience. Heated swimming pool, whirlpool. Restaurant. Information: Best Western Rio Grande Inn, 1015 Rio Grande Northwest, Albuquerque, New Mexico 87104; (505) 843–9500 or (800) 959–4726; fax (505) 843–9238; www.riograndeinn.com. Moderate.

Brittania and W. E. Mauger Estate Bed and Breakfast. This historic Victorian home, only 10 blocks from Old Town, has been thoroughly renovated to its previous splendor and is now a wonderfully comfortable inn. Built in 1897, it is one of the oldest homes of this style in Albuquerque. There are eight air-conditioned rooms (one suite), each with private bath and shower. A full continental breakfast is served in the handsome and spacious public rooms. Information: Brittania and W. E. Mauger Estate Bed and Breakfast, 701 Roma Northwest, Albuquerque, New Mexico 87102; (505) 242–8755 or (800) 719–9189;

fax (505) 842–8835; www.mauge bb.com. Moderate to expensive.

Monterey Motel. This fifteen-unit, air-conditioned motel is just 2 blocks from Old Town on Central Avenue (from I–40 take the Rio Grande Boulevard exit). The price is right for families or budget travelers. Color TVs and queen-size beds are available in all rooms, and a coin-operated laundry is on the premises. Heated swimming pool. Many Old Town restaurants are nearby. Information: Monterey Motel, 2402 Central Southwest, Albuquerque, New Mexico 87104; (505) 243–3554 or (877) 666–8379; fax (505) 243–9701. Inexpensive.

Hacienda Antigua Bed and Breakfast. Easy to get to from I–25 (take exit 230 and travel Osuna Road, taking a right to 6708 Tierra Drive Northwest) and located in a quiet residential area. This 200-year-old adobe hacienda with all the modern amenities offers yards and yards of Southwest charm with its beautifully furnished public rooms. Breakfast is taken on the cozy courtyard with its well-kept gardens and Mexican fountain. The four comfortable rooms and four suites and swimming pool offer the southwestern relaxation many are seeking. Information: Hacienda Antigua Bed and Breakfast, 6708 Tierra Drive Northwest, Albuquerque, New Mexico 87107; (505) 345–5399 or (800) 201–2986; www.haciendantigua.com. Moderate.

La Posada de Albuquerque. If the rebuilt, modern glass and steel high-rise core of downtown Albuquerque has a heart and soul, it resides in the ten-story hotel at 125 Second Street Southwest. There Conrad Hilton built his pride and joy in 1939. You get there from I–25 by taking the Central exit and traveling Central to Second Street. The Albuquerque Hilton, as La Posada de Albuquerque was known in those days, saw the famous and the soon-to-be famous enter its stunning New Mexican–style lobby. Conrad Hilton honeymooned with Zsa Zsa Gabor in room 821. Jimmy Stewart checked in on weekends when he was stationed at the nearby air base during World War II. And Lucille Ball, along with a host of other movers and shakers, made pilgrimages to this most elegant hotel, which soon became the center of Albuquerque's social life. Today this restored hotel with its spacious territorial-style lobby with pueblo deco motifs is popular with locals and visitors alike. Conrad's, a stylish contemporary restaurant, is located just off the lobby. The 109 air-conditioned rooms and three suites are also decorated in southwestern style with Spanish-style bedsteads and wall art of the region. Located only about ten minutes from Old Town Plaza. Parking fee. Information: La Posada de Albuquerque, 125 Second Street Northwest, Albuquerque, New Mexico 87102; (505) 242–9090 or (800) 777–5732; fax (505) 242–1945; www.laposada~abq.com. Moderate.

Le Baron Courtyard and Suites. A large, conveniently located motel near the junction of U.S. I–40 and Highway 25 at 2120 Menaul Northeast. There are 200 air-conditioned units, pool, and coin-operated laundry. Restaurants nearby. Take the Carlisle Boulevard exit from I–40. Information: Le Baron Courtyard and Suites, 2120 Menaul Boulevard Northeast, Albuquerque, New Mexico 87107; (505) 884–0250 or (800)

444–7378; fax (505) 883–0594; www.lebaroncourtyard.com. Inexpensive.

Fairfield Inn by Marriott. Conveniently located at the junction of I–25 and I–40 is this handsome but basic motel in the Marriott chain that features an indoor pool, sauna, Jacuzzi, complimentary continental breakfast, and airport transportation. The 188 smallish rooms are comfortable and have all the amenities. Information: Fairfield Inn by Marriott, 1760 Menaul Boulevard Northeast, Albuquerque, New Mexico 87102; (505) 889–4000 or (800) 228–2800; fax (505) 872–3094; www.fairfieldinn.com. Inexpensive.

Amberley Suite Hotel. This large three-story motor hotel is located north of Albuquerque just off the main route to Santa Fe, I–25. Take exit 231 from I–25 and follow the frontage road to Pan American Freeway Northeast. All of the 170 units are suites, each having two rooms plus bath. The living area includes a kitchen with a full-size refrigerator, microwave oven, and built-in coffeemaker. Heated pool, whirlpool bath, sauna bath, health club, coffee shop. And don't miss the landscaped courtyard with fountains. Information: Amberley Suite Hotel, 7620 Pan American Freeway Northeast, Albuquerque, New Mexico 87109; (505) 823–1300 or (800) 333–9806; fax (505) 823–2896; www.amberley suite.com. Moderate.

Los Poblanos Inn. Located in the village of Los Ranchos de Albuquerque in North Valley on 5 acres of gardens, ponds, orchards, and fields with knockout views of the Sandia Mountains is this historic John Gaw

Meem adobe on the site of a nineteenth-century rancho. There are three rooms and two suites around a charming interior courtyard, and a larger detached guest house. New Mexico antiques and art work adorn every corner of this pleasant hostelry. Gourmet breakfast and afternoon snacks included. Handy to Old Town and downtown. Information: Los Poblanos Inn; 4803 Rio Grande Boulevard Northwest; Village of Ranchos de Albuquerque, New Mexico 87107; (505) 344–9297; fax (505) 342–1302; www.lospoblanos.com. Moderate to expensive.

Sarabande Bed and Breakfast. Situated on Rio Grande Boulevard in an enviable location out in North Valley about halfway between Old Town and Corrales, this five-room restful stop has some rooms situated around the garden. This modern home is beautifully furnished Southwest style, as are the public rooms, where a full breakfast is served. Information: Sarabande Bed and Breakfast, 5637 Rio Grande Boulevard Northwest, Albuquerque, New Mexico 87107; (505) 345–4923 or (888) 506–4923; www.sarabandebb.com. Moderate to expensive.

Casita Chamisa Bed and Breakfast. Located in Albuquerque's cottonwood-shaded North Valley not far from the Rio Grande is this very southwestern B&B. There's a separate two-bedroom guesthouse with private bath, kitchenette, and fireplace, or you may choose a spacious room with a fireplace and private bath in the owner's home. Enclosed pool and hot tub are available to guests. Homemade breakfasts. There is a 700-year-old Pueblo Indian village that has been excavated on the property under the auspices of the Maxwell Museum of Anthropology. Fifteen minutes from Old Town and museums. Nearby walking and jogging trails. Call for directions. Information: Casita Chamisa Bed and Breakfast, 850 Chamisal Road Northwest, Albuquerque, New Mexico 87107; (505) 897–4644; www.casitachamisa.com. Moderate.

Around Albuquerque to the North—West of the Rio Grande

Corrales is a charming, still somewhat rural community—all the more precious as rural Albuquerque slowly recedes—set amidst orchards, fertile fields, and the cottonwood forests along the Rio Grande. There are walking and jogging trails beside the *acequias* (or water ditches), as well as alongside the mother river. Interesting shops and restaurants make Corrales a pleasant destination. To reach Corrales from U.S. I–40, take the Rio Grande (Old Town) exit and travel north 6.5 miles through North Valley and the village of Los Ranchos de Albuquerque, turning left onto Alameda Road to cross the Rio Grande. In less than a mile, turn right at the first major intersection onto Corrales Road. From I–25 exit west onto Alameda Boulevard (New Mexico Highway 528).

Yours Truly Bed and Breakfast. Wonderfully situated out in the countryside on a high hill (just above Corrales) that offers unending, magnificent views of the Rio Grande Valley and the Sandia Mountains is this modern, ranch-style home with four guest rooms, each with a private bath.

The hospitable owners make this seem like a real bed-and-breakfast place. Spa, spacious view patio, walking trails. Owners are hot air balloon enthusiasts. Full breakfast inside or on the patio. Information: Yours Truly Bed and Breakfast, 160 Paseo de Corrales, P.O. Box 2263, Corrales, New Mexico 87048; (505) 898–7027 or (800) 942–7890; fax (505) 898–9022; www.yourstrulybb.com. Inexpensive to moderate.

The Nora Dixon Place Bed and Breakfast. B&B on the north side of Corrales has three charming rooms with private baths. Information: The Nora Dixon Place Bed and Breakfast, 312 Dixon Road, Corrales, New Mexico 87048; (505) 898–3662 or (888) 667–2349; fax (505) 898–6430. Inexpensive to moderate.

Sandhill Crane Bed and Breakfast. A restful establishment that has two rooms with private baths and one two-bedroom suite. Information: Sandhill Crane Bed and Breakfast, 389 Camino Hermosa, Corrales, New Mexico 87048; (505) 898–2445 or (800) 375–2445; fax (505) 898–1189; www.bbonline.com/nm/sandhill. Inexpensive to moderate.

Hyatt Regency Tamaya Resort and Spa. Owned by the Santa Ana tribe on their reservation north of Corrales, not far from I–25 at **Bernalillo,** New Mexico, is the Albuquerque area's most luxurious place to stay. Snugged discreetly into the west bank of the Rio Grande with drop-dead views of the Sandia Mountains and readily accessible walking and jogging trails in the cottonwood forest along the river, this 350-room hotel twenty minutes from central Albuquerque and forty minutes from Santa Fe has a to-die-for collection of American Indian art, a golf course, tennis courts, three heated outdoor swimming pools, horseback riding, full-service spa, two restaurants, and a handy deli. Although you'll rub shoulders with convention-goers, this spacious property has room enough for everyone. Search out discounted rates. Information: Hyatt Regency Tamaya Resort and Spa, 1300 Tuyuna Trail, Santa Ana Pueblo, New Mexico 87004; (505) 867–1234 or (800) 554–9288; fax (505) 771–6180; www.tamayahyatt.com. Very expensive.

Camping

Albuquerque Central K.O.A. Campground. Located east of downtown. 157 paved sites. Cabins and kitchens available. Hot tub, showers, laundry, and rest rooms. Information: Albuquerque Central K.O.A. Campground, 12400 Skyline Road Northeast, Albuquerque, New Mexico 87123; (505) 296–2729 or (800) 562–7781.

Albuquerque North K.O.A. Out a little north of Albuquerque in Bernalillo, New Mexico, is this quiet setting among large trees with seventy-plus sites, forty-one with full hookups. Pleasant tent area, shaded pool. Information: Albuquerque North K.O.A., 555 Hill Road, Bernalillo, New Mexico 87004; (505) 867–5227 or (800) 562–3616.

Food

Pueblo Harvest Cafe. Located 1 block north of U.S. I–40 West at 2401 Twelfth Street Northwest. From I–40 West take the Sixth and Twelfth

Streets exit, and turn right at second stoplight onto Twelfth Street Northwest. From Old Town take Rio Grande Boulevard north, pass under I–40 West, and turn right onto Indian School Road, which becomes Menaul Boulevard. Turn right from Menaul Boulevard onto Twelfth Street Northwest. Located in the Indian Pueblo Cultural Center; (505) 843–7270, ext. 327 or (800) 766–4405; www.indian pueblo.com. This restaurant, open for breakfast and lunch, is a must if you are new to this area. It is the place to "break in" on the foods of the region. The menu includes many native southwestern American Indian dishes, as well as a large variety of New Mexican specialties. Open daily.

La Placita Dining Room. In Old Town on San Felipe Street, across from the plaza; (505) 247–2204. This establishment has been serving travelers and locals for several decades. Built in 1706, its thick adobe walls, once enclosing one of the first Spanish homes in Albuquerque, wrap around an inner courtyard that is now covered for year-round use. The other rooms of this hacienda make up the rest of the restaurant. The food is basic regional fare, such as tamales, enchiladas, *chilies rellenos,* and sopaipillas. Standard American fare is also served. Historically and architecturally this 275-year-old building is worth a visit by itself. Music some nights. Open for lunch and dinner. Moderate.

La Hacienda Restaurant. Located just down the street from La Placita at 302 San Felipe Northwest (505–243–3131) are the dining rooms of this longtime visitors' favorite in a large, turn-of-the-twentieth-century hacienda. In the attractive, no-nonsense,

Mexican-style dining rooms or outside on the porch, you can have a fine enchilada, *chilies rellenos,* or other regional specialties, along with sopaipillas, for a modest price. **Casa Fiesta Mexican Grill,** a sister enterprise, is a more contemporary version of La Hacienda, located just down the block and across the street on the south side of the Plaza at 2004 South Plaza Northwest; (505) 248–0110. Both restaurants open daily for lunch and dinner except for major holidays. Moderate.

Casa de Ruiz Church Street Cafe. Situated in a historic residence, the Casa de Ruiz—at 2111 Church Street Northwest, right behind the church in Old Town—is a pleasant restaurant offering both inside and patio dining; (505) 247–8522. For lunch you'll dine on traditional New Mexican fare such as *carne adovada al horno* (oven-cooked pork marinated in red chili), green chili chicken soup, vegetarian or pork tamales, and sopaipillas. But there are salads and sandwiches as well. Breakfast and lunch daily. Dinner some weekend summer evenings. Open daily till 4:00 p.m. Inexpensive.

La Crepe Michel. Tucked back in the corner of a tree-shaded courtyard in Old Town just off San Felipe Northwest is this French restaurant (505–242–1251) that may appeal if you've been having too many spicy, regional meals. You can dine indoors or out for lunch or dinner and be very pleased with the freshness and quality of the food here, which ranges from crepes to complex fresh fish and veal dishes. Excellent desserts. Espresso. Dinner reservations recommended. Moderate.

Chef du Jour. Here's one near Old Town you shouldn't miss. One long block east of Rio Grand Boulevard and down Central Avenue past the post office, take a right onto San Pasqual Avenue Southwest. There hidden away in a small nondescript strip mall at 119 San Pasqual Southwest is this stellar lunch restaurant (505–247–8998). Enjoy a starter of fire-roasted spicy tomato basil soup followed by a grilled chicken and sharp white cheddar cheese quesadilla with carmelized shallots and chipotle barbecue sauce. Wine and beer list. Lunch Monday through Friday. Call for dinner hours. Moderate.

Seasons Rotisserie and Grill. For a lunch or dinner that veers toward nouveau Mediterranean rather than Mexican or Southwest, seek out this restaurant—open for lunch or dinner—just across Mountain Road Northwest from Old Town in San Felipe Plaza; (505) 766–5100. Spit-roasted chicken with roasted garlic mashed potatoes or grilled local sweet Italian sausage with grilled polenta in a spicy tomato-veal sauce are but a few of the tasty offerings. Soups, salads, and bread (with the requisite dipping oils) are excellent. And don't forget the tiramisu or fruit cobbler for dessert. Dine inside or out or catch views from the second floor. Dinner daily. Lunch Monday through Saturday; www.seasonsthenet.com. Moderate.

Duran Central Pharmacy. Just a hop, skip, and a jump from Old Town (about 3 blocks) is this unique cafe (505–247–4141) at 1815 Central Northwest, a local lunch favorite situated in one end of a drugstore. Go early or late to avoid the lines. The popular red sauce may be just what the doctor ordered. Try it on the blue corn enchiladas, *carne adovada,* stuffed sopaipillas, or *huevos rancheros.* Breakfast, too. Soft drinks and shakes. Inexpensive.

Monroe's. Also located close to Old Town (a short drive or a long walk), at 1500 Lomas Northwest, is this egalitarian breakfast, lunch, and dinner establishment (505–242–1111), where your craving for well-prepared New Mexican food can also be sated. Inexpensive.

Rio Grande Cantina. Located just a short distance from Old Town, at 901 Rio Grande Boulevard Northwest in the Rio Grande Plaza, is this local lunch and dinner favorite (505–242–1777), open daily, where you can dine or drink either inside or out on a patio with its own fireplace. Here they grow their own chilies for their popular fresh salsa. New Mexican regional specialties star here, but you can get a hamburger or fresh fish too, as well as a dish of tantalizing *sopa de lima* (lime soup). Excellent margaritas and beer selection. Inexpensive to moderate.

M and J Restaurant and Sanitary Tortilla Factory. Located at 403 Second Street Southwest; (505) 242–4890. This mecca of native Mexican food has received rave national reviews. Sometimes the best is the simplest, and that is what you have at the very plain but equally authentic M and J. Go easy on the hot sauce unless you know your limits. Tortillas are made on the premises, and freshly prepared chips with homemade salsa are but a few of the joys here. A burrito filled with *carne adovada* is a specialty, and the *chilies rellenos* are outstanding, as are most of the other regional entrees, which are served with a homemade red or green chili sauce. Sopaipillas and honey are the antidote in this "picante" haven. Children's menu. Breakfast (especially *huevos rancheros*) and lunch until 3:30 P.M. Closed Saturday and Sunday and major holidays. Inexpensive.

Artichoke Cafe. Located at 424 Central Avenue Southeast; (505) 243–0200; www.artichoke.com. If you are looking for good New American, French, and Italian cooking in Albuquerque, this is the place to come. Fresh food is the byword in this very nice corner bistro cafe, a handsome, comfortable, intimate place with just the right touch of elegance. The tantalizing array of specialties includes fresh fish entrees and numerous outstanding veal, lamb, beef, and pasta dishes. Excellent desserts. Wine list. Lunch and dinner. Open for lunch Monday through Friday. Dinner Monday through Saturday. Sunday dinner in season. Moderate.

Starz. Downtown between the Convention Center and Old Town at 918 Central Southwest (adjacent to Silver Moon Lodge; 505–848–7827) is this contemporary American diner, compliments of the Spanish tapas gurus on Santa Fe's Canyon Road. Open for breakfast, lunch, and dinner, serving traditional American favorites and tapas, of course. Inexpensive to moderate.

66 Diner. Located on old Highway 66 at 1405 Central Avenue Northeast is this 1950s-style diner (505–247–1421) that is a real kick. At lunch or dinner daily you can get just about anything you want at the 66, including malts, shakes, sodas, and phosphates at the fountain and blue-plate specials featuring old-time favorites like chicken pot pie, beef stew and cornbread, and pot roast. Also hotdogs, hamburgers a la every kind (green chili cheeseburger), soups, and salads. Breakfast Saturday and Sunday. Inexpensive.

Monte Vista Fire Station. Out by the University of New Mexico in the Nob Hill area in a renovated unique old pueblo-revival fire station at 3201 Central Avenue is this popular and innovative restaurant; (505) 255–2424. Noveau Southwest is the culinary theme for a wide array of well-prepared fish, pasta, duck, lamb, and pork dishes. The bar where you can catch views of mountain sunsets is upstairs. Dinner nightly. Lunch Monday through Friday. Moderate.

Flying Star Cafe. Located in the Nob Hill area at 3416 Central Southeast; (505) 255–6633; and also in Los Ranchos de Albuquerque at 4026 Rio Grande Northwest; (505) 344–6714. This busy cafe—with a huge selections of magazines for sale—is worth a visit if you're in the area. Scrumptious breakfast pastries, excellent coffees, Italian sodas, and a good gelato selection bring the customers in. But their quiches, soups, sandwiches, salads, and desserts are invariably delicious, making this a worthwhile destination for lunch or a light dinner. Outside dining. Open daily.

Scalo Northern Italian Grill. A veteran up on flourishing Nob Hill at 3500 Central Southeast; (505) 255–8781; www.scalonm.com. This popular and very good lunch and dinner restaurant continues to please. The excellent soups, salads, pasta dishes, succulent grilled meats, and fresh fish entrees are the reasons why. Commendable Italian wine list,

Western red-tailed hawk

desserts. Moderate.

Barelas Coffee House. Just south of the downtown Civic Plaza area at 1502 Fourth Southwest near the Barelas Bridge; (505) 843–7577. This down-home, native food cafe has legendary green chili sauce. In addition to *huevos rancheros* and enchiladas (maybe slathered in some of that green sauce), burritos, and *carne adovada,* you can also order that Pueblo Indian favorite *posole.* Hamburgers. Fresh tortillas are made on the premises, as are the dessert empanadas. Or you can soothe your membranes with a deliciously smooth and cooling rice pudding. Breakfast and lunch until 3:00 P.M. Closed Sunday.

Sadie's Dining Room. Located at 6230 Fourth Street Northwest; (505) 345–5339. This very popular restaurant, with its outdoor patios, features well-prepared, consistently good New Mexican food. Many dishes come with *papitas*—tasty, diced Spanish-style potatoes—which help offset the spicy and delicious *carne adovada, chilies rel-*

lenos, and enchiladas slathered with red or green chili sauce. Beer and wine. Open daily for lunch and dinner. Inexpensive to moderate.

Le Cafe Miche. Located in northeast Albuquerque at 1431 Wyoming Boulevard Northeast (505– 299–6088) is this very good Zagat-rated traditional French restaurant with a bistro flair. You can start with a particularly tasty onion soup or escargot and move on to veal piccata or one of the other signature veal dishes, lamb, fresh fish, or pork. Excellent wine list. Homemade desserts. Moderate.

El Pinto Restaurant. Located at 10500 Fourth Street Northwest, 9 miles north of Old Town in Albuquerque's North Valley; (505) 898–1771. This handsome, territorial-style restaurant is set on spacious landscaped grounds. Meals are served either in the nicely appointed dining rooms or outdoors on the garden patio. New Mexican food is the specialty of the house. Included are *carne adovada, tamales, chilies rellenos,* burritos, and very good enchiladas, along with puffy sopaipillas. To get to El Pinto from I–40, take the Rio Grande Avenue exit, and drive north 6.5 miles to Alameda Road. Turn right onto Alameda, and drive about 1 mile to the junction with Fourth Street Northwest, New Mexico Highway 313. Turn left onto Fourth Street, and drive about 1 mile to the restaurant on the right side of the road. Lunch and dinner daily. Inexpensive to moderate.

Terra American Bistro. Located on the east side of the Rio Grande out by Corrales at 1119 Alameda Northwest; (505) 792–1700; terrabistro. com. This very nice lunch and dinner restaurant offers up some of the more creative new American fare in the city. Start with baby spinach with imported gorgonzola cheese, hot sweet vinaigrette, and candied pecans, and follow with the signature entree: mushroom-crusted beef tenderloin. Wines, dessert, Sunday brunch. Closed Monday. Moderate.

Jim White's Casa Vieja. At 4541 Corrales Road (505–890–5234) is this historic hacienda and pleasant place to eat, either indoors or out, weather permitting. Its American grill menu features mixed grill kabobs with a green chili aioli, sauteed Sweetwoods chicken breast filled with local goat cheese, and numerous New Mexican specialties. Moderate.

Indigo Crow Cafe. Located at 4515 Corrales Road; (505) 898–7000. Lunch or dinner inside or out under the cottonwoods is always a treat here. Start with the French onion soup gratine or soup of the day. Move on to apple jack quesadillas or blue corn–encrusted rainbow trout. Wine and beer lists, desserts. Sunday brunch. Closed Monday. Moderate.

Tours and Activities

Walk in Time Tours. Discover the Old Town Territorial period history on a two-hour narrated walking tour; (505) 232–7010 or (888) 921–TOUR; www.geocities.com/ abqwalkingtours.

Rio Grande Super Tours and All-star Limousine. Step-on guides as well as daily tours around Albuquerque; (505) 790–0246.

Jane Butel's Cooking School. This vacation cooking school at the La Posada de Albuquerque Hotel is a tour de force with the talented culinary wizard Jane Butel in charge. This editor of multiple Southwest cookbooks has weekend and weeklong classes. Information: Jane Butel Cooking School, La Posada de Albuquerque, 125 Second Avenue, Albuquerque, New Mexico 87102; (505) 243–2622 or (800) 472–8229; www.janebutel.com.

Old Town Bicycles. Bicycle rentals and service and mountain bike tours. Information: Old Town Bicycles, 2209-B Central Northwest, Albuquerque, New Mexico 87104; (505) 247–4926; www.oldtownbicycles.com.

Horseback Riding

The Stables at Tamaya. Located at the Hyatt Regency Tamaya Resort and Spa on the Santa Ana Indian Reservation north of Bernalillo, New Mexico. Trail rides or carriage rides along the Rio Grande. Information: 1300 Tamaya Trail, Santa Ana, Pueblo; (505) 867–1234 or (800) 554–9288; www.tamaya.com.

Fairs, Festivals, and Fiestas

For up-to-date event information: (505) 842–9918 or (800) 284–2282; www.itsatrip.org.

The National Fiery Foods and Barbecue Show. Where better to celebrate hot food and spicy products but in Albuquerque? Held annually the first week of March in the Albuquerque Convention Center; (505) 298–3835; www.fiery-foods.com.

Annual Rio Grande Arts and Crafts Festival and Show. This juried fine arts and crafts event featuring a couple of hundred artists from across the nation is held at the New Mexico State Fairgrounds on a weekend early in March. Demonstrations, entertainment, food, and fun; (505) 292–7457; www.riogrande festivals.com.

American Indian Week Celebration. This week filled with Indian music, dance, food, and fun is held the last week of April at the Indian Pueblo Cultural Center; (505) 843–7270 or (800) 766–4405; www.indianpueblo.org.

Gathering of Nations Pow Wow and Miss Indian World Competition. This event, held the last weekend in April, involves 3,000 dancers and singers from the United States and Canada; (505) 843–7270, (505) 836–2810 or (800) 766–4405; www.indianpueblo.org.

Annual Rio Grande Celtic Festival. The Celtic Festival and Highland Games, held one day in mid-May at Menaul School (between Broadway and University), offers food, dance, music, attire, and athletic events of the Celtic Heritage.

Annual New Mexico Arts and Crafts Fair. This colossal event, involving several hundred craftspersons from New Mexico, is held the last weekend in June at the state fairgrounds, 5500 San Mateo Northeast. The participants, who include some of New Mexico's best Spanish, Indian, and Anglo artists, bring their finest ceramics, fiber arts, glass, sculptures, and more for the largest event of this kind in New Mexico; (505) 884–9043.

Magnifico—Art of Albuquerque. This premier juried exhibition of

Albuquerque area artists showcases both emerging and established artists from mid-August through mid-September at the Albuquerque Museum; (505) 242–8244 or 243–7255; www.magnifico.org.

New Mexico State Fair. This popular event is held over a two-week period in September, starting the weekend after Labor Day. In addition to the usual displays at most state fairs, this one includes exhibits of Navajo rugs, Spanish weaving, Indian pottery and jewelry, and many other crafts. And there is entertainment in the Indian Village and Villa Hispanic replicas, with native music, dances, songs, and costumes. There is also horseracing and a rodeo. Held in the fairgrounds at Central Avenue and San Pedro; (505) 265–1791.

Albuquerque International Balloon Fiesta. This event, held nine days spanning the first two weekends in October, has been important in putting Albuquerque on the map. Most Americans and many Europeans have by now seen magazine or newspaper pictures of hundreds of hot air balloons as they ascend above the desert over Albuquerque. Although balloons go up all week, the mass rising occurs only at sunrise on the first and last weekends; (888) 422–7277; www.balloonfiesta.com.

Southwest Arts Festival. This large exhibition of arts and crafts from the Southwest as well as across the nation is an invitational, juried show held in early- to mid-October. Displayed work for sale at the New Mexico State Fairgrounds, 1554 Don Felipe Road Southwest; (505) 898–1594; www.southwestartsfestival.net.

Weems Artfest. In early November this knock-your-eyes-out exhibition of several hundred artists and craftspeople from New Mexico and seventeen other states and award-winning Children's ArtMart is held at the New Mexico State Fairgrounds; (505) 293–6133.

Shopping

There are many excellent shops in Albuquerque that sell both traditional Indian and contemporary crafts from this region. Many of the better shops are in the Old Town area in west Albuquerque. The shops listed here have been favorites over the years and have a reputation of dependability and reliability. Generally speaking you will get what you pay for in these shops.

Gift Shops at the Indian Pueblo Cultural Center. Located at 2401 Twelfth Street Northwest; (505) 843–7270. In these shops you will find a wide variety of carefully chosen Indian pottery, basketry, weaving, and jewelry from the nineteen participating pueblos. Also a large selection of Southwest American Indian books.

Adobe Gallery. Located at 413 Romero Street Northwest; (505) 243–8485 or (800) 821–5221; www.adobegallery.com. A collector's paradise and a casual shopper's delight. The owner of this spacious Old Town, museum-quality gallery and his staff know their stuff, having had many years of contact with Southwest Indian artists and craftspeople. Contemporary and historic Pueblo Indian pottery is a specialty here, but there are also old and new Hopi kachina dolls, Navajo rugs, and ceremonial sashes, as well as Southwest Indian paintings, baskets, old Indian jewelry, and antique Mission furniture. In addition to the tastefully displayed craft and art pieces, the gallery also sells Southwest American Indian art books.

R. C. Gorman/Nizhoni Gallery. Located at 323 Romero Street Northwest #1 in Old Town; (505) 843–7667 or (800) 399–2970; www.rcgorman-nizhoni.com. This gallery is the authorized representative of Navajo artist R. C. Gorman. It is a showcase for many of his paintings, prints, and sculpted pieces. Other contemporary artists are also shown.

Christmas Shop. Located at 400 Romero Street Northwest; (505) 843–6744. There are Christmas shops, and then there is this truly original store that sells high-quality Christmas decorations reflecting the Indian and Spanish heritage of the Southwest, as well as Mexico and the Americas. Ingenious is the word for the wax candle luminarias and chili pepper Christmas light covers.

Old Town Card Shop. Located at 1919 Old Town Road Northwest in a small shopping complex about ½ block east of the Old Town plaza; (505) 247–9634. Some of the most unusual and beautiful greeting cards from all over the world are gathered together here. In addition to a wide selection of Southwest regional cards, the shop prints its own very fine silk-screened cards, depicting Southwest Christmas scenes, Rio Grande Pueblo pottery, and Navajo rug patterns.

Andrews Pueblo Pottery and Art Gallery. Located in Plaza Don Luis at 303 Romero Northwest, Old Town;

(505) 243–0414 or (800) 606–0543; www.andrewspueblopottery.com. This well-established Southwest Indian art gallery is worth a stop. But the stop may be a long one, as this gallery's selection of kachina dolls, fetishes, paintings, Doug West's serigraphs, other graphics, and baskets is extensive and outstanding. Also you will see rare old Pueblo pottery. Open daily.

Hispaniae. Located at 2032 South Plaza Northwest; (505) 244–1533. In this folk art gallery you will find moderately priced items from Mexico and the Americas. In a sister gallery **John Isaac Antiques** several doors down the street and upstairs at 2036 South Plaza Northwest (505–842–6656), there are many Latin American, American Indian, and Country American pieces of great interest and high quality.

Cranes and Crows Birding and Nature Shop. Located at 400 B San Felipe Street; (505) 242–0800. At this birding and nature shop, you can either read up on or gear up for birding in the Southwest. Bird art and special gifts as well.

Casa Talavera. Located at 621 Rio Grande Boulevard Northwest; (505) 243–2413. If you have an interest in handmade tiles from Talavera, Mexico, and other areas across the border, do not miss this shop. It carries every size, shape, and configuration of handmade glazed and unglazed tiles. In addition, it has a fine selection of Mexican handicrafts.

Wide Open Spaces Bookstore. This Public Lands bookstore and information outlet at 6501 Fourth Street Southwest (505–345–9498) has just about every regional hiking and outdoor recreation title you may be looking for. Detailed maps as well.

Palms Trading Company. Located at 1504 Lomas Boulevard Northwest; (505) 247–8504. This store sells Southwest Indian jewelry, pottery, sandpaintings, Navajo rugs, and much more. You will browse among authentic American Indian crafts as well as curio look-alikes made elsewhere. Ask questions to be sure you are buying what you intend. The final price may be less than the ticket price.

Bookworks. Located in the Dietz Farm Plaza at 4022 Rio Grande Boulevard Northwest; (505) 344–8139. This excellent full-service bookstore offers a wide selection of regional Southwest titles, as well as titles in just about every other category. Unusual titles often not found elsewhere can be found here.

Museum Shop–Maxwell Museum of Anthropology. University of New Mexico campus. Located on University Boulevard, just north of Martin Luther King Boulevard; (505) 277–4405 or (505) 277–3700; unm.edu/~maxwell. This small shop carries folk crafts and jewelry from the region and beyond. The book section is wide ranging and encompasses local as well as worldwide ethnic and cultural subjects. The museum also sells its own books, such as *Southwestern Weaving* and *Seven Families in Pueblo Pottery*, classics in the craft field. Also a children's gift section.

Mariposa Gallery. Located in the Nob Hill district at 3500 Central Avenue Southeast; (505) 268–6828; www.mariposagallery.com. If your interest is fine contemporary crafts, you should not miss this gallery. It is one of the best in the Southwest. The selection of contemporary ceramics, glass, fabric, and mixed-media pieces is cutting edge and of the highest quality. There is an extensive and very good selection of contemporary jewelry.

Dartmouth Street Gallery. While you're in the Nob Hill/University area, take time to visit this gallery with its rotating shows of wall art, sculpture, weavings, and other forms of fine art by contemporary New Mexican artists. Information: Dartmouth Street Gallery, 3011 Monte Vista Northeast, Albuquerque, New Mexico 87106; (505) 266–7751 or (800) 474–7751; www.dsg-art.com.

Bound to be Read. Located in Northeast Albuquerque just off I–25 at 6300 San Mateo Boulevard Northeast; (505) 828–3500 or (800) 688–4041. This large, very good independent bookstore has a coffee shop and cafe. This home for readers features a fine selection of general, children's, and Southwest regional books.

Page One. Located in northeast Albuquerque at 11018 Montgomery Northeast; (505) 294–2026 or (800) 521–4122. This large, dynamic— always busy—full-service, general adult and children's bookstore has an excellent Southwest selection.

Telephone Numbers

New Mexico Sno-Phone. (505) 984–0606.

Road and Weather Conditions. (800) 432–4269.

National Forest Service, Southwestern Region. (505) 842–3292.

Alamo Rent-a-Car. (505) 842–4057 or (800) 462–5266.

Budget Rent-a-Car. (505) 344–7196 or (800) 527–0700.

Hertz Rent-a-Car. (505) 842–4235 or (800) 654–3131.

Thrifty Car Rental (also vans and four-by-fours). (505) 842–8733 or (800) 367–2277.

Taxi service. (505) 842–5292 or (505) 883–4888.

Sun Tran and Sun Trolley (City of Albuquerque bus service). (505) 843–9200.

Airport Shuttle Albuquerque. To the airport from any place in Albuquerque. (505) 765–1234 or (800) 395–7680.

Airport bus service to Taos. (505) 751–1201 or (800) 654–9456.

Greyhound TNM&O (commercial services to Santa Fe, Taos, and other New Mexico, Texas, and Oklahoma destinations). (505) 242–4998; www.tnmo.com.

Sandia Peak Ski Area. (505) 242–9052.

Chamisa Hills Golf and Country Club. (505) 892–5813.

Santa Ana Pueblo Golf Club. (505) 867–9464.

Amtrak Rail Station. (505) 842–9650 or (800) 872–7245.

Albuquerque's Sunport International Airport Shuttle Services to Santa Fe and Taos, Etc. Sandia Shuttle Express, (505) 474–5696 or (888) 775–5696; **Herrera/Santa Fe Shuttle,** (888) 833–2300; **Twin Hearts Express,** (505) 751–1201;

(800) 654–9456; **Pride of Taos Transportation,** (505) 758–8340; and **Faust's Transportation, Inc.,** (505) 758–7359 or (888) 830–3410.

Santa Fe

If you are flying into the area, you will quickly find that Santa Fe does not have a major airport. Most visitors fly into Albuquerque's Sunport International Airport and then either rent a car or take one of the convenient, modern shuttle buses that carry travelers daily to and from Albuquerque and Santa Fe on a regular schedule. Amtrak offers passenger rail service to Lamy, New Mexico, which is 18 miles south of Santa Fe. Transportation to Santa Fe daily via the Lamy Shuttle Service; (505) 982–8829. There is air service via small plane (fewer than twenty passengers) from Denver International Airport by United Express; (505) 473–4118 or (800) 241–6522. Long-distance bus service is provided by Greyhound and TNM&O Coaches, 858 Saint Michael's Drive; (505) 471–0008 or (800) 231–2222 (reservations).

In Santa Fe it is possible to eat and sleep in settings that fulfill your fantasies about the area without totally breaking your pocketbook, although prices in Santa Fe's downtown historic area are some of the highest of those listed in this book. And if you wish to go first-class, you will find that your wish can be fulfilled in several of America's most distinctive hotels and resorts and in some of the High Southwest's finest restaurants. Over the years Santa Fe has become more and more crowded during the spring and fall shoulder seasons and especially in the summer, as its reputation has spread through the many magazine and newspaper articles, both here and abroad, that have sung its praises. In recent years just about every music, art, and craft magazine has featured the artistic boom that is going on there, from opera and chamber music to painting and ceramics. Background photographs of Santa Fe often appear in glossy fashion magazines. And home-decorating magazines and books have repeatedly featured the "Santa Fe style" of living, many elements of which have been duplicated in homes throughout the United States. With more affluent, sophisticated travelers coming to Santa Fe, the character of the downtown area is changing rapidly. Most of the locally owned utilitarian shops and stores along the plaza, faced with increasingly high rents and congested traffic, have moved off the plaza to other downtown locations or to outlying shopping centers. They have been replaced by upscale boutiques, galleries, and trendy restaurants, some of which have national affiliations.

But the plaza and its surrounding streets do not represent the only shopping area for travelers. For many years **Canyon Road,** southeast of the plaza, has been a visitors' favorite, with its many interesting galleries and restaurants. And two other favorite shopping areas are the **Guadalupe/Sanbusco District,** centered around the Sanbusco Market Center shopping mall, stretching along South Guadalupe Street from the Santuario de Guadalupe Church to Montezuma Avenue, and the **Guadalupe/Railyard District,** centered around the former terminus of the Chili Line Railway, extending from Montezuma

Avenue toward Paseo de Peralta. Shoppers and diners may also find it rewarding to explore the streets east of South Guadalupe Street like Aztec, Montezuma, Garfield, Read, and Manhattan Streets as far as Sandoval Street or Cerrillos Road, where the multiuse marketplace pavilion **Design Center** and **Hotel Santa Fe** are located.

After the ski seasons ends, the Santa Fe "season" begins in April and lasts until late October. Reservations for lodging in the place of your choice are necessary during most of those months, particularly between Memorial Day and Labor Day. In fact, to get any decent reservations during the major summer holidays, such as Memorial Day, or during special weekends, such as Indian Market in late August, reserve far in advance of your arrival and be prepared to pay up to one-third more for a hotel room. In the winter things slow down a bit, but then there is Christmas in Santa Fe, a unique time of the year there that has been popularized by national television specials. And, of course, there is both downhill and cross-country skiing in the nearby mountains, keeping an increasing level of activity going all winter. All of this does not mean that you cannot find a place to stay if you arrive impromptu. But if you want anything special—a room with a view, an adobe fireplace, or a patio—then you had better try to tie your wishes down a few months ahead of time. Many of the restaurants take reservations. For those that do it is wise to call the day before or the morning of your projected visit to make a reservation.

Almost all of the accommodations in Santa Fe that evoke the spirit of the region are in the downtown historic area within a 5- or 6-block radius of the plaza. With the exception of a few rooms in some of the bed and breakfasts and a few of the larger establishments, most of the accommodations downtown are in the expensive to very expensive range, and some (check when you make a reservation) now charge guests daily parking fees. But the convenience of the downtown inns and hotels to the major sights and the Santa Fe scene is truly a plus. If, however, you require less expensive accommodations, you must, unfortunately, leave the city's historic center and drive out to the busy "strip," Cerrillos Road. Most of the motels there are quite adequate, but with one or two exceptions they do not offer the charm or convenience that visitors seek when they come to Santa Fe. For the increasing number of return visitors to the area and for those who for one reason or another do not choose to stay in the city, a number of options are available. Besides the one luxury resort just north of town, a number of more modest, somewhat less expensive accommodations are cropping up outside of Santa Fe in the form of bed-and-breakfast inns. Some are located within a few miles of the city, while others are about thirty minutes or more out, in towns such as Galisteo to the south and Chimayó to the north. (See Lodging: "Around Santa Fe."). They offer a different, quieter, more pastoral scene in charmingly renovated historic old adobes in rural locations.

Santa Fe is truly a city of wonderful museums. The four Museums of New Mexico (the Palace of the Governors, Museum of Fine Arts, Museum of International Folk Art, and Museum of Indian Arts and Culture), operated by the state of New Mexico's Office of Cultural Affairs, are all superb. (For a recorded announcement of hours, fees, and current exhibits, telephone day or night, call 505–827–6463.) Try to allow time to see them, for they, along with the Wheelwright Museum of the American Indian, should not be missed. (There is a description of each of these museums, along with their telephone numbers, in the "See the Spanish Rio Grande Country: Santa Fe" section of this book. In this section of the book, there are several other museums listed under "Tours," including the Institute of American Indian Arts Museum, and the Santa Fe Children's Museum.)

Brochures in French, German, Japanese, and Spanish are available at the Santa Fe Convention and Visitors Bureau. In addition, budget accommodations are available for both international travelers and Americans in a dormitory setting at the Santa Fe International Hostel, 1412 Cerrillos Road (505–988–1153; www.santafe. org. Those needing to exchange foreign currency for dollars should do so in Albuquerque before coming to Santa Fe at one of the Bank of America walk-in locations there. For the closest branch check at the Albuquerque visitor center information desk in the baggage area at Sunport International Airport.

And all visitors can receive last-minute, up-to-date information on lodging, activities, and events from the visitor information booth located in the summer across the street from the west side of the plaza or year-round at the information desk of the **Santa Fe**

Convention and Visitors Bureau, (Sweeney Center, corner of West Marcy and Grant Streets, P.O. Box 909, Santa Fe, New Mexico 87504; (505) 955–6200 or (800) 777–2489; www.santafe.org.

For those interested in municipal facilities or relocation to Santa Fe, contact the **Santa Fe County Chamber of Commerce** in De Vargas Mall at 510 North Guadalupe; (505) 983–7317; www.santafe chamber.com.

During many times of the year, parking space can be tight in downtown Santa Fe. For available public and private paid parking venues, see "Parking," which precedes "Shopping" this section.

Restaurant closure times listed are applicable to high season only. These may change during the shoulder and winter seasons.

Lodging

La Fonda Hotel. One of the questions you may be asked by friends when you return home from your trip to Santa Fe is whether you stayed at La Fonda, the gem of a hotel that reveals the signature of both John Gaw Meem and Mary Colter. Over the years that venerable old adobe inn has been as much a part of the scene as the plaza and many of the area's historical sights. Grand and impressive as it is, it is not really that old. The present hotel was constructed during the period of Pueblo architectural revival in the 1920s. Previous to that other hotels had profited from the same location at the end of the Santa Fe Trail. Today's rambling, much renovated but commanding old adobe has a wide range of accommodations,

from "standard" rooms to fifth-story suites with adobe fireplaces, furnished with fine examples of Spanish colonial furniture, crafts, and accessories.

The hotel and its welcome parking garage (fee) cover 1 full city block and are the best situated of all Santa Fe's lodgings for seeing the city. But be warned. In midsummer the hotel and the streets around it are the most congested in this capital city. The beautiful old lobby, with its white plastered walls and heavy, ornate beams and tile floors, always buzzes with activity. The lobby contains an excellent display of old paintings by some of Santa Fe's prominent artists of the past fifty years. The **newsstand** in the lobby carries a wide variety of newspapers from all over the United States and an excellent supply of local and regional magazines. In addition, there are several shelves jammed full of books about the region. On the ground floor of the hotel is a variety of shops. The inner courtyard of the hotel has been enclosed to create the dining area, **La Plazuela,** which serves three meals a day in a very pleasant, informal atmosphere. The beautiful hand-painted glass windows there are well worth seeing. And high up on the fifth floor (high up for Santa Fe anyway) in the bell tower is the **Patio Bell Tower Bar,** where you can catch great views of the city and wonderful mountain panoramas, especially at sunset. The 167 rooms and suites are air-conditioned and have TVs and phones. There is a heated swimming pool. Information: La Fonda Hotel, 100 East San Francisco Street, Santa Fe, New Mexico 87501; (505) 982–5511 or (800) 523–5002; fax (505) 988–2952; www.lafondasantafe.com. Very expensive.

La Fonda, Santa Fe

Inn at Loretto. If you want the adobe ambience but in a more modern hotel, head straight for this five-story hotel. Located on grounds that formerly belonged to the Sisters of Loretto, 1 block south of the plaza, this modern, Pueblo-style structure harmoniously and tastefully echoes the architecture of La Fonda Hotel to the north. Built in the shape of an L, the building's walls enclose a large sun-drenched area on the east side, where you will find a pleasant patio and heated swimming pool. The dining room, with the traditional *viga* and *latia* ceiling members and corner adobe fireplace, is a handsome room and a pleasant place for breakfast or lunch. The multilevel bar with its large fireplace is also attractive. There are many upscale shops lining the first-floor corridor. The 140 air-conditioned rooms are nicely furnished with modern fixtures. A few rooms have fireplaces, king-size beds, and patios. On-site fee parking. Information: The Hotel Loretto, 211 Old Santa Fe Trail, Santa Fe, New Mexico 87501; (505) 988–5531 or (800) 727–5531; fax (505) 984–7988; www.hotelloretto.com. Very expensive.

Hotel Santa Fe. It's a pleasant walk (5 to 6 short blocks) to the Downtown Historic District from this handsome, larger, yet intimate and warm, Pueblo and territorial-style hostelry with 163 units (including 35 ultralux ury rooms and suites in the adjacent *hacienda*). This is Santa Fe's only American Indian–owned hotel, in partnership with the Picuris Pueblo. Easily one of the most pleasing hotels in Santa Fe, it is a favorite of many veteran Santa Fe travelers. The public rooms are handsomely decorated in Southwest style, displaying the works of Southwest Indian artists like sculptor Allan Houser. A small gift shop routinely sells Picuris pottery and other crafts. More than ninety of the rooms are one- and two-bedroom suites that have well-selected Southwest decor, like the other rooms. Some room safes and microwaves. Swimming pool and hot tub. Free guest shuttle to and from the Plaza. Free parking. Information: Hotel Santa Fe, 1501 Paseo de Peralta at Cerrillos, Santa Fe, New Mexico 87501; (505) 982–1200 or (800) 210–6441; fax (505) 984–2211; www.hotelsantafe. com. Expensive to very expensive.

Old Santa Fe Inn. Located 3 blocks from the plaza and close to the South Guadalupe–Sanbusco shopping area is this modern Santa Fe–style forty-three-room one-story inn with on-site parking. The nicely appointed rooms and suites are spacious enough, and the suites have fireplaces, jetted tubs, refrigerators, and microwaves. Exercise room. Continental breakfast included. Information: Old Santa Fe Inn, 320 Galisteo, Santa Fe, New Mexico 87501; (505) 995–0800 or (800) 745–9910; www.oldsantafeinn. com. Expensive.

Hotel St. Francis. Commanding one of the best downtown locations just 1 block from the plaza yet one step removed from the crowds and congestion is this pleasant hotel. The tan stucco building creates a distinctly Spanish, Old World atmosphere with its rounded Moorish arches, tiled floors, and wrought-iron work. Although the eighty-three nicely decorated rooms and suites vary in size, most have high ceilings, and many are equipped with small refrigerators as well as lock boxes for valuables. Dine inside or outdoors on the tree-shaded garden patio. Afternoon tea is served daily in the lobby and on the veranda. Parking provided. Information: Hotel St. Francis, 210 Don Gaspar Avenue, Santa Fe, New Mexico 87501; (505) 983–5700 or (800) 529–5700; fax (505) 989–7690; www.historicfrancis. com. Moderate to expensive.

Eldorado Hotel. If you enjoy the ambience, comfort, and prestige of the best big-city hotels, the five-story Eldorado will make you feel right at home. In an enviable location a little more than 2 blocks from the plaza, this multistoried hotel blends amazingly well into its historic site. Not only is it Santa Fe's largest hotel, it is also one of the most elegant.

From the spacious, atriumlike lobby with its lounge and cafe, where you can eat breakfast, lunch, or dinner or drink your favorite libation, to the rooftop outdoor heated swimming pool, which offers unparalleled views of Santa Fe and vistas of the surrounding mountains, you will appreciate this landmark hotel. There are 219 large rooms and suites, most with stocked bar refrigerators and some with fireplaces, wet bars, Jacuzzi tubs, and balconies. The air-conditioned rooms are spacious, quiet, and very comfortable, and the attractive decor is southwestern. Through the hotel you can also book a condominium unit with full kitchen, at a nearby location. Besides the lobby-atrium bar, the Eldorado Court, there is an elegant, formal restaurant, the **Old House.** Shopping arcade. Information: Eldorado Hotel, 309 West San Francisco Street, Santa Fe, New Mexico 87501; (505) 988–4455 or (800) 955–4455; fax (505) 995–4555; www.eldoradohotel.com Very expensive.

La Posada de Santa Fe Resort and Spa. These 159 luxurious rooms and suites, a RockResort, are located on East Palace Avenue just across Paseo de Peralta on 6 acres of landscaped grounds, within 2 long blocks of the plaza. This reincarnation of La Posada with its large Meeting and Conference Center, Avanyu Spa, exercise facilities, and underground parking makes it one of the toniest of the downtown hotels. The rooms have all the amenities, and there's a Southwest flair almost everywhere you look. The **Staab House Lounge and Cafe** and **Fuego Restaurant** occupy the historic house on the property by the same name. Information: La Posada de Santa Fe Resort and Spa, 330 East Palace Avenue, Santa Fe, New Mexico

87501; (505) 986–0000 or (800) 727–5276; fax (505) 982–6850; www.rockresorts.com. Very expensive.

Hilton Inn of Santa Fe. Conveniently located at the west end of San Francisco Street about 3 blocks from the plaza, this large territorial-style hotel with more than 150 air-conditioned units offers all the amenities in pleasant surroundings. Heated swimming pool in a very pleasant courtyard area. Dining room and coffee shop. No charge for children accompanied by their parents and in the same room. Information: Hilton Inn of Santa Fe, 100 Sandoval Street, Santa Fe, New Mexico 87504; (505) 988–2811 or (800) 336–3676; fax (505) 986–6435; www.hilton.com. Expensive to very expensive.

La Tienda Inn and Duran House. Just 4 blocks from the plaza at the corner of West San Francisco Street and Park Avenue, this bed-and-breakfast inn occupies a renovated historic building compound. The eleven spacious guest rooms (one suite) with antiques and hand-built furniture speak Spanish and American Indian Southwest at every turn. Some rooms with fireplaces—all overlooking the garden. A generous continental breakfast in your room or in the garden. Afternoon tea in the Old Store Common Room. Parking. Information: La Tienda Inn, 445–447 West San Francisco Street, Santa Fe, New Mexico 87501; (505) 989–8259 or (800) 889–7611; www.latiendabb. com. Moderate to expensive.

Garrett's Desert Inn. In that it looks like a motel almost anywhere, it seems strange that this inn is right in the center of the historic district alongside the Santa Fe River, 2 blocks south of the plaza. Nevertheless it is, and that fact, besides its being extremely well run and priced right, with plenty of parking, is why it is almost always full. The eighty-two spacious, air-conditioned rooms are decorated in motel modern. Heated outdoor swimming pool. Restaurant with outside dining. Information: Garrett's Desert Inn, 311 Old Santa Fe Trail, Santa Fe, New Mexico 87501; (505) 982–1851 or (800) 888–2145; fax (505) 989–1647; www.garrettsdesertinn.com. Moderate.

Inn on the Alameda. Well situated near Canyon Road's shops and yet just 3 blocks from the plaza is this charming adobe inn, which functions with all the amenities and personal service of a small and elegant European B&B. And it is just across from the shady Alameda, which borders the Santa Fe River. The sixty-nine air-conditioned rooms with private baths and cable TVs are beautifully furnished with southwestern decorative touches. Some rooms have private balconies. A gourmet continental breakfast is served in your room or in the handsomely decorated country dining area downstairs, adjacent to the comfortable living room-library area with its kiva fireplace. Fitness center. Two Jacuzzi tubs. Free parking. Information: Inn on the Alameda, 303 East Alameda, Santa Fe, New Mexico 87501; (505) 984–2121 or (800) 506–9204; fax (505) 986–8325; www.inn-alameda.com. Expensive to very expensive.

El Paradero Bed and Breakfast. This delightful adobe is just a short walk from the state capitol and just a few more blocks to the historic district. It offers much Santa Fe ambience. There are fourteen well-designed, nicely furnished adobe-style rooms, several with adobe fireplaces. Some rooms have private baths, while in others tastefully designed baths are shared. This place, with its delightful homey atmosphere, is run by an owner-manager family who live on the premises. The breakfast, included in the price, varies from eggs Benedict to home-baked goods, sausages, and pancakes. Pets allowed. Information: El Paradero Bed and Breakfast, 220 West Manhattan Street, Santa Fe, New Mexico 87501; (505) 988–1177; www.elparadero.com. Inexpensive to moderate.

Pueblo Bonito Bed and Breakfast Inn. Take an historic two-story adobe complex near the state capitol and a short walk to the historic district, on landscaped, tree-shaded grounds, slowly renovate it over the years, and soon you have a hostelry that, while not luxurious, is comfortable enough and a little easier on the pocketbook than some. The twenty rooms and suites are eclectic in their furnishings, some very modest, others more decorous. Two of the rooms have fireplaces, while six of the larger units have kitchens. An expanded continental breakfast buffet is served in the mornings. Afternoon tea and drinks and snacks in the communal area. Hot tub. Parking. Information: Pueblo Bonito Bed and Breakfast Inn, 138 West Manhattan at Galisteo, Santa Fe, New Mexico 87501; (505) 984–8001 or (800) 461–4599; fax (505) 984–3155; www.pueblobonito.com. Moderate.

The Madeleine (Bed and Breakfast). One of Santa Fe's old, late-1800s Victorian-style homes that is conveniently situated 3 blocks from the plaza on a quiet street 1 block north of La Posada de Santa Fe. Some of the eight rooms have private baths, while the others have shared baths. The rooms are nicely furnished and beautifully renovated. Some have fireplaces. Continental breakfast included. Information: The Madeleine, 106 Faithway Street, Santa Fe, New Mexico 87501; (505) 982–3465 or (888) 877–7622; www.madeleineinn.com. Moderate to expensive.

Grant Corner Inn (Bed and Breakfast). Advantageously located 1 block from the New Mexico Museum of Fine Arts and less than 2 blocks from the plaza is this beautifully restored, three-story, historical colonial manor home with warm stucco exterior and red-tiled roof. Its eight guest rooms and two suites are tastefully decorated and comfortable. Southwest artifacts grace the hallways and the downstairs living areas, shared by all the guests. And then there's breakfast, a not-to-be-missed gourmet's delight, served to all the guests and open to the public by reservation. Afternoon tea, also open to the public, is equally delicious. The owners are gracious hosts, careful to attend to your needs. Information: Grant Corner Inn, 122 Grant Avenue, Santa Fe, New Mexico 87501; (505) 983–6678 or (800) 964–9003; www.grantcornerinn.com. Moderate to expensive.

Spencer House Bed and Breakfast Inn. This 1920s adobe house with Mediterranean features is enviably situated close to the convention center and the Georgia O'Keefe Museum. The thoroughly restored inn has four very nicely appointed rooms with British Isles themes and a

The Madeleine, bed-and-breakfast inn, Santa Fe

detached casita with fireplace out back. Parking. Full breakfast. Information: Spencer House Bed and Breakfast Inn, 222 McKenzie Street, Santa Fe, New Mexico 87501; (505) 988–3024 or (800) 647–0530; fax (505) 984–9862; www.spencerhse-santafe.com. Moderate to expensive.

Adobe Abode Bed and Breakfast. Just 3 blocks from the plaza is this pleasant historic home and detached casita with six very nice rooms, all with private baths and a contemporary Southwest decor. Secluded, fenced, outdoor patio. Full gourmet breakfasts. Information: Adobe Abode Bed and Breakfast, 202 Chapelle, Santa Fe, New Mexico 87501; (505) 983–3133; fax (505) 986–0972; www.adobeabode.com. Moderate to expensive.

Sunterra Resort Villas de Santa Fe. This large, multistory all-suites hotel is located on Santa Fe's northwest side just off Paseo de Peralta,

making it an easy 5- or 6-block walk along Griffin Street to West Palace Avenue and the Downtown Historic District. The ninety comfortable suites feature one or two bedrooms plus living quarters with an equipped kitchen and dining area, swimming pool, exercise room, executive center, Laundromat, and convenience store. Continental breakfast buffet. Information: Sunterra Resort Villas de Santa Fe, 400 Griffen Street, Santa Fe, New Mexico 87501; (505) 988–3000 or (800) 869–6790; fax (505) 988–4700; www.sunterra.com. Expensive.

Territorial Inn. Located 2 blocks from the plaza up on a quiet section of Washington Avenue is this historic two-story territorial-style home converted to a B&B and a nearby annex. From the handsome public rooms to the twenty-three nicely decorated guest rooms (a few with shared bath) to the tree-shaded garden area with gazebo-enclosed hot tub, this inn charms. Continental-plus breakfast. Parking. Information: Territorial Inn, 215 Washington Avenue, Santa Fe, New Mexico 87501; (505) 989–7737 or (800) 745–9910; fax (505) 986–9212; www.territorialinn.com. Expensive.

Fort Marcy Hotel Suites. About 6 blocks from the plaza up on a hill with sweeping vistas is this eighty-six-suite complex with an indoor pool and hot tub. Coin laundry. The one-, two-, and three-bedroom units have a variety of amenities, including fireplaces and kitchens. Continental breakfast included. Information: Fort Marcy Hotel Suites, 320 Artist Road, Santa Fe, New Mexico 87501; (505) 982–6636 or (800) 745–9910; fax (505) 984–8682; www.santafeinformation.com. Moderate to expensive.

Santa Fe Motel. The closest (about 5 blocks) to the plaza of the more modest lodging establishments out near Cerrillos Road, this twenty-three-room motel has, in addition to humdrum standard motel rooms (some with kitchenettes)—surprise—eight pleasant adobe casita rooms in two renovated adobe houses with viga ceilings and patio entrances on a quieter side of the property. Information: Santa Fe Motel, 510 Cerrillos Road, Santa Fe, New Mexico 87501; (505) 982–1039 or (800) 745–9910; fax (505) 986–1275; www.santafe hotels.com. Moderate.

Santa Fe Plaza Travelodge. This motel, part of a large chain, is at the intersection of Guadalupe Street and Cerrillos Road, 6 blocks from the plaza and only 3 blocks from the many shops and restaurants along Guadalupe Street. It is one of the most conveniently situated to down-town of all the motels on Cerrillos Road. In this complex there are forty-eight air-conditioned units with a heated pool. Information: Santa Fe Plaza Travelodge, 646 Cerrillos Road, Santa Fe, New Mexico 87501. Telephone: (505) 982–3551 or (800) 578–7878; fax (505) 983–8624; www.travelodge.com. Moderate.

Santa Fe Budget Inn. This large, plain motel with 160 air-conditioned units is located along Cerrillos Road close to the Travelodge and the intersection of Guadalupe Street and Cerrillos Road. As the shops and restaurants along Guadalupe move farther and farther south, this inn and the Travelodge become closer to the action. TV in each room. Heated swimming pool. Information: Santa Fe Budget Inn, 725 Cerrillos Road, Santa Fe, New Mexico 87501; (505) 982–5952 or (800) 288–7600; fax (505) 984–8879. Inexpensive.

El Rey Inn. Although located along busy Cerrillos Road, this very attractive, air-conditioned adobe-style inn is situated on more than 3 acres of beautifully landscaped grounds, isolating it from all the hubbub and making it a peaceful haven. Ten of the eighty-six nicely furnished Santa Fe–style rooms and suites are deluxe and are situated around a lovely Spanish Colonial–style courtyard. And there are twenty nice but less expensive rooms around the north courtyard. The remaining rooms are traditional El Rey rooms and suites, a few situated on the terrace by the large outdoor heated swimming pool. Some kiva fireplaces. Coin-operated laundry. Ample parking and children's play areas. Just 2 miles from the plaza, this is your best bet if everything downtown is full or if you want southwestern ambience at a lower price. Complimentary continental breakfast in lovely European-style breakfast room. Whirlpool. Information: El Rey Motel, 1862 Cerrillos Road, Box 4759, Santa Fe, New Mexico 87502–4759; (505) 982–1931 or (800) 521–1349; fax (505) 989–9249. Inexpensive to moderate.

Around Santa Fe

The Bishop's Lodge. Located 3.5 miles north of Santa Fe on Bishop's Lodge Road (New Mexico Highway 590) is this resort, which provides enough southwestern atmosphere, comfort, and services to empty most pocketbooks in a few days. The "Bishop" in the lodge's name was Santa Fe's Bishop Lamy. He loved this place as Joseph Pulitzer and his family did when they purchased this property after Lamy's death. Lamy's chapel is still on the grounds. The 111 air-conditioned rooms are spread among a half-dozen or so Pueblo-style adobe buildings on this 1,000-acre ranch. Some rooms have adobe-style fireplaces. Others have more modern furnishings and Southwest decor. Full horseback riding program (fee) and a series of trails where you can walk through gardens and orchards or hike into the surrounding pine-clad foothills. Fishing is available (fee). There are four tennis courts (fee), and a large heated swimming pool. There are also saunas, whirlpool baths, a children's playground, outdoor patio open to the public, and a social program for kids. The dining room serves American food and is open to the public. Modified American Plan available. Information: Bishop's Lodge, P.O. Box 2367, Santa Fe, New Mexico 87504; (505) 983–6377 or (800) 732–2240; fax (505) 989–8739; www.bishops.lodge.com. Very expensive.

Galisteo Inn. Located 25 miles south of Santa Fe, taking U.S. Highway 285 South, then New Mexico Highway 41, in the quaint village of Galisteo. This impressive historic adobe inn is set on 8 acres with its landscaped grounds ringed by stone walls. Everywhere this lovely and tranquil inn echoes New Mexico, New Mexico. The twelve throughly updated rooms are comfortable and sensibly reflect the decor of the region. The *ramada* (covered porch) out front with its cane rocking chairs overlooks a pristine New Mexico countryside that takes you back a generation or two. A full breakfast is served in the handsome dining room, which in the evening is a fine dinner restaurant, frequented by many Santa Feans. (See "Food: Around Santa Fe.") Heated swimming pool. Mountain bikes. Horseback riding (fee). Box lunches (fee). Information: The Galisteo Inn, HC 75 Box 4, Galisteo, New Mexico 87540; (505) 466–8200; fax (505) 466–4008; www.galisteoinn.com. Moderate to expensive.

Rancho Jacona. In an idyllic setting near San Ildefonso Pueblo, about twenty minutes north out of Santa Fe (about 0.5 mile north off New Mexico Highway 502, the route to Los Alamos), is a compound of five handsome adobe casitas (studio units) and a house, once part of a large country estate. All have fireplaces and complete kitchens. Clothes washers and dryers available. There is plenty of room to roam and walk the country roads here in the Pojaque River Valley or to just sit out under the giant old cottonwood trees. Heated outdoor swimming pool. Call for directions. Information: Rancho Jacona, Route 5, Box 250, Santa Fe, New Mexico 87501; (505) 455–7948; www.rancho jacona.com. Rates variable depending on length of stay. Moderate.

Rancho Manzana. A thirty-five-minute drive from Santa Fe takes you back a century or two as you arrive at this delightful 250-year-old, territorial-style adobe farmhouse set amidst lavender fields and apple orchards on historic Plaza del Cerro in old Chimayó, New Mexico. (For directions see "Seeing the Spanish Rio Grande Country: A Day Traveling through Spanish New Mexico: A Narrative Account.") The two spacious and thoughtfully appointed rooms in the main house open up to a sitting room and library, which access Chimayó Plaza. Two more rooms are in newer cottages overlooking the lavender fields and the pink hills. The rancho's large kitchen is often used for cooking classes. The breakfasts are out of this world. Walk out the front door and hike trails through the pink New Mexico hills. Information: Rancho Manzana, HCR 64, P.O. Box 18, 26 Camino De Mision (County Road 94E), Chimayó, New Mexico 87522; (505) 351–2227 or (888) 505–2227; fax (505) 351–2223; www.taoswebb.com/ manzana. Moderate.

Hacienda Rancho de Chimayó. Across the road from the popular restaurant of the same name is this seven-room bed and breakfast inn located in a one-hundred-year-old home. The rooms face a central courtyard and are filled with regional antiques. Continental breakfast is served in your room, outdoors, or in one of the public rooms. Often closed in January. (For directions, see Rancho de Chimayó listing under "Food," this section.) Information: Rancho de Chimayó, P.O. Box 11, Chimayó, New Mexico 87522; (505) 351–2222 or (888) 270–2320; www.hacienda ranchodechimayo.com. Moderate.

Inn at the Delta. Located in Española and associated with the restaurant Anthony's at the Delta is this luxury bed-and-breakfast inn that exudes Southwest charm at every turn. Kiva fireplaces. Jacuzzi tubs. Each of the ten oversized rooms is decorated with hand-carved fixtures by local artisans. Continental breakfast. Information: Inn at the Delta, 228 Onata Northwest, Española, New Mexico 87532; (505) 753–9466 or (800) 995–8599; www.cybermesa. com/~delta. Moderate to expensive.

The Abiquiu Inn. Just off U.S. Highway 84 in a green oasis surrounded by pink cliffs is this very nice and charming, well-run inn about half a mile from the **Georgia O'Keeffe** home and next door to the Georgia O'Keeffe Foundation office, where minibus tours depart for the artist's home. The nineteen pleasant rooms and several larger casitas (some with courtyard, fireplace, or views) make for a pleasant stay in a parklike setting. Some kitchens. **Cafe Abiquiu** (along with a gift shop and regional art gallery) occupies much of the main lodge and serves up northern New Mexican specialties as well as Mediterranean and Middle Eastern dishes. Information: Abiquiu Inn, P.O. Box 120, Abiquiu, New Mexico 87510; (505) 685–4378 or (800) 447–5621; www.abiquiuinn.com. Inexpensive to moderate.

Camping

Hyde Memorial State Park.
Located just off the road to the ski
area (New Mexico Highway 475 or
Hyde Park Road), approximately 11
miles northeast of the plaza. From the
northeast corner of the plaza, travel
0.5 mile north on Washington
Avenue, then east on Artist Road to
New Mexico Highway 475 or Hyde
Park Road. Seventy sites on 350 acres;
(505) 983–7175.

Black Canyon. This National Forest
Service campground is located
approximately 10 miles northeast of
the plaza off New Mexico Highway
475. Follow the directions to Hyde
Memorial State Park, above. Forty-
one sites on 16 acres at an elevation
of 8,400 feet. For information: (505)
753–7331 or for reservations: (877)
444–6777.

Rancheros de Santa Fe Camping.
Located approximately 10.5 miles east
of the plaza off Frontage Road, which
parallels I–25 as it heads toward Las
Vegas, New Mexico, 736 Old Las
Vegas Highway. One hundred and
twenty sites on 122 acres. Reservation
deposit required; (505) 466–3482;
www.ranchos.com.

Santa Fe K.O.A. Located in Apache
Canyon just 11 miles from the plaza,
934 Old Las Vegas Highway. Many
tent sites, full hookups, and pull-
throughs; (505) 466 1419.

Food

Shed. 113½ East Palace Avenue,
Prince Plaza at Sena Plaza Complex;
(505) 982–9030. Here you'll dine
inside one of Santa Fe's old adobes or
outdoors on the patio. Soups and
sandwiches, delicious charbroiled
hamburgers, and the savory Pueblo
Indian dish *posole* as well as a specialty
of the house, blue corn tortillas,
which are used to make tasty, stacked
red chili and blue corn enchiladas.
Good homemade desserts too. Open
for lunch (you may have to stand in
line) and dinner (reservations). Closed
Sundays. Moderate.

La Casa Sena. 125 East Palace
Avenue. Located 1 block east of the
plaza in Sena Plaza courtyard at 20
Sena Place; (505) 988–9232. Nicely
situated adjacent to the Sena Plaza
gardens, this elegant restaurant serves
up innovative American Southwest
specialties for lunch and dinner in the
handsomely refurbished interior of
the historic old Sena House and in
season on the lovely outdoor garden
patio. From lamb chops with
habanero-papaya sauce to the bittersweet chocolate and raspberry frozen
souffle, you can't go wrong. And then
there is La Cantina, which provides
entertainment by strolling troubadour
waiters singing many popular and
favorite songs while you eat and sip a
glass of wine from the extensive wine
list. Open daily. Expensive.

Burrito Company. Just ½ block
north of the plaza at 111 Washington
Avenue (505–982–4453) is this always
busy, informal, fun, egalitarian eatery
with its numerous outdoor tables
spread out in front. A good stop for a
quick lunch, a snack, or just a good
cold drink on a hot day. Many New
Mexican specialties prepared with red
chilies from Chimayó and green
chilies from Hatch, New Mexico.
Breakfast, lunch, and dinner served.
Takeout food available.

Paul's Restaurant. Tucked into a

small, inconspicuous storefront location at 72 West Marcy Street (505–982–8738) is this outstanding lunch and dinner venue where some of the best cooking in Santa Fe goes on. Excellent soups and salads as well as several complex, creative dishes for lunch. On the dinner menu you might find wild mushroom and feta ravioli in a pepper tomato sauce, baked salmon in pecan herb crust and sorrel sauce, or red chili duck wontons with soy ginger sauce. Mouthwatering desserts as well. Carefully selected wine list. Lunch and dinner daily. Moderate.

Santacafe. 231 Washington Avenue; (505) 984–1788; www.santacafe.com. Located just beyond Marcy Street in the historic Padre Gallegos House several blocks from the hustle and bustle of downtown. If you seek some of the best-prepared food an area has to offer, then you should make a reservation here fast for lunch or dinner. The setting is remarkable for the blend of old territorial-style architecture on the outside and the elegant contemporary treatment of the superb restaurant inside. Carefully prepared from the freshest of ingredients are innovative dishes fusing Southwest, American, European, and Asian flavors that are just outstanding, if not ambrosial. The eclectic freewheeling menu offers a variety of dishes: appetizers like shiitake and cactus spring rolls with green chili salsa and shrimp and spinach dumplings with tahini sauce; dinner entrees like pan-seared salmon with spring pea risotto and lovage butter; as well as other expertly prepared pasta, beef, and fresh fish entrees await you at this excellent restaurant. The dessert menu is equally tantalizing. If the weather permits, eat outdoors in the lovely courtyard for lunch or dinner. Inside guests may see the old water well, covered and lighted for viewing. Reservations highly recommended. Expensive.

Grant Corner Inn. 112 Grant Avenue; (505) 983–6678. This centrally located B&B, situated about 2 blocks west of the plaza, serves breakfast daily and Sunday brunch. You can eat inside in the dining room of the lovely renovated historic home or on the porch in the summer. Featuring dishes like blue corn waffles, Dutch babies, eggs Benedict, and *huevos rancheros,* along with mouth-watering, flaky homemade pastries and fresh fruit frappés, the Grant Corner Inn knows how to do breakfast! Reservations accepted.

Palace Restaurant. 142 West Palace Avenue; (505) 982–9891. This Santa Fe lunch and dinner restaurant has been at it for decades and still draws crowds. The most recent reincarnation is eclectic Mediterranean—grilled asparagus and goat cheese or crab cakes with summery orange relish. The outdoor patio is a very pleasant place for lunch in the summertime, and the bar is a favorite watering hole for many Santa Feans. Reservations advised. Lunch/dinner daily. Moderate to expensive.

Cafe Paris. Located on historic Burro Alley between Palace Avenue and West San Francisco Street at 31 Burro Alley; (505) 986–9162. This casual cafe does well with the kinds of traditional French dishes that you have come to love: fresh croissants plain or stuffed, crepes, omelettes, waffles, and French toast for breakfast; onion soup, eggs Benedict, salad Niçoise, and crepes for lunch; steamed mussels, confit de canard, ris de veau, steak frites, and the cafe's popular apple tart for dessert. An informal, fun kind of a place. Wine and beer. Closed Sunday. Moderate.

Tulips. 222 North Guadalupe; (505) 989–7340. Only a few blocks from the Georgia O'Keeffe Museum and the El Dorado Hotel is this quiet, cozy, intimate dining spot reminiscent of a previous, more relaxed Santa Fe. There are several dining rooms in this early-twentieth-century home, each simply but carefully decorated; but it's the fresh ingredients and how they're put together that brings you here. Start with a grilled beet and goat cheese quesadilla, then move on to roasted New Mexico lamb shoulder with carrot vegetable couscous and creamy leek feta cheese relish. Well-selected wine list. Good desserts. A fine evening. Closed Monday. Reservations advised. Expensive.

The Old House. Located at the Eldorado Hotel at 309 West San Francisco Street; (505) 988–4455, ext. 130. Here experience the complexity of French, American, and Southwest cooking. In a stunningly beautiful Southwest style dining room, start with dishes like pan-seared Alaskan halibut with potato and lobster cake and pepper tomato jam. Finish with desserts like warm liquid-center chocolate cake or bourbon vanilla crème brûlée. Dinner nightly. Reservations advised. Expensive.

San Francisco Street Bar and Grill. 114 West San Francisco Street; (505) 982–2044. A chic gourmet short-order house might be a good description of this popular and very good modern-style restaurant downstairs at the **Plaza Mercado** (across

Desert cottontail rabbits

the street from El Paseo Theater). Open for lunch and dinner daily with many specials but regularly featuring superb hamburgers, sandwiches, homemade soups, and salads. Homemade sausages served with herbs and green chilies. Inexpensive.

La Plazuela. In La Fonda Hotel, San Francisco Street and Old Santa Fe Trail Road; (505) 982–5511. This enclosed, roofed courtyard or patio is an excellent place for breakfast, and it serves lunch and dinner as well. You can have traditional or continental breakfast or regional specialties, like *huevos rancheros.* Very pleasant atmosphere. Superb views are available on the fifth floor in the **Bell Tower Bar,** where you can sip your drink as the sun slips behind the mountains. Moderate.

French Pastry Shop and Crêperie. La Fonda Hotel; (505) 983–6697. San Francisco Street side. This busy place serves croissants and other French delights for breakfast. Good soups, sandwiches, and quiches for lunch. A favorite breakfast spot if you do not mind the crowds. Revel in these authentic and delicious French pastries as you remember the history of the cathedral just down the street, the one that was so heavily influenced by French priests in the 1800s (see "History"). Breakfast and lunch daily.

Cafe Pasqual's. 121 Don Gaspar at Water Street; (505) 983–9340 or (800) 722–7672. Just a little more than 1 block south of the plaza. This centrally located restaurant with its festive Mexican decor is an ideal place to stop at mealtime. As one of several Santa Fe restaurants that has produced a cookbook, it has consistently honed its south-of-the-border and New Mexican fare over the years and now encompasses other regions. Breakfast is very popular here, as is lunch (tasty breakfast burritos and quesadillas). For dinner their chicken mole Puebla with Mexican rice and squash tamales can't be beat. Outstanding smaller plates include grilled bananas and poblano corn pudding. Delicious salads and soups. Excellent baked goods. Wine and beer. Espresso drinks. Breakfast, lunch and dinner. Reservations for dinner only. Moderate to expensive.

Blue Corn Cafe. Located upstairs in a bright cheerful space at 133 Water Street (corner of Water and Galisteo Streets) is this popular luncheon stop that is also open for dinner; (505) 984–1800. The fare is mostly northern New Mexican but with some different and innovative touches; whole-wheat sopaipillas and the vegi-fajita burritos come to mind, but the tamales and blue corn enchiladas are excellent as well. Don't miss dessert: the flan, the piñon cheesecake, or the sopa—a bread pudding baked with raisins and cinnamon. Inexpensive.

Coyote Cafe. 132 West Water Street; (505) 983–1615. A little more than 2 blocks southwest of the plaza and up one long nicely designed flight of stairs is a fun and innovative restaurant. Architecturally the dining room is a work of art that should not be missed. Its high ceiling and sparsely but elegantly decorated stucco walls give a sense of openness to the room not unlike the wide-open spaces around Santa Fe itself. The creative interior decor is a delight. But this is no coyote's trick. The decor is no more pleasing or inventive than the food created by a nationally known chef-restaurateur with seven cookbooks under his belt. Dishes like Moroccan spiced quail, tuna relleno, and cowboy-cut ribeye steaks with jalapeno skillet bread and green chili salsa are typical of the fare here. (Lighter fare for lunch and dinner and in-between is available daily upstairs in Coyote's **Rooftop Cantina,** offering city views.) The main dining room is open daily for dinner and Friday through Sunday for brunch. Expensive.

Zele Coffee and Cafe. Located 2 blocks southwest of the plaza at 201 Galisteo at Water Street (505–982–7835) is this casual establishment where you can quaff delicious espresso drinks and pastries. Good spot for breakfast (burritos, pastries, granola) on the run or lunch (soups, salads, panini).

Pink Adobe Restaurant and Dragon Room Bar. 406 Old Santa Fe Trail; (505) 983–7712. A trip to Santa Fe is not complete without a visit to this venerable old restaurant located in one of the oldest districts in Santa Fe. You will dine in an atmosphere that evokes northern New Mexico and the Spanish Southwest. New Mexican, Creole, and continental specialties are served. Excellent homemade desserts are also part of the scene. The Dragon Room Bar across the driveway is a beauty and a good place to catch a before- or after-dinner drink. Lunch Monday through Friday. Dinner daily. Reservations advised. Moderate to expensive.

Guadalupe Cafe. Located at 422 Old Santa Fe Trail; (505) 982–9762. Here's another popular breakfast and lunch place (dinner, too) thick with southwestern atmosphere. The *huevos rancheros* and *migas* (eggs, chilis, and cheese all mixed up) are wonderful, as are the baked goods. At lunch, the *chalupas* (corn tortilla baskets containing various fillings), the enchildada and burrito plates, stuffed sopaipillas, and chimichangas (a fried, filled flour tortilla) are all done well. Also sandwiches, homemade soups, hamburgers, and delicious desserts. Open daily except Monday. Patio dining. Parking behind the building. Inexpensive.

Downtown Subscription. 376 Garcia Street; (505) 983–3085. About 1 block or so off Canyon Road on Garcia is this newsstand and espresso-pastry bar that not only has most out-of-town newspapers (including many international editions) and a huge selection of magazines but also serves up a wide variety of espresso drinks and pastries for breakfast. The local scene is thick here, both in the nice sit-down cafe and out on the patio.

Celebrations. 613 Canyon Road; (505) 989–8904. Either out on the patio or inside the rambling old adobe, this casual dining establishment offers a wide-ranging, tasty breakfast menu and serves excellent soups, salads, and sandwiches for lunch and dinner—as well as northern New Mexican specialties. Open daily. Dinner Wednesday through Sunday. Sunday brunch. Moderate.

Geronimo. 724 Canyon Road; (505) 982–1500. This luncheon and dining establishment is located in the historic 235-year-old Borrego House, where beautifully prepared global fusion–Southwest entrees reign. You'll find a selection of elk, duck, beef, pork, and seafood entrees, including dishes like broiled lobster bisque with grilled shiitake mushrooms, peppery elk tenderloin, and seared yellow tuna with wasabi potato puree. Nice wine list. Good desserts. Outdoor dining as well in season. Lunch daily except Monday. Reservations advised. Expensive.

The Compound. Located a short walk off the main throughfare in a grove of cottonwoods at 653 Canyon Road; (505) 982–4353. Designed by Alexander Girard, architect and famed folk art collector, this is one of the handsomest dining rooms, with a garden patio that is equally pleasing. With a more formal attitude than most of its competitors, you should still be able to relax enough to enjoy the outstanding food here, which includes creative dishes like cast iron–seared halibut with Parmesan soft polenta and spring peas, fava bean relish and chardonnay butter, or muscovy duck steak with creamy grits, figs, and sangiovese. Expensive wine list. Lunch Monday through Friday; dinner daily. Reservations advised. Expensive.

El Farol. 808 Canyon Road; (505) 983–9912. Superb cold and hot Spanish tapas and gourmet entrees in this popular, very atmospheric restaurant and bar. Paella is a favorite. This is a popular watering hole for local artists. Informal live music in the evening may vary from folk and country to flambuoyant flamenco. Outdoor dining in the summer. Lunch and dinner daily. Bar open nightly. Reservations for dinner advised. Moderate to expensive.

Ristra. Located at 548 Agua Fria; (505) 982–8608. The front entrance faces Sanbusco Market Center. This consistently outstanding, intimate dinner restaurant, occupying a historic home with a tented outdoor patio, cooks French with a dose of New American and New Mexican flavors. You can start with something like pear and watercress salad with apple and potato chips, smoked bacon, and apple cider vinaigrette; moving on to an entree like roasted minted rack of lamb accompanied by potato gratin with piquillo pepper coulis, baby carrots, haricot verts, and natural jus. Excellent wine list by glass or bottle. Good desserts. Friendly, efficient service. Reservations advised. Expensive.

El Encanto. 416 Aguia Fria Street; (505) 988–5991. Located in an historic adobe across from the Guadalupe mission church is this lovely restaurant/gallery whose magnificent contemporary art on the walls transports you immediately to the heart of Mexico City. Open for both lunch and dinner, the nuevo cocino Mexican dishes are outstanding. Try the ensenada abalone in lime chipotle sauce, then move on to either one of the succulent fresh fish entrees or lamb wrapped in banana leaves cooked overnight in a pit. Good wine and beer list. Delicious

desserts. Reservations advised. Closed Sunday. Moderate to expensive.

Zia Diner. 326 South Guadalupe Street; (505) 988–7008; bakery telephone: (505) 988–5155. Modern American cooking in this one-hundred-year-old adobe warehouse. Art deco 1950s interior with patio dining in the summer is the scene for lunch and dinner. Excellent soups and meals your mother used to make. And for your sweet tooth, there are homemade pies as well as old-fashioned soda fountain delights. Espresso. Open daily. Inexpensive to moderate.

Tomasita's. 500 South Guadalupe Street; (505) 983–5721. This New Mexican restaurant located in the old Chili Line Railway freight depot is a bustling place with a lot of charm. Local Santa Feans out for a night of margaritas and good New Mexican food mingle and rub shoulders with the travelers who find this spot. But no matter where you are from, you will have to wait for a table in the evenings. The price is right, and the food is always good. Also open for lunch. Inexpensive.

Saveur. Located at 204 Montezuma Avenue, a short walk from South Guadalupe or from the downtown historic shopping area; (505) 989–4200. Living up to the magazine of the same name, this informal gourmet lunch spot should be savored. With a salad bar that looks as delectable as a color photo out of the magazine and with delicious soups that offer a complexity most mothers couldn't imitate, this place is a winner whether you eat in or take food out for a picnic. Also pasta dishes and plat du jour. Specialty coffees, desserts. Wine and beer.

Tamale Molly. 323 Aztec Street; (505) 989–4500 or (877) 509–1800; www.tamalemolly.com. Carry out these freshly prepared, hand-tied vegetarian tamales, or eat them inside or out on the patio—just enjoy these unique tamales, the best in Santa Fe, knowing that all profits fight hunger. Tamales with squash, tomato, and fresh oregano; blue corn with mixed fresh herbs; and goat cheese with mint are but a few you can choose from. Picnic takeout all day. Lunch 11:30–5:30. Closed Sunday and Monday.

Andiamo! The Guadalupe–Sanbusco area touts a fine Italian dinner restaurant too, located in a renovated older home at 322 Garfield Street; (505) 995–9595. In this warm, intimate setting you can savor traditional yet upscale Italian food at affordable prices. Start with bruschetta with goat cheese, roasted red pepper, and watercress or an antipasto or a small pizza. Entrees like farfalle with grilled chicken, green beans, spinach, scallions, and asiago as well as a variety of other pasta dishes predominate. Excellent wine and beer list. Dinner nightly. Moderate.

Corn Dance Cafe. Located in the Hotel Santa Fe between South Guadalupe Street and Cerrillos Road at 1501 Paseo de Peralta; (505) 982–1200. In the warmth of the exceptionally well-designed dining area at this American Indian–owned hotel, it only stands to reason that Native American food dominates the menu. You can start with grilled ear of corn with chipotle oil or Indian triad salad of marinated corn, beans, and squash. Then choose a "little big pie," a flat bread with a variety of zesty toppings, before moving on to entrees like grilled ribeye of American bison, Tlinglit salmon, or grilled venison medallions with chokecherry sauce. For a special celebration, buy a Tee Pee Experience in the big tee pee outside on the lawn where you can arrange by reserving ahead a Prairie Feast or a Traditional Picuris Pueblo Meal complete with warm Indian bread coming from the nearby horno. Call for details. Wine and beer list. Moderate to expensive.

Sage Bakery. Located across the street from Hotel Santa Fe, at 535 Cerrillos Road; (505) 820–7243. In back is a large bakery that provides Santa Fe's better restaurants with their baked goods. Up front in the very small retail bakery and eatery, at breakfast you can treat yourself to the best scones you've ever had. Ditto for lunch the breads, brownies, cookies, and even the sandwiches, quiches, and salads. Good place to pick up picnic items. Specialty coffees. Patio.

Tiny's Restaurant and Lounge. Southeast corner of St. Francis and Cerrillos Road in the Pen Road Shopping Center; (505) 983–9817. At first you think you're in Akron or maybe Topeka. But then you bite into the fajitas, seafood enchiladas, *posole*, beans, or any of the other northern New Mexican specialties and realize you are in Santa Fe heaven. There's hardly a coyote to be seen, just a lot of Santa Fe regulars who don't need the trappings to tell them where they are. Live band on the weekend, so you can dance off a few pounds on the postage-stamp-size floor before returning to Tiny's tasty desserts. Also steaks. Patio dining available. Lunch Monday through Friday. Dinner daily except Sunday. Reservations advised. Inexpensive to moderate.

Tecolote Cafe. 1203 Cerrillos Road; (505) 988–1362. If you are staying out on Cerrillos Road, this is a convenient place to stop in for breakfast or lunch. The breakfasts are famous at this family-run restaurant, where you will feel right at home. From the New Mexican specialties such as the breakfast burrito to western favorites like flapjacks, you will start the morning right here. Closed Monday.

Old Mexico Grill. 2434 Cerrillos Road; (505) 473–0338. Located out on Cerrillos Road on the south side of the College Plaza Shopping Center. This very nicely appointed lunch and dinner establishment is popular with many New Mexicans who want a taste of Old Mexico. The open grill, fueled by mesquite, and the rotisserie cook the meats for the excellent beef and chicken fajitas and the *tacos al carbón*, a soft taco with a beef, chicken, or sausage filling. There are also *chilies rellenos*, quesadillas, carne asada, and mole poblano done the way they do them south of the border. Freshly baked flan for dessert and a selection of Pañafiel soda pop, a delightfully different fruit-based soda pop made in Mexico. Many varieties of beer. Lunch and dinner daily. Moderate.

Around Santa Fe

Tesuque Village Market. Located at the junction of New Mexico Highway 591 and Bishop's Lodge Road in Tesuque, north of Santa Fe; (505) 988–8848 (for directions to Tesuque see "A Day Traveling through Spanish New Mexico: A Narrative Account"). This is an art gallery, restaurant, delicatessen, wine shop, and grocery store all rolled into one. Breakfast, lunch, and dinner (northern New Mexican cuisine) are served daily, and, of course, there are lots of goodies to carry out for picnics. Homemade breads and muffins, as well as delectable desserts, are specialties. Homemade soups, sandwiches, and enchiladas for lunch. Inexpensive to moderate.

El Nido. Located 7 miles north of Santa Fe in Tesuque; (505) 988–4340. Take New Mexico Highway 590 from downtown Santa Fe. For many years this local favorite has been known as a steak house worth patronizing. Not only is the drive pleasant, but the southwestern ambience is thick. It is a large restaurant and almost always seems busy and full of life. In addition to quality cuts of aged beef, seafood and a variety of New Mexican specialties are served. Dinner only. Closed Monday. Reservations advised. Moderate.

Harry's Roadhouse. Located 1 mile east of Old Pecos Trail on Old Las Vegas Highway; (505) 989–4629. Only a short drive from the historic area, this eclectic breakfast, lunch, and dinner house also offers outdoor dining in season on a pine-shaded patio beside a stream. The wide-ranging menu offers everything from turkey meatloaf and corn chowder to blue corn enchiladas, stir fry, and Manchego cheese frittatas. You can get just about anything you want for breakfast, lunch, and dinner at Harry's very nice roadhouse and bar. Open daily. Moderate.

Bobcat Bite. Located 2 miles east of Harry's Roadhouse at 420 Old Las Vegas Highway; (505) 983–5319. Why drive out of town this far in the countryside to end up standing in line? You should go and find out. The ordinary hamburger here beats most any other burger you've ever tasted, and the green chili cheeseburger may be the best in the state. The quality of the meat is the thing. Ribeye steaks are also legendary. Lunch and dinner. No reservations. Inexpensive to moderate.

The Galisteo Inn Restaurant.
Located South of Santa Fe (see "Lodging: Around Santa Fe") in Galisteo; (505) 466–8200. The pleasant dining room in this historic adobe serves sophisticated cuisine like you find in Santa Fe. You could start your prix fixe dinner with ginger chicken soup with avocado, lime, and crispy tortillas or a field green salad with Maytag blue cheese vinaigrette, then proceed to an entree like seared beef tenderloin with currant balsamic jus or stuffed poblano chili with golden raisin couscous, ancho mole, and mint pesto. The grapefruit custard tart with pecan crust is one way to finish the meal. Lunch and dinner, Wednesday through Sunday. Menu changes weekly. Prix fixe dinner. Reservations required. Expensive.

El Paragua Restaurant. Located 24 miles north of Santa Fe just off Highway 64 and 285 along New Mexico Highway 76 to Santa Cruz; 603 Santa Cruz Road; (505) 753–3211. In this venerable stone building set among the trees, this very traditional Northern New Mexican restaurant serves up some items like sopaipillas that are as good as they get. Besides carne adovado, tamales, and enchiladas, there are also tantalizing dishes like garlic shrimp. Traditional natilla is one of the desserts served. Some traditional American specialties as well. Wine and beer. Margaritas. Open daily. Moderate.

Right next door to El Paragua is its little sister, **El Parasol,** a highly popular Northern New Mexican takeout specializing in crisp grilled chicken, guacamole tacos, and much more; (505) 753–8852.

Rancho de Chimayó. Approximately a thirty-minute drive from Santa Fe to the north. (See "A Day Traveling through Spanish New Mexico: A Narrative Account" for directions.) A more direct alternate route is to take U.S. Highway 285 north approximately 15 miles. Then just beyond the Los Alamos exit, take New Mexico Highway 503 east through Nambe 7.5 miles. Turn left onto County Road 98, and continue a few miles to the Rancho on the right; (505) 351–4444 or (800) 477–1441. Breakfast served Saturday and Sunday. Lunch and dinner daily. Closed Monday November through April. If you'd like to eat New Mexican regional food in a truly southwestern setting, you should visit the rancho (see detailed description of interior in "A Day Traveling through Spanish New Mexico: A Narrative Account"). There in one of the area's longest-running restaurants, the well-prepared New Mexican specialties carry the day. Try the Chimayó cocktail for starters, then follow that with one of the entrees, which include pork *adovada,* enchiladas, tamales, and *sopaipilla rellenos.* Also steaks and trout. Reservations advised. Moderate.

Rio Grande Cafe. In Española at the Los Alamos turnoff, 1 block south of U.S. Highway 84 intersection at 101 Los Alamos Southwest; (505) 753–2125. If you are in or around

Española at lunch- or dinnertime, do not miss this family-owned and -run regional cafe that has been serving up excellent New Mexican specialties since 1948. At this restaurant the food is called "native" food. Informal, cafelike, very clean, and very authentic. Closed Saturday and Sunday. Inexpensive.

Anthony's at the Delta. One of the most aesthetic restaurants in the Santa Fe area is along the river in Española. Anthony's, family-owned and -operated, is worth seeing whether you're hungry or not. You will find it by driving north from Santa Fe to Española. There look for the Chama Highway, U.S. Highway 84, and the Delta Bar sign. The restaurant is located just off the highway at 228 Onate Northwest; (505) 753–9466 or (800) 995–8599. In numerous, beautifully appointed dining rooms decorated with Hispanic and Native American art and fronting on exquisite adobe-walled courtyards filled with fragrant fresh flowers and exotic plants, you will dine on well-prepared entrees of fresh fish, prime rib, and steaks. Outdoor dining, weather permitting. Reservations advised. Dinner only; open daily. Moderate.

Tours, More Museums, and Activities

For more information, see www.santafe.org.

Georgia O'Keeffe Museum. 217 Johnson Street; (505) 995–0785; www.okeeffemuseum.org. In a wonderfully bright and airy space across from El Dorado Hotel is this must-see museum displaying an outstanding collection of the work of the region's premiere artist. The collection includes oil paintings and watercolors as well as works on paper and sculpture. The images range from still lifes and nudes to abstractions and landscapes. Rotating shows of art relevant to the Georgia O'Keeffe period. Fee.

Santa Fe Museums. Consult the "Seeing the Spanish Rio Grande Country, Santa Fe" for a review of Santa Fe's major museums and telephone numbers. And see this listing for still more museums. The Museums of New Mexico museum infoline is (505) 827–6463.

Indian Arts Research Center at the School of American Research. 660 East Garcia Street; (505) 954–7205. This prestigious group of scholars has gathered together one of the finest collections of traditional American Indian work, particularly ceramics, baskets, and fabrics, that you will find anywhere. The collection may be viewed by appointment only once weekly under the direction of a tour guide. Fee. Call for tour dates and times. In addition, the grounds of the school are particularly attractive.

Institute of American Indian Arts (IAIA) Museum. 108 Cathedral Place; (505) 988–6211 or 983–8900. You may take a self-tour of this prestigious museum, which focuses on contemporary art of American Indians from the Southwest and throughout the nation. Fee. In addition to seeing the works of well-known American Indian artists, you will also view the work of many of the talented students at the IAIA. Perhaps they will follow in the path of many successful former students like Fritz Scholder and T. C. Cannon. Well-selected items in gift shop.

Santa Fe Children's Museum.
1050 Old Pecos Trail. Adjacent to the old Santa Fe armory; (505) 989–8359. The development of special museums for children around the country has not escaped Santa Fe. This excellent, hands-on, tuned-into-the-senses museum will delight most children.

Plan B-Evolving Arts. 1050 Old Pecos Trail; (505) 982–1338. This art venue hosts lectures, films, and performances, as well as contemporary art exhibitions.

Site Santa Fe. Out on Paseo de Peralta is this large exhibit gallery that places Santa Fe squarely on the contemporary international art circuit. Docent tours available. Fee. Information: Site Santa Fe, 1606 Paseo de Peralta, Santa Fe, New Mexico 87501; (505) 989–1199; www.sitessantafe.org.

El Museo de Cultural de Santa Fe. See this museum located in the Guadalupe/Railway District for a better understanding of Hispanic culture of Northern New Mexico. Looks for art shows, performances, lectures, demonstrations, and special events. Information: El Museo de Cultural de Santa Fe, 1615-B Paseo de Peralta, Santa Fe, New Mexico 87501; (505) 992–0591; www.museocultural.org.

Lensic Performing Arts Center. Located downtown at 211 West San Francisco Street; (505) 988–1234; www.lensic.com. This revival 1931 pseudo-Spanish and Moorish architectural gem warms the hearts of all Santa Feans. It's comfortable, updated, and high-tech state-of-the-art interior is the venue for lectures and live music, dance, and theatre productions.

Santa Maria de La Paz. Although not a museum, this contemporary church south of I–25, across from Santa Fe Community College, houses a rich collection of traditional Hispanic and American Indian art executed by some of the very best artists in the region. It is best to call ahead before visiting this beautiful church whose dedicated members lovingly developed this site. Information: Santa Maria de la Paz, 11 College Way, Santa Fe, New Mexico 87505; (505) 473–4200.

The Planetarium at Santa Fe Community College. Come to this planetarium for numerous scheduled programs centered around the celestial universe, including ones featuring American Indian story-tellers and others who reveal the creation legends of various American Indian tribes and their beliefs about how the stars got in the sky. Also children's programs. Fee; 6401 South Richards Avenue; call (505) 428–1677 for schedules and hours.

Georgia O'Keeffe Home Tours. Tour Georgia O'Keeffe's home in Abiquiu, overlooking the surrounding hills and the Chama River Valley, which she lovingly painted so that the world knew the New Mexico landscape without ever visiting there. The home is much the way it was when O'Keeffe died in 1986. Don't plan to drive the 50 miles from Santa Fe to Abiquiu unless you already have a tour reservation. Tours of the home are strictly regulated and may be solidly booked months in advance. Call several months ahead of time for booking. Fee. Information: The Georgia O'Keeffe Foundation, P.O. Box 40 Abiquiu, New Mexico 85710; (505) 685–4539.

Behind Adobe Walls Tours. House and garden tours of Santa Fe, sponsored by the Santa Fe Garden Club, are given the last two Tuesdays in July and the first two Tuesdays in August; (505) 982–5464. Here is your chance to see the Santa Fe style at its peak as you tour some of Santa Fe's most interesting and beautiful adobe homes and gardens. Fee.

Walking Tours. There are a variety of one- to two-hour walking tours of Santa Fe. Some of the better-known guide services are as follows: Downtown Walking Tours, sponsored by Friends of the Palace of the Governors (schedule posted on the blue gate on the Lincoln Street side of the Palace of the Governors), (505) 476–5109; Afoot in Santa Fe Tours, (505) 983–3701; and Aboot About Santa Fe Walks and Tours, (505) 988–2774.

Santa Fe Southern Railway Tours. Take a train trip out through the New Mexico high desert to Lamy, New Mexico. Round-trips offered on a variable schedule year-round with sunset dinner runs on Fridays between May and October. Information: Santa Fe Southern Railway Depot, 410 South Guadalupe Street, Santa Fe, New Mexico 87501; (505) or (888) 989–8600; www.sfsr.com.

Santa Fe School of Cooking. Take a tour through the kitchen of this popular cooking school, where you will be led step-by-step as you learn how to cook Southwest style. Extended culinary tours also available. Information: Santa Fe School of Cooking, 116 West San Francisco Street, Santa Fe, New Mexico 87501; (505) 983–4511; www.santafeschool ofcooking.com.

Public Lands Information Center. Customize your own tour of the great outdoors by visiting this multiagency outdoor information center to get help planning an outing to nearby national parks, wildlife refuges, Bureau of Land Management lands, state parks, and game and fish hot spots. This is where you get a detailed map of the outdoors, guide books to various recreational activities, licenses and permits, and directions for local hiking trails, campgrounds, and wilderness trails. Information: Public Lands Information Center, 1474 Rodeo Road, Santa Fe, New Mexico 87505; (505) 438–7542; fax (505) 438–7582; www.publiclands.org.

Ten Thousand Waves Japanese Health Spa. The City Different lives up to its reputation with this popular spa, a blend of American technology and Japanese hot-tub traditions. With literally dozens of masseuses on board, traditional therapeutic massage is a big thing but so also are aquatic massage, East Indian cleansing treatments, herbal wraps, facials, and salt glows. Also, saunas, steam rooms, and a Waterfall Tub. Find this spiritual mecca of relaxation about 4 miles from downtown Santa Fe, in the pine-clad foothills rising to the Santa Fe Ski Basin. Reservations essential. Information: Ten Thousand Waves Japanese Health Spa, 3451 Ski Basin Road, P.O. Box 10200, Santa Fe, New Mexico 87504; (505) 992–5025 (information) or (505) 982–9304 (reservations); fax: (505) 989–5077; www.tenthousandwaves.com.

Santa Fe Detours, Rivers, Rails, Trails, and Tours. Besides walking tours of Santa Fe, this eclectic tour operator offers scenic railway journeys, white-water rafting, horseback riding, guide service, wilderness hikes and overnights, and air and land adventures around Santa Fe. Individuals or groups. Information: Santa Fe Detours, 54½ East San Francisco Street, 87501; (505) 983–6565 or (800) 338–6877; fax (505) 986–0214; www.sfdetours.com.

Rojo Tours and Services. This tour and service group also offers a wide range of personalized tours for individuals or groups, from walking and driving tours of the city to tours to Taos and Taos Pueblo. Information: Rojo Tours and Services, P.O. Box 15744, Santa Fe, New Mexico 87501; (505) 474–8333; fax (505) 474–2992; www.rojotours.com.

Outback Jeep Tours. This organization offers four-wheel-drive, half-, full-, and multiday safaris to prehistoric ruins, petroglyph sites, and ghost towns. Hikes can be arranged as well as natural history trips. Information: Outback Jeep Tours, P.O. Box 961, Santa Fe, New Mexico 87504–0961; (505) 820–6101; fax (505) 820–0830; www.outbacktours.com; www.out backtours.com.

Sun Mountain Bike Company. Regional mountain bike tours for all levels. Also sunset tours. Information: Sun Mountain Bike Company, (505) 820–2902; www.sunmountain bike.com.

New Wave Rafting. Raft the Rio Grande, Chama, or other regional rivers with these guides. Pick up and return to Santa Fe. Half-day, full-day, and overnight trips. Information: New Wave Rafting, 107 Washington Avenue, Route 5, Box 302 A, Santa Fe, New Mexico 87501; (505) or

(800) 984–1444; www.newwave rafting.com.

Horseback Riding

Bishop's Lodge Stables. (See "Lodging" for directions to the lodge.) You can take trail rides into the Sangre de Cristo Mountains; lodge guests have first priority, however; (505) 983–6377/819–4013 or (800) 732–2240.

Galarosa Stables. Located in rural New Mexico about 23 miles southeast of Santa Fe off New Mexico Highway 41; (505) 466–4654.

Events

Check www.santafe.org or call (505) 955–6200 or (800) 777–2489 for full up-to-date listings of concerts, plays, art shows, and other current events.

Santa Fe Opera. One of the best-known opera companies in the United States performs from early July through late August in an impressive outdoor theater with a unique sweeping roof system. Located 7 miles north of Santa Fe just off U.S. Highways 84 and 285. Take warm clothing and rain gear. Performances (late June through late August) begin at 9:00 P.M. and later in the season at 8:30 P.M. Arrive thirty minutes early to avoid all the congestion. Cameras, recording equipment, food, and beverages are not allowed inside. Information: Santa Fe Opera, P.O. Box 2408, Santa Fe, New Mexico 87504–2408; for ticket purchases: (505) 986–5900 or (800) 280–4654. (In the summer tickets can be purchased at the Lensic Performing Arts Center. It is wise to reserve as far in advance as possible.) Fax: (505) 995–3030; www.santafeopera.org.

Santa Fe Chamber Music Festival. The prestigious Santa Fe Chamber Music Festival is held from around mid-July to around mid-August. During this five- or six-week period, the performances are held at the New Mexico Museum of Fine Arts, the Lensic Performing Arts Center, and SITE Santa Fe. Noon concerts (ticket purchase required) are given at the St. Francis Auditorium, and daily open rehearsals are given free to the public (call 505–983–2075 for dates and locations). A jazz series is also associated with the festival. Tickets can be purchased at the festival office at 239 Johnson Street; St. Francis Auditorium; or at the Lensic Performing Center box office, 225 West San Francisco Street. Information: Santa Fe Chamber Music Festival, P.O. Box 2227, Santa Fe, New Mexico 87504; (505) 982–1890; www.sfcmf.org.

Santa Fe Desert Chorale. This professional vocal ensemble performs from mid-June through late August in the Santuario de Guadalupe on the corner of Agua Fria and Guadalupe. This fine group presents a wide range of choral music. Information: Santa Fe Desert Chorale, 500 Montezuma, Santa Fe, New Mexico 87501; (505) 988–7505; www.desertchorale.org.

Shakespeare in Santa Fe. Presented under the stars at St. John's College on certain July and August weekends. Free; (505) 982–2910; www.shakespearesantafe.org.

Santa Fe Stages. Throughout the year this organization brings to Santa Fe a packed series of international dance and theater companies and entertainers offering some of the finest entertainment in the country. Performances at the Firestone Plaza and Lensic Performing Arts Center. Information: Santa Fe Stages, 100 North Guadalupe, Suite 107, Santa Fe, New Mexico 87501; (505) 982–6683; www.santafestages.org.

Santa Fe Playhouse This well-established drama group (now more than sixty years old) gives performances throughout the summer. From hilarious melodramas to sophisticated contemporary dramas, this experienced group of local players does an outstanding job. Information: Santa Fe Community Theatre, 142 East DeVargas Street, Santa Fe, New Mexico 87501; (505) 988–4262; www.santafeplayhouse.org.

Greer Garson Theatre. Located on the campus of the College of Santa Fe, this theater, named for the illustrious actress who for many years called the Santa Fe area home, stages a number of excellent drama productions throughout the year. The season starts after school begins and continues throughout the winter and spring. Information: Greer Garson Theatre, College of Santa Fe, 1600 Saint Michael's Drive, Santa Fe, New Mexico 87501; (505) 473–6511.

Maria Benítez Teatro Flamenco. Throughout the summer this outstanding flamenco dancer and her talented Estampa Flamenca Spanish dance company perform to enthusiastic audiences. The dancer is touted as one of the most outstanding performers of this style of dance in the United States; the evening shows at Santa Fe Radisson, 750 North St. Francis Drive, are usually jammed. For venue and reservations telephone (505) 982–1237 or (800) 905–3315 after June 15; www.mariabenitez.com.

Horseracing, Santa Fe Downs. The Santa Fe Downs racetrack is 5 miles south of town, just off I–25. The season is from April until Labor Day; (505) 471–3311.

Fairs, Fiestas, and Studio Tours

Santa Fe Century Bicycle Event. This annual May event for pedalheads attracts nearly 2,000 or more riders on a course through Santa Fe, Galisteo, and south along the Turquoise Trail; (505) 982–1282.

La Conquistadora Procession. June, the Sunday after Corpus Christi Feast Day, or the ninth Sunday after Easter. During this annual event *La Conquistadora Madonna* is taken from the old North Chapel of St. Francis Cathedral and carried in procession to the Rosario Chapel northwest of the city in the cemetery by the same name, which was built for the purpose of receiving the Madonna (see "History"). This was the approximate location of the De Vargas encampment prior to retaking Santa Fe. After a novena of masses, the statue is returned to the cathedral the following Sunday.

Rodeo de Santa Fe. Three days centering on the second weekend in July. This large, colorful event is augmented by a parade and entertainment at the rodeo grounds; (505) 471–4300 or (888) 737–6336; www.rodeosantafe.org.

Annual Traditional and Contemporary Spanish Markets. Usually held the last weekend in July, this is the place to see and buy the best of fine art and traditional crafts by New Mexico's Hispanic citizens. Wood carving (*bultos, retablos,* furniture) and *colcha* embroidery are but a few of the crafts represented. The **traditional** Spanish Market is held on the plaza, while the **contemporary** Spanish Market is held on Lincoln Avenue next to the Plaza. The **Winter Spanish Market** is held the first weekend in December at the Sweeney Convention Center. Information: Spanish Colonial Arts Society, (505) 982–2226; www.spanishcolonial.org.

Annual Santa Fe Indian Market. This annual event, held the third weekend in August, is a nationally famous Indian art fair and market. Indians from around the Southwest and beyond bring their crafts to the plaza and fill it with display and sales booths. You will see many fine crafts there; moreover, you will have the opportunity to see and meet some of the best-known Indian potters, sculptors, weavers, painters, and basket makers in the country. Information: Southwestern Association for Indian Arts, Inc., P.O. Box 969, Santa Fe, New Mexico 87504–0969; (505) 983–5220; fax (505) 983–7647; www.swaia.org.

Fiesta de Santa Fe. First weekend after Labor Day. Labeled as the oldest community celebration of its kind in the United States, this four-day celebration commemorates the Spanish reconquest of New Mexico by De Vargas (see "History"). During this event a giant 40-foot-tall effigy of Zozobra ("Old Man Gloom"; see Glossary) is burned. In addition, parades and a candlelight procession, mariachi music, Spanish colonial dancers, and musicians perform daily in the plaza. Information: Santa Fe Convention and Visitors Bureau, P.O. Box 909, Santa Fe, New Mexico 87504–0909; (505) 988–7575, (505) 988–7575, or (800) 777–2489; www.santafe.org.

Christmas in Santa Fe. For the very special and unique events held during the Christmas season in Santa Fe and the pueblos and villages in the area, call the Santa Fe Convention and Visitors Bureau; (800) 777–2489.

San Antonio Feast Day Corn Dance. San Ildefonso, Tesuque, and Santa Clara Pueblos. Often the second Sunday in June.

San Juan Feast Day. San Juan Pueblo. Held the third weekend in June. Buffalo and Comanche dances at San Juan (see "Revisiting the Plaza and a Day with the Pueblo Indians North of Santa Fe: A Narrative Account") and Corn Dance in Taos, same weekend.

San Pedro Feast Days. The last weekend in June. Corn Dance at Santa Ana Pueblo.

Fiesta del Valle de Española. Three days over the second weekend of July. In Española. Commemorating the Spaniard Oñate's expedition to northern New Mexico. The celebration includes raft races on the Rio Grande, a torch run from Santuario de Chimayó, fireworks, and mariachi music in this Hispanic town. Information: Española Valley Chamber of Commerce, 417 Big Rock Center, Española, New Mexico 87532; (505) 747–6100.

San Buenaventura Feast Day. Cochiti Pueblo. Corn Dance. The second weekend in July.

Enpic Arts and Crafts Show. The eight Northern Indian Pueblos hold this event the third week of July to showcase their artists and well as Indian artists from around the country. It is the only American Indian–owned art show in the United States. Originally rotating among the pueblos, the show will soon be held in a permanent multiuse facility several miles north of Española, just east off New Mexico Highway 68. Information: (505) 852–4265 or (800) 793–4955; www.8northern.org.

Santo Domingo Feast Day. Santo Domingo Pueblo. Held the first weekend in August. Features the Corn Dance. This is probably the granddaddy of them all, with more than 500 dancers participating. Full of pageantry, beauty, and mystery. In spite of the heat and crowds, it is worth every minute of the hassle.

Santa Clara Feast Days. Santa Clara Pueblo. The second weekend in August. A variety of important and beautiful dances at this ancient Rio Grande pueblo.

For more complete and up-to-date information about the Pueblo Indian ceremonies, dances, and other inquiries you may have, contact the Rio Grande pueblos listed under "Indian Pueblo Telephone Numbers" at the end of "Santa Fe: Staying There." A central telephone number for most of the pueblos north of Santa Fe is (505) 852–4265, or (800) 793–4955; www.8northern.org.

Parking

Santa Fe has strictly enforced metered street parking. Pay fines promptly. The following pay parking areas are within a few blocks of the plaza. The rates may vary from location to location. These lots are marked PUBLIC PARKING. Look for both commercial and hotel parking garages that may offer public parking.

• Two lots bounded by Bishop's Lodge Road and Old Taos Highway just north off Paseo de Peralta and west off Bishop's Lodge Road.

• Lot bounded by East Water and Don Gaspar Streets, across from the Hotel St. Francis and west of El Centro Mall.

• Lot bounded by West Marcy and Sheridan Streets, and the lot adjacent to Sweeney Convention Center on Marcy Street.

• Parking garage bounded by Sandoval and West Water Streets, across from the Hilton Hotel.

• Three lots east of the Loretto Chapel and the Hotel Loretto between Cathedral Place and Paseo de Peralta north of Alameda.

When parking on the street, note these colored curb markings to avoid a ticket: yellow curb, no parking (heavily enforced); blue curb, handicapped zone; green curb, commercial and passenger loading zones; red curb, fire zone; pink curb, bus loading, unloading.

Shopping

Museum of New Mexico Shop Branches. Each of the museums operated by Museum of New Mexico has a site-specific shop, each with inventory representing the focus of the museum. All have excellent regional book selections: Palace of the Governors Shop, (505) 988–3454; Museum of Fine Arts Shop, (505) 982–1131; Museum of Indian Arts and Culture Shop, (505) 982–5057; and Museum of International Folk Art Shop, (505) 982–5186.

Montez Gallery. 125 East Palace Avenue, No. 33 (on the west side of Sena Plaza Courtyard); (505) 982–1828; www.montezgallery.com. From *santos* and *retablos* to tin work and weaving, this gallery brings together many of the masterpieces of Hispanic New Mexican art.

LewAllen and LewAllen Jewelry. 105 East Palace Avenue; (505) 983–2657. Ross LewAllen is one of the Southwest's best-known contemporary jewelers. His "earcuffs" are legendary. Working in sterling silver and gold, he has produced many unique earrings and bracelets evoking Southwest themes. New Mexico safari bracelets and a series of pieces that use folk images of trout and snakes are also in his repertoire. His daughter is the second LewAllen.

Davis Mather. 141 Lincoln Avenue; (505) 983–1660. This museum-quality shop stocks a nice selection of crafts from Mexico and the Southwest that evoke the Santa Fe style. Particularly prominent here from time to time are wood carvings of rabbits, chickens, and other hand-carved images of regional animals. Well-selected handicrafts from some of Mexico's finest craftspeople as well.

LewAllen Contemporary Gallery. 129 West Palace Avenue; (505) 988–8997; www.lewallenart.com. Representing fifty artists, this gallery has an excellent selection of contemporary paintings, glass, sculpture— even a special ceramics nook—and photography. A must-see gallery in Santa Fe.

Zozobra, Fiesta de Santa Fe

Cline Fine Art. 135 West Palace Avenue and 526 Canyon Road; (505) 982–5328; www.clinefineart.com. These two well-known galleries feature twentieth-century American art with focus on early modernism and regionalism.

Riva Yares Gallery. 123 Grant Avenue; (505) 984–0330. Modern and contemporary art and sculpture in a space the size of a supermarket, which allows the showing of larger works. Represents more than sixty major American and international artists.

Dewey Galleries Ltd. 53 Old Santa Fe Trail, second floor; (505) 982–8632; www.deweyltd.com. This gallery represents the work of the late, legendary Allan Houser and other icons. Design pieces of Mies van der Rohe, Isamu Noguchi, and Florence Knoll are in their collection of modern furniture.

Owings-Dewey Fine Art. 76 East San Francisco Street; (505) 982–6244; www.owingsdewey.com. This large upstairs gallery shows the work of nineteenth- and twentieth-century American artists. **Owings-Dewey North,** in the Healy Building, north of the plaza at 120 East Marcy Street, Suite 7 (505–986–9088) offers interesting contemporary American art and sculpture.

The Clay Angel. 125 Lincoln Avenue; (505) 988–4800. In this large gallery are an unbelievable number of high-quality ceramics from Spain, France, and Italy. If Mediterranean pottery is your passion, you could browse here for an hour or so.

Andrew Smith Gallery, Inc. 203 West San Francisco Street; (505) 984–1234; www.andrewsmith gallery.com. This gallery's commitment to exhibiting the best photographic work available anywhere is deserving of your attention. Shows have included Eliot Porter's 35-millimeter color photographs of New York and the works of Annie Lebovitz.

Andrea Fisher Gallery. 221 West San Francisco Street; (505) 986–1234. Lovers of fine Pueblo Indian pottery will think they have died and gone to heaven here. There are the older works of Maria Martinez and then shelf after shelf of the very best in recently produced Pueblo pottery from Hopi and Navajo to Ácoma and Santa Clara. Also a very fine selection of well-made pottery from Mata Ortiz, Mexico, including works by the master himself, Juan Quezada.

Nambe Showrooms. 104 West San Francisco Street and 924 Paseo de Peralta; (505) 471–2912. These retail outlets offer a truly useful and beautiful handcrafted product. Nambeware, as it is called, is freezeproof, ovenproof ware, sand-cast from a special alloy that has the appearance of fine silver. A unique, easy-care product made in Santa Fe. Seconds and firsts available in the outlets.

Origins. 135 West San Francisco Street; (505) 988–2323. A large shop carrying an unbelievably wide selection of traditional ethnic clothing from around the world, as well as some locally made clothes.

Collected Works Bookstore. 208B West San Francisco Street; (505) 988–4226 or (877) 988–4226; www.collectedworksbookstore.com. In business for many years and anchoring the west end of San Francisco Street is this excellent bookstore, with a wide selection of general books as well as mystery and Southwest regional titles, including guidebooks, cookbooks, maps, and books about the Indian and Spanish cultures of the area.

La Fonda Newsstand. La Fonda Hotel lobby; (505) 988–1404. Good selection of magazines and out-of-town newspapers as well as many southwestern books, including history, archaeology, and regional arts and crafts titles. Nice selection of regional greeting and postcards.

Senor Murphy Candymaker. Located at the La Fonda Hotel. Candy made from the wonderful piñon nuts, a local delicacy grown also in Spain and Portugal. Roasted and salted piñon nuts for cooking are also available, as are red and green chili jellies.

Handwoven Originals. 211 Old Santa Fe Trail Road, in the Inn at Loretto; (505) 982–4118. Original jewelry by one of the area's finest

contemporary jewelry artists, Richard Lindsay. Unique silver and gold pieces featuring a menagerie of animals, including folk rabbits, trout, cats, and his now-famous road-killed animals series. Necklaces, pins, drops, and earrings are all made by this talented artist. Also featured are beautiful handwoven clothing, including ponchos, and other southwestern favorites and creative accessories.

Cristof's. 420 Old Santa Fe Trail; (505) 988–9881; www.cristofs.com. Another showcase gallery with an excellent selection of Navajo rugs, Hopi kachina dolls, and many fine contemporary American Indian paintings. Also an outstanding selection of both contemporary and traditional fine jewelry.

The Chile Shop. 109 East Water Street; (505) 983–6080. There are enough unique items of the region gathered together under one roof here to fill several homebound suitcases with gifts and mementos. Unique chili lights for the Christmas tree and all the blue corn, chili products, and native herbs and condiments you'll ever need. In addition, chili greeting cards, folk art gourds, handmade tabletop accessories (salsa jars, chip-and-dip platters), table and door decorations made with dried native plant materials, and chili *ristras* and wreaths are all available, plus replicas of the Old Santa Fe Railway dining car china with its interesting *mimbres* decorations.

Foreign Traders (Old Mexico Shop). 202 Galisteo Street, on the corner of Galisteo and Water Streets. This large shop carries handcrafted items from Mexico and Central America. Merchandise ranges from

Guatemalan fabrics to large pieces of furniture from Mexico. Information: Foreign Traders, P.O. Box 1967, Santa Fe, New Mexico 87501; (505) 983–6441 or (866) 530–9080.

Artesanos Imports of Mexico. 222 Galisteo Street; (505) 983–1743. All in all, this is one of the most interesting large shops to browse through in Santa Fe. The owner, originally from Mexico, has an excellent selection of Mexican crafts, from furniture and textiles to baskets and tiles. The outdoor courtyard carries some outstanding, large sculpted stone garden pieces from Michoacan, Mexico. If you are interested in Mexican pottery tiles and glassware, do not miss this shop.

James Kelly Contemporary. 1601 Paseo de Peralta; (505) 989–1601; www.jameskelly.com. In a former warehouse site across Paseo de Peralta from SITE Santa Fe is this very good contemporary gallery with rotating exhibits on two floors. The emphasis here is on cutting-edge mixed-media work and painting.

Travel Bug. 328 South Guadalupe Street, Suite E; (505) 992–0418; www.mapsofnewmexico.com and www.booksense.com. Santa Fe is lucky to have this richly stocked travel bookstore that many larger cities don't have. Besides an excellent selection of travel books covering the globe, their regional selection stands out—plus you can find USGS and BLM maps of New Mexico and detailed maps of Colorado.

Borders Books. 500 Montezuma Avenue in Sanbusco Center; (505) 954–4707. This large chain bookstore has a wide selection of general and regional books.

High Desert Angler. 435 South Guadalupe; (505) 98–TROUT; www.highdesertangler.com. Those coming to New Mexico to fish will find all they need from flies to outdoor clothing here. You can also arrange guided fly-fishing trips locally and worldwide.

Cookworks. 316 and 318 South Guadalupe Street; (505) 988–7676. There are a lot of kitchen stores around these days but few with the scope and quality of this one housed in three separate but adjacent buildings. There are plenty of useful items for the kitchen all right, but here there is also a good supply of both regional and general cookbooks, numerous gourmet spices and condiments, and many gift items.

Santa Fe Pottery. 323 South Guadalupe Street; (505) 989–3363. Santa Fe Pottery is a retail gallery, selling functional pottery from the region and beyond. From utilitarian pottery lamps and tableware to many other accessories for home and kitchen, this pottery gallery consistently displays high-quality ware.

Rainbow Gate. 310 Johnson Street; (505) 983–8892; www.rainbowgate.com. Just down the street a short distance from the Georgia O'Keeffe Museum near the intersection of Johnson Street and North Guadalupe Street is this large studio, gallery, and retail space directed by two well-known, highly talented New Mexican ceramic artists. The artfully designed and colorful dinnerware and ceramic tiles are just the beginning. In the gallery are Jenny Lind's knock-out ceramic sculpture pieces. Not to be missed.

Nedra Matteucci Galleries. 1075 Paseo de Peralta; (505) 982–4631 and at 555 Canyon Road, **Nedra Matteucci Fine Art;** (505) 983–2731; www.matteuci.com. When native Santa Feans take guests to see a showplace gallery in town that captures the essence of the fine arts of the Southwest, they often take them here. There are many fine historic western paintings for sale from such prestigious artists as Nicolai Fechin and Leon Gaspard, as well as monumental sculpture and contemporary southwestern paintings. The sculpture garden is worth a visit.

Gerald Peters Gallery. 1011 Paseo de Peralta; (505) 954–5700; www.gpgallery.com. The hype surrounding this gallery notwithstanding, this is a place you shouldn't miss. Spanning most of the art of the twentieth century yet offering rotating shows of contemporary art in its large exhibit space, this gallery doesn't miss much. There's also an outdoor sculpture garden worth viewing.

Adobe Gallery. 221 Canyon Road; (505) 955–0550; www.adobegallery. com. This is one of the first galleries that you will see as you enter Canyon Road, and it offers a warm welcome. It is the Santa Fe branch of a highly respected Albuquerque Old Town Southwest American Indian Gallery. The emphasis is on historic Southwest Indian pottery and textiles, but there is also Southwest wall art, a fine collection of Indian arts and crafts books, and a good selection of antique Mission-style furniture. This gallery hosts a variety of rotating shows featuring the works of renowned pueblo potters like Maria Martinez, or of Southwest landscape artists like Russ Tanner.

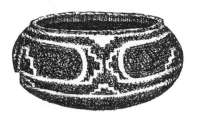

Santa Clara bowl

Pachamama. 223 Canyon Road; (505) 983–4020. Specializing in antique and traditional folk art from Latin America, this intriguing gallery carries everything from folk toys to furniture (with retablos, milagros, and santos in between) and is very satisfying.

Munson Gallery. 225 Canyon Road; (505) 983–1657; www.mun songallery.com. This well-established, well-run, handsome art gallery is well worth a visit as you begin your cruise up Canyon Road. It exhibits a fine selection of Southwest contemporary painting, sculpture, and graphics.

McLarry Fine Art. 225 Canyon Road; (505) 988–1161; www.mclarry fineart.com. This gallery specializes in landscapes and art of Western America, representing outstanding landscape artists like Donna Clair and still-life artists like Chuck Sabatino.

Photo-Eye Gallery and Photo-Eye Bookstore. Gallery: 370 Garcia Street; bookstore: 376 Garcia Street; (505) 988–5152 or (800) 277–6941; www.photoeye.com. Just one very long block south of Canyon Road are these two locations that are a photographer's dream. On the one hand there's the contemporary photography gallery, featuring nationally and internationally known artists while on the other hand there's a fine art photography in-print and out-of-print bookstore you might expect to find only in Manhattan, representing titles from around the world.

Garcia Street Books. 376 Garcia Street; (505) 986–0151. This spacious bookstore, with a good selection of general books as well as Southwest regional titles, is just 1 very long block off Canyon Road.

Morning Star Gallery. 513 Canyon Road; (505) 982–8187; www.morn ingstar.com. If you have time to see just one Canyon Road gallery featuring American Indian arts, see this one. It is devoted to securing the very finest historical and contemporary Native American art from across America. From southwestern textiles and pottery to jewelry, sculpture, and paintings, you probably will not find such a large and complete collection anywhere else but a museum. Here you will also see Northwest Coast Indian masks and Plains Indian artifacts. The handsome gallery-showrooms are well designed, and the staff is knowledgeable and helpful.

Allene Lapides Gallery. 558 Canyon Road; (505) 984–0191. In this spacious gallery the finest in abstract and contemporary paintings, sculpture, and ceramics are handsomely exhibited.

Running Ridge Gallery. 640 Canyon Road; (505) 988–2515; www.collectorsguide.com/running ridge. This is another gallery on the leading edge of the American craft movement. If you are walking out on Canyon Road, take a look at the gallery's contemporary ceramics from around the United States, as well as its

excellent selection of glass, graphics, jewelry, and other art forms.

Bellas Artes. 653 Canyon Road; (505) 983–2745. Next door to the Compound Restaurant. Here you will find contemporary painting, drawing, clay, ceramic, glass, fiber, and textile art from some of the best-known names in the international contemporary art community. And that's not all. This gallery also exhibits and sells outstanding pieces of African and pre-Hispanic art from Central and South America.

Case Trading Post. 704 Camino Lejo; (505) 982–4636; casetrading post.com. Wheelwright Museum (see driving instructions in "A Three-Quarters-of-a-Day Auto Tour of Southeastern Santa Fe"). This excellent shop is downstairs from the gallery of the Wheelwright Museum of the American Indian. In addition to a large selection of Navajo rugs, Navajo, Hopi, and Ácoma pottery, you will find a good selection of regional Indian jewelry, pottery, basketry, and weaving. Some contemporary crafts by Indian artists in the area are also showcased. Also regional books. As at the other museum shops, the dependability and reliability are high.

Santa Fe Area Farmer's Market. Outdoors in the Railyard District just south of Sanbusco Market Center; (505) 983–4098. Farmers from the farms and villages around Santa Fe bring in their produce to sell on Saturday mornings (and some Tuesdays) from early May to early November. Not to be missed in September, when truckloads of fresh chilies are brought in.

Jackalope. 2820 Cerrillos Road; (505) 471–8539 or (800) 753–7757;

www.jackalope.com. This very large emporium, which is a cross between a curio shop, souvenir store, and folk arts store, has many items both large and small from Mexico, Central America, and South America, as well as from throughout New Mexico and throughout the world. Some claim their visit to Santa Fe wouldn't be complete without a visit here.

Shidoni Sculpture Gallery and Foundry and Fine Arts and Crafts Gallery. Five miles north of Santa Fe located on 8 acres between Santa Fe and Tesuque just off New Mexico Highway 590 or Bishop's Lodge Road; (505) 988–8001; www.shidoni.com. This indoor and outdoor sculpture gallery is in a beautiful location that serves as a fine natural background for the contemporary, unique sculpture work produced here. Most of the pieces are bronze or steel fabrications. There are bronze tours open to the public every Saturday. Besides the sculpture there's the outstanding arts and crafts gallery on the premises; it is the repository of some of the region's (and beyond) finest contemporary, mixed-media art.

Flea Market. Located 5.5 miles north of Santa Fe next to the Santa Fe Opera on U.S. Highway 84/285; (505) 995–8626. This is the largest flea market in New Mexico and highly popular. It is operated by the Tesuque Pueblo and has more than 300 permanent vendors offering Indian arts and crafts, antiques, and collectibles. The Pueblo Cafe is on the premises.

Linda Durham Contemporary Art. 12 La Vega, Galisteo; (505) 466–6600; www.lindadurham.com. This prestigious gallery represents

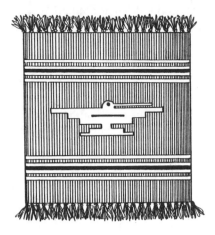

Chimayó weaving

engaging, beautiful, and often controversial work by many New Mexico–based artists.

Oke Oweenge Crafts Cooperative. San Juan Pueblo; (505) 852–2372. (See "Revisiting the Plaza and a Day with the Pueblo Indians North of Santa Fe: A Narrative Account.") Beautiful handwoven San Juan rain sashes, ribbon shirts, pottery, painted gourds, and jewelry made from corn, squash, and watermelon seeds, as well as other materials, are but a few of the excellent, high-quality crafts found in this large, most reliable, and friendly shop, where prices are reasonable.

Herman Valdez Fruit Stand. No. 1 R.A., County Road 60 or P.O. Box 218, Velarde, New Mexico 87582; (505) 852–2129. Do not miss this bastion of Spanish crafts located on the west side of New Mexico Highway 68, 14 miles north of Española on the "low road" to Taos. The art of weaving peppers, corn, gourds, pomegranates, and pine cones into decorative wreaths and table centerpieces is at its peak in this shop. In addition, if you have been hankering for a *ristra* (long strips of chili peppers or corn cobs) to hang from your door, this is a good place to buy one.

Sopyn's Fruit Stand. Located in Rinconda, just north of the Dixon junction on New Mexico Highway 68, the road to Taos; (505) 579–4223. This unpretentious fruit stand on the west side of New Mexico Highway 68 is where you will find many of those unusual dried chili and corn decorations for door and table that you see decorating restaurants and shops. The talented artisan has an excellent eye and a good touch when it comes to making a unified decoration from the regional dried flowers, vegetables, grasses, and weeds. And what's more, the prices for these expertly done pieces are very reasonable.

Trujillo's Weaving Shop. Chimayó, New Mexico. Located on the west side of New Mexico Highway 76, the high road to Taos, just before that road intersects with County Road 98 to Rancho de Chimayó and Santuario de Chimayó. Information: Trujillo's Weaving Shop, Box 18A, Chimayó 87522; (505) 351–4457. See members of this talented Spanish family, at work weaving beautiful blankets and rugs in the classic contemporary and historical styles of the region. The quality of the weaving is excellent. Special orders are taken. In addition, there is a very good selection of local Spanish wood carving for sale, as well as a few other crafts indigenous to the area.

Ortega's Weaving Shop and Galeria Ortega. Chimayó, New Mexico;

(505) 351–4215. Located just off the high road to Taos on County Road 98, the highway to Santuario de Chimayó and Rancho de Chimayó. This large shop has many Chimayó blankets and rugs for sale, as well as a large selection of Spanish wood carvings.

Centinela Traditional Arts. Located on Highway 76 just a short distance northwest of the junction with County Road 98; (505) 351–2180. This large weaving shop has a wide variety of traditional weavings in the Rio Grande, Satillo, Vallero, and Chimayó styles as well as many utiliarian woven items.

Hand Artes Gallery. Truchas, New Mexico. Follow the main street through Truchas until you see the sign; (505) 689–2243. This excellent shop/gallery in a striking rural setting features Southwest fine art paintings by regional artists, textiles, wood, clay, and glass. Also local Hispanic wood carvings and quality crafts from Mexico.

Indian Pueblo Telephone Numbers

Acoma. (505) or (800) 747–0181.

Cochiti. (505) 465–2244.

Nambe. (505) 455–2036.

Picuris. (505) 587–2519 or 587–2957.

Santa Clara. (505) 753–7330 or 753–7326.

Santo Domingo. (505) 465–2214.

San Ildefonso. (505) 455–3549 or 455–2273.

San Juan. (505) 852–4400 or 852–4210.

Taos. (505) 758–1028.

Tesuque. (505) 983–2667.

Pojaque. (505) 455–3460 or 455–2278.

Isleta. (505) 869–3111.

Other Telephone Numbers

Santa Fe Convention and Visitors Bureau. (505) 955–6200 or (800) 777–2489; www.santafe.org.

Santa Fe Central Reservations (does not represent all accommodations). (505) 983–8200 or (800) 776–7669; www.santafecentral res.com.

University of New Mexico Extended University. (505) 428–1234.

College of Santa Fe Visual Arts Center. (505) 473–6011.

Santa Fe Art Institute. (505) 424–5050; www.sfai.org.

Historic Santa Fe Foundation. (505) 983–2567.

Santa Fe Opera. (505) 986–5900 or (877) 999–7499.

American Automobile Association. (505) 471–6620 or (800) 881–7585.

New Mexico Highway Hot Line. (800) 432–4269.

New Mexico Office of Tourism. (800) 827–7400 or (800) 733–6396; www.newmexico.org.

New Mexico Parks and Recreation. (505) 827– 7173.

National Park Service, Southwest Regional Office. (505) 988–6004.

BLM Public Lands Information Center. (505) 438–7542; www.public lands.org.

Santa Fe National Forest. (505) 438–7840.

Golf, Santa Fe Country Club. (505) 471–2626.

Quail Run Golf Course. (505) 986–2255.

Marty Sanchez Links de Santa Fe (golf). (505) 955–4400.

Shellaberger Tennis Center. (505) 473–6144.

Fishing Information and Licenses. (505) 827–7911.

Santa Fe Ski Area. (505) 982–4429.

Ski-snow report. (505) 983–9155; www.skisantafe.com.

Santa Fe Trails bus system. (505) 955–2001 or 955–2003.

Sante Fe Municipal Airport. (505) 955–2900.

Taxicab Service. (505) 438–0000.

Avis Rent-a-Car. (505) 471–5892.

Hertz Rent-a-Car. (505) 471–7189.

Weather and Road Conditions. (800) 432–4269.

TNM&O Greyhound Bus Depot. (505) 471–0008.

Amtrak Rail Station, Lamy depot. (505) 466–4511.

Lamy Depot (Amtrak) Shuttle. (505) 982–8829.

Taos

While the winter and spring seasons in Taos are busy with skiing and white-water rafting, it is still the summer season—four months jam-packed with events and festivals in town and out at Taos Pueblo—that creates all the excitement. And then, of course, there are Taos's museums and art galleries, which attract visitors like a magnet year-round. (Many of these are described in the several walking and automobile tours detailed in the section of the book "Seeing the Spanish Rio Grande Country," "Taos.")

Taos is long on good accommodations, many having the kind of ambience that brought you to New Mexico in the first place. Lodging rates are generally the highest during the ski season and holidays. But if you need basic digs, they can be found ten miles northeast of Taos on New Mexico Highway 150, in Arroyo Seco, at the Abominable Snowmansion Hostel (AYH), P.O. Box 3271, Taos; (505) 776–8298. Hostel facilities are also available at the Taos Motel; (505) 758–2524. The restaurant scene is neither as good nor as varied as in Santa Fe, but then Taos is a town of just more than 6,000, with just 30,000 in all Taos County, and receives fewer visitors than Santa Fe and its more than 65,000 residents. Nonetheless you will not starve in Taos. In fact in several restaurants you will eat some fine continental, regional, and New American dishes that are just about equal to any in the region. With several exceptions, many of the accommodations and restaurants are within a few blocks of the plaza, making Taos an excellent walking town.

Like Santa Fe but on a smaller scale, Taos has had its problems with traffic. As the University of New Mexico–Taos campus grows and the Las Vegas–style casino at Taos Pueblo prospers, the traffic congestion will likely increase year-round. The prime bottleneck is just east of the plaza along the major north-south arterial. This has become a particular problem because of the development of numerous large motels along that arterial south of the plaza. They are just far enough out from the plaza that most visitors feel compelled to drive into the city center. But they don't have to. The Town of Taos Transit (The Chili Line); 505–751–4459), provides an option, operating buses six days a week, stopping at many of the major motels and inns along the main route from Taos Pueblo in the north via the Plaza, going all the way south to Rancho de Taos.

For pathfinding purposes it's helpful to note as you read this book and travel through town that the following streets—either due to local usage or due to the use of Spanish rather than English (or vice versa)—have two names: Camino de la Placita, also known as Placitas Road; Paseo del Pueblo Norte, also known as North Pueblo Road (U.S. Highway 64); and Paseo del Pueblo Sur (South Pueblo Road), also known as Santa Fe Road or South Santa Fe Road (New Mexico Highway 68).

The helpful **Taos County Chamber of Commerce** is housed in the easily accessible Taos Visitor Center on the main highway, New Mexico Highway 68 (Paseo del Pueblo Sur) south of the plaza on the southwest corner of Paseo del Pueblo Sur and Paseo del Canon (New Mexico Highway 585, U.S. Highway 64 bypass). Information: Taos County Chamber of Commerce and Visitor Center, P.O. Drawer I, Taos, New Mexico 87571; (505) 758–3873, (800) 732–8267 or (800) 732–1516; www.taoschamber.com.

Lodging

If lodging is heavily booked during the time you will be in Taos and you've exhausted the recommendations in this book, contact Taos Central Reservations, representing some but not all properties in Taos; (505) 758–9767 or (800) 821–2437; fax (505) 758–1875; www.taoswebb. com/plan/tcr. Or contact Taos Association of Bed and Breakfasts; (505) 758–7301 or (800) 939–2215; www.taos-bandb-inns.com.

The Historic Taos Inn. This attractive, adobe hostelry right in the center of town is overflowing with the region's Spanish charm. Its location, just 1½ blocks north of the plaza, and its unbeatable ambience make it one of the best places to stay in Taos. The lobby is where the courtyard used to be 750 years ago, and in the middle of it, preserved for all to see, is the site of the old Taos water well. Today the lobby, like the well in days gone by, seems to serve as a gathering place for both visitors and Taos natives. Some of the thirty-six rooms are in the three-story adobe structure that fronts on Pueblo Road; others, many with fireplaces, are out back around a delightful courtyard. The rooms are tastefully furnished Southwest style. Just off the lobby is the hotel restaurant, **Doc Martin's,** and bar. The ever-busy **Adobe Bar,** on the other side of the lobby, is a friendly place, popular with visitors as well as locals. Just off the dining room is an outdoor dining patio for breakfast, lunch, or dinner. Beyond that are a heated swimming pool and an indoor Jacuzzi, which front a grassy, open courtyard circled by numerous secluded rooms. Information: Historic

Taos Inn, 125 Paseo del Pueblo Norte, Taos, New Mexico 87571; (505) 758–2233 or (888) 519–8267; fax (505) 758–5776; www.taosinn. com. Inexpensive to expensive.

Fechin Inn. Snuggling up to the handsome, historic Nicolai Fechin home adjacent to Kit Carson Park are several equally appealing buildings that house the eighty-four well-appointed rooms of the Fechin Inn, within easy walking distance of the plaza. The inn's construction was lovingly directed by the artist's family and is decorated Southwest style with many touches reminiscent of the talented Fechin, who was as adept working with wood as painting on canvas. The attractive rooms notwithstanding, there are also aesthetically pleasing public rooms; the lounge, the library, and the courtyards particularly come to mind. But there are other amenities as well: some minirefrigerators, a fitness center, and an open-air whirlpool. You can also purchase a breakfast buffet. Information: Fechin Inn, 227 Paseo del Pueblo Norte, Taos, New Mexico 87571; (505) 751–1000 or (800) 811–2933; fax (505) 751–7338; www-fechin-inn.com. Moderate to expensive.

La Posada de Taos. This B&B has a location just 2½ blocks west of the plaza, at 309 Juanita Lane. Six charming rooms with private baths in a handsomely renovated older adobe house and an adobe casita. From adobe fireplaces and wood-burning stoves to some rooms with Jacuzzi bathtubs, the amenities are many. The main public room is a warm, pleasant living space decorated southwestern style with comfortable reading chairs and good lighting. Breakfast is served

Historic Taos Inn

in a sunny location at the far end of this room. Truly a full breakfast, with many New Mexican touches. Call for directions. Information: La Posada de Taos, P.O. Box 1118, Taos, New Mexico 87571; (505) 758–8164 or (800) 645–4803; fax (505) 751–4696; www.laposadadetaos.com. Moderate to expensive.

Inn on La Loma Plaza. Enviably located at the corner of Ranchitos Road and Valdez (within easy walking distance—3 blocks—of the plaza) and nestled in a quiet area amid shade trees and gardens on a knoll that offers grand views of the valley and mountains is this beautifully restored, historic two-story adobe hacienda. Some of the walls of the original house were built in 1800 and served as part of the fortifications of La Loma Plaza, a historic Taos residential plaza. Each of the seven rooms (some with views, patios, or fireplaces) is a winner. The spacious public room—the gallery, with its fountain and fireplace—has a wall of windows offering sweeping views of the mountains and opens to a large outdoor terrace. Full breakfast is served. Outdoor hot tub. Parking on the property. Information: Inn on La Loma Plaza, 102 La Loma Plaza, Box 4159, Taos, New Mexico 87571; (505) 758–1717 or (800)

530–3040; fax (505) 751–0155; www.taos-nm.net. Moderate to expensive.

Casa Europa Bed and Breakfast Inn and Gallery. Located out in beautiful, peaceful countryside (offering territorial views) just off Ranchitos Road and less than 2 miles out of town is this restored historic home, whose helpful, knowledgeable owners know how this sort of place should be run. Wonderful charm and ambience abide here, where Europe meets the Southwest. The upstairs sitting room is extraordinarily handsome. But then so are the beautifully and individually decorated six rooms and one apartment suite—each with private bath and featuring a kiva fireplace and/or Jacuzzi or whirlpool bath—or the nicely appointed, simpler rooms that offer either garden or territorial views. The attractive dining room is the setting for a full gourmet breakfast. A sales gallery features regional Southwest art. Outside hot tub and Swedish sauna. Reservation deposit required. Information: Casa Europa, 840 Upper Ranchitos Road, H.C. 68 Box 3F, Taos, New Mexico 87571; (505) 758–9798 or (888) 758–9798; www.casaeuropa.com. Moderate to expensive.

La Doña Luz Inn. Centrally located, just ½ block from the plaza behind the oldest trading post in Taos by the same name and under the same family ownership is this very charming B&B, which exudes southwestern ambience. The fourteen nicely decorated rooms (some smallish), all with private baths, many with fireplaces, Jacuzzi bath tubs and two with kitchenette units, are on three different levels of several adobes. Some have views, some have a terrace or a patio. Two have hot tubs. All of the rooms are handsomely decorated, and most have TVs with VCRs. The continental breakfast is taken downstairs in the dining room or out on the patio, weather permitting. And it is only a short walk to galleries and restaurants. Information: La Doña Luz Inn, 114 Kit Carson Street, Taos, New Mexico 87571; (505) 758–4874 or (800) 759–9187; fax (505) 758–4541; www.ladonaluz.com. Inexpensive to moderate.

Hotel La Fonda de Taos. Conveniently located right on the plaza, this charming, historic, but extensively renovated and upscaled 1937 hotel takes you back to an earlier time. The handsome lobby/mezzanine with its intriguing art-deco/Southwest look is worth a peek even if you're not staying there. Ask at the desk to see the rare collection of D. H. Lawrence paintings on the premises. The comfortable nineteen rooms and five suites (all with private bathrooms) vary in size, and some have fireplaces. Exercise and massage rooms. Open air hot tub. Information: La Fonda de Taos, 108 South Plaza, Taos, New Mexico 87571; (505) 758–2211 or (888) 833–2211; fax (505) 758–8508; www.hotellafonda.com. Expensive.

Casa Benavides. Just about 1 block away from the plaza is this compound of older adobe homes carefully renovated into a very charming B&B with thirty-three rooms and suites, each decorated Southwest style. Also some studios with kitchens. All have private baths, and many have fireplaces and handcrafted accessories. The very nicely furnished dining area is the scene for a huge but nicely concocted gourmet breakfast in the mornings; the fare includes dishes like granola, Mexican eggs, homemade tortillas, and pancakes. Hot tub. Information: Casa Benavides, 137 Kit Carson Road, Taos, New Mexico 87571; (505) 758–1772 or (800) 552–1772; fax (505) 758–5738; www.taos-casabenavides.com. Moderate.

Mabel Dodge Luhan House. This B&B is located at the end of Morada Road (see "Three-Quarters-of-a-Day Walking Tour of Taos") about 0.5 mile northeast of the plaza. In addition to the modern guesthouse nearby having eight rooms with private baths, nine rooms in this historic home are available to travelers, including Mabel's bedroom, which is the most expensive except for one two-bedroom cottage with kitchen. Beautiful setting overlooking Taos Indian reservation lands and the Sangre de Cristo Mountains. Shared or private bath. The home is used for other functions, which makes rooms scarce during certain times of the year. So make inquiries at least three months ahead of your stay. Information: Mabel Dodge Luhan House, 240 Morada Lane, P.O. Box 558, Taos, New Mexico 87571; (505) 751–9686 or (800) 846–2235; fax (505) 737–0365; www.mabeldodgeluhan.com. Moderate.

American Artists Gallery House.
This adobe-style bed-and-breakfast home, situated behind a low-lying adobe wall in a quiet spot about 1.5 miles from the plaza, provides beautiful unobstructed views of Taos Mountain from its patio and some of the rooms. There is art on the walls throughout the ten nicely appointed guest rooms and the attractive public rooms, and there are sculptural pieces sharing the garden with the hollyhocks and roses. Most of the art is for sale in this gallery-house. All ten rooms have traditional fireplaces as well as private baths. There is a hot tub outdoors and three Jacuzzi suites. A gourmet, full breakfast. Call for directions. Information: American Artists Gallery House, 132 Frontier Road, P.O. Box 584, Taos, New Mexico 87571; (505) 758–4446 or (800) 532–2041; fax (505) 758–0497; www.taosbedandbreakfast.com. Inexpensive to expensive.

Ramada Inn de Taos. Located a little more than 1 mile south of the plaza, just off New Mexico Highway 68 (Santa Fe Road South), is this 124-unit, modern, two-story, harmoniously designed structure, which blends features of the historic adobes of the region with more contemporary elements. The comfortable, spacious rooms are nicely decorated with Southwest touches, and guests have available to them a heated indoor pool with Jacuzzi. Most rooms have views of the mountains. Air-conditioned. Information: Ramada Inn, Box 6257, Taos, New Mexico 87571; (505) 758–2900 or (800) 659–8267; fax (505) 758–1662. Inexpensive.

Holiday Inn Don Fernando de Taos. Located several miles south of the plaza on Paseo del Pueblo Sur, this Holiday Inn offers 126 air-conditioned units divided among a large complex of six two-story buildings. The buildings are nicely spaced on the roomy property, with its grassy yards and gardens. Many of the rooms offer views, and some have fireplaces. Heated swimming pool. Whirlpool. Indoor tennis court. Pets (deposit). Restaurant. Information: Holiday Inn Don Fernando de Taos, 1005 Paseo del Pueblo Sur, Taos, New Mexico 87571; (505) 758–4444 or (800) 759–2736; fax (505) 758–0055; www.holiday-taos.com. Moderate to expensive.

Sagebrush Inn and Conference Center. The Sagebrush Inn is located 3 miles south of the plaza on the west side of New Mexico Highway 68. This adobe inn was built in 1929. Over the years it has hosted many of Taos's famous and near-famous guests, including Georgia O'Keeffe. There are fine views of Taos Mountain and the rest of the Sangre de Cristo Mountains. Pleasant, tree-shaded patios, atmospheric *ramadas,* heated swimming pool, Jacuzzi, as well as condominium units, are all part of the scene. Two dining rooms. Lobby bar with live music at times. Seventy of the one hundred rooms have traditional fireplaces. There is a slightly worn, comfortable-as-an-old-shoe quality in some of the rooms. Complimentary breakfast. Information: Sagebrush Inn, 1508 Paseo del Pueblo Sur, P.O. Box 557, Taos, New Mexico 87571; (505) 758–2254 or (888) 782–8267; fax (505) 758–5077; www.sagebrushinn.com. Inexpensive to expensive.

Sagebrush Inn and Conference Center, Taos

Adobe and Pines Inn. Located 3 miles south of the Plaza, just south of Rancho de Taos in the shelter of a grove of pine trees is this bed-and-breakfast inn situated in a renovated 150-year-old adobe home with views of Taos Mountain. The nine units, all with either kiva or corner fireplaces, are handsomely decorated. Some have whirlpool baths and one has a sauna and soaking tub. A full breakfast is served in the bright, sunny breakfast room. Weddings and small conferences are sometimes held here. Information: Adobe and Pines Inn, P.O. Box 837, Ranchos De Taos, New Mexico 87557; (505) 751–0947 or (800) 723–8267; fax (505) 758–8423; www.adobepines.com. Moderate to expensive.

El Pueblo Lodge. Located just off busy U.S. Highway 64 at 412 Paseo del Pueblo Norte, 0.5 mile (about 4 long blocks) north of the plaza, is this pueblo-style motel with sixty rooms. Some of the rooms have kitchens or efficiencies, and some have fireplaces. You can choose between either modern or southwestern-style rooms. Condominium units also available. Heated swimming pool. Information: El Pueblo Lodge, 412 Paseo del Pueblo Norte, Taos, New Mexico 87571; (505) 758–8700 or (800) 433–9612; fax (505) 758–7321; www.elpueblolodge.com. Inexpensive.

Best Western Kachina Lodge de Taos. One of the oldest motels in Taos, this busy large pueblo, territorial-style place, with its art deco interior and its 118 rooms upgraded just enough, still has loads of charm and is within walking distance (about 0.5 mile) of the plaza. With lots of parking, considerable open space, a large heated swimming pool and hot tub, and a grassy courtyard, the lodge is as good for families now as it was thirty or forty years ago. And Kit Carson Park is just down the road. Handsome public rooms, outdoor patios, coffee shop, and dining rooms. And as in days gone by, Indian dances are held at night May through October. Information: Best Western Kachina Lodge de Taos, 413 North Pueblo Road, Box NN, Taos, New Mexico 87571; (505) 758–2275 or (800) 522–4462; www.kachinalodge.com. Inexpensive to moderate.

Hacienda del Sol. This B&B is located about 1 mile north of the plaza, just off U.S. Highway 64 (North Pueblo Road). Although just a short distance off the busy highway at 109 Mabel Dodge Lane, the hacienda rests peacefully under the largest cottonwood trees you may ever see on 1 acre of ground offering views out over Taos Indian reservation lands to the mountains. There are ten rooms—some have whirlpool baths and most have fireplaces—in this historic adobe. Creative homemade breakfasts in the handsomely decorated, southwestern-style dining room. Outdoor hot tub. Call for directions. Information: Hacienda del Sol, Box 177, Taos, New Mexico 87571; (505) 758–0287 or (866) 333–4459; fax (505) 758–5895; www.taoshaciendadelsol.com. Moderate to expensive.

Touchstone Inn. Located at 110 Mabel Dodge Lane (see previous listing), this historic adobe is set at the edge of Taos Pueblo lands on 2 acres with views of Taos Mountain. It's a comfortable sort of place and an art gallery besides. There's art on the walls wherever you look. The nine rooms and one suite are handsomely done

Southwest style, some with fireplaces, intimate patios, a few with whirlpool baths. Small pets allowed (deposit). Information: Touchstone Inn, 110 Mabel Dodge Lane, P.O. Box 1885, Taos, New Mexico 87571; (505) 758–0192 or (800) 758–0192; fax (505) 758–3498; www.touch stoneinn.com. Moderate to expensive.

Quail Ridge Inn Resort. Out on the sage plain, 6 miles northeast of the plaza on Ski Valley Road (New Mexico Highway 150), is this tastefully designed, two-story, contemporary southwestern-style resort-lodge, which has all the amenities, including tennis (six outdoor and two indoor courts), swimming (covered pool), racquetball (four courts), volleyball, and a fitness center. The 110 spacious rooms and suites, with some elements of southwestern decor, have fireplaces and balconies or patios; more than half have fully equipped kitchens. Outstanding views of the high sage plain and Sangre de Cristo Mountains. Information: Quail Ridge Inn Resort, P.O. Box 707, Taos, New Mexico 87571; (505) 776–2211 or (800) 624–4448; fax (505) 776–2949; www.quailridgeinn. com. Moderate to expensive.

Cottonwood Inn. This bed-and-breakfast inn is located northeast of Taos at the junction of New Mexico Highways 150 and 230 in a peaceful garden setting with fine views. The seven rooms in this large two-story adobe home are nicely appointed, some having kiva fireplaces and exterior entrances. Outdoor hot tub. Information: Cottonwood Inn, HCR 7B, Box 24609, El Prado-Taos, New Mexico 87529; (505) 776–5826 or (800) 324–7120; www.taos-cotton wood.com. Inexpensive to expensive.

Mountain Light Bed and Breakfast and Gallery. Located 12 miles north of Taos on New Mexico Highway 522, on a hill overlooking the village of Arroyo Hondo, New Mexico, this attractive adobe home is owned by a photographer-artist. And it offers views over the countryside that won't stop. The three rooms have shared bathroom facilities, and the common kitchen may be used by the guests (fee). But the full breakfast comes with the territory here at the region's oldest B&B. The gallery features the work of the owner and other regional photographers. Information: Mountain Light Bed and Breakfast, Box 241, Taos, New Mexico 87571; (505) 776–8474; fax (505) 776–8050; www.mtnlight.com. Inexpensive.

Camping

Around Taos there are many trails to hike and places to camp. Beyond the limited listing below, visit or call Carson National Forest Headquarters, 208 Cruz Alta Road, Taos, New Mexico 87571; (505) 758–6200; www.fs.fed.us/r3/carson.

Taos Valley RV Park. Located just off New Mexico Highway 68, 3 miles south of the plaza. Ninety-two sites on 12 acres; (505) 758–4469 or (800) 999–7571.

Taos Motel and RV Park. Located on New Mexico Highway 68, 3.4 miles south of the plaza at 1800 Paseo del Pueblo Sur. A Good Sampark site with twenty-two full hookups and seven grassy sites with water; (505) 758–2524 or (800) 323–6009.

Capulin. This National Forest Service campground is located 5.6 miles east of Taos on U.S. Highway 64. Ten sites on 6 acres. Reservation deposit required; (505) 758–6200.

La Sombra. This National Forest Service campground is located 6 miles east of Taos on U.S. Highway 64. Thirteen sites on 3 acres. River fishing; (505) 758–6200.

Rio Grande Gorge State Park. Located approximately 16 miles southwest on New Mexico Highway 68 near Pilar, New Mexico. Sixteen sites on 1,300 acres. River fishing. No telephone.

Food

Apple Tree Restaurant. This restaurant, located in an old adobe at 123 Bent Street, 1 block from the plaza, is a good bet for lunch, dinner, or Sunday brunch; (505) 758–1900; apple treerestaurant.com. On nice days lunch and dinner are served in the comfortable outdoor patio shaded by several old apple trees. The inside dining room in the old adobe is also very pleasant. Regional specialties sprinkle the somewhat international menu. The excellently prepared New American and New Mexican food includes many unique variations of seafood, chicken, and gourmet vegetarian dishes. Picnic lunches to go. Superb apple juice. Outstanding wine list (wine bar upstairs). Desserts and espresso. Sunday brunch. Reservations for dinner advised. Moderate.

Bent Street Deli and Cafe. Smack-dab in the middle of Bent Street is this useful eatery good for breakfast, a quick lunch, or a dinner; (505) 758–5787. The choices are many and good for breakfast, while lunch offers several tasty soups, appetizers, salads, and sandwiches for your consideration. Wine and beer. Heated patio dining in the cool season. Moderate.

Taos Trading Co. 212 North Plaza; (550) 758–3012. Sometimes on a hot day, it is nice to know of a place to get an ice-cream cone or a cold drink. The old-fashioned soda fountain at the Taos Trading Co. provides the answer, with its malts, milkshakes, and soda fountain drinks. Also cards and T-shirts.

Taos Tea Room. At 246B Ledoux just south of the plaza; (505) 751–0211. Just beyond the Harwood Museum is this inviting space offering great teas, sweets, snacks, and soups. Call for hours.

Ogelvie's Bar and Grille. Enviably located on the east side of and overlooking Taos Plaza; (505) 758–8866. In this lively restaurant you can sate your lunch or dinner appetite with good sandwiches, southwestern regional dishes, and fresh seafood selections. The bar is as popular as the restaurant, and live music is provided on some weekends. Dinner reservations accepted. Moderate.

Caffee Tazza. East of the plaza at 122 Kit Carson Road (505–758–8706) is this all-day-and-into-the-night, inside-or-out-on-the-large-patio, coffee-tea-and-light-food (including pastries) venue. Out-of-town newspapers and magazines are sold here, and many evenings there is live music.

Caffe Renato. 133 Paseo Del Pueblo Norte; (505) 758–0244; located downtown just next door to the Taos Inn. Inside is an elegant but small breakfast and dining area across from the Farnsworth Art Gallery, or you can dine in the garden. For breakfast try the homemade baked goods, freshly squeezed juice or fresh fruit, or perhaps the breakfast quiche. For lunch a variety of fresh salads, panini, and sandwiches. Graze here for picnics too.

Lambert's of Taos. 309 Paseo del Pueblo Sur; (505) 758–1009. Located in a lovely historic-home-turned-restaurant, this is a very good, chic but casual dinner establishment. The menu is contemporary American and may include dishes like pork tenderloin with chipotle cream sauce or jumbo scallops on angel hair pasta, as well as quail, lamb, beef, and chicken dishes. Desserts such as chocolate mousse with raspberry sauce grace the menu. Very good wine and beer menu. Espresso. Dinner nightly. Reservations recommended. Moderate to expensive.

Doc Martin's. This restaurant is located in the Taos Inn just ½ block up North Pueblo Road (U.S. Highway 64) from the plaza; (505) 758–1977. Thick, old adobe walls provide a quiet but informal setting, which includes an outdoor patio. Regional specialties on the menu are numerous and good. A nice variety of meat and seafood dishes completes the dinner bill of fare. A highly varied and good breakfast menu. Also open for lunch. Moderate.

Michael's Kitchen. Located 0.25 mile north of the plaza on North Pueblo Road (U.S. Highway 64); (505) 758–4178. This establishment, which has grown from a bakery and breakfast place, serves three meals a day. Both regional and American food are served in an informal, lively atmosphere. Good place for families.

The food is good and reasonably priced. Best for breakfast and lunch. Inexpensive.

Orlando's. Located in El Prado at 1114 Don Juan Valdez Lane (505–751–1450), just off Paseo Del Pueblo Norte, 1.8 miles north of the plaza. You feel that you've stepped way south into Mexico at this popular little New Mexican cafe where the tasty smothered burritos, shrimp plates, Baja fish tacos, and blue corn enchiladas are authentically prepared. Dine inside or out on the patio. Lunch and dinner. Inexpensive.

Antonio's. Also in El Prado just off Paseo Del Pueblo Norte (505–758–9889; www.taostorreon.com), in the remodeled historic El Torreon Hacienda is this upscale Mexican dining venue with its prominent fireplace. The menu features dishes from Yucatan, Puebla, Veracruz, Mexico City, and Tampico. Lovely views of the mountains and patio dining in season. Moderate.

Villa Fontana. Located 5 miles north of Taos on Highway 522; (505) 758–5800. You will be rewarded by driving a few miles north to this excellent dinner restaurant focusing on the dishes of northern Italy. The setting is pleasantly elegant but also friendly and informal. Fresh mushrooms appear frequently on this wide-ranging menu flavored by herbs from the garden. With fresh ingredients and skill in the kitchen, this place doesn't disappoint. You can start with cream of wild mushroom soup and then raise the ante with osso buco (braised veal shank), fresh fish, and game dishes. Excellent wine selection. Desserts and espresso. Closed Sunday. Moderate to expensive.

Momentitos de la Vida. Located in a historic adobe building on the way out to the ski valley on New Mexico 150 (Ski Valley Road) just outside of Arroyo Seco (505–776–3333; www.vidarest.com). The menu is New American, and you can dine either in the handsome dining room or more intimately near the fireplace in the bar. You could start with house corn chowder with roasted green chili, then proceed to diver scallop beggar's purses with sweet pea broth. Good wine list. Desserts include a selection of cheeses. Moderate to expensive.

Bravo. Located south of the plaza at 1353-A Paseo del Pueblo Sur (505–758–8100) is this casual gourmet-to-go and pleasant dining spot, specializing in salads, sandwiches, burgers, and soups. But there's more too at this wine bar restaurant—a delicious array of complex and tasty appetizers as well as a children's menu. A wide selection of microbrew beers as well.

Trading Post Cafe. Still farther south at Rancho de Taos is this excellent lunch and dinner establishment at 4179 New Mexico Highway 68; (505) 758–5089. You'll dine in style in a nicely refurbished old trading post building where the upscale menu reads more northern California and northern Italy than northern New Mexico. Minestrone or Trading Post chicken noodle soup might get you started. Then you might choose roast duck in apple chutney, Frangelico sauce, or crispy garlic pork loin chop, or New Zealand lamb chops with tomato–mint salsa. Desserts. Espresso. Wine and beer list. Open daily. Moderate.

Ranchos Plaza Grill. Located at No. 8 Saint Francis Plaza, Ranchos de Taos; (505) 758–5788. If you're visiting the old church at Rancho de Taos, you might want to stop in here for breakfast, lunch, or dinner. Dine inside or out on the tree-shaded patio. Breakfast, served all day long, is quite a treat here, the many choices ranging from eggs Benedict to breakfast burritos and hard-to-beat just plain old pancakes. Hamburgers and sandwiches for lunch as well as soups and green salads. Inexpensive to moderate.

Stakeout. Located 8 miles south of Taos on New Mexico Highway 68; (505) 758–2042. If you are a sunset aficionado and you want to see a "ten" sunset, this is the place to come. Viewing a sunset from this location may make you feel like you have died and gone to heaven barefoot, for the sunset view, which stretches for more than 100 miles, will knock your socks off. And while you are there, you might have a drink in the bar or dinner in this antiques-filled adobe house. Entrees include duck, lobster, lamb, veal, fresh pasta, and, of course, a long list of steaks, which gave this place its name (if you like to play on words, that is). Moderate.

Tours, More Museums, and Activities

For additional information check taosmuseums.org or taoschamber.com.

Taos Transit–The Chili Line. If you are without wheels or do not want to drive into the plaza, ride the Taos Transit. This local bus service stops at most major motels north and south of the plaza, as well as at some of the parking lots; (505) 751–4459.

Taos Walks. Historic Walking Tours leaves from the Taos Inn lobby (505–758–2233 or 758–4020). Other walking tours are also available: All Aboard Step-On Guide and Walking Tours (505–758–9368) and Spiritland Walking Tours (505–737–3030).

Harwood Museum of Art. Located at 238 Ledoux Street (505–758–9826; www.harwood.unm.edu) is this University of New Mexico museum. The historic pueblo revival compound features a gallery of early twentieth-century art, featuring the works of the Taos Society of Artists; the Hispanic Traditions Gallery, with many *santos* and *bultos* donated by Mabel Dodge Luhan; a mid-twentieth-century gallery; a late-twentieth-century gallery; and the world-class Agnes Martin Gallery. There are rotating shows as well.

Van Vechten–Linberry Taos Museum. Located on beautiful secluded grounds on the way out to Taos Pueblo at 501 Paseo del Pueblo Norte (505–758–2690) is this repository of historic regional art. Every member of the Taos Society of Artists, they claim, is represented here—all under one roof. Closed Monday and Tuesday.

Nicolai Fechin House. For details about this outstanding attraction, see description in "A Three-Quarters-of-a-Day Walking Tour of Taos" earlier in this section. Also shown are changing exhibits of other artists; (505) 758–1710.

Taos County Farmers Market.
Located northwest of the plaza on
the grounds of the town hall across
from the public library at 400
Camino de la Placita. This active
marketplace comes alive on Saturday
mornings throughout the summer.

Historic Taos Trolley Tours. From
the summer trolley enjoy the sights of
historic Taos during a seventy-minute,
narrated tour. Two tours daily in the
summer. Also Albuquerque airport
service; (505) 751–0366 or (800)
273–8340; www.taostrolleytours.com.

Faust's Transportation. This group
provides not only taxi service in Taos
and tours of the "High Road," Santa
Fe, and Taos, but also shuttle service
to Albuquerque International Airport;
(505) 758–3410 or (888) 830–3410.

Twin Hearts Express. This transportation company connects Taos,
Española, and Santa Fe to the Albuquerque airport and other destinations
in New Mexico and southern Colorado; (505) 751–1201 or (800)
654–9456.

Taylor Streit Flyfish Service. This
fellow either is full of himself or is
indeed one of the region's most
sought-after guides, as many anglers
have testified. Tours led by this very
knowledgeable guide to the Rio
Grande, Chama, and the Red River as
well as small streams. It seems like he
fishes almost all year; (505) 751–1312;
www.streitflyfishing.com.

Taos Mountain Outfitters. Located
on the south side of the plaza, 114
South Taos Plaza (505–758–9292;
www.taosmountainoutfitters.com),

this full-service outdoor store rents
and sells mountain bikes and, with a
wide selection of outdoor maps, can
tell you where to go. Also rental and
sale of outdoor hiking and backpacking equipment, white-water expeditions, and mountain-climbing
instruction classes. The shop additionally sells some of the best-known
brands of outdoor clothing.

At **Cottam's Ski and Outdoor
Store,** 207 Paseo del Pueblo Sur
(505–758–2822) or at **Gearing Up,**
129 Paseo del Pueblo Sur (505–751–
0365), you can rent or buy a bicycle.

Rio Grande Raft Trips. For one-
day raft trips through the exciting
Taos Box or the Lower Gorge and for
two- and three-day trips through the
Rio Grande Wild and Scenic River
area, contact Rio Grande River Tours
(505–758–0762 or 800–525–4966;
www.rivertours.com); Los Rios River
Runners (505) 776–8854; or Far
Flung Adventures (505–758–2628 or
800–359–2627; www.farflung.com).

**Cumbres and Toltec Scenic Rail-
road.** From Taos you can drive to
either Chama, New Mexico, or
Antonito, Colorado, for a seven-hour-
long, round-trip steam narrow-gauge
railway trip into the Sangre de
Cristos. The tracks are part of the
Denver and Rio Grande system built
for the mining booms of the 1880s.
Information: Cumbres and Toltec
Scenic Railroad, P.O. Box 789,
Chama, New Mexico 87520; (888)
286–2737; www.cumbrestoltec.com.
Or write P.O. Box 668, Antonito,
Colorado 81120.

Horseback Riding

Taos Indian Horse Ranch. Located at Taos Pueblo. This well-established stable offers hour-long rides for novices at the pueblo, as well as two-hour rides for intermediate and advanced riders. Also available are overnight trips into the Rio Grande Gorge and the Sangre de Cristo Mountains. Information: Taos Indian Horse Ranch, P.O. Box 3019, Taos, New Mexico 87571; (505) 758–3212 or (800) 659–3210.

Events, Fairs, Festivals, and Fiestas

To fine-tune dates and obtain a complete listing of Taos events, fairs, and festivals, contact the Taos County Chamber of Commerce at (800) 732–8267 or www.taoschamber.com/calendar.shtml/.

To confirm dates of festivals and dances at Taos Pueblo, it is best to check with the **pueblo visitors center;** (505) 758–1028; taospueblo.com.

Taos Talking Pictures Festivals. This fine art film festival in early April with its workshops and screenings is a big hit here. (505) 751–0637.

Santa Cruz Day. Close to the first weekend in May. Green Corn Dance at Taos Pueblo.

Taos Spring Arts Celebration. During the month of May this festival features the visual, performing, and literary arts of Taos. Besides a major art show there are many special gallery and museum shows as well; (808) 816–1516.

Taos Inn's Meet the Artist Series. This series, wherein the public has a chance to participate in informal sessions with Taos-based artists and beyond, is held at the Taos Inn. It includes studio tours, lectures, and demonstrations and is held twice a year. The first session is in May and early June. The second session is in September; (505) 758–2233.

Taos Poetry Circus. A poetry competition among well-known poets in early June. (505) 758–1800.

San Antonio Feast Day. Second weekend in June. Corn Dance at Taos and Picuris Pueblos.

San Juan Feast Day. Midweek, around the fourth week in June. Corn Dance at Taos Pueblo.

Taos School of Music Annual Chamber Music Festival. Midweek beginning around the third week in June. In addition to the concerts staged by professional musicians, there are student chamber music concerts held throughout June, July, and the first week of August. Sponsored by the Taos School of Music and held in the Taos Community Auditorium, as well as at Ski Valley. Information: Taos School of Music Annual Chamber Music Festival, Box 1897, Taos, New Mexico 87571; (505) 776–2388.

Annual Taos Pueblo Powwow. Around the second weekend in July, costumed Indian dancers from around the United States gather for this major powwow and dance competition held on reservation land behind the Overland Sheepskin Co. north of town. Arts and crafts booths and many, many traditional dances. A festive event well worth seeing. Special Native American foods; (505) 758–1028.

Las Fiestas de Taos. Along about the third weekend in July comes the largest summer celebration in Taos, celebrating the feast days of Santa Ana and Santiago (James). There are street dances, an arts and crafts fair, Spanish-style entertainment, a fiesta mass, and a candlelight procession from one of the churches, like Our Lady of Guadalupe Church, to the plaza. The next week Taos Pueblo celebrates these saints' days with Corn Dances on two different days.

Taos County Fair. Third week in August; (800) 816–1516.

Annual Taos Fall Arts Festival. The last two weeks in September and most of October. Large, juried show of arts and crafts. Retrospective exhibition of famous Taos artists over the years. Studio tours, theater, and music performances; (800) 816–1516.

Old Taos Trade Fair. Held during the last week in September as a major part of the Taos Fall Arts Festival, this gala affair is a re-creation of the early-nineteenth-century trade fairs held in this remote outpost. Sponsored by the people who should know more about this kind of thing than anybody else, the Kit Carson Foundation really captures the spirit of former times as it stages traditional-style caravans complete with Indian, Spanish settler, and mountain men look-alikes. Craft demonstrations, native foods, and authentic Spanish music and dances at Hacienda de los Martinez; (505) 785–0505 or (800) 758–0505.

San Geronimo Eve Vespers Dance. The last week in September at Taos Pueblo. This two-day occasion begins with a ceremonial dance at sunset on the first day, followed by more dances, war games, foot races, and an arts and crafts fair the next day.

Wool Festival. Part of the Taos Fall Arts Festival held during the first weekend in October at Kit Carson Park, weavers from the region and beyond gather to talk shop, give educational demonstrations, put on weaving exhibits, sell their wares, and who knows what else—maybe even gather wool; (505) 751–0306.

Taos Mountain Balloon Rally. Held the third weekend in October, this hot air balloon festival includes parades, dances, and an arts and crafts fair; (800) 816–1516.

Christmas in Taos. Christmas in northern New Mexico is often a unique experience, and certainly Taos is no exception. Out at the pueblo there are the Procession of the Virgin and Matachines Dance on Christmas Eve and either Deer or Matachines Dances on Christmas Day. But before making the trip, check with Taos Pueblo or Taos Information for details and any last-minute changes; (505) 758–1028 or (800) 732–8267; www.taospuelbo.com.

Parking

You will find municipal parking lots in the following locations. These lots are not visible from the major pedestrian and auto byways.

- Lot bounded by Bent Street (just south of Bent Street) and Placitas Road (Camino de la Placitas). Behind the shops that border the north side of the plaza.
- Lot immediately west of the Plaza bounded by Camino de la Placitas and Don Fernando Street.

- Lot a few blocks east on Kit Carson Road where Kit Carson intersects Morada and Quesnel Roads.
- Lot entered from North Pueblo Road. Turn east onto the first road just north of the Taos Center for the Arts (133 Paseo del Pueblo Norte) and the Farnsworth Gallery. There is parking just north of the Taos Center for the Arts around the back in the Taos Community Auditorium parking lot.

Shopping

Blue Rain Gallery. Located just off the Plaza at 117 South Taos Plaza; (505) 751–0066; www.BlueRain Gallery.com. If you want to see the best in Southwest Indian pottery, wall art, and jewelry, pay a visit here. The work of today's contemporary Indian artists is absolutely stunning and displayed beautifully in this gallery, which has Native American roots.

Fernandez de Taos Bookstore. Located on the north side of the plaza; (505) 758–4391. A conveniently located general bookstore featuring magazines, posters, and film, as well as a good selection of general and Southwest regional books.

Navajo Gallery. 210 Ledoux Street; (505) 758–3250; www.rcgorman gallery.com. This beautiful gallery is located in an old adobe, formerly the home of talented and famous Navajo artist R. C. Gorman. It is an interesting gallery containing many of Gorman's paintings, prints, sculptures, and painted ceramic pieces. The artist has given many personal decorative touches to the gallery. If you are a Gorman fan, you will find a wide selection of his work for sale there.

Robert L. Parsons Fine Art. At 131 Bent Street down by Ranchitos Road; (505) 751–0159 or (800) 613–5091; www.parsonsart.com. Visit this handsome gallery, enjoy its architectural charm, and view antique Navajo textiles, old beadwork and pottery, and early paintings of the Southwest. Rotating exhibits as well.

Moby Dickens Bookshop. 124A Bent Street, #6 Dunn House; (505) 758–3050. This large bookshop covers a broad range of titles and has especially fine offerings in art, children's, and regional selections: Southwest archaeology, art, and rare and out-of-print books. A very good general bookstore.

G. Robinson Old Prints and Maps. 124D Bent Street; (505) 758–2278. Step into this antique map and prints shop (sixteenth to nineteenth century) and find yourself fascinated with early maps of the city or state you hail from. Catalogs issued.

Alexandra Stevens Gallery of Fine Art. 115 Bent Street; (505) 758–1399; www.alexandra stevens.com. Come here to see one of the most intriguing and wide-ranging selections of fine art painting in Taos. The eclectic selection is refreshing.

Dwellings Revisited. 107 Bent Street. Located near the corner of Bent Street and North Pueblo Road; (505) 758–3377. For anyone interested in the Santa Fe or Mexican style of decorating, this intriguing gallery is fun to browse. Besides antiques of the region and a melange of folk art and oddities, you'll see primitive worn furniture and numerous architectural items—all with a Southwest flair.

Morgan Gallery. 4 Bent Street; (505) 758–2599; www.edmorgangallery.com. Ed Morgan is a master engraver, and that is quite evident from the exquisitely beautiful work that is the central focus of this gallery. His highly unusual, very complex, colorful embossed prints are stunning. Many Southwest themes are explored in his work. The gallery also features one-of-a-kind and limited-edition jewelry and other fine art of the region.

Farnsworth Gallery. Located next to the Taos Inn at 133 Paseo Del Pueblo Norte; (505) 758–0776; www.johnfarnsworth.com. This gallery, which opens into Cafe Renato, features the representational work of John Farnsworth, whose striking depictions of horses and dogs and other images are for sale here along with folk art from the region.

Stephen Kilborn Pottery. Located across the street from the Taos Inn (505–758–5760 or 758–0135) is this gallery that specializes in the work of its artist owner, one of New Mexico's most evocative potters. Functional and handmade pottery that echoes Southwest and many more popular themes is what you will find here.

Brodsky Bookshop. 226-A Paseo del Pueblo Norte; (505) 758–9468 or (888) 223–8730. If you're eating or shopping up on North Pueblo Road, drop in at this bookshop, which, in addition to a wide selection of general books, has an in-depth selection of regional titles.

Fenix Gallery. 228-B Paseo Del Pueblo Norte; (505) 758–9120; www.taoswebb.com/fenix. This gallery displays an impressive body of work of the region's contemporary painters and sculptors and sometimes beyond the region. Well worth a visit.

Weaving Southwest Gallery and Rio Grande Weavers Supply. 216-B Paseo del Pueblo Norte; (550) 758–0433; fax (505) 758–5869. Located about 1 block north of the plaza is this contemporary weaving gallery, which features weavings by artists of three cultures of New Mexico. Custom-designed weavings can be ordered. Also equipment and supplies for weavers. Well worth a look.

El Rincon. 114 Kit Carson Road; (505) 758–9188. Located just ½ block east of the plaza on Kit Carson Road. Probably the oldest trading post in Taos, this excellent shop is a fine place to buy Indian jewelry (some jewelry made on the premises), Spanish wood carvings, and many fine Indian crafts, both old and new. This shop has an interesting museum section in the back.

Bryans Gallery. 121 Kit Carson Road; (505) 758–9407; www.bryansgallery.com. This eclectic Southwest gallery has evocative works (wooden masks, jewelry, fetishes, and wall art) that are well selected and evince the spirit of the region.

The Parks Gallery. 140 Kit Carson Road; (505) 751–0343; www.parksgallery.com. This contemporary painting and sculpture gallery offers well-selected pieces, many with a Southwest theme.

Carson House Shop. On Kit Carson Road next to the Kit Carson House Museum; (505) 758–0113. In this location for many years, this shop carries a nice selection of local and regional Indian crafts. Indian moccasins, as well as Taos drums, Hopi kachina dolls, Navajo rugs, and Pueblo pottery, can be purchased there.

Taos Book Shop. 122-D Kit Carson Road. About ½ block east of the plaza; (505) 758–3733. A fine old established Taos landmark with a large general book section, as well as special sections on D. H. Lawrence, Taos, New Mexico, and the Southwest. Old and rare out-of-print books relating to the Southwest. Magazines of regional interest. In addition, this shop has a good selection of children's books.

Total Arts Gallery, Inc. 122-A Kit Carson Road; (505) 758–4667; www.totalartsgallery.com. Here you'll wander through a series of gallery rooms where piece after piece of well-selected fine art, from traditional to modern, pleases, including the works of Doug West.

Gallery Elena. 111 Morada Lane; (505) or (888) 758–9094; and 103 Bent Street; (505) 751–3680; www.GalleryElena.com. These two galleries specialize in contemporary works of art such as those of the Vigil dynasty of painters: Veloy, Dan, and Michael.

Lumina Fine Art, Lumina Gardens North. Located at #11 State Road 230, West off Highway 150; (505) 776–0123; (877)–558–6462; www.luminagallery.com. This easy to access gallery (eight minutes north of Taos Plaza) on the Taos Ski Valley Road near Arroyo Seco, is a "must" destination for fine art devotees. The art gallery itself is a work of art situated on three acres of gardens with numerous water features in an enclosed patio that contains sculptural pieces from around the globe. Equally outstanding is the fine selection of painting, ceramics, and photography.

Nichols Taos Fine Arts Gallery. 403 North Pueblo Road; (505) 758–2475; www.nicholsgallery.com. This spacious gallery, about 4 blocks north of the plaza, has an outstanding selection of traditional western art and Southwest impressionism in watercolor, oils, bronze, and sculpture.

Millicent Rogers Museum Shop. North of Taos; (505) 758–2462. (For directions see "A One-Day Auto Tour around Taos: A Narrative Account.") This excellent shop, with reasonable prices and buyers who know what they are doing, has a wide variety of Pueblo, Four Corners, and Navajo Indian crafts, as well as a fine selection of Spanish wood carvings. The bookstore there is also well worth a visit for its good selections of books on regional subjects.

Big Sun. Located on the church plaza of historic San Francisco Church in Rancho De Taos; (505) 758–3100; www.bigsungallery.com. This gallery's emphasis on devotional art and New Mexican folk art including the whimsical sculptural works of the popular Navajo family, the Herberts—is well worth a stop.

Telephone Numbers

Weather and Road Conditions. (800) 432–4269.

Snow Report. (505) 776–2916.

Taos County Chamber of Commerce. (505) 758–3873 or (800) 732–8267.

Taos Bed and Breakfast Association. (505) 758–7301 or (800)

939–2215; www.Taos-BandB-inns.com.

Taos Central Reservations. (800) 821–2437.

Faust's Transportation (taxi). (505) 758–3410 or (888) 830–3410.

Twin Hearts Express. (505) 751–1201 or (800) 654–9456.

Enterprise Rent-a-Car. (505) 737–0514.

Dollar Rental Car. (505) 758–3500 or (800) 800–4000.

Rio Grande Air. Albuquerque-Taos commuter service; (877) 435–9742; www.riograndeair.com.

Taos Ski Valley. (800) 347–7414; www.TaosSkiValley.com or www.ski taos.org.

Enchanted Forest Cross Country Ski Area. (505) 754–2374.

Red River Ski Area. (505) 754–2223; www.RedRiverSkiArea.com.

Angel Fire Resort (ski, golf). (505) 377–6661 or (800) 633–7463; www.angelfireresort.com.

Carson National Forest (camping and so on). (505) 758–6200 or 758–6390.

Taos Don Fernando Swim Pool. (505) 737–2622 or (505) 758–4160; www.taosgov.com.

Golf at Taos Country Club. (888) TAOSGOLF or 826–7465.

TNM&O and Greyhound Station. (505) 758–1144 or (800) 231–2222.

PRACTICAL HINTS

There are two variables you may wish to consider before planning a trip to the High Southwest: the weather and the crowds.

Weather

Winter in the High Southwest can be severe, with below-freezing temperatures and sudden **snowstorms**, often of blizzard proportions, that can turn the landscape and roads into a slippery, dangerous mess in minutes. If you plan to ski, then, of course, winter is the time to visit the High Southwest. But if you are visiting to see the sights, it is best to wait until the weather settles, usually sometime in April or early May. By then the snow is mostly gone, even from the higher elevations listed in this book, and late spring is breaking in all of its glory with sunshine, warmth, and high-desert wildflowers. Although it is possible to be caught in a freak snowstorm at higher elevations in early May, that risk diminishes considerably by the middle of the month. During that time of year, if it is cold and raining at one location and you are planning to drive to a higher location, be certain to check with the highway patrol to be sure the road is free of snow. It can be raining in Moab, elevation 4,000 feet, while it is snowing to the south at Monticello, elevation 7,000 feet.

June is often a dry month, sometimes hot and windy. In July and August the daily **heat,** which may reach one hundred degrees Farenheit in some of the lower areas but seldom exceeds ninety degrees in the higher elevations, is dramatically broken by afternoon thunderstorms that clear the air and cool it. Although the days are often hot in the summer, the air is so dry and the elevation is so high that if you get out of the sun into the shade, you will experience immediate relief. Even though it is hot in the High Southwest in the summer, it is comfortable compared with temperatures in the lower deserts to the south and west and plains states to the east and the south. For many who live in other parts of the United States, the High Southwest is the best place to escape the unrelenting summer heat and humidity.

The heat in the High Southwest varies considerably with the **elevation**. Most of the towns and cities in this book range from 4,000 feet elevation to more than 9,000 feet elevation. It is generally accepted that the temperature goes down three degrees Fahrenheit for every 1,000 feet of increase in elevation. Consequently if it is ninety-five degrees in Moab, Utah, elevation 4,000 feet, it is probably going to be eighty-three degrees at the rim of Bryce Canyon or eighty-six degrees in Santa Fe, New Mexico. But almost everywhere in the High Southwest, there is a

cooling effect when the sun goes down so that nights are considerably cooler. In many higher locales like Santa Fe, New Mexico, air-conditioning is not essential to a good night's sleep. But in towns at a lower elevation, most of the facilities are air-conditioned.

The fall through mid-October is also an excellent time to travel the High Southwest. But beyond the middle of September, there is an increased likelihood of an occasional early snowstorm at the higher elevations. The weather is usually sunny and warm in the daytime, but the nights become very cool as the aspen leaves begin to turn and reveal their golden fall foliage. After mid-October the chance of capricious unfavorable winter weather increases.

Crowds

Some people flock to the High Southwest in the summer to seek relief from the heat in their home states, while others choose that time of year to travel because it is the only time they can bring their children to see this beautiful and educational part of the United States. July and August are the **peak travel months.** April, May, June, September, and October are less crowded. You will particularly notice the summer crowds in the Santa Fe area, especially when there is a special event going on. Flagstaff, Durango, Mesa Verde, and Bryce Canyon are also crowded in the summer, while Moab can be crowded in spring and fall. In most of the other areas covered by this book, the crowds are not so thick that even in the peak summer months you can't find some of the solitude for which this area is famous.

Preparing to Go There

During the best travel months, from May through September, plan on **sunny, warm-to-hot days.** If you are accustomed to covering up in the sun, then bring a hat with a brim, plenty of sunscreen, and lightweight long-sleeved shirts and pants. For comfort's sake these garments should be made of lightweight cotton or a cotton-polyester blend that is nearly half cotton. (Most polyester fabrics do not breathe, so they tend to trap the heat next to your body.) If you feel comfortable in the sun with fewer clothes rather than more, bring cutoffs, shorts, sleeveless blouses, cool skirts, and so on, plus a good supply of your favorite sunscreen. Unless you want to bring more formal clothes, casual, informal dress is usually the order of the day and night in most of the towns and cities covered by this book. The exceptions to this general rule, depending on what you want to do there, may be Santa Fe and Albuquerque, where some travelers choose to dress more formally in the evening.

The air is dry in the Southwest, a fact that contributes to many of its more favorable climatic conditions. But it is so dry that it can chap and crack your lips in less than a day, especially if it is windy. So bring along a Chapstick or lip balm to prevent this uncomfortable condition. Other useful items to bring along are insect repellent (for mosquitoes and flies), binoculars, sunglasses, and a pair of good sturdy walking shoes, tennis shoes, or boots with soles that offer good traction. These will get you by for walking the short trails listed here. But if you plan to do more extensive hiking either on or off the trails, you should unquestionably wear high-top boots with good Vibram or traction soles. Also be certain to bring a lightweight rain jacket in case you get caught in a sudden cloudburst out in the open. A small day pack is an excellent item to bring along to tote water, snacks, cameras, and other necessities as you hike some of the scenic trails this book describes. To carry water you may want to bring along several plastic or poly bottles or one-quart canteens. Water not only tastes good on the trails but is also a refreshing aid as you drive through arid, isolated stretches of high desert without facilities offering cold drinks. It is very easy to get dehydrated in the High Southwest. So if you plan to do a full day of hiking during the hot summer, carry along one gallon of water per person for each full day of hiking, just as the park rangers suggest.

And, of course, do not forget your camera. When you buy your film, take into account that the light is very intense in the High Southwest and extremely bright.

Getting There

It is possible to reach the High Southwest by driving your family auto or by taking a plane, train, or bus from most parts of the United States. But once you get there, you should have a car. The major sights are miles apart, and the accommodations are equally isolated from one another. **Rental cars** are available at most entry points. If, however, you are just touring a small area covered by this book, you may be able to do without a car. For instance, visitors making Santa Fe their base will find they can tour many points of interest north and south of there by making use of the public bus system (to Taos and Albuquerque) or by joining tour groups to more specific sites. In northern Arizona several bus and van tours depart Flagstaff for many of the nearby attractions. Similarly the Durango and Mesa Verde area can be toured without a car, since tour buses regularly leave Durango for both Mesa Verde and the towns of the Silver Circle. But the remaining areas covered by this book are best seen by car.

Being There

Driving

Be certain your car is in good operating condition before you leave home or depart from the rental car agency. Because towns are far apart and a few of the areas are fairly remote, you want to be sure you have a good spare tire and equipment to change tires if you need to. Also it helps to have tires with good treads, since you will be traveling in hot weather and occasionally over dirt or graveled roads.

In the summer **air-conditioning** is definitely a plus, especially if you are not used to hot climates or if you have children who do not tolerate the heat. Driving without air-conditioning in the summer, especially at the lower elevations of 4,000 to 6,000 feet, can be very fatiguing, for the hot dry air coming in through open windows seems to sap every bit of energy you have. But if you do drive without air-conditioning, you should consider sun shades or screens for at least some of the windows. These are often available at auto supply or trail supply stores.

They reflect the sun's rays but let you see out. They are also helpful in cars with air-conditioning. If you have a choice of automobiles to drive, try to get a light-colored one. White is best. Light colors reflect the sun's rays, while dark ones absorb them. Now you know why the Bedouins wear white robes! You may also want to try to schedule the longest drives in your unair-conditioned car during the early morning hours or early evening hours when it is cooler.

Whether you have an air-conditioned car or not, you should carry plenty of cold water, pop, and juice to drink. Small, inexpensive ice chests are available at most discount and hardware stores, and they are ideal for cooling your drinks or keeping picnic lunches from spoiling in the heat. These little ice chests will literally save the day for you when temperatures are soaring in the high desert to one hundred degrees and your spirits are flagging in the dehydrating heat. You may also want to bring an old blanket or tablecloth to spread under the shade of a piñon tree for an inexpensive lunch in one of the many excellent picnic areas along the way.

All of the roads mentioned in this book can be driven by the average driver in the average family car, except for those few that are listed for four-wheel-drive vehicles only. Of course, if you have a four-wheel-drive vehicle and are comfortable operating it under adverse conditions, there are many jeep trails open to you that are not available to the average motorist.

The only truly mountainous driving you will find routed in this book is the stretch of road between Durango and the old mining towns to the north. On those high mountain roads, be certain to stay toward the center of the road and drive slowly, taking care not to pass over the yellow center stripe as you make the curves. At higher altitudes your car will lose some of its power, especially if you are going uphill. On the way down use your brakes, of course, but also shift into lower gear, which helps slow you down without placing too much wear on your brakes. Do not slip into neutral gear on the way down. Coasting is very dangerous. Before you start out on a mountainous stretch, be certain that you have plenty of water in your radiator and that your water hoses are in good shape. The altitude and grade can heat an engine up rapidly. If your car stalls at higher altitudes, it may be suffering from vapor lock, a condition that may be remedied by placing a damp cloth over the fuel pump to cool it down. If that does not work, keep the hood up to signify distress, put on your emergency blinkers, and get back in your car to await help from either the highway patrol or helpful fellow travelers (vapor lock rarely occurs these days.)

Most of the roads you will travel are good, paved, two-lane highways. But a few of the highways are not elevated and follow the lay of the land. Certain stretches of these roads are marked with signs like FLASH FLOODS NEXT 5 MILES or ROAD SUBJECT TO FLOODING NEXT 5 MILES or DO NOT ENTER IF RAINING. Do heed these signs. In the High Southwest an afternoon thunderstorm can let loose an unbelievable amount of water in just a few minutes, flooding absolutely dry gullies and washes so that they become raging rivers before you realize it. These gully washers have been known to wash both people and cars away.

If you are driving and you enter a rain or dust storm that diminishes your visibility so you cannot see, look for a safe place to turn off the road. Stop there until the storm abates. But do not stop in soft sand or at the mouth of a wash or gully.

It is generally advised to wait the storm out with your lights off. Those dramatic blinding storms are typically over in five to fifteen minutes, usually rewarding you with cool air, rainbows, and sunshine. If there is lightning associated with the storm, do not touch anything metal in your car, and turn your radio off. Do not seek protection under a tree during a lightning storm, as trees attract lightning. If you are worried about a storm or the road conditions ahead, look for roadside signs giving information about where to turn your radio dial to receive updated **storm alerts.**

If you have need to pull off some of the roads without shoulders, be certain you are not pulling into a sandy area. But if you happen to find yourself getting stuck in sand or deep mud, do not allow the car to stop until you are out of it. Do not, though, accelerate rapidly or you will just dig yourself in more. Apply steady, slow pressure while in low gear, just as you would in snow. If that does not get you out, rock back and forth by switching from drive to reverse and back again, pressing gently on the accelerator. If this fails, you can try deflating your tires somewhat and then attempting to drive out. If you have a shovel, you can dig the sand or mud away from the tires and then place tree limbs or other materials in front of all four tires to give you sufficient traction to pull out. If all else fails, wait for a park ranger or the highway patrol.

Some perfectly good dirt and clay roads become slippery when wet. So slow down under wet conditions. If you begin to slide, treat your car as if you were on snow.

Occasionally you will see signs warning you of high winds. If the winds are high as you drive through these areas, just slow down until your car feels firm and steady in its forward progress and then proceed.

When you drive at night, look for critters on the road in the unfenced areas or where you see a warning sign with the picture of a deer on it. In the High Southwest deer share the road with you in the evenings, but hitting a deer can be fatal to both you and the deer. But deer are not all you will see on the highways. On the Indian reservations, where there are few fences, cattle, sheep, and goats often roam the highway at night, so be careful.

Be certain to obey the speed limits in the small towns you will travel through. In one small town in New Mexico, at a point that some would consider a wide place in the road of little consequence, a sign on the road going into town used to say DRIVE SLOWLY AND SEE THE TOWN, DRIVE FAST AND SEE THE JUDGE. And be especially careful about observing speed limits on the Indian reservations in towns like Kayenta and Tuba City, for they are strictly enforced. If driving 10 or 15 miles per hour seems ridiculous to you, just wait to see what your reaction is to a $75 speeding ticket.

When you leave your car in a parking area to walk a trail, be sure to lock it. And if you are going to be beyond viewing distance of your car for a while, be certain to **put everything out of sight.** In some places you may even want to take anything of great value along with you. Yes, even the remote High Southwest suffers from theft and vandalism.

Distances between towns and gas stations can sometimes be great, so be sure you have plenty of gas in the tank and know where you can fill up again. Except

Colorado River Bridge, Moab, Utah

for Mesa Verde National Park, none of the national parks or monuments listed in this book offers automobile services.

If you are planning to visit a half-dozen or so national parks and monuments, you may find it worthwhile to purchase a **Golden Eagle National Park Pass,** a **Golden Age Pass** (a much discounted pass for those sixty-two years or older), or a Golden Access Pass, a free pass available for residents of the U.S. who have certain disabilities.

Hiking

For hiking the trails listed in this book, very little special equipment is needed. But there are some practices you should try to observe. First, stay on the designated trail, and in areas of switchbacks do not make your own trail by cutting through from one level to another. This causes erosion of the trail. Also do not throw rocks upon the trail or from canyon or mesa rims. Someone like yourself may be hiking far below you. If you have young children, do not let them run ahead to a rim or a viewing point. Some rims are fenced and protected, but many others are open. It is often a long way to the bottom. Also be careful about standing on mesa edges or rims when you take photographs. More than one would-be photographer has walked over the rim while his eye was glued to his range finder. Sandstone ledges at cliff rims are often undermined by erosion of softer rocks underneath. Your weight may be enough to aid nature's erosional forces by splitting the rim rock and widening the canyon. And, of course, do not walk up dry streambeds, washes, or arroyos if it is raining or about to rain.

People often wonder about snakes in the High Southwest. Most travelers will visit there and may hike many trails without ever seeing a sign of a live snake. But there are plenty of dead ones along the highways to let you know they are there. Many, however, like the garter and bullsnake, are harmless. The poisonous ones are generally of the rattlesnake variety and can vary from 12 to 14 inches to 20 to 24 inches. Believe it or not, they are more afraid of you than you are of them. Given

TRAVEL ACCESS

Arrival Point	Interstate Highways	*Air Service	Train
Denver, Colorado	76, 70, 25	Commercial and commuter	Amtrak
Albuquerque, New Mexico	40, 25	Commercial and commuter	Amtrak
Santa Fe, New Mexico	25	Shuttle flights to and from Denver (nineteen-passenger, two-engine)	Amtrak to nearby Lamy, New Mexico
Salt Lake City, Utah	80, 15	Commercial and commuter	Amtrak
Phoenix, Arizona	17, 10	Commercial and commuter	Amtrak
Green River, Utah	70	None	Amtrak****
Grand Junction, Colorado	70	Commuter or shuttle flights from Denver and Salt Lake City	Amtrak
Telluride, Montrose, Colorado	None	Commuter or shuttle flights from Denver and Phoenix	None
Durango, Colorado	None	Commuter or shuttle flights from Denver and Phoenix	None
Flagstaff, Arizona	40, 17	Commuter or shuttle flights from Phoenix	Amtrak
Winslow, Arizona	40	None	Amtrak
Las Vegas, Nevada	15	Commercial and commuter	

*Commercial jet service utilizes larger jets usually carrying more than one hundred passengers. Commuter or shuttle services utilize much smaller planes carrying sixty passengers or fewer.
** Numerals correspond to Sections 1–4 of the book.
*** Mileages greater than 400 miles not listed.
**** For shuttle service to Moab, see page 97.

Bus	Car Rentals (National Companies)	Destination**	Approximate Miles to Destination***
Yes	Yes	4—Santa Fe	310
		3—Durango	350
		1—Moab	390
Yes	Yes	4—Santa Fe	60
		2—Hopi reservation	255
Yes (plus hourly shuttle buses from the Albuquerque airport	Yes	3—Durango	225
Yes	Yes	1—Moab	240
		2—Monument Valley	386
		3—Durango	398
Yes	Yes	2—Hopi reservation	281
Yes Yes****	No	1—Moab	40
		2—Monument Valley	186
		3—Durango	200
Yes	Yes	1—Moab	115
		3—Durango	168
		2—Monument Valley	261
Telluride No Montrose Yes	Yes	3—Durango	108
		1—Moab	175
Yes	Yes	2—Moab	158
		2—Canyon de Chelly	170
		4—Santa Fe	230
Yes	Yes	2—Navajo reservation	55
		2—Hopi reservation	130
		4—Santa Fe	384
		2—Moab	330
		3—Durango	325
Yes	Yes	2—Flagstaff	60
		2—Hopi reservation	65
Yes	Yes	1—Bryce Canyon	240
		2—Flagstaff	350

the least opportunity to run from your approaching footsteps if they sense your presence, their immediate instinct is to flee. If you hike the trails described in this book, you will probably never see a snake, much less hear one slithering away from you in the grass. But hiking cross-country you may well encounter the sounds of snakes as they attempt to avoid you. In either circumstance do not stick your hands in rock crevasses or on rock ledges without first seeing what is on top. And if you walk through thick grass, go slowly, making as much noise as you can with your feet. Snakes, sluggish from their sunbaths on rock ledges, may not sense your approach, and if your hand interrupts their nap they may get irritated. In a like fashion if you do any walking at night along the highway still warm from the afternoon's sun, carry a flashlight so you do not accidentally interrupt a snake taking a snooze on its warm pad. In addition to snakes you will see many lizards, all harmless in the High Southwest. You will hear a lot of talk about scorpions, insects that can sting something fierce when they attack you with their stinger tail. Generally they will not be a problem unless you are camping. Shake out your boots before putting them on, and place mosquito netting over your tent entrance, securing it at the bottom of the opening, and you should never have to suffer the pain of a scorpion bite. Rattlesnake bites and the bites of some scorpions demand professional attention right away. A single antivenin good for all types of poisonous snakes is generally available throughout the Southwest, but should a problem develop and you need further advice about a poisonous bite, you can call one of the **Arizona Poison Control Centers** twenty-four hours a day. In Arizona (800) 362–0101. In New Mexico (800) 432–6866. In Utah (800) 456–7707; or dial 911 wherever you are.

Throughout the book you will see the term *slickrock*. Most of the sandstone you will be walking over is a form of slickrock. The rock really is not slick unless it is wet. Nonetheless it does not offer the traction of cement or asphalt, because the grains of sand act as roller bearings and could send you tumbling if you are wearing smooth leather soles. Tennis shoes, walking shoes, and boots with good treads all offer safety on dry slickrock. If it is wet, though, you should exert caution even with good footgear. If you plan to do a lot of cross-country hiking, you should definitely wear high-top hiking boots with thick Vibram soles or the equivalent. Not only will the high tops help to keep dirt and sand away from your feet, but they will offer additional support and traction on the rougher, steeper ground away from the trails.

The average summer travelers who want to hike some of the trails may want to consider doing their hiking in the morning during the season of afternoon thunderstorms, which can start as early as late June and last through July and August. This way you avoid the danger of flash floods, slippery rock, and the discomfort of becoming thoroughly soaked. Another alternative is to plan some hiking after the daily showers in the late afternoon. In both instances the temperatures are cooler, and you will enjoy your hike more. Plan to take a siesta during the afternoon thundershowers, or sit it out in a protected place where you can enjoy these beautiful and dramatic storms.

Try to allow time to see the various sights at their best. Do not plan such a busy schedule that you are constantly rushing from one place to another. Slow

Sample Altitudes in the High Southwest

Place	Altitude above Sea Level
Bryce Canyon National Park	8,000 feet
Capitol Reef National Park, visitor center	5,400 feet
Moab, Utah	4,000 feet
Arches National Park	5,000 feet
Monument Valley	5,000 feet
Hopi mesas—Second Mesa	6,300 feet
Canyon de Chelly	5,500 feet
Mesa Verde	7,000 feet
Durango, Colorado	6,500 feet
Silverton, Colorado	9,032 feet
Telluride, Colorado	8,744 feet
Santa Fe, New Mexico	7,000 feet
Albuquerque, New Mexico	5,300 feet

down a bit to nature's pace and you will enjoy your trip more. If you find yourself getting overheated while you are hiking, seek a shaded area and rest for a few minutes. It is cool in the dry air at these higher altitudes when you are out of the sun.

Health-Disabled Travelers

The High Southwest is a healthy environment for most, but for those with certain types of heart disease or disabling lung conditions, the altitude can be a detriment. If you have one of these conditions, you may wish to travel the lower parts of the High Southwest. The table on the previous page lists some of the elevations you may want to take into consideration or use to consult with your physician.

Most everyone has some temporary reaction to the higher elevations above 6,000 feet, a reaction that is often more noticeable if the person has flown into the High Southwest rather than traveled there by surface. But do not worry. Your body's initial reactions of sluggishness and shortness of breath will diminish as you adjust to the altitude in a matter of hours or within a day or two of your arrival. Some visitors find that cutting down their alcohol intake the first day and drinking more water than usual helps make the adjustment easier.

People often ask, "Is it safe to drink the **water?**" Absolutely. The same high standards that apply to public water supplies in the rest of the United States prevail in the High Southwest and on the Indian reservations. But it is not safe to drink water from streams, ponds, creeks, and other natural sources. Seek the advice of the U.S. Forest Service or National Park Information Services about the specific area you are going to.

Rabies is a problem in certain areas of the High Southwest, especially in northern New Mexico. If you should be bitten by any animals—dogs, squirrels, chipmunks, or bats—be sure to contact a local physician in that area or seek help immediately at one of the nearby ranger stations. Travelers with disabilities may wish to consult the following book: *Easy Access to National Parks: The Sierra Club Guide for People with Disabilities* by Wendy Roth and Michael Tompane (San Francisco: Sierra Club Books, 1998).

Meeting the Indians

Your contact with American Indians in the Southwest will most likely be pleasant and rewarding. As with many people who live in small towns and rural areas, there is generally an attitude of openness and a desire to be helpful. But there are a few sensitivities you should be aware of before entering Indian Country.

After reading this book you will be aware of some of the historical roots that have affected the relationship between the whites and the Indians in the High Southwest. Many of the negative aspects of these roots have extended into modern times when twenty-first-century white tourists and visitors have on occasion roused the ire of the Indians. Not too many years ago, well-meaning but insensitive fortune seekers plundered ancient ruins that seemed to belong to no one, carting off the relics and selling them for profit. (Even today—in spite of strict laws—bands of professional, profiteering "thieves of time" continue to ruthlessly exploit remote ruin sites.) Not too many years later, intrusive visitors with **cameras** would snap photos of the Indians and sell them for profit to be used on postcards or for other commercial enterprises. Later when the Indians discovered what had been done, they were infuriated. Once again it seemed the white man had profited from the Indian.

The Hopi banned cameras from their ceremonies in 1907, and the Taos Indians have carefully regulated white visitors for decades. The ban or regulation on cameras is still present today and in fact has been extended to include sketching, drawing, tape-recording, videotaping, and all other mechanical means of reproducing a real-life situation. The Hopi are probably the most adamant today about the use of cameras, recorders, even sketches, and the like. Most Hopi will not give permission to have their pictures taken, and village chiefs will not give permission for you to bring your camera into the villages. For all practical purposes the camera and all devices like it are banned on the Hopi reservation. So the best place for your camera when you visit the Hopi villages is in the glove compartment of your car, not around your neck or in your hands. And, of course, these devices are strictly banned at the ceremonial dances.

The Rio Grande Pueblo people are a little more tolerant. In most instances they regulate rather than ban image-making equipment. The procedure there is to ask the village chief for permission to take pictures of the village. You may have to pay a fee to do so. The Taos Indians have different fees for the different kinds of equipment you want to bring in. It costs more to obtain a permit for a video camera than a 110 still camera. Nonetheless, with a permit and the inevitable restrictions that go along with it, you may still be able to take pictures of some of the Rio Grande Pueblos and their ceremonial dances. If you involve individuals other than those in a crowd scene, you should ask for their permission. They may turn you down, charge you a fee, or just say "OK." The Navajo seem to be more tolerant than the Hopi. Because they live in widely spread family clusters, you must negotiate with each family or individual whose picture you may want to take. Again, you will probably be asked to pay a fee to take a picture.

In general I would suggest that you just put your camera away and work on formulating visual images in your memory. Much of what you see is so dramatic and strikingly different that it will leave an indelible imprint far more true than any photo or slide that you may take.

Not infrequently you will see travelers drive into a village, park, and embark on an aggressive sight-seeing tour, including cupping their hands and looking in the windows of houses. It is doubtful that these people would do the same thing in their own town or city or in a neighboring town. So treat and respect the privacy of the Native Americans as you would your own. Be courteous and remember you are a guest visiting them. Do not stand and point at people or things. As intriguing as they are, stay away from the sacred kivas and do not let children climb on kiva ladders. Respect these religious objects. If you need information or help, do ask someone in the village. Local residents are almost always helpful in this situation. If you plan more than just a brief visit to a village, be sure to obtain approval at the **village headquarters.**

In conversations with Native Americans, do not ask questions relating to their **religious or ceremonial life.** If you do, you will be rebuffed quickly, for most Native Americans believe that their religion is none of your business no matter how good your intentions are. For many whites who often talk openly and easily about their religion, this difference is particularly hard to understand. But it makes perfectly good sense to the Indian people, whose religion is very private and does not condone proselytism.

You should also be warned that the American Indians of the High Southwest come from an ancient and timeless culture where the concern about timeliness and punctuality is not the same as it is in the white culture. In order for you not to be disturbed by this, you will find yourself having to slow your reaction time to the pace of their culture, rather than expect the opposite to happen. Perhaps in being patient rather than angry, the lesson learned is that their culture has been in existence for more than 900 years. The white American culture has been at it for only a little more than 200 years.

Many High Southwest Indians will sell their crafts directly to visitors from their homes. You may get a better price or you may not, but the selection may be different than in a shop or trading post, and you also have the opportunity to custom-order something you might want. So visit the artist who has made an object you have seen in a shop that has caught your eye. Or if you are visiting a village, ask someone who makes kachina dolls or pottery or who does weaving. You will be directed to an artisan's door. You may very well be invited to watch the craftsperson work. If you do not find what you want to buy, do not feel bad. A sincere "thank you" will suffice to let the artist know that you are just looking.

You will seldom see traditional Southwest American Indian adults wearing shorts in their villages. In fact shorts are banned at many of the Hopi ceremonial dances. One hot summer afternoon our daughter was wearing shorts as we left the car and headed for the plaza where a dance was to be performed. After parking outside the village, we got out of the car. Immediately we were face-to-face with a Hopi policeman who gently and sensitively informed us that our daughter would not be permitted at the ceremony wearing shorts. She quickly changed in the car, and we were then given a warm smile and nod from the Hopi policeman and proceeded to the ceremony.

When visiting Indian or public lands in the Southwest, it is wise to remember that the **Federal Antiquities Law** passed in 1906 is still in effect and was reinforced by the Archaeological Protection Act of 1979. And some states ban taking artifacts from private lands. It is against the law to remove any Indian relics or artifacts from these lands. To do so could result in stiff fines as well as imprisonment in some cases. It is interesting to note that the Native American Graves Protection and Repatriation Act, which became law in 1990, has resulted in many institutions that receive federal monies returning important religious artifacts, as well as skeletal remains and burial objects, to the tribes.

Camping

Although this book does not pretend to be a camping guide, numerous campsites are listed for areas where camping seems particularly enjoyable. Some of the campsites at lower elevations are plagued with heat, dust, and bugs, whereas higher-elevation campsites are more pleasant. Details on these campsites and others are outlined in several books on the market, including Woodall's *Campground Directory,* Western Edition, and the American Automobile Association's *Southwest Campbook Guide.*

Campers (and hikers)should be aware that since the early 1990s, a small number of residents living in the rural areas of the High Southwest and other parts of the country have been afflicted with a potentially life-threatening disease, hantavirus infection—sometimes knows as adult respiratory distress syndrome.

While most tourist activities pose little or no risk that would expose travelers to the hantavirus, there are some precautions hikers and campers especially should take to avoid contact with rodents (deer mice, house mice, chipmunks, rock squirrels, and pack rats), their burrows, and their urine, saliva, or pelletlike fecal excreta. For example, do not sleep directly on the dirt. Pitch tents with floors (or use ground cloths) away from areas like woodpiles and garbage dumps that may shelter rodents. And do not sweep or kick the dust and dirt from the ground into the air since the disease is primarily carried in air-borne particles.

Tips for International Visitors (and Others)
Some Things Your Travel Agent May Not Have Told You

Welcome to the American Southwest. Now that you're in the High Southwest, there are some things you should know to make your travels easier. For your convenience this book lists in the "Staying There" part of each section (just before "Lodging") information about traveler's checks and where to exchange foreign money (bills only) and gives the location of hostels (AYH [American Youth Hostels], some of which honor International Youth Hostel Federation memberships, and AAIH [American Association of International Hostels]). Under "Shopping" you may find listings of bookstores and newsstands that stock international newspapers and magazines; under "Telephone Numbers" you'll find for each area the names and telephone numbers of specific car rental agencies. A rough sketch of train, bus, and car rental services throughout the High Southwest is on pages 520–21. Further orientation follows.

Language. Some of the larger national parks print their basic orientation materials in German, French, Spanish, and Japanese. Inquire at the visitor center of each park. In cities like Santa Fe, visitor centers have orientation materials in several languages. It's instructive for international visitors to know that there are not many U.S. citizens in the Southwest who speak German, French, or Japanese. Spanish, however, is the most frequent second language spoken by Southwest natives.

Up Close and Personal. Along the interstate highways are rest areas with toilet facilities, although they are seldom clean; bring some paper seat covers with you. Fast-food outlets and gasoline service stations also have free facilities; the former are often clean (and as a way of saying thank you, I usually purchase a cold drink before I leave). In towns and cities there are usually public facilities in visitor centers. The same is true for the national parks and monuments.

If you are camping and need a shower, you should stay at one of the larger national park campgrounds (like Morefield Campground at Mesa Verde) or at one of the private, fee-charging campgrounds (K.O.A. or Good Sam Park) listed in this book. Most National Forest Service campgrounds do not have shower facilities.

Although you may not drink much water at home, when you are in the arid Southwest you must consume considerably more to avoid dehydration. Up to a gallon per person per day is recommended in the heat of the summer if you are backpacking, walking, or hiking all day. The water from all municipal public sources (usually treated under demanding standards) is safe to drink and bottled water (flat water recommended) is readily available. But do not drink from any creeks, streams, rivers, or lakes, no matter how clear the water looks, since almost all natural water sources in the Southwest are contaminated with the microorganism *Giardia lamblia*.

The United States is quickly becoming a nonsmoking country. If you're a smoker and don't want to be sneered at (people feel strongly about this), you should be courteous and observe the NO SMOKING signs. Most restaurants have both smoking and nonsmoking sections, but some prohibit smoking altogether.

For safety reasons hitchhiking is not recommended in the United States, and it is prohibited on the interstate highways. And do not pick up hitchhikers—that's not a safe practice in this country.

Getting Around. Public transportation by rail (800–872–7245; www.amtrak.com) or bus (800–231–2222; www.greyhound.com) in this part of the United States is often substandard and doesn't reach many points of interest listed in this book. Renting a car is highly recommended. This can be done if you are of age (usually twenty-five years old but sometimes, depending on the location, twenty-one years old) and have a valid driver's license from your country and a major credit card (see the list under "Money Matters," following). Without a major credit card, you may find it either impossible to rent from some companies or more complex to rent from others (often an up-front cash deposit of hundreds of dollars is required and additional personal documentation needed). If your driver's license is not printed in English, it's advisable to obtain an international driver's license from your local automobile association or travel agent before leaving home.

Rental cars (also four-wheel-drive trucks, recreational vehicles, and so on) can be rented less expensively here than in most other countries. Most of these vehicles use unleaded gas and come with air-conditioning. Gasoline is comparatively cheap in the United States, especially if you use the self-serve pumps. Our gallon (3.785 liters) is smaller than the imperial gallon (4.546 liters). United Kingdom and Irish visitors also need to be aware that we drive on the right side of the road.

If your car has a radio, do tune into the local stations for a slice of small-town southwestern life hard to get any other way, and to the Navajo Nation radio station KTNN, 660 on the AM channel, for authentic Native American music. By chance you will probably find the occasional station beaming music across the border to the United States from Mexico. A radio is also handy for listening to up-to-date road conditions. Watch for signs along the highway telling you how to tune in.

If you are member of an automobile club like ADAC in Germany or AA in the United Kingdom and France, you can use the American Automobile Association's emergency road service by calling, toll free in the United States, (800) 222–4357 or (800) 955–4TDD (hearing impaired).

The landmass this book covers is about the size of the former West Germany. Although there are fast interstate highways with a speed limit varying from 65 miles per hour to 75 miles per hour (but sometimes only 55 miles per hour, or about 90 kilometers per hour, through cities), they do not penetrate much of the area you will be traveling. Usually you will be driving two-lane roads with a speed limit of around 55 to 65 miles per hour. Because of the winding, twisting nature of some roads and heavy or slow traffic on others, you may average only 50 miles per hour. In spite of this nation's efforts to convert to the metric system, you will still find most highway distances expressed in miles and elevations in feet (1 foot equals 0.3 meter). To make a quick but approximate conversion of miles to kilometers, divide miles by six and move the decimal point one place to the right.

When you park, be certain to **lock your car** at all times. Put anything of value out of sight. And **do not leave anything of value in the car** at night when you check into a hotel or motel. Even though the High Southwest is relatively remote and sparsely populated, there are still car thieves who may escape with your rental car to Mexico and petty thieves who may steal anything of value they see in your car. Be that as it may, after traveling in the Southwest for many years, I have never had my car stolen or anything taken from it. But others have, as rangers in the national parks know so well.

As you travel through the four states covered by this book, the borders are wide open, but at the California border, drivers may periodically be stopped at agricultural inspection stations. It is illegal to bring most fruits and vegetables into California.

Money Matters. Banking hours vary but are usually 9:00 A.M. to 4:00, 5:00, or 6:00 P.M. daily, and some banks are open on Saturday until 2:00 P.M. Banks are closed on these major holidays: New Year's Day (January 1), Martin Luther King Jr. Day (third Monday in January), President's Day (third Monday in February), Memorial Day (last Monday in May), Independence Day (July 4), Labor Day (first Monday in September), Columbus Day (second Monday in October), Thanksgiving (fourth Thursday in November), and Christmas Day (December 25).

Only a few banks in the Southwest offer convenient foreign-exchange services. The ones that do will exchange traveler's checks at the current exchange rate, usually, but not always, without an extra charge. You will definitely be charged a special fee to exchange foreign cash (paper only) at these banks. You can avoid exchanging money altogether by purchasing traveler's checks in U.S. dollars before you leave home (purchase mostly twenties and a few fifties, the latter for larger purchases only) to use in restaurants, stores, and so on. Traveler's checks in $100 denominations will probably have to be cashed at a bank. Better yet, you can use either a credit card in restaurants and hotels and even some B&Bs. Check with the issuer of the card you hold to see whether you can use your card in this country and whether you can use it at ATM or cash machines (available in most Southwest cities and towns) or to receive a cash advance from a bank. Banks in this country that display a MasterCard or VISA symbol in the window are usually able to offer cash advances. For all over-the-counter banking transactions, you will need your passport and/ or visa.

Time. The High Southwest is on mountain time, two hours earlier than eastern time and one hour later than western time. Daylight savings time (clocks are set forward one hour from standard time from the first Sunday in April through the last Saturday in October) is observed by Colorado, New Mexico, and the Navajo reservation in Arizona. The rest of Arizona, including the Hopi reservation, does not observe daylight savings time.

In the United States we tell time on the twelve-hour clock rather than the twenty-four-hour clock. We call 12:00 at night "midnight" and the hour following that "1:00 A.M." (ante meridien). We call 12:00 in the daytime "noon" and the hour following that "1:00 P.M." (post meridien) not "1300 hours."

Telephones. To place local calls and to access directory assistance from public or pay phones in some areas, you will need 35 cents. Reach local directory assistance by dialing 411 or for directory assistance throughout the state 1–411. If these numbers don't work, try 1, then the area code you are in, plus 555–1212. Directory assistance from outside the state you are calling from cannot be accessed from a coin deposit phone. But using a public phone that accepts major credit cards, telephone credit cards, or prepaid calling cards (available in denominations up to U.S. $50 at convenience stores and some mail depots), for information dial 1 (the area code), then 555–1212. For international information dial 00 and follow the prompts for International Information.

For **emergencies** dial (depending on the community) either **911** or **0** for the operator—no coins needed.

For international calls dial 011 instead of 1, the country code (France, 33; Federal Republic of Germany, 49; United Kingdom, 44; Japan, 81), then the city code followed by the local number. If the city code has a 0 in front of it, omit it when you dial. The operator will intercept the call to tell you how much money to deposit before the call can be completed. Travelers from Japan and most countries in Europe (except Germany) can use the same procedure as that outlined in the previous paragraph to make collect calls and some credit card calls. The cheapest rates for international calls are usually from 6:00 P.M. to 7:00 A.M., U.S. time.

For information about toll-free telephone numbers within the United States, see page xviii. Usually no coins are needed to make these calls from public phones, but you must dial a 1 before dialing the 800, 888, 877, 866, etc. number.

Mail. It will cost you 23 cents to mail a postcard and 37 cents to mail a letter weighing one ounce or less anywhere in the United States. You can send a postcard to Canada for 50 cents and a one-ounce letter for 60 cents. To send mail abroad (Europe or Japan), it will cost you 70 cents for a postcard, 80 cents for a one-ounce letter, and 70 cents for an aerogram. For international airmail pieces you must attach a sticker that says "airmail" (available free of charge at most U.S. post offices) or write "airmail" on the envelope.

Post offices are generally open weekdays from 8:00 or 8:30 A.M. to 5:00 or 5:30 P.M. Saturday hours are highly variable but in larger towns are usually from 9:00 A.M. to noon. Post offices in most towns and cities sell shipping boxes, wrapping tape, and so on. Their staff will also assist you in the proper way to address a letter being sent within the United States or outside it. Before you leave home, you should write down the mailing address and phone number of your country's embassy in this country in case any of your important documents are lost.

Health. There is no national health insurance in the United States. If you get sick, you must have your own health and hospital insurance. Be certain that you are insured while traveling in this country. If you are not, ask a travel agent before you leave home about a special health insurance policy to cover you while you're traveling.

The quickest way to get medical attention in the United States is to present yourself in the emergency room of a hospital, with documentation of your health insurance and its validity in this country. Pharmacies—located in drugstores and in large grocery stores called supermarkets—often have extended hours. Dial **911** in most communities for medical emergencies.

Tipping. After your meal in a cafe or restaurant, ask the waitperson for the check or the bill. The tip is generally not included in the total. It is customary in this country to tip the waitperson around 15 to 20 percent of the total food bill. Americans generally do not tip at fast-food outlets or where there is no table service.

Alcoholic Beverages. The wide-open Southwest is not so wide open when it comes to liquor. The legal drinking age in this country is twenty-one. Alcohol (either possession or consumption of it) is illegal on Indian reservations. Utah has some mighty peculiar liquor laws that are outlined in the "Staying There" section for Southeastern Utah. In New Mexico you can't buy a drink until after noon on Sunday, and the sale of bottled alcohol is prohibited altogether on Sunday.

Tax. The tax you see added on the merchandise you purchase is usually local tax and is nonrefundable. It is not a VAT tax. You can expect a 10 percent tax or more to be added to the listed rates for motels, hotels, and B&Bs. Local taxes are also added to restaurant and rental bills.

Store Hours. Many grocery stores are open long hours seven days a week and on weekends. Small convenience stores, which stock basic grocery, sundry, and first-aid items, are open twenty-four hours a day. Most towns and some motels and private, fee-charging campgrounds have coin-operated laundry facilities.

Bits and Pieces. We use 110- to 115-volt, 60-cycle current. You will probably need a transformer to operate your electric appliances. You will also need a different style of plug. Outlets here use two thin rectangular prongs. For larger appliances there is a third, round prong centered above the two rectangular ones.

We use the Fahrenheit scale for temperature. To convert to Centigrade, subtract thirty-two from the Fahrenheit temperature, then multiply by five and divide by nine. Freezing in Fahrenheit is thirty-two degrees, while in centigrade it is zero degrees.

Volume measurements equate like this: One quart equals 0.946 liter. There are thirty-two ounces (one ounce equals 29.5 milliliters) in one quart, and there are four quarts in a gallon.

For linear measurements, 1 inch equals 25 millimeters. There are 12 inches in a foot, 3 feet in a yard, and 5,280 feet in a mile.

BIBLIOGRAPHY

1. Southeastern Utah: Canyon Country

General Descriptive / Historical / Cultural

Abbey, Edward. *Desert Solitaire: A Season in the Wilderness.* New York: Ballantine Books, 1968.

Abbey, Edward, and Hyde, Philip. *Slickrock: The Canyon Country of Southeast Utah.* San Francisco: Sierra Club, 1979. (pictorial book in color)

Adkinson, Ron. *Utah's National Parks: Hiking, Camping, and Vacationing in Utah's Canyon Country.* Berkeley, Calif.: Wilderness Press, 1991.

Bakker, Elna, and Lillard, Richard G. *The Great Southwest: The Story of a Land and Its People.* The Great West Series. Palo Alto, Calif.: American West Publishing Co., 1972.

Barnes, F. A. *Canyon Country Scenic Roads.* Salt Lake City: Wasatch Publishers, Inc., 1977.

"Canyonlands National Park." *Plateau,* Magazine of the Museum of Northern Arizona 52 (1980): 1–32. (entire issue)

Crampton, C. Gregory. *Standing Up Country: The Canyon Lands of Utah and Arizona.* New York: Alfred A. Knopf/University of Utah Press, 1965.

Findley, Rowe. "Canyonlands: Realm of Rock and the Far Horizon." *National Geographic* 140 (July 1971): 71–91.

Folsom, Franklin. *America's Ancient Treasures.* New York: Rand McNally and Co., 1974.

Grant, Campbell. *Rock Art of the American Indian.* New York: Promontory Press, 1967.

Hafen, Leroy R., and Hafen, Ann W. *Old Spanish Trail.* Glendale, Calif.: Arthur H. Clark Co., 1954.

Lavender, David. *Colorado River Country.* New York: E. P. Dutton, Inc., 1982.

Leigh, Rufus Wood. *Five Hundred Utah Place Names.* Salt Lake City: Desert News Press, 1961.

Roylance, Ward J. *Seeing Capitol Reef National Park: A Guide to the Roads and Trails.* Salt Lake City: Wasatch Publishers, Inc., 1979.

———. *Utah Part 2. A Guide to the State.* Salt Lake City: A Guide to the State Foundation, 1982.

Stegner, Wallace. "The High Plateaus." *Sierra* 66 (1981): 9–17.

Stegner, Wallace, and Stegner, Page. *American Places.* New York: Elsevier-Dutton Publishing Co., 1981.

Sunset Books and Sunset Magazine Editors. *National Parks of the West.* Menlo Park, Calif.: Lane Publishing Co., 1980.

Trimble, Stephen. *The Bright Edge.* Flagstaff: Museum of Northern Arizona Press, 1979.

Natural History

Baars, Donald L. *Red Rock Country: The Geologic History of the Colorado Plateau.* Garden City, N.Y.: Doubleday/Natural History Press, 1972.

———. *Canyonlands Country: Geology of Canyonlands and Arches National Parks.* Lawrence, Kan.: Cañon Publishers Ltd., 1992.

Barnes, F.A. *Canyon Country Geology for the Layman and Rockhound.* Salt Lake City: Wasatch Publishers, Inc., 1978.

Bezy, John. *Bryce Canyon: The Story behind the Scenery.* Las Vegas: K. C. Publications, 1981.

Dodge, Natt N. *Roadside Wildflowers of Southwest Uplands.* Globe, Ariz.: Southwest Parks and Monuments Association, 1963.

Fremont Indian petroglyph

Doolittle, Jerome, and the editors of Time-Life Books. *Canyons and Mesas.* New York: Time-Life Books, 1974.

Hinchman, Sandra. *Hiking the Southwest's Canyon Country,* 2d ed. Seattle: The Mountaineers Books, 1999.

Hintze, Lehi F. *Geologic History of Utah.* Brigham Young University Geology Studies, vol. 20, pt. 3. Provo, Utah: Brigham Young University Press, n.d.

Hoffman, John F. *Arches National Park: An Illustrated Guide and History.* San Diego: Western Recreational Publications, 1981.

Knighton, José. *Canyon Country's La Sal Mountains Hiking and Nature Handbook.* Moab, Utah: Canyon Country Publications, 1995.

Lamb, Samuel H. *Woody Plants of the Southwest.* Santa Fe: Sunstone Press, 1977.

Olson, Virgil J. *Capitol Reef: The Story behind the Scenery.* Las Vegas: K. C. Publications, 1975.

Redfern, Ron. *Corridors of Time.* New York: Times Books, 1980.

Rigby, Keith J. *Northern Colorado Plateau.* K/H Geology Field Guide Series. Dubuque, Iowa: Kendall/Hunt Publishing Co., 1976.

Stokes, William Lee. *Scenes of the Plateau Lands and How They Came to Be.* Salt Lake City: Publishers Press, 1969.

Trimble, Stephen. *The Hickman Natural Bridge Trail.* Torrey, Utah: Capitol Reef Natural History Association, n.d.

Tweit, Susan. *The Great Southwest Nature Factbook.* Seattle: Alaska Northwest Books, 1992.

Welsh, Stanley L., and Ratcliffe, Bill. *Flowers of the Canyon Country.* Provo, Utah: Brigham Young University Press, 1977.

Worster, Donald. *A River Running West: The Life of John Wesley Powell.* New York: Oxford University Press, 2001.

Yundell, Michael D., ed. *Photographic and Comprehensive Guide to Zion and Bryce Canyon.* Casper, Wyo.: National Parks Division of Worldwide Research and Publishing Co., 1972.

Information about and/or purchase of the aforementioned books and related books may be obtained from the following sources:

Capitol Reef Natural History Association, Capitol Reef National Park, Torrey, Utah 84775; (435) 425–3791, ext. 115.

Western National Parks Association, 12880 North Vistoso Village Drive, Tucson (Oro Valley), Arizona 85737; (520) 622–6014 or (888) 569–7762; www.wnpa.org.

Canyonlands Natural History Association, 3031 South Highway 191, Moab, Utah 84532; (435) 259–6003 or (800) 840–8978; www.cnha.org.

Bryce Canyon Natural History Association, Bryce Canyon Natural Park, Bryce Canyon, Utah 84717; (435) 834–4603.

Maps

Southeastern Utah, Utah Multipurpose Map, Utah Travel Council.
Southeastern–Central Utah, Utah Multipurpose Map, Utah Travel Council.
American Automobile Association Maps: Western States, Utah-Nevada, and A Guide to Indian Country.
Grand Staircase–Escalante National Monument Illustrated Map. Southwest Natural and Cultural Heritage Association and the Bureau of Land Management.

The Utah multipurpose regional maps, helpful brochures, and other useful, generally free information can be obtained by writing the Utah Travel Council, Council Hall/Capitol Hill, Salt Lake City, Utah 84114; (801) 538–1030 or (800) 200–1160; www.utah.com. Maps are available without charge to AAA members at the California State Automobile Association at 560 East 500 South Street, Salt Lake City, Utah 84102; (801) 364–5615 or (800) 541–9902.

Additional site and trail maps as well as general information brochures, updated entrance fee rates, and visitor center opening and closing hours can be obtained from the following:

Utah Division of Parks and Recreation, Information Services, 1636 West North Temple, Salt Lake City, Utah 84116; (801) 537–3100.

Bureau of Land Management, 82 East Dogwood, Moab, Utah 78532; (801) 259–2196; www.UT.blm.gov.

National Park Service brochures and some general information about parks in Utah, Colorado, and Arizona can be obtained free from the National Park Service, 12795 West Alameda Parkway, P.O. Box 25287, Denver, Colorado 80225–0287; (303) 969–2000 or 969–2020; www.nps.gov.

You may obtain detailed maps of the national parks throughout the High Southwest by writing for a copy of the U.S. Geological Survey index map, which lists availability of topographic maps for each park. Index and maps can be ordered from USGS Denver-Federal Center, Box 25286, Federal Center, Denver, Colorado 80225; (303) 202–4700; www.usgs.gov.

2. Northeastern Arizona: Indian Country

Background Information: The Indians on the Colorado Plateau

Adler, Michael A., ed. *The Prehistoric Pueblo World A.D. 1150–1350*. Tucson: University of Arizona Press, 1996.

Arizona Highways. "A Special 46-Page Salute in Color to Canyon de Chelly." *Arizona Highways* 53 (March 1977): 1–48. (entire issue)

———. "Special Edition: Touring the Navajo Nation." *Arizona Highways* 55 (1979): 1–48. (entire issue)

———. "The Hopi Tricentennial." *Arizona Highways* 56 (September 1980): 1–48. (entire issue)

Arnold, David A. "Pueblo Artistry in Clay." *National Geographic* 162 (November 1982): 593 605.

Bahti, Tom. *Southwestern Indian Ceremonials*. Las Vegas: K. C. Publications, 1970.

Bates, Caroline. "Pueblo Indian Breads." *Gourmet Magazine* 37 (November 1977): 48–53, 120–24, 130–34.

Belknap, William Jr. "20th-Century Indians Preserve Cliff Dwellers' Customs." *National Geographic* 125 (February 1964): 196–211.

Bishop, James Jr. "Bones of Contention." *High Country News* (October 1999): 8–9.

Bowman, Eldon. "Beale's Historic Road: By Camel, from the Zuni Villages to the Rio Colorado." *Arizona Highways* 60 (July 1984): 2–10 and 15.

Canby, Thomas Y. "Search for the First Americans." *National Geographic* 156 (September 1979): 330–63.

———. "The Anasazi: Riddles in the Ruins." *National Geographic* 162 (November 1982): 554–92.

De Lauer, Marjel. "A Century of Indian Traders and Trading Posts." *Arizona Highways* 51 (March 1975): 6–14.

———. "The Bi-Millennium of the Southwest." *Arizona Highways* 52 (January 1976): 3–9.

Dutton, Bertha P. *The Rancheria Ute and Southern Paiute Peoples: Indians of the American Southwest*. Englewood Cliffs, N.J.: Prentice Hall, Inc., 1976.

Eggan, Fred. *Social Organization of the Western Pueblos*. Chicago: University of Chicago Press, 1950.

Harjo, Joy, and Bird, Gloria, with Blanco, Patricia, Cuthand, Beth, and Martinez, Valerie. *Reinventing the Enemy's Language: Contemporary Native Women's Writings of North America*. New York: W.W. Norton and Company, 1999.

Hillerman, Tony. *The Blessing Way*. New York: Harper and Row, 1970.

———. *Dance Hall of the Dead*. New York: Harper and Row, 1973.

———. *Fallen Man*. New York: Harper and Row, 1997.

———. *The Fallen Eagle*. New York: Harper-Collins, 1998.

———. *Listening Woman*. New York: Harper and Row, 1978.

———. *A Thief of Time*. New York: Harper and Row, 1988.

Hodge, Carl. "Arizona's First Farmers." *Arizona Highways* 52 (November 1976): 2–6.

———. "Museum of Northern Arizona." *Arizona Highways* 58 (June 1982): 12–17.

Jacka, Jerry. "The Miracle of Hopi Corn. *Arizona Highways* 54 (March 1978): 3–15.

Klinck, Richard E. *Land of Room Enough and Time Enough.* Salt Lake City: Peregrine Smith Books, 1984.

"The Land of the Hopi and the Navajo." *Sunset Magazine* (May 1987): 96–109.

Laughter, Albert. "Our People, Our Past." *National Geographic* 156 (July 1979): 81–85.

Lipe, William D. "The Southwest." Chap. 8 in *Ancient Native Americans,* edited by Jesse D. Jennings, 327–401. San Francisco: W. H. Freeman and Company, 1978.

Lister, Robert H., and Lister, Florence C. *Those Who Came Before.* Albuquerque: University of New Mexico Press, 1994.

Looney, Ralph. "The Navajos." *National Geographic* 142 (December 1972): 740–81.

Lowenkopf, Anne N., and Katz, Michael W. *Camping with the Indians.* Los Angeles: Sherbourne Press, Inc., 1974.

Marquis, Arnold. *A Guide to America's Indians: Ceremonials, Reservations, Museums.* Norman: University of Oklahoma Press, 1960.

May, Karl. *Winnetou: A Novel.* Translated by Michael Shaw. New York: Seabury Press, 1977.

McAllester, David P., and McAllester, Susan W. *Hogans, Navajo Houses, and House Songs.* Irvington, N.Y.: Columbia University Press, 1980.

Muench, David, and Pike, Donald. *Anasazi: Ancient People of the Rock.* Palo Alto, Calif.: American West Publishing Co., 1974.

Nelson, Lisa. "Electricity Lights Up Lives of Navajo Families." *Winds of Change: A Magazine for American Indians* 1 (December 1986): 15–16.

Nequatewa, Edmund. *Truth of a Hopi.* Flagstaff, Ariz.: Northland Press, 1967.

Noble, David Grant. *Ancient Ruins of the Southwest.* Flagstaff, Ariz.: Northland Press, 2000.

Olin, George. *Mammals of the Southwest Mountains and Mesas.* Globe, Ariz.: Southwest Parks and Monuments Association, 1961.

Page, Jake, and Page, Suzanne. "Inside the Hopi Homeland." *National Geographic* 162 (November 1982): 607–29.

———. *Hopi.* New York: Harry N. Abrams, 1982.

Rigby, J. Keith. *Southern Colorado Plateau.* K/H Geology Field Guide Series. Dubuque, Iowa: Kendall/Hunt Publishing Co., 1977.

Rock Point Community School. *Between Sacred Mountains: Navajo Stories and Lessons from the Land.* Chinle, Ariz.: Rock Point Community School, 1983.

Romero, Manny. "Flagstaff: One Century Old." *Arizona Highways* 52 (July 1976): 16–20.

Schaafsma, Polly. *Indian Rock Art of the Southwest.* Santa Fe: School of American Research, 1980.

Scully, Vincent. *Pueblo/Mountain, Village, Dance.* New York: Viking Press, 1975.

Supplee, Douglas, and Anderson, Barbara. *Canyon de Chelly: The Story behind the Scenery,* rev. ed. Las Vegas: K. C. Publications, 1981. Reprint, New York: Penguin Books, 1982.

"Wapatki-Sunset Crater." *Plateau* 49 (2): 1–33. (entire issue)

Weaver, Thomas, ed. *Indians of Arizona: A Contemporary Perspective.* Tucson: University of Arizona Press, 1979.

Webb, William, and Weinstein, Robert A. *Dwellers at the Source: Southwestern Indian Photographs of A. C. Vroman, 1895–1904.* New York: Grossman Publishers, 1973.

Widdison, Jerold G., ed. *The Anasazi/Why did they leave? Where did they go?* Albuquerque, N. Mex.: Southwest Natural and Cultural Heritage Association, 1991.

Wilson, Maggie. "Men, Myths, and Rituals." *Arizona Highways* 55 (September 1979): 2–9.

———. "The Sacred Mountains." *Arizona Highways* 56 (May 1980): 12–33.

Witherspoon, Gary. *Navajo Kinship and Marriage.* Chicago: University of Chicago Press, 1975.

Wormington, H. M. *Prehistoric Indians of the Southwest.* Denver, Colorado: Denver Museum of Natural History, 1973.

Art Including Navajo and Hopi Crafts

Allen, Laura Graves. *Contemporary Hopi Pottery.* Flagstaff: Museum of Northern Arizona, 1984.

Arizona Highways. "Turquoise Attitude." *Arizona Highways* 50 (January 1974): 1–48. (entire issue)

———. "Prehistoric Pottery of Arizona." *Arizona Highways* 50 (February 1974): 1–48. (entire issue)

———. "Southwestern Pottery Today." (Special Edition) *Arizona Highways* 50 (May 1974): 1–48. (entire issue)

———. "Indian Weaving." (Special Edition) *Arizona Highways* 50 (July 1974): 1–48. (entire issue)

———. "Indian Jewelry." *Arizona Highways* 50 (August 1974): 1–48. (entire issue)

———. "American Indian Basketry." (Special Edition) *Arizona Highways* 51 (July 1975): 1–47. (entire issue)

———. American Indian Artists Series. *Arizona Highways* 52 (August 1976): 1–48. (entire issue)

———. "Collector's Edition: The New Look in Indian Jewelry." *Arizona Highways* 55 (April 1979): 1–48. (entire issue)

———. "The New Individualists: A Spectacular Visual Journey through the Realm of Native American Fine Art." *Arizona Highways* 62: (May 1986): 1–47. (entire issue)

Bahti, Mark. *A Consumer's Guide to Southwestern Indian Arts and Crafts.* Tucson, Ariz.: Bahti Indian Arts, 1975.

Bahti, Tom. *Southwestern Indian Arts and Crafts.* Flagstaff, Ariz.: K. C. Publications, 1966.

Berke, Arnold. *Mary Colter: Architect of the Southwest.* New York: Princeton Architecture Press, 2002.

Collins, John E. *Hopi Traditions in Pottery and Painting.* Alhambra, Calif.: NuMasters Gallery, 1977.

Deedra, Don. *Navajo Rugs: How to Find, Evaluate, Buy, and Care for Them.* Flagstaff, Ariz.: Northland Press, 1975.

Edison, Carol A., ed. *Willow Stories: Utah Navajo Baskets.* Salt Lake City: Utah Arts Council, 1996.

Gertzwiller, Steve. *The Fine Art of Navajo Weaving.* Tucson, Ariz.: Ray Manley, 1984.

"Hopi and Hopi-Tewa Pottery." *Plateau* (winter 1977): 1–32. (entire issue)

James, H. L. *Posts and Rugs: The Story of Navajo Rugs and Their Homes.* Globe, Ariz.: Southwest Parks and Monuments Association, 1977.

Lister, Robert H., and Lister, Florence C. *Anasazi Pottery*. Albuquerque: University of New Mexico Press, 1978.

Maxwell, Gilbert S. *Navajo Rugs—Past, Present, and Future*. Santa Fe: Heritage Art, 1984.

McCoy, Ron. "Naalye he Bahooghan: Where the Past Is Present" (Indian Country Trading Posts)," *Arizona Highways* 63 (June 1987): 6–15.

Mercurio, Giari, and Pechel, Maxymilian L. *The Guide to Trading Posts*. Cortez, Colo.: Lonewolf Publishing, 1994.

Mora, Joseph. *The Year of the Hopi: Paintings and Photographs 1904–06*. With essays by Tyrone Stewart, Frederick Dock Stader, and Barton Wright. New York: Rizzoli International Publications, Inc., 1979.

Rosnek, Carl, and Stacey, Joseph. *Skystone and Silver: The Collector's Book of Southwest Indian Jewelry*. New York: Prentice Hall, 1976.

Tanner, Clara Lee. *Prehistoric Southwestern Craft Arts*. Tucson: University of Arizona Press, 1976.

Trimble, Stephen. *Talking with the Clay: The Art of Pueblo Pottery*. Santa Fe: School of American Research, 1987.

Washburn, Dorothy K., ed. *Hopi Kachina: Spirit of Life*. San Francisco: California Academy of Sciences, 1980.

Wright, Barton. *Hopi Kachinas: The Complete Guide to Collecting Kachina Dolls*. Flagstaff, Ariz.: Northland Press, 1977.

Wright, Barton, and Roat, Evelyn. *This Is a Hopi Kachina*. Flagstaff: Museum of Northern Arizona, 1973.

Wright, Margaret. *Hopi Silver: The History and Hallmarks of Hopi Silversmithing*. Flagstaff, Ariz.: Northland Press, 1972–74.

Maps

Guide to Indian Country, Automobile Club of Southern California. To order the for-sale edition, contact Western National Parks Association, 12880 North Vistoso Village Drive, Tucson (Oro Valley), 85737; (520) 622–6014 or (888) 569–7762. For members many branches of the American Automobile Association also carry this invaluable map or it can be ordered online from amazon.com.

Maps plus general tourist information are available from the Arizona Office of Tourism, 2703 North Third Street, Suite 4015, Phoenix, Arizona 85004; (602) 230–7733 or (800) 520–3434; www.Arizonaguide.com. Maps and information can also be obtained, free of charge to AAA members, from the Arizona Automobile Association, 3144 North Seventh Avenue, Phoenix, Arizona 85013; (602) 274–1116.

Public Lands Information Center, 1474 Rodeo Road, Santa Fe, New Mexico 87505; (505) 627–0210; www.publiclands.org.

3. Southwestern Colorado and Northwestern New Mexico: Rocky Mountain Frontier Country

General Descriptive/Historical

Beckner, Raymond M. *Guns along the Silvery San Juan.* Cannon City, Colo.: Masber Printers, distributed by Raymond M. Beckner, 1975.

Brown, Robert. *An Empire of Silver. History of San Juan Silver Rush.* Caldwell, Idaho: Caxton Printers Ltd., 1965.

Chronic, Halka. *Roadside Geology of Colorado.* Missoula, Mont.: Mountain Press Publishing Co., 1980.

Dawson, Frank J. *Place Names in Colorado.* Denver: Golden Bell Press, 1954.

Eichler, George R. *Colorado Place Names.* Boulder, Colo.: Johnson Publishing Co., 1977.

Elliott, Melinda. *Great Excavations: Tales of Early Southwestern Archaeology 1888–1939.* Santa Fe: School of American Research Press, 1995.

Elmore, Francis H. *Shrubs and Trees of the Southwest Uplands.* Globe, Ariz.: Southwest Parks and Monuments Association, 1976.

Fisher, Vardis, and Holmes, Opal Laurel. *Gold Rushes and Mining Camps of the Early American West.* Caldwell, Idaho: Caxton Printers Ltd., 1968.

Goetzmann, William H. *Exploration and Empire.* New York: W. W. Norton & Co., Inc., 1966.

Johnson, Robert Neil. *Southwestern Ghost Town Atlas.* Susanville, Calif.: C. Y. Johnson and Son, 1977.

Landi, Val. *The Great American Countryside.* New York: Macmillan, Inc., 1982.

Lavender, David. *The Rockies.* Lincoln: University of Nebraska Press, 1968.

————. *The Telluride Story.* Boulder, Colo.: Wayfinder Press, 1987.

Lister, Robert H., and Lister, Florence C. *Those Who Came Before: Southwestern Archaeology in the National Park System,* 2d ed. Tucson, Ariz.: Southwest Parks and Monuments Association, 1994.

Miller, Millie. *Kinnikinnick: The Mountain Flower Book.* Boulder, Colo.: Johnson Publishing Co., 1980.

Newberry, Friederica. *Specialty of the House.* Durango, Colo.: Sojourner Press, 1979.

Nord, Myrtle. *Durango Early Times,* vol. 1. Durango, Colo.: TriState Printing Co., n.d.

Osborne, Douglas. "Solving the Riddles of Wetherill Mesa." *National Geographic* 125 (February 1964): 155–95.

Osterwald, Doris B. *Cinders and Smoke.* Lakewood, Colo.: Western Guideways, 1965.

Silverton Standard and the Miner. *Silverton–San Juan Vacation Guide 1980–1981 and 1982.* Silverton, Colo: Silverton Standard and the Miner, 1980.

Smith, Duane Allen. *Mesa Verde National Park: Shadows of the Centuries.* Lawrence: University Press of Kansas, 1988.

————. *Rocky Mountain Mining Camps: The Urban Frontier.* Bloomington: Indiana University Press, 1967.

————. *Colorado Mining: A Photographic History.* Albuquerque: University of New Mexico Press, 1977.

Sprague, Marshall. *The Great Gates.* Lincoln: University of Nebraska Press, 1964.

Panning for gold

Sumner, David. *Colorado/Southwest: The Land, the People, the History.* Denver: Sanborn Souvenir Co., Inc., 1973.

Weber, David J. *Taos Trappers.* Norman: University of Oklahoma Press, 1971.

Wenger, Gilbert R. *The Story of Mesa Verde.* Denver: Mesa Verde Museum Associates, Inc., 1980.

Wolle, Muriel Sibell. *From Stampede to Timberline.* Chicago: Sage Books, 1949.

————. *Timberline Tailings.* Chicago: The Swallow Press, Inc., 1977.

Young, Michael D., ed. *National Parkway Photographic and Comprehensive Guide to Mesa Verde and Rocky Mountain National Parks.* Casper, Wyo.: Worldwide Research and Publishing Co., 1975.

Zwinger, Ann. *Beyond the Aspen Grove.* 1970. Reprint, New York: Harper and Row, 1981.

————. *Land above the Trees. A Guide to American Alpine Tundra.* New York: Harper and Row, 1972.

Maps

A free Colorado state map can be obtained from the Colorado Tourism and Travel Authority, 1625 Broadway, Suite 1700, Denver, Colorado 80202; (800) 265–6723; www.colorado.com. If you are an AAA member, you can receive free maps of the region from the American Automobile Association at either of the following locations: 8601 West Cross Drive #B1, Denver, Colorado 80123; (303) 753–8800 or (800) 238–5222; or 2454 U.S. Highway 6 and 50, Suite 109, Grand Junction, Colorado 81505; (970) 245–2236 or (800) 283–5222.

Another excellent source for books and maps related to Colorado history and lore and Indian Country is the Southwest Natural and Cultural Heritage Association's mail order bookstore. Information: SNCHA Bookstore, Anasazi Heritage Center, 27501 Highway 184, Dolores, Colorado 81323; (970) 882–4811; fax (970) 882–7035; www.co.blm.gov/ahc/hmepge.htm.

4. North Central New Mexico: The Spanish Rio Grande Country

General Descriptive/Historical

Armstrong, Ruth, and New Mexico Magazine Staff. *New Mexico Magazine's Enchanted Trails.* Santa Fe: New Mexico Magazine Press, 1980.

Austin, Mary. *The Land of Journey's Ending.* New York: Century, 1924.

Bowman, Jon. "Los Alamos and Española." *New Mexico Magazine* 65 (1987) 10: 63–71.

Chronic, Halka. *Roadside Geology of New Mexico.* Missoula, Mont.: Mountain Press Publishing Co., 1987.

DeWitt, Dave, and Wilan, Mary Jane. *The Food Lover's Handbook to the Southwest.* Rocklin, Calif.: Prima Publishing, 1992.

Ellis, William S. "A Goal at the End of the Trail: Santa Fe." *National Geographic* 161 (March 1982): 323–45.

Flint, Richard, and Flint, Shirley Cushing. *The Coronado Expedition to Tierra Nueva: The 1540–1542 Route across the Southwest.* Niwot, Colo.: University Press of Colorado, 1998.

Hagan, Bob. "West Mesa Petroglyphs." *New Mexico Magazine* 65, no. 2 (1987): 16–21, 59–60.

Hazen-Hammond, Susan. "Farmington." *New Mexico Magazine* 64, no. 5 (1986): 54–55, 58–60.

Hillerman, Tony, ed. *The Spell of New Mexico.* Albuquerque: University of New Mexico Press, 1976.

Jamison, Cheryl Alters, and Jamison, Bill. *The Borders Cookbook.* Boston: The Harvard Common Press, 1995.

Julyan, Robert. *The Place Names of New Mexico.* Albuquerque: University of New Mexico Press, 1996.

Kuhn, I. C. "Christmas in Santa Fe." *Gourmet Magazine* 38 (December 1979): 20–24, 82–88.

Lawrence, D. H. *Mornings in Mexico and Etruscan Places.* Middlesex: Penguin Books, 1967.

———. "New Mexico." *Survey Graphics* 1 May 1931. Also collected in *Phoenix: The Posthumous Papers of D. H. Lawrence,* edited by Edward McDonald. New York: Viking, 1936.

Laxalt, Robert. "New Mexico: The Golden Land." *National Geographic* 138 (September 1970): 299–345.

———. "New Mexico's Mountains of Mystery." *National Geographic* 154 (September 1978): 416–36.

Muench, David, and Hillerman, Tony. *New Mexico.* Portland, Ore.: Charles H. Belding, 1974.

O'Keeffe, Georgia. *Georgia O'Keeffe.* 1976. Reprint. New York: Penguin Books, 1977.

Roach, Archibald W. *Outdoor Plants of the Southwest.* Dallas: Taylor Publishing Co., 1982.

Sagar, Keith, ed. *D. H. Lawrence and New Mexico.* Salt Lake City: Gibbs M. Smith, Inc., 1982.

Sutton, George Miksch. *Oklahoma Birds.* Norman: University of Oklahoma Press, 1967.

Thompson, Waite, and Gottlieb, H. Richard. *The Santa Fe Guide.* Santa Fe: Sunstone Press, 1980.

Young, John V. *The State Parks of New Mexico.* Albuquerque: University of New Mexico Press, 1984.

Historical / Cultural

Anaya, A. Rudolfo. *Bless Me, Ultima.* Berkeley, Calif.: Tonatiuh International, Inc. 1972.

Cather, Willa. *Death Comes for the Archbishop.* New York: Random House, Inc., 1971.

Dutton, P. Bertha. *Let's Explore Indian Villages Past and Present.* Santa Fe: Museum of New Mexico Press, 1962.

Fergusson, Erna. *New Mexico: A Pageant of Three Peoples.* Albuquerque: University of New Mexico Press, 1964.

Historic Santa Fe Foundation. *Old Santa Fe Today.* Albuquerque: University of New Mexico Press, 1982.

Hogan, Paul. *The Heroic Triad.* New York: World Publishing, 1970.

Jenkins, Myra Ellen, and Schroeder, Albert H. *A Brief History of New Mexico.* Albuquerque: University of New Mexico Press, 1974.

La Farge, Oliver. *Santa Fe.* Norman: University of Oklahoma Press, 1959.

Langseth-Christensen, Lillian. "The Kitchens of El Rancho de las Golondrinas." *Gourmet Magazine* 34 (August 1979): 44–48, 94.

Lavender, David. *The Southwest.* New York: Harper and Row, 1980.

Morrill, Claire. *A Taos Mosaic: Portrait of New Mexico Village.* Albuquerque: University of New Mexico Press, 1973.

Nichols, John, and Davis, William. *If Mountains Die: A New Mexico Memoir.* New York: Alfred A. Knopf, 1979.

Querry, Ronald B. *Growing Old at Willie Nelson's Picnic and Other Sketches of Life in the Southwest.* College Station: Texas A & M University Press, 1983.

Simmons, Marc. *The Last Conquistadore: Juan de Oñate and the Setting of the Far Southwest.* Norman: University of Oklahoma Press, 1992.

Shishkin, K. H. *The Palace of the Governors.* Santa Fe: Museum of New Mexico Press, 1972.

Smith, Griffin, Jr. "The Mexican Americans: A People on the Move." *National Geographic* 157 (June 1980): 780–809.

Stein, Rita. *A Literary Tour Guide to the United States: South and Southwest.* New York: William Morrow & Co., Inc., 1979.

Weber, J. David. *The Taos Trappers.* Norman: University of Oklahoma Press, 1968.

Fine Arts and Traditional Arts and Crafts

Babcock, Barbara A., and Monthan, Guy and Doris. *The Pueblo Storyteller: Development of a Figurative Ceramic Tradition.* Tucson: University of Arizona Press, 1986.

Barry, John W. *American Indian Pottery,* 2d ed. Florence, Ala.: Books Americana, 1984.

Boyd, E. *Popular Arts of Spanish New Mexico.* Santa Fe: Museum of New Mexico Press, 1974.

Broggs, L. Charles. *The Wood Carvers of Cordova, New Mexico.* Knoxville: University of Tennessee Press, 1980.

Dickey, F. Roland. *New Mexico Village Arts.* Albuquerque: University of New Mexico Press, 1949.

Dittert, Alfred E. Jr., and Plog, Fred. *Generations in Clay.* Flagstaff, Ariz.: Northland Press, 1980.

Jacka, Jerry. *Pottery Treasures.* Portland: Graphic Arts Center Publishing Co., 1976.

Jeter, James, and Juelke, Paula Marie. *The Saltillo Serape.* Santa Barbara, Calif.: New World Arts, 1978.

Kent, Kate Peck. *Pueblo Indian Textiles: A Living Tradition.* Seattle: University of Washington Press, 1983.

Truchas, New Mexico

Lambert, Marjorie F. *Pueblo Indian Pottery: Materials, Tools and Techniques.* Santa Fe: Museum of New Mexico Press, 1966.

LeFree, Betty. *Santa Clara Pottery Today.* Albuquerque: University of New Mexico Press, 1975.

Lister, H. Robert, and Lister, C. Florence. *Anasazi Pottery.* Albuquerque: University of New Mexico Press, 1978.

Marriott, Alice. *Maria: The Potter of San Ildefonso.* Norman: University of Oklahoma Press, 1948.

Martinez, Levi. *What Is a New Mexico Santo?* Santa Fe: Sunstone Press, 1978.

Mather, Christine, and Woods, Sharon. *Santa Fe Style.* New York: Rizzoli International Publications, 1986.

Maxwell Museum of Anthropology. *Seven Families in Pueblo Pottery.* Albuquerque: University of New Mexico Press, 1974.

Monthan, Guy, and Monthan, Doris. *Nacimientos.* Flagstaff, Ariz.: Northland Press, 1979.

Trenton, Patricia, ed. *Independent Spirits: Women Painters of the American West, 1890–1945.* Berkeley: University of California Press, 1995.

Wilder, Kathryn, ed. *Walking the Twilight: Women Writers of the Southwest.* Flagstaff, Ariz.: Northland Publishing, 1994 (vol. 1) and 1996 (vol. 2).

Worth, William, ed. *Hispanic Crafts of the Southwest.* Colorado Springs: Colorado Springs Fine Arts Center (Taylor Museum), 1977.

Zeigler, George M. *Art in Santa Fe.* Chicago: Lake Shore Press, 1987.

Maps

Free maps and tourist information are available from the New Mexico Department of Tourism, 491 Old Santa Fe Trail, Santa Fe, New Mexico 87503; (505) 827–7400 or (800) 733–6396; www.newmexico.org/. Additionally maps are available without charge to members of the American Automobile Association at both of the following addresses: 10501 Montgomery Boulevard Northeast, Albuquerque, New Mexico 87111; (505) 291–6611 or (800) 846–0377; 1644 St. Michaels Drive, Santa Fe, New Mexico 87505; (505) 471–6620 or (800) 881–7585. The American Automobile Association map "A Guide to Indian Country" is excellent for much of north central New Mexico. (See Section 2 of the bibliography for sources.)

Still another source for maps, books, licenses, permits, passes and detailed information about national forests, parks, wilderness areas and BLM lands in New Mexico and Indian Country is the Public Lands Information Center, 1474 Rodeo Road, Santa Fe, New Mexico 87505; (505) 627–0210; www.publiclandsinfo.org.

GLOSSARY

acequia	irrigation ditch
adovado	the name of a sour seasoning paste for meat made of ground chilies, herbs, and vinegar
arrastra	a rudimentary mill for pulverizing ores containing valuable minerals like gold
arroyo	the wide, water-carved, flat-floored channel of an intermittent stream in dry country
barrio	a district or section of a town
biscochitos	traditional cookies created by Spanish settlers in New Mexico based on earlier recipes from Mexico
bolillo	a small, elongated, oval bread roll, often with a slightly sweet taste
brujo	a witch or sorcerer who performs black magic and is capable of influencing others adversely
bulto	a three-dimensional, carved figure or statue, often of a saint
cacique	a word brought to the Southwest by the Spanish from Cuba, meaning "chief"; it was applied to the religious leaders of the pueblos
cairn	a pile of stones, usually in conical shape, raised as a landmark
curandera	a healer who is skilled in the use of herbs but who is also endowed with certain powers to counteract the evil influence of the *brujo*
Diné	a word used by the Navajo to refer to themselves; it means "The People"
fetish	a natural object or a man-made object resembling a natural object and believed to hold a spirit that will protect or aid its owner
fonda	an inn or restaurant
frijoles	beans
hogan	a Navajo house
horno	a beehive or inverted cone-shaped outdoor oven of Moorish-Arabic origin, brought to the Southwest by the Spanish
Indian fry bread	large, round, puffy flatbread made from a dough of flour, salt, and baking powder (like sopaipilla dough) that is deep-fried in vegetable oil in a large skillet, often over an open fire

kachina (*katsina*)	a supernatural Hopi deity; there are more than 300 kachinas, representing the various forms of life that reside in the San Francisco Peaks; dolls are often made in their image
kikmongwi	a village leader in a Hopi village
kiska	a covered passageway in a Hopi village between the buildings, connecting part of the village to the plaza
kiva	Pueblo Indian ceremonial chamber that is sometimes underground or partially underground
latia (*latillas*)	small peeled poles of juniper or aspen used in the construction of ceilings in adobe buildings
mariachi	a group of folk musicians (including a guitarist, a violinist, and singers) that had its origin in Mexico
nacimiento	a representation of the Nativity scene through one of several media, including clay or carved wood figures
pahaana	the Hopi word for a white person
Pai tribes	Two Pai tribes indigenous to Northern Arizona are the Havasupai, located in an isolated area in the westernmost part of the Grand Canyon, and the Hualapai, who live in Western Arizona on a high plateau near the Utah border.
pan dulce	sweet roll
paraje	a stopping place for travelers
parroquia	a parish church, as opposed to a mission church
Penitente	short for Los Hermanos Penitentes, the Penitente Brothers, a religious order of laymen known for their severe religious practices
petroglyph	an image that has been pecked, carved, scratched, or abraded on the face of a stone
pictograph	an image that has been painted on the surface of a stone
placer	a gravel or sand deposit, usually along a streambed, that contains small particles of gold or other valuable minerals washed down from larger deposits upstream
placita	a small courtyard, square, or plaza located either in the center of a private home or in the center of a complex of buildings
portal	a long covered porch supported by vertical posts
posada	an inn or place of lodging; also a Christmas festivity lasting nine days
posole	the name given to a soup or stew of meat and corn, as well as the name of the special corn used in the stew that is prepared by boiling it in limewater until it is free of hulls
potsherd	a fragment or broken piece of fired pottery
pregonero	a crier in Pueblo villages who announces the time to open the irrigation ditches and other important events

rancho   a small ranch

rebozo   a shawl made of cotton or silk

reredos   an altar screen

retablo   a religious picture, usually painted on wood or tin or other flat surfaces

ristra   a string of chilies, corn, or garlic, hung up to dry or strung for ornamental purposes

santero   a local craftsperson or artist who makes religious statues or paintings

santuario   a sanctuary

shard   a fragment of a broken pottery vessel; also called a potsherd

sing   a Navajo ceremonial occasion where, in addition to social dancing, there are healing ceremonies presided over by a Navajo medicine man or "singer" whose singing and chanting is an important part of the ceremony

sipaapuni   a small hole in the floor of a kivas that, in the Hopi religion, symbolizes the place of man's emergence from the earth

tailings   the mounds of accumulated waste debris from ore-processing mills

talus   piles of fallen, broken rock that accumulate at the base of a ridge or a cliff

viga   a log used as a ceiling beam in adobe houses

villa   an early-day Spanish town or city that served as an administration center

zaguan   a covered passageway joining separate buildings, often serving as an entryway to a *placita*

Zozobra   a Spanish word meaning "foundering," "sinking," or "worry"; the term has been used to name a 40-foot-tall puppet figure representing Old Man Gloom that is burned every September at fiesta time in Santa Fe

INDEX

Boldface numerals indicate pages on which illustrations appear.

Blue Corn Cafe, 474
Blue doors, **405**
Bluegrass, and Acoustic, Music Festival,
    Annual, 329
Blue Lake, 371, 438
Blue Lake Ranch, 302
Blue Mountains. *See* Abajo Mountains
Blue Rain Gallery, 510
Blue, significance of, 339, 406
Blue spruce, 244, **267**
Bluffs, Utah, 32, 98
Blumenschein, Ernest L., 372, 429, 438
Blumenschein Memorial Home,
    Ernest L., 429
Bobcat Bite, 478–79
Boca Negra Canyon, 378
Bonito Campground, 218
Bon Ton Restaurant, 316, 319
Bookworks, 331, 458
Bootlegger campgrounds, 218
Borders Books, 490
Borrego House, 400
Bosque, 377
Bosque Redondo, 133, 152, 155
Boston Party, 140
Bötteger Koch Mansion Bed and
    Breakfast, 446
Bottle plant, **38**
Boulder Mountain, 4, 16, 62, 65, 71, 79,
    103, 244, 267
Boulder Mountain Lodge and Hell's
    Backbone Grill, 103
Boulder Utah, 16, 31, 80, 103, 125
Bound to be Read, 458
Bowtie Arch, 57
Box Canyon Falls, 318
Box Canyon Lodge and Hot Springs, 318
Box Canyon Park, 271
Boyle House, 398
Bradbury Science Museum, 410
Branigar/Chase Discovery Center, 144
Brass band festival, 315
Bravo, 505
Brett, Lady Dorothy, 436, 437
Brewer's blackbirds, 264
Bridal Veil Falls, 275
Bridge, swinging, 38
Bridges, natural, **27**, 75–**77**
Brigham's Tomb, 160
Brink's Burgers, 101
Bristlecone Loop Trail, 86
Bristlecone pine, 86
Brittania and W.E Mauger Estate Bed and
    Breakfast, 446
Broad Arch, 76

Brodsky Bookshop, 511
Brothers of the Light. *See* Penitentes
Brown Bear Cafe, 313
Brunot Agreement, 248
Bryan's Gallery, 511
Bryan, William Jennings, 257, 275, 322
Bryce Canyon Lodge, 85, 104; western
    cabins, **106**
Bryce Canyon National Park, 4, 5, 10, 13,
    31, 74, **83**–88; uplift and formation, **17**;
    rock formation, 21; Wall Street Gorge,
    86, 87; western cabin, **106**; lodging and
    food, 104–6; campgrounds, 106–7;
    tourists at, 5, 31, 83; travel access to,
    520–21
Bryce Canyon Pines, 105
Bryce, Ebenezer, 9
Bryce Point, 85
Bryce Temple, 86
Buck's Grill House, 93–94
Buckskin Booksellers, 321
Budget Host Saga Motel, 216
Budget Rent-A-Car, 97, 225, 331, 459
Buen Tiempo Restaurant, 319
Buffaloberry, roundleaf, **75**
Buffalo Dance, **411**
Buffalo hide shields, 64
Bultos, 366, **367,** 370, 383, 419, **420, 422,**
    434, 485
Bureau of Indian Affairs, 135, 137
Bureau of Land Management, 290, 291;
    exhibit, 46
Bureau of Reclamation, 291
Burgwin, Captain John, 367, 425, 438
Burrito Company, 471
Burros, **364**
Burro Alley, 392
Burr Trail Road, 81
Buster's, 218–19
Butch Cassidy Days, 97
Butterflies, Monarch, 72
Butterfly Dance, 204
Buttes, **18,** 19, 45

Cabeza de Vaca, Alvar Nuñéz, 351
Cabin, early settler's, 247
Cache Valley Overlook, 37
Cactus: fishhook, **38**; prickly pear, 39, 75
Cafe Diablo, 101
Cafe Espress Cafe-Bakery, 220
Cafe Paris, 472–73
Caffe Renato, 504
Cafe Pasqual's, 474
Caffee Tazza, 504
Caineville, Utah, 26, 73, 78, **100**

Le Papillon Bakery and Dog and Burger Bar, 319
Le Rendezvous Swiss Bakery, 304
LewAllen and LewAllen Jewelry, 487
LewAllen Contemporary Gallery, 487
LewAllen, Ross, 487
Liberty Bell mine, 251, 274
Lightner Creek Campground, 303
Lilies, sego or mariposa, **84**
Limestone, 13
Liquor laws, 89
Little America Hotel, 216
Little Bryce Canyon, 182
Little Colorado River, 170, 182
Little Colorado River Gorge, 149
Little Giant Gold Mine, 248
Little River of the Beans, 409
Lizard, **39**
Lizard Head Pass, 276–77
Lizard Head Peak, **277**
Lockett Fine Arts Gallery, 144
Lodestar Astonomy Center and Star Theater, 376
Lodging prices and reservations, xvii–xviii
Logwood Bed and Breakfast, 301–2
Loloma, Charles, 434
Lomaki, 147
Long House (Wetherill Mesa), 281, 282
Long House Ruin (Bandelier), 410
Long Walk, 133, 188, 190
Lopez, George, 424
Lopez, José Dolores, 424
Lopez, Nasario, 424
Loretto Chapel, 369, **395**
Los Alamos Historical Museum, 410
Los Alamos Ranch School, 372
Los Moros y Los Cristianos, 358, 419
Los Poblanos Inn, 448
Louisiana Purchase, 363
Lowell, Amy, 141
Lowell Observatory, 141, 144
Lowell, Percival, 141
Lower Calf Creek Falls, **82**
Lowry Pueblo National Historic Landmark, 164, 280, 288–92, **289, 290**; painted wall, **290**
Luhan, Mabel Dodge, 372, 430, 431, 437, 499
Luhan, Tony, 431
Lukachukai Mountains, 281
Lumina Fine Art, Lumina Gardens North, 512
Luminarias, 441
Lynn's Inn B&B, 215

Maasaw, 171; doll, **174**
Macomb, Captain J. N., 44, 48, 247
Mabel Dodge Luhan House, **431,** 432, 499
Madeline Inn Bed and Breakfast, 466, **467**
Madrid, New Mexico, 381
Maggie Gulch, 248
Magnifico!, 455
Magpies, 67, 166, **265**
Main Avenue Arts Festival, 309
Main Street Brewery, 333
Malone, Bill, 234
Mancos Canyon Indian Park,333
Mancos, Colorado, 278, 334
Mancos Ranch, Lake, 335
Mancos River, 335
Mancos River Valley, 255
Mancos shale, 20, 36, 78, 109
M and J Restaurant and Sanitary Tortilla Factory, 452
Manhattan Atomic Bomb Project, 389
Manitou Lodge Bed and Breakfast, 324
Mano, **288**
Manor Bed and Breakfast, The, 316
Manti—La Sal Mountains, 14, 36, 40, 46, 47, 50
Many Farms, 200
Many Horses, 188
Maraw, 175
Marcos, Fray, 352
María Benítez Teatro Flamenco, 484
Maria's Book Shop, 311
Marin, John, 372
Mariposa Gallery, 458
Marsh Pass, 163, 166
Martin and Roll Gallery, 310
Martinez, Hacienda de Don Antonio Severino, 433–34
Martinez, José, 369
Martinez, Julian, 283
Martinez, Maria, 283, 406; museum, 434
Martinez, Padre, 430
Maseeba, 179
Mason, Charles, 256
Masonry, 123–24, **124**
Massacre Cave, 199
Masterson, Bat, 240, 268
Mather, Davis, 487
Matterhorn Campground, 326
Mauger Estate Bed and Breakfast, W. E., 446
Maxwell Museum of Anthropology, 379, 449, 458
May, Karl, 194
Mayflower Gold Mill, 314
Maze, the, 48

ABOUT THE AUTHOR

Robert L. Casey has traveled the High Southwest for five decades,
inheriting his curiosity and boundless enthusiasm for the region from his
parents, who were visitors there early in the twentieth century. The author
currently resides in Seattle, Washington, where he is at work on a Sonoran
Desert memoir based on the years he lived in Tucson, Arizona.